Lecture Notes in Artificial Intelligence 9250

Subseries of Lecture Notes in Computer Science

More information about this series at http://www.springer.com/series/1244

Yike Guo · Karl Friston
Aldo Faisal · Sean Hill
Hanchuan Peng (Eds.)

Brain Informatics and Health

8th International Conference, BIH 2015
London, UK, August 30 – September 2, 2015
Proceedings

 Springer

Editors

Yike Guo
Data Science Institute
Imperial College London
London
UK

Karl Friston
Institute of Cognitive Neuroscience
University College London
London
UK

Aldo Faisal
Imperial College London
London
UK

Sean Hill
École Polytechnique Fédérale de Lausanne
Campus Biotech
Geneva
Switzerland

Hanchuan Peng
Allen Institute for Brain Science
Seattle
USA

ISSN 0302-9743   ISSN 1611-3349   (electronic)
Lecture Notes in Artificial Intelligence
ISBN 978-3-319-23343-7   ISBN 978-3-319-23344-4   (eBook)
DOI 10.1007/978-3-319-23344-4

Library of Congress Control Number: 2015946771

LNCS Sublibrary: SL7 – Artificial Intelligence

Printed on acid-free paper

Springer International Publishing AG Switzerland is part of Springer Science+Business Media
(www.springer.com)

Preface

This volume contains the papers selected for the 2015 International Conference on Brain Informatics and Health (BIH 2015), which was held at the Royal Geographical Society, London, UK, 30th August – 2nd September 2015. BIH 2015 was organized by Imperial College London, together with other co-organizers from the Allen Institute for Brain Science, École polytechnique fédérale de Lausanne, University College London, University of Kent, Maebashi Institute of Technology, and the Web Intelligence Consortium.

Brain research is rapidly advancing with the application of big data technology to neuroscience as can be seen in major international initiatives in the USA, Europe, and Asia. The paradigm of Brain Informatics is becoming mainstream and crosses the disciplines of neuroscience, cognitive science, computer science, signal processing, and neuroimaging technologies as well as data science. Brain Informatics investigates essential functions of the brain, in a wide range from perception to thinking, and encompassing areas such as multi-perception, attention, memory, language, computation, heuristic search, reasoning, planning, decision-making, problem-solving, learning, discovery, and creativity. The current goal of Brain Informatics is to develop and demonstrate a systematic approach to achieving an integrated understanding of working principles of the brain from the macroscopic to microscopic level, by means of experimental, computational, and cognitive neuroscience studies, not least utilizing advanced web intelligence-centric information technologies.

The series of Brain Informatics Conferences had started with the First WICI International Workshop on Web Intelligence meets Brain Informatics (WImBI'06), held in Beijing, China in 2006. The 2nd, 3rd, and 4th Conferences on Brain Informatics (BI09, BI10, and BI11) were jointly held with the International Conferences on Active Media Technology (AMT09, AMT10, and AMT11), in Beijing, China; Toronto, Canada; and Lanzhou, China, respectively. The 5th Conference on Brain Informatics was held jointly with other international conferences (AMT12, WI12, IAT12, and ISMIS12) in Macau, China, in 2012. The 2013 International Conference on Brain and Health Informatics was held in Maebashi-City, Japan, and it was the first conference specifically dedicated to the interdisciplinary research in Brain and Health Informatics. The BIH 2014 conference was held in Warsaw, Poland. Following the success of past conferences in this series, BIH 2015 placed a strong emphasis on emerging trends of big data analysis and management technology for brain research, behavior learning, and real-world applications of brain science in human health and wellbeing.

BIH 2015 aimed to give a common thesis of Informatics for Human Brain, Behavior, and Health. The conference gathered people who are doing cutting edge research in the field of Brain Informatics, bringing together researchers and practitioners from neuroscience, cognitive science, computer science, data science, and neuroimaging technologies with the purpose of exploring the fundamental roles, interactions, as well as practical impacts of Brain Informatics. BIH 2015 involved a great number of world leaders in brain research, including our keynote speakers Allan Jones, the Chief Executive Officer of the Allen Institute for Brain Science; Karlheinz Meier, Professor of Universität Heidelberg; David C. Van Essen, Alumni Endowed Professor at Washington University School of Medicine; and our feature speakers Giorgio A. Ascoli, founding director of the Center for Neural Informatics at the Krasnow Institute for Advanced Study of George Mason University; Henry Kennedy, Director of Research at the Stem-cell and Brain Research Institute; Barbara Sahakian, Professor in the Department of Psychiatry at the University of Cambridge; Nelson Spruston, Janelia Group Leader and Scientific Program Director at Howard Hughes Medical Institute; Paul Matthews, Edmond and Lily Safra Chair of Translational Neuroscience and Therapeutics and Head of the Division of Brain Sciences in the Department of Medicine of Imperial College London; and Paul Verschure, ICREA Research Professor, Head of the SPECS research group at Universitat Pompeu Fabra. BIH 2015 also included a panel discussion among the leaders of the big brain initiatives in the world, moderated by Sarah Caddick from the Gatsby Charitable Foundation.

Here we would like to express our gratitude to all members of the Conference Committee for their instrumental and unfailing support. BIH 2015 had a very exciting program with a number of features, ranging from keynote and feature talks, technical sessions, satellite symposiums, to social programs. This would not have been possible without the generous dedication of the Program Committee members in reviewing the papers submitted to BIH 2015, the BIH 2015 workshop and special session chairs and organizers in organizing the satellite symposiums and special sessions, and our keynote and feature speakers in giving outstanding talks at the conference. BIH 2015 could not have taken place without the great team effort of the Exhibition/Sponsorship Committee and the Local Organizing Committee.

Special thanks go to the Steering Committee Co-chair, Ning Zhong, for his help in organizing and promoting BIH 2015. We would also like to thank Juzhen Dong for her support with the CyberChair submission system. We are grateful to Springer Lecture Notes in Computer Science (LNCS/LNAI) for their generous support. We thank Springer for their help in coordinating the publication of this special volume in an emerging and interdisciplinary research field.

August 2015   Yike Guo
                                                                                          Karl Friston
                                                                                          Aldo Faisal
                                                                                          Sean Hill
                                                                                       Hanchuan Peng

Conference Organization

Conference General Chairs

Karl Friston — University College London, UK
Yike Guo — Data Science Institute and Imperial College London, UK

Program Chairs

Aldo Faisal — Imperial College London and MRC Clinical Science Centre, UK
Sean Hill — EPFL, Switzerland
Hanchuan Peng — Allen Institute for Brain Science, USA

Workshop/Special-Session Chairs

Andreas Holzinger — Medical University Graz and Center for Biomarker Research, Austria
Zhisheng Huang — Vrije University of Amsterdam, The Netherlands
David Powers — Flinders University of South Australia, Australia

Publicity Chairs

Jessica Turner — Georgia State University, USA
Juan D. Velasquez — University of Chile, Chile
Yi Zeng — Institute of Automation, Chinese Academy of Sciences, China

Local Organizing Chairs

Thomas Heinis — Imperial College London, UK
Kai Sun — Imperial College London, UK
Chao Wu — Imperial College London, UK

Exhibition/Sponsorship Chair

Caroline Li — University of Kent, UK

Steering Committee Co-chairs

Ning Zhong — Maebashi Institute of Technology, Japan
Hanchuan Peng — Allen Institute for Brain Science, USA

Program Committee

Tonio Ball	Bernstein Center Freiburg, Germany
Jan Bazan	University of Rzeszow, Poland
Anil Anthony Bharath	Imperial College London, UK
Howard Bowman	University of Kent, UK
Mirko Cesarini	University Milano-Bicocca, Italy
W. Art Chaovalitwongse	University of Washington, USA
Amir Chaudhry	University of Cambridge, UK
Kang Cheng	RIKEN Brain Science Institute, Japan
Yiu-ming Cheung	Hong Kong Baptist University, China
Frank D. Hsu	Fordham University, USA
Massimo Ferri	University Bologna, Italy
David Fortin	Université de Sherbrooke, Canada
Philippe Fournier-Viger	University of Moncton, Canada
Richard Frackowiak	University of Lausanne, Switzerland
Yong He	Beijing Normal University, China
Kazuyuki Imamura	Maebashi Institute of Technology, Japan
Shuiwang Ji	Old Dominion University, USA
Tianzi Jiang	Chinese Academy of Sciences, China
Colin Johnson	University of Kent, UK
Hanmin Jung	Korea Institute of Science and Technology Information, South Korea
Ferath Kherif	CHUV/UNIL, Switzerland
Margarita Kotti	Imperial College London, UK
Abbas Z. Kouzani	Deakin University, Australia
Nikolaus Kriegeskorte	MRC CBU Unit, UK
Arvind Kumar	KTH Royal Institute of Technology, Sweden
Renaud Lambiotte	University of Namur, Belgium
Ilse Lamers	University Hasselt, Belgium
Nada Lavrac	Joszef Stefan Institute, Slovenia
Robert Leech	Imperial College London, UK
Yan Li	University of Southern Queensland, Australia
Peipeng Liang	Xuanwu Hospital, Capital Medical University, China
Xiaohui Liu	Brunel University, UK
Paul Matthews	Imperial College London, UK
Mariofanna Milanova	University of Arkansas at Little Rock, USA
Antonio Moreno-Ribas	University Rovira i Virigili, Spain
Kazumi Nakamatsu	University of Hyogo, Japan
Jan Paralic	Technical University of Kosice, Slovakia
Marcello Pelillo	University of Venice, Italy
Esther Rodriguez-Villegas	Imperial College London, UK
Constantin Rothkopf	Technical University Darmstadt, Germany
Helge Ritter	University of Bielefeld, Germany
Daniel Rueckert	Imperial College London, UK

Contents

Brain-inspired Technologies, Systems and Applications

Special Session on Neuroimaging Data Analysis and Applications

Special Session on Interactive Machine Learning with the Human-in-the-Loop: Cognitive Computing at its best

Symposium on Computational Psychophysiology

Symposium on Modelling Brain Information

Thinking and Perception-Centric Investigations of Human Information Processing System (HIPS) and Computational Foundations of Brain Science

Eye Tracking and EEG Features for Salient Web Object Identification

Gino Slanzi, Claudio Aracena, and Juan D. Velásquez[✉]

Department of Industrial Engineering, Universidad de Chile,
Av. República 701, P.O. Box: 8370439, Santiago, Chile
{gslanzi,caracena}@ing.uchile.cl, jvelasqu@dii.uchile.cl

Abstract. We propose a biological-based feature comparison for identifying salient Web objects. We compare several features extracted from
eye tracking and EEG data with a baseline given by mean fixation impact
introduced by Buscher. For this, we performed an experiment with 20
healthy subjects in which gaze position, pupil size and brain activity were
recorded while browsing in a Web site adaptation. Our results show that
there are EEG features that could be related to Web user attention in
objects. In particular the Gamma Band RMS and the EEG Variance
indicate that the longer subjects view a web object (more attention),
the less brain signal disturbance appears. We also discarded pupil size
features due to low correlation with baseline. These results suggest that
EEG features could be used to identify salient objects without using the
time users spent on them as done in previous methodologies.

1 Introduction

The penetration of the Web has changed people's behaviour over time. For
example, when any sort of information or product is required, people usually,
and almost naturally, check the Web. Thus, companies and organizations have
wanted to get presence in this network and increase their sales and market position. To achieve effectiveness in their goals it is necessary to design web sites
that can attract more customers than competitors' web sites.

However, designing and implementing attractive websites require knowledge
about customer behavior and preferences. For that purpose there are several
techniques for discovering customer experience while browsing a website, including polls, surveys, weblog analysis, etc. In addition to those techniques several
modern methodologies such as mouse tracking have been developed in order to
extract more objective patterns from web user behavior.

In this study we compare different types of data analysis from web user
behavior, including eye tracking, pupil size and electroencephalography. The
aim is to find out what the most relevant objects on a web site are depending
on the different data analyses. In addition, we discuss the salient web object
identification differences between each analysis.

This comparison is interesting due to the fact that each biological response
can explain different human behaviors. For instance, eye fixations have been

© Springer International Publishing Switzerland 2015
Y. Guo et al. (Eds.): BIH 2015, LNAI 9250, pp. 3–12, 2015.
DOI: 10.1007/978-3-319-23344-4_1

related with attention in the focus area [1], pupil size has been related with cognitive load or mental activity [4] and EEG signals have been related with many phenomena, in particular, emotional or cognitive states [7].

To achieve our objective, we performed an experiment where the gaze movements, pupil size and EEG signals were recorded for 20 subjects. The task consisted of browsing 32 web pages of the MBA program of the University of Chile's web site.

The paper is organized as follows, first we present some related research, and then describe our approach for identifying salient objects and features from biological signals used as comparison measures. After specifying the experimental setup, we will attempt to answer the data processing and research questions. Next, the results are shown along with their pertinent discussion, and finally we conclude our study and propose future work.

2   Related Work

One remarkable line of salient web object identification was developed by Buscher et al. The main motivation comes from the need to understand how people allocate visual attention on Web pages, taking into account its relevance for both web developers and advertisers. In 2009, authors implemented an eye-tracking-based analysis in which 20 users were shown 361 pages while performing information foraging and inspection tasks [1]. The main assumption was that gaze data could represent a proxy of attention. From that, an analysis framework was developed by first generating a tool that allows DOM elements to be characterized and a mapping performed between gaze data and the DOM elements. The second part involves the use of the extracted web features in a machine-learning setting to predict salient elements on a web page.

Another relevant contribution by Buscher et al. is the introduction of the concept of *fixation impact*. It allows the identification of the set of elements that are under the gaze of the user at a certain time. It follows empirical studies that show that human vision is characterized by a narrow window of high acuity along with the standard gaze area. Thus, when visualizing an element, it means that other elements in the surroundings are also being considered. Therefore, given a fixation point, a DOM area is selected in order to identify every element under it. A distance score is given to each element based on its coverage, assuming a Gaussian distribution. The fixation impact is computed using this distance and also incorporating a time dimension, which means the fixation duration.

A methodology to extract salient web objects was developed by Velásquez et al. This methodology started with the analysis of plain text for identifying the *Website Keywords*, defined as *"word or possibly set of words that is used by visitors in their search process and characterizes the content of a given web page or web site"* [10]. Afterwards, the methodology was extended, defining a *web object* as *"any structured group of words or multimedia resource within a web page that has metadata to describe its content"* and a *Website Keyobject* as *"the web object or group of web objects that attracts web users' attention and that characterizes the content of a given web page or web site.*" Thus the main objective of the methodology turned into identifying *Website Keyobjects* instead of *Website Keywords* [9]. One problem presented in the methodology was the application of a survey for collecting information about user preferences, thus acquiring subjective results. To solve this problem, eye-tracking technology was incorporated, with the result that the time spent on each object was able to be extracted in a more precise and objective way [8].

Dimpfel and Morys in [2] used quantitative features from EEG to analyze five websites and an eye-tracking device was added, mainly for tracking gaze movements. These features first tried to measure attention and activation and then results were compared with a typical survey. The results show that using EEG features can be helpful in website analysis, but more studies are needed to confirm if this kind of research could be helpful in other scenarios, such as advertising.

Khushaba et al. [5] have been researching consumer neuroscience, in particular, user preferences using EEG and ET data. Their studies aim to find interdependencies among the EEG signals from cortical regions in a decision-making environment, and also a way to quantify the importance of different product features such as shape, color, texture, etc., in these decisions. Results showed there was a clear and significant change in the EEG power spectral activities taking place mainly in the frontal, temporal, and occipital regions when participants indicated their preferences.

3   Proposed Approach

The main goal of this study is to investigate salient Web object identification using different biological features that we describe in this section. In particular, we propose a comparison of eye gaze, pupil dilation and electroencephalogram features for identifying these relevant Web objects.

3.1   Web Object Identification

The initial element of analysis is the *web object*, which is defined as any combination of DOM elements that comprises an idea or a concept. For example, the combination between an image and an adjacent text paragraph could represent a defined block on which the user focuses his attention. The decision of using an aggregated representation and not the original DOM elements resides in our observation that *(a)* DOM objects are usually too small to satisfy the level of granularity the visual attention provides. Since fixation usually encompasses a set of elements, *(b)* using an aggregated representation provides a better understanding of the user interest, as the level of information that can be extracted from the semantic combination is richer.

The task of grouping DOM elements into web objects is not a trivial process, since several criteria could be used, leading to different sets. In our case, the selection task consists of presenting all the Web pages in the Web site to the expert in a sequential order. For each page, the expert is asked to arrange the elements into groups, and write down a unique identifier. The criteria for grouping is left to the expert, therefore no specific requirement is requested. Finally, through a DOM manipulation process, the web object is fully identified and its characteristics, such as size and position, are extracted.

3.2   Comparison Measures

There are several ways to estimate and rank which elements capture the attention of users, such as post-navigation surveys and questionnaires. Although these approaches are easy to perform, they do not provide a robust response because each user has different perceptions for each web element, hence, these kinds of responses are not representative of the real degree of relevance a user gave to each Web object.

An experiment was performed where an eye-tracking device was used to capture subjects' gaze movements and measure pupil size. In parallel we included the brain signal recording with an electroencephalogram device. Thus, it allowed us to have a triple data stream of biological signals.

As we collected the raw data, we extracted relevant features included in the state of the art for providing an objective comparison. For each data type it is possible to obtain several features that we discuss below.

Eye Gaze Measures. We used a type of eye tracking that allowed us to obtain a reliable spectrum of the visual activity for each Web page and for each Web element. Then, having this recording as a stream of data with an associated time component, we identified interest points, formally called *fixations*, which consist of periods of time in which the user was focused on a defined point. Each fixation is preceded and followed by a *saccade*, which is a transition between elements.

As a quantitative metric for fixation time, we followed the approach by Buscher et al. [1], namely the *mean fixation impact* (MFI). In that sense, we take into account that as human vision has a narrow window of high acuity, called *fovea*, when fixating on a specific area, the user is also gathering information from its surroundings. If the user is focusing on a Web object, attention resources are also being distributed to other elements as well. To capture that phenomenon, it is assumed that the attention allocation follows a Gaussian distribution of volume 1. This forms a circle around the fixation point and for all Web elements that intersect, an attention score is computed.

One particular element can receive attention from several fixations during a Web session, so the score is defined as the addition of all the contributions. This represents the attention based on an information foraging task on a specific page. Formally, given F_{pu} the set of fixations the user u produced on page p, the aggregated fixation impact for the Web object o is

$$I(o,p) = \sum_{u \in U} \sum_{f \in F_{pu}} \Phi(f,o) \tag{1}$$

where $\Phi(f, o)$ computes the proportion of attention based on the Gaussian distribution for a given fixation f on the element o.

Pupil Dilation Measures. Pupil size has been related with different cognitive processes since it is closely linked with the sympathetic and parasympathetic systems. For instance, Hess et al. [4] studied the relation of pupil size and mental activity in simple problem solving and Goldinger et al. [3] studied this response related with memory retrieval, among others.

Since it is not a straightforward task to define a measure that can express all the underlying patterns present in pupil size, we used two measures based on studies of pupil size and its relationships.

- **mean pupil size:** This metric is calculated as the mean of pupil size while subjects are fixating their gaze on a particular web object. Then, for each object a grand average considering all subjects is calculated. This measure indicates a level of pupil size for each object and can lead to different interpretations according to object characteristics, for example, it would be different if the object corresponds to plain text or an image.
- **mean delta indicator:** A pupil size versus time wave is generated when users browse the Web page. This signal can be described as a smooth continuous curve. In most cases, this curve has a unique maximum and minimum and the difference between them, called *delta indicator*, can show a strong or soft biological reaction depending on its value. A possible interpretation of this measure can be the arousal level, which means that if there is a large *delta indicator* it could indicate that an object provokes a higher level of attention in users. As well as mean pupil size, the *delta indicator* is calculated for each object considering a grand average among all users.

Electroencephalogram Measures. We include brain activity analysis by means of an EEG recording. For each object, a mean EEG signal is calculated and transformed into different parameters. In order to use brain activity as a measure for identifying user interest of each Web object, we propose the following features:

- **Frequency Band Features:** A useful way to analyze EEG waves is to separate them into different frequency bands. A possible way is to use *Wavelet Transform*, in which each of these bands coincide with the standard EEG frequency bands (*Delta* $0 - 4$ Hz, *Theta* $4 - 8$ Hz, *Alpha* $8 - 16$ Hz, *Beta* $16 - 32$ Hz, *Gamma* $32+$ Hz). Then for each band the energy, RMS and power were computed.
- **Typical Statistics:** Mean, variance and standard deviation was calculated for each object signal, in order to analyze if these values could be useful as a quantifier of users' attention, focus or interest in objects.

3.3 Research Questions

In order to compare the previously-defined features, we will consider the MFI as a baseline for comparison, due to its relevance as a proxy of user attention [1].

As we anticipate, for establishing an objective comparison between our baseline and the other features, we propose the following research questions:

1. **Which features can be discarded due to low correlation with the baseline feature, and which ones could be considered the most similar?**
2. **Among the most similar features, what are the differences regarding Web object type and structure?**

4   Experimental Setting

In order to obtain the data, an experiment was performed considering different aspects that allowed the reproduction of user Web browsing, while monitoring and recording eye gaze position, pupil dilation and EEG. This experimental stage took place at the Neurosystems Laboratory of the Faculty of Medicine of the University of Chile.

Participants. We used 20 healthy subjects, 3 females and 17 males aged between 22 and 25 years old (mean $= 24.2$, variance $= 1.64$). All subjects declared having normal or corrected-to-normal vision and did not have any neurological or psychiatric illness. All participants had to sign an informed consent approved by the *Ethical Committee of the Faculty of Medicine of the University of Chile*.

Design. We used a website adaptation based on an MBA program website offered by the University of Chile. Thirty-two web pages containing 359 objects were transformed to images. Objects were extracted according to the process described in subsection 3.1. Each image was divided depending on its length to generate sub-pictures of 1600 x 900 pixels. The experiment consisted of a website simulation made up of images, where subjects could move below, above and forward at will. The instruction that was given was **Browse the site freely, with no time limits (minimum nor maximum) on each page. Use the keyboard up and down arrows for scrolling and right arrow to show the next page**.

Instrumentation. Image presentation was controlled by the *Experiment Builder* software by *SR Research*. Pictures were displayed on a 32″ LG screen located in the experimental room, at a distance of 80 cms from the subject. Pupil size and gaze position was recorded using an *EyeLink 1000* eye tracker by *SR Research*, this device recorded both eyes at a rate of 500 Hz during all the experiment. Subjects' heads were adjusted by a chin support that helped to keep the head steady. For brain activity data, the *BioSemi Active 2* EEG system was used at a 2000 Hz sampling rate. 32 scalp electrodes were placed according to the $10 - 20$ international system, in addition to 8 external electrodes placed in the ocular and mastoid zone. The experimental room had no light on during recording sessions.

5   Results and Discussion

Once the data was fully acquired, some treatments were performed in order to answer the research questions proposed in 3.3. This section describes this treatment and gives a solution to those questions and the respective discussion.

Data Pre-processing and Transformation. The eye tracking and EEG data were preprocessed separately. For the eye-tracking data, the pupil dilation signal was taken and preprocessed by linearly interpolating blinks and fixing saccade offsets. Additionally, a low-pass filter of 2 Hz was used to remove noise. Ocular positioning was used to determine what object was being seen and the time spent on each one.

For the EEG data, first of all, the sampling rate was reduced from 2000 to 500 Hz, for synchronization with the eye-tracking data. Then the data was filtered with a $1 - 60$ Hz bandpass filter. Blinks, saccades and other irregularities were removed using the Matlab toolbox Eeglab.

Considering a time window of 300 ms for the minimum fixation, a mean signal was calculated for each object. This was done for both pupil dilation and EEG signal (for the average of the 32 scalp electrode signals). As mentioned in 3.2 a series of features were obtained for these signals: Merging the Web object identification and the eye tracking and EEG data allowed us to characterize each object according to the eye gaze, pupil dilation and EEG features. Particularly, for EEG frequency band features, the Daubechies-5 wavelet function in addition to a 6 level decomposition were used, in order to have 6 scales of details (d1-d6) and a final approximation (a6), since the sampling rate was set at 500 Hz.

RQ1 - Feature Comparison. The set of Web elements defined for the study Web site was arranged in decreasing order according to their MFI values. Buscher et al. used this feature as a proxy for users' visual attention, thus based on this evidence, we can have a list of ordered Web elements as a comparison baseline. In this sense, it is important to say that every object within the complete Web site was considered unique. That is, if object $ID1$ was present on pages 1, 2, and 3, in the baseline list this object would appear three times, together with its respective impact value and page. In the end the baseline list consisted of 1014 elements.

In the same way, for each object we computed the proposed features and proceeded to order them without considering objects with respective EEG feature values equal to 0. We also noticed that sorting elements decreasingly, yielded no relationship at all, whereas the increasing sorting had *high* levels of similitude with the baseline for some variables. Then, to obtain a comparison measure, we took the first 100 objects of both baseline and EEG features, and counted the repeated objects.

Accordingly, we found EEG-based features that allow the identification of approximate users' attention in a similar way to the MFI. There were also variables that did not have any relation with the baseline, which were then discarded for further analysis, for example the *mean*.

We performed an analogous procedure for the pupil dilation features, *mean pupil size* and *mean delta* of each object, finding that these variables could not represent users' attention in the same way as the baseline, having no correlation with it at all. Thus, pupil size variables were discarded as well. In Table 1 is an example set of features compared with the baseline, where variables can be seen with both high and low correlation to it.

Table 1. Example of EEG and ET feature comparison performance

Feature	γ Power	γ Energy	γ RMS	MeanEEG	Var	DeltaInd	MeanPupil
Matching	74	79	80	2	79	32	5

From not discarded features, we chose those that could represent in a better way relations with the MFI. In the previous analysis, *Energy*, *RMS* and *Power* features for all bands have analogous numbers of salient web objects compared with our baseline. Nevertheless, it is possible to observe that the *RMS of Gamma band* have a slightly better performance in most of the cases. Another relevant feature is the *EEG Variance* which shows good performance too.

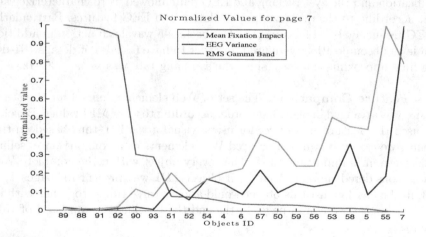

Fig. 1. Normalized values of *Mean fixation impact*, *EEG Variance* and *RMS of Gamma band* for page 7.

For comparing, graphs were constructed to show how the features behave versus our baseline. These graphs depict feature values per ID object on a particular page, while for display purposes we just included 20 objects as a maximum and range normalized values in [0,1]. Figure 1 shows the graph for MFI, *EEG Variance*, and *RMS of Gamma band* for page 7. As seen, objects are in descending order according to MFI values. A negative correlation exists between baseline

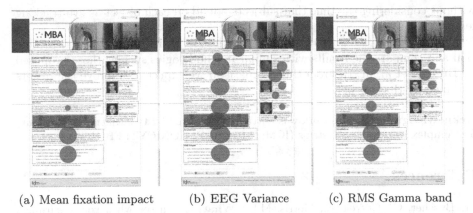

(a) Mean fixation impact   (b) EEG Variance   (c) RMS Gamma band

Fig. 2. Attention maps for selected features for page 7.

features and the others (R = −0.41 for *EEG Variance* and R = −0.61 for *RMS of Gamma band*). This finding could suggest that the longer subjects view a web object, that is, the more attention given, the less brain signal disturbance appears. This fact can be supported with evidence from [6], where it was found that a lower signal amplitude level is related to an attention/learning state.

RQ2 - Web Objects Difference Analysis. We constructed attention maps for each feature under study, thus the differences between them can be graphically observed. The way to build the attention map is to depict a red circle on each web object, where the bigger the circle is, the more attention was attracted to it. Since *EEG Variance* and *RMS of Gamma band* has a negative correlation with MFI a conversion was made, in which small values in *EEG Variance* and *RMS of Gamma band* correspond to large circles on maps.

Figure 2 shows attention maps. The MFI map presents more attention on web objects with text as we expected, because it is necessary to spend more time to get an idea about them, unlike with pictures. However, if we look at the *EEG Variance* and *RMS of Gamma band* maps, we can observe that pictures and text objects have a similar amount of attention. This evidence could suggest that these features are a proxy of attention independent of the amount of time spent on web objects.

6   Conclusion and Future Work

In this work we studied the relationship between EEG and eye-tracking features in order to improve and obtain a more objective method of salient web object identification. We conducted an experiment where EEG and eye-tracking data were recorded while subjects were surfing on a web site. Then, features were extracted and compared in order to determine which was more closely related to our baseline feature, *mean fixation impact*. The results suggest that *Gamma band RMS* and the *EEG variance* features can help to identify salient objects without considering the time that subjects spend on each object as eye-tracking features do.

As future work we want to use EEG features for salient web object identification and compare the results with similar methodologies such as those proposed by Buscher et al. in [1]. From this comparison we expect to improve the results obtained by that author.

Acknowledgments. This work was partially supported by the Millennium Institute on Complex Engineering Systems (ICM: P-05-004-F, CONICYT: FBO16).

References

1. Buscher, G., Cutrell, E., Morris, M.R.: What do you see when you're surfing?: using eye tracking to predict salient regions of web pages. In: Proceedings of the SIGCHI Conference on Human Factors in Computing Systems, pp. 21–30. ACM (2009)
2. Dimpfel, W., Morys, A.: Quantitative objective assessment of websites by neurocode-tracking in combination with eye-tracking. Journal of Behavioral and Brain Science **4**, 384–395 (2014)
3. Goldinger, S.D., Papesh, M.H.: Pupil dilation reflects the creation and retrieval of memories. Current Directions in Psychological Science **21**(2), 90–95 (2012)
4. Hess, E.H., Polt, J.M.: Pupil size in relation to mental activity during simple problem-solving. Science **143**(3611), 1190–1192 (1964)
5. Khushaba, R.N., Wise, C., Kodagoda, S., Louviere, J., Kahn, B.E., Townsend, C.: Consumer neuroscience: Assessing the brain response to marketing stimuli using electroencephalogram (eeg) and eye tracking. Expert Systems with Applications **40**(9), 3803–3812 (2013)
6. Li, X., Hu, B., Zhu, T., Yan, J., Zheng, F.: Towards affective learning with an eeg feedback approach. In: Proceedings of the First ACM International Workshop on Multimedia Technologies for Distance Learning, pp. 33–38. ACM (2009)
7. Pastor, M.C., Bradley, M.M., Löw, A., Versace, F., Moltó, J., Lang, P.J.: Affective picture perception: emotion, context, and the late positive potential. Brain research **1189**, 145–151 (2008)
8. Velásquez, J.D.: Combining eye-tracking technologies with web usage mining for identifying website keyobjects. Engineering Applications of Artificial Intelligence **26**(5), 1469–1478 (2013)
9. Velásquez, J.D., Dujovne, L.E., LHuillier, G.: Extracting significant website key objects: A semantic web mining approach. Engineering Applications of Artificial Intelligence **24**(8), 1532–1541 (2011)
10. Velásquez, J.D., Weber, R., Yasuda, H., Aoki, T.: A methodology to find web site keywords. In: 2004 IEEE International Conference on e-Technology, e-Commerce and e-Service, EEE 2004, pp. 285–292. IEEE (2004)

Cognitive Task Classificaiton from Wireless EEG

Shuvo Kumar Paul, M.S.Q. Zulkar Nine, Mahady Hasan, and M. Ashraful Amin[(✉)]

Computer Vision and Cybernetics Group, CSE, Independent University Bangladesh,
Dhaka, Bangladesh
{shuvo.k.paul,engrbiruni}@gmail.com, mahadyh@yahoo.com,
aminmdashraful@iub.edu.bd

Abstract. Human brain uses a complex electro-chemical signaling pattern that creates our imagination, memory and self-consciousness. It is said that Electroencephalography better known as EEG contains signatures of various tasks that we perform. In this paper we study the possibility of categorizing tasks conducted by humans from EEG recordings. The novelty of this study mainly lies in the use of very cost effective consumer grade wireless EEG devices. Three cognitive tasks were considered: text reading and writing, Math problem solving and watching videos. Twelve subjects were used in this experiment. Initial features were calculated from Discrete Wavelet Transform (DWT) of raw EEG signals. After application of appropriate dimensionality reduction, Support Vector Machine (SVM) was used for classification of tasks. DWT + Kernel PCA with SVM based classifier showed 86.09 % accuracy.

Keywords: BCI · HCI · EEG · Signal processing · DWT

1   Introduction

Brain is by far the most complex structure known in the whole universe with its trillions of neural connections and their complex electro-chemical signaling. The secondary electrical field due to brain activity can be measured by Electroencephalographic (EEG) system. This micro-volt range temporal signal fascinated researchers over decades to understand the brain activity and it opens the opportunity to interact with machines by only using such signals.

Obermaier et al. [1] proposed the information transfer rate, given in bits per trial, to evaluate measurement in a brain–computer interface (BCI). Three subjects performed four motor-imagery (left hand, right hand, foot, and tongue) and one mental-calculation task. Classification of the electroencephalogram (EEG) patterns was based on band power estimates and hidden Markov models (HMMs). Hsu et al. [2] proposed an analysis system for single-trial classification of EEG data. They used SVM for the discriminant of wavelet-based AM features. Nigam and Graupe [3] presented a technique that uses a multistage non-linear pre-processing filter in combination with an Artificial Neural Network (ANN) for the automated detection of epilepsy. In another study Kannaathal et. al. [4] different types of entropies were used to analyze the same

© Springer International Publishing Switzerland 2015
Y. Guo et al. (Eds.): BIH 2015, LNAI 9250, pp. 13–22, 2015.
DOI: 10.1007/978-3-319-23344-4_2

dataset. Adaptive Neuro Fuzzy Inference System (ANFIS) was used for classification. Sadati et al. [5] used an Adaptive Neuro Fuzzy network (ANFN) to detect epileptic seizures. Subasi [6] used the Discrete Wavelet Transform (DWT) coefficients of normal and epileptic EEG segments in a modular neural network called Mixture of Experts (ME).

A hybrid framework that uses Fast Fourier transform based features in a DT classifier was presented by Polat and Guenes [7]. Srinivasan et al [8] proposed a neural-network-based automated epileptic EEG detection system which uses approximate entropy (ApEn) as the input feature.

In this work we acquired EEG signals using a consumer grade wireless EEG device from twelve subjects while they were asked to perform three tasks: i) reading and writing, ii) mathematical problem solving, and iii) vi) watching video. Our intention was to be able to discriminate the EEG signals according to the task performed. For this purpose first we calculated the features using Discrete Wavelet Transform (DWT) and then relevant features are extracted using dimensionality reduction techniques. Then finally classification is performed using SVM.

2   Implementation and Experimentation

2.1   The Device

This experiment used MindWave headset [16], a consumer grade wireless EEG device. Fig. 1 provides an illustration of the headset. Adjustable headset is used to fix the device over the head. Sensor tip is dry and easy to use and suitable to extract signals from Fp1 point of the brain. The device is completely safe and designed with passive biosensors. A reference sensor is placed in A1 position which act as a reference sensor for the main sensor.

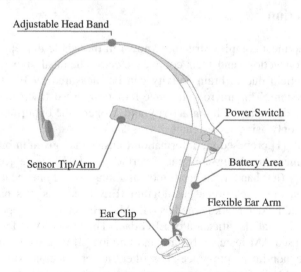

Fig. 1. MindWave Headset [16]

2.2   Experimental Setup and Data Collection

Twelve student aged between 20 to 24 years volunteered and participated in the data collection. We used a controlled environment to perform our experiments. For this reason we have used a closed room at the Independent University, Bangladesh.

EEG data is collected using our software that is able to properly synchronize the audio-visual event with the EEG signal supplied by the MindWave headset. For each user, data is recorded for three tasks: i) text reading (from LED monitor) and writing (using computer keyboard), solving math (using pen & paper), and watching video.

First the subject read a Wikipedia article then he/she writes a summary. Then he read an online news and writes a summary.

In the math solving part he/she is given a 2x3 by 3x3 matrix multiplication problem.

In the video viewing section they were shown two videos one is a video about Tesla from TED talks and other is a short documentary about nature.

After data is collected for each subject first task is to preprocess data and make it suitable for feature extraction and machine learning applications.

2.3   Preprocessing: Equal Interval Patch Creation

First each subjects EEG recording is segmented into three different categories, text reading and writing EEG, math EEG and video EEG. Then each of the segments are farther subdivided into several equal interval patches. EEG signals contain highly dense temporal data. To extract detailed features from the signal we logically divide the signal into patches as shown in Fig. 2. Then Features are calculated from each of the patch.

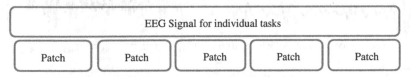

Fig. 2. EEG sample is segmented into patches

2.4   Feature Extraction: Frequency Domain

Fourier Transform is very popular strategy to extract features in the frequency domain, however, it does not work well on non-stationary signals like EEG. Thus we used a multi-resolution analysis called Discrete Wavelet Transform (DWT). The main feature of DWT is multi-scale representation of a function. By using wavelets, given function can be analyzed at various levels of resolution. An illustration is provided in fig. 3.

DWT can analyze different frequencies in different resolutions. It can provide good time resolution and poor frequency resolution at high frequencies, and good frequency resolution and poor temporal resolution at low frequencies. The main principle of wavelet transform is to split the signal into a number of signals. Those split signals are the same signals as the original ones, however, they are corresponding to different frequency bands. In our experiment we split the signal into eight different frequency bands. Then we have computed the band power of each signal. Fig. 4 shows such representations for a single patch.

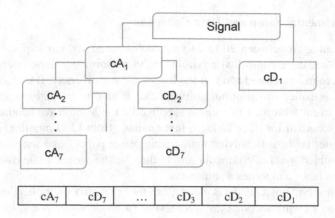

Fig. 3. Discrete wavelet transform

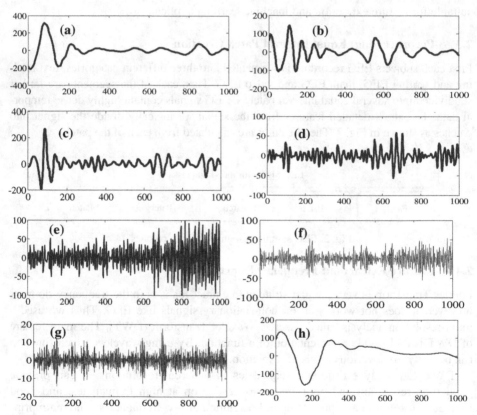

Fig. 4. (a) Detail D7, (b) Detail D6, (c) Detail D5, (d) Detail D4, (e) Detail D3, (f) Detail D2, (g) Detail D1, and (h) Approximation A7.

Then the band power of each frequency bin is computed using Parserval's theorem which states that energy of the distorted signal can be partitioned at different levels. Mathematically it can be expressed as

$$ED_i = \sum_{j=1}^{n} ||D_{ij}||^2 \tag{1}$$

$$EA_l = \sum_{j=1}^{n} ||A_{ij}||^2 \tag{2}$$

Where i = 1 .... l. is the wavelet decomposition levels. ED_i is the energy at decomposition level i and EA_l is the energy of the approximate at decomposition level l. Finally, a 5k dimensional feature vector space is computed whose reduced dimensional version is used later to train a non-linear classifier. Table 1 shows band power of each of the decomposition level as shown in figure 4.

Table 1. Computed Band power in each decomposition level

Decomposition	Computed Band Power
A7	3976.14812830952
D1	6631.52398523541
D2	1719.86749363561
D3	2418.81393945169
D4	239.709913971939
D5	926.077564745012
D6	255.730639344208
D7	18.4974850194762

2.5 Relevant Feature Extraction: Dimensionality Reduction

Though DWT is a good way to capture multiresolution characteristics of a signal, often it comes with a lot of irrelevant features. Thus it is a common practice to use dimensionality reduction techniques to extract relevant and useful features from DWT representation of a signal.

Along with traditional linear techniques like – PCA [9], factor analysis, classical scaling, a rich variety of non-linear approaches have been proposed in the last few decades. We have investigated performance of seven different dimensionality reduction techniques – PCA [9], Kernel PCA [10], Isomap [11], Local Linear Embedding (LLE) [12], Laplacian Eigen map [13], Sammon mapping [14], and Local Linear Coordination (LLC) [15].

2.6 Signal Classification

For signal classification we have used K-Nearest Neighbor (KNN) classifier and Support Vector Machine (SVM). EEG signal for each data points in the dataset were vectorized to 750 dimensions. Then seven methods – PCA, Kernel PCA, Isomap, LLE, Laplacian Eigenmap, Sammon mapping, LLC were implemented and optimized for the task.

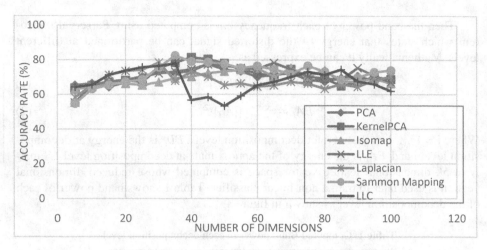

Fig. 5. Classification rates of various dimensionality reduction methods against reduced number of dimension in range $5 \leq dimension \leq 100$ with SVM.

3   Performance Evaluation

Individual has his/her own brain signal patterns and an overall system that can classify same task of different people is not suitable. So we have created classifier that can classify single person's brain signals. To do so we have to train each classifier every time when the cognitive tasks of a new subject needs to be classified. Then we performed a ten-fold cross validation. Average of all those accuracy for each type of model is shown in the Table 2.

Table 2. Overall accuracy of each model

Models	Avg. Accuracy (%)
KPCA + SVM	**86.09**
Laplacian Eigenmap + SVM	84.14
LLE + SVM	83.86
PCA + SVM	83.41
Isomap + SVM	82.40
Sammon Mapping + SVM	82.36
LLC + SVM	82.08
PCA + KNN	73.12
KPCA + KNN	70.38
Sammon Mapping + KNN	69.93
LLE + KNN	69.41
Isomap + KNN	69.30
LLC + KNN	68.71
Laplacian Eigenmap + KNN	67.48

It can be seen that kernel PCA with SVM shows the highest accuracy. As we can see that accuracy for the SVM models show superior performance than the models with KNN classifier. One important aspect of the observation is that SVM can classify better than KNN because it projects the data in higher dimensional Hilbert space where classification is simpler then the lower dimensional feature space. Unlike the KNN that uses only neighborhood information to classify new instances.

Accuracy is not the only measure of how good a classifier can work. We can use confusion matrix to estimate false positives and true negatives, so that we can really understand, how efficient the model is. Here we have generated confusion matrix for all SVM based models as they have the highest accuracy over the KNN based models. Table 3 to Table 9 shows the confusion matrices. We have total 1465 instances for text processing, 1629 instances for math solving and 2794 instances for video watching for all subjects.

We can see the PCA and SVM based models have overall 83.41% accuracy, however, it misclassified 290 text processing instances as math solving instances and 86 as watching video instances. It can be seen that misclassification increased between text processing and math solving instances. It also misclassified 278 math solving instances as text processing instances. However, the classification error between watching video and math solving is minimal. This is also true for watching video and text processing.

Table 3. Confusion Matrix of PCA+SVM model

	Text	Math	Video
Text	1089	290	86
Math	278	1275	76
Video	108	138	2548

KPCA + SVM model have shown highest accuracy. If we analyze the confusion matrix we can see that it classifies text, math and video with higher accuracy. Still its confusion increases between the text processing and math problem solving. False positive and true negatives are in much better shape.

Table 4. Confusion Matrix of KPCA+SVM model

	Text	Math	Video
Text	1172	198	95
Math	155	1389	85
Video	127	165	2502

Table 5. Performance measure of Isomap+SVM model

	Text	Math	Video
Text	980	311	174
Math	158	1385	86
Video	179	134	2481

The model with isomap + SVM is not that much efficient in text classification it misclassified 311 text processing instances to Math solving instances. However, the confusion between the math and watching video is minimum. This might be the reason that watching videos are more relaxing and solving math problems need more conscious awareness of brain.

Table 6. Performance measure of LLE+SVM model

	Text	Math	Video
Text	1026	361	78
Math	203	1403	23
Video	162	129	2503

Table 6 shows the confusion matrix of the model with LLE and SVM which shows that it misclassified 361 text processing instances to Math solving instances. The confusion between the math and watching video is minimum like the previous one. However, it has greater accuracy rate than the isomap model.

Table 7. Confusion Matrix of Laplacian Eigenmap+SVM model

	Text	Math	Video
Text	1198	198	69
Math	210	1368	51
Video	213	198	2383

Table 7 shows the confusion matrix of Laplacian Eigenmap and SVM which has overall accuracy of 84.16% which is actually the second highest accuracy among the models. However, its misclassification increases in the cases between Math and Text, and Video and text. It also shown poor result in classifying watching video.

Table 8. Confusion Matrix of Sammon mapping+SVM model

	Text	Math	Video
Text	889	511	65
Math	398	1208	23
Video	29	18	2747

The confusion matrix of the model with Sammon Mapping and SVM is shown in Table 8. Sammon Mapping model has overall accuracy of 82.36 %. However, it has a high misclassification rate between text processing and math solving instances. It misclassified 511 instances of the text processing instance as math problem solving. However, its video classification rate is high and it can be seen that it confuses only a nominal amount of watching video instances with text processing and Math solving.

Table 9. Confusion Matrix of LLC+SVM model

	Text	Math	Video
Text	1142	165	158
Math	189	1278	162
Video	206	181	2407

The confusion of LLC + SVM model is shown in table 9. It has merely similar overall accuracy as the Sammon Mapping + SVM model, however, its misclassification rates moderately lower than the previous one. Misclassification is higher between Watching Video instance and text processing instances. As a whole it is better model than the Sammon Mapping + SVM model, even if they have same overall accuracy.

4   Conclusion and Future Work

Even a decade ago it might have deemed as a fairy-tale to even think about controlling something using only our mind. However, research in BCI has shown that it is possible if we can correctly classify the brain signals. Individual brain signals does not have any meaning. It just the raw electro-chemical signal transfer between the regions of brain. However, this signals can generate a pattern which can be extracted using a non-invasive sensor. This sensor only captures the signal pattern on the brain scalp. We can use a supervised learning algorithm and train it to learn the specific pattern for task assigned to the subject. We can use that trained model to classify the task again when the subject performs the task. To do so we asked our subjects to do three different tasks like text processing, math solving and watching video. We proposed a novel model that can classify those tasks with high accuracy. As high temporal data density exist in EEG signals, we need a proper dimensionality reduction technique that can address the problem of the curse of dimensionality. To do so we have tested seven dimensionality reduction techniques and two non-linear classifier – SVM and KNN. Then we have evaluated their performance based on accuracy and confusion matrix. Our experiment shows that Kernel PCA + SVM model shows the highest accuracy and with a sound confusion matrix with low confusion rates between the tasks.

Recently as the advent of non-invasive dry sensor EEG devices opens new opportunities for research in the BCI field with low operational budget. Because of the low cost and easy to use properties of the devices in can be easily used to operate with mobile apps. It opens the research to correctly classify the brain signals, so that it can generate commands with the brain signal. Various mobile apps controlled by classifying the brain signal is possible to design.

Acknowledgements. This work is supported by a grant from Independent University, Bangladesh.

References

1. Obermaier, B., Neuper, C., Guger, C., Pfurtscheller, G.: Information transfer rate in a five-class brain-computer interface. IEEE Transactions on Neural Systems and Rehabilitation Engineering **9**(3), 283–288 (2001)
2. Hsu, W.Y., Lin, C.H., Hsu, H.J., Chen, P.H., Chen, I.R.: Wavelet-based envelope features with automatic EOG artifact removal: Application to single-trial EEG data. Expert Systems with Applications **39**(3), 2743–2749 (2012)

3. Nigam, V.P., Graupe, D.: A neural-network-based detection of epilepsy. Neurological Research **26**(1), 55–60 (2004)
4. Kannathal, N., Choo, M.L., Acharya, U.R., Sadasivan, P.K.: Entropies for detection of epilepsy in EEG. Computer methods and programs in biomedicine **80**(3), 187–194 (2005)
5. Sadati, N., Mohseni, H.R., Maghsoudi, A.: Epileptic seizure detection using neural fuzzy networks. In: 2006 IEEE International Conference on Fuzzy Systems. IEEE (2006)
6. Subasi, A.: EEG Signal classification using wavelet feature extraction and a mixture of expert model. Expert Systems with Applications, pp. 1084–1093 (2007)
7. Polat, K., Güneş, S.: Classification of epileptic form EEG using a hybrid systems based on decision tree classifier and fast Fourier transform. Applied Mathematics and Computation **32**(2), 625–631 (2007)
8. Srinivasan, V., Eswaren, C., Sriraam, N.: Approximate entropy-based epileptic EEG detection using artificial neural network. IEEE Transaction on Information Technology in Biomedicine **11**(3), 288–295 (2007)
9. Hotelling, H.: Analysis of a complex of statistical variables into principal components. Journal of Educational Psychology, 417–441 (1933)
10. Schölkopf, B., Smola, A., Müller, K.R.: Nonlinear component analysis as a kernel eigenvalue problem. Neural Computation, 1299–1319 (1998)
11. Balasubramanian, M., Schwartz, E.L.: The Isomap algorithm and topological stability. Science, 7 (2002)
12. Roweis, S.T., Lawrence, K.S.: Nonlinear dimensionality reduction by Locally Linear Embedding. Science **290**(5500), 2323–2326 (2000)
13. Belkin, M., Niyogi, P.: Laplacian eigenmaps and spectral techniques for embedding and clustering. NIPS **14** (2001)
14. Sammon, J.W.: A nonlinear mapping for data structure analysis. IEEE Transactions on computers **18**(5), 401–409 (1969)
15. The, Y.W., Roweis, S.T.: Automatic alignment of hidden representations. In: Advances in Neural Information Processing Systems, pp. 841–848 (2002)
16. MindWave Headset. Neurosky Inc., San Jose (2014). http://store.neurosky.com/products/mindwave-1 (accessed 3 Jan 2014)

Identifying the Computational Parameters Gone Awry in Psychosis

Gerit Pfuhl[1,2(✉)], Kristin Sandvik[2], Robert Biegler[2], and Håkon Tjelmeland[3]

[1] Department of Psychology, UiT the Artic University of Norway, Tromsø, Norway
gerit.pfuhl@uit.no
[2] Department of Psychology, Norwegian University of Science and Technology, Trondheim, Norway
[3] Department of Mathematical Sciences, Norwegian University of Science and Technology, Trondheim, Norway

Abstract. Probabilistic inference is assumed to be aberrant in deluded patients. Here, we present two novel tasks, designed to measure these computational parameters. Our shape precision task measures the precision of visual short term memory and perceived precision (confidence judgement). This provides a direct assessment of the prediction error. Our probability task is a modification of the "beads in a jar" task. Our version asks for probability estimates after each bead drawn. We derived the mathematical optimal solution and compared it to the estimates of the participants. 15 healthy subjects and 15 patients diagnosed with psychosis played the tasks. Results: patients think their memory is better than it actually is. Further, their probability judgment is worse than that of healthy controls. There was a strong correlation between perceived precision and the probability judgements. Thus, both tasks may measure the same underlying statistical inference mechanism – which is disturbed in deluded patients.

1 Introduction

Mental disorders are currently detectable only after onset of the pathology. This is due to the multidimensional nature of mental disorders insufficiently captured by current diagnosis criteria, i.e. multiple aetiologies converge on the same symptoms. Importantly, the underlying computational parameters causing the symptoms are just beginning to be unraveled. Among these computational parameters are those relevant to statistical inference. All sensory information is subject to measurement error, and patterns of sensory data often have multiple possible causes. Thus knowledge of the real world is imprecise and often ambiguous [1-4]. At least some of the parameters of the computations involved in interpreting sensory data must be relevant to the abnormal perceptions that are hallucinations and possibly also the abnormal beliefs that are delusions. The problem lies in identifying and measuring those computational parameters. We examine decision threshold, weighting of evidence, and the perceived precision of information. With our novel experimental tasks we try to measure whether prediction error and probability judgments are linked.

© Springer International Publishing Switzerland 2015
Y. Guo et al. (Eds.): BIH 2015, LNAI 9250, pp. 23–32, 2015.
DOI: 10.1007/978-3-319-23344-4_3

1.1 Prediction Errors and Types of Uncertainties

Fletcher & Frith [5], Pellicano & Burr [6] and van de Cruys et al. [7] all suggested that one relevant computational parameter is the perceived precision of sensory information, as compared to the real precision. The background to that idea is that a fundamental problem in making inferences about the world is to distinguish the effects of our own actions from the effects of other causes. A solution is to predict the effects of our own actions, and to attribute any large enough deviation from that prediction to other causes. Because the prediction itself can never be perfect, that deviation must be defined statistically: how large is the deviation compared to the expected variation in prediction? This may be expressed as Cohen's d: how many standard deviations is the current measurement from the expected average? That calculation depends on knowing those standard deviations, yet they are themselves estimates, and may not match reality. If the estimated standard deviations of the data are too small, then perceived precision is greater than real precision. If people believe their predictions to be more precise than they really are, then normal deviations seem large compared to the expected variation, and therefore surprising.

[5-7] all proposed that systematic distortion in perceived precision is linked to either schizophrenia or autism, but they differ in which psychopathology they link with which kind of distortion, and they differ in how they link the distortion in perceived precision with the symptoms of the psychopathology. [5] explain the same symptoms as do [6], but by reference to opposite biases in the same parameter. [5] and [7] agree on the bias, but disagree on which symptoms follow. We have not noticed these authors substantially disagreeing on the interpretation of specific data, yet they disagree fundamentally on theory. That suggests to us that more of the same kind of data will not help much, but that a somewhat different approach might be useful. That approach requires a closer look at kinds of prediction error and kinds of uncertainty.

We can conceive of four different kinds of prediction errors, arising from applying either a scalar or a statistical metric to either sensorimotor or internally generated information.

1. A sensorimotor error in a scalar metric, for example units of distance, direction, force etc., can be used to recalibrate erroneous estimations or to correct movements.
2. A scalar prediction error in units of how much an event is liked or disliked directly drives learning, i.e. it determines how much the weight of an association is changed, in certain models of learning [8, 9].
3. The statistical effect size of a sensorimotor prediction error is a measure of how surprising the error is. A sufficiently surprising error could indicate the influence of unaccounted external factors in instrumental learning. For example, an arrow going wider off the mark than usual could be a sign of an unnoticed cross breeze somewhere along its flight path.
4. The statistical effect size of prediction error in liking, of how surprisingly enjoyable or aversive an event is, indicates whether new learning is advisable. This effect depends on the corresponding scalar changes, motivation, and on the precision of

knowledge. For example, if in the last 5 years a patch of blueberries yielded 1 ± 0.1 kg/day, then a reduction to 0.7 kg on the first day of the new harvesting season suggests something has changed for the worse, future yields may also be reduced, and a new food source may be needed. If the patch yielded 1 ± 0.5 kg/day, then a reduction to 0.7 kg is within normal variation and a poor predictor of yields later in the season. The meaning of the same scalar change depends on the precision of knowledge. And if the blueberries suddenly make you ill, that could also be a good reason to eat something else.

The need to distinguish between the scalar and the statistical metric of prediction error is well established [2, 10-14].

The need to distinguish surprising change from normal variation led Yu and Dayan [14] to introduce the distinction between unexpected and expected uncertainty. Later work further divided expected uncertainty into risk and parameter estimation uncertainty, and other researchers added more. We know of six different kinds of uncertainty: 1) risk or how well can I predict an individual event; 2) parameter estimation uncertainty or how precisely do I know the probability of a class of events; 3) unexpected uncertainty or what is the probability that a class of events has changed suddenly; 4) volatility, or does the probability of events change often; 5) structural uncertainty or do I know the processes that generate probabilities; and 6) sample space ignorance, or do I know all possible outcomes [12,14,15].

We have found no data or discussion of whether a bias to perceive predictions as more precise than they really are would generalise to parameter estimation uncertainty, the closest analogue to precision in this list. If the bias does generalise, then we should expect that people who show this bias in predictions of liking or of sensorimotor information would also be biased to believe they know probabilities more precisely than sample size justifies. That in turn would bias them to see changes in the probabilities that generate observed events. We test this idea by measuring the perceived precision of memory in the sensory domain, and correlating that to a bias to perceive a change in probability.

1.2   Improving the Beads Task – Measuring Parameter Estimation Uncertainty and Unexpected Uncertainy

Jumping to conclusions, as measured by the beads task, correlates with being prone to delusions [16,17]. Participants are asked to imagine that beads are drawn one at a time, with replacement, from one of two jars. One contains, for example, 85 black and 15 white beads, the other 15 black and 85 white beads. In the simplest, draws to decisions version of the beads task, participants can ask for another bead to be drawn until they are sure they have enough evidence to work out from which jar the beads came. Decisions based on fewer beads are associated with being prone to delusions. What change in which computational parameters leads to those quick decisions is still being debated. Moritz et al. [18] also asked their participants to provide a subjective probability estimate after each bead was drawn, and discovered that patients and controls found the evidence equally persuasive; they changed their probability estimates at the same rate. The patients, though, needed less extreme probability levels to feel sure they knew from which jar the beads came. Moritz et al. thus conclude that patients differ from controls in needing less evidence to adopt a belief.

Moutoussis et al. [19] interpret such data differently. Their analysis relies on developing mathematical models of the decision making process. They propose two paths to an early decision: first, the more someone dislikes the effort of taking in new information, compared to being wrong, the earlier that person will make a decision. Thus if patients require less extreme probabilities than controls to decide that they know from which jar the beads came at, that could reflect a greater dislike of sampling, rather than a difference in an explicit threshold. Second, there is a noise term which represents the tendency to choose randomly between saying there are more black beads, more white beads, or to continue sampling. Greater noise increases the chances of deciding early. The authors [19] found that patients differed from controls only in the best fitting models having larger noise terms. However, their definition of the noise term predicts that if there were more than two jars, noise should cause even faster decisions. Yet when [18] tried that, the change in procedure abolished the difference between patients and controls, instead of magnifying the difference as predicted by applying the model of [19].

Regardless of which of these computational biases leads people to jump to conclusions in the beads task, the changes in computational parameters we discussed can explain why people who are prone to delusions would accept beliefs that most would find implausible. However, none of these specific changes in computational parameters can explain the persistence of delusions. The proposed changes should lead to quick decisions no matter what the starting point. Patients should relatively easily abandon a delusion for another belief. Indeed, [20] found just such a pattern in a new version of the beads task. They presented participants with a series of 38 beads in which the first half of the sequence exactly mirrored the second half, as if the jar from which the beads were drawn had been switched halfway through. Yet, participants were told that all beads in the whole sequence came from the same jar. Those who nevertheless changed their belief regarding the source of the beads scored higher on a measure of delusional ideation. As those who are prone to delusions change their minds easily in this task, the reason why delusions are resistant to contradictory evidence must be sought elsewhere.

Meanwhile, pushing [20]'s procedure a bit further, it becomes possible to introduce unexpected uncertainty into the beads task and test whether choices in the beads task correlate with distortions in perceived precision. We told participants that the source of beads could change, but that we would switch the jar from which the beads were drawn in only some of the sequences. That allows us to measure both sensitivity to a change in probability, and bias to see such a change. In the sensorimotor domain, a bias to perceive change can be caused by believing predictions to be more precise than they really are. Measuring perceived precision directly lets us correlate it with bias to see change in our modified beads task. Further, in the sensorimotor domain, precision that is perceived to be greater than is justified makes each new piece of evidence more persuasive than it should be; probability estimates should change faster than is mathematically correct, and faster than in people who lack this bias. In the probability domain, if parameter estimation uncertainty is similarly biased, such that probabilities are thought to be known more precisely than is justified by the number of samples, then people with this bias would also have a lower threshold for believing that small variations indicate changes in the underlying probabilities. If the same processes were to bias parameter estimation uncertainty and the perceived precision of sensorimotor predictions, then [5] would be right in arguing that a single mechanism underlies the adoption of erroneous beliefs. High perceived precision in the sensorimotor domain should be accompanied by fast changes in subjective probability estimates in a beads task. Such fast changes were not found in the patients in [18], but the direct comparison has not yet been made. We present that here. A null result would suggest the existence of more than one statistical inference mechanism that is related to the adoption of delusions.

2   Methods

2.1   Participants and Procedure

15 patients diagnosed with schizophrenia (F20 or F22 according to DSM-IV, APA 1996) were recruited from the St. Olavs hospital, Trondheim. 15 age-matched healthy subjects were recruited for the control group. The study was approved by the regional ethical committee (REK-131107). We were interested in whether the performance in the beads task related to perceived precision measured with the precision task. We therefore administered both experimental tasks, lasting about 25 min with instructions. All participants did first the precision task before playing the beads task. For a thorough model fit in the beads task far more trials would have been needed. However, our aim here was to see whether these two novel task tap into similar cognitive mechanisms.

2.2   The Precision Task

We have examined how knowledge of precision and of probability affects optimal behaviour in cache search [23]. In the current task, we kept the probability constant since we were mainly interested in the precision of memory and how confident people judge their memory to be. On a computer screen a squiggly shape was displayed for 1 sec. The shape was drawn from a pool of 360 continuously modified shapes. After a retention interval of 3 seconds, a circle appears with 30 shapes uniformly aligned (see Fig. 1). The participant indicates his/her best estimate of which shape was shown by pointing at it. Thereafter the participant draws a confidence wedge centered at the best guess. We explained a priori that one gets only points if the wedge was wide enough to include the correct shape and one lost points for any surplus area. We measured the precision, the width of the confidence wedge, whether the wedge was wide enough (as proportion target included). There was also the option to go directly to the next trial if one had forgotten the shape. We provided feedback after each trial and a few demo trials to ensure a person understood the task. We examine whether the width of the confidence wedge is primarily controlled by perceived precision, which secondarily affects the proportion of targets included, or whether that proportion represents a decision criterion that secondarily affects the width of the confidence wedge.

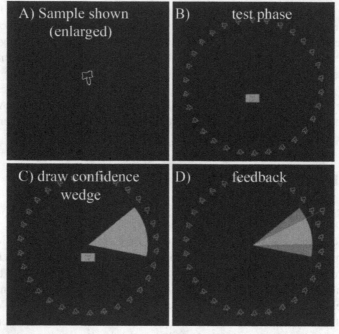

Fig. 1. Shape precision task. A) First a squiggly shape is shown. B) In the test phase one can either abort the trial or indicate which of the shapes comes closest to the one seen in the sample phase. C) The confidence interval is drawn and D) feedback provided with the correct shape and the excess area.

2.3   Modified Beads Task

The classical beads task present the subject with two jars A and B, filled with white and black beads. In jar A the fraction of white beads is p, whereas in jar B the fraction of white beads is 1-p. One bead at a time is drawn (with replacement) and presented to the participant. The task is to think about the underlying cause, i.e. from which jar the bead was drawn. As soon as one thinks to know the answer, one declares it. Thus the main outcome is the draws to decisions. The task has been modified to ask for a confidence judgment after each bead. We expand on this here.

In our version participants are asked to indicate their probability or belief that the drawn bead has come from jar A or B. This is done with the help of a slider bar, ranging from 0 = absolute sure it comes from jar A, to 1 = absolute sure it comes from jar B in 101 steps. There are two crucial aspects. First, participants had a maximum of 10 seconds for their decision. Second, we told them that the jar from which beads are drawn can change. This probability was q and we explained that in half of the trials the jar will change. 5 trials of 20 beads drawn (20 beads are 1 sequence) were played. The drawing was random and hence each participant received different sequences.

We derived a mathematical optimal solution of the task beforehand. Briefly, we modelled the optimal probabilities after having seen a bead drawn given that the jar from which the bead was drawn can change several times in one sequence. The optimal decision should be based on $P(x_n|z_1,...,z_n)$ where x_n is either jar A or jar B and z_n is either drawing a white or black ball, respectively. The optimal decision is to guess on jar A if $P(x_n = 0|z_1,...,z_n) > \frac{1}{2}$, and jar B otherwise. The probability of the jars changing is q. The prior distribution over q is $f(q)$. Thus, we have to estimate:

$$P(x_n|z_1,...,z_n) = \int_0^1 P(x_n|q,z_1,...,z_n)f(q|z_1,...,z_n)dq$$

This mathematical derivation of the optimal probability requires numerical integration (the code is freely available from the authors). We assumed in model 1 a uniform distribution of q, or being ignorant; and in model 2 we set the value to .04. This is equivalent to "for every bead there is a 50% chance of a change in jar" which was what we told participants.

Accordingly, we compared the participants' probability judgments to two models. We calculated the absolute difference between the participant's estimate and the models' value for each bead. That is, for each sequence we calculated the slope or difference in probability between the previous bead and the current bead. That was done for the theoretical models and for the estimates from the participant. We then calculated the differences. Finally, we averaged those values over the 20 beads and the 5 trials (Table 1). A positive difference represents an overestimation of the changes whereas a negative difference means an underestimation of the changes.

To investigate a group difference we used GLM with age and sex as nuisance regressors. Two patients did not do the beads task.

3   Results

Table 1 provides a summary of the patients diagnosed with psychosis (PP) and healthy controls (HC) performance in the two tasks.

Table 1. Demographics and performance in the two novel tasks

demographics			Shape precision task				beads task	
			precision in degrees	Confidence interval	Prop. target found	Conf/prec ision	Model 1 q ignorant	Model 2 (q=.04)(
	N	age (stdev)	(SE)	(SE)	(SE)	(SE)	(SE)	SE)
HC	15 (7 f)	24.13 (2.6)	26.68 (2.14)	23.6 (1.82)	.57 (.03)	6.04 (3.9)	-.021 (.016)	.134 (.012)
PP	15 (3 f)	24.93 (4.4)	45.1 (4.69)	29.91 (3.67)	.44 (.04)	2.55 (1.6)	.040 (.028)	.197 (.024)

3.1   Precision Task

Psychotic patients had a worse visual short-term memory than HC: $F(1,26) = 13.644$, $p = .001$, $\eta^2 = .344$. PP drew slightly larger confidence intervals but this was not significantly different from the HC group: $F(1,26) = 3.156$, $p = .087$, $\eta^2 = .108$. The target was more often included in HC than PP: $F(1,26) = 4.762$, $p = .038$, $\eta^2 = .155$. The PP lost points whereas HC had a positive gain, resulting in a large group difference: $F(1,26) = 8.095$, $p = .009$, $\eta^2 = .237$. Importantly, the ratio of confidence interval (perceived precision) to real precision differed significantly between the groups, $F(1,26) = 8.021$, $p = .009$, $\eta^2 = .0236$. Neither age nor sex were significant contributors in any of the five GLMs. The average difference between target and memory correlated with the average width of the confidence wedge ($r = .486$, $p = 0.007$) and with the proportion of targets included in confidence wedges ($r = -.518$, $p = .003$). The absolute values of these correlations did not differ ($t = -0.157$).

3.2   Modified Beads Task and Correlation with Precision Task

For model 1, which assumes an uniform distribution for the chance of the jar changing, the groups differed: $F(1,24) = 5.146$, $p = .033$, $\eta^2 = .177$. For model 2 which incorporates a belief of the jar changing according to our instructions, the groups did also differ, $F(1,24) = 6.756$, $p = .016$, $\eta^2 = .22$. All but three HC underestimated the slopes in model 1 whereas 7 of 13 PP overestimated the slope. This difference did not reach significance, $\chi^2 = 3.475$, $p = .062$. Next, we checked for each of the two groups whether their slopes were significantly different from those prescribed by the models. The probability judgment did not significantly differ from model 1 for both HC and PP group, independent t-tests, both p's > .1. However, both groups deviated strongly from model 2, HC: $t(1,14) = 11.217$, $p < .001$; PP: $t(1,12) = 8.672$, $p < .001$.

Finally, we looked at whether a participant's performance in the precision task was associated with the beads task performance. We found that a person's precision correlated with the probability judgment in the beads task, i.e. slope differences; model 1: Pearson's $r = .506$, $p = .006$, model 2: $r = .426$, $p = .024$. The confidence intervals made did also correlate with the probability judgments, model 1: $r = .538$, $p = .003$, and model 2: $r = .382$, $p = .045$. However, the ratio of confidence interval and precision did not correlate with the slopes, model 1: $r = -.199$, $p = .283$; model 2: $r = -.320$, $p = .080$. There was also a negative relationship between the probability judgments and the proportion of targets included and the gain, but it did not reach significance, smallest $p = .079$.

4   Discussion

We have developed two novel tasks with the aim to identify the cognitive mechanisms underlying psychosis and delusions. The precision task yielded a significant group difference with psychotic patients being worse at judging their own memory. The patients' confidence wedges suggest that patients think their memory is better than it actually is, yet to be sure of that we must consider whether the patients perhaps differ in the decision criterion they apply. If people with equally precise memory differ in the confidence they indicate because they differ in perceived precision, and the proportion of targets included is secondarily affected, then the correlation between precision and the size of the confidence wedge should be greater than the correlation between precision and the proportion of targets included. The lack of a difference does not let us decide this question.

In our modified beads task, we looked at probability judgment and parameter estimation uncertainty. We found that patients were less able to judge the optimal probabilities than controls. But despite our instructions, the fit for both groups was better for a model where one is ignorant of the probability that the jar changes. Further, there was a significant relationship between a participant's precision and confidence judgment in the precision task and the probability judgment in the beads task. This suggests that the two tasks, estimating perceived precision and judging probabilities given parameter estimation uncertainty, measure similar computational parameters in the human brain. That relationship should constrain future theorising over the contribution of cognitive biases to psychosis and delusion. As the example of the conflicting interpretations of the beads task illustrates [17-19], it is difficult to go beyond mere description when attempting to characterise parameters through only one task.

It would also help to extend the investigation to autistic spectrum disorders, to find out whether they really are, in some respect, the opposite of psychosis. Given many more trials in our beads task, we could have measured people's sensitivity and bias in detecting a change in the source of beads, or we might have developed and compared more detailed models of the underlying cognitive processes [see 12]. However, it is difficult to motivate participants, especially patients, to invest the required time and effort, and the difficulty grows when asking people to complete other tasks as well. Yet correlating results from our two tasks with clinically proven measurements will be necessary to find out what exactly we measure and when it matters.

Acknowledgements. We thank S. Klæbo Reitan for recruiting patients.

References

1. Adams, W.J., Graf, E.W., Ernst, M.O.: Experience can change the 'light-from-above' prior. Nature Neurosci **7**(10), 1057–1058 (2004)
2. Ernst, M.O., Banks, M.S.: Humans integrate visual and haptic information in a statistically optimal fashion. Nature **415**, 429–433 (2002)
3. Kersten, D., Mamassian, P., Yuille, A.: Object perception as Bayesian inference. Annual Rev. Psychol. **55**, 271–304 (2004)
4. Sinha, P., Poggio, T.: Role of learning in three-dimensional form perception. Nature **384**, 460–463 (1996)
5. Fletcher, P.C., Frith, C.D.: Perceiving is believing: a Bayesian approach to explaining the positive symptoms of schizophrenia. Nature Rev. Neurosci. **10**(1), 48–58 (2009)
6. Pellicano, E., Burr, D.: When the world becomes 'too real': a Bayesian explanation of autistic perception. Trends Cogn. Sci. **16**(10), 504–510 (2012)

7. Van de Cruys, S., Evers, K., van der Hallen, R., van Eylen, L., Boets, B., de Wit, L., Wagemans, J.: Precise minds in uncertain worlds: predictive coding in autism. Psychol. Review **121**(4), 649–675 (2014)
8. Rescorla, R.A., Wagner, A.R.: A theory of Pavlovian conditioning: variations in the effectiveness of reinforcement and nonreinforcement. In: Black, A.H., Prokasy, W.F. (eds.) Classical Conditioning II: Current Theory and Research. Appleton-Centiry-Crofts, New York (1972)
9. Sutton, R.S., Barto, A.G.: Time-derivative models of Pavlovian reinforcement. In: Gabriel, M., Moore, J. (eds.) Learning and Computational Neuroscience: Foundations of Adaptive Networks, pp. 497–537. MIT Press, Cambridge (1990)
10. Atkins, J.E., Fiser, J., Jacobs, R.A.: Experience-dependent visual cue integration based on consistencies between visual and haptic percepts. Vision Res. **41**, 449–461 (2001)
11. Fiser, J., Berkes, P., Orban, G., Lengyel, M.: Statistically optimal perception and learning: from behavior to neural representations. Trends Cogn. Sci. **14**(3), 119–30 (2010)
12. Payzan-LeNestour, E., Bossaerts, P.: Risk, unexpected uncertainty, and estimation uncertainty: Bayesian learning in unstable settings. PLoS Computational Biology **7**, 1–14 (2011)
13. Yu, A.J., Dayan, P.: Expected and unexpected uncertainty: ACh and NE in the neocortex. In: Becker, S.T.S., Obermayer, K. (eds.) Advances in Neural Information Processing Systems 15. MIT Press, Cambridge (2003)
14. Yu, A.J., Dayan, P.: Uncertainty, neuromodulation and attention. Neuron **46**, 681–692 (2005)
15. Bland, A.R., Schaefer, A.: Different varieties of uncertainty in human decision making. Front Neurosci. **6**, 85 (2012)
16. Huq, S.F., Garety, P.A., Hemsley, D.R.: Probabilistic judgments in deluded and non-deluded subjects. Q. J. Exp. Psychol. A **40**(4), 801–12 (1988)
17. McKay, R., Langdon, R., Coltheart, M.: Need for closure, jumping to conclusions, and decisiveness in delusion-prone individuals. J. Nerv. Ment. Diseas. **194**(6), 422–426 (2006)
18. Moritz, S., Woodward, T.S., Lambert, M.: Under what circumstances do patients with schizophrenia jump to conclusions? A liberal acceptance account. Br. J. Clin. Psychol. **46**, 127–137 (2007)
19. Moutoussis, M., Bentall, R.P., El-Dredy, W., Dayan, P.: Bayesian modelling of Jumping-to-conclusion bias in delusional patients. Cogn. Neuropsychiatry **16**, 422–447 (2011)
20. Rodier, M., Prévost, M., Renoult, L., Lionnet, C., Kwann, Y., Dionne-Dostie, E., Chapleu, I., Debruille, J.B.: Healthy people with delusional ideation change their minds with conviction. Psychiat. Res. **189**, 433–439 (2011)
21. Peters, E.R., Moritz, S., Schwannauer, M., Wiseman, Z., Greenwood, K., Scott, J., Beck, A.T., Donaldson, C., Hagen, R., Ross, K., Veckenstedt, R., Ison, R., Williams, S., Kuipers, E., Garety, P.A.: Cognitive biases questionnaire for psychosis. Schizophr Bull **40**(2), 300–313 (2014)
22. Roets, A., Van Hiel, A.: Item selection and validation of a brief, 15-item version of the need for closure scale. Personal Individ. Diff. **50**(1), 90–94 (2011)
23. Pfuhl, G., Tjelmeland, H., Molden, S., Biegler, R.: Optimal cache search depends on precision of spatial memory and pilfering, but what if that knowledge is not perfect? Anim. Beh. **78**(4), 819–828 (2009). doi:10.1016/j.anbehav.2009.06.014

Morphologic and Functional Connectivity Alterations in Patients with Major Depressive Disorder

Yang Yang[1,3,4], Changqing Hu[5,6], Kazuyuki Imamura[1], Xiaojing Yang[2,3,4],
Huaizhou Li[2,3,4], Gang Wang[5,6], Lei Feng[5,6], Bin Hu[7], Shengfu Lu[2,3,4],
and Ning Zhong[1,2,3,4(✉)]

[1] Maebashi Institute of Technology, Maebashi, Japan
yang@maebashi-it.org, {imamurak,zhong}@maebashi-it.ac.jp
[2] International WIC Institute, Beijing University of Technology, Beijing, China
[3] Beijing International Collaboration Base on Brain Informatics
and Wisdom Services, Beijing, China
[4] Beijing Key Laboratory of MRI and Brain Informatics, Beijing, China
[5] Mood Disorders Center, Beijing Anding Hospital,
Capital Medical University, Beijing, China
coannhu@126.com
[6] China Clinical Research Center for Mental Disorders, Beijing, China
[7] Ubiquitous Awareness and Intelligent Solutions Lab, Lanzhou University, Lanzhou, China

Abstract. In order to obtain a panorama of structural and functional brain abnormalities as well as the association between the anatomic and functional alterations and clinical symptoms in patients with major depressive disorder (MDD), integrated magnetic resonance imaging (MRI) measures were implemented on 21 MDD patients and 21 healthy controls, to facilitate the multimodality of voxel-based morphometry (VBM) analysis, resting-state functional connectivity analysis, and symptom rating. MDD patients showed significantly decreased gray matter volume (GMV) in the rostral part of anterior cingulate cortex (rACC), precuneus, and superior parietal lobule in the right hemisphere. By using the above morphologic deficits areas as seed regions, functional connectivity analysis revealed reduced coupling in the limbic-cortical and fronto-parietal networks, respectively. Subsequent correlation analyses revealed that GMV in the rACC negatively correlated with the depressive symptom severity and anxiety level. Our findings provide evidence supporting both morphologic and functional deficits in the limbic-cortical and frontal-parietal areas in MDD patients which could account for their dysfunctions on emotional regulation and cognition. Moreover, the neural changes found in rACC could be possible state markers for evaluating effects of anti-depressive treatment and anxiety level.

1 Introduction

Neuroimaging studies, especially magnetic resonance imaging (MRI) studies, have played an important role in the identification of brain abnormalities in major depressive disorder (MDD) [1]. Differences resulted from comparisons between

Y. Yang and C. Hu—These authors contributed equally to this work.

Y. Guo et al. (Eds.): BIH 2015, LNAI 9250, pp. 33–42, 2015.
DOI: 10.1007/978-3-319-23344-4_4

MDD patients and healthy controls might represent biomarkers underlying the etiology of MDD, as well as reveal some important meanings for its clinical symptoms [2].

Brain abnormalities in MDD reported in previous studies were primarily localized in brain regions involved in emotional processing, such as prefrontal cortex, limbic system, and basal ganglia [3]. Besides functional deficits, brain structural changes were also revealed in MDD. Voxel-based morphometry (VBM) [4] is a user-independent, fully automated method for detecting potentially unsuspected brain structure abnormalities, and has been widely used for finding differences in patients with neuropsychiatric disorders such as obsessive-compulsive disorder (OCD), and bipolar disorder [5, 6]. With the help of VBM, many MRI studies focusing on structural abnormalities in MDD have found evidence of volume reductions in the anterior cingulate cortex (ACC), orbitofrontal cortex, hippocampus, amygdala, as well as caudate and putamen [7, 8]. Furthermore, it has been found that the gray matter volume (GMV) in MDD patients was positively correlated with their executive performance and the effect of treatment with cognitive behavioral therapy [9]. Therefore, a growing consensus is being achieved on the importance of structure changes as biomarkers related to MDD.

However, evidence on how the abnormal GMV affects brain functions and symptomatic progression is still insufficient. In addition, increasing evidence exhibits that the disturbances in MDD are unlikely to be the results of a single region with abnormal function and / or structure, MDD could be considered as a disorder with distributed brain networks [10]. Resting-state functional MRI provides a promising approach to discover useful imaging endophenotypes associated with MDD. Studies with resting-state functional connectivity showed increased connectivity and nodal centralities within the default mode network (DMN) which indicated hyperactivity for self-referential and disruption to emotional modulation in MDD patients [11]. On the other hand, decreased activation found within fronto-parietal network during cognitive control-related tasks after MDD patients were shown negative self-referential statements implicated their inability to shift attention away from self-related stimuli [12].

Although abundant results about brain abnormalities in MDD have been yielded in neuroimaging using multiple structural and functional imaging modalities, these investigations have invariably been conducted independently, and the interrelationships among structural, functional abnormalities and the clinical symptoms variables are thus poorly understood. Therefore, in the present study we combined VBM and resting-state functional connectivity analysis in order to perform a comprehensive evaluation of the neural circuitry of MDD, and explored the relationship among structural deficits, functional connectivity, and symptom severity in MDD patients.

2   Materials and Methods

2.1   Participants

Twenty-one right-handed MDD patients (9 males and 12 females) were recruited among outpatients from Beijing Anding Hospital, China, and 21 healthy controls matched for gender, age, and years of education with MDD patients were recruited from community. Diagnostic assessments for all participants were performed by clinically trained and experienced raters (T. Tian and B. Fu) using the Mini International Neuropsychiatric Interview 6.0 (MINI 6.0) [13] based on DSM-IV. Clinical symptom severity of depression and anxiety level were evaluated for patients using Hamilton Depression Rating Scale 17 items (HDRS-17)   and Trait Anxiety Inventory (T-AI), respectively (see Table 1). The exclusion criteria were: (1) depressive patients with any mania episode or history of any comorbid major psychiatric illness on Axis I or Axis II; (2) concurrent serious medical illness or primary neurological illness; (3) history of head injury resulting in loss of consciousness; (4) abuse of or dependence on alcohol or other substances; (5) and contraindication for MRI. All subjects signed the informed consent and this study was approved by the Ethics committee of Beijing Anding Hospital, Capital Medical University.

2.2   MRI Data Acquisition

A 3.0 T MRI system (Siemens Trio Tim; Siemens Medical System, Erlanger, Germany) and a 12-channel phased array head coil were employed for the scanning. Foam padding and headphone were used to limit head motion and reduce scanning noise. 192 slices of structural images with a thickness of 1 mm were acquired by using a T1 weighted 3D MPRAGE sequence (TR = 1600 ms, TE = 3.28 ms, TI = 800 ms, FOV = 256 × 256 mm^2, flip angle = 9°, voxel size = 1 × 1 × 1 mm^3). Functional images were collected through a T2 gradient-echo EPI sequence (TR = 2000 ms, TE = 31 ms, flip angle = 90°, FOV = 240 × 240 mm^2, matrix size = 64 × 64). Thirty axial slices with a thickness of 4 mm and an interslice gap of 0.8 mm were acquired.

2.3   Voxel-Based Morphometric Analysis

The voxel-based morphometric analysis was performed using SPM8 software (Statistical Parametric Mapping; http://www.fil.ion.ucl.ac.uk/spm/) and the VBM 8 toolbox (http://dbm.neuro.uni-jena.de/vbm/). All T1 structural images were bias-corrected and segmented into gray matter (GM), white matter (WM), and cerebrospinal fluid (CSF) using the Maximum A Posterior spatial probability segmentation approach. The deformations that best aligned the images together were estimated by iteratively registering the imported images with their average through the Diffeomorphic Anatomical Registration Through Exponential Lie Algebra (DARTEL) algorithm [14]. Then the images were normalized to the standard Montreal Neurological Institute (MNI) brain template using the parameters obtained in the DARTEL's template normalization to MNI template. The voxel values of segmented and normalized gray matter images were modulated by the Jacobian determinants obtained from non-linear normalization steps. Finally, all wrapped modulated gray matter images were smoothed with an 8 mm Gaussian kernel.

Comparisons of GM volume between the MDD and control groups were performed using two-sample t tests. Age, gender, years of education, and total intracranial volume were modeled as covariates of no interest. The statistical significance of group differences in each region was set at uncorrected p < 0.001 with a minimum cluster size of k > 50. The average values of gray matter volume for all the voxels in abnormal areas revealed by VBM were extracted and correlated with the HDRS-17 and T-AI scores using Pearson correlation analysis, to identify the association between gray matter abnormalities and clinical characteristics.

Table 1. Demographic and clinical characteristics of MDD patients and healthy controls.

Characteristics	MDD Patients (n = 21)	Controls (n = 21)	p -Value
Gender (male: female)	9 : 12	9 : 12	1
Mean age (years)	33.8 ±9.1	29.9 ±7.7	0.15
Education level (years)	13.1 ±3.1	11.9 ±2.4	0.18
HDRS-17 Total Score	19.2 ±6.3	-	-
T-AI Total Score	52.9 ±10.6	-	-

Abbreviation: HDRS-17: Hamilton Depression Rating Scale 17 items, T-AI : Trait Anxiety Inventory

2.4 Functional Connectivity Analysis

The preprocessing of resting-state fMRI data was implemented with SPM8. The first 10 volumes have been discarded to allow the magnetization to approach dynamic equilibrium. Slice timing was applied to the rest of EPI images, then a series of stages followed: realignment that aimed at identifying and correcting redundant body motions, co-registration that merged the high resolution structural image with the mean image of the EPI series, normalization that adjusted the structural image to the MNI template and applied normalization parameters to EPI images, smoothing that had fMRI data smoothed with an 8 mm FWHM isotropic Gaussian kernel. After normalization, all volumes were resampled into $3{\times}3{\times}3$ mm^3 voxels. Head movement was less than 2 mm and 2 degree in all cases.

Functional connectivity was analyzed using a seed-oriented correlation approach with the REST software package (http://www.restfmri.net). Regions with gray matter abnormalities that resulted from voxel-based morphometric analysis were utilized as the seeds. Several possible spurious sources of variances, including the estimated head motion parameters and average signals from the cerebrospinal fluid and white matter, were removed from the data through linear regression. Time courses were extracted from each voxel after linear detrend and bandpass filtering (0.01 - 0.08 Hz). Based on the corrected time courses, we computed the Pearson correlation coefficients between one seed and the rest parts of the brain voxel-by-voxel. Differences in functional connectivity between the MDD patients and healthy control group were compared by using two-sample t-tests. Age, gender, years of education, and total gray matter volume were entered as covariates of no interest. The significance level of group differences was set at a $p < 0.05$ with the AlphaSim correction (combined height threshold of a $p < 0.001$ and a minimum cluster size of 22 voxels).

3 Results

3.1 Morphometric Analysis

Compared with healthy control group, MDD patients showed reduced gray matter volume (GMV) in the rostral part of anterior cingulate cortex (rACC), precuneus, and superior parietal lobule (SPL) in the right hemisphere (see Table 2 and Figure 1). No significantly increased GMV was found in MDD patients relative to healthy controls.

Table 2. Regions of gray matter reduction in MDD patients compared to healthy controls. All regions survived at the statistical threshold of p < 0.001 (uncorrected), cluster size k > 50 voxels.

Region	BA	Cluster	Talairach Coordinates			T-score
			x	y	z	
R. rACC	32	56	11	41	9	6.61
R. Precuneus	7	146	1	-73	41	4.49
R. SPL	7	76	35	-56	55	3.84

Abbreviation: rACC: rostral part of anterior cingulate cortex, SPL: superior parietal lobule, R: right, BA: Brodmann Area.

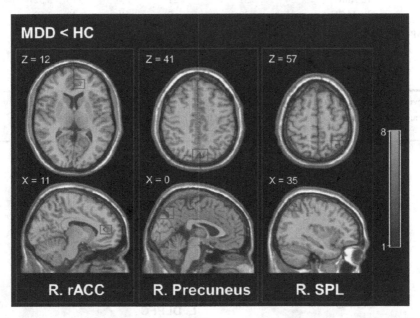

Fig. 1. Gray matter differences between MDD patients and healthy controls (HC). Cold color denotes the brain regions having significantly decreased gray matter volume in MDD patients compared with healthy controls. Maps threshold were set at p<0.001 (uncorrected), cluster size k > 50 voxels.

3.2   Resting-State Functional Connectivity Analysis

Seed-oriented functional connectivity analyses were performed based on seeds corresponding to R. rACC (11, 41, 9), R. Precuneus (1, -73, 41), and R. SPL (35, -56, 55) that showed abnormalities in MDD patients in the above VBM analysis. As results of two-sample t-tests, MDD patients exhibited a general pattern with decreased connectivity between seeds and several emotion or cognition-related brain regions. When the seed was located in the R. rACC, patients showed decreased connectivity mainly in the right amygdala, dorsal anterior cingulate cortex (dACC), as well as the left fusiform gyrus. When the seed was located in the R. SPL, patients showed decreased connectivity in the left insula, dACC, and bilateral dorsolateral prefrontal cortex (DLPFC) (see Table 3 and Figure 2). No significant group difference was found when the seed was located in the right precuneus.

Table 3. Brain regions with significantly altered functional connectivity in patients with MDD. All regions survived at the threshold of p < 0.05 with the AlphaSim correction (combined height threshold of a p < 0.001 and a minimum cluster size of 22 voxels).

Seed	Connected Region	BA	Cluster	Talairach Coordinates			T-score
				x	y	z	
R. rACC	L. FFG	37	42	-45	-37	-15	4.32
	R. Amy	34	31	21	4	-10	3.52
	R. dACC	31	37	3	-29	40	3.69
R. SPL	L. Insula	47/13	48	-33	16	-3	4.33
	L. DLPFC	10	53	-39	42	17	4.65
	L. dACC	32	37	-9	17	18	4.13
	R. DLPFC	6	70	21	4	55	4.87

Abbreviation: rACC: rostral anterior cingulate cortex, SPL: superior parietal lobule, FFG: fusiform gyrus, Amy: amygdala, dACC: dorsal anterior cingulate gyrus, DLPFC: dorsolateral prefrontal cortex.

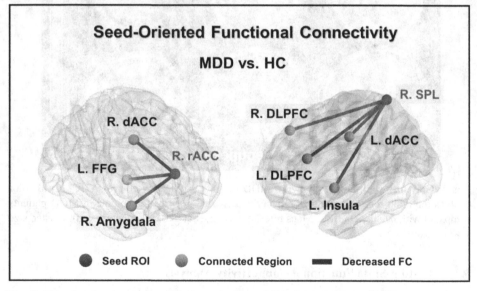

Fig. 2. Functional connectivity differences between MDD patients and healthy controls (HC). The blue line denotes the reduced functional connectivity between seeds and connected regions in MDD patients. Maps threshold were set at the threshold of p < 0.05 with the AlphaSim correction.

3.3   Brain-Symptom Associations

The average gray matter volume values of abnormal brain regions in MDD patients were extracted and correlated with the MDD symptom severity and anxiety level. As shown in Figure 3, significant negative correlations were only observed between gray matter volume in the rostral part of the anterior cingulate cortex and HDRS-17 total score (r = -0.51, p < 0.05), as well as T-AI total score (r = -0.65, p < 0.01). No significant correlations were found between other brain regions and clinical symptoms.

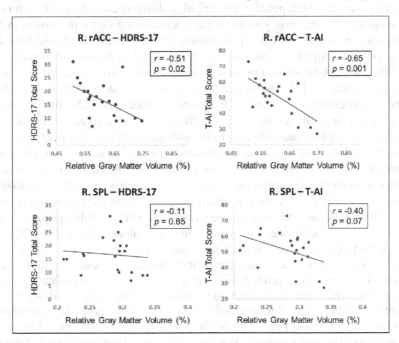

Fig. 3. Negative correlation between brain gray matter volume and total scores of HDRS-17 as well as T-AI. Significant negative correlations were observed in R. rACC (upper panel). Although R. SPL showed both structural and functional deficits in patients, correlations between R. SPL and clinical symptoms were not significant (bottom panel).

4   Discussion

The present study revealed an overall perspective about structural and functional abnormalities in patients with major depressive disorder (MDD) based on three aspects: gray matter volume (GMV) deficits, decreased resting-state functional connectivity between GMV deficits areas and other emotion or cognition-related regions, and the negative correlations between GMV and clinical symptom severity. Through the investigations using multiple structural and functional imaging modalities, we have not only verified the consistency of rostral part of anterior cingulate cortex (rACC) as the morphologic focal region for MDD, but also found out the functional changes and clinical characteristics that were related to the regions with morphologic abnormalities.

4.1   rACC and State-Dependent Morphologic Biomarker

Despite an incomplete understanding of the neural circuitry underlying MDD, there is growing consensus that some specific brain areas are significant to depression. Many studies have identified reduced grey matter volume (GMV) in anterior cingulate cortex (ACC) of MDD patients' brains [15].   Three independent meta-analyses also revealed a robust relationship between MDD and the grey matter loss in ACC [2, 8, 16]. Especially, a recent meta-analysis study, using signed differential mapping approach which can reconstruct both positive and negative differences in the same map (signed map), suggested that the most consistent region exhibiting GMV reductions in MDD patients were located in rACC [17]. Although mass of studies have also focused on hippocampus and amygdala which are strongly related to depression as well, it was implied that, amygdalar reductions were more associated with untreated or comorbid depressive patients [7, 17], and hippocampal reductions can be only found subtly in patients with stress-related recurrent depressive episodes [18]. Our finding of rACC GMV reductions in MDD is consistent with the previous investigations. The decreased volume in this area has been indicated to be associated with an abnormal reduction of cerebral blood flow (CBF), glucose metabolism, and glial cells that were observed by PET studies [19]. These findings have demonstrated that the rACC is robust to act as a focal region which showed neurophysiological abnormalities in MDD. Moreover, GM reductions were also found in the posterior parietal cortex in the current study, including the right precuneus and superior parietal lobule (SPL). Although less evidence could be found on the association between affective abnormalities and PPC, it was likely that the PPC deficits were related to the cognitive dysfunctions in MDD.

We also computed the correlation coefficients between regions with GMV deficits and symptom severity. It turned out that only the rACC showed significantly negative correlationship with depressive symptom severity (p = 0.02). The result suggests high sensitivity of GMV in rACC to depressive severity, and the potential association between GMV in rACC and prediction of disease progression. This is in line with the previous study [19], and illustrates that the rACC may be a candidate for the state-dependent biomarker that can evaluate responses to anti-depressive treatments. Furthermore, the rACC appeared more sensitivity to anxiety level (p = 0.001) which presented a feasibility to predict anxiety level in MDD.

4.2   Disrupted Limbic-Cortical and Fronto-Parietal Networks in MDD

rACC is considered as a critical node in the limbic-cortical network and known to control emotional regulation by inhibiting the activity of limbic regions such as the hippocampus and the amygdala [8]. In the present study, the decreased resting-state functional connectivity between the right   rACC and amygdala demonstrated a disrupted connection between the two regions which could account for the neuropathology underlying the disability to control negative emotions in MDD. MR spectroscopic studies detected an abnormal relationship between GABAergic-mediated neural inhibition as well as glutamatergic-mediated neural excitation in rACC in MDD [20]. These observations pointed in the direction of an imbalance in MDD between excitation and inhibition in the rACC and provided further explanations for understanding the decreased functional connectivity observed in the present study. Moreover, reduced coupling of right rACC was also found in the connections to the left fusiform gyrus and the right dorsal anterior cingulate cortex (dACC). These results may reflect perturbations in neural networks related to social functioning and cognitive processing, due to the roles of the relevant regions in facial recognition and cognitive task achievement, respectively.

On the other hand, when the seed was located in the right SPL, MDD patients showed decreased functional connectivity in the left insula, dACC, and bilateral dorsolateral prefrontal cortices, which depicted a decoupling fronto-parietal network. The fronto-cingulo-parietal regions are believed to act as important nodes involved in the "task-positive" network that responds with activation increases to attention-demanding tasks. The deceased activation and impaired cognitive functions discovered in MDD patients might be elicited by the break-down of the fronto-parietal network [12].

5   Conclusion

In conclusion, the present study applied morphometry analysis and resting-state functional connectivity to examine the structural and functional integrity changes in MDD patients. Our findings provide evidence supporting both morphologic and functional deficits in the limbic-cortical and frontal-parietal areas in MDD patients that can lead to dysfunctions on emotional regulation and cognition. Especially the potential of rACC was revealed as a possible state marker for evaluating the MDD disease progression, effect of anti-depressive treatment, and even the anxiety level, because of its convergence of gray matter volume abnormality, altered functional connectivity and sensitivity to the symptom severity. Nevertheless, it is unclear whether brain abnormalities in rACC can be also found in other psychiatric patients, such as patients with bipolar disorder. To figure out the specificity of rACC changes to MDD, comparison between MDD and other psychiatric patients will be necessary in the future study.

Acknowledgements. This work was funded by National Basic Research Program of China (2014CB744600), International Science & Technology Cooperation Program of China (2013DFA32180), National Natural Science Foundation of China (61420106005, 61272345), JSPS Grants-in-Aid for Scientific Research of Japan (26350994), and Beijing Natural Science Foundation (4132023), and supported by Beijing Municipal Commission of Education, and Beijing Xuanwu Hospital.

References

1. Li, B., Liu, L., Friston, K.J., Shen, H., Wang, L., Zeng, L.L., Hu, D.: A treatment-resistant default mode subnetwork in major depression. Biological psychiatry **74**, 48–54 (2013)
2. Graham, J., Salimi-Khorshidi, G., Hagan, C., Walsh, N., Goodyer, I., Lennox, B., Suckling, J.: Meta-analytic evidence for neuroimaging models of depression: state or trait? Journal of affective disorders **151**, 423–431 (2013)

3. Ressler, K.J., Mayberg, H.S.: Targeting abnormal neural circuits in mood and anxiety disorders: from the laboratory to the clinic. Nature neuroscience **10**, 1116–1124 (2007)
4. Ashburner, J., Friston, K.J.: Voxel-based morphometry–the methods. NeuroImage **11**, 805–821 (2000)
5. Hou, J., Song, L., Zhang, W., Wu, W., Wang, J., Zhou, D., Qu, W., Guo, J., Gu, S., He, M., Xie, B., Li, H.: Morphologic and functional connectivity alterations of corticostriatal and default mode network in treatment-naive patients with obsessive-compulsive disorder. PloS one **8**, e83931 (2013)
6. Adler, C.M., DelBello, M.P., Jarvis, K., Levine, A., Adams, J., Strakowski, S.M.: Voxel-based study of structural changes in first-episode patients with bipolar disorder. Biological psychiatry **61**, 776–781 (2007)
7. Hamilton, J.P., Siemer, M., Gotlib, I.H.: Amygdala volume in major depressive disorder: a meta-analysis of magnetic resonance imaging studies. Molecular psychiatry **13**, 993–1000 (2008)
8. Koolschijn, P.C., van Haren, N.E., Lensvelt-Mulders, G.J., Hulshoff Pol, H.E., Kahn, R.S.: Brain volume abnormalities in major depressive disorder: a meta-analysis of magnetic resonance imaging studies. Human brain mapping **30**, 3719–3735 (2009)
9. Fujino, J., Yamasaki, N., Miyata, J., Sasaki, H., Matsukawa, N., Takemura, A., Tei, S., Sugihara, G., Aso, T., Fukuyama, H., Takahashi, H., Inoue, K., Murai, T.: Anterior cingulate volume predicts response to cognitive behavioral therapy in major depressive disorder. Journal of affective disorders **174**, 397–399 (2015)
10. Damasio, A.R.: Neuropsychology. Towards a neuropathology of emotion and mood. Nature **386**, 769–770 (1997)
11. Zhang, J., Wang, J., Wu, Q., Kuang, W., Huang, X., He, Y., Gong, Q.: Disrupted brain connectivity networks in drug-naive, first-episode major depressive disorder. Biological psychiatry **70**, 334–342 (2011)
12. Wagner, G., Schachtzabel, C., Peikert, G., Bar, K.J.: The neural basis of the abnormal self-referential processing and its impact on cognitive control in depressed patients. Human brain mapping (2015)
13. Sheehan, D.V., Sheehan, K.H., Shytle, R.D., Janavs, J., Bannon, Y., Rogers, J.E., Milo, K.M., Stock, S.L., Wilkinson, B.: Reliability and validity of the Mini International Neuropsychiatric Interview for Children and Adolescents (MINI-KID). The Journal of clinical psychiatry **71**, 313–326 (2010)
14. Ashburner, J.: A fast diffeomorphic image registration algorithm. NeuroImage **38**, 95–113 (2007)
15. Depping, M.S., Wolf, N.D., Vasic, N., Sambataro, F., Thomann, P.A., Christian Wolf, R.: Specificity of abnormal brain volume in major depressive disorder: a comparison with borderline personality disorder. Journal of affective disorders **174**, 650–657 (2015)
16. Zhao, Y.J., Du, M.Y., Huang, X.Q., Lui, S., Chen, Z.Q., Liu, J., Luo, Y., Wang, X.L., Kemp, G.J., Gong, Q.Y.: Brain grey matter abnormalities in medication-free patients with major depressive disorder: a meta-analysis. Psychological medicine **44**, 2927–2937 (2014)
17. Bora, E., Fornito, A., Pantelis, C., Yucel, M.: Gray matter abnormalities in Major Depressive Disorder: a meta-analysis of voxel based morphometry studies. Journal of affective disorders **138**, 9–18 (2012)
18. Warner-Schmidt, J.L., Duman, R.S.: Hippocampal neurogenesis: opposing effects of stress and antidepressant treatment. Hippocampus **16**, 239–249 (2006)
19. Drevets, W.C., Savitz, J., Trimble, M.: The subgenual anterior cingulate cortex in mood disorders. CNS spectrums **13**, 663–681 (2008)
20. Northoff, G., Sibille, E.: Why are cortical GABA neurons relevant to internal focus in depression? A cross-level model linking cellular, biochemical and neural network findings. Molecular psychiatry **19**, 966–977 (2014)

A Cognitive Model for Understanding Chinese Character

Qingsheng Li[✉], Qinxia Wu, and Feng Gao

School of Computer & Information Engineering,
Anyang Normal University, Anyang, Henan, China
aylqs@163.com

Abstract. Much experimental evidence has supported the idea that the brain is organized into processing streams, but how these streams are determined and how they interact to generate behavior is still a topic of active research. Based on cognitive functionalities in human vision processing, this paper propose a computational cognitive model for Chinese character understanding with detailed algorithmic descriptions. The contribution of this paper is of two folds. Firstly, we present a systematic review on psychological and neurophysiological studies, which provide collective evidence for a distributed representation of Chinese character in the human brain. Secondly, we present a computational model which simulates the distributed mechanism of object vision pathway. Experimental results show that the presented computational cognitive model outperforms other stander Chinese character vision understanding algorithms in computer science research.

Keywords: Distributed cognition · Computational model · Chinese character understanding · Human vision system

1 Introduction

Compare with image retrieval, text retrieval is often more convenient and fast. From the view of understanding of machine, it is the simple coding and representation reason that make the Chinese characters calculate becomes very difficult, the representation of 0 and 1 may be suitable computing, but not for understanding. It is illustrated by the plate diagram (Fig.1), data that are saved to the store device (such as document files) are called "insiders." Data that are not saved to the store device are called "outside." Compare person to understand the outside information, It is more difficult to understand the inside information to machine.

To improve the level of Chinese character cognitive and understanding, the computer must provide more knowledge storage, more knowledge representation and more scientific method of calculation, which means to have more storage space, more knowledge and greater accumulation range suitable for the cognitive.

In today's internet era, it is possible to describe Chinese character in more detail. First and foremost is, of course, the rapid increase in computing power and distributed storage technology. More description Chinese character to our saved document can now be conveniently be performed on internet or cloud server, while others, for

© Springer International Publishing Switzerland 2015
Y. Guo et al. (Eds.): BIH 2015, LNAI 9250, pp. 43–53, 2015.
DOI: 10.1007/978-3-319-23344-4_5

example large-scale clustering of characters, can be came out on supercomputers. It is illustrated by the plate diagram in Figure.2.

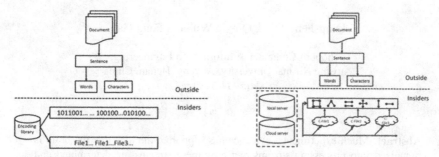

Fig. 1. Outside and inside, Character font and file system

Fig. 2. Outside and inside, storage and distributed storage

Chinese character understanding is one of fundamental tasks in computer vision. Many recognition algorithms have been proposed in computer science area. While the CPU processing speed can now be reached at 109 Hz, the human brain has a limited speed of 100 Hz at which the neurons process their input. However, compared to coding-of-the-character computational algorithms for Chinese character understanding, human brain has a distinct advantage in character recognition, i.e., human being can accurately recognize one from unlimited variety of objects within a fraction of a second, even if the object is partially occluded or contaminated by noises. Thus, it is much desired to explore computational cognitive models of how human brain recognizes Chinese Character, in both areas of computer vision and cognitive computation.

A modern view of the relation between brain and mind is based on the neuroscience paradigm [1], according to which the architecture of the brain is determined by connections between neurons, their inhibitory or excitatory character and also by the strength of the connections. Human brain displays a great plasticity, synapses are perpetually formed (but also deleted) during a learning process. It can be stated, that an ability of brain to perform not only cognitive activities, but also to serve as memory and control center for our motoric activities, is fully encoded by its architecture. The metaphor of a human brain as a computer should be therefore formulated in such a way, that a computer is a parallel distributed computer (containing many billions of neurons, elementary processors interconnected into a complex neural network). A program in such a parallel computer is directly encoded in the architecture of the neural network, i.e. human brain is a single-purpose parallel computer represented by a neural network, which can't be reprogrammed without a change of its architecture.

Based on the summarized cognitive model, we present a computational implementation of the cognitive model (also called computational cognitive model in this paper) for Chinese character understanding. A computational model of human cognition can be defined in several different senses. In this paper, we present a model which is quantitative in a programmable way. By utilizing cognitive functionalities in the human brain, our model is distinct from existing computational algorithms in computer science area. We further use Chinese character dynamic description library (CCDDL) to demonstrate that the presented computational cognitive model outperforms other computer algorithms for Chinese character understanding. We make the following two contributions in this paper:

A. We present a systemic review on font description and generation studies with converging evidences, to uncover cognitive mechanisms of Chinese character understanding in the human brain.
B. Based on these cognitive mechanisms, we present a computational cognitive model for Chinese character understanding. The presented model utilizes distributed local features which are defined as Chinese stroke element patterns and are similarity-invariant. By utilizing a learning process characterized by a Markov chain model, the features are clustered into abstract representations stored in memory traces, which form the partial representations of the Chinese character.
C. Based the computational cognitive model we propose a Dynamic Description Algorithm (DDA) for Chinese characters understanding. Use DDA Algorithm we can add some special symbol to currently Chinese character.

The organization of this paper is as follows. Section 2, we classify and discuss a number of popular Chinese character depiction methods, existing algorithms and the lack of their application in machine's cognitive. Section 3 illustrates a dynamic description model for generating Chinese characters based on Chinese character description algorithm. Section 4 describes our experiment. Section 5 shows the conclusion of our work and the future and direction.

2   Chinese Characters Description

Chinese characters are pictographs, which stroke and parts have certain of semantic information, however, as Chinese character encoding methods in information processing is whole operations, it is very difficult to decompose the strokes and components from a Chinese character, so that should have been playing a role in the calculation of semantic components of Chinese characters lose its unique significance to the research and development of Chinese information technology. In today's lightning- speed information and the big data in a wide range of data represents era, this issue has attracted more and more concern and attention in many domestic and foreign scholars [2].

2.1   Description of Words, Phrases and Sentences for Corpus and Language Knowledge Base Development

Corpus and knowledge building is normal method for the research of Natural Language Processing (NLP), in which all data in the corpus are electronically labeled. It is the electronic labels makes unstructured text easy to understand. Electronic labels can be viewed as a description of unstructured text for linguistic knowledge.

At present, there are many resources help system deal with the unstructured text in Chinese language information processing, which is more representative of the people's daily, the corpus, which have. Language knowledgebase is represent language knowledge with structure of description through records language and character, it is the directly resources for language information processing system, language knowledgebase of typical representative is "How Net" [3]. In addition, there are number of other knowledge base, for example, Chinese semantic dictionary, phrasal structure knowledge base, the Chinese concept of modern Chinese dictionary, Chinese Treebank and so on. In recent years, in linguistic knowledge resources research filed, Institute of Information Science, Academia Sinica does a solid job, such as "the Chinese sentence structure tree database", and "Chinese network (Word Net)" [4], are two relatively complete Web services functionality in Chinese semantic knowledge base.

2.2   Description for Components and Strokes of Chinese Characters

The stroke of Chinese character comes from Chinese traditional calligraphy, which is one of the most important aspects of Chinese culture. The stroke of a Chinese character carries more latent topic, as like as text mining attempts to add structure to an unstructured document corpus, Chinese character latent topic mining attempts to extract semantically meaningful information from Chinese character, components and stokes. Numerous works on simulation of Chinese calligraphies and paintings have reported, Chu [5] developed a physically-based 3D brush model with spreading bristles and rendering strokes in real time. The users are able to create much aesthetic brushworks with this virtual brush. Also, Lee [6], proposed a method to simulate real-time dynamic of ink diffusion in absorbent paper for art creation. Additionally, Xu and Lau [7] proposed an intelligent system to create calligraphy artwork of various styles through an interpolation process using input samples of trained font style as knowledge sources. T.S.Wong [8] and Wong, P.Y.C. [9] proposed a methodology to study Chinese calligraphic for automatically estimating the set of geometric and writing model.

2.3   Description for Special Chinese Characters

Strokes-segment-mesh glyph depiction model [10],which are addressed by Beijing language and Culture University, and Inner Mongolia Normal University song and Lin research team, is one of the special Chinese characters description method, it has defined limited direction segments—strokes as basic depiction unit to descript Chinese character. This method is an input tool for both uncommon characters and wrongly written characters.

CDL and HanGlyph[11] description method, which are based on the arrangement of the strokes, is first used to describe the Chinese character by operators, XML and expressions. It captures the topological relation of the strokes without specifying precise geometric information. The primitives of the language are the strokes. A character is composed by applying a sequence operation on the strokes.

Stroke-Elements and Stroke-Segments-Vector dynamically description methods, which is proposed by report [12], is first used to described by automatic generation of glyphs at Jiaguwen (Oracle Bones Script),   in which an effective multi-word, dynamic description methods ware proposed, Not only the Jiaguwen character but also the variant forms of the modern Chinese characters, irregular characters, merging characters and misprints can use this method to dynamically describe.

3   Chinese Characters Dynamic Description Model for Chinese Character Understanding

In this section, we propose a model of Chinese Characters Dynamic Description (CCDD) and make it successful theoretic and practical, which includes Chinese character description algorithm and Chinese character dynamic generation method based on the Chinese characters strokes-elements. We discuss the experimental technique in normal document and understanding document that we used to obtain in our results, including a stander output and special output experiments. Finally, we describe the Chinese character dynamic generation method from the point of view of text document protection, a text document protection technique based on Chinese characters description library.

3.1   Strokes Feature Points and Stroke-Element

3.1.1   Strokes-Elements and Hidden-Strokes-Elements

Definition 1. A Strokes-Elements (SE) is an object consisting of two sets called its Strokes-Segments-Points (SSP) and its Strokes-Segments-Vector (SSV) set. The SSP set is a non-empty finite set, the SSV set, may be empty, but otherwise its elements are ordered two-element subset of the SSP set.

Chinese character can be described by SE, each SE represented by an array of co-ordinate points (x_i, y_i) and A SSV. A SSV can be described by S_{ij}:

$$S_{ij} = (x_i, y_i, x_j, y_j) \qquad\qquad i, j \in N, \; j \geq i \qquad\qquad (1)$$

Equation (1) is a directed line segment, where (x_i, y_i) and (x_j, y_j) are the start-point and end-point of S_{ij}, respectively. A Stroke-Element can be described:

$$E_n = (S_{i_1j_1}, S_{i_2j_2}, \ldots, S_{i_nj_n}) \qquad\qquad n \in N, \; j \geq i \qquad\qquad (2)$$

Equation (2) is a complete stroke structure which consists of n stroke-segments-vectors, where n is a positive integer. For any integer k with $1 \leq k \leq n$, let $S_k = S_{i_kj_k}$. Then

$$E_n = (S_1, S_2, \ldots, S_n) \qquad\qquad n \in N \qquad\qquad (3)$$

The start-point of S_1 is called the start-point of E_n and the end-point of S_n is called the end-point of E_n.

Definition 2. A Hidden-Strokes-Elements is a special Strokes-Elements which SSP called Hidden-Strokes-Segments-Points (HSSP), SSV called Hidden-Strokes-Segments-Vector (HSSV), they are all included by S_{ij} in Equation (1). A HSSV can be described by HS_{ij}:

$$HS_{mn} = (hx_m, hy_m, hx_n, hy_n) \qquad\qquad m, n \in N, \; m \geq n$$

The relationship between SE and HSE can be illustrated by fig.3.

A SE is a part of a stroke in Chinese characters. The number of the SE of a Chinese character is relevant to the character's structure. Since the SSV has directions, a SE may have many description methods. According to the modern Chinese characters' writing rules, we describe every stoke element obeying the left-right, top-down, out-side-inside rules. Due to there are many different typeface in Chinese character font, We categorize the stroke elements of Chinese characters into three groups, i.e., (BSE).Combination Strokes Elements (CSE) and Export Strokes Elements(ESE),BSE used to describe simple Chinese character stroke , CSE used to describe complex stroke and ESE used to generate other special Chinese character stroke.

A HSE play an important role in Chinese character security due to it can be added and extracted by Chinese character description and generation algorithm.

3.1.2   Base Strokes Elements
Base Strokes Elements (Table 1) usually consists of one stroke-segments-vectors, where

$$S_{12} = (x_1, y_1, x_2, y_2), \quad n = 2.$$

For example, Horizontal (H), that is means Hen in Chinese, Vertical (V), that is means Shu in Chinese, right-falling (Pie) and left-falling (Na), that are means Pie and Na in Chinese. All they are represented by one stroke-segments-vector. Dian stroke is a special stroke segments in this description, it can be defined as any one of other four of stroke-segments-vectors.

Table 1. Feature Point and Base Strokes Elements

No	Stroke Elements	Feature Point		Graph	Vector Graph
1	Hen (H)	v_1	v_2		
2	Shu (V)	v_1	v_2		
3	Pie (R_L)	v_1	v_2		
4	Na (L_R)	v_1	v_2		
5	Dian (H)	v_1	v_2		

BSE's stroke-segments-vectors can be seen in fig.4.

Fig. 3. Strokes-Elements and Hidden-Strokes-Elements

Fig. 4. BSE's stroke-segments-vectors

Fig. 5. BSE's stroke-segments-vectors

3.1.3 Combination Strokes Elements

Combination Strokes Elements (Table 2) usually consists of n stroke-segments-vectors, where $n \geq 2$. For example, CPie and CNa is composed of two or more Strokes Elements, the number of its feature points may be 3, 4, 5, 6... and so on, the feature expression of   CPie is:

$$CPie = Pie_1 + Pie_2 + ... + Pie_i \qquad (4)$$

And CNa is:

$$CNa = Na_1 + Na_2 + ... + Na_i \qquad (5)$$

CSE's stroke-segments-vectors can be seen in fig.5.

Table 2. Feature point of Combination Strokes Elements

No	Stroke Elements	Feature Point	Feature Expression
1	CHen (H)	v_1 v_2... v_i	$CHen = Hen_1 + Hen_2 + ... + Hen_i$
2	CShu (V)	v_1 v_2... v_i	$CShu = Shu_1 + Shu_2 + ... + Shu_i$
3	CPie (R_L)	v_1 v_2... v_i	$CPie = Pie_1 + Pie_2 + ... + Pie_i$
4	CNa (L_R)	v_1 v_2... v_i	$CNa = Na_1 + Na_2 + ... + Na_i$
5	CDian	v_1 v_2... v_i	$CDian = Dian_1 + Dian_2 + ... + Dian_i$

3.2   Dynamic Description Algorithm for Chinese Characters

We propose a Dynamic Description Algorithm (DDA) for Chinese characters. Combining this algorithm with the description methods introduced in Section 3.1, one can deal with all the Chinese characters aided by computers. The steps of the algorithm are as follows.

Algorithm DDA

Step 1: Encode Chinese characters using one of the methods introduced in Section 3.1
   In this step, we don't consider the variant forms of any Chinese character.
Step 2: Create a Chinese characters stroke library according to the encoding scheme.
Step 3: Victories every Chinese character's stroke in the Chinese stroke library. Thus, we will obtain a stroke description library.
Step 4: Encode each variant form of every Chinese character and find a mapping from the Chinese character stroke library to the stroke description library.
Step 5: Input and output Chinese characters using the dynamically created stroke description library.

End DDA

The above steps except Step 3 are easy to implement. The implement of Step 3 is relative to the operations of transforming Chinese characters to graphs and transforming graphs to Chinese characters.

Human is involved in the transforming, i.e., human will adjust and edit the strokes according to his individual viewpoint. Therefore, it is required to describe Chinese characters by human-computer dynamic way.

4   Experiment and Analysis

4.1   Experiment in Chinese Character and Chinese Document Output

As shown in Fig.6, a normal document entering the understanding system is decomposed into its special characters and words, removing all coding-words in the understanding document by description algorithm. Next, a Chinese character generated algorithm come from cloud server or local server, is applied to convert all special characters and words to an appropriate form based on the user's demand.(e.g., 'standard or general output' and 'special or feather output').

The result of experiment briefly described in table 3 and table 4, which come from our experiments system.

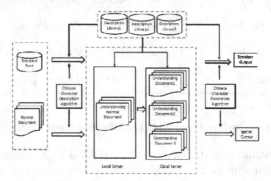

Fig. 6. Illustration of the Chinese character document dynamic generation model

Table 3. Experiment of Chinese characters output

No	Level 1	Level 2	...	Level n
Character1	矮	矮	...	矮
Character 2	碍	碍	...	碍
Character 3	爱	爱	...	爱

Table 4. Experiment of Chinese characters documents output

No	Documents
Document 1	啊 阿 埃 挨 哎 唉 哀 皑 癌 蔼 矮 艾 碍 爱 隘 0 1 2 3 4 5 6 7 8 9 10 11 12 13 14 鞍 氨 安 俺 按 暗 岸 胺 案 肮 昂 盎 凹 敖 熬 15 16 17 18 19 20 21 22 23 24 25 26 27 28 29 翱 袄 傲 奥 懊 澳 芭 捌 扒 叭 吧 笆 八 疤 巴 30 31 32 33 34 35 36 37 38 39 40 41 42 43 44
Document 3	啊 阿 埃 挨 哎 唉 哀 皑 癌 蔼 矮 艾 碍 爱 隘 0 1 2 3 4 5 6 7 8 9 10 11 12 13 14 鞍 氨 安 俺 按 暗 岸 胺 案 肮 昂 盎 凹 敖 熬 15 16 17 18 19 20 21 22 23 24 25 26 27 28 29 翱 袄 傲 奥 懊 澳 芭 捌 扒 叭 吧 笆 八 疤 巴
Document 3	啊 阿 埃 挨 哎 唉 哀 皑 癌 蔼 矮 艾 碍 爱 隘 0 1 2 3 4 5 6 7 8 9 10 11 12 13 14 鞍 氨 安 俺 按 暗 岸 胺 案 肮 昂 盎 凹 敖 熬 15 16 17 18 19 20 21 22 23 24 25 26 27 28 29 翱 袄 傲 奥 奥 懊 澳 芭 捌 扒 叭 吧 笆 八 疤 30 31 32 33 34 35 36 37 38 39 40 41 42 43 44

4.2   Experiment in Hidden Information

In this experiment, we also test the information carrying capacity by 3D data view. We find the Stroke Element play an important role in information carrying capacity. The more Stroke Element Chinese character defined, the more information would be hidden. The result of our experiment is shown in table 5

Table 5. Information and hidden information data view

Stroke Elements	SSV	Data map	HSSV	Data map
SE_1	-8 -6 -8 4		-8 -4 -8 0 -8 0	
SE_2	-8 -6 -5 -6 -5 5		-5 -4 -5 0	
SE_3	-8 4 -5 4		2 -3 2 0	
SE_4	-3 -6 1 -6 0 -3 -1 -1 0 1 1 2 1 3 -1 5 -3 4		4 -3 4 0	
SE_5	-3 -6 -3 8		6 -4 6 0	
SE_6	1 -6 8 -6		None	
SE_7	6 -6 6 7 4 8		None	
SE_8	2 -4 2 3		None	
SE_9	2 -4 4 -4 4 4		None	
SE_{10}	2 3 4 3		None	

5   Conclusions and Future Directions

In this paper, we present a systemic review on font description and generation studies with converging evidences, to uncover cognitive mechanisms of Chinese character understanding in the human brain. Based on these cognitive mechanisms, we present a computational cognitive model for Chinese character understanding. Based the computational cognitive model we propose a dynamic description algorithm for Chinese characters understanding.

Our experiment revealed that our methods performed very well in generating a set of Chinese character understanding in client. Despite some initial successful applications of selected Chinese character for Chinese character understanding, there are numerous research directions that need to be pursued before we can develop a robust solution to Chinese character understanding system. We believe this research has shed light on the feasibility and usefulness of the newer content-based text and document description methods for Chinese information understanding. However, more extensive and systematic studies of structure and non-structure document for large scale, real-time, application in information understanding techniques are needed. We hope by incorporating into more detail, more content, and more knowledge-based techniques for information understanding, improve information understanding strategy.

Acknowledgments. This work is supported by the National Natural Science Foundation of China (60973051). Science and Technology Department of Henan province key scientific and technological project (112102210375).

References

1. Davis, P.J.: Circulant Matrices. Chelsea Publishing, New York (1999)
2. Qiu, X., Jia, W.: A font style learning and transferring method based on strokes and structure of Chinese characters. In: Computer Science & Service System (CSSS), 2012 International Conference on Digital Object Identifier, Beijing (2012)
3. HowNet. http://www.keenage.com 2014.2.20 visit
4. knowledge-based language processing systems, Institute of Information Science, Academia Sinica. http://TreeBank.sinica.edu.tw 2014.2.20 visit
5. Chu, N.S.-H., Tai, C.-L.: Real-time Painting with an Expressive Virtual Chinese Brush. IEEE Computer Graphics and Applications 24(5), 76–85 (2004)
6. Lee, J.: Diffusion Rendering of Black Ink Painting using New Paper and Ink Models. Computer and Graphics 25(2), 295–308 (2001)
7. Xu, S., Lau, F.C.M., Cheung, W.K., Pan, Y.: Automatic Generation of Artistic Chinese Calligraphy. IEEE Computer Society, pp. 32–39 (2005)
8. Wong, S.T.S., Leung, H.: Device Model-based analysis of Chinese calligraphy images. Computer Vision and Image Understanding 109, 69–85 (2008)
9. Hira, T., Iida, K.: A study of calligraphic skill by virtual brush-writing with haptic device—hidden Markov modeling of writing strokes. In: International Conference on Control, Automation and Systems, pp. 1751–1754, October 27–30, 2010

10. Wong, W.: HanGlyph–a Chinese character description language(C). In: Proceedings of the Seventeenth International Conference on Computer Processing of Oriental Languages, Hong Kong (1997)
11. Lin, M., Song, R., Ge, S.-L.: A Research on the Stroke-Segment-Mesh (SSM) Glyph Depiction Method of Chinese Character. Advanced Language Processing and Web Information Technology, pp. 269–278 (2008)
12. Li, Q., Yang, Y.: A human-computer interactive dynamic description method for Jiaguwen characters. In: 2012 International Workshop on Information and Electronics Engineering (IWIEE), Harbin (2012)

Information Technologies for Curating, Mining, Managing and Using Big Brain Data

Identification of Gender Specific Biomarkers for Alzheimer's Disease

Dragan Gamberger[1](✉), Bernard Ženko[2], Alexis Mitelpunkt[3],
and Nada Lavrač[2,4] for the Alzheimer's Disease Neuroimaging Initiative

[1] Rudjer Bošković Institute, Bijenička 54, 10000 Zagreb, Croatia
dragan.gamberger@irb.hr
[2] Jožef Stefan Institute, Ljubljana, Slovenia
[3] Tel Aviv University, Tel Aviv, Israel
[4] University of Nova Gorica, Nova Gorica, Slovenia

Abstract. The paper presents experiments with a novel clustering methodology that enables identification of subpopulations of the
Alzheimer's disease patients that are homogeneous in respect of both
clinical and biological descriptors. It is expected that recognition of relevant connections between clinical and biological descriptors will be easier within such subpopulations. Our dataset includes 317 female and 342
male patients from the ADNI study that are described by a total of
243 biological and clinical descriptors recorded at baseline evaluation.
The constructed clusters clearly demonstrate differences between female
and male patient subpopulations. An interesting result is identification
of a cluster of male Alzheimer's disease patients that are, surprisingly,
characterized by increased intracerebral and whole brain volumes. The
finding suggests existence of two different biological pathways for the
Alzheimer's disease.

1 Introduction

Identification of connections between biological and clinical characteristics of
Alzheimer's disease patients is a long term goal that could significantly improve
the understanding of the Alzheimer's disease (AD) pathophysiology, improve
clinical trial design, and help in predicting outcomes of mild cognitive impairment [1]. In line with the approach proposed in [2], our work aims at finding
homogeneous subpopulations of AD patients in which it will be easier to identify statistically and logically relevant relations between clinical and biological
descriptors. This is not an easy task because we are looking for homogeneous
clusters in a noisy domain with a large set of descriptors with unreliable values of

ADNI—Data used in preparation of this article were obtained from the Alzheimers
Disease Neuroimaging Initiative (ADNI) database (adni.loni.usc.edu). As such, the
investigators within the ADNI contributed to the design and implementation of
ADNI and/or provided data but did not participate in analysis or writing of this
report. A complete listing of ADNI investigators can be found at: http://adni.loni.
usc.edu/wp-content/uploads/how_to_apply/ADNI_Acknowledgement_List.pdf

© Springer International Publishing Switzerland 2015
Y. Guo et al. (Eds.): BIH 2015, LNAI 9250, pp. 57–66, 2015.
DOI: 10.1007/978-3-319-23344-4_6

the clinical data and with biological data that may depend on various biological processes, including those not related to AD.

The distinguishing property of our multi-layer clustering methodology is that the constructed clusters are homogeneous in both biological and clinical layers simultaneously [3]. Preliminary results with the same methodology demonstrated that it enables construction of coherent clusters of AD patients with biological properties that are interesting for expert medical evaluation [4]. In this work we continue the research by using a significantly extended dataset, especially with regard to the number of included clinical and biological properties of patients.

The main novelty of the presented experiments is that we use a gender specific approach. The motivation arose from the preliminary experiments with the same dataset that resulted in some clusters characteristic for either male or female subpopulations. Our primary goal is not the detection of gender related differences in respect of incidence rate or severity of AD, but elimination of gender related characteristics that potentially interfere with the properties related to the dementia. It must be noted that it could be useful to eliminate other sources of variability in biological and clinical data in the same way (e.g., age or ethnic group), but this inevitably reduces the size of populations being analysed. We have therefore concentrated on gender specific analysis only.

The rest of the paper is structured as follows. Section 2 describes the data set and the multi-layer clustering methodology. Section 3 presents the results and statistical comparison of two selected clusters constructed for the male population. Finally, in Section 4 we analyse medical relevance of the results.

2   Data and Methodology

All experiments were performed on the data from the Alzheimer's Disease Neuroimaging Initiative (ADNI) database[1]. From the ADNIMERGE dataframe we have extracted the baseline evaluation data for 317 female and 342 male patients. The patients are described by 56 biological and 187 clinical properties. Some numerical values were transformed in order to avoid highly nonlinear variables. Biological descriptors include ABETA peptides, TAU and PTAU proteins, the APOE4 related genetic variations, PET imaging results FDG-PET and AV45, MRI volumetric data (Ventricles, Hippocampus, WholeBrain, Entorhinal, Fusiform gyrus, Middle temporal gyrus (MidTemp)), intracerebral volume (ICV), and results of various laboratory measurements like red blood cells and total bilirubin. Clinical descriptors include Alzheimer's Disease Assessment Scale (ADAS13), Mini Mental State Examination (MMSE), Rey Auditory Verbal Learning Test (RAVLT immediate, learning, forgetting, percentage

---

[1] The ADNI was launched in 2003 by the National Institute on Aging (NIA), the National Institute of Biomedical Imaging and Bioengineering (NIBIB), the Food and Drug Administration (FDA), private pharmaceutical companies and non-profit organizations. The Principal Investigator of this initiative is Michael W. Weiner, MD, VA Medical Center and University of California, San Francisco. More information can be found at http://www.adni-info.org and http://adni.loni.usc.edu.

of forgetting), Functional Assessment Questionnaire (FAQ), Montreal Cognitive Assessment (MOCA) and Everyday Cognition, which is a cognitive functions questionnaire filled out by patients (ECogPt) and their study partners (ECogSP) (Memory, Language, Visuospatial Abilities, Planning, Organization, Divided Attention and the Total score), Neuropsychiatric Inventory Questionnaire, Modified Hachinski Ischemia Scale, and Geriatric Depression Scale. As an indication of the medical diagnosis we have used global clinical dementia rating score that is interpreted as clinically normal (CN value 0), mild cognitive impairment (MCI value 0.5) and Alzheimer's disease (AD value 1).

2.1   Multi-layer Clustering

Clustering is a standard machine learning approach but it still suffers from problems such as optimal selection of the distance measure and the number of resulting clusters. Typically, the obtained clusters are unstable because they significantly depend on user selectable parameters. This is especially true for noisy domains and domains with statistically related descriptors (attributes). Recently, a novel approach called *multi-layer clustering* has been developed that successfully solves some of these basic problems [3]. In this approach, the quality of the resulting clusters is ensured by the constraint that clusters must be homogeneous simultaneously in two or more data layers, i.e., two or more sets of distinct data descriptors. By defining the clinical descriptors as one data layer and biological descriptors as the second layer, one can expect not only more reliable clusters, but clusters which will be potentially good candidates for the detection of relevant relations between the clinical and biological descriptors.

The multi-layer clustering consists of two steps. In the first step, for each data layer separately, pair-wise similarity of examples is estimated. In the second step these similarity estimations are used in order to construct clusters. The example similarity table (EST) is an $N \times N$ symmetric matrix, where N is the number of examples. One EST is constructed for each layer by defining an artificial binary classification problem, which needs to distinguish between original data examples and some randomly generated ones. These artificial problems are solved with a supervised machine learning algorithm such as decision trees or rules. These types of models enable us to determine if two examples were classified in the same way, i.e., if they fall in the same leaf or are covered by the same rule. An EST is constructed by counting how many times a pair of original examples is classified in the same way, and these counts represent a similarity estimation between the two examples. In the final EST the counts are normalized.

The second step of the algorithm is the agglomerative clustering. It starts with each example being in a separate cluster and then the algorithm iteratively tries to merge clusters together. In each iteration for each possible pair of clusters the potential variability reduction, based on the EST values that can be obtained by merging the clusters, is computed. Let x_{ij} be the similarity between examples i and j from the EST matrix. The CRV score of a single example i from cluster C is the sum of within cluster and outside of cluster components: $\text{CRV}(i) = \text{CRV}_{\text{wc}}(i) + \text{CRV}_{\text{oc}}(i), i \in C$. The two components are sums of squared deviations

Table 1. List and short descriptions of constructed clusters.

Cluster ID	Number of patients	Distribution of CD diagnoses AD / MCI / CN	Clinical status	Biological properties (with z-score versus cognitive normal)	
Clusters for female patients					
F1	46	18 / 24 / 4	Significant cognitive problems (high ADAS13, high FAQ, high MMSE)	low FDG high AV45 low Entorhinal low MidTemp low Fusiform high TAU	9.25 7.66 7.58 7.45 6.89 6.84
F0	18	0 / 4 / 14	Mild or no dementia	Nothing specific	
Clusters for male patients					
M1	20	12 / 8 / 0	Significant cognitive problems	low FDG low Hippocampus low MidTemp high TAU low Entorhinal low Whole brain	6.52 5.52 5.26 5.24 5.08 4.89
M2	18	13 / 3 / 2	Significant cognitive problems	low FDG high AV45 low Hippocampus high ICV high Ventricles high APOE4	5.70 4.95 3.96 3.76 3.61 3.57
M0	20	0 / 1 / 19	Mild or no dementia	Nothing specific	

from the mean value within (or outside of) cluster C: $\mathrm{CRV}_{\mathrm{wc}}(i) = \sum_{j \in C}(x_{ij} - \overline{x_{i,wc}})^2$ and $\mathrm{CRV}_{\mathrm{oc}}(i) = \sum_{j \notin C}(x_{ij} - \overline{x_{i,oc}})^2$. Finally, the CRV score of cluster C is the mean value of $\mathrm{CRV}(i)$ values of all examples in the cluster: $\mathrm{CRV}(C) = \sum_{i \in C} \mathrm{CRV}(i)/|C|$. In each iteration for each possible pair of clusters we compute the potential variability reduction that can be obtained by merging the clusters. The variability reduction of joining clusters C_1 and C_2 is computed as: $\mathrm{DIFF}(C_1, C_2) = (\mathrm{CRV}(C_1) + \mathrm{CRV}(C_2))/2 - \mathrm{CRV}(C_2 \cup C_2)$. The pair of clusters with the largest variability reduction in all layers is then merged together. The iterative process repeats until no pair of clusters exists for which the variability reduction is positive. More details on the algorithm can be found in [3].

3   Clustering Results

Table 1 presents the clusters constructed with the multi-layer clustering, independently for the populations of 317 females and 342 males. For the female population we have one large cluster F1 in which the majority of patients have significant problems with dementia. Out of the 46 included patients, 18 have the diagnosis of AD while 24 have been diagnosed with mild cognitive impairment. In the entire dataset there are 22 patients with AD diagnosis and 18 of them are included into this cluster. The clinical properties of these patients are high ADAS13, FAQ, MMSE scores, and all types of cognitive problems. The biological properties of these patients are also typical for AD patients, e.g., low FDG values, high AV45 values, and significantly decreased Entorhinal volume. A statistical comparison with a population of all 145 female patients with cognitive normal status in the dataset has been used to identify the most distinguishing biological properties of the cluster. The last column of Table 1 presents the most significant properties in respect of the highest z-score values of the Mann-Whitney test. The values are very high denoting that differences between cognitive normal patients and those included in the cluster are very significant.[2] It is surprising that, according to the global clinical dementia rating score, besides 18 AD patients, the cluster also includes 24 patients with the mild cognitive impairment and even 4 cognitive normal patients.

The second cluster F0 constructed for the female population includes 18 patients that are typical patients with no or early mild dementia and have no biological properties that are significantly different from cognitive normal patients. Interestingly, the cluster is relatively small compared to the previous female cluster F1, especially if we take into account that there are 145 cognitive normal female patients in the data set. A probable explanation could be that among ADNI patients diagnosed as cognitive normal there are also patients that are not completely healthy, but their subjective or objective problems are either not severe enough or their problems are in discrepancy with typical clinical profiles.

The bottom part of Table 1 presents clusters for the male population. First, we have a cluster of cognitive normal patients (M0) that is very similar in size and properties to the female cluster F0. The most significant difference to the female population is that there are two male clusters of AD patients (M1 and M2) that have clinical properties of typical AD patients. In the first one (M1) there are 20 patients, 12 of them with AD and 8 with mild cognitive impairment. In the second cluster (M2) there are 18 patients, 13 of them with AD diagnosis.

Although that at the first glance the biological properties characterizing patients in clusters M1 and M2, in contrast to the cognitive normal patients, seem similar, there are substantial differences between these two clusters. Biological and clinical properties that most significantly differ between the clusters according to the Mann-Whitney test are listed in Table 2.

4   Analysis of the Results

Cluster M2 deserves special attention due to the fact that the average values of ICV and whole brain volume for patients in M2 are higher than average values for the set of all 124 cognitive normal male patients. The result is surprising because it is in contradiction with common knowledge that atrophy of human brain is related with cognitive problems and in contradiction with results of structural

---

[2] A value of a z-score higher than 3.29 denotes statistical significance of $P < 0.001$.

Table 2. Biological and clinical properties that are most significantly different for patients in clusters M1 and M2.

Property	Average value for cognitive normal males	Average value for M2	Average value for M1	Mann-Whitney z-score M1 versus M2
Biological properties				
ICV (*1000)	**1576**	**1728**	**1457**	4.14
Whole brain (*1000)	**1109**	**1154**	**961**	3.95
MidTemp	21640	19748	17000	3.38
Fusiform	19600	18237	16175	3.20
TAU	60	86	126	2.53
Red blood cells	62	159	215	2.17
Hippocampus	7792	6565	5684	2.06
Clinical properties				
Abstraction_moca	1.81	1.78	1.15	2.69
MMscore	29.01	24.5	22.35	2.53
Naming_moca	2.92	2.94	2.25	2.38
Q4score (Delayed Word Recall)	3.35	7.83	9.30	2.34
FAQTV	0.10	1.67	3.00	2.19
RAVLT.immediate	44.15	26.28	19.90	2.02

MRI that for AD patients typically show a pattern of decreased grey matter in different regions of the brain [5]. The differences are statistically significant, average ICV values are 1576 and 1728 for cognitive normal and M2 patients, respectively (z-score 3.76, $P < 0.001$), while average whole brain volumes are 1109 and 1154 (z-score 1.99, $P < 0.05$).[3] When comparing patients in cluster M2 with patients in M1, who also have typical AD symptoms but, as expected, decreased ICV and whole brain volumes, then the differences are even more statistically significant (see Table 2).

The importance of the discovery is manifold. First, it indicates gender specific differences because such a cluster with similar properties is not detected in the female population. Second, for a domain in which biological processes with opposite manifestations (decrease and increase of ICV) may result in similar clinical consequences (dementia), segmentation of the patient population is suggested before other analyses aimed at the discovery of relations between biological and clinical properties of patients are performed. Finally, the result is intriguing in respect of its biological and medical interpretation.

It is possible that the increased ICV and whole brain volumes are a consequence of an artefact in data collection procedures, feature extraction from images, or data post-processing (normalization). The assumption may stimulate careful evaluation of the ADNI data, especially for patients in cluster M2. But the result may also suggest the existence of a different biological pathway

---

[3] Actual absolute values for ICV and whole brain volume are 1000 times larger.

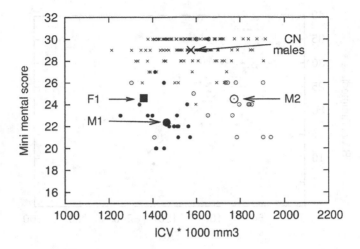

Fig. 1. Patients in cluster M1 (black circles), M2 (white circles), and cognitive normal males (×-marks) presented in respect of intracerebral volume (ICV) and Mini Mental total score values. The large circles and ×-mark denote median values of these clusters and of the cognitive normal male population, respectively. The large black square denotes the mean of female AD patients in cluster F1.

for the male population, resulting in serious dementia problems that are often diagnosed as Alzheimer's disease but with less expressed clinical symptoms (see bottom part of Table 2). In the scientific literature we have found no support for such explanation except that the study devoted to gender related differences [6] concluded that "AD pathology is more likely to be clinically expressed as dementia in women than in men". Fig. 1 illustrates the differences among patients in clusters M1 and M2 and cognitive normal male patients in respect of measured ICV values and Mini Mental scores.

Two male clusters M1 and M2 together include 25 (71%) of a total of 35 male patients with AD diagnosis in the data set. In contrast, the female cluster F1 includes 18 female patients with AD diagnosis (82%) of a total of 22 present in the data set. From the fact that we have one large female cluster and two small

Table 3. Most correlated biological-clinical pairs of properties for various patient populations.

Population	Number of patients	Biological property	Clinical property	Spearman correlation r_s
All	659	FDG	MOCA	−0.51 (df=645, $P < 0.001$)
Female	317	FDG	ADAS13	−0.56 (df=307, $P < 0.001$)
Male	342	Hippocampus	ADAS13	−0.58 (df=289, $P < 0.001$)
F1	46	MidTemp	ADAS13	−0.62 (df=35, $P < 0.001$)
M1	20	TAU	RAVLT.immediate	−0.79 (df=14, $P < 0.01$)
M2	18	ABETA	RAVLT.forgetting	−0.69 (df=9, $P < 0.05$)

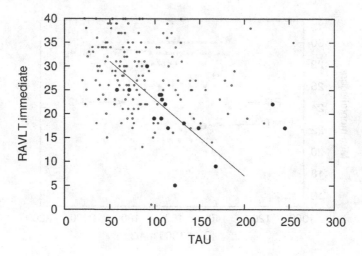

Fig. 2. Patients in cluster M1 (big black circles) and all male patients (small white circles) presented in respect of TAU values and RAVL.immediate scores.

male clusters that together still include a smaller proportion of a population with AD diagnosis than the female one, we can conclude that the male population with serious dementia problems is significantly less homogeneous than the female population. Additionally, the majority of patients in male clusters have AD diagnosis (70% and 80% for M1 and M2, respectively) in contrast to the female cluster F1 in which only 40% of patients have AD diagnosis. The majority of patients in the female cluster have diagnosis of mild cognitive impairment, in spite of the fact that the average values of clinical symptoms are high and biological properties are very different from the cognitive normal female population. This is a surprising finding that is potentially interesting for further analysis, especially in respect of the current diagnostic practice.

One of the stated ADNI goals is to improve clinical trial design through detection of biomarkers that could be used as approximate measures of the severity of dementia. This is known as a difficult task that is still far from a satisfactory solution. If the constructed clusters are really more homogeneous than the complete population, then it may be expected that identification of dementia disease markers should be an easier task for each cluster separately than it is for the complete population. Table 3 presents the best pairs of one biological and one clinical property that can be identified for the complete population, for the female population only, for the male population only, and finally for clusters F1, M1, and M2. The best pairs are identified with the Spearman rank-order correlation coefficient r_s that is computed for all possible pairs of properties. The result confirms that for constructed clusters there exist more strongly correlated biological-clinical relations. The maximal value is detected for cluster M1.[4] The

---

[4] Only the absolute value is important, the negative sign means an inverse correlation.

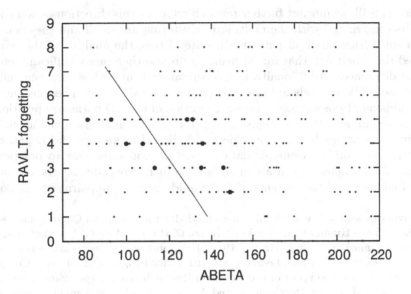

Fig. 3. Patients in cluster M2 (big black circles) and all male patients (small white circles) presented in respect of ABETA values and RAVL.forgetting scores.

correlation is illustrated in Fig. 2 in which patients from cluster M1 and the complete male population are plotted according to their TAU values and RAVLT immediate memory scores. The plotted line is a linear interpolation for patients from cluster M1. In Fig. 3 we present a similar plot of the corresponding best biological-clinical relation for cluster M2. It must be noted that in spite of higher correlation coefficient values, the statistical significance of correlations for small clusters is smaller than for the large cluster because of their size. The result means that detected high correlations are not so reliable and that they have to be confirmed by further experiments. Additionally, it is worth noting the differences between properties that participate in the best pairs. As expected, FDG is the most useful biological property for the general patient population and the result is in agreement with previously reported research [7]. MidTemp, TAU, and ABETA properties are most useful for F1, M1, and M2 clusters, respectively. Also interesting is that RAVLT memory related problems are selected as the most appropriate clinical indicators for both M1 and M2 clusters and that they are correlated with protein specific variables.

5   Conclusions

The presented results confirm that novel machine learning approaches to clustering can indeed be a useful tool for identifying homogeneous patient subsets in various medical knowledge discovery tasks. The applied multi-layer clustering technique and its combination with the gender related separation of the population of patients is definitely not the only possible approach but its results are promising. Still, significant further research effort in this direction is necessary. Clusters constructed with the multi-layer clustering are small and they contain only a small fraction of all patients. In spite of this, the analysis of the results enabled the conclusion that for Alzheimer's disease there are significant gender specific differences. Additionally, a male subpopulation with a surprising effect of increased ICV and whole brain volume has been detected. The existence of these subpopulations suggests that segmentation of the AD patient population is strongly recommended as a preprocessing step for any analysis aimed at understanding of relations between biological and clinical properties of AD patients, however, based on the available data we still do not know how to practically perform the segmentation in a non ad-hoc manner, especially for the cognitive normal patients and the patients with the mild cognitive impairment diagnosis.

Acknowledgments. We would like to acknowledge the European Commission's support through the Human Brain Project (Gr. no. 604102), MAESTRA project (Gr. no. 612944) and InnoMol project (Gr. no. 316289), support of the Croatian Science Foundation (Pr. no. 9623: Machine Learning Algorithms for Insightful Analysis of Complex Data Structures) and support of the Slovenian Research Agency (program Knowledge Technologies and project Development and Applications of New Semantic Data Mining Methods in Life Sciences). Data collection and sharing for this project was funded by the Alzheimer's Disease Neuroimaging Initiative (ADNI) (National Institutes of Health Grant U01 AG024904) and DOD ADNI (Department of Defense award number W81XWH-12-2-0012). ADNI is funded by the National Institute on Aging, the National Institute of Biomedical Imaging and Bioengineering, and through generous contributions from many private pharmaceutical companies and non-profit organizations.

References

1. Weiner, M.W., et al.: The Alzheimer's Disease Neuroimaging Initiative: A review of papers published since its inception. Alzheimer's & Dem. **9**(5), e111–e194 (2013)
2. Galili, T., Mitelpunkt, A., Shachar, N., Marcus-Kalish, M., Benjamini, Y.: Categorize, cluster, and classify: a 3-c strategy for scientific discovery in the medical informatics platform of the human brain project. In: Džeroski, S., Panov, P., Kocev, D., Todorovski, L. (eds.) DS 2014. LNCS, vol. 8777, pp. 73–86. Springer, Heidelberg (2014)
3. Gamberger, D., Mihelčić, M., Lavrač, N.: Multilayer clustering: a discovery experiment on country level trading data. In: Džeroski, S., Panov, P., Kocev, D., Todorovski, L. (eds.) DS 2014. LNCS, vol. 8777, pp. 87–98. Springer, Heidelberg (2014)
4. Gamberger, D., Ženko, B., Mitelpunkt, A., Lavrač, N.: Multilayer clustering: biomarker driven segmentation of Alzheimer's disease patient population. In: Proc. of the International Conference IWBBIO 2015, pp. 134–145 (2015)
5. Hample, H.L., et al.: Biomarkers for Alzheimer's disease: academic, industry, and regulatory perspectives. Nature Reviews Drug Discovery **9**, 560–574 (2010)
6. Barnes, L.L., et al.: Sex differences in the clinical manifestations of Alzheimer disease pathology. Archives of General Psychiatry **62**(6), 685–691 (2005)
7. Langbaum, J.B., et al.: Categorical and correlational analyses of baseline fluorodeoxyglucose positron emission tomography images from the Alzheimer's Disease Neuroimaging Initiative (ADNI). Neuroimage **45**(4), 1107–1116 (2009)

BRAINtrinsic: A Virtual Reality-Compatible Tool for Exploring Intrinsic Topologies of the Human Brain Connectome

Giorgio Conte[1], Allen Q. Ye[2], Angus G. Forbes[1], Olusola Ajilore[2], and Alex Leow[2]([✉])

[1] Department of Computer Science,
University of Illinois at Chicago, Chicago, IL, USA
{gconte2,aforbes}@uic.edu
[2] Department of Psychiatry and Bioengineering,
University of Illinois at Chicago, Chicago, IL, USA
allenye2@uic.edu, {oajilore,aleow}@psych.uic.edu

Abstract. Thanks to advances in non-invasive technologies such as functional Magnetic Resonance Imaging (fMRI) and Diffusion Tensor Imaging (DTI), highly-detailed maps of brain structure and function can now be collected. In this context, brain connectomics have emerged as a fast growing field that aims at understanding these comprehensive maps of brain connectivity using sophisticated computational models. In this paper we present BRAINtrinsic, an innovative web-based 3D visual analytics tool that allows users to intuitively and iteratively interact with connectome data. Moreover, BRAINtrinsic implements a novel visualization platform that reconstructs connectomes' intrinsic geometry, i.e., the topological space as informed by brain connectivity, via dimensionality reduction. BRAINtrinsic is implemented with virtual reality in mind and is fully compatible with the Oculus Rift technology. Last, we demonstrate its effectiveness through a series of case studies involving both structural and resting-state MR imaging data.

Keywords: Connectomics · Connectome datasets · Intrinsic geometry · Neuroimaging

1 Introduction

Magnetic resonance (MR) imaging techniques such as *functional Magnetic Resonance Imaging* (fMRI) and *diffusion weighted imaging* (DWI) enable neuroimagers to collect and derive data about how different brain regions connect from both a structural and a functional point of view [15]. Analogous to the concept of *genome* for genetic data, a brain *connectome* is a whole-brain comprehensive map of neural connections [20]. As neural connections exhibit complex patterns of function and structure, the field of brain connectomics has emerged in order to understand these imaging big data. The brain connectome is typically mathematically represented using connectivity matrices that describe the interaction

© Springer International Publishing Switzerland 2015
Y. Guo et al. (Eds.): BIH 2015, LNAI 9250, pp. 67–76, 2015.
DOI: 10.1007/978-3-319-23344-4_7

among different brain regions. To date, most connectome study designs use brain connectivity matrices to compute summary statistics on either a global or a nodal level [21].

In the current work, we introduce an innovative visualization technology with the ability to reconstruct and analyze the *intrinsic geometry* of brain data, that is, the topological space where brain connectivity natively resides (independent of anatomy). Understanding this intrinsic geometry could not only lead to a greater distinction of differences in clinical cohorts, but also help track longitudinal changes in individual brains in order to better deliver precision medicine. To the best of our knowledge, no such tool currently exists that effectively addresses these needs.

2   Intrinsic Geometry

The proposed *intrinsic geometry* represents the brain connectome after non-linear multidimensional data reduction techniques are applied. This means that the position of each node does not correspond to its anatomical location, as it does in the original brain geometry. Instead, its position is based on the strength of the interaction that each region has with the rest of the brain, whether structural or functional. To put into context why intrinsic geometry may be a better space to understand brain connectivity data, for decades cartographers have mapped quantitative data onto world maps to create unique, informative visualizations. For example, by resizing countries according the Gross Domestic Product (GDP), the viewer can easily appreciate that the United States has the largest GDP. Similarly, dimensionality reduction techniques remap the brain according to network properties. In the intrinsic geometry we are more interested in the shape the brain connectome assumes independent of the anatomical distances between nodes. Thus, the space in which the intrinsic geometry is plotted in is called a *topological space* [4].

Linear dimensionality reduction techniques such as multidimensional scaling (MDS) [2] and principal component analysis (PCA) [14] have been previously used in unrelated fields of medicine as a way to distinguish clinical cohorts through biomarkers, although it can be argued that they are not suitable for complex high-dimensional connectome data [13,22]. To the best of our knowledge, this study represents the first comprehensive application of non-linear dimensionality reduction techniques in the ever-expanding field of brain connectomics. This intrinsic geometry concept provides a connectomic visualization that is not obscured or constrained by the brains anatomy. Indeed, visualizing connectivity information within an anatomical representation of the brain can potentially limit one's ability to clearly understand the complexity of a human brain connectome; some meaningful patterns of structure or function may be much easier to appreciate in a topological space.

2.1 Data Acquisition and Intrinsic Geometry Reconstruction

Structural and diffusion-weighted imaging data were acquired from 46 healthy control subjects (HC, mean age: 59.7±14.6, 20 males). Resting-state functional MRI data were additionally acquired on a subset of healthy controls ($n = 10$). To obtain DTI-informed structural brain connectome, we used a pipeline reported previously [9]. Functional connectomes were generated using the resting state fMRI toolbox, CONN.[1] In brief, raw EPI images were realigned, co-registered, normalized, and smoothed before analyses. Confounding effects from motion artifact, white matter, and CSF were regressed out of the signal. Using the same 82 cortical/subcortical gray-matter labels as the structural brain networks [7], functional brain networks were derived using pairwise fMRI signal correlations.

These 82 anatomical regions were then further upsampled using an algorithm that continuously bisected each region across all subjects at an identical angle until the average region size reached a certain threshold. Previous studies using similar algorithms have shown that up-sampling regions into higher-resolution voxels maintains network connectivity [11]. The resulting parcellation converted 82 regions into 620 sub-regions for the structural data and 739 for the functional data. Brain networks formed by either the fiber tract counts or the functional correlations between up-sampled gray matter regions were generated using an in-house program in Matlab. These up-sampled regions were also re-registered to original subcortical/cortical regions in preparation for nonlinear dimensionality reduction. All networks were examined to ensure that all regions were directly connected to at least one other region preventing the formation of any isolated "islands". To compensate for inter-subject variations, we averaged individual subjects' networks together to obtain a group average network.

2.2 Intrinsic Geometry Reconstruction

Representing Functional and Structural Connectomes as High-dimensional Data. Before any dimensionality reduction can be applied, we need a representation of the connectome data in a high-dimensional space where a distance metric can be properly computed (such that a neighborhood could be defined). In the case of fMRI BOLD signal time series correlations, we propose to first transform inter-regional correlations (r) using the transformation: $s_{i,j} = log(\frac{1}{|r_{i,j}|})$. Here $r_{i,j}$ represents the correlation coefficient between i and j. Note this non-negative transformation yields $s = 0$ if two nodes are completely coupled (i.e., $r = 1$ or -1), and infinity when completely decoupled ($r = 0$). This transformation provides the building block for representing functional data in a high-dimensional space. To this end, we first note that for any brain region the n-dimensional vector $S_* = (s_{*,1}, s_{*,2}, s_{*,3} \ldots, s_{*,n})$ now encodes the pattern of coupling between this region and the entire brain (n denotes the total number of brain regions or nodes; $n = 739$ in our resting state imaging data). In the intrinsic geometry one would thus want to embed two nodes i and j next to each other if they exhibit very similar coupling patterns, i.e., the Euclidean distance $|S_i - S_j| = \sqrt{\sum_n (s_{i,n} - s_{j,n})^2}$

---

[1] http://www.nitrc.org/projects/conn

is small, where $S_i = (s_{i,1}, s_{i,2}, s_{i,3} \ldots, s_{i,n})$ and $S_j = (s_{j,1}, s_{j,2}, s_{j,3}, \ldots, s_{j,n})$. This intuitive example illustrates that we could simply represent functional connectome data in a $n = 739$ dimensional Euclidean space, with node k having the following coordinates, $S_k = (s_{k,1}, s_{k,2}, s_{k,3}, \ldots, s_{k,739})$. In the case of structural connectome (whose connectivity matrix codes the strength of white matter tracts) we propose, with similar rationale, to represent structural connectivity data in a $n = 620$ Euclidean space with node k placed at the following coordinates: $S_k = (GraphDist_{k,1}, GraphDist_{k,2}, \ldots, GraphDist_{k,620})$; here $GraphDist$ codes the shortest path length (i.e., graph distance) connecting two nodes; graph distances are usually computed by defining edge length as the inverse of the edge strength (i.e., fiber counts) followed by applying Dijkstra's algorithm [5]. Figure 1 visualizes these two different transformations for both the structural and functional connectivity matrices.

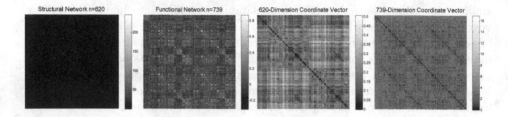

Fig. 1. The figure shows the adjacency matrices for both the structural and the functional group-averaged connectome. The (i,j) element represents the tractography-based fiber count or the BOLD fMRI signal correlation between brain regions i and j. The resulting n-dimensional row vectors describing the Euclidean coordinates of high-dimensional connectome data are shown on the right. See Section 2.2 for more details.

Constructing 3-Dimensional Embedding. To promote uniformity throughout the analyses, we used the dimensionality reduction toolbox introduced by van der Maaten for all reductions [17]. The number of dimensions was reduced from 620 and 739 to 3, for the structural and functional connectome respectively. We used the compute_mapping routine, with the "Isomap" and the "k-nearest neighbor" options. The number of nearest neighbors (i.e., k) during local neighborhood construction was increased iteratively such that all points were included in the embedding. For structural connectome, k was determined to be 17, and for functional 27.

3   Design Features of BRAINtrinsic

A range of interesting approaches to visualizing the human brain connectome are available. Some recent connectome visualization tools include a 3D node-link representation to provide meaningful spatial information relative to the real anatomical position [10, 16, 24]. However, in these tools, the overall visual clutter tends to increase in large networks with dense interconnections between nodes. In this context, interaction helps limit the potential visual clutter that may occur when visualizing the human brain connectome. A possible solution is to let the user easily choose the level of details of the exploration within a Virtual Reality (VR) environment.

Since the advent of this technology, VR systems have been used for visualizing scientific datasets [19]. Additionally, recent VR tools have provided new ways to interact with and explore complex datasets effectively. For example, Ware et al. evaluates the effectiveness of 3D graph visualization when using high resolution stereoscopic displays [23]. Recently, Forbes et al. presents a stereoscopic system to visualize temporal data of the brain activity responding to external stimuli [8], providing new insights when dealing with the temporal dimension in a 3D environment. Broadly speaking, multi-purpose immersive VR environments, such as the CAVE2 [6], enable a more engaging and effective exploration of complex datasets.

Although, the effectiveness of utilizing 3D for representing data has been debated [18], recent work by Alper et al. [1] has shown that in some situations visualizing 3D networks can outperform 2D static visualization, especially when considering complex tasks. To the best of our knowledge, *BRAINtrinsic* presents the first dynamic and interactive VR-compatible visualization platform for connectome representation and exploration.

3.1 Design and Functionality

BRAINtrinsic uses an interactive 3D node-link diagram to visualize connectome data. The individual nodes represented different brain regions and are visualized using circular glyphs, while edges representing a functional or a structural connection between these regions are displayed using lines.

A main concern with the use of node-link diagrams is the potential for visual clutter when displaying a highly interconnected graph. Instead of showing all the connections simultaneously, by default BRAINtrinsic only shows nodes while hiding all links unless explicitly required. Through interaction, users are able to display or hide connections according to their preferences and current needs. We also allow the user to view the connections only within a particular sub-graph. This edges-on-demand technique allows exploration tasks to be performed by showing only the connections starting from a specific region that is currently being interrogated. The user can pin the connections in the scene by simply clicking on the node itself. We use varying degrees of transparency to visually encode the strength of edge weights; stronger connections are represented using opaque lines while weaker edges are more transparent. Transparency is scaled relative to only the currently displayed edges.

Colors are used to highlight the neuroanatomical membership of each node in the brain. Here, each glyph belongs to one of the 87 neuroanatomical gray matter regions as defined by Freesurfer [7]. However, the data structure is flexible enough to accept any membership or affiliation definition. Additionally, we implemented a range of user interactions to support visual analysis including the following:

- Dynamically display the nodal strength for any node being interrogated [3];
- Dynamically create the shortest-path tree rooted in the node selected by the user;
- Visualize the shortest path between any two nodes;
- Select or deselect any regions in any topological space (anatomy versus intrinsic) during visualization;

We again used Dijkstra's algorithm [5] to create the shortest path tree. The user can filter the shortest path tree according to two different measures: graph distance and number of intermediate nodes or "hops". In the first case the user can filter the tree according to the relative distance with respect to its farthest node. Given a threshold t, all the nodes that satisfy the following inequality are drawn: $d(r, i) \leq maxDistance(r) \cdot t$, where r is the root node, i is the node considered, $maxDistance(r)$ is the distance between the root node and the farthest node, and t is the threshold chosen by the user. If $t = 0$ then only the root node is displayed, while if $t = 1$ the entire shortest path tree is drawn. In the latter case, the user is able to filter out nodes that are not reachable within a certain number of nodes from the root.

Following the computation of the shortest-path tree, the user then can proceed to select a second "destination" node and visualize the shortest route connecting this node to the root. In this case, we display all the nodes in the network to provide the overall perspective of the route course.

3.2 System Details

BRAINtrinsic was developed in *Javascript* using the *threejs* library (http://threejs.org) an open source wrapper for the hardware accelerated graphics functionality provided by *WebGL* (http://webgl.com). BRAINtrinsic was designed to be fully compatible within a virtual reality environment, and has been specifically calibrated for use with the Oculus Rift VR headset (http://oculus.com). Through stereographic rendering, we emulate the way human eyes perceive the real world, creating a natural navigation for the user. The code developed is open source and publicly available at the authors' code repository [2].

4 Results

4.1 Visualizing the Intrinsic Geometry and Simulated Rich-club Removal

Figure 2 visualizes the intrinsic geometry of the structural and the functional group-averaged connectome, as well as illustrates the rich-club property of the human connectome (second row). The basic concept behind the rich club property is the tendency for nodes with high nodal strengths to form tightly interconnected groups [12]. Mathematically speaking, given a graph N and the parameter

---

[2] https://github.com/CreativeCodingLab/BRAINtrinsic

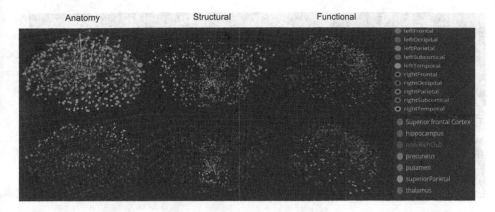

Fig. 2. This figure visualizes the intrinsic geometry of the tractography-derived structural and the resting-state fMRI connectome (middle and right panel, respectively), as well as the locations of rich-club regions in these spaces (second row). For comparison, their corresponding locations in the original neuroanatomical space are also shown (left panel).

k which defines a nodal strength cut off, the rich club property is defined as

$$\phi(k) = \frac{2E_{>k}}{N_{>k}(N_{>k} - 1)} \tag{1}$$

where $E_{>k}$ is the number of edges in N between the nodes of nodal strength greater than k and $N_{>k}$ is the number of nodes in N with nodal strength greater than k. Visually and intuitively, it is clear that rich-club nodes form the center of the structural connectome's intrinsic geometry (lower middle panel). To further appreciate the power of BRAINtrinsic, we demonstrate gross changes in the shape of the structural connectome's intrinsic geometry when rich-club nodes are removed.

Figure 3 (top left) again visualizes the bowl-like shape of the complete structural connectome, while the connectome without rich club nodes (top right) shows a ring-like structure with a "hole" in the middle. Visually, rich-club nodes thus keep the entire network intact by forming the center. When they are removed, remaining brain regions are now topologically dispersed and less coupled. Similar simulations were further conducted by removing an equal number of nodes with respect to the following criteria: a) nodal strength (high to low), b) clustering (low to high), c) nodal path length (low to high), and d) random removal. While random removal(top middle) as expected only induces subtle changes to the intrinsic geometry, interestingly removing nodes based on clustering (lower left) also minimally changes the overall shape, supporting the fundamental differences in what local properties such as clustering capture relative to global properties. The immersive VR environment provided by BRAINtrinsic helps user better appreciate the differences mentioned above. BRAINtrinsic

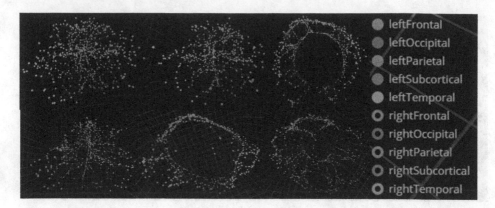

Fig. 3. This figure compares the intrinsic geometry of the structural connectome when different node removal strategies are applied. Top Row (from left): the first image depicts the connectome in its entirety, the second visualizes the intrinsic geometry when a 20% random-removal procedure is applied, and the last when rich-club nodes are removed (20% of all nodes). Bottom Row (from left) depicts the intrinsic geometry after removing nodes ranked within the bottom 20% with the respect to the clustering coefficient, bottom 20% with respect to the nodal path length and top 20% with respect to the nodal strength.

is particularly effective when experts aim at understanding and comparing the overall shape of the entire connectome.

4.2   Resting State Functional Connectome

The right panel of Figure 2 visualizes the intrinsic geometry of resting-state fMRI connectome, which exhibits a very different pattern compared to its structural counterpart. Due to the strong inter-hemispheric fMRI connectivity between homologous regions, here one does not see the left-right symmetry as in the

Fig. 4. Exploring connectome data using BRAINtrinsic within the Oculus Rift environment.

structural case; instead homologous regions now coalesce into a single cluster. More interestingly, while rich-club regions are located at the center of structural connectome's intrinsic geometry, this is no longer the case for functional connectome. BRAINtrinsic allows for such an appreciation to easily occur when exploring functional datasets. The choice of using different glyphs and colors to encode different regions-of-interests coupled with effective VR rendering provides a clear understanding of the underlying neuroanatomy even in this topological space.

5 Discussion and Conclusion

This paper introduced *BRAINtrinsic*, a novel VR-compatible visualization application that enables users to interactively explore the human brain connectome and its intrinsic topology. Since in the intrinsic space, spatial vicinity equates to stronger connectivity, the user is able to explore freely and easily the terrain of brain connectivity, either functional or structural. Indeed, the real advantage of exploring in the intrinsic space (especially when coupled with virtual-reality technology), is the ability to understand the connectivity relationship among a number of brain regions as neuroimagers unfold complex high-dimensional connectivity data into easily understandable and relatable configurations in 3D (Figure 4). By representing structural or functional connectomes using high-dimensional data followed by dimensionality reduction, this visualization software creates a "road map" of the human brain. While the actual connectivity matrix can be parsed much like knowing the distance to any stop of a road trip it is hard to comprehend these strict numerical quantities without a map to help guide relative locations. BRAINtrinsic facilitates this appreciation and further provides methods for interacting with individual nodes to discover highly integrated circuits in both functional and structural connectomes.

References

1. Alper, B., Hollerer, T., Kuchera-Morin, J., Forbes, A.: Stereoscopic highlighting: 2d graph visualization on stereo displays. IEEE Transactions on Visualization and Computer Graphics **17**(12), 2325–2333 (2011)
2. Borg, I., Groenen, P.J.: Modern multidimensional scaling: Theory and applications. Springer Science & Business Media (2005)
3. Bullmore, E., Sporns, O.: Complex brain networks: graph theoretical analysis of structural and functional systems. Nature Reviews Neuroscience **10**(3), 186–198 (2009)
4. Bullmore, E.T., Bassett, D.S.: Brain graphs: graphical models of the human brain connectome. Annual review of clinical psychology **7**, 113–140 (2011)
5. Dijkstra, E.W.: A note on two problems in connexion with graphs. Numerische mathematik **1**(1), 269–271 (1959)
6. Febretti, A., Nishimoto, A., Thigpen, T., Talandis, J., Long, L., Pirtle, J., Peterka, T., Verlo, A., Brown, M., Plepys, D., et al.: Cave2: a hybrid reality environment for immersive simulation and information analysis. In: IS&T/SPIE Electronic Imaging, pp. 864903–864903. International Society for Optics and Photonics (2013)

7. Fischl, B.: Freesurfer. Neuroimage **62**(2), 774–781 (2012)
8. Forbes, A., Villegas, J., Almryde, K.R., Plante, E.: A stereoscopic system for viewing the temporal evolution of brain activity clusters in response to linguistic stimuli. In: IS&T/SPIE Electronic Imaging, pp. 90110I–90110I. International Society for Optics and Photonics (2014)
9. GadElkarim, J.J., Schonfeld, D., Ajilore, O., Zhan, L., Zhang, A.F., Feusner, J.D., Thompson, P.M., Simon, T.J., Kumar, A., Leow, A.D.: A framework for quantifying node-level community structure group differences in brain connectivity networks. In: Ayache, N., Delingette, H., Golland, P., Mori, K. (eds.) MICCAI 2012, Part II. LNCS, vol. 7511, pp. 196–203. Springer, Heidelberg (2012)
10. Gerhard, S., Daducci, A., Lemkaddem, A., Meuli, R., Thiran, J.P., Hagmann, P.: The connectome viewer toolkit: an open source framework to manage, analyze and visualize connectomes. Frontiers in Neuroinformatics **5**(3) (2011). http://www.frontiersin.org/neuroinformatics/10.3389/fninf.2011.00003/abstract
11. Hagmann, P., Cammoun, L., Gigandet, X., Meuli, R., Honey, C.J., Wedeen, V.J., Sporns, O.: Mapping the structural core of human cerebral cortex. PLoS biology **6**(7), e159 (2008)
12. van den Heuvel, M.P., Sporns, O.: Rich-club organization of the human connectome. The Journal of neuroscience **31**(44), 15775–15786 (2011)
13. Howells, S., Maxwell, R., Peet, A., Griffiths, J.: An investigation of tumor 1h nuclear magnetic resonance spectra by the application of chemometric techniques. Magnetic resonance in medicine **28**(2), 214–236 (1992)
14. Jolliffe, I.: Principal component analysis. Wiley Online Library (2002)
15. Jones, D.K.: Diffusion MRI: Theory, methods, and applications. Oxford University Press (2010)
16. LaPlante, R.A., Douw, L., Tang, W., Stufflebeam, S.M.: The connectome visualization utility: Software for visualization of human brain networks. PLoS ONE **9**(12), e113838 (2014). http://dx.doi.org/10.1371%2Fjournal.pone.0113838
17. van der Maaten, L.J., Postma, E.O., van den Herik, H.J.: Dimensionality reduction: A comparative review. Journal of Machine Learning Research **10**(1–41), 66–71 (2009)
18. Munzner, T.: Process and pitfalls in writing information visualization research papers. In: Kerren, A., Stasko, J.T., Fekete, J.-D., North, C. (eds.) Information Visualization. LNCS, vol. 4950, pp. 134–153. Springer, Heidelberg (2008)
19. Robertson, G.G., Mackinlay, J.D., Card, S.K.: Cone trees: animated 3d visualizations of hierarchical information. In: Proceedings of the SIGCHI conference on Human factors in computing systems, pp. 189–194. ACM (1991)
20. Sporns, O.: The human connectome: a complex network. Annals of the New York Academy of Sciences **1224**(1), 109–125 (2011)
21. Sporns, O., Tononi, G., Kötter, R.: The human connectome: a structural description of the human brain. PLoS computational biology **1**(4), e42 (2005)
22. Vujovic, S., Henderson, S., Presneau, N., Odell, E., Jacques, T., Tirabosco, R., Boshoff, C., Flanagan, A.: Brachyury, a crucial regulator of notochordal development, is a novel biomarker for chordomas. The Journal of pathology **209**(2), 157–165 (2006)
23. Ware, C., Mitchell, P.: Visualizing graphs in three dimensions. ACM Transactions on Applied Perception (TAP) **5**(1), 2 (2008)
24. Xia, M., Wang, J., He, Y.: Brainnet viewer: a network visualization tool for human brain connectomics. PloS one **8**(7), e68910 (2013)

Sleep Stages Classification from Electroencephalographic Signals Based on Unsupervised Feature Space Clustering

Iosif Mporas[✉], Anastasia Efstathiou, and Vasileios Megalooikonomou

Multidimensional Data Analysis and Knowledge Management Laboratory, Department of Computer Engineering and Informatics, University of Patras, 26500 Rion-Patras, Greece
imporas@upatras.gr

Abstract. In this article we present a methodology for the automatic classification of sleep stages. The methodology relies on short-time analysis with time and frequency domain features followed by unsupervised feature subspace clustering. For each cluster of the feature space a different classification setup is adopted thus fine-tuning the classification algorithm to the specifics of the corresponding feature subspace area. The experimental results showed that the proposed methodology achieved a sleep stage classification accuracy equal to 92.53%, which corresponds to an improvement of approximately 3% compared to the best performing single classifier without applying clustering of the feature space.

Keywords: Sleep stages · Electroencephalography · Clustering

1   Introduction

The modern lifestyle at work as well as at off-work daily activities, especially in the case of developed countries, is frequently characterized as stressful, which can result in mental distress. Population suffering from sleep problems is increasing and sleep disordering becomes one of the popular health problems. This affects the physical and mental health of people, in contrast to effective sleep which results to comfort and relief from stress. The quality of sleep is more important than the quantity and the falling asleep period is important in obtaining good quality sleep [1]. The inability either to sleep or to stay awake is a significant health problem which may result in an abnormal everyday living.

In order to diagnose and offer appropriate therapy to sleep disorders, the understanding of the brain and body mechanism during sleep is necessary. Sleep is a losing state as temporary, partial, and periodic in the form of that can be returned with various forced stimulus of the communication of the organism with the environment [2]. It can also be defined by the decreasing of motor activity, the decreasing of response with stimulus, and to be easy recycling as behavioral [3, 4].

Neuroscientists have described the human sleep, more than one century ago after studies using electroencephalography (EEG), as a succession of five recurring stages. These stages are the rapid eye movement stage (REM) and the non-rapid eye movement stages (NREM), which are distinguished in N1, N2, N3 and N4 NREM stages.

© Springer International Publishing Switzerland 2015
Y. Guo et al. (Eds.): BIH 2015, LNAI 9250, pp. 77–85, 2015.
DOI: 10.1007/978-3-319-23344-4_8

The awake status is considered as a separate stage and is not included in the above five ones. These stages are characterized by rapid changes in the amplitude and the frequencies (rhythms) of the electroencephalographic (EEG) signal [5]. Specifically, N1 presents a frequency transition of the brain from alpha waves (approx. 8–13 Hz, common in the awake state) to theta waves (approx. 4-7 Hz). N2 is characterized by sleep spindles (approx. 11-16 Hz) and K-complexes [6]. In N3 stage a minimum of 20% delta waves (approx. 0.5-2 Hz) appear, having a peak-to-peak amplitude of more than 75 μV, while in N4 stage delta waves reach 50%. REM stage accounts for 20–25% of total sleep time duration in most human adults and presents a rapid low-voltage EEG (higher frequency saw-tooth waves). The study and the analysis of the sleep stages from sleep scientists is essential for the treatment and therapy of sleep related disorders. It typically results in a hypnogram [23], i.e. a form of polysomno-graphy (PSG) that graphically represents the stages of sleep as a function of time.

The analysis and evaluation of sleep is performed by expert neurologists using EEG signals. Sleep recordings usually last approximately 6-8 hours and thus visual investigation of the EEG signals manually by a sleep scientist is quite tedious and time-consuming. Moreover, manual investigation of the EEG sleep recordings may result to biased/subjective analysis conclusions since it will rely on the degree of ex-perience of the sleep expert. Additionally, the need for sleep experts sets manual analysis of sleep recordings as an expensive solution. Due to the above mentioned disadvantages of manual analysis of sleep recordings, computer-based solutions for the automatic sleep stage scoring have been proposed based on the recent advances in information technology and specifically in the areas of statistical signal modeling, pattern recognition and machine learning.

Most methodologies found in the literature are based on short-time decomposition of the EEG signals to frames (or epochs). The epochs are represented by spectral analysis methods [2, 12, 14, 15], wavelet transformation [7, 8], autoregressive analy-sis [5, 11], band-specific energy [9, 10], entropy [10, 13], etc. Except from the EEG signal, several studies report analysis of sleep stages using electrocardiogram (ECG) [1, 9, 16] signals. Furthermore, in [10, 15] the study of sleep and wakefulness was performed using polysomnographic (PSG) data, i.e., concurrent recordings of multiple sensors including EEG, ECG, electro-oculogram (EOG) and electromyogram (EMG). For the automatic scoring of sleep stages each epoch is labeled with one of the sleep stage classes by classifying the corresponding feature vectors. Several well-known machine learning algorithms for classification have been used in this task, such as the support vector machines (SVMs) [9, 13], the artificial neural networks (NNs) [7, 8, 10, 12, 16], the decision trees (DTs) [2] and other classification methods such as the Gaussian mixture models (GMMs) [14], the hidden Markov models (HMMs) [17], the Kullback-Leibler divergence (KL) [5] the Bayesian classifier (BN) and the k-nearest neighbors (knn) [10].

In this article we present a methodology for automatic classification scoring of the sleep stages from electroencephalographic data, based on feature subspace clustering and use of cluster-specific classifiers for the sleep stage scoring. The remaining of this article is organized as follows: In Section 2 we explain the proposed methodology for automatic sleep stage classification. In Section 3 we offer a description of the data used in the evaluation and describe the experimental setup. In Section 4 we describe the experimental results and conclude in Section 5.

2　Sleep Stages Classification Using Feature Space Clustering

The proposed methodology for sleep stage classification is based on the use of time and frequency based EEG signal features in order to exploit the differences in the frequencies and the amplitudes of the EEG signal among the sleep stages, as described in Section 1. In particular, during the training phase of the methodology we perform short-time analysis of the EEG signal using widely used time-domain and frequency-domain features and perform unsupervised clustering of the feature vector space. Moreover for a number of dissimilar classifiers we examine their discriminative ability per cluster and assign the best-performing classifier per cluster. In the test phase, each EEG epoch is represented by the time-domain and frequency-domain features used in training and is classified to one of these feature space clusters as they were modeled during training. Subsequently, the corresponding cluster-specific classifier is used to assign a sleep stage score to the corresponding EEG epoch. The concept of the proposed methodology is illustrated in Figure 1.

As can be seen in Figure 1, during the training phase a bootstrap set of EEG data with known hypnogram labeling, i.e., known time intervals per sleep stage is used. The training EEG signal is initially preprocessed with frame blocking of constant length w samples and time-shift $t \le w$ samples, thus decomposing the EEG signal to a sequence of N epochs $X = \{x_n\}$, $x_n \in \mathbb{R}^w$, with $1 \le n \le N$. Here we consider single channel EEG analysis. Each epoch is processed by time domain

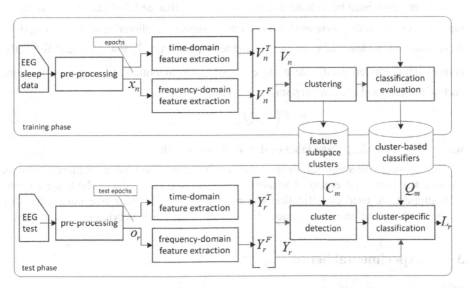

Fig. 1. Block diagram of the proposed methodology for sleep stage classification from EEG data with unsupervised feature space clustering.

parameterization algorithms producing a corresponding feature vector, $V_n^T \in \mathbb{R}^{|V_n^T|}$, $1 \leq n \leq N$, and by frequency domain parameterization algorithms producing a corresponding feature vector, $V_n^F \in \mathbb{R}^{|V_n^F|}$, $1 \leq n \leq N$. The time and frequency domain feature vectors of each epoch are concatenated into a common feature vector, i.e. $V_n^T || V_n^F = V_n \in \mathbb{R}^{|V_n^T| + |V_n^F|}$, $1 \leq n \leq N$. Subsequently, unsupervised clustering of the feature vector space to M subspace clusters, C_m, $1 \leq m \leq M$, is applied using a clustering algorithm. For each of the M subsets of epochs belonging to the m-th cluster, we evaluate K dissimilar classification algorithms, S_k, $1 \leq k \leq K$, in order to extract the best performing, Q_m, classifier per cluster, i.e.

$$Q_m = \arg \max_k \left(C_m, S_k \right) \tag{1}$$

where $Q_m \in \{S_k\}$.

During the test phase a test EEG sleep signal recording, O, with unknown sleep stage annotation is preprocessed similarly to the training phase. The corresponding epochs, $O = \{o_r\}$, $1 \leq r \leq R$, $o_r \in \mathbb{R}^w$, are processed by time-domain and frequency-domain feature extraction algorithms, identical to the training phase, producing the feature vectors Y_r^T and Y_r^F, respectively. The concatenated test feature vectors $Y_r^T || Y_r^F = Y_r \in \mathbb{R}^{|V_n|}$ are subsequently processed by a cluster detector, which classifies each test vector, Y_r, to one of the M clusters, as they were modeled from the unsupervised clustering of the training data. After assigning a cluster label to each of the test epochs, i.e. $Y_r \in C_m$, $1 \leq r \leq R$, the corresponding cluster-specific sleep stage classification algorithm, Q_m, is used to score each of the test epochs with a sleep stage label, i.e.

$$L_r = f \left(Y_r, Q_m \right), \ Y_r \in C_m \tag{2}$$

where L_r is the sleep stage label of the r-th test epoch.

The above architecture for sleep stage scoring can be extended to more channels without any loss of generality. The use of unsupervised clustering of the feature space may support the used classification engines in fine-tuning their free parameters for sleep stages separation in a subspace of the features with less varying characteristics.

3   Experimental Setup

The sleep stage classification architecture presented in Section 2 was evaluated using "The Sleep EDF Database" [18] provided by Physionet [19]. It is a collection of 61 polysomnograms (PSGs) with accompanying hypnograms. The recordings were obtained from Caucasian males and females (21 - 35 years old) without any medication and they contain bipolar Fpz-Cz and Pz-Oz EEG channels according to the 10-20 system [24], sampled at 100 Hz. The labeling of the electrodes indicate the position of the EEG electrodes: the letters F, T, C, P and O stand for frontal, temporal, central, parietal, and occipital lobes, respectively, a "z" (zero) refers to an electrode placed on the midline, even numbers (2,4,6,8) refer to electrode positions on the right hemisphere, whereas odd numbers (1,3,5,7) refer to those on the left hemisphere. The Fpz-Cz channel was used here. Hypnograms were manually scored according to Rechtschaffen & Kales based on Fpz-Cz/Pz-Oz EEG channels.

During pre-processing the EEG recordings were frame blocked to epochs of 15, 30, 45 and 60 seconds length, without time-overlap between successive epochs. For each epoch well-known and widely used time and frequency domain features were extracted [20]. In particular, the EEG waveform was parameterized using the following features: (i) time-domain features: minimum value, maximum value, mean, variance, standard deviation, percentiles (25%, 50%-median and 75%), interquartile range, mean absolute deviation, range, skewness, kyrtosis, energy, Shannon's entropy, logarithmic energy entropy, number of positive and negative peaks, zero-crossing rate, and (ii) frequency-domain features: 6-th order autoregressive-filter (AR) coefficients, power spectral density, frequency with maximum and minimum amplitude, spectral entropy, delta-theta-alpha-beta-gamma band energy, discrete wavelet transform coefficients with mother wavelet function Daubechies 16 and decomposition level equal to 8, thus resulting to a feature vector of dimensionality equal to 55.

For the clustering step we used the expectation-maximization (EM) algorithm. Both for the training and the test phase classification we relied on dissimilar algorithms in order to maximize complementarity. Specifically, we used the k-nearest neighbors classifier with linear search of the nearest neighbor and without weighting of the distance also known as instance based classifier (IBk), the pruned C4.5 decision tree (C4.5) with 3 folds for pruning and 7 for growing the tree, the multilayer perceptron neural network (MLP) with an architecture of 3-layers, and the support vector machine (SVM) using the sequential minimal optimization algorithm and radial basis function kernel. The values of the parameters C and γ for the kernel were empirically set to 15 and to 0.1 respectively after grid search. For the implementation of the algorithms we relied on the WEKA toolkit implementations [21].

4   Experimental Results

The sleep stage classification methodology using unsupervised feature space clustering presented in Section 2 was evaluated following the experimental setup described in Section 3. In order to evaluate the performance of the proposed methodology we examined the percentage of correctly classified epochs. We followed a ten-fold cross validation setup, in order to avoid overlap between training and test datasets.

As a first step, we examined the performance of the four evaluated classification algorithms with different size, w, of frame length (epoch). The results (in percentages) are tabulated in Table 1. The best performing setup is shown in bold. In all evaluated epoch sizes there is no overlap between successive epochs.

Table 1. Sleep stage classification accuracy for different classification algorithms using different epoch lenghts.

Classifier	w =15s	w =30s	w =45s	w =60s
IBk	85.94	87.50	87.10	86.32
C4.5	84.13	86.31	85.92	84.73
SVM	87.66	**89.44**	88.84	88.31
MLP	87.12	88.02	87.63	87.09

As can be seen in Table 1, the best performing algorithm is the SVM with best achieving accuracy equal to 89.44%. The best performing SVM is followed by the second discriminative algorithm, MLP, with an accuracy of 88.02%. The other two algorithms achieved worse performance. With respect to the size to the epoch, the 30 seconds length achieved the best performance across all evaluated classification algorithms. The experimental results show that the use of longer epochs slightly decreases the performance, while the use of shorter epochs significantly increases the error rate. The superiority of SVMs is probably owed to the fact that these classifiers circumvent the "curse of dimensionality" and the fact that SVM training always finds a global solution [22], in contrast to other classifiers (e.g. neural networks) where many local minima usually exist and thus are sensitive to the distributional specifics of the training data. More than 65% of the misclassified epochs were found close to the transitions of the sleep stages and mainly at the beginnings of each sleep stage. The most misclassified is the sleep stage N1 followed by N3, which is in agreement with [2, 7, 8, 12]. Although due to different data and experimental setup no direct comparison to the reported in the literature sleep stage classification performance (varying approximately from 80% to 95% [2, 5, 7, 8, 10]) can be done, the above reported baseline performance is comparable to the literature.

In a second step we examined the performance of the sleep stage classification methodology with unsupervised feature clustering. Specifically, we applied the EM clustering algorithm for 2 up to 4 clusters. The performance of the cluster-based methodology was evaluated using the best performing 30 seconds epoch size. The experimental results are tabulated in Table 2. The best sleep stage classification performance is indicated in bold. The results of Table 1, which correspond to the case of M=1 cluster (i.e. without clustering) are duplicated in Table 2. The last row corresponds to the results for sleep stage classification using the best per cluster classifier.

Table 2. Sleep stage classification accuracy for different classification algorithms using different number M of feature space clusters.

Classifier	M=1	M=2	M=3	M=4
IBk	87.50	89.33	90.58	89.96
C4.5	86.31	88.79	89.47	89.04
SVM	89.44	91.56	92.39	91.30
MLP	88.02	91.31	92.26	91.28
Best Cluster-based	-	91.60	**92.53**	91.63

The experimental results in Table 2 show a significant improvement of the sleep classification accuracy when using feature subspace clusters compared to the results of single classification algorithms without clustering shown in the first column. In detail, the best performance was achieved when clustering the feature space to 3 subspaces. The accuracy in this case was equal to 92.53%, which results to an improvement of 3.09% in terms of absolute performance. The increase of the number of clusters was not followed by an increase in the sleep stage classification accuracy. To some degree, this is probably owed to the amount of data, since by increasing the number of clusters the available data for training the cluster-based classification models are decreasing. Moreover, the use of many clusters increases the test feature vectors that are incorrectly assigned to clusters. Except for the best per cluster performing algorithm (in the last row of Table 2), the use of feature space clustering increased the sleep stage classification performance for all evaluated algorithms. Specifically, the SVM classifier, which was the best performing algorithm when no clustering was applied, improved its performance by approximately 3%. The MLP algorithm was improved by approximately 4% and both the IBk and C4.5 algorithms by approximately 3%. In all evaluated cases the use of feature space clustering resulted in less misclassifications around the sleep stage transitions, while the improvement comparing to the baseline setup was not found significant for the middle of each sleep stage. This is probably owed to the fact that the application of feature space clustering restricts the classification to a less varying subspace area, which is more intense close to the sleep stage transitions.

The evaluation showed that in all cases the use of feature space clustering before training the sleep stage classification algorithms results in more robust models. When the training data are restricted to a subarea of the feature space the free parameters of the classifier are better fine-tuned to the diversity among the sleep stages and not to other potential variations of the feature vectors. This results to classification models with better discriminative ability among the EEG sleep stages.

5   Conclusion

We presented a methodology for the robust classification of sleep stages from EEG signals. The methodology exploits time-domain and frequency-domain features and trains sleep stage classification models on subareas of the feature space, after unsupervised clustering of the training data. The experimental results showed the validity of the proposed methodology, since the accuracy was improved by more than 3% when using cluster-specific sleep stage classification models instead of models trained with data from the whole feature vector space.

The use of clusters of the feature space offers advantage to the classification algorithms to fine-tune their free parameters to the specific characteristics of each cluster, i.e. to space areas which typically will have lower variation and will be less sparse. Finally, the specific and dissimilar characteristics of the feature data within each cluster can better be modeled by different classification algorithms.

Acknowledgment. The research reported in the present paper was partially supported by the ARMOR Project (FP7-ICT-2011-5.1-287720) "Advanced multi-paRametric Monitoring and analysis for diagnosis and Optimal management of epilepsy and Related brain disorders", co-funded by the EC under the 7th Framework Programme and the BioMed-Mine Project "Mining Biomedical Data and Images: Development of Algorithms and Applications" funded through the Operational Program "Education and Lifelong Learning" of the NSRF-Research Funding Program: Thales. Investing in knowledge society through the European Social Fund.

References

1. Hagiwara, H.: Estimation of sleep stage in the falling asleep period using a Lorenz plot of ECG RR intervals. In: Proc. of the 31st Annual International Conference of the IEEE EMBS, pp. 2510–2513 (2009)
2. Gunes, S., Polat, K., Yosunkaya, S.: Efficient sleep stage recognition system based on EEG signal using k-means clustering based feature weighting. Expert Systems with Applications **37**, 7922–7928 (2010)
3. Polat, K., Yosunkaya, S., Gunes, S.: Comparison of different classifier algorithms on the automated detection of obstructive sleep apnea syndrome. J. of Medical Systems **32**(3), 243–250 (2008)
4. Rechtschaffen, A., Kales, A.: A manual of standardized terminology, techniques and scoring system for sleep stages of human subject. US Government Printing Office, National Institute of Health Publication, Washington (1968)
5. Zhovna, I., Shallom, I.D.: Automatic detection and classification of sleep stages by multichannel EEG signal modeling. In: Proc. of the 30th IEEE EMBS Conference (2008)
6. Mporas, I., Tsirka, V., Zacharaki, E.I., Koutroumanidis, M., Megalooikonomou, V.: Online seizure detection from EEG and ECG signals for monitoring of epileptic patients. In: Likas, A., Blekas, K., Kalles, D. (eds.) SETN 2014. LNCS, vol. 8445, pp. 442–447. Springer, Heidelberg (2014)
7. Chiu, C.-C., Hai, B.H., Yeh, S.-J.: Sleep stages recognition based on combined artificial neural network and fuzzy system using wavelet transform features. In: Toi, V.V., Toan, N.B., Dang Khoa, T.Q., Lien Phuong, T.H. (eds.) 4th International Conference on Biomedical Engineering in Vietnam. IFMBE Proceedings, vol. 40, pp. 72–76. Springer, Heidelberg (2013)
8. Ebrahimi, F., Mikaeili, M., Estrada, E., Nazeran, H.: Automatic sleep stage classification based on EEG signals by using neural networks and wavelet packet coefficients. In: Proc. of the 30th IEEE EMBS Conference (2008)
9. Yu, S., Chen, X., Wang, B., Wang, X.: Automatic sleep stage classification based on ECG and EEG features for day time short nap evaluation. In: Proc. of the 10th World Congress on Intelligent Control and Automation (2012)
10. Zoubek, L., Charbonnier, S., Lesecq, S., Buguet, A., Chapotot, F.: Feature selection for sleep/wake stages classification using data driven methods. Biomedical Signal Processing and Control **2**, 171–179 (2007)
11. Zhovna, I., Shallom, I.: Multichannel Analysis of EEG Signal Applied to Sleep Stage Classification. Recent Advances in Biomedical Engineering (2009). ISBN: 978-953-307-004-9

12. Kerkeni, N., Alexandre, F., Bedoui, M.H., Bougrain, L., Dogui, M.: Automatic classifcation of sleep stages on a EEG signal by artificial neural networks. In: Proc. of the 5th WSEAS International Conference on Signal, Speech and Image Processing, WSEAS SSIP 2005 (2005)
13. Aboalayon, K.A.I., Ocbagabir, H.T., Faezipour, M.: Efficient sleep stage classification based on EEG signals. In: Proc. of the IEEE Systems, Applications and Technology Conference, LISAT (2014)
14. Acharya, U.R., Chua, E.C., Chua, K.C., Min, L.C., Tamura, T.: Analysis and automatic identification of sleep stages using higher order spectra. Int. J. Neural Syst. **20**(6), 509–521 (2010)
15. Estevez, P.A., Held, C.M., Holzmann, C.A., Perez, C.A., Perez, J.P., Heiss, J., Garrido, M., Peirano, P.: Polysomnographic pattern recognition for automated classification of sleep-waking states in infants. Med Biol Eng Comput. **40**(1), 105–113 (2002)
16. Noviyanto, A., Arymurthy, A.M.: Sleep stages classification based on temporal pattern recogniton in neural network approach. In: Proc. of IEEE World Congress on Computational Intelligence (WCCI) (2012)
17. Langkvist, M., Karlsson, L., Loutfi, A.: Sleep stage classification using unsupervised feature learning. Advances in Artificial Neural Systems (2012)
18. Kemp, B., Zwinderman, A.H., Tuk, B., Kamphuisen, H.A.C., Oberye, J.J.L.: Analysis of a sleep-dependent neuronal feedback loop: the slow-wave microcontinuity of the EEG. IEEE Transactions on Biomedical Engineering **47**(9), 1185–1194 (2000)
19. Goldberger, A.L., Amaral, L.A.N., Glass, L., Hausdorff, J.M., Ivanov, P.C., Mark, R.G., Mietus, J.E., Moody, G.B., Peng, C.-K., Stanley, H.E.: PhysioBank, PhysioToolkit, and PhysioNet: Components of a New Research Resource for Complex Physiologic Signals. Circulation **101**(23) (2000)
20. Mporas, I., Tsirka, V., Zacharaki, E.I., Koutroumanidis, M., Richardson, M., Megalooikonomou, V.: Seizure detection using EEG and ECG signals for computer-based monitoring, analysis and management of epileptic patients. Expert Systems with Applications **42**(6), 3227–3233 (2015)
21. Witten, I.H., Frank, E.: Data mining: practical machine learning tools and techniques, 2nd edn. Morgan-Kaufman Series of Data Management Systems. Elsevier, San Francisco (2005)
22. Burges, C.: A tutorial on Support Vector Machines for Pattern Recognition. Data Mining and Knowledge Discovery **2**(2), 121–167 (1998)
23. Silber, M.H., Ancoli-Israel, S., Bonnet, M.H., Chokroverty, S., Grigg-Damberger, M.M., et al.: The visual scoring of sleep in adults. J. of Clinical Sleep Medicine **3**(2), 121–131 (2007)
24. Jasper, H.H.: The ten-twenty electrode system of the International Federation. Electroencephalography and Clinical Neurophysiology 371–375 (1958)

Identifying Distinguishing Factors in Predicting Brain Activities – An Inclusive Machine Learning Approach

Jürgen Ommen and Chih Lai[✉]

Graduate Program in Software, University of St. Thomas, Saint Paul, MN 55105, USA
omme0003@stthomas.edu, clai@sthomas.edu

Abstract. The human brain forms a large-scale, interconnected network when performing different activities. To compare networks extracted from different subjects, they are first converted into sparse graphs with similar densities to reveal topological differences. Graph analysis is then applied to the sparse graphs to extract global and local graph invariants for quantitative comparisons. However, many previous works not only studied global and local graph invariants separately, but also created only one single sparse graph for each subject, potentially excluding important factors in connectome analysis. In this work, we adopt a more inclusive approach: generating multiple graphs using different density thresholds for each subject; and describing each graph with both global and local graph invariants. A machine learning approach is then applied to analyze these comprehensive datasets. We show that our inclusive approach can help machine learning methods to automatically identify most discriminating factors in predicting brain activities with much higher accuracy than the previous exclusive approaches.

1 Introduction

The average human brain consists of more than 85 billion neurons. Each connects to about 10,000 other neurons, making it the most complex yet unknown part of human body [1]. Therefore, analyzing human brain networks, frequently referred to as connectomes [11, 20], has become a central and challenging topic in computational neuroscience.

Recent studies have shown that analyzing functional connectomes is necessary to understand many higher cognitive functions like memory, planning, and social interactions [17]. Each such connectome can be represented as symmetric correlation matrix among all pairs of brain regions. A density threshold is then applied to the matrix to generate a sparse graph to preserve the connections with strong correlations. This often leads to different network topologies that enable the comparison between different connectomes [9].

To quantitatively describe the features of a network, global (i.e. graph diameter, radius) and local graph invariants (i.e. node centrality, node betweenness) are extracted from a sparse graph. Results from previous studies show a very interesting direction in analyzing connectomes using graph invariants [7, 9, 13, 18, 21–23].

© Springer International Publishing Switzerland 2015
Y. Guo et al. (Eds.): BIH 2015, LNAI 9250, pp. 86–95, 2015.
DOI: 10.1007/978-3-319-23344-4_9

However, most of the previous works not only considered global and local graph invariants separately, but also created only one single sparse graph for each connectome, potentially excluding important factors in connectome analysis.

Our approach, instead, utilizes a multi-layer graph analysis technique that computes various graph invariants from graphs generated with different density thresholds. This inclusive set of graph invariants is then analyzed by an ensemble machine learning method to automatically identify the most discriminating factors in predicting different brain tasks. We demonstrate in this paper that our more inclusive approach is able to predict several brain activities with very high accuracy.

2   Related Work

Several methods have been proposed to analyze and classify brain activities using graph-based connectome analysis [7]. For instance, a study in [4] used classification methods to predict different motor tasks by extracting frequent subgraphs from functional connectomes.

Another approach is to analyze the graph invariants that are summarized from the connectome. For example, studies and surveys in [9, 13, 18, 21–23] used various graph invariants to describe the distinctive features of the connectomes. While the approach in [22] utilized graph invariants to compare the effects of neurological disorders for strokes patients, studies in [13, 18, 23] took a step further to train classification models for various predictions based on graph invariants. For example, the study in [13] trained their classification models based on local graph invariants to automatically differentiate between male and female brains. Robinson et al. [18] not only used machine learning techniques to classify subjects based on patterns in structural connectomes, their analyses also identified key discriminating features in different subject groups.

3   Methods

3.1   Data

Our work is based on the task-related functional MRI (task fMRI) data that were processed and provided by the Human Connectome Project (HCP) [3, 10]. More specifically, the data consists of grayordinate time series for 100 unrelated and healthy subjects, each performing seven different tasks in different scans. Our study analyzes several events occurred in each task. The tasks and events are described in [3] which we briefly summarize below:

- **Emotion:** Subjects were presented with different shapes or emotional face expressions of fear or anger. They were further asked to match similar shapes or faces.
- **Gambling:** Subjects played a card game to guess the number on a card.
- **Language:** Subjects were presented with different math and story problems. They were then asked to answer certain questions.

- **Motor:** Subjects were asked to perform various motor tasks such as tapping their left or right fingers, squeezing their left or right toes, or moving their tongue.
- **Relational:** Subjects were presented with different shapes filled with different textures. They were then asked to match pairs of objects against shape or texture.
- **Social:** Subjects were presented videos of moving objects. They were then asked to decide if the objects move randomly or interact with each other.
- **Working Memory:** Subjects were presented with pictures of different objects. They were then asked to memorize objects in the pictures.

Note that unlike many previous studies that compared subjects in heterogeneous groups (e. g. male vs. female, healthy vs. patient groups, and young vs. old groups), subjects in our dataset are highly homogeneous (e.g. mixed genders, similar ages or similar health status).

3.2 Event Graphs

All event graphs are created separately for each subject with the Connectome Workbench version 1.0[1]. We first demean and variance normalize the time series data and then parcellate it into 148 cortical (74 for each left and right hemisphere) with the Destrieux brain atlas (aparc.a2009s) [8] and 19 sub-cortical brain regions.

The HCP dataset also provides the periods in which individual events occurred during the fMRI scans. Based on these periods, temporal masks are created in order to extract the time series data of each target event. We then generate a correlation matrix among all the parcellated time series. Finally, these correlation coefficients are normalized to support better inter-connectome comparability by converting them to z-values using Fisher's r-to-z transformation. Since negative correlations have ambiguous biological explanations, we restrict our analysis to positive correlations only [6].

After generating the correlation matrices, a density threshold converts them to sparse graphs to preserve only the connections with strong correlations. Since many graph invariants are highly sensitive to the density of the graph, this conversion process also guarantees that all the output graphs have the same density.

Most of the existing connectome studies relied on a single threshold to generate one graph for each subject. Unfortunately, it is unclear how to choose a threshold such that a single sparse graph can capture all the appropriate features of a connectome. It is also unclear how the accuracy of an analysis will be influenced by the combined effects of different thresholds and various graph invariants. To avoid those uncertainties, we utilize a multi-layer graph analysis technique that represents each graph by its invariants at 9 density thresholds $\kappa \in \{0.1, 0.15, 0.2, ...0.5\}$. These invariants are then analyzed together by an ensemble machine learning method (to be discussed later) to automatically identify the most discriminating factors in predicting task events.

Table 1 shows the number of graphs generated from various events under different tasks and the length of the time series used to generate these graphs.

---

[1] http://humanconnectome.org/software/workbench-command.php

Table 1. Number of graphs generated from events under different tasks and the length of each time series used to generate those graphs.

Task	Event	#Graphs	#Frames
Emotion	Face	600	26
Emotion	Shape	600	26
Gambling	Loss event	2,900	5-6
Gambling	Win event	2,900	5-6
Language	Math	1,865	11-22
Language	Story	800	29-42
Motor	L. foot	400	17-18
Motor	L. hand	400	17-18
Motor	R. foot	400	17-18
Motor	R. hand	400	17-18
Motor	Tongue	400	17-18
Relational	Match	600	23-24
Relational	Relation	600	23-24
Social	Mental	500	33
Social	Random	500	33
Working Memory	Correct	14,141	5-6
Working Memory	Error	1,859	5-6

3.3   Graph Invariants

Graph analysis is applied to the event graphs to extract several graph invariants for quantitative comparisons between different connectomes. We extract the following 7 global graph invariants in this study to describe the features of the entire graph: diameter, radius, average node degree, average path length, mean clustering coefficient, s-metric and assortativity. Invariants that describe the features of each graph node are local graph invariants. In this study, we extract the following 6 local graph invariants: betweenness, closeness, eccentricity, node strength, cluster coefficients, and eigenvector centrality. We use a slightly modified version of the brain connectivity toolbox [19] to obtain those graph invariants and refer readers to [19] for their mathematical definitions.

Since each graph has 167 nodes (brain parcels), we have $167 \times 6 + 7 = 1,009$ invariants for each graph generated from one density threshold. By using 9 different thresholds to generate graphs with different densities, each event will be represented by 9,081 attributes.

The next section describes how to apply a machine learning approach to the analysis these comprehensive datasets and automatically identify most discriminating factors in predicting brain activities with very high accuracy.

4   Classification Models

4.1   Learning Classification Models

The goal of this study is to train a machine learning model to gain insights from the 9,081 graph invariants extracted for each connectome, and automatically identify discriminating factors that can predict which event a subject is performing. Since an ensemble machine learning approach consists of multiple classification models, it has better capability in identifying discriminating factors from many variables, and achieves higher predictive accuracy than a single model approach [2, 15]. Hence, we choose the random forest [5] approach which consists of many decision trees.

Specifically, we build a random forest of 400 trees to analyze the data extracted from each event. Each random forest is trained on events performed by 75% of randomly selected subjects; with the rest of 25% being used to test the prediction accuracy of the forest. This process is repeated 30 times for each event for later hypothesis testing. To measure the prediction accuracy of the single threshold method, the same process was executed for each of the graphs generated by one of the 9 different thresholds.

4.2   Analysis of Prediction Results

Table 2 summarizes the prediction accuracy of the single and multiple threshold approach, respectively. Note that the accuracy is averaged over all 30 rounds of predictions as described previously. Moreover, the accuracy of the single threshold method is the highest average among each of the 9 thresholds we used. As the table demonstrates, the classification models based on multiple thresholds improve the accuracy of some event predictions by 10% to 30%, compared to those based on a single threshold. However, the accuracies of both methods in predicting events under the motor and social tasks are about the same. The t-tests and p-values in table 2 reject the null hypothesis that the multiple threshold method does not improve the prediction accuracy.

Table 2. Mean accuracy of the classification models ± standard deviation.

Task	Single threshold	Multiple threshold	p-value	#Events
Emotion	71.31 ± 1.85 %	95.01 ± 1.60 %	7.09e-33	2
Gambling	53.29 ± 0.93 %	67.33 ± 1.98 %	6.29e-25	2
Language	97.22 ± 0.83 %	97.66 ± 0.90 %	7.12e-03	2
Motor	35.86 ± 1.66 %	38.33 ± 2.05 %	1.33e-06	5
Relational	60.79 ± 1.97 %	91.93 ± 2.77 %	2.49e-28	2
Social	68.89 ± 2.52 %	71.35 ± 3.57 %	1.01e-02	2
Working Memory	71.75 ± 1.40 %	80.00 ± 1.24 %	1.69e-23	2

We further analyze the receiver operating characteristic (ROC) curves for predictions based on either the single (dashed line) or the multiple threshold method (solid line) in fig. 1. The ROC curve plots the true positive rate (TPR) against the false positive rate (FPR) at various prediction confidences [12]. Fig. 1 shows that as we gradually reduce the confidence level, more events were classified correctly (TPR) or incorrectly (FPR). The decreasing confidence level in the ROC curve is encoded in color and ranges from blue (high confidence) to red (low confidence).

As we can see in fig. 1, the multiple threshold method generates a much larger area under the curve (AUC) [12] than the other one that uses only a single threshold. Hence, the multiple threshold approach is able to predict the events much more precisely. From the colors (confidence level) in fig. 1, we also know that, in most cases, the multiple threshold approach has a higher confidence in making predictions than the single threshold method.

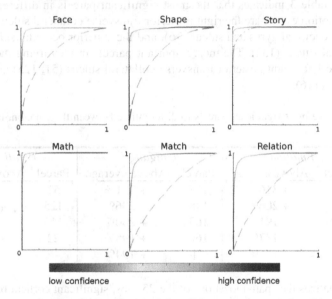

Fig. 1. ROC curves for the emotion (face and shape), language (story and math), and relational (match and relation) tasks. Y-axis = TPR. X-axis = FPR. The dashed lines = ROC curves from single threshold. The solid lines = ROC curves from multiple thresholds (best viewed in color).

4.3   Analysis of Classification Models

In this section, we analyze the multiple threshold classification models in order to identify top discriminating factors in predicting different events. It is done by measuring the increase in misclassification rate of the entire ensemble by randomly permuting the values of a single attribute across the test data. This process is repeated for each attribute [5]. A higher prediction error produced by this permutation indicates greater sensitivity or significance of this attribute to the predictions. The importance of brain parcels and graph invariants is then aggregated over the 9 thresholds used in our multiple threshold approach.

Since our models are much more accurate in predicting events under the emotion, language and relational tasks, the top discriminating factors in those tasks are more reliable. Hence, we focus our further discussion on these three tasks in this report. Significant factors under other tasks can be found in [16].

Most Significant Brain Parcels. After sorting the permutation error of the 167 brain parcels in descending order, we identify the top five most significant parcels in characterizing the neural connectivity during different events and list them in table 3. The relative importance of each top parcel is also compared to the average importance of all the 167 parcels. For example, we observe that the left / right accumbens (157, 166) and the right pallidum (163) are highly important in distinguishing between the math and story events in the language task. Interestingly, these sub-cortical regions, especially the accumbens, are known for being indicators of math-anxiety in individuals with deficits in performing math tasks as pointed out in [14].

Similarly, table 3 indicates that the most significant parcels in differentiating between the emotion events are the right posterior transverse collateral sulcus (125), the right inferior occipital gyrus and sulcus (76), and the superior occipital sulcus / transverse occipital sulcus (132). The most important parcels in identifying the relational events are the left / right posterior transverse collateral sulcus (51, 125) and the right occipital pole (116).

Table 3. Top five most significant parcels to differentiate between the emotion, language and relational events

Top	Emotion		Language		Relational	
	Parcel	Above average	Parcel	Above average	Parcel	Above average
1	125	+ 316%	157	+ 221%	51	+ 381%
2	76	+ 206%	148	+ 206%	125	+ 351%
3	132	+ 191%	163	+ 200%	116	+ 282%
4	116	+ 187%	166	+ 195%	22	+ 261%
5	95	+ 186%	74	+ 194%	42	+ 248%

Fig. 2 visualizes the spatial locations of the 25 most significant cortical brain parcels without considering sub-cortical ones. It shows that the distinguishing brain parcels for the emotion and relational events mostly concentrate on the frontal lobe. In contrast, the important distinguishing parcels for the language events are more spread across different parts of the brain. Moreover, we see that the significance of the cortical parcels in the relational task is highly synchronized between the left and right hemisphere.

Most Significant Graph Invariants. The top and bottom bar charts in fig. 3 show the importance of the 13 graph invariants (6 local invariants and 7 global invariants) in distinguishing different events under certain tasks. We observe that while the important invariants are similar for the emotion and language tasks, they are very different in the relational task. More specifically, while the node eccentricity is the most significant local invariant in the emotion and language tasks, it plays only a minor role in the relational task. Furthermore, the mean clustering coefficient is the top driving global invariant in classifying the events under the relational task, but it has nearly no influence in classifying the emotion and language events.

We also analyze the most significant combinations of local invariants and parcels in predicting different tasks. To conserve space, we refer readers to [16] for details.

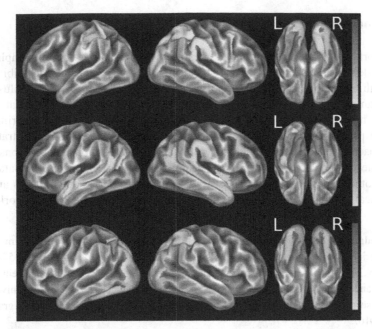

Fig. 2. Shows the top 25 most important cortical brain parcels identified by our method in performing different tasks: emotion (top), language (middle) and relational (bottom). The color encodes the increasing importance from yellow to red (best viewed in color).

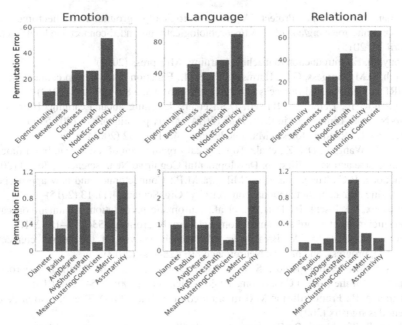

Fig. 3. Importance of the local (top) and global (bottom) graph invariants in distinguishing between events under the emotion, language and relational task.

5   Conclusion

In this work, we adopted a more inclusive approach: generating multiple graphs using different density thresholds from a connectome of each event; and describing each graph with both global and local graph invariants. We showed that our inclusive approach can generate a comprehensive dataset with various graph invariants for an ensemble machine learning method to automatically identify the most discriminating factors in predicting brain activities with high accuracy. We also demonstrated that our approach is able to correctly identify the sub-cortical brain parcels responsible for math-anxiety. We plan to perform further analyses on our comprehensive dataset and discover other types of frequent patterns. We intend to verify our findings and their neurological implications with neuroscientists as another important future work.

Acknowledgment. Data were provided by the Human Connectome Project, WU-Minn Consortium (Principal Investigators: David Van Essen and Kamil Ugurbil; 1U54MH091657) funded by the 16 NIH Institutes and Centers that support the NIH Blueprint for Neuroscience Research; and by the McDonnell Center for Systems Neuroscience at Washington University.

This research work is also supported by Amazon Cloud Computing Research grant from 2015 to 2016.

References

1. Human Connectome Project A neurobiologically grounded connectome. http://humanconnectome.org/about/project/neurobiologically-grounded-connectome.html (accessed April 15, 2015)
2. Alpaydin, E.: Introduction to machine learning. MIT press (2014)
3. Barch, D.M., Burgess, G.C., Harms, M.P., et al.: Function in the human connectome: task-fMRI and individual differences in behavior. Neuroimage **80**, 169–189 (2013)
4. Bogdanov, P., Dereli, N., Bassett, D.S., et al.: Learning about Learning: Human Brain Sub-Network Biomarkers in fMRI Data (2014). arXiv preprint arXiv:1407.5590
5. Breiman, L.: Random forests. Machine learning **45**(1), 5–32 (2001)
6. Cao, M., Wang, J., Dai, Z., et al.: Topological organization of the human brain functional connectome across the lifespan. Developmental Cognitive Neuroscience **7**, 76–93 (2014)
7. Craddock, R.C., Tungaraza, R.L., Milham, M.P.: Connectomics and new approaches for analyzing human brain functional connectivity. GigaScience **4**(1), 13 (2015)
8. Destrieux, C., Fischl, B., Dale, A., et al.: Automatic parcellation of human cortical gyri and sulci using standard anatomical nomenclature. Neuroimage **53**(1), 1–15 (2010)
9. Fornito, A., Zalesky, A., Breakspear, M.: Graph analysis of the human connectome: promise, progress, and pitfalls. Neuroimage **80**, 426–444 (2013)
10. Glasser, M.F., Sotiropoulos, S.N., Wilson, J.A., et al.: The minimal preprocessing pipelines for the Human Connectome Project. Neuroimage **80**, 105–124 (2013)
11. Hagmann, P.: From diffusion MRI to brain connectomics. Ph.D. Thesis, Institut de traitement des signaux (2005)
12. Hastie, T., Tibshirani, R., Friedman, J., et al.: The elements of statistical learning, vol. 2. Springer (2009)

13. Kulkarni, V., Pudipeddi, J.S., Akoglu, L., et al.: Sex differences in the human connectome. In: Brain and Health Informatics, pp. 82–91. Springer (2013)
14. Lyons, I.M., Beilock, S.L.: Mathematics anxiety: Separating the math from the anxiety. Cerebral Cortex: bhr289 (2011)
15. Marsland, S.: Machine learning: an algorithmic perspective. CRC press (2014)
16. Ommen, J.: Analytics of Human Brain Connectome Networks. Master Thesis (draft under preparation), University of St. Thomas (2015)
17. Reijneveld, J.C., Ponten, S.C., Berendse, H.W., et al.: The application of graph theoretical analysis to complex networks in the brain. Clinical Neurophysiology 118(11), 2317–2331 (2007)
18. Robinson, E.C., Hammers, A., Ericsson, A., et al.: Identifying population differences in whole-brain structural networks: a machine learning approach. Neuroimage 50(3), 910–919 (2010)
19. Rubinov, M., Sporns, O.: Complex network measures of brain connectivity: uses and interpretations. Neuroimage 52(3), 1059–1069 (2010)
20. Sporns, O., Tononi, G., Kötter, R.: The human connectome: a structural description of the human brain. PLoS computational biology 1(4), e42 (2005)
21. Wijk, V., Bernadette, C.M., Stam, C.J., Daffertshofer, A.: Comparing brain networks of different size and connectivity density using graph theory. PloS one 5(10), e13701 (2010)
22. Wang, L., Yu, C., Chen, H., et al.: Dynamic functional reorganization of the motor execution network after stroke. Brain 133(4), 1224–1238 (2010)
23. Zhou, J., Gennatas, E.D., Kramer, J.H., et al.: Predicting regional neurodegeneration from the healthy brain functional connectome. Neuron 73(6), 1216–1227 (2012)

Classification Analysis of Chronological Age Using Brief Resting Electroencephalographic (EEG) Recordings

Miaolin Fan[1](✉), Vladimir Miskovic[2], Chun-An Chou[1,2], Sina Khanmohammadi[1], Hiroki Sayama[1,2], and Brandon E. Gibb[2]

[1] Department of Systems Science and Industrial Engineering,
State University of New York at Binghamton, Binghamton, NY, USA
mfan4@binghamton.edu
[2] Center for Affective Science, State University of New York at Binghamton,
Binghamton, NY, USA

Abstract. The present study aims to build a classification model that discriminates between chronological ages of subjects based on resting-state electroencephalography (EEG) data collected from a community sample of 269 children aged 7 to 11. Specifically, spectral power densities in four classical frequency bands: Delta (0.5–3 Hz), Theta (4–7 Hz), Alpha (8–12 Hz) and Beta (14–25 Hz) were extracted for each electrode as features, and fed to three classification algorithms including logistic regression (LR), support vector machine (SVM), and least absolute shrinkage and selection operator (Lasso). In addition, principal component analysis (PCA) was used to reduce the dimensions of the feature space. The results demonstrated that SVM and Lasso evidenced better performance (maximal accuracy = 80.68 ± 2.01% by SVM and 77.82 ± 2.11% by Lasso) when applied to original feature space, but LR yielded the best performance with PCA (80.72 ± 1.73%). The accuracy of binary classification exhibited a decreasing trend with diminishing chronological gaps between the groups.

Keywords: Electroencephalography · Brain development · Adolescence · Machine learning · Pattern classification

1 Introduction

Brain electrical activity, as measured by non-invasive electroencephalography (EEG), undergoes a protracted maturational trajectory from infancy to adulthood [1]. Spectral decomposition of EEG time domain signals reveals that normative brain development from infancy to late adolescence/young adulthood is best summarized by dramatic decreases in slow-wave density (~ 0.5 to 7 Hz) along with a redistribution of relative power in the higher frequency ranges [2-7]. Furthermore, the dominant posterior frequency typically shifts towards a higher peak frequency during neural development, which appears to be related to myelination and increases in the efficiency of cortico-cortical wave propagation [3, 6]. The redistribution of EEG

© Springer International Publishing Switzerland 2015
Y. Guo et al. (Eds.): BIH 2015, LNAI 9250, pp. 96–104, 2015.
DOI: 10.1007/978-3-319-23344-4_10

spectra likely reflects age-related changes in neuronal structure and function, e.g., neutrophil reduction and grey matter thinning along with linear increases in white matter density [8].

In recent decades, the advent of machine learning techniques, with their capability for processing large multivariate data sets, has created the possibility of using neural time series data to predict chronological age, and by extension, the brain's maturational state [10]. There has long been an interest in using such an approach to make sensitive predictions of brain maturation (a so-called "brain electric maturation scale" [12]) for putative diagnostic and prognostic uses [13]. In particular, since EEG recordings are non-invasive, easy to obtain in pediatric populations and increasingly ambulatory, it represents a modality that is uniquely suited for this goal (unlike expensive fMRI scans, for example). Data-driven predictions about individual brain maturation using a machine learning approach has considerable diagnostic and prognostic value as it creates the possibility of identifying individuals exhibiting developmental delays or lags.

The present study adopts a data-driven machine learning framework in order to predict chronological age using EEG spectral indices obtained from brief resting (eyes-closed) recordings. Logistic regression (LR), least absolute shrinkage and selection operator (Lasso), and support vector machine (SVM) were employed to discriminate between children of different age groups based on spectral density of classical EEG frequency bands. Moreover, their performance was compared to examine 1) whether the EEG patterns of different age groups are distinguishable, and 2) the fitness for classification tasks based on whole-brain EEG biomarkers of those algorithms employed in this study.

2   Method

Fig.1 depicts the framework of our study in schematic format. The feature space included spectral density in four classical frequency bands: Delta (0.5-3 Hz), Theta (4-7 Hz), Alpha (8-12 Hz) and Beta (14-25 Hz), and from 33 electrodes located on the scalp as well as the IAF for each subject, yielding a total of 133 features. Since there are 5 age groups (age 7, 8, 9, 10 and 11) in this classification problem, 10 binary classifiers need to be trained to distinguish subjects between every two groups. Since it may introduce viability with random split of the training and test set, this entire procedure was repeated for k ($k = 100$) replications and the statistics of performance was collected and discussed in the result section. Student's t-test was used for testing the significance of differences between performances of selected algorithms.

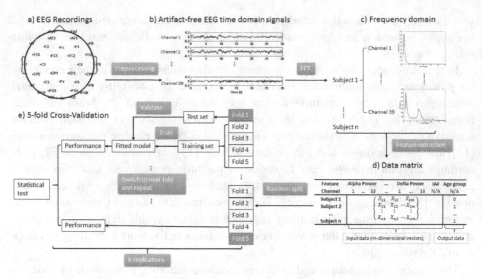

Fig. 1. A flowchart of the methodological framework. The raw EEG signals were recorded from 39 channels and preprocessed off-line. After the artifact removal, the clean time domain signals were submitted to FFT for a spectral analysis. Next, the feature extraction was performed to obtain the spectral density and IAF. The input data was re-arranged such that each subject was represented by an m-dimensional vector, where each feature was represented by one dimension of the vector. Finally, we run the 5-fold CV using this dataset for k (k=100) replications and collect the statistics of performance.

2.1   Participants

A total of 269 subjects aged 7-11 years old (Mean = 9.40, SD = 1.46) were grouped into 7 years old (32 males and 29 females), 8 years old (29 males and 26 females), 9 years old (20 males and 30 females), 10 years old (33 males and 24 females) and 11 years old (29 males and 17 females) according to their chronological age.

2.2   EEG Recording, Preprocessing and Feature Extraction

For each subject, one minute of resting-state EEG was collected using a custom cap and BioSemi ActiveTwoBio system with a 64-bit resolution at 512 Hz sampling rate, while subjects were instructed to remain still and keep eyes closed. The EEG activity was recorded using 34 sintered Ag/AgCI active scalp electrodes based on the International 10/20 system, and an active Common Mode Sense (CMS) and a passive Driven Right Leg (DRL) electrode were also placed to drive an average potential of a subject through a feedback loop. Furthermore, Electrooculography (EOG) was also measured to capture the vertical and horizontal eye movements during recordings, which helped visual inspection of artifact removal afterwards.

The EEG time domain signals were processed off-line using the EEGLAB toolbox [14] (http://sccn.ucsd.edu/eeglab/) and custom scripts in Matlab (The MathWorks Inc., R2014a). The raw signals were re-referenced to Cz and band-pass filtered using a two-way least squares finite impulse response (FIR) filter with a range of 0.5-35 Hz. Manual artifact removal was performed on the filtered data by trained observers. For each subject, a minimum of 30 seconds of artifact-free EEG signals were required for further spectral analysis. The artifact-free EEG signals were then detrended and decomposed using the Welch periodogram method with Hanning tapered of 2 seconds duration and with 50% overlap, yielding a frequency resolution of 0.50 Hz. The EEG spectral densities were aggregated into four frequency bands: Delta (0.5-3 Hz), Theta (4-7 Hz), Alpha (8-12 Hz) and Beta (14-25 Hz) and then converted into decibel (dB) units.

To detect the individual alpha frequency (IAF), we averaged the spectral density across a cluster of posterior electrodes (O1, O2, Oz, PO7, PO8, PO3 and PO4). Next, an automated peak detection algorithm was used to identify each individual's maximum within the 7 to 14 Hz range.

2.3 Classification Analysis

Suppose that we have input vectors $x = \{x_1, x_2, \dots x_N\}$ with the corresponding outcomes $Y = \{Y_1, Y_2, \dots Y_N\}$, where Y_i represents a binary state or value to be predicted. In our study, the predictor is defined to be which age group this subject belongs to.

Classifiers

Three algorithms including LR, Lasso and SVM were used in this study. A Matlab toolbox *glmnet* (http://web.stanford.edu/~hastie/glmnet_matlab/) was used for implementing Lasso, and the other two algorithms were implemented using the built-in Matlab functions.

Logistic Regression

The objective of logistic regression for binary classification is to model the likelihood that the ith output Y_i belongs to one of the possible categories given the input vector x_i. Arbitrarily, we labeled subjects in the younger group as 0 and the elders as 1. The likelihood in a binary classification problem is modeled based on the sigmoid function, which is defined as follows:

$$h_\theta(x) = \frac{1}{1+e^{-(\theta_0+\theta^T x)}} \tag{1}$$

where θ_0 and θ^T denote the intercept and the transposed vector of coefficients, respectively, and x represents the input vector. If the estimated likelihood $h_\theta(x)$ is greater than a pre-determined threshold (typically 0.5 in binary classification problems), then the corresponding outcome Y_i for the ith sample will be predicted to be the chosen category, otherwise it will be predicted as the other. The classification problem then is to be solved by finding an optimal θ and θ_0 such that

$$arg\ min_\theta \left\{ \frac{1}{n}\sum_{i=1}^{n}(-Y_i \log(h_\theta(x_i)) - (1-Y_i)\log(1-h_\theta(x_i))) \right\} \tag{2}$$

Lasso

In problems with a large number of features, Lasso tries to build a regression model while selecting a smaller subset of features with strongest effects [15]. It automatically removes the less important features by shrinking their coefficients to be zero. The original definition of Lasso is to estimate parameter vector θ and intercept θ_0 such that for a linear regression model is formulated as follows:

$$arg\ min_{\theta}\{\Sigma_{i=1}^{N}(y_i - \theta_0 - \theta^T x)^2\},\ s.t.\ \Sigma_i|\hat{\theta}_i| \leq \lambda \tag{3}$$

where λ is a tuning parameter to control the degree of penalty.

In the present study, we applied an adaptation of Lasso to fit the binary classification problem [15]. It solves the problem by replacing the least squared error term in linear regression $\Sigma_{i=1}^{N}(y_i - \theta_0 - \theta^T x)^2$ with the cost function of logistic regression, whereas the constraint of problem remains the same.

Support Vector Machine

In SVM-based classification problems, the objective is to find an optimal decision boundary between classes such that the margin (defined as the smallest distance between the decision boundary and the closest sample points) is maximized [16]. These closest sample points involved in determining the decision boundary are referred to as support vectors. In a multi-dimensional space, this decision boundary is represented by a hyper-plane that separates the regions of different classes in a way such that the geometric distance between the support vectors and decision boundary is maximized. In our study, a linear kernel was used in SVM.

Let the hyper-plane be defined by $h(x) = 0$, where $h(x)$ follows the form of $h(x) = \theta_0 + \theta^T x$. For a particular point x_n, the distance from x to the hyper-plane is given by $|h(x_n)|/\|\theta\|$. Suppose that for input vectors $x_1, x_2, ..., x_N$, the corresponding outcomes are $Y_1, Y_2, ..., Y_N$, where $Y_i \in \{-1, 1\}$. Then for all points correctly classified, it always yields $Y_n h(x_n) > 0$. Therefore, the optimal solution is given by solving

$$arg\ \max_{\theta_0, \theta}\left\{\frac{1}{\|\theta\|} min_n[Y_n(\theta_0 + \theta^T x)]\right\} \tag{4}$$

Since solving the original problem directly is very complex, the problem is reformulated as an equivalent problem as follows:

$$arg\ min_{\theta_0, \theta} \frac{1}{2}\|\theta\|^2,$$

$$s.t.\ Y_n(\theta_0 + \theta^T x) \geq 1, n = 1, ..., N, \tag{5}$$

which gives the definition of hard margin SVM.

However, recall that we assumed all data points are grouped correctly in the beginning, and this case is not realistic in most real-life problems. Therefore, a so-called "soft margin" SVM is formulated by introducing a slack variable ξ as follows:

$$arg\ min_{\theta_0, \theta} \frac{1}{2}\|\theta\|^2 + C \Sigma_{n=1}^{N} \xi_n,$$

$$s.t.\ Y_n(\theta_0 + \theta^T x) \geq 1 - \xi_n, n = 1, ..., N. \tag{6}$$

In order to evaluate the generalizability of this classification model, a nested 5-fold cross-validation scheme was used, as suggested in Lemm's paper [10]. In the outer loop, the dataset was split randomly into 5 folds where one was chosen as test set and the others were used for training. In the inner loop, the training set was further divided into 5 folds in order to cross-validate the tuning parameters in SVM and Lasso algorithms.

Dimensionality Reduction
Principal component analysis (PCA) is a common technique of dimensionality reduction. It aims to convert the original data points into a set of orthogonal projections such that the maximal variance of original data is explained. Since in the present study, we had a total of 133 features, we employed PCA to 1) reduce the dimensionality of feature space to build a more precise model; 2) remove the possibly correlation between input variables. Furthermore, to evaluate the effect of dimension reduction, PCA was also applied to the original dataset, and the classification models built on the basis of principal components were considered as alternative models. Principal components were ranked in descending order of the explained variance and selected until cumulative explained variance is sufficient (exceeding 80% of total variance of original dataset) or the variance explained by individual principal component is small (lower than 2%).

3   Results and Discussion

Using the original dataset, the LR performed close to random level (accuracy $\approx 50\%$) in most circumstances. SVM and Lasso demonstrated better performance ($p < 0.0001$ in one-sided paired t-test) than LR, whereas no significant difference was found between the overall performances of SVM and Lasso. Fig.2 shows the classification accuracy of selected algorithms across all binary classifications. From this figure it is evident that the classification accuracy increases as the gap between the two respective age groups widens. The most successful classification was between age 7 and age 11, where Lasso and SVM yielded $77.82 \pm 2.11\%$ and $80.68 \pm 2.01\%$ accuracy respectively, suggesting distinguishable patterns of EEG spectral densities for these two groups. The low accuracy in classification between age 7 vs. 8 (ranging from 49.51% to 56.32% in all models), age 8 vs. 9 (46.42% to 50.31%), age 9 vs. 10 (49.28% to 63.74%) and age 10 vs. 11 (48.78% to 60.14%) implies that it would be difficult to distinguish between subjects from two groups with only one year difference. Since an individual's chronological development continuously changes on a continuum, and given that the variability in development could be large across individuals, there may exist many overlapping areas between adjacent categories.

Another issue that deserves consideration is dimensionality reduction. Given the large number of features, it is costly and unnecessary to build classification models on the basis of original feature space. Accordingly, PCA was employed in our study to reduce the dimensionality of the feature space by creating projections of original data points that best explained the total variance. After PCA was applied to the original dataset, 7 principal components were selected with 77.50% of total variance explained (Fig.3). Consequently, the performance of LR-based classifiers was significantly improved in all classification tasks ($p < 0.0001$) except for age 8 vs. 9 and reached accuracy levels comparable to the other two algorithms. Following PCA dimensional reduction, LR-based classifiers achieved the highest performance when classifying between 7 and 11 age groups (accuracy =80.72 ± 1.73%). These results may imply that with dimensionality reduced dataset, LR has the potential to obtain a comparable classification accuracy to even more sophisticated learning algorithms, which opens an interesting topic to be further explored in the future.

However, for SVM-based classifiers the improvement of performance after applying PCA was only significant in the following classification tasks: age 9 vs. 11 (p < 0.0001), age 10 vs. 11 (p < 0.0001), age 8 vs. 9 (p = 0.0047) and age 7 vs. 8 (p = 0.0013). Besides, there was a decrease (p < 0.0001) in performance of SVM-based classification between age 8 vs. 11, age 7 vs. 10, age 9 vs. 10 and age 7 vs. 9. It was also found that PCA decreased the performance of Lasso-based classifications significantly (p < 0.0001) except for age 7 vs. 11, age 10 vs. 11, and age 8 vs. 9. This is probably due to the property of L1 regularization that it performs feature selection within learning algorithm; usually it is a desired property especially in high-dimensional-small-sample problems to prevent overfitting. It is not preferred, nevertheless, to be employed in combination with PCA, as shown by our experimental results. One probable reason might be that many redundant variables in the original feature space has been eliminated by PCA; as a result, removing any of the remaining variables may cause a loss of useful information in terms of classification.

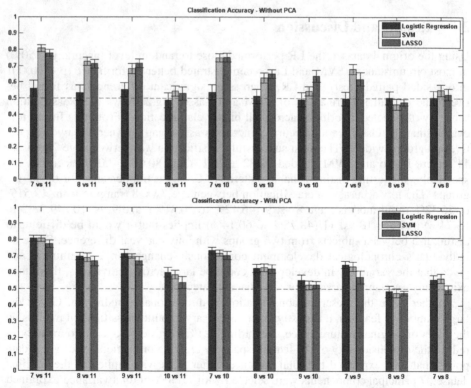

Fig. 2. Classification performance with/without PCA. The dashed red line marked 50% accuracy level.

It should be noted that, since we focused on binary classification between two age groups in the present study, the age-dependent changes of EEG spectral patterns across 7 to 11 years old were not directly examined. Notwithstanding this limitation, our results showed that the classification approach performs better when discriminating between subjects with larger age differences, and vice versa, which may imply a continuous, developmental change in EEG patterns that are recognizable for selected pattern classification algorithms. Thus, our future study will also include support vector regression (SVR), a modified regression-based algorithm to make a prediction of individual brain maturity based on real-valued age. On the other hand, the three learning algorithms chosen in the present study classify patterns of different age groups depending on EEG spectral densities. The best performance that can be achieved, however, also relies on the quality of feature engineering. More attention can be paid to derive features that contain sufficient information with regards to age differences from original signals.

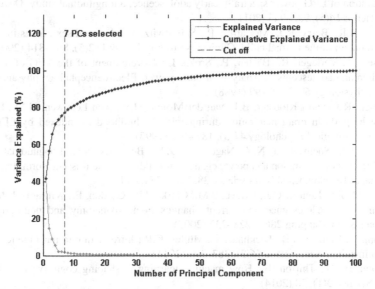

Fig. 3. Principal component analysis. The blue line and green line give the cumulative explained variance and variance explained by each individual principal component respectively, and we selected seven PCs as the individual explained variance was below 2% after the seventh PC.

4   Conclusion and Future Work

Overall, our study has demonstrated the feasibility of applying SVM and Lasso to classify age-dependent differences on the basis of resting EEG spectral content obtained from relatively brief duration recordings. LR has a limited performance when employing a high-dimensional feature space, but when used in combination with PCA it performs at a comparable level to the other two algorithms. Future improvement possibly involves 1) building a regression model to predict the chronological age using brain-based measures of maturational state and; 2) using EEG biomarkers to identify subjects with developmental delay who might be at elevated risk for psychiatric and cognitive difficulties; 3) comparing the performances of other learning algorithms that can develop features independently, such as deep learning or so, to examine if feature extraction has an effect on classification accuracy.

References

1. Segalowitz, S.J., Santesso, D.L., Jetha, M.K.: Electrophysiological changes during adolescence: a review. Brain and Cognition **72**(1), 86–100 (2010)
2. Benninger, C., Matthis, P., Scheffner, D.: EEG development of healthy boys and girls. Results of a longitudinal study. Electroencephalography and Clinical Neurophysiology **57**(1), 1–12 (1984)
3. Cragg, L., Kovacevic, N., McIntosh, A.R., Poulsen, C., Martinu, K., Leonard, G., Paus, T.: Maturation of EEG power spectra in early adolescence: a longitudinal study. Developmental Science **14**(5), 935–943 (2011)
4. Clarke, A.R., Barry, R.J., McCarthy, R., Selikowitz, M.: Age and sex effects in the EEG: development of the normal child. Clinical Neurophysiology **112**(5), 806–814 (2001)
5. Gasser, T., Verleger, R., Bächer, P., Sroka, L.: Development of the EEG of school-age children and adolescents. I. Analysis of band power. Electroencephalography and Clinical Neurophysiology **69**(2), 91–99 (1988)
6. Somsen, R.J., van't Klooster, B.J., van der Molen, M.W., van Leeuwen, H.M., Licht, R.: Growth spurts in brain maturation during middle childhood as indexed by EEG power spectra. Biological Psychology **44**(3), 187–209 (1997)
7. Soroko, S.I., Shemyakina, N.V., Nagornova, Z.V., Bekshaev, S.S.: Longitudinal study of EEG frequency maturation and power changes in children on the Russian North. International Journal of Developmental Neuroscience **38**, 127–137 (2014)
8. Whitford, T.J., Rennie, C.J., Grieve, S.M., Clark, C.R., Gordon, E., Williams, L.M.: Brain maturation in adolescence: concurrent changes in neuroanatomy and neurophysiology. Human Brain Mapping **28**(3), 228–237 (2007)
9. Lemm, S., Blankertz, B., Dickhaus, T., Müller, K.R.: Introduction to machine learning for brain imaging. Neuroimage **56**(2), 387–399 (2011)
10. Varoquaux, G., Thirion, B.: How machine learning is shaping cognitive neuroimaging. GigaScience **3**(1), 28 (2014)
11. Dosenbach, N.U., Nardos, B., Cohen, A.L., Fair, D.A., Power, J.D., Church, J.A., Nelson, S.M., Wig, G.S., Vogel, A.C., Lessov-Schlaggar, C.N., Barnes, K.A., Dubis, J.W., Feczko, E., Coalson, R.S., Pruett, J.R., Barch, D.M., Petersen, S.E., Schlaggar, B.L.: Prediction of individual brain maturity using fMRI. Science **329**(5997), 1358–1361 (2010)
12. Wackermann, J., Matoušek, M.: From the 'EEG age' to a rational scale of brain electric maturation. Electroencephalography and clinical Neurophysiology **107**(6), 415–421 (1998)
13. Bresnahan, S.M., Anderson, J.W., Barry, R.J.: Age-related changes in quantitative EEG in attention-deficit/hyperactivity disorder. Biological Psychiatry **46**(12), 1690–1697 (1999)
14. Delorme, A., Makeig, S.: EEGLAB: an open source toolbox for analysis of single-trial EEG dynamics including independent component analysis. Journal of Neuroscience Methods **134**(1), 9–21 (2004)
15. Tibshirani, R.: Regression shrinkage and selection via the lasso. Journal of the Royal Statistical Society. Series B (Methodological), 267–288 (1996)
16. Bishop, C.M.: Pattern recognition and machine learning, vol. 4, no. 4. Springer, New York (2006)

Identification of Discriminative Subgraph Patterns in fMRI Brain Networks in Bipolar Affective Disorder

Bokai Cao[1]([⊠]), Liang Zhan[2], Xiangnan Kong[3], Philip S. Yu[1,4],
Nathalie Vizueta[5], Lori L. Altshuler[5], and Alex D. Leow[6]

[1] Department of Computer Science, University of Illinois, Chicago, IL, USA
{caobokai,psyu}@uic.edu
[2] Laboratory of Neuro Imaging, Department of Neurology,
UCLA, Los Angeles, CA, USA
zhan.liang@gmail.com
[3] Department of Computer Science, Worcester Polytechnic Institute,
Worcester, MA, USA
xkong@wpi.edu
[4] Institute for Data Science, Tsinghua University, Beijing, China
[5] Department of Psychiatry and Behavioral Sciences, UCLA Semel Institute
for Neuroscience and Human Behavior, Los Angeles, CA, USA
nathalievizueta@ucla.edu, laltshuler@mednet.ucla.edu
[6] Department of Psychiatry, University of Illinois, Chicago, IL, USA
alexfeuillet@gmail.com

Abstract. Using sophisticated graph-theoretical analyses, modern magnetic resonance imaging techniques have allowed us to model the human brain as a brain connectivity network or a *graph*. In a brain network, the nodes of the network correspond to a set of brain regions and the link or edges correspond to the functional or structural connectivity between these regions. The linkage structure in brain networks can encode valuable information about the organizational properties of the human brain as a whole. However, the complexity of such linkage information raises major challenges in the era of big data in brain informatics. Conventional approaches on brain networks primarily focus on local patterns within select brain regions or pairwise connectivity between regions. By contrast, in this study, we proposed a graph mining framework based on state-of-the-art data mining techniques. Using a statistical test based on the G-test, we validated this framework in a sample of euthymic bipolar I subjects, and identified abnormal subgraph patterns in the rsfMRI networks of these subjects relative to healthy controls.

Keywords: Data mining · Bipolar disorder · Brain network · Subgraph pattern · Feature selection

1 Introduction

To correctly diagnose and properly treat neuropsychiatric disorders, many different diagnostic tools and techniques have been developed over the last decade,

© Springer International Publishing Switzerland 2015
Y. Guo et al. (Eds.): BIH 2015, LNAI 9250, pp. 105–114, 2015.
DOI: 10.1007/978-3-319-23344-4_11

often yielding a large amount of data measurements. Especially, recent advances in neuroimaging technology have provided an efficient and noninvasive way of studying the structural and functional connectivity of the human brain, either in a normal or a diseased state [16]. This can be attributed in part to advances in magnetic resonance imaging (MRI) capabilities [13]. Functional MRI (fMRI) is a functional neuroimaging procedure that identifies localized patterns of brain activation by detecting associated changes in cerebral blood flow [3,14,15].

fMRI scans consist of activations of tens of thousands of voxels over time, among which a complex interaction of signals and noise is embedded [7]. Using relevant spatio-temporal brain activity tensor data from these scans, the underlying brain network, here also called a connectome [17], can be computed. The functional connectome provides a graph-theoretical viewpoint to investigate the collective pattern of functional activity across all brain regions, and has been shown to be abnormal in neuropsychiatric disorders [10]. Indeed, brain networks, both structural and functional, have been increasingly studied in recent years [1,5,17], with potential applications to the early detection of brain diseases [19].

To date, conventional network approaches primarily focus on local patterns at the level of brain regions [9,24] or pairwise connectivities [25]. Ye et al. presented a kernel-based method for selecting biomarkers or brain regions from multiple heterogeneous data sources that may play more important roles than others in confirming an Alzheimer's disease (AD) diagnosis [24]. Similarly, Huang et al. introduced a sparse composite linear discriminant analysis model for identifying disease-related brain regions in AD [9].

In contrast to detecting single brain regions as biomarkers, Zalesky et al. proposed a network-based statistic approach to identify a collection of pairwise connections, some forming subnetworks, that is abnormal in patients with schizophrenia [25]. Here, thresholding was applied to pairwise connections, thus requiring each candidate link to be statistically significant under pre-defined criteria. However, links may not be discriminative by themselves until they form a component. Moreover, only connected components present in the set of suprathreshold links were examined in [25]. However, a component may lose its significance by incorporating links that are uncorrelated with other links in the component. Therefore, a full set of candidate components need to be investigated, including those with separately insignificant links and those with a subset of significant links. In this study, we focus on integrating statistical analysis and graph mining algorithms to identify subgraph patterns that distinguish rsfMRI networks obtained from two diagnostic groups (subjects with bipolar disorder versus healthy controls).

2   Method

We use a subgraph mining algorithm to analyze discriminative patterns in fMRI brain networks, which are also referred to as graphs hereafter.

Definition 1 (Binary Graph). *A binary graph is represented as $G = (V, E)$, where $V = \{v_1, \cdots, v_{n_v}\}$ is the set of vertices, $E \subseteq V \times V$ is the set of deterministic edges.*

Let $\mathcal{D} = \{(G_i, y_i)\}_{i=1}^n$ denote a graph dataset. All graphs in the dataset share a given set of nodes V, which corresponds to a specific brain parcellation scheme. Each graph G_i is associated with a label y_i based on the diagnosis of this subject. Here, if a subject has bipolar disorder, the corresponding graph is labeled positive. By contrast, if a subject is in the control group, the graph is labeled negative.

2.1 Subgraph Patterns in Brain Networks

In brain network analysis, the ideal patterns we want to mine from the data should balance local with global graph topological information. Subgraph patterns are a desired option, which can simultaneously model the network connectivity patterns among nodes and still capture changes on a local scale [13].

Definition 2 (Subgraph). *Let $G' = (V', E')$ and $G = (V, E)$ be two binary graphs. G' is a subgraph of G (denoted as $G' \subseteq G$) iff $V' \subseteq V$ and $E' \subseteq E$. If G' is a subgraph of G, then G is supergraph of G'.*

A subgraph pattern, in a brain network, represents a collection of brain regions and their connections. In other fields, mining subgraph patterns from graph data has been extensively studied by many researchers [4,11,18,23]. In general, a variety of filtering criteria are proposed. A typical evaluation criterion is frequency, which aims at searching for frequently appearing subgraph patterns in a graph dataset satisfying a pre-specified value as minimum support. Most of the frequent subgraph mining approaches are unsupervised such that the discrimination power of identified subgraph patterns can not be guaranteed.

In contrast to frequent subgraph patterns, we want to mine discriminative patterns that can be used to distinguish subjects with bipolar disorder from normal controls. For example, as shown in Fig. 1, three brain regions (red nodes) may work collaboratively for normal people and abnormal connections between them can result in a diseased state (*e.g.*, bipolar disorder). Thus, it is valuable to understand which connections collectively play a significant role subserving the underlying disease mechanisms by finding discriminative subgraph patterns.

In this study, we use the G-test as the selection criterion for a subgraph pattern. It tests the null hypothesis that the frequency of a pattern in the positively-labeled (*i.e.*, bipolar disorder) graph fits its distribution in the negatively-labeled (*i.e.*, normal controls) counterparts. Rejecting the null hypothesis indicates a significant pattern with discrimination power. G-test score is defined as follows [23]:

$$t(g, \mathcal{D}) = 2m(p \cdot ln\frac{p}{q} + (1 - p) \cdot ln\frac{1 - p}{1 - q})$$

where m is the number of positive graphs, and p and q are the frequency of the subgraph pattern g in positive graphs and negative graphs, respectively,

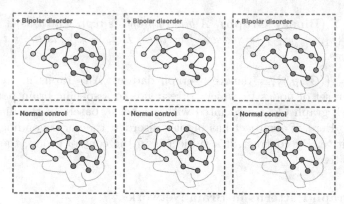

Fig. 1. An example of discriminative subgraph patterns (connections between red nodes) in brain networks.

in the dataset $\mathcal{D}$. From the G-test score of a subgraph pattern, its statistical significance (*i.e.*, p-value) can be calculated using the chi-square distribution χ^2 with 1 degree of freedom in our case.

However, given that edges in fMRI brain networks are inherently weighted (correlations of time series), it is ambiguous to define whether a subgraph pattern is contained in such network, thereby difficult to determine p and q. Hence, the uncertainty information on weighted edges should be accounted for.

2.2 Mining fMRI Brain Networks

Conventional graph mining approaches are best suited for binary edges, where the structure of graphs is deterministic, and the binary edges represent the presence or absence of linkages between the nodes [13]. In fMRI brain network data however, there are inherently weighted edges in the graph linkage structure, as shown in Fig. 2 (left). A straightforward solution is to threshold weighted networks to yield binary networks. However, such simplification will result in potentially a great loss of information. By regarding the positive correlation of time series between two brain regions as a probability of existence for the corresponding edge, Kong et al. model fMRI brain networks as weighted graphs [12].

Definition 3 (Weighted Graph). *A weighted graph is represented as $\widetilde{G} = (V, E, p)$, where $V = \{v_1, \cdots, v_{n_v}\}$ is the set of vertices, $E \subseteq V \times V$ is the set of nondeterministic edges, and $p : E \to (0, 1]$ is a function that assigns a probability of existence to each edge in E.*

For a weighted graph $\widetilde{G}(V, E, p)$, each edge $e \in E$ is associated with a probability $p(e)$ indicating the likelihood of whether this edge should exist or not. It is assumed that $p(e)$ of different edges in a weighted graph are independent from each other. Therefore, by enumerating the possible existence of all the edges in a weighted graph, we can obtain a set of binary graphs. Formally, we denote G

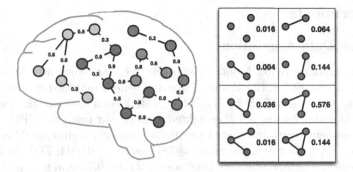

Fig. 2. An example of fMRI brain networks (left) and all the possible instantiations of linkage structures between red nodes (right).

implied from $\widetilde{G}$ as $\widetilde{G} \Rightarrow G$ with a probability, as follows [12]:

$$\Pr(\widetilde{G} \Rightarrow G) = \prod_{e \in E(G)} p(e) \prod_{e \in E(\widetilde{G}) - E(G)} (1 - p(e)) \tag{1}$$

For example, in Fig. 2 (right), consider the three red nodes and links between them as a weighted graph. There are $2^3 = 8$ binary graphs that can be implied with different probabilities, computed using Eq. (1).

Suppose we are given a weighted graph dataset $\widetilde{\mathcal{D}} = \{(\widetilde{G}_i, y_i)\}_{i=1}^n$. For each weighted graph $\widetilde{G}_i \in \widetilde{\mathcal{D}}$, a binary graph G_i can be implied, i.e., $\widetilde{G}_i \Rightarrow G_i$. Then a binary graph dataset $\mathcal{D} = \{(G_i, y_i)\}_{i=1}^n$ is said to be implied from the weighted graph dataset $\widetilde{\mathcal{D}}$, i.e., $\widetilde{\mathcal{D}} \Rightarrow \mathcal{D}$, iff $\forall i \in \{1, \cdots, n\}, \widetilde{G}_i \Rightarrow G_i$. All the possible instantiations of a weighted graph dataset $\widetilde{\mathcal{D}}$ are referred to as worlds of $\widetilde{\mathcal{D}}$, denoted as $\mathcal{W}(\widetilde{\mathcal{D}}) = \{\mathcal{D} | \widetilde{\mathcal{D}} \Rightarrow \mathcal{D}\}$, where each world corresponds to an implied binary graph dataset $\mathcal{D}$. Intuitively, $|\mathcal{W}(\widetilde{\mathcal{D}})| = \prod_{i=1}^n 2^{E(\widetilde{G}_i)}$. By assuming that different weighted graphs are independent from each other, we have the probability of a binary graph dataset $\mathcal{D} \in \mathcal{W}(\widetilde{\mathcal{D}})$ being implied by $\widetilde{\mathcal{D}}$:

$$\Pr(\widetilde{\mathcal{D}} \Rightarrow \mathcal{D}) = \prod_{i=1}^n \Pr(\widetilde{G}_i \Rightarrow G_i) \tag{2}$$

Thus, the expected G-test score of a subgraph pattern over the weighted fMRI brain networks can be computed as follows:

$$\mathrm{Exp}\left(t(g, \widetilde{\mathcal{D}})\right) = \sum_{\mathcal{D} \in \mathcal{W}(\widetilde{\mathcal{D}})} \Pr(\widetilde{\mathcal{D}} \Rightarrow \mathcal{D}) \cdot t(g, \mathcal{D})$$

By leveraging the fact that $t(g, \mathcal{D})$ can only take a limited number of values (no more than n^2) and the moderate-size of our brain network dataset (a small n), we can use dynamic programming proposed in [12] to efficiently compute the expected G-test score.

3   Experiments

3.1   Image Data Acquisition

Our sample consists of 52 bipolar I subjects who are currently in euthymia (23 females; age = 40.8 ± 12.84) and 45 age and gender matched healthy controls (18 females; age = 40.15 ± 10.77). The rsfMRI scan was acquired on a 3T Siemens Trio scanner using a T2*-weighted echo planar imaging (EPI) gradient-echo pulse sequence with integrated parallel acquisition technique (IPAT), with TR = 2 sec, TE = 25 msec, flip angle = 78, matrix = 64x64, FOV = 192 mm, in-plane voxel size = 3x3 mm, slice thickness = 3 mm, 0.75 mm gap, and 30 total interleaved slices. To allow for scanner equilibration, two TRs at the beginning of the scan were discarded. The total sequence time was 7 min and 2 sec, with 208 volumes acquired.

3.2   Brain Network Construction

Functional connectomes were generated using the rsfMRI toolbox, CONN[1] [21]. In brief, raw EPI images were realigned, co-registered, normalized, and smoothed before analyses. Confound effects from motion artifact, white matter, and CSF were regressed out of the signal. Using the 82 labels Freesurfer-generated cortical/subcortical gray matter regions, functional brain networks were derived using pairwise BOLD signal correlations. The constructed connectivity maps are shown in Fig. 3. Here, due to the sheer amount of pairwise connections, visually it is hard to discern local differences between groups.

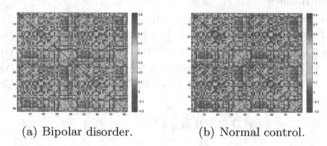

(a) Bipolar disorder.   (b) Normal control.

Fig. 3. Connectivity maps constructed from fMRI data. Here, the partitioning of the network is based on neuroanatomy.

3.3   Discriminative Subgraph Patterns

The most significant 10 subgraph patterns identified from these fMRI brain networks were visualized with the BrainNet Viewer[2] [22], as shown in Fig. 4

---

[1] http://www.nitrc.org/projects/conn
[2] http://www.nitrc.org/projects/bnv

where p-values are presented for each pattern. Considering our discriminative subgraph patterns were selected from a large number of candidate frequent subgraph patterns ($62,776$ in our dataset), multiple comparisons were accounted for by following the Benjamini-Hochberg procedure [2] to control the false discovery rate (FDR). Results indicated that these top-10 patterns would be significant with a FDR of 17.10%. Note that in contrast to the more than $60,000$ subgraphs identified and tested here, conventional pairwise comparisons result in only $\binom{82}{2} = 3,321$ comparisons.

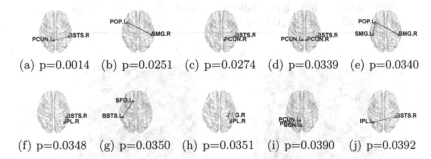

(a) p=0.0014   (b) p=0.0251   (c) p=0.0274   (d) p=0.0339   (e) p=0.0340

(f) p=0.0348   (g) p=0.0350   (h) p=0.0351   (i) p=0.0390   (j) p=0.0392

Fig. 4. Discriminative subgraph patterns in the rsfMRI networks of euthymic bipolar subjects versus healthy controls. Patterns with higher frequency in bipolar subjects are shown in red (all except for b and e), while patterns with higher frequency in controls are shown in blue. See Table 1 for node abbreviations.

We observed that the patterns in Fig. 4(b) and Fig. 4(e) are shown to be more frequent in the control group while usually absent in the subjects with bipolar disorder; other patterns in Fig. 4 are present more frequently in subjects with bipolar disorder while less so in the control group. Particularly, we identified patterns in Fig. 4(d), Fig. 4(e) and Fig. 4(i) which are composed of 3 nodes, while pairwise (*i.e.*, 2 nodes) patterns have been studied before in [25]. By contrast, we investigated a full set of candidate components, including those with separately insignificant links and those with a subset of significant links.

Table 1 lists the names of the nodes contributing to the top-10 discriminative subgraph patterns in Fig. 4. To better visualize the different connectivity patterns, the 18-by-18 subnetwork formed by these significant brain regions are additionally shown in Fig. 5.

4   Discussion

Thanks to recent advent of connectomics, global topological information can now be probed using state-of-the-art graph-theoretical analyses by modeling comprehensive patterns of brain connectivity as a network. In contrast to conventional connectome approaches that focus on local connectivity patterns among select regions-of-interest, in this study we proposed to employ sophisticated graph mining techniques to identify and quantify subgraph patterns in brain networks, and

Table 1. Node abbreviations.

Abbreviations	Nodes
BSTS.L(R)	left(right)-Banks of the superior temporal sulcus
PCUN.L(R)	left(right)-Precuneus
SMG.L(R)	left(right)-Supra-marginal
IPL.L(R)	left(right)-Inferior parietal
POP.L(R)	left(right)-Pars opercularis
CUN.L(R)	left(right)-Cuneus
PCAL.L(R)	left(right)-Peri-calcarine
SFG.L(R)	left(right)-Superior frontal
FFG.L(R)	left(right)-Fusiform

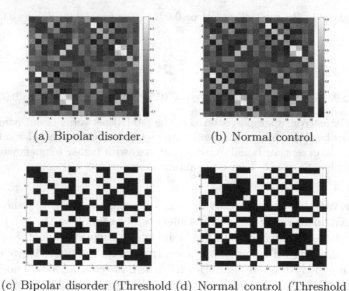

(a) Bipolar disorder.   (b) Normal control.

(c) Bipolar disorder (Threshold   (d) Normal control (Threshold
    = 0.1).   = 0.1).

Fig. 5. 18-by-18 rsfMRI subnetwork showing the connectivity between the 18 brain regions listed in Table 1 (nodes 1-9 are regions in the left hemisphere, while nodes 10-18 in the right hemisphere; nodes are listed following the same order as in Table 1).

applied them to rsfMRI data acquired from a sample of subjects with bipolar disorder.

While we used the G-test to detect between-group differences in subgraph patterns, an alternative approach to determine statistical significance is bootstrapping by randomizing assignment of subjects into different diagnostic groups. However, such an approach would now render the two groups significantly different in gender and age, which would then need to be taken into account when interpreting subsequent results.

While the results presented here require further validation in the future, many of the identified regions that distinguished bipolar subjects from healthy controls are known regions important for mood regulation and self-referential operations in the temporal and parietal lobes. For example, as integral part of the default mode network, the inferior parietal lobule and the precuneus are known to be instrumental for the self-referential operations (thinking about self) human brains engage in at rest (but disengage during tasks) [8]. The default mode network thus is considered a task-negative network, whose function has been shown to be abnormal in both unipolar depression and bipolar disorder [6].

In the future, the technique proposed here can be easily adapted and applied to multi-modal imaging data thanks to the existence of a variety of neuroimaging techniques that characterize the brain structure and/or function from different yet complementary perspectives: diffusion tensor imaging (DTI) yields local microstructural characteristics of water diffusion; structural MRI can be used to delineate brain atrophy; fMRI records BOLD response related to neural activity; PET measures metabolic patterns [20]. Based on such a multi-modality representation, it is thus desirable to find useful patterns with rich semantics (*e.g.*, it is important to know which connectivity between brain regions is significantly altered in the context of both structure and function). Moreover, by leveraging the complementary information embedded in a multi-modality representation, better performance (*i.e.*, higher sensitivity and specificity) on disease diagnosis can be expected.

Acknowledgments. This work is supported in part by NSF through grants CNS-1115234.

References

1. Ajilore, O., Zhan, L., GadElkarim, J., Zhang, A., Feusner, J.D., Yang, S., Thompson, P.M., Kumar, A., Leow, A.: Constructing the resting state structural connectome. Frontiers in Neuroinformatics **7** (2013)
2. Benjamini, Y., Hochberg, Y.: Controlling the false discovery rate: a practical and powerful approach to multiple testing. Journal of the Royal Statistical Society. Series B (Methodological), 289–300 (1995)
3. Biswal, B., Yetkin, F.Z., Haughton, V.M., Hyde, J.S.: Functional connectivity in the motor cortex of resting human brain using echo-planar MRI. Magnetic Resonance in Medicine **34**(4), 537–541 (1995)
4. Cheng, H., Lo, D., Zhou, Y., Wang, X., Yan, X.: Identifying bug signatures using discriminative graph mining. In: ISSTA, pp. 141–152. ACM (2009)
5. Craddock, R.C., James, G.A., Holtzheimer, P.E., Hu, X.P., Mayberg, H.S.: A whole brain fMRI atlas generated via spatially constrained spectral clustering. Human Brain Mapping **33**(8), 1914–1928 (2012)
6. GadElkarim, J.J., Ajilore, O., Schonfeld, D., Zhan, L., Thompson, P.M., Feusner, J.D., Kumar, A., Altshuler, L.L., Leow, A.D.: Investigating brain community structure abnormalities in bipolar disorder using path length associated community estimation. Human Brain Mapping **35**(5), 2253–2264 (2014)

7. Genovese, C.R., Lazar, N.A., Nichols, T.: Thresholding of statistical maps in functional neuroimaging using the false discovery rate. Neuroimage 15(4), 870–878 (2002)
8. Greicius, M.D., Krasnow, B., Reiss, A.L., Menon, V.: Functional connectivity in the resting brain: a network analysis of the default mode hypothesis. Proceedings of the National Academy of Sciences 100(1), 253–258 (2003)
9. Huang, S., Li, J., Ye, J., Wu, T., Chen, K., Fleisher, A., Reiman, E.: Identifying Alzheimer's disease-related brain regions from multi-modality neuroimaging data using sparse composite linear discrimination analysis. In: NIPS, pp. 1431–1439 (2011)
10. Jie, B., Zhang, D., Gao, W., Wang, Q., Wee, C., Shen, D.: Integration of network topological and connectivity properties for neuroimaging classification. Biomedical Engineering 61(2), 576 (2014)
11. Jin, N., Young, C., Wang, W.: GAIA: graph classification using evolutionary computation. In: SIGMOD, pp. 879–890. ACM (2010)
12. Kong, X., Ragin, A.B., Wang, X., Yu, P.S.: Discriminative feature selection for uncertain graph classification. In: SDM, pp. 82–93. SIAM (2013)
13. Kong, X., Yu, P.S.: Brain network analysis: a data mining perspective. ACM SIGKDD Explorations Newsletter 15(2), 30–38 (2014)
14. Ogawa, S., Lee, T., Kay, A., Tank, D.: Brain magnetic resonance imaging with contrast dependent on blood oxygenation. Proceedings of the National Academy of Sciences 87(24), 9868–9872 (1990)
15. Ogawa, S., Lee, T.-M., Nayak, A.S., Glynn, P.: Oxygenation-sensitive contrast in magnetic resonance image of rodent brain at high magnetic fields. Magnetic Resonance in Medicine 14(1), 68–78 (1990)
16. Rubinov, M., Sporns, O.: Complex network measures of brain connectivity: uses and interpretations. Neuroimage 52(3), 1059–1069 (2010)
17. Sporns, O., Tononi, G., Kötter, R.: The human connectome: a structural description of the human brain. PLoS Computational Biology 1(4), e42 (2005)
18. Thoma, M., Cheng, H., Gretton, A., Han, J., Kriegel, H.-P., Smola, A.J., Song, L., Philip, S.Y., Yan, X., Borgwardt, K.M.: Near-optimal supervised feature selection among frequent subgraphs. In: SDM, pp. 1076–1087. SIAM (2009)
19. Wang, X., Foryt, P., Ochs, R., Chung, J.-H., Wu, Y., Parrish, T., Ragin, A.B.: Abnormalities in resting-state functional connectivity in early human immunodeficiency virus infection. Brain Connectivity 1(3), 207–217 (2011)
20. Wee, C.-Y., Yap, P.-T., Zhang, D., Denny, K., Browndyke, J.N., Potter, G.G., Welsh-Bohmer, K.A., Wang, L., Shen, D.: Identification of mci individuals using structural and functional connectivity networks. Neuroimage 59(3), 2045–2056 (2012)
21. Whitfield-Gabrieli, S., Nieto-Castanon, A.: Conn: a functional connectivity toolbox for correlated and anticorrelated brain networks. Brain Connectivity 2(3), 125–141 (2012)
22. Xia, M., Wang, J., He, Y.: Brainnet viewer: a network visualization tool for human brain connectomics. PloS One 8(7), e68910 (2013)
23. Yan, X., Cheng, H., Han, J., Yu, P.S.: Mining significant graph patterns by leap search. In: SIGMOD, pp. 433–444. ACM (2008)
24. Ye, J., Chen, K., Wu, T., Li, J., Zhao, Z., Patel, R., Bae, M., Janardan, R., Liu, H., Alexander, G., et al.: Heterogeneous data fusion for alzheimer's disease study. In: KDD, pp. 1025–1033. ACM (2008)
25. Zalesky, A., Fornito, A., Bullmore, E.T.: Network-based statistic: identifying differences in brain networks. Neuroimage 53(4), 1197–1207 (2010)

Two-Dimensional Enrichment Analysis for Mining High-Level Imaging Genetic Associations

Xiaohui Yao[1,2], Jingwen Yan[1,2], Sungeun Kim[1], Kwangsik Nho[1],
Shannon L. Risacher[1], Mark Inlow[3], Jason H. Moore[4], Andrew J. Saykin[1],
and Li Shen[1,2(✉)], for the Alzheimer's Disease Neuroimaging Initiative

[1] Radiology and Imaging Sciences, Indiana University School of Medicine,
Indianapolis, IN, USA
shenli@iu.edu
[2] School of Informatics and Computing, Indiana University Indianapolis,
Indianapolis, IN, USA
[3] Mathematics, Rose-Hulman Institute of Technology, Terre Haute, IN, USA
[4] Biomedical Informatics, School of Medicine, University of Pennsylvania,
Philadelphia, PA, USA

Abstract. Enrichment analysis has been widely applied in the genome-wide association studies (GWAS), where gene sets corresponding to biological pathways are examined for significant associations with a phenotype to help increase statistical power and improve biological interpretation. In this work, we expand the scope of enrichment analysis into brain imaging genetics, an emerging field that studies how genetic variation influences brain structure and function measured by neuroimaging quantitative traits (QT). Given the high dimensionality of both imaging and genetic data, we propose to study Imaging Genetic Enrichment Analysis (IGEA), a new enrichment analysis paradigm that jointly considers meaningful gene sets (GS) and brain circuits (BC) and examines whether any given GS-BC pair is enriched in a list of gene-QT findings. Using gene expression data from Allen Human Brain Atlas and imaging genetics data from Alzheimer's Disease Neuroimaging Initiative as test beds, we present an IGEA framework and conduct a proof-of-concept study. This empirical study identifies 12 significant high level two dimensional imaging genetics modules. Many of these modules are relevant to a variety of neurobiological pathways or neurodegenerative diseases, showing the promise of the proposal framework for providing insight into the mechanism of complex diseases.

Keywords: Imaging genetics · Enrichment analysis · Genome wide association study · Quantitative trait

L. Shen—This work was supported by NIH R01 LM011360, U01 AG024904 (details available at http://adni.loni.usc.edu), RC2 AG036535, R01 AG19771, P30 AG10133, and NSF IIS-1117335 at IU, and by NIH R01 LM011360, R01 LM009012, and R01 LM010098 at UPenn.
Data used in preparation of this article were obtained from the Alzheimer's Disease Neuroimaging Initiative (ADNI) database (adni.loni.usc.edu). As such, the investigators within the ADNI contributed to the design and implementation of ADNI and/or provided data but did not participate in analysis or writing of this report. A complete listing of ADNI investigators can be found at: http://adni.loni.usc.edu/wp-content/uploads/how_to_apply/ADNI_Acknowledgement_List.pdf.

© Springer International Publishing Switzerland 2015
Y. Guo et al. (Eds.): BIH 2015, LNAI 9250, pp. 115–124, 2015.
DOI: 10.1007/978-3-319-23344-4_12

1   Introduction

Brain imaging genetics is an emerging field that studies how genetic variation influences brain structure and function. Genome-wide association studies (GWAS) have been performed to identify genetic markers such as single nucleotide polymorphisms (SNPs) that are associated with brain imaging quantitative traits (QTs) [15,16]. Using biological pathways and networks as prior knowledge, enrichment analysis has also been performed to discover pathways or network modules enriched by GWAS findings to enhance statistical power and help biological interpretation [5]. For example, numerous studies on complex diseases have demonstrated that genes functioning in the same pathway can influence imaging QTs collectively even when constituent SNPs do not show significant association individually [13]. Enrichment analysis can also help identify relevant pathways and improve mechanistic understanding of underlying neurobiology [6,10,11,14].

In the genetic domain, enrichment analysis has been widely studied in gene expression data analysis and has recently been modified to analyze GWAS data. GWAS-based enrichment analysis first maps SNP-level scores to gene-level scores, and then test whether a pre-defined gene set S (e.g., a pathway) is enriched in a set of significant genes L (e.g., GWAS findings). Two strategies are often used to compute enrichment significance: threshold-based [3,4,8,19] and rank-based [17]. Threshold-based approaches aim to solve an independence test problem (e.g., chi-square test, hypergeometric test, or binomial z-test) by treating genes as significant if their scores exceed a threshold. Rank-based methods take into account the score of each gene to determine if the members of S are randomly distributed throughout L.

In brain imaging genetics, the above enrichment analysis methods are applicable only to genetic findings associated with each single imaging QT. Our ultimate goal is to discover high level associations between meaningful gene sets (GS) and brain circuits (BC), which typically include multiple genes and multiple QTs. To achieve this goal, we propose to study Imaging Genetic Enrichment Analysis (IGEA), a new enrichment analysis paradigm that jointly considers sets of interest (i.e., GS and BC) in both genetic and imaging domains and examines whether any given GS-BC pair is enriched in a list of gene-QT findings.

Using whole brain whole genome gene expression data from Allen Human Brain Atlas (AHBA) and imaging genetics data from Alzheimer's Disease Neuroimaging Initiative (ADNI) as test beds, we present a novel IGEA framework and conduct a proof-of-concept study to explore high level imaging genetic associations based on brain-wide genome-wide association study (BWGWAS) results. For consistency purpose, in this paper, we use GS to indicate a set of genes and BC to indicate a set of regions of interest (ROIs) in the brain. The proposed framework consists of the following steps (see also Figure 1): (1) use AHBA to identify meaningful GS-BC modules, (2) conduct BWGWAS on ADNI amyloid imaging genetics data to identify SNP-QT and gene-QT associations, (3) perform IGEA to identify GS-BC modules significantly enriched by gene-QT associations using threshold-based strategy, and (4) visualize and interpret the identified GS-BC modules.

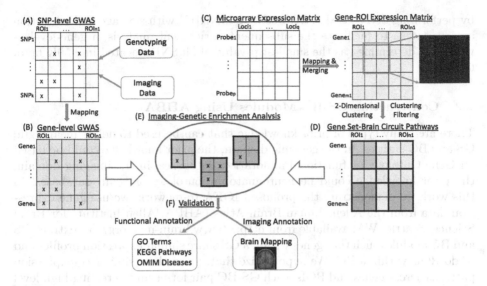

Fig. 1. Overview of the proposed Imaging Genetic Enrichment Analysis (IGEA) framework. (A) Perform SNP-level GWAS of brain wide imaging measures. (B) Map SNP-level GWAS findings to gene-level. (C) Construct gene-ROI expression matrix from AHBA data. (D) Construct GS-BC modules by performing 2D hierarchical clustering, and filter out non-significant 2D clusters. (E) Perform IGEA by mapping gene-level GWAS findings to identified GS-BC modules. (F) For each enriched GS-BC module, examine the GS using GO terms, KEGG pathways, and OMIM disease databases, and map the BC to the brain.

2   Methods and Materials

2.1   Brain Wide Genome Wide Association Study (BWGWAS)

The imaging and genotyping data used for BWGWAS were obtained from the Alzheimer's Disease Neuroimaging Initiative (ADNI) database (adni.loni.usc.edu). One goal of ADNI has been to test whether serial magnetic resonance imaging (MRI), positron emission tomography (PET), other biological markers, and clinical and neuropsychological assessment can be combined to measure the progression of mild cognitive impairment (MCI) and early AD. For up-to-date information, see www.adni-info.org. Preprocessed [18F]Florbetapir PET scans (i.e., amyloid imaging data) were downloaded from adni.loni.usc.edu, then aligned to each participant's same visit scan and normalized to the Montreal Neurological Institute (MNI) space as $2 \times 2 \times 2$ mm voxels. ROI level amyloid measurements were further extracted based on the MarsBaR AAL atlas. Genotype data of both ADNI-1 and ADNI-GO/2 phases were also downloaded, and then quality controlled, imputed and combined as decribed in [9]. A total of 980 non-Hispanic Caucasian participants with both complete amyloid measurements and genome-wide data were studied. Associations between 105 (out of a total 116) baseline amyloid measures and 5,574,300 SNPs were examined by performing SNP-based GWAS using PLINK[12] with sex, age and education as covariates. To facilitate the subsequent enrichment analysis, a gene-level p-value was determined as the smallest p-value of all SNPs located in ±50K bp of the gene.

2.2   Constructing GS-BC Modules Using AHBA

There are many types of prior knowledge that can be used to define meaningful GS and BC entities. In the genomic domain, the prior knowledge could be based on Gene Ontology or functional annotation databases; in the imaging domain, the prior knowledge could be neuroanatomic ontology or brain databases. In this work, to demonstrate the proposed IGEA framework, we use gene expression data from the Allen Human Brain Atlas (AHBA, Allen Institute for Brain Science, Seattle, WA; available from http://www.brain-map.org/) to extract GS and BC modules such that genes within a GS share similar expression profiles and so do ROIs within a BC. We hypothesize that, given these similar co-expression patterns across genes and ROIs, each GS-BC pair forms an interesting high level imaging genetic entity that may be related to certain biological function and can serve as a valuable candidate for two-dimensional IGEA.

The AHBA includes genome-wide microarray-based expression covering the entire brain through systematic sampling of regional tissue. Expression profiles for eight health human brains have been released, including two full brains and six right hemispheres. One goal of AHBA is to combine genomics with the neuroanatomy to better understand the connections between genes and brain functioning. As an early report indicated that individuals share as much as 95% gene expression profile [21], in this study, we only included one full brain (H0351.2001) to construct GS-BC modules. First all the brain samples ($\sim$ 900) were mapped to MarsBaR AAL atlas, which included 116 brain ROIs. Due to many-to-one mapping from brain samples to AAL ROIs, there are > 1 samples for each ROI. Following [20], samples located in the same ROI were merged using the mean statistics. Probes were then merged to genes using the same strategy. Finally the preprocessed gene-ROI profiles were normalized for each ROI. As a result, the expression matrix contained 16,097 genes over 105 ROIs.

We performed a 2D cluster analysis on the gene-ROI expression matrix to identify interesting GS-BC modules. First, we calculated the distance matrices for both genes and ROIs, respectively. In other words, we computed the dissimilarity between each pair of genes, and the dissimilarity between each pair of ROIs, using Equation (1).

$$\text{Dissimilarity} = \left(1 - \text{Pearson's Correlation Coefficient}\right)/2 \qquad (1)$$

Two dendrograms were constructed by applying hierarchical clustering to two distance matrices separately, using the UPGMA (Unweighted Pair Group Method with Arithmetic Mean) algorithm. As most enrichment analyses placed constraints on genetic pathways of sizes from 10 to 400 [13], we cut the dendrogram at half of its height to build genetic clusters (i.e., GSs) whose sizes are mostly within the above range. For the imaging domain, we also employed the same parameter to construct ROI clusters (i.e., BCs).

We tested the statistical significance of each GS-BC pair based on a null hypothesis that the expression level of a gene is independent from the expression level of other genes across relevant brain ROIs in the same GS-BC module, assuming that the average Pearson's correlation coefficients (PCCs) of gene expression levels for genes in the GS-BC module are higher than the ones from random GS-BC modules. Thus, for each GS-BC module, we constructed another GS-BC module with the same number of randomly selected genes and ROIs, and calculated its average PCC (avgPCC), This procedure was repeated $N = 1000$ times and the empirical p-value of original GS-BC module was calculated using the following equation, where I is an indicator function [7].

$$\text{p-value} = \frac{1}{N} \sum_{i=1}^{N} I(\text{avgPCC}_{\text{original}} < \text{avgPCC}_{\text{random}}(i)) \tag{2}$$

2.3 Imaging Genetic Enrichment Analysis (IGEA)

Pathway enrichment analysis has been extensively employed to genomic domain to analyze the genetic findings associated with a specific imaging QT. In this study, our goal is to identify high level associations between gene sets and brain circuits, which typically include multiple genes and multiple QTs.

In this study, we propose the threshold-based IGEA by extending the existing threshold-based enrichment analysis. SNP level findings have been mapped to gene level findings in Section 2.1. The GWAS findings are a list L of $N = N_G \times N_B$ gene-QT associations, where we have a set G_d of $N_G = |G_d|$ genes and a set B_d of $N_B = |B_d|$ QTs in our analysis. From Section 2.2, significant GS-BC modules, where relevant genes share similar expression profiles across relevant ROIs, have been constructed. Given an interesting GS-BC module with gene set G_k and QT set B_k, IGEA aims to determine whether the target GS-BC module $T = \{(g, b) | g \in G_d \cap G_k, b \in B_d \cap B_k\}$ is enriched in L.

Now we describe our threshold-based IGEA method. We have N gene-QT pairs from GWAS. Out of these, $n = |A|$ pairs (the set A) are significant ones with GWAS p-value passed a certain threshold. We also have $m = |P|$ (the set P) gene-QT pairs from a given GS-BC module, and k significant pairs are from P. Using Fisher's exact test for independence, the enrichment p-value for the given GS-BC module is calculated as:

$$\text{p-value} = Pr(|A \cap P| \geq k) = \sum_{i \geq k} \frac{\binom{m}{i} \times \binom{N-m}{n-i}}{\binom{N}{n}} \tag{3}$$

2.4 Evaluation of the Identified GS-BC Modules

For evaluation purpose, we tested the statistical significance of the IGEA results. We hypothesize that the gene-QT associations from BWGWAS of the original

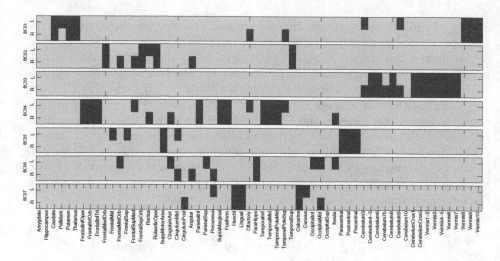

Fig. 2. Seven unique brain circuits (BCs) identified from IGEA. ROIs belonging to each BC are colored in red.

data should be overrepresented in certain GS-BC modules, and the BWGWAS results on permuted data should not be enriched in a similar number of GS-BC modules. We performed IGEA analyses on 50 permuted BWGWAS data sets, and estimated the distribution of the number of significant GS-BC modules. The distribution appeared to be normal. Using this normal distribution, we estimated an empirical p-value for the number of significant GS-BC modules discovered from the original data.

To determine the functional relevance of the enriched GS-BC modules, we also tested whether genes from each module are overrepresented for specific neurobiological functions, signaling pathways or complex neurodegenerative diseases. We performed pathway enrichment tests using gene ontology (GO) biological process terms, KEGG pathways and OMIM (Online Mendelian Inheritance in Man) database.

3   Results and Discussions

3.1   Significant GS-BC Modules from AHBA

By performing hierarchical clustering on both genetic and imaging domains, 275 out of 357 genetic clusters (only those with size ranging from 10 to 400) and 8 imaging clusters (with size ranging from 4 to 23, no clusters are excluded) were identified. 2200 GS-BC modules were generated by combining each pair of genetic and ROI clusters. After performing 1000 permutation tests, 610 modules were kept with a p-value ≤ 0.05. We did not use extremely stringent statistical thresholds for the selection, to avoid the exclusion of potentially interesting candidates. For the BWGWAS results, we obtained $21,028 \times 105 = 2,207,940$

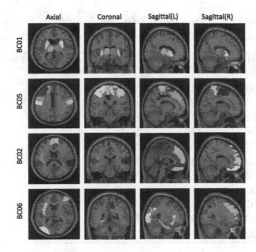

Fig. 3. Brain maps of four brain circuits (BCs) identified from IGEA.

gene-QT associations after mapping SNP-based p-values to genes. Out of these, 1679 gene-QT associations passed the BWGWAS p-value of 1.0E-5.

All 610 constructed GS-BC modules were tested for whether they could be enriched by BWGWAS results using IGEA, and 12 of them turned out to be significant after Bonferroni correction (see Table 1). We also tested the significance of the number of identified GS-BC modules. Compared to permuted results, the analysis on the original data yielded a significantly larger number of enriched GS-BC modules with empirical p-value = 2.6E-2, indicating that imaging genetic associations existed in these enriched GS-BC modules.

Across all 12 identified modules, there are 5 and 7 unique GS and BC entities respectively. Table 2 lists the 5 unique GSs with gene symbols. Figure 2 shows the 7 unique BCs with corresponding ROI names, and Figure 3 maps four of those onto the brain. For example, BC01 involves structures responsible for motivated behaviors (e.g., caudate, pallidum, putamen) and sensory information processing (e.g., thalamus). BC02 involves various frontal regions responsible for executive functions. BC06 includes structures that are major spots for amyloid accumulation in AD (e.g., cingulum, precuneus). Details of all 12 modules are listed in Table 1. We can find that some modules share common gene sets with different brain circuits, and some share the same brain circuits with different gene sets. This illustrates the complex associations among multiple genes and multiple brain ROIs.

3.2   Pathway Analysis of Identified GS-BC Modules

To explore and analyze functional relevance of our identified GS-BC modules, we performed pathway analysis from three aspects including biological processes, functional pathways and diseases using Gene Ontology, KEGG pathways and OMIM diseases databases, respectively.

Table 1. Twelve significantly enriched GS-BC modules from IGEA. See also Table 2 and Figure 2 for details about relevant GSs and BCs respectively.

Module ID	BC ID	# of ROIs	GS ID	# of genes	Corrected P-value
01	BC02	13	GS01	59	1.83E-12
02	BC01	14	GS01	59	8.46E-07
03	BC05	12	GS02	18	1.58E-02
04	BC02	13	GS03	107	1.08E-04
05	BC06	11	GS03	107	9.17E-09
06	BC07	10	GS03	107	6.99E-07
07	BC03	18	GS03	107	2.96E-09
08	BC04	23	GS03	107	7.42E-06
09	BC06	11	GS04	50	4.51E-02
10	BC07	10	GS04	50	2.88E-02
11	BC03	18	GS04	50	4.56E-03
12	BC02	13	GS05	52	1.25E-07

Table 2. Five unique gene sets (GSs) identified from IGEA.

GS ID	Gene symbols
GS01	AASDHPPT, APOC1, APOC4, ARHGAP1, ARMC2, BCR, C16orf74, CHST11, COL25A1, DCLK3, DNAH6, DNAI1, DOCK4, DRD1, ELMOD1, ERLIN1, EXD2, EYA1, FAM107A, FAM118B, FZD2, GNAL, GPR6, GPR88, GSTM3, HTR4, HYDIN, IL17D, ITPK1, KLF5, MFN2, MIPEP, MLLT3, MMD2, MTHFD1, MYB, NCKAP1, NSUN3, PALM, PDE1B, PDYN, PFDN6, PHF21B, PPP1R1A, RAP1GAP, RGS14, RGS20, RNF44, SLC17A8, SLC2A4, STYXL1, TRIM69, UBQLN4, UBR7, VAX1, WNT8A, ZC3HAV1L, ZMAT2, ZNF883
GS02	ACSS1, CPLX1, CSMD2, DDX4, ITGB3, LRIG1, METTL7A, NDRG2, NPAS4, PDIA6, PLA2G5, POTED, PPARGC1A, PSD2, PXDNL, TFCP2L1, USH2A, VEGFA
GS03	ADPRHL2, ADRM1, AKR1A1, ANAPC2, AP4M1, AP5Z1, APBB1, APBB3, ARFGAP3, ARMC6, ASL, ATP5B, AUP1, AURKAIP1, B4GALT3, C17orf59, CAPN1, CCS, CCT3, CDIPT, COG4, CPNE1, CSNK2B, CSTF1, DAPK3, DDX21, DECR2, DEPDC5, DHPS, DHX16, DHX38, DNAJC30, EIF2B4, EIF2B5, ELOF1, ERAL1, FAM50B, FAM96B, FLII, GALK1, GGNBP2, GPAA1, GPATCH3, GPI, GPR137, HEXIM2, HN1, HOOK2, HPS6, IFFO1, KAT5, KHK, KLHL22, LDLR, LRSAM1, LZTR1, MAF1, MAGEF1, MFSD10, MMS19, MRPL38, MRPL54, NARFL, NCAPH2, NCLN, NISCH, NRBP1, NTHL1, PHB2, PI4KB, PIH1D1, POLD2, POLG, PPOX, PRDX2, PRMT1, PRPF31, PTBP2, PTOV1, RABGGTA, RALY, RPS19BP1, RRN3, SH2B1, SLC25A42, SLC41A3, SMPD1, SNRPA, SSNA1, STK19, STUB1, SULT1A1, TCEA2, TCEB3, TMED3, TMEM106C, TMEM161A, TOMM40, TRMU, TRPC4AP, TTC27, TUSC1, TXN2, TXNL4B, UBR4, YTHDF2, ZFAND2B
GS04	AIPL1, AP1M2, ARRDC5, CD1C, CST1, DEFB113, DEFB126, EPGN, FBP2, FGF19, FNDC7, FRG2, GPRC5D, IL22, INMT, KCNK18, KIF18A, KLRG2, KRT79, MBD3L2, MMP7, MS4A1, MS4A3, MSMB, NEIL3, OR13C3, OR1M1, OR4F15, OR51I2, OR5AN1, OR5AR1, OR5M1, OR7G3, PDZK1IP1, PRAMEF8, PTCHD3, RLN1, SIRPD, TBX20, TEDDM1, TGM3, TIAF1, TIMD4, TM4SF19, TM4SF20, TMC1, TPD52L3, WFDC13, XDH, ZFP42
GS05	ALDH9A1, ANKFN1, APOE, ATP6V0A4, BIN1, C11orf65, C15orf52, C1orf64, CD81, CDH1, CNN3, ECSCR, EDNRB, ENG, FAM84B, GGT5, GIMAP5, GPR137B, GREM1, GSTM2, GTF2F2, HRASLS2, ID1, LMO2, MAPKAPK3, MARCH10, PARP4, PAWR, PGR, PHF10, PLSCR4, PMAIP1, POLI, PRDX1, RAB13, RGS22, SDS, SLC2A1, SLC40A1, SMAD9, STX18, SULT1C4, SVOPL, TIE1, TM4SF18, TMEM204, TRIP6, TST, WASF2, WFDC3, WRB, WWC2

Most identified GSs have a significant functional enrichment, and several can be related to the neurodegenerative disease and its development. For instance, calcium signaling pathway (from Module #01 and #02) playing key role in short- and long-term synaptic plasticity, has shown abnormality in many neurodegenerative disorders including AD, Parkinson's disease, amyotrophic lateral sclerosis, Huntington's disease, spinocerebellar ataxias and so on [1]. There are also several enriched pathways related to oxidative stress, which is a critical factor for a range of neurodegenerative disorders. For example, DNA polymerase (from Module #04-08) deficiency can lead to neurodegeneration and exacerbates AD phenotypes by reducing repair of oxidative DNA damage [18]; glycolysis and gluconeogenesis (from Module #04-08) are associated with hypoxia, ischemia, and AD [2]; others like adherens junction (from Module #12) and focal adhesion (from Module #03) have also been shown disorder-related by indirectly affecting oxidative stress. For the enriched disease results, we also find some neurodegeneration-related (like anomalies from Module #01 and #02, neuropathy from module #04-08), while a large part of them are cancer-related (like prostate cancer from Module #09, #10 and #11). A large body of studies have focused on investigating the relationship between cancer and neurodegeneration, with abnormal cell growth and cell loss in common. For the GO Biological Process enrichment, various Biological Process terms are enriched and can be grouped to 5 categories including cellular process, cell cycle, metabolic process, neurological system process and response to stimulus. Most of these terms have direct or indirect relationships with neurodegenerative diseases or phenotypes.

4   Conclusions

We have presented a two dimensional imaging genetic enrichment analysis (IGEA) framework to explore the high level imaging genetic associations by integrating whole brain genomic, transcriptomic and neuroanatomic data. Traditional pathway enrichment analysis focused on investigating genetic findings of a single phenotype one at a time, and relationships among imaging QTs could be ignored. Such approach could be inadequate to provide insights into the mechanisms of complex diseases that involve multiple genes and multiple QTs. In this paper, we have proposed a novel enrichment analysis paradigm IGEA to detect high level associations between gene sets and brain circuits. By jointly considering the complex relationships between interlinked genetic markers and correlated brain imaging phenotypes, IGEA provides additional power for extracting biological insights on neurogenomic associations at a systems biology level.

References

1. Bezprozvanny, I.: Calcium signaling and neurodegenerative diseases. Trends Mol. Med. **15**(3), 89–100 (2009)
2. Butterfield, D., Lange, M.: Multifunctional roles of enolase in Alzheimer's disease brain: beyond altered glucose metabolism. J. Neurochem. **111**(4), 915–933 (2009)
3. Draghici, S., Khatri, P., et al.: Global functional profiling of gene expression. Genomics **81**(2), 98–104 (2003)

4. Draghici, S., Khatri, P., et al.: Onto-tools, the toolkit of the modern biologist: Onto-express, onto-compare, onto-design and onto-translate. Nucleic Acids Res. **31**(13), 3775–3781 (2003)
5. Hirschhorn, J.N.: Genomewide association studies-illuminating biologic pathways. N. Engl. J. Med. **360**(17), 1699–1701 (2009)
6. Hong, M.G., Alexeyenko, A., et al.: Genome-wide pathway analysis implicates intracellular transmembrane protein transport in Alzheimer disease. J. Hum. Genet. **55**(10), 707 (2010)
7. Jin, D., Lee, H.: A computational approach to identifying gene-microRNA modules in cancer. PLoS Comput. Biol. **11**(1), e1004042 (2015)
8. Khatri, P., Draghici, S.: Ontological analysis of gene expression data: current tools, limitations, and open problems. Bioinformatics **21**(18), 3587–3595 (2005)
9. Kim, S., Swaminathan, S., et al.: Influence of genetic variation on plasma protein levels in older adults using a multi-analyte panel. Plos One **8**(7) (2013)
10. Lambert, J.C., Grenier-Boley, B., et al.: Implication of the immune system in Alzheimer's disease: evidence from genome-wide pathway analysis. J. Alzheimers Dis. **20**(4), 1107–1118 (2010)
11. O'Dushlaine, C., Kenny, E., et al.: Molecular pathways involved in neuronal cell adhesion and membrane scaffolding contribute to schizophrenia and bipolar disorder susceptibility. Mol. Psychiatry **16**(3), 286–292 (2011)
12. Purcell, S., Neale, B., et al.: Plink: a tool set for whole-genome association and population-based linkage analyses. Am. J. Hum. Genet. **81**(3), 559–575 (2007)
13. Ramanan, V., Shen, L., et al.: Pathway analysis of genomic data: concepts, methods, and prospects for future development. Trends Genet. **28**(7), 323–332 (2012)
14. Ramanan, V.K., Kim, S., et al.: Genome-wide pathway analysis of memory impairment in the Alzheimer's Disease Neuroimaging Initiative (ADNI) cohort implicates gene candidates, canonical pathways, and networks. Brain Imaging Behav. **6**(4), 634–648 (2012)
15. Saykin, A.J., Shen, L., et al.: Alzheimer's Disease Neuroimaging Initiative biomarkers as quantitative phenotypes: Genetics core aims, progress, and plans. Alzheimers Dement. **6**(3), 265–273 (2010)
16. Shen, L., Thompson, P.M., et al.: Genetic analysis of quantitative phenotypes in AD and MCI: imaging, cognition and biomarkers. Brain Imaging Behav. **8**(2), 183–207 (2014)
17. Subramanian, A., Tamayo, P., et al.: Gene set enrichment analysis: A knowledge-based approach for interpreting genome-wide expression profiles. Proc. Natl. Acad. Sci. USA **102**(43), 15545–15550 (2005)
18. Sykora, P., Misiak, M., et al.: Dna polymerase beta deficiency leads to neurodegeneration and exacerbates Alzheimer disease phenotypes. Nucleic Acids Res. **43**(2), 943–959 (2015)
19. Ulitsky, I., Maron-Katz, A., et al.: Expander: from expression microarrays to networks and functions. Nature Protocols **5**(2), 303–322 (2010)
20. Yan, J., Du, L., et al.: Transcriptome-guided amyloid imaging genetic analysis via a novel structured sparse learning algorithm. Bioinformatics **30**(17), i564–i571 (2014)
21. Zeng, H., Shen, E.H., et al.: Large-scale cellular-resolution gene profiling in human neocortex reveals species-specific molecular signatures. Cell **149**(2), 483–496 (2012)

Minimum Partial Correlation: An Accurate and Parameter-Free Measure of Functional Connectivity in fMRI

Lei Nie[1,2], Xian Yang[1], Paul M. Matthews[3], Zhiwei Xu[2], and Yike Guo[1,4(✉)]

[1] Department of Computing, Imperial College London, London, UK
y.guo@imperial.ac.uk
[2] Institute of Computing Technology, Chinese Academy of Sciences, Beijing, China
[3] Department of Medicine, Imperial College London, London, UK
[4] School of Computer Engineering and Science, Shanghai University, Shanghai, China

Abstract. Functional connectivity, a data-driven modelling of spontaneous fluctuations in activity in spatially segregated brain regions, has emerged as a promising approach to generate hypotheses and features for prediction. The most widely used method for inferring functional connectivity is full correlation, but it cannot differentiate direct and indirect effects. This disadvantage is often avoided by fully partial correlation, but this method suffers from Berkson's paradox. Some advanced methods, such as regularised inverse covariance and Bayes nets, have been applied. However, the connectivity inferred by these methods usually depends on crucial parameters. This paper suggests minimum partial correlation as a parameter-free measure of functional connectivity in fMRI. An algorithm, called elastic PC-algorithm, is designed to approximately calculate minimum partial correlation. Our experimental results show that the proposed method is more accurate than full correlation, fully partial correlation, regularised inverse covariance, network deconvolution algorithm and global silencing algorithm in most cases.

Keywords: fMRI · Functional connectivity · Partial correlation · PC-algorithm

1 Introduction

Functional connectivity, which is defined as measurable temporal dependences among spatially segregated brain areas, does not rest on any generative models about brains [10]. Although functional connectivity does not necessarily reveal mechanisms about how the brain works, it is expected to imply true links (i.e. direct causal effects) between regions of interest as accurately as possible. Such studies are motivated by the belief that more accurate descriptions of functional connectivity may generate more reliable hypotheses of brain organizations [3] and provide a better basis for predictions [6], such as in decoding cognitive states [18], or in evaluating brain diseases or their severity [12].

© Springer International Publishing Switzerland 2015
Y. Guo et al. (Eds.): BIH 2015, LNAI 9250, pp. 125–134, 2015.
DOI: 10.1007/978-3-319-23344-4_13

The accuracy of functional connectivity is typically evaluated from three aspects: the skeleton, directionality and strength. This paper focuses on inferring the skeleton, which is to determine whether a link between two ROIs (i.e. nodes) exists or not. Smith et al. [19] systematically investigated the accuracy of many methods for skeleton inference using 28 synthetic networks and their corresponding BLOD signals generated from the dynamic causal model [11]. Their results show that the top-3 methods are regularised inverse covariance (ICOV), fully partial correlation and Bayes net, which are followed by full correlation.

Among the above four methods, full correlation is the most widely used method. It has been demonstrated that full correlation offers deep insights into brain structures [13] and powerful features for brain decoding [22]. Full correlation is robust and parameter-free, but there is an intrinsic limitation to differentiation of direct and indirect effects. Fig. 1(A) shows an example of differentiating direct and indirect effects in the network where Node 1 → Node 2→ Node 3. The full correlation between Node 1 and Node 3 is as high as 1.0, but there is no real link between the two nodes.

Fully partial correlation [15] often successfully identifies the direct effects by controlling the intermediate nodes. The fully partial correlation of two nodes is their correlation when all other nodes in the network are controlled. It is worth noting that "fully partial correlation" is called "partial correlation" in previous studies about functional connectivity. Mathematically, partial correlation is also used to express the correlation when any subset of nodes are controlled. To avoid ambiguity, fully partial correlation and partial correlation are explicitly distinguished in this paper. In [19], fully partial correlation performs excellently. However, this strategy sometimes causes two independent nodes to become conditionally dependent, which is known as Berkson's paradox [2]. As illustrated by Fig. 1(B), there is no link between Node 1 and Node 2, but the fully partial correlation between these two nodes is very close to 1.0.

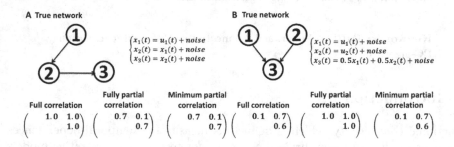

Fig. 1. (A) An example of differentiating direct and indirect effects. (B) An example of Berkson's paradox.

ICOV is a regularised version of fully partial correlation, which tends to reduce the number of non-zero elements of the precision matrix [9, 25]. Hinne et al. [14] extended ICOV to incorporate both functional and diffusion imaging data. ICOV may correct Berkson's paradox if the regularisation parameter is set to an appropriate value. The main drawback of ICOV is that its accuracy highly depends on the regularisation parameter. One possible way to overcome this drawback is to use cross-validation for automatically adjusting the regularisation parameter. For real datasets, the cross-validation scores were usually calculated based on the accuracies of predicted BOLD signals rather than inferred links [25], because the real links are unknown. However, the validity of tuning the regularisation parameter in this way is still in doubtful for two reasons. One reason is that a value of the parameter that results in accurate prediction (e.g. BOLD signals) is not usually same as the one that is likely to recover the true model (e.g. real links) [16]. The other reason is that functional connectivity is data summarization rather than a generative model [10], so it is not reasonable to use functional connectivity to produce BOLD signals for cross-validation.

This paper suggests minimum partial correlation as a measure of functional connectivity in fMRI. The minimum partial correlation between two nodes is the minimum of all absolute values of partial correlations by controlling on all possible subsets of other nodes. Fully partial correlation, which controls all other nodes rather than a proper subset of other nodes, can be regarded as an approximation of minimum partial correlation. Under the faithfulness and Gaussian assumptions, the minimum partial correlation between two nodes is zero if and only if there is no link between the two nodes in the corresponding causal Bayesian network [20]. It is time-consuming to calculate minimum partial correlation, since the number of all possible controlling subsets grows exponentially with the number of nodes. We modify the PC-algorithm to approximate minimum partial correlation, which called elastic PC-algorithm. Unlike the PC-algorithm and its other variations, the elastic PC-algorithm is not based on a specific significance threshold. Within a given time budget, the elastic PC-algorithm can approach the minimum partial correlation as possible. Furthermore, we evaluate and illustrate the elastic PC-algorithm using the NetSim dataset [19] and resting-state fMRI data from the Human Connectome Project [24].

2   Methods

2.1   Preliminaries

Given a directed acyclic graph (DAG) $\mathcal{G} = (V, E)$, which consists of a node set $V = \{r_1, r_2, \cdots, r_N\}$ and an edge set E. Each node denotes a random variable and each directed edge represents a causal effect from one random variable to another one. A causal model represented by $\mathcal{G}$ generates a joint probability distribution over the nodes, which is denoted as $P(V)$. The DAG $\mathcal{G}$ and the distribution P satisfy the causal Markov condition if and only if for every node $r \in V$, the node r is independent of $V \backslash (Descendants(r) \bigcup Parents(r))$ given $Parents(r)$ [20].

When the causal Markov condition is satisfied, the conditional independence relations in the generated distribution P are entailed in the DAG $\mathcal{G}$ using the concept called d-separation. For a 3-node path $r_1 \rightarrow r_2 \leftarrow r_3$, the middle node

r_3 is called collider. A path is said to be d-separated by a node set Z if and only if at least one non-collider is in Z or at least one collider and all its descendants are not in Z; two nodes are said to be d-separated by a node set Z if and only if all path between the two nodes are d-separated by Z [20].

If two nodes r_i and r_j in the DAG $\mathcal{G}$ are d-separated by a node set Z, then r_i and r_j are conditionally independent in the distribution P given Z. Here we only emphasis that there is no edge between nodes r_i and r_j if and only if they can be d-separated by some node set. This means that the nodes r_i and r_j are conditionally independent in the distribution P given some node set, if there is no edge in the DAG $\mathcal{G}$ between the two nodes. However, the reverse statement is not true. For some DAG $\mathcal{G}$ and distribution P that satisfy the causal Markov condition, the conditional independence between two nodes r_i and r_j does not necessarily imply the absence of the edge between r_i and r_j. In order to exclude these cases, two equivalent concepts, faithfulness [20] and stability [17] , are introduced. A distribution P is faithful to a DAG $\mathcal{G}$ if all and only the conditional independence relations in P are entailed by $\mathcal{G}$ [20]. In other words, there is an edge between two nodes r_i and r_j in $\mathcal{G}$ if and only if r_i and r_j are conditionally dependent in P given any node set.

2.2 Minimum Partial Correlation

In this paper, we assume the mechanism that generates BOLD signals can be represent by a DAG $\mathcal{G} = (V, E)$, where $V = \{r_1, r_2, \cdots, r_N\}$. The node r_i denotes the random variable of the ith region of interest (ROI). The random variable r_i generates T samples of the BOLD signals of the ith ROI, which are denoted as $X_i = \{x_i^1, x_i^2, \cdots, x_i^T\}$. All random variables generate the same number of samples. The Pearson's correlation coefficient $\rho_{i,j}$ between r_i and r_j can be estimated from samples as follows:

$$\hat{\rho}_{i,j} = \frac{\sum_{t=1}^{T}(x_i^t - \bar{x}_i)(x_j^t - \bar{x}_j)}{\sqrt{\sum_{t=1}^{T}(x_i^t - \bar{x}_i)^2 \sum_{t=1}^{T}(x_j^t - \bar{x}_j)^2}} \tag{1}$$

where $\bar{x}_i$ and $\bar{x}_j$ are sample means of random variables r_i and r_j. The Pearson's correlation coefficient is also called full correlation.

Full correlation counts both direct and indirect effects between two random variables. To remove indirect effects, we can calculate the second order correlation between r_i and r_j by removing the effects of a node set $Z \subseteq (V - \{r_i, r_j\})$. This second order correlation is called the partial correlation $\rho_{i,j\cdot Z}$ controlled the node set Z. Similarly, partial correlation can be estimated from samples:

$$\hat{\rho}_{i,j\cdot Z} = \frac{\sum_{t=1}^{T}(\varepsilon_{i\cdot Z}^t - \bar{\varepsilon}_{i\cdot Z})(\varepsilon_{j\cdot Z}^t - \bar{\varepsilon}_{j\cdot Z})}{\sqrt{\sum_{t=1}^{T}(\varepsilon_{i\cdot Z}^t - \bar{\varepsilon}_{i\cdot Z})^2 \sum_{t=1}^{T}(\varepsilon_{j\cdot Z}^t - \bar{\varepsilon}_{j\cdot Z})^2}} \tag{2}$$

where $\{\varepsilon_{i\cdot Z}^t\}$ is a set of the residuals of the linear regression with r_i as the response variable and Z as the predictor variable set. So is $\{\varepsilon_{j\cdot Z}^t\}$. The sample partial correlation is the sample full correlation on the residuals when some controlling factors are regressed out.

The partial correlation between two nodes varies with the controlling set. For a node set V, the minimum partial correlation (MPC) between two nodes is the minimum of all absolute values of partial correlations by controlling all possible subsets of other nodes, which is formally defined as follows:

Definition 1. *Given two nodes r_i and r_j in a node set V, the minimum partial correlation $\omega_{i,j}$ between the two nodes is:*

$$\omega_{i,j} = \min\{|\rho_{i,j\cdot Z}|\,|\,Z \in 2^{(V-\{r_i,r_j\})}\} \tag{3}$$

where $\rho_{i,j\cdot Z}$ is the partial correlation between r_i and r_j by controlling on the node set Z; $2^{(V-\{r_i,r_j\})}$ represents all subsets of the set $V - \{r_i, r_j\}$. A controlling set Z that satisfies $\rho_{i,j\cdot Z} = \omega_{i,j}$ is called a minimum controlling set for nodes r_i and r_j.

Next, we will discuss an important property of minimum partial correlation that implies that it is a good measure of the existence of functional connectivity.

Proposition 1. *Assuming the distribution P of the nodes V in a DAG $\mathcal{G}$ is multivariate Gaussian and faithful to $\mathcal{G}$, there is an edge between the two nodes r_i and r_j in $\mathcal{G}$ if and only if the minimum partial correlation $\omega_{i,j} \neq 0$.*

According to Proposition 1, minimum partial correlation is a measure of the existence of functional connectivity (i.e. the links in functional networks). Because minimum partial correlation is symmetrical, it cannot infer the directions of functional connectivity. According to Definition 1, minimum partial correlation can be calculated only based on partial correlation. Thus, minimum partial correlation can be estimated from samples, which is denoted as $\hat{\omega}_{i,j}$.

We denote the cardinality of the controlling node set Z as $|Z|$. According to [8], the distribution of the estimated partial correlation $\hat{\rho}_{i,j\cdot Z}$ is the same as the full correlation estimated from $T - |Z|$ samples. Under the hypothesis that $\rho_{i,j\cdot Z} = 0$, the z-score $\tilde{\rho}_{i,j\cdot Z}$ of the estimated partial correlation $\hat{\rho}_{i,j\cdot Z}$ can be calculated as follows:

$$\tilde{\rho}_{i,j\cdot Z} = \frac{1}{2} \log(\frac{1 + \hat{\rho}_{i,j\cdot Z}}{1 - \hat{\rho}_{i,j\cdot Z}})\sqrt{T - |Z| - 3}. \tag{4}$$

However, the distribution of estimated minimum partial correlation is unknown. In this paper, we approximate the absolute value of z-score $\tilde{\omega}_{i,j\cdot Z}$ of the estimate minimum partial correlation $\hat{\omega}_{i,j\cdot Z}$ as follows:

$$\tilde{\omega}_{i,j\cdot Z} = \min\{|\tilde{\rho}_{i,j\cdot Z}|\,|\,Z \in 2^{(V-\{r_i,r_j\})}\}. \tag{5}$$

Given the BOLD signal samples from all ROIs of a brain, we can calculate the estimated value or the absolute value of its z-score of the minimum partial correlation for each pair of ROIs. These estimated values or absolute values of z-scores form a symmetric matrix Ω. The matrix Ω represents the skeleton of functional connectivity in a fractional way. Given a directed graph $\mathcal{G}$, its skeleton is an undirected graph by stripping away all arrowheads from its links and getting rid of redundant undirected links. A pair of ROIs with higher estimated minimum partial correlation value or absolute value of the z-score is more likely to have a link between them. The matrix Ω is therefore a parameter-free measure of functional connectivity, which can be used for decoding cognitive states, evaluating brain disease, and etc.

2.3   Elastic PC-algorithm

It is in polynomial time to estimate partial correlation by controlling a given node set. However, we need to enumerate all possible controlling sets in order to estimate minimum partial correlation; the number of all possible controlling sets is exponential. Several algorithms for causal inference can be easily modified to calculate minimum partial correlation, such as SGS [20], PC [20], TPDA [4], MMHC [21] and TPMB [26]. This paper proposes an algorithm, called elastic

---

Algorithm 1.. Elastic PC-algorithm (EPC)

Input: signal samples $\{x_i^t \| t \in [1 : T], i \in [1 : N]\}$, significance threshold α, previous
    significance threshold β, previous s-cube $\mathcal{D}$ for β
Output: s-cube $\mathcal{C}$ for α
1: **for each** ordered node pair (x_i, x_j) **do**
2:     $\mathcal{C}(i, j, 0 : (N - 2)) \leftarrow |\tilde{\rho}_{i,j}|$
3: **end for**
4: **for** $k = 1 : (N - 2)$ **do**
5:     initialize the referenced skeletons $\mathcal{S}_\alpha$ and $\mathcal{S}_\beta$ as complete undirected graphs
6:     **for each** unordered node pair (x_i, x_j) **do**
7:         **if** $\mathcal{C}(i, j, k - 1) \leq N^{-1}(1 - \frac{\alpha}{2})$ **then**
8:             delete the undirected edge (x_i, x_j) from the referenced skeleton $\mathcal{S}_\alpha$
9:         **end if**
10:        **if** $\mathcal{D}(i, j, k - 1) \leq N^{-1}(1 - \frac{\beta}{2})$ **then**
11:           delete the undirected edge (x_i, x_j) from the referenced skeleton $\mathcal{S}_\beta$
12:        **end if**
13:     **end for**
14:     $\mathcal{C}(:, :, k) \leftarrow \mathcal{D}(:, :, k)$
15:     **for each** ordered node pair (x_i, x_j) that satisfies $|adj(\mathcal{S}_\alpha, x_i)\backslash\{x_j\}| \geq k$ **do**
16:         **for each** controlling node set $Z \subseteq adj(\mathcal{S}_\alpha, x_i)\backslash\{x_j\}$ that satisfies $|Z| = k$
        and $Z \bigcup\{x_j\} \not\subseteq adj(\mathcal{S}_\beta, x_i)$ **do**
17:            **if** $\mathcal{C}(i, j, k) > |\tilde{\rho}_{i,j \cdot Z}|$ **then**
18:               $\mathcal{C}(i, j, k : (N - 2)) \leftarrow |\tilde{\rho}_{i,j \cdot Z}|$
19:               $\mathcal{C}(j, i, k : (N - 2)) \leftarrow |\tilde{\rho}_{i,j \cdot Z}|$
20:            **end if**
21:         **end for**
22:     **end for**
23: **end for**

PC-algorithm (EPC), to approximately calculate the absolute value of the z-score of minimum partial correlation.

The elastic PC-algorithm is based on PC-stable algorithm [5]. Different from the PC-algorithm, PC-stable and other variants, the elastic PC-algorithm is not based on a given significant threshold, but automatically increases the significant threshold within a given time budget in order to approach the minimum partial correlation as possible. Moreover, the proposed algorithm can avoid repeatedly calculating same partial correlation. The key of the elastic PC-algorithm is a data structure that called skeleton cube or s-cube for short. A s-cube is a 3D array. Its dimension is $N \times N \times (N - 1)$, where N is the number of nodes. The referenced skeleton in the kth stage can be calculated by using the kth slice of the s-cube. Referenced skeletons are used to reduce the number of possible controlling sets.

The elastic PC-algorithm is presented in Algorithm 1. The symbol $N^{-1}(\cdot)$ represents the inverse of the standard normal CDF. The z-score of full correlation $\tilde{\rho}_{i,j}$ and the z-score of partial correlation $\tilde{\rho}_{i,j \cdot Z}$ can be calculated according to Equation 4. To compute the absolute value of the z-scores of minimum partial correlation for a DAG, we start from a small significance threshold and use the EPC to calculate its corresponding s-cube. Based on the s-cube for the previous significant threshold, we use the EPC again to calculate a new s-cube for a larger significant threshold. According to Line 16 in Algorithm 1, the EPC does not calculate the z-scores of partial correlation that have been calculated in the previous significant threshold. The EPC is repeatedly executed within the given time budget. Due to the space limitation, the details and discussions of the elastic PC-algorithm will be presented in the full version of this paper.

3 Results

The NetSim dataset [19] was used to evaluate the proposed method. There were 28 simulated brain networks with different properties in the NetSim dataset. The signals of brain networks were generated using dynamic causal models with nonlinear balloon models for the vascular dynamics [11]. For each network, 50 simulated subjects were generated by slightly changing the values of parameters. Following [19], we used c-sensitivity of skeleton inference to measure the accuracy. For the details of the NetSim dataset and the definition of c-sensitivity, please refer to [19]. We compared the elastic PC-algorithm with full correlation, fully partial correlation, ICOV [9], network deconvolution (ND) algorithm [7] and global silencing (GS) algorithm [1]. For the elastic PC-algorithm, the initial significant threshold was set to 0.05 and the step size was set to 0.05. Ten steps were executed. For ICOV, the regularisation parameter was set to 5 and 100 [19].

Table 1 shows the results of the 28 simulations in the NetSim dataset. The figures highlighted by yellow in Table 1 are the highest c-sensitivity scores in their corresponding simulations. Generally speaking, the elastic PC-algorithm (EPC) performed best. The EPC gained highest c-sensitivity in 24 simulations, full correlation (full) in 1 simulation, fully partial correlation (FP) in 2 simulations,

ICOV-5 in 3 simulations, ICOV-100 in 1 simulation, network deconvolution (ND) in 3 simulations, and global silencing (GS) in 4 simulations. The c-sensitivity values of the EPC were above 0.85 for 19 simulations.

Table 1. Summary of c-sensitivity results over simulations and methods.

ID	Full	FP	ICOV-5	ICOV-100	ND	GS	EPC
1	84.00	92.40	93.60	89.60	92.80	92.00	95.60
2	80.00	86.73	88.36	88.18	91.45	88.18	93.82
3	80.67	82.56	84.78	88.00	88.00	71.22	89.44
4	91.51	77.02	82.95	91.48	91.34	45.97	90.16
5	97.20	99.60	100.00	99.60	100.00	100.00	100.00
6	94.00	99.64	99.82	99.27	99.82	99.64	100.00
7	98.80	100.00	100.00	100.00	100.00	100.00	100.00
8	47.20	65.20	65.20	58.40	62.40	60.40	67.20
9	57.60	81.20	81.20	69.20	74.80	76.00	80.00
10	80.00	96.80	96.80	95.20	95.20	90.80	97.20
11	14.91	11.45	12.91	13.64	13.82	15.27	12.18
12	76.00	83.64	84.55	86.00	87.64	84.73	88.55
13	61.20	61.20	62.00	61.20	64.00	63.20	65.20
14	81.20	94.00	94.40	90.00	93.20	94.80	94.40
15	59.20	89.20	90.00	84.80	80.00	78.00	95.20
16	69.14	85.71	86.57	80.57	86.86	83.14	86.86
17	87.64	92.18	93.27	96.73	96.73	80.18	97.45
18	81.60	91.60	91.60	89.20	92.40	91.60	94.40
19	86.00	94.00	94.40	94.80	95.20	94.80	96.40
20	87.20	95.60	97.20	95.20	98.00	96.00	98.80
21	82.40	89.60	90.40	87.60	90.80	89.20	92.80
22	61.20	74.00	73.60	68.40	72.80	66.80	76.80
23	46.40	73.20	78.00	63.20	70.40	69.20	80.40
24	32.00	41.20	41.60	24.80	38.40	42.40	45.60
25	65.60	68.00	67.20	69.60	72.00	71.60	73.60
26	51.20	53.60	54.00	57.60	57.60	52.80	60.00
27	65.20	68.00	69.20	71.20	74.00	61.60	75.60
28	74.40	83.20	84.00	84.00	84.40	83.20	87.60

We illustrated the proposed method using the resting-state fMRI data of 10 unrelated subjects from the Human Connectome Project [24]. The 10 subjects were healthy, six females and four males. There were 2 subjects in the 22-25 age range, 3 subjects in the 26-30 age range, and 5 subjects in the 31-35 age range. For each subject, the functional data were acquired in four approximate-15-minute runs, which were carried out in two separate sessions. The AAL atlas [23] was used to parcel a whole brain into to 116 ROIs, which are 90 regions in cerebrum and 26 regions in cerebellum. The time series of a ROI were defined to be the average time series of all voxels in this ROI.

Due to the space limitation, we only summarized the results of this empirical study. Details of this study will be presented in the full version of this paper.

With the increase of the significance threshold, the matrix inferred by the EPC algorithm became sparser. Comparing with full correlation, fully partial correlation, ICOV, network deconvolution algorithm and global silencing algorithm, the results of the EPC algorithm were sparest. The matrices inferred by the EPC algorithm seemed denoised versions of the matrices inferred by fully partial correlation. Many elements of the matrices inferred by the EPC algorithm are much smaller that the corresponding elements of the matrices inferred by fully partial correlation. This is because the EPC algorithm tried to minimize partial correlations and shrinks the absolute value of elements.

We analysed the top 1% links inferred by the EPC algorithm. In these strongest 67 links, there were 26 links that connected two homotypic functional regions in different hemispheres; there were 40 links that connected two heterotypic functional regions in same hemispheres; interestingly, there were only 1 links that connected two heterotypic functional regions in different hemispheres. This asymmetrically inter-hemispheric link connected the the superior occipital gyrus of the left hemisphere with the cuneus in the right hemisphere.

4   Conclusions

We proposed an alternative measure, minimum partial correlation, to infer the skeleton of functional connectivity using fMRI data. We designed an algorithm, called elastic PC-algorithm, to approximate the minimum partial correlation. The experimental results demonstrated the capability of the proposed method to improve the accuracy of skeleton inference.

References

1. Barzel, B., Barabási, A.L.: Network link prediction by global silencing of indirect correlations. Nature Biotechnology **31**(8), 720–725 (2013)
2. Berkson, J.: Limitations of the application of fourfold table analysis to hospital data. Biometrics Bulletin, pp. 47–53 (1946)
3. Buckner, R.L., Krienen, F.M., Yeo, B.T.: Opportunities and limitations of intrinsic functional connectivity mri. Nature Neuroscience **16**(7), 832–837 (2013)
4. Chenga, J., Greinera, R., Kellya, J., Bellb, D., Liub, W.: Learning bayesian networks from data: an information-theory based approach. Artificial Intelligence **137**, 43–90 (2002)
5. Colombo, D., Maathuis, M.H.: Order-independent constraint-based causal structure learning. Journal of Machine Learning Research **15**, 3741–3782 (2014)
6. Craddock, R.C., Jbabdi, S., Yan, C.G., Vogelstein, J.T., Castellanos, F.X., Di Martino, A., Kelly, C., Heberlein, K., Colcombe, S., Milham, M.P.: Imaging human connectomes at the macroscale. Nature Methods **10**(6), 524–539 (2013)
7. Feizi, S., Marbach, D., Médard, M., Kellis, M.: Network deconvolution as a general method to distinguish direct dependencies in networks. Nature Biotechnology **31**(8), 726–733 (2013)
8. Fisher, R.A.: The distribution of the partial correlation coefficient. Metron **3**, 329–332 (1924)

9. Friedman, J., Hastie, T., Tibshirani, R.: Sparse inverse covariance estimation with the graphical lasso. Biostatistics **9**(3), 432–441 (2008)
10. Friston, K.J.: Functional and effective connectivity: a review. Brain Connectivity **1**(1), 13–36 (2011)
11. Friston, K.J., Harrison, L., Penny, W.: Dynamic causal modelling. Neuroimage **19**(4), 1273–1302 (2003)
12. Hawellek, D.J., Hipp, J.F., Lewis, C.M., Corbetta, M., Engel, A.K.: Increased functional connectivity indicates the severity of cognitive impairment in multiple sclerosis. Proceedings of the National Academy of Sciences **108**(47), 19066–19071 (2011)
13. Hermundstad, A.M., Bassett, D.S., Brown, K.S., Aminoff, E.M., Clewett, D., Freeman, S., Frithsen, A., Johnson, A., Tipper, C.M., Miller, M.B., et al.: Structural foundations of resting-state and task-based functional connectivity in the human brain. Proceedings of the National Academy of Sciences **110**(15), 6169–6174 (2013)
14. Hinne, M., Ambrogioni, L., Janssen, R.J., Heskes, T., van Gerven, M.A.: Structurally-informed bayesian functional connectivity analysis. Neuroimage **86**, 294–305 (2014)
15. Marrelec, G., Krainik, A., Duffau, H., Pélégrini-Issac, M., Lehéricy, S., Doyon, J., Benali, H.: Partial correlation for functional brain interactivity investigation in functional mri. Neuroimage **32**(1), 228–237 (2006)
16. Murphy, K.P.: Machine Learning: a Probabilistic Perspective. MIT press (2012)
17. Pearl, J.: Causality: Models, Reasoning and Inference. Cambridge University Press (2000)
18. Shirer, W., Ryali, S., Rykhlevskaia, E., Menon, V., Greicius, M.: Decoding subject-driven cognitive states with whole-brain connectivity patterns. Cerebral Cortex **22**(1), 158–165 (2012)
19. Smith, S.M., Miller, K.L., Salimi-Khorshidi, G., Webster, M., Beckmann, C.F., Nichols, T.E., Ramsey, J.D., Woolrich, M.W.: Network modelling methods for fmri. Neuroimage **54**(2), 875–891 (2011)
20. Spirtes, P., Glymour, C.N., Scheines, R.: Causation, Prediction, and Search. MIT press (2000)
21. Tsamardinos, I., Brown, L.E., Aliferis, C.F.: The max-min hill-climbing bayesian network structure learning algorithm. Machine Learning **65**(1), 31–78 (2006)
22. Turk-Browne, N.B.: Functional interactions as big data in the human brain. Science **342**(6158), 580–584 (2013)
23. Tzourio-Mazoyer, N., Landeau, B., Papathanassiou, D., Crivello, F., Etard, O., Delcroix, N., Mazoyer, B., Joliot, M.: Automated anatomical labeling of activations in spm using a macroscopic anatomical parcellation of the mni mri single-subject brain. Neuroimage **15**(1), 273–289 (2002)
24. Van Essen, D.C., Smith, S.M., Barch, D.M., Behrens, T.E., Yacoub, E., Ugurbil, K., Consortium, W.M.H., et al.: The wu-minn human connectome project: an overview. Neuroimage **80**, 62–79 (2013)
25. Varoquaux, G., Gramfort, A., Poline, J.B., Thirion, B.: Brain covariance selection: better individual functional connectivity models using population prior. In: Advances in Neural Information Processing Systems, pp. 2334–2342 (2010)
26. Wang, Z., Chan, L.: Learning bayesian networks from markov random fields: an efficient algorithm for linear models. ACM Transactions on Knowledge Discovery from Data **6**(3), 10 (2012)

A Model-Guided String-Based Approach
to White Matter Fiber-Bundles Extraction

Claudio Stamile[1], Francesco Cauteruccio[2], Giorgio Terracina[2],
Domenico Ursino[3](✉), Gabriel Kocevar[1], and Dominique Sappey-Marinier[1]

[1] CREATIS, CNRS UMR5220, INSERM U1044, Université de Lyon,
Université Lyon 1, INSA-Lyon, Lyon, France
{stamile,kocevar}@creatis.insa-lyon.fr,
dominique.sappey-marinier@univ-lyon1.fr
[2] DEMACS, University of Calabria, Arcavacata, Italy
{cauteruccio,terracina}@mat.unical.it
[3] DIIES, University Mediterranea of Reggio Calabria, Reggio Calabria, Italy
ursino@unirc.it

Abstract. In this paper we present a new model-guided approach to
extracting anatomically plausible White Matter fiber-bundles from the
high number of streamlines generated by tractography algorithms. Our
approach is based on: *(i)* an approximate shape model of certain fiber-
bundles constructed by an expert operator; *(ii)* a particular string representation of fibers; *(iii)* a new string similarity metric. It transforms
the fiber-bundles of both the model and the tractography streamlines
into strings and uses the string similarity metric for comparison and
extraction tasks.

Keywords: Brain imaging · Segmentation · Diffusion MRI · Magnetic
resonance imaging

1 Introduction

Reconstructing and visualizing *in vivo* White Matter (WM) fibers is a challenging
issue in the investigation of brain. For instance, the knowledge of these fibers is
useful to understand and predict the effects of some neurodegenerative patholo-
gies, like multiple sclerosis [1]. The most accurate method to perform this task is
tractography [2], which is based on the analysis of the main diffusion directions
of the water molecules estimated by Diffusion Tensor Imaging (DTI) [3]. From
an anatomic point of view, particular sets of fibers (called fiber-bundles) represent different WM structures [4]. In order to analyze WM structures, it is crucial
to isolate subsets of fibers belonging to the WM regions into consideration. This
task is often performed manually by expert neuroanatomists, who define inclusion and exclusion criteria in such a way as to delineate regions of interests and
isolate specific WM fiber-bundles [5]. However, this way of proceeding is time consuming and cannot be applied on large cohorts of subjects where an automated
or, at least, semi-automated approach is in order. Actually, different automated

© Springer International Publishing Switzerland 2015
Y. Guo et al. (Eds.): BIH 2015, LNAI 9250, pp. 135–144, 2015.
DOI: 10.1007/978-3-319-23344-4_14

approaches to isolate and extract WM fiber-bundles have been proposed in the past literature [6,7]. They generally perform the extraction of fiber-bundles by clustering the fibers into examination on the basis of their layout in the three-dimensional space. However, all of them suffer several limitations. For instance, the approach described in [6] depends on a complex and time consuming supervision performed by an expert. This task is carried out through a "try-and-check" activity. Specifically, the parameters are iteratively selected until they correctly separate the different fiber-bundles. The parameter selection method should be as general as possible to avoid the need of re-executing supervision on each new set of data. The approach of [7], instead, is fully unsupervised. Thanks to this feature, it can strongly increase the extraction speed; however, extracted fibers could not represent anatomically plausible fiber-bundles.

In this paper, we aim at providing a contribution in this setting. In particular, we propose a semi-automated model-guided approach to extracting WM fiber-bundles from the high number of streamlines generated by tractography algorithms. Our approach is based on: (i) the usage of an approximate model, constructed by an expert, which represents the shape of the fiber-bundles we want to extract; (ii) a new string-based formalism that allows a simplified description of fiber-bundles; (iii) a new string similarity metric, well suited for this application context. Specifically, the first component and the core of our approach is the fiber-bundle model constructed with the support of an expert. It represents an approximate shape of the fiber-bundle to extract. The second "ingredient" of our approach consists in a new way of representing a fiber as a sequence of m voxels in the three-dimensional space. Initially, we assume that all the fibers have the same number of voxels. It is possible to associate a color with each voxel, specifying its space orientation. As a consequence of this notation, a fiber can be represented as a sequence of colors, each expressed in the RGB color space. Finally, by discretizing this last space, a fiber can be represented by means of a string. Thanks to this fiber representation, our WM fiber-bundles extraction problem reduces to a string similarity one, which is much simpler to face. The third component of our approach consists in a new string similarity metrics. Thanks to it, the extraction of WM fiber-bundles reduces to: (i) computing the dissimilarity between the model fiber-bundles and the real fibers; (ii) selecting the real fiber-bundles having a dissimilarity degree w.r.t. the model fiber-bundles less than a given threshold. Interestingly, our similarity metrics allows the integrated analysis of data flows, which are very heterogeneous but provide a multi-view representation of a certain event. Thanks to our metrics, all these measures can be analyzed simultaneously and compared in such a way as to evidence possible correlations.

In order to verify the suitability of our approach, we have performed an experimental campaign. Obtained results are very satisfying, as will be illustrated below.

This paper is structured as follows. In Section 2, we provide a detailed description of our approach. In Section 3, we present our experimental campaign. Finally, in Section 4, we draw our conclusions.

2   Description of the Proposed Approach

In this section, we illustrate the three steps of our approach, one step per subsection.

2.1   The WM Fiber-Bundles Reference Model

The first "ingredient" of our approach is a model defining the approximate shape of the fiber-bundle to extract. It could be obtained in two different ways, namely: (i) by exploiting a spline curve to draw the profile of the fiber-bundle of interest; (ii) by importing the mean-line profile of the fiber-bundle of interest from an atlas of pre-labeled fiber-bundles. Interestingly, the approximate model adopted to extract a specific fiber-bundle could be exploited to extract the same filter-bundle from other images with different resolutions, possibly acquired from other subjects. Indeed, the representation of our model is based on its shape and is independent of its spatial location.

2.2   The Fiber Representation Formalism

The second component of our approach is a fiber representation technique. Consider a set $F = \{f_1, f_2, \ldots, f_n\}$ of fibers. The generic fiber $f_i \in F$ is defined as a sequence $f_i = (v_1, v_2, \ldots, v_m)$ of voxels in the three-dimensional space. Initially, we assume that all the fibers of F have the same number m of voxels. Thanks to this representation, each fiber f_i could be represented as a curve in $\mathbb{R}^3$. A color can be associated with each voxel $v_j \in f_i$, derived from its orientation in the space [8]. Following the standard color code defined in [8], a voxel parallel to the x (resp., y, z) axis is red (resp., green, blue). If the orientation of a particular voxel v_j is not perfectly parallel to one of the three axes, its color will be computed by a weighted mix of the colors corresponding to those axes such that v_j has a component parallel to each of them. With this notation a fiber $f_i \in F$ could be represented by using the colors associated with its voxels. More in detail, $f_i = (c_1, c_2, \ldots, c_m)$, where c_k is a color expressed in the RGB color space. In order to represent each fiber f_i as a string, we need to discretize the RGB color space. Therefore, it is necessary to define a map:

$$\Psi : RGB \to \Sigma$$

where $\Sigma \subset \mathbb{N}_0$ and $|\Sigma| = s$. We compute the map relation Ψ by using the algorithm described in [9]. With this map a generic fiber f_i could now be expressed as a string in Σ^m. Using this transformation, we can create a new set T derived from F, where each element $t_i \in T$ is a string of Σ^m corresponding to the fiber $f_i \in F$.

2.3   The Proposed String Similarity Metric

Classical string-based distance metrics (like the Hamming or the Levenshtein distance [10], also known as edit distance) could not work properly in our application context. In fact, they are based on the assumption that one-to-one correspondences between the symbols of the two strings into consideration are implicitly determined simply by means of identity relationship.

However, since, in our context, strings represent multi-view data, such an assumption would be quite reductive and could lead to either imprecise or wrong results. In fact, different symbols may express similar concepts. For instance, treating as not matchable a symbol representing an horizontal voxel and a symbol representing a slightly oblique one, may lead to a possible error if this different representation comes from an approximation during discretization. Analogously, it could be highly significant being able to match an horizontal voxel with both another horizontal and/or a slightly oblique one; however in order to avoid over-matchings, it could be important to limit the amount of such "exceptions". Finally, there may exist symbol pairs which clearly should not match (think, for instance, of an horizontal and a vertical voxel). In these cases, constraining invalid matches should be taken into account.

In this paper we exploit a more general Semi-Blind Edit Distance (SBED, for short). It addresses the observations outlined above and allows the computation of the minimum edit distance between two strings, provided that finding the optimal matching schema, under a set of constraints, is part of the problem.

Intuitively, given two sequences of symbols (strings) s_1 and s_2, defined over two (possibly disjoint) sets of alphabets Π_1 and Π_2, a $\langle \pi_1, \pi_2 \rangle$-matching schema defines which symbols of Π_1 can be considered as matching with symbols of Π_2, provided that each symbol of Π_1 (resp., Π_2) can match at most π_1 (resp., π_2) symbols of Π_2 (resp., Π_1). In some contexts, a specific set χ of constraints can be identified to specify symbol matchings to be avoided; in this case, we talk about constrained matching schemas $M_{\langle \pi_1, \pi_2, \chi \rangle}$.

Definition 1 (Match and Distance). Let $\langle \bar{s}_1, \bar{s}_2 \rangle$ be an alignment (in classical terms) for s_1 and s_2, let $M_{\langle \pi_1, \pi_2, \chi \rangle}$ be a $\langle \pi_1, \pi_2, \chi \rangle$-matching schema. We say that $\langle \bar{s}_1, \bar{s}_2 \rangle$ has a match at j if either: (i) $\bar{s}_1[j] \in \Pi_1$, $\bar{s}_2[j] \in \Pi_2$ and $\bar{s}_1[j] = \bar{s}_2[j]$, or (ii) $\bar{s}_1[j]$ and $\bar{s}_2[j]$ match, according to $M_{\langle \pi_1, \pi_2, \chi \rangle}$. The *distance* between $\bar{s}_1$ and $\bar{s}_2$ under $M_{\langle \pi_1, \pi_2, \chi \rangle}$ is the number of positions at which $\langle \bar{s}_1, \bar{s}_2 \rangle$ does not have a match.

Definition 2 (Semi-Blind Edit Distance - SBED). Given two integers π_1 and π_2, such that $0 < \pi_1 \leq |\Pi_2|$ and $0 < \pi_2 \leq |\Pi_1|$, the $\langle \pi_1, \pi_2, \chi \rangle$-edit distance between s_1 and s_2 ($\mathcal{L}_{\langle \pi_1, \pi_2, \chi \rangle}(s_1, s_2)$ for short) is the minimum edit distance that can be obtained according to any $\langle \pi_1, \pi_2, \chi \rangle$-matching schema and over any string alignment $\langle \bar{s}_1, \bar{s}_2 \rangle$ of s_1 and s_2.

Example 1. Let $s1 = $ AAABCCDCAA and $s2 = $ EEFGHGGFHH, which determines $\Pi_1 = \{$A,B,C,D$\}$ and $\Pi_2 = \{$E,F,G,H$\}$. For $\pi_1 = \pi_2 = 1$ and the constraint $\chi = \{\langle A, E \rangle\}$, the best alignment that can be computed is:

$$s_1 : \text{AAABCCDDCAA} \rightarrow \text{AAABC-CDDCAA}$$
$$s_2 : \text{EEFGHGGFHH} \rightarrow \text{--EEFGHGGFHH}$$
$$\text{**} \quad \text{*****}$$

which gives $\mathcal{L}_{\langle 1,1,\chi \rangle}(s_1, s_2) = 5$ with the optimal matching schema {A}-{H}, {B}-{E}, {C}-{F}, and {D}-{G}.

The general problem of computing $\mathcal{L}_{\langle \pi_1,\pi_2,\chi \rangle}(s_1, s_2)$ is NP-Complete. In order to provide a feasible solution, we designed a heuristic which iteratively searches for the optimal matching schema. Our heuristic is based on a *random-restart steepest ascent hill climbing algorithm*. This is a generic metaheuristic capable of efficiently locating a good approximation to the global optimum of a given function in a large search space.

The heuristic works by iterative refinements of the matching schema. Intuitively, at step 0, a valid matching schema M^0 is first chosen, and a global edit distance is computed. At each iteration i, the neighbors of the current matching schema M^i are considered, and the edit distance that can be obtained with it is computed. The one allowing to obtain the lowest edit distance is set as the matching schema M^{i+1} for the next step. This phase stops when the edit distance cannot be further improved. When this happens, the current edit distance is returned as the result. A neighbor of a matching schema is a perturbation exchanging only one pair of symbols in the same partition.

In order to increase the chances of finding the optimal alignment, a certain number of random restarts, each characterized by a new randomly selected matching schema, are subsequently carried out.

The algorithm COMPUTE-SBED, shown below, performs the computation of $\mathcal{L}_{\langle \pi_1,\pi_2,\chi \rangle}(s_1, s_2)$.

At the end of the description of the proposed approach, we would like to point out the following remarks:

- In Section 2.2, we specified that we assume that all the fibers of F have the same number of voxels. Now, after having described our technique in all details, we can show that this assumption is not reductive. Indeed, the intrinsic complexity of computing $\mathcal{L}_{\langle \pi_1,\pi_2,\chi \rangle}(s_1, s_2)$ relies on the size of the alphabet on which strings are defined. As a matter of fact, by examining the algorithm COMPUTE-SBED, it is possible to see that the hardest computational effort of the approach is required for finding the best matching schema. By contrast, the alignment and the computation of the edit distance, performed by the function $editdistance(\cdot, \cdot, \cdot)$, which are strictly related to the string length, can be carried out in a quadratic time (see [14]). This last time is not comparable with the time necessary to perform the other tasks of COMPUTE-SBED. As a consequence, the assumption of a fixed length for the strings is not reductive.
- We decided to use SBED, instead of a spatial metric, because the models into consideration for fiber bundles do not present spatial coordinates that could be used as reference points. As a consequence, in order to compute the distance between models, it is not possible to adopt the euclidean distance or other spatial metrics analogous to it. Actually, our SBED-based approach provides an easy way to create models, whether this task is performed by an expert or not, without the need of information regarding spatial location.

Input : String s_1 and s_2 over Π_1 and Π_2, a set of constraints χ and three
            integers π_1, π_2 and T
Output: $\mathcal{L}_{\langle \pi_1, \pi_2, \chi \rangle}(s_1, s_2)$
Data : M, M': two $\Pi_1 \times \Pi_2$ boolean matrices representing matching
            schemas; *improved*: boolean; t, *mindist*, *globaldist*: integer
begin
    $t = 0$;
    initialize(M,χ);
    mindist = *editdistance*(s_1, s_2, M);
    globaldist = *mindist*;
    improved = TRUE;
    while improved **do**
        improved = FALSE;
        n = neighbors(M, χ);
        foreach M' **in** n **do**
            if *editdistance*(s_1, s_2, M') <*mindist* **then**
                mindist = *editdistance*(s_1, s_2, M');
                improved = TRUE;
                $M = M'$;
            end
        end
        if *not improved* **then**
            if *mindist* < *globaldist* **then**
                globaldist = *mindist*;
                improved = TRUE;
                $t = 0$;
            else if $t < T$ **then**
                $t = t + 1$;
                improved = TRUE;
                $M = randomSelect(M, \chi)$;
                mindist = *editdistance*(s_1, s_2, M);
            end
        end
    return *globaldist*
end

Algorithm 1. COMPUTE-SBED

As a further positive feature of SBED, when compared with spatial metrics, it avoids the matching of two unrelated symbols representing different orientations, such as a strictly horizontal voxel and a strictly vertical one.

3   Experimental Campaign

In this section, we show the results we have obtained by running several tests on both synthetic and real data sets. These have been carried out to assess the effectiveness of the proposed approach both qualitatively and quantitatively.

3.1   Validation of the in Silico Fiber-Bundles Extraction Algorithm

The input dataset consists of a virtual diffusion MR phantom that accurately simulates the brain complexity with the fiber geometry used in the 2nd HARDI Reconstruction Challenge (ISBI 2013). Data has been generated with Phantomas [11]. In order to obtain the ground truth, experts segmented all the fiber-bundles in the phantom manually. Then, approximate shapes of these fiber-bundles were defined so as to identify 17 models. These are illustrated in Figure 1b.

In order to quantitatively assess the effectiveness of our approach, we measured the distance between each of the 17 models and each fiber in the phantom, by applying both SBED and the classic edit distance. Distances below a given threshold stated a match. Each result was compared with the ground truth, and Precision, Recall and F-measure [12] were computed for both SBED and the edit distance. Table 1 shows obtained results for a threshold equal to 30% of fiber lengths (i.e., $Th = 15$). For each model, Table 1 shows the results provided by SBED and the difference (Δ) between them and the ones provided by the edit distance. A positive Δ states a better performance of SBED. Table 1 also presents the average Precision (resp., Recall, F-measure) and the average Δ obtained over all models.

Before going through the analysis of results, it is important to observe that, in our reference context, Precision should be privileged over Recall because the number of fibers generated by tractography algorithms usually does not reflect the number of real fibers of a human brain. From the analysis of results it is possible to observe that: *(i)* SBED obtains a very high average Precision (i.e., 83.78%); *(ii)* Recall reaches a satisfying average result (i.e., 36.37%) with peaks of 92%; *(iii)* the average Precision of SBED is higher than the one of the edit distance (i.e., +29.33%); an analogous trend can be observed for the average Recall (i.e., +5.67%) *(iv)* SBED has, on average, a better F-measure than the edit distance with the worst difference being -16.32% and the best one being +64.64%; *(v)* there are few models, e.g. 3 and 17, where both SBED and the edit distance do not work properly; these models need further analyses to correct the behavior of both the techniques.

We also studied how Precision, Recall, and F-measure varied depending on the threshold Th used for SBED. Results, averaged over all available models, are shown in Figure 1a. First of all, this figure shows that F-measure is not characterized by a clear peak indicating the best trade-off between Precision and Recall. In fact, for a very low Th, Precision is really high (i.e., near to 90%) but Recall is correspondingly very low (near to 20%). Conversely, for increasing values of Th (after 15), Precision decreases with a slope significantly higher than the increase of Recall. These results also justify the choice of $Th = 15$ adopted in our previous analysis (recall that, in our application context, Precision is more important than Recall). However, it is important to point out that our approach is flexible enough to satisfy different needs; as an example, if a higher Recall would be needed in an application scenario, the threshold could be tuned to get a sufficient number of results without degrading too much their quality.

Table 1. Comparison of results obtained with SBED and the edit distance on 17 models

		Model								
		AVG	1	2	3	4	5	6	7	8
SBED	Precision	83.78	100	100	20.81	40.69	100	51.94	94.12	94.74
	Recall	36.37	2.20	11.11	77.01	63.44	48.86	65.05	35.56	34.62
	F-measure	40.31	4.3	20	32.76	49.58	65.64	57.76	51.61	50.70
Δ	Precision	29.33	100	100	−15.21	−0.74	100	−0.82	−5.88	−5.26
	Recall	5.67	2.20	11.11	0	1.08	48.86	0	0	1.92
	F-measure	7.78	4.30	20	−16.32	−0.21	65.64	−0.50	−0.85	1.43

		9	10	11	12	13	14	15	16	17
SBED	Precision	73.33	66.89	100	100	100	100	97.97	100	0
	Recall	92.445	66.89	5.77	1.98	11.54	1.55	74.72	25.53	0
	F-measure	81.78	66.89	10.91	3.88	20.69	3.06	84.78	40.68	0
Δ	Precision	0	−2.83	0	100	100	0	0	0	0
	Recall	0	0	3.85	1.98	11.54	−0.44	0	14.89	−0.7
	F-measure	0	−1.38	7.14	3.88	20.69	−0.86	0	21.44	0

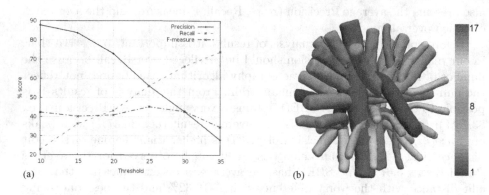

(a)   (b)

Fig. 1. a. SBED results for different threshold values; **b.** Virtual phantom

3.2   Application on Human Brain Data

Our approach was applied to a healthy volunteer, who underwent a MR examination on a 3 Teslas Siemens Prisma MR System (64 channels head-coil). Diffusion protocol consisted on the acquisition of 100 slices in the AC-PC plane, TR/TE = 13700/69 ms, FOV = 160 × 160, with a spatial resolution of 1.5 mm^3 along 45 gradient directions ($b = 3000$ $s.mm^{-2}$). Orientation Distribution Function (ODF) and probabilistic tractography were computed using the algorithms of MRtrix [13].

An expert operator was asked to draw approximate shapes to extract three fiber-bundles, namely Cortico-Spinal Tact (CST) - Figure 2a - and Corpus Callosum (CC) forceps major and minor - Figure 2c. Since our approach is currently unable to distinguish symmetrical fibers, we asked also to draw the axis of symmetry for each model.

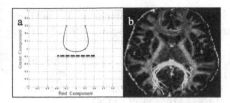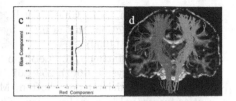

Fig. 2. a. Approximate shape of Corpus Callosum (CC) and its axis of symmetry (black dotted line) drew by the operator; **b.** Extracted force major (yellow) and minor (blue) of CC fibers; **c.** Approximate shape of Cortico-Spinal Tract (CST) and its axis of symmetry (black dotted line) drew by the operator; **d.** Extracted left (red) and right (green) CST fibers.

Both input models and fibers obtained from tractography were transformed in strings using the formalism described in Section 2.2. String similarity between models and fibers were computed using SBED and a $Th = 25$ was exploited in this case. The extracted fibers are visible in Figure 2b,d. An anatomical analysis of the fibers extracted with our method (b) suggests how both forceps major and minor of CC are well extracted with our method. Similarly fibers belonging to left and right CST (d) are well isolated.

4 Conclusion

In this paper we have proposed a string-based approach to the extraction of WM fiber-bundles. Interestingly, our approach overcomes different limitations of the related ones already presented in the literature. For instance, it allows an easy improvement of the integration of the a priori information given by a neuroanatomist. Indeed, the usage of a string model, representing the shape of a particular fiber-bundle, allows an easy extraction of just the fibers having the same structure as the input model.

As for future work, we plan to operate in two directions. The former is further improving our approach. We plan to discriminate short and long fibers by normalizing string length w.r.t. fiber length. Furthermore, we plan to further extend our approach in such a way as to make it completely automatic by using pre-labeled fiber-bundle atlases containing the model of the fiber-bundles of interest.

Acknowledgments. Claudio Stamile is funded by an EU-funded FP7-PEOPLE-2012-ITN project 316679 TRANSACT. Domenico Ursino is partially supported by Aubay Italia S.p.A.

References

1. Wilson, M., Tench, C.R., Morgan, P.S., Blumhardt, L.D.: Pyramidal tract mapping by diffusion tensor magnetic resonance imaging in multiple sclerosis: improving correlations with disability. J. Neurol Neurosurg Psychiatry **74**(2), 203–207 (2003)

2. Mori, S., Crain, B.J., Chacko, V.P., van Zijl, P.C.: Three-dimensional tracking of axonal projections in the brain by magnetic resonance imaging. Ann. Neurol. **45**(2), 265–269 (1999)
3. Basser, P.J., Mattiello, J., LeBihan, D.: Mr diffusion tensor spectroscopy and imaging. Biophys. J. **66**(1), 259–267 (1994)
4. Catani, M., Thiebaut de Schotten, M.: A diffusion tensor imaging tractography atlas for virtual in vivo dissections. Cortex **44**(8), 1105–1132 (2008)
5. Mårtensson, J., Nilsson, M., Ståhlberg, F., Sundgren, P.C., Nilsson, C., van Westen, D., Larsson, E.-M., Lätt, J.: Spatial analysis of diffusion tensor tractography statistics along the inferior fronto-occipital fasciculus with application in progressive supranuclear palsy. MAGMA **26**(6), 527–537 (2013)
6. Zhang, S., Correia, S., Laidlaw, D.H.: Identifying white-matter fiber bundles in dti data using an automated proximity-based fiber-clustering method. IEEE Trans. Vis. Comput. Graph. **14**(5), 1044–1053 (2008)
7. Garyfallidis, E., Brett, M., Correia, M.M., Williams, G.B., Nimmo-Smith, I.: Quickbundles, a method for tractography simplification. Front Neurosci. **6**, 175 (2012)
8. Le Bihan, D., Mangin, J.F., Poupon, C., Clark, C.A., Pappata, S., Molko, N., Chabriat, H.: Diffusion tensor imaging: concepts and applications. J. Magn. Reson. Imaging **13**(4), 534–546 (2001)
9. Arvo, J.: Graphics gems II. Elsevier (1994)
10. Levenshtein, V.: Binary codes capable of correcting deletions, insertions, and reversals. Soviet Physics-Doklady **10**(8), 707–710 (1966)
11. Caruyer, E., Daducci, A., Descoteaux, M., Houde, J.-C., Thiran, J.: Phantomas: a flexible software library to simulate diffusion mr phantom. In: ISMRM, Milan, Italy, May 2014
12. Powers, D.: Evaluation: From precision, recall and f-factor to roc, informedness, markedness & correlation (tech. rep.), Adelaide, Australia (2007)
13. Tournier, J., et al.: MRtrix: Diffusion tractography in crossing fiber regions. IJIST **22**(1), 53–66 (2012)
14. Needleman, S.B., Wunsch, C.D.: A general method applicable to the search for similarities in the amino acid sequence of two proteins. Journal of Molecular Biology **48**(1), 443–453 (1970)

Towards the Identification of Disease Signatures

Tassos Venetis[1]([⊠]), Anastasia Ailamaki[2], Thomas Heinis[3],
Manos Karpathiotakis[2], Ferath Kherif[4],
Alexis Mitelpunkt[5], and Vasilis Vassalos[1]

[1] Athens University of Economics and Business, Athens, Greece
avenet@aueb.gr
[2] Ecole Polytechnique Fédérale de Lausanne, Lausanne, Switzerland
[3] Imperial College of London, London, UK
[4] CHUV University of Lausanne, Lausanne, Switzerland
[5] Tel Aviv University, Tel Aviv, Israel

Abstract. The identification of biological signatures of diseases will enable the development of new biologically grounded classifications of brain diseases, leading to a new systematic understanding of their causes, and new diagnostic tools. In this paper we present the challenges and steps taken towards the identification of disease signatures, through the Medical Informatics Platform of the Human Brain Project, that will expedite diagnosis and lead to more accurate prognosis and objective diagnosis.

Keywords: Medical data · Data integration · Data mining

1 Introduction

Throughout history doctors diagnose their patients. To do so they use the patients history, the symptoms presented and the signs seen in the physical examination. Especially in neurology and psychiatry the signs and symptoms still have a major role in the determination of the diagnosis. However, technology developments allow physicians to have more information on the patients condition as well as new knowledge on the process of disease.

The current diagnosis of Alzheimers disease (AD) [23] consists of the following elements of dementia: 1. Interference with the ability to function at work or at usual activities; 2. Decline from previous levels of functioning; 3. Not explained by other psychiatric disorder; 4. Cognitive impairment is detected and diagnosed through a combination of (a) history-taking and (b) an objective cognitive assessment; 5. The cognitive or behavioral impairment involves a minimum of two cognitive domains. A probable diagnosis of AD also has to present an insidious onset over months or years; clear-cut history of worsening of cognition; and in the most common syndromic presentation of AD the initial and most prominent cognitive deficits are Amnestic (Memory and learning). It is thus obvious that diagnosis is mostly based on symptoms which has led to a large diagnosis error rate, near 20%, in AD [5]. Additional information, such as biological markers, is mentioned in the most updated recommendation but

© Springer International Publishing Switzerland 2015
Y. Guo et al. (Eds.): BIH 2015, LNAI 9250, pp. 145–155, 2015.
DOI: 10.1007/978-3-319-23344-4_15

again only as supporting the diagnosis, even though there is a growing amount of information on patient through imaging studies, genetic data and other biological markers (proteins, pathology, electroencephalography (EEG) etc.) gathered in hospitals and research studies.

This information can be of great assistance in the diagnosis procedure, hence, we need to seek for more precise relations between clinical presentation and biological markers. Each relation of a clinically based cluster with a group of potential biomarker can be referred as *disease signature*. The connection of biomarkers to a more homogenous clinical cluster of patients allows the interpretation of results to physicians, translation process and advancement to targeted research for validation and implementation of the results to medical progress. The biological signature of brain diseases will thus form the basis for a new multidimensional brain disease space, facilitating scientific investigation, permitting personalised medicine and hence leading to expedite diagnosis, more accurate prognosis and new types of drug discovery for development of new medicines.

Our approach towards the identification of disease signatures includes the development of a platform, called the Medical Informatics Platform (MIP) (section 3), under the Human Brain Project (HBP). This platform will integrate clinical data, such as genetics, imaging and other, currently locked in hospital and research archives, aiming to make them available to relevant research communities, while guaranteeing protection for sensitive patient information as imposed by national legislation and institutional ethics. Sophisticated data mining algorithms and techniques will be employed on the data made available by the platform to identify biological signatures of diseases related to the brain. Projects similar to MIP are VPH-share,[1] p-medical,[2] and @neurIST.[3] Integrating [4,20,25,26] as well as performing data mining on medical data [4,17,30] have gained a lot of attention in the literature.

In this paper we present the challenges we are confronted with as well as the approaches adopted towards the identification of disease signatures utilizing data from a single hospital. While the overall scope of HBP includes scaling to multiple hospitals, our proposed approach can yield results by exploiting the wealth of clinical data available within a hospital, and this is our current focus. The power and challenges induced by putting the information of multiple hospitals is out of the scope of this paper. In section 2 we emphasize on our goals and challenges. In section 3 we present the proposed MIP architecture, while in sections 4 and 5 we present our approaches for data integration and data mining, respectively. Finally, section 6 concludes our paper.

2   Goals and Challenges

Our goal is to allow the identification of biological mechanisms that explain the complex nature of brain diseases and to create a new disease space that

---

[1] http://www.vph-share.eu/
[2] http://p-medicine.eu/
[3] http://www.aneurist.org/

neuroscientists and clinicians can explore. This space will help explain etiological, diagnostic, and pathogenic observations as well as treatment effects and can be largely achieved by the identification of disease signatures.

To identify disease signatures we incorporate advanced data mining algorithms that will be applied on a vast, and thus representative, amount of medical data. The first step towards the identification of disease signatures is to create a platform that will be able to collect clinical data and make them available as research data in a unified manner, while at the same time preserving patients' privacy. These are disparate data, output of proprietary medical systems, as well as databases, that might exist autonomously in hospitals or research centers.

The large volume of data and the required variety imply they originate from a large number of hospitals and research centers, while protection of patient privacy imposes that they may not leave each hospital's servers, apart from being anonymized. The use of divergent schemata, to store these data, and the possibly different references to same objects indicate we need to deal with syntactic, value and semantic heterogeneities and inconsistencies, to share the data through an as much as possible common platform schema. Additionally, in order to be universal an effort needs to be undertaken that the data conform to international standards, indicating data standardization as another major challenge. Moreover, to be able to standardise and transform the original data to the common schema mapping transformations as well as a data exchange engine [7] (that will apply these transformations) are necessary. Finally, due to the vast volume of data each data provider (hospital or research center) needs to employ an efficient storing mechanism. To fully exploit the available hospital data to create disease signatures we face an additional challenge that is data federation, i.e. the ability to answer queries and perform analysis using the totality of available information from all hospitals (while preserving privacy). This however adds extra overhead, hence in this paper we focus on a single hospital.

Concerning data mining, first of all, even though it is widely accepted that expert medical knowledge is extremely valuable, current diagnosis might be misleading. Diagnosis is usually a rough criteria, while the actual clinical situation is more complex and sophisticated. Therefore, it is essential to have a way to use the medical knowledge and also incorporate it into the data mining process. Another challenge is that compensatory mechanisms obscure the linkage between biological markers (i.e. imaging, pathology, genetics) and disease manifestation, making it more difficult to discover. For example, two people with the same brain pathology or brain images do not necessarily share the same clinical manifestation. It is not only the complexity of the disease and inefficiency of the marker, but the fact that the compensatory mechanisms may differ from one person to the other.

Moreover, trying to find relations between a marker to a large heterogeneous population (e.g. all dementia patients) decreases the chance to find a marker that is relevant only to a part of that population because of decreased signal to noise ratio. Hence, another major challenge is identifying ways to tailor treatment to each patient specifically, i.e., personalize solutions to heterogeneous populations.

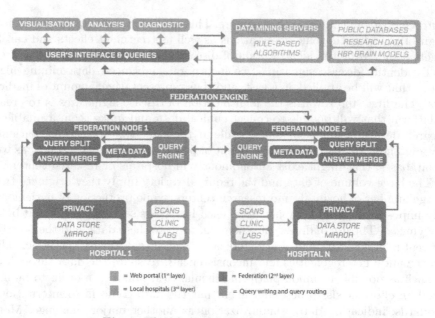

Fig. 1. The Medical Informatics Platform

Finally, as the volume of the available data increases an inherent arising problem is the danger that a large proportion of the few results selected to be interesting are actually irrelevant and appear to be interesting by mere chance due to the extensive search [21].

3   Medical Informatics Platform Architecture

The first step towards identification of disease signatures is the design of a platform that aims at federating clinical data stored in hospitals and research centers to make them available for analysis. The federation of these data, unlike another approach where the data could be collected in a centralized repository, is imposed by the privacy preserving constraints of patient information as well as by the large amount of data. This platform is the MIP shown in Figure 1. It is composed of three different layers.

The first, called the Web portal is the user interface of the platform, where users depending on their access rights will be able to perform epidemiological exploration and interactive analysis queries as well as complex data mining tasks.

The second layer, called the Federation layer features two basic components: the federation engine and the local data store mirror (LDSM). The federation engine is the access point for all queries coming from the Web portal. It is responsible for translating queries posed over the Web portal to proper queries that can be answered from each individual hospital's LDSM as well as for collecting their aggregate responses and merging their results. The LDSM makes local data accessible for queries arriving from the federation engine.

Hospital data are collected at the LDSM of each hospital at the Local layer. The data that populate each hospital's LDSM originate from that hospital's servers and databases and are processed to fit to the same schema/model used across local data stores and the Web portal.

4 Creating a Homogeneous Local Data Store Mirror

The first challenge addressed towards the creation of the LDSM for each hospital is the creation of its schema. At its current state, it consists of thirteen tables, that describe information regarding patients, diagnostics, diseases, laboratory examinations, genetic information as well as brain information. Additionally, these tables describe meta-data, such as annotations and provenance information. Schema creation is tightly connected with variable extraction, a collaborative effort between computer scientists and medical experts identifying variables that play a prominent role in the supported MIP services. Moreover, an effort is undertaken for the LDSM schema of each hospital to be similar to each other and to that of the Web portal. An efficient way to achieve this is if the variables of the schema are standardized. So, another challenge is the standardization of the extracted variables and their values. Note, that these are challenges also addressed at the Web portal.

Our approach, regarding (data and query) standardization, concerns using variables (query terms) from the Logical Observation Identifier Names and Codes (LOINC) [9] ontology. LOINC provides a universal code system for reporting laboratory and other clinical observations and contains more than 30,000 different observations. For each observation the LOINC database includes a code, a long formal name, a "short" name as well as synonyms. For example, the *diagnosis* variable is represented by code 52797-8, with a long (and short) name "Diagnosis ICD code", and synonyms "International Classification of Diseases", "DX ICD code" and other.

Additionally, in order to capture the MRI image processing pipelines we have employed the Cortical Labeling Protocol [16] atlas that identifies brain regions. Region examples are "Right Cerebellum Exterior", "Left Hippocampus" and others and corresponding values are estimated volumes in cc produced by a feature extraction process [3]. Moreover, regarding genetic data, we focus on Single Nucleotide Polymorphisms (SNPs) that represent the difference in a pair of nucleotides from the general population. SNPs are probably the most important category of genetic changes influencing common diseases, since they have been shown to influence disease risk, drug efficacy and side-effects, provide information about ancestry, and predict aspects of how humans look and even act. Queries use rs names provided by dbSNP [28] or information about genes and chromosomes that each SNP appears in, that dbSNP provides. For example, rs2075650 is an example of an SNP found on gene TOMM40 of chromosome 19 associated with high risk of Alzheimer disease. Each SNP is represented by a value from the range of $\{0, 1, 2\}$, where 0 means that the two nucleotides are the same as the reference, 1 means that one of them is different, while 2 that both are different.

While the above standards capture variables used when issuing a query, standardization is also needed to provide query constant values as well as to capture answers of queries. Our queries and answers utilize International Classification of Diseases ICD-10 codes [24] that refers to classification of mental and behavioral disorders. For example, *Alzheimer disease with early onset*, represented by code G30.1, is a subcategory of *Alzheimer disease*, represented by code G30.

Another major challenge is the creation of schema mappings that ensure necessary transformations will be applied on the original hospital data to translate them to a uniform coherent representation, i.e., the common platform schema. These transformations will be performed to all but imaging data and include cleaning, normalizing and integrating/merging the input data. In order to specify these transformations we use declarative mappings, under the formalisms of TGDs [1], that are executed using an appropriate data exchange (chase) engine [7]. Use of declarative mappings is heavily based on the fact that mappings are formal, easily reusable, even by non computer experts, and that chase engines can be highly efficient. For the creation and execution of all these TGDs we have developed a visual mapping tool, called MIPMap that extends the open source mapping tool ++Spicy [22] in order to meet the needs of HBP. MIPMap, also includes an improved mapping execution engine to deal with the complexity and size of HBP data transformations. For example, the following formula is a TGD (that also contains user defined functions) that joins tuples of tables *hbp_diags* and *hbp_patients* on *hid* and populates the *diagnostic* table (of the common hospitals' schema) with values of the *pid*, *code*, *type*, and *date* variables. Moreover "$CHUV$" is a constant, while newID is a function that produces a unique identification number for each tuple.

$$hbp\_diags(hid, \textbf{date}, \textbf{code}, \ descr, \textbf{type}), hbp\_patients(hid, \textbf{pid}, \ldots) \rightarrow$$
$$diagnostic(\textsf{newID}(), \textbf{pid}, \textbf{code}, \textbf{type}, \textbf{date}, \text{``}CHUV\text{''})$$

Imaging data will undergo a different process. More precisely, they will be fed into a feature extraction process that will produce volume measurements for the brain regions identified at the Cortical Labeling Protocol [16].

All the data produced by the previous translation process will be stored in raw files, possibly CSV, that will reside at the LDSM of each hospital, following the common schema. To query this homogenized collection of information at the LDSM we use a system called RAW [2,15], with some uniquely useful characteristics. It avoids ingestion or import of data: instead of converting data into a proprietary file format to suit the database/query execution engine, the raw data is left as it is, in-situ at the hospital where it is queried by an execution engine that adapts to the data. While executing queries on raw data is typically associated with considerable overheads (for parsing etc.), RAW uses several strategies to avoid the overhead of accessing raw data and to ensure efficient and quick execution of queries on raw data. RAW uses positional maps [2] to index the raw data to reduce data parsing overhead, uses monoid comprehensions to enable uniform access to different underlying data models and compiles access paths to raw data to optimize for the underlying hardware [14]. Hence, RAW essentially adapts itself to the data layout and hardware used.

Experimental results [14] comparing RAW to three popular approaches of integrating data stored in heterogeneous formats, converting and importing all data into a relational DBMS, into document stores or combining traditional DBMSs with document stores, clearly demonstrates that query execution with RAW is no slower than with a DBMS. RAWs query execution time indeed is similar as the fastest traditional approach (converting and importing into a relational DBMS), but does not require any costly conversion or import step. Measuring the entire data-to-result time, the time it takes to go from being given the data to obtaining a result, RAW is consequently considerably faster without moving the data from where they reside and thus without compromising privacy.

Privacy of the data is further ensured on two different levels: (a) the data made available in the LDSM and (b) the queries permitted. First, and most importantly, only de-identified data is made available through the local stores. Upon exporting the data from the hospital systems and before importing it into the LDSM, all personal identifiers are stripped (names, phone numbers and other unique identifiers) from the data. Second, we only allow aggregate queries on the local stores through the federated platform. By only allowing the execution of aggregate queries we ensure that no individual records can be retrieved. Whether queries do not return individual information, i.e., they only retrieve aggregates, is tested at the federation engine but also every local store tests incoming queries. Queries not conforming to the format are discarded. Additionally, before returning any query results to the federation engine (and ultimately to the user), personal identifiers are removed from the query result should there be any before it leaves the local store. Stronger privacy guarantees in the form of differential privacy [8] are the subject of future work.

5   Data Mining Towards Disease Signatures

Following the bottom up approach of our presentation (Figure 1), and bypassing the federation challenges, that as presented earlier are out of scope of this paper, we now present our approach towards the data mining challenges. We have developed a three-stage process (Categorize, Cluster & Classify) named the 3-C strategy for Brain Health Informatics [10,11] that we describe in the following.

Step 1 - Categorization of Variables. The goal of the categorization step is to distinguish variables relevant to determination of the clinical representation of the disease and the functional state of the patient from other variable. During this stage we use expert medical knowledge to categorize the variables, which incorporates this information not only as diagnosis labels but in much deeper and fine insights. All available variables are categorized into three types:

1. The first category is the disease diagnosis variable as assigned in the electronic health record (EHR). This assigned diagnosis for example in dementia could be: Cognitively Normal (CN), Mild Cognitive Impairment (MCI), Alzheimers disease (AD).

2. The second category is of clinical measurements that reflect the patients condition and functionality of the patient. They encompass scores of different cognitive and psycho-neurological tests and ratings, according to clinical assessment and patients or partners' report. This battery of cognitive and functional assessment scores might include: Clinical Dementia Rating (CDR), Alzheimer's disease assessment scale (ADAS), minimental state examination (MMSE), Rey Auditory Verbal Learning Test (RAVLT), Family history questionnaire (FAQ) Montreal Cognitive Assessment (MoCA), Everyday Cognition (Ecog).

3. The third category includes measurements of potential biological markers, which were proposed to have a predictive value for disease risk, for deterioration, or for severity. These markers are either proteins levels measured in the cerebrospinal fluid (CSF) such as ApoE4 [12] or imaging data from different modalities: AV45 PET [13], FDG-PET [18] and MRI. These will be referred to as potential biomarkers (PB).

Step 2 - Feature Selection and Clustering. The intention of this step is to find homogenous sub-groups of patients. Creating clinical measurements based classes that are medically easy to interpret, as well as addressing the challenge of big data and adjusting the process to multiple comparisons requires a methodological solution. Therefore a feature selection procedure is performed on all potential clinical measurements. Using algorithms such as Random Forest [19], Stepwise selection with false discovery rate (FDR) control [6] or other methods that may prove as useful or even more.

We then cluster the data based on the selected subset of clinical measurements using an algorithm like k-means, hierarchical clustering, predictive clustering [29] or others. In any such algorithm, the number of clusters is a crucial parameter. We chose to combine statistical information with medical perspectives. According to the latter, there is a natural lower bound to the number of clusters: the measured clinical data should represent the different classes of clinical manifestation including patients' medical history, background, symptoms, etc. From the literature [27] and knowledge about dementia we know that within the clinical spectrum that could be lines from Normal to AD there are some sub-classes of patients. It is reasonable to consider at least 8 subclasses of disease manifestation: AD with a rapid progression and dysfunction; AD with slower progression course; Cognitive Normal that will not develop dementia; Cognitive Normal that will develop dementia; MCI that will later develop AD; MCI that will develop other irreversible cause (i.e. FrontoTemporal Degeneration or vascular); MCI that will develop other irreversible cause (i.e. Dementia of Lewy Bodies - DLB); MCI that will not deteriorate and will stay with a stable impairment status.

Step 3 - Classifying with Potential Biomarkers. At this stage we seek relations between a subsets of potential biomarkers and each of the homogenous clusters found in the previous step and by that increasing the chances of discoveries. We classify the new diagnosis classes using the set of potential biomarkers. In principle this stage also consists of two parts. First, using importance analysis by, say, random forests, a promising subset of the biomarkers is selected Then, the final classification step is done using hierarchical decision trees, or other rule based analysis, utilizing the selected subset. This is essential in order to give easy interpretation to the diagnosis process. In the envisioned application to hospital data the number of potential biomarkers may increase to thousands, before incorporating genomic information. Thus, the subset selection stage may be crucial.

6 Conclusion

In this paper we have presented challenges and approaches followed towards the identification of disease signatures from medical data coming from a single hospital or research center. Our approach involves the design of a platform, that with advanced data mining and data integration techniques as a basis, provides dedicated services for researchers to carry out neuro-epidemiological and biological investigations on clinical data. The first participating hospital is in the process of contributing its data and we are already working on applying our methodology and techniques to this hospital and research data to get preliminary results. The platform is expected to derive unique data driven biological signatures of brain disease by transforming medical records into research data, extracting knowledge and building models of brain diseases. Inference from these models will move forward the field of medicine from descriptive symptomatology towards diagnostic, predictive and prescriptive personalised medicine.

Acknowledgments. The research leading to these results has received funding from the European Union Seventh Framework Programme (FP7/2007-2013) under grant agreement no. 604102 (Human Brain Project).

References

1. Abiteboul, S., Hull, R., Vianu, V.: Foundations of Databases. Addison-Wesley (1995)
2. Alagiannis, I., Borovica, R., Branco, M., Idreos, S., Ailamaki, A.: NoDB: efficient query execution on raw data files. In: Proceedings of the 2012 ACM SIGMOD International Conference on Management of Data, pp. 241–252. ACM (2012)
3. Ashburner, J., Friston, K.J.: Diffeomorphic registration using geodesic shooting and Gauss-Newton optimisation. NeuroImage **55**(3), 954–967 (2011)
4. Astakhov, V., Gupta, A., Santini, S., Grethe, J.S.: Data integration in the biomedical informatics research network (BIRN). In: Ludäscher, B., Raschid, L. (eds.) DILS 2005. LNCS (LNBI), vol. 3615, pp. 317–320. Springer, Heidelberg (2005). http://dx.doi.org/10.1007/11530084_31
5. Beach, T.G., Monsell, S.E., Phillips, L.E., Kukull, W.: Accuracy of the clinical diagnosis of alzheimer disease at national institute on aging alzheimer's disease centers, 2005–2010. Journal of Neuropathology and Experimental Neurology **71**(4), 266 (2012)

6. Benjamini, Y., Hochberg, Y.: Controlling the false discovery rate: a practical and powerful approach to multiple testing. Journal of the Royal Statistical Society. Series B (Methodological), 289–300 (1995)
7. Doan, A., Halevy, A.Y., Ives, Z.G.: Principles of Data Integration. Morgan Kaufmann (2012)
8. Dwork, C., Roth, A.: The algorithmic foundations of differential privacy. Theoretical Computer Science 9(3–4), 211–407 (2013)
9. Forrey, A., et al.: Logical observation identifier names and codes (LOINC) database: a public use set of codes and names for electronic reporting of clinical laboratory test results. Clinical Chemistry 42(1), 81–90 (1996)
10. Galili, T., Mitelpunkt, A., Shachar, N., Marcus-Kalish, M., Benjamini, Y.: Categorize, cluster, and classify: a 3-c strategy for scientific discovery in the medical informatics platform of the human brain project. In: Džeroski, S., Panov, P., Kocev, D., Todorovski, L. (eds.) DS 2014. LNCS, vol. 8777, pp. 73–86. Springer, Heidelberg (2014)
11. Galili, T., Mitelpunkt, A., Shachar, N., Marcus-Kalish, M., Benjamini, Y.: Categorize, cluster & classify - the 3c strategy applied to alzheimer's disease as a case study. In: Proceedings of the International Conference on Health Informatics, pp. 566–573 (2015)
12. Gupta, V., Laws, S.M., Villemagne, V.L., Ames, D., Bush, A.I., Ellis, K.A., Lui, J.K., Masters, C., Rowe, C.C., Szoeke, C., et al.: Plasma apolipoprotein E and Alzheimer disease risk The AIBL study of aging. Neurology 76(12), 1091–1098 (2011)
13. Hinrichs, C., Singh, V., Xu, G., Johnson, S.C., Initiative, A.D.N., et al.: Predictive markers for ad in a multi-modality framework: an analysis of mci progression in the adni population. Neuroimage 55(2), 574–589 (2011)
14. Karpathiotakis, M., Alagiannis, I., Heinis, T., Branco, M., Ailamaki, A.: Just-in-time data virtualization: lightweight data management with vida. In: CIDR 2015, Asilomar, CA, USA, January 4–7, 2015, Online Proceedings (2015)
15. Karpathiotakis, M., Branco, M., Alagiannis, I., Ailamaki, A.: Adaptive query processing on RAW data. PVLDB 7(12), 1119–1130 (2014)
16. Klein, A., Tourville, J.: 101 labeled brain images and a consistent human cortical labeling protocol. Frontiers in neuroscience 6 (2012)
17. Kohannim, O., Hua, X., Hibar, D.P., Lee, S., Chou, Y.Y., Toga, A.W., Jack, C.R., Weiner, M.W., Thompson, P.M., Initiative, A.D.N., et al.: Boosting power for clinical trials using classifiers based on multiple biomarkers. Neurobiology of Aging 31(8), 1429–1442 (2010)
18. Langbaum, J.B., Chen, K., Lee, W., Reschke, C., Bandy, D., Fleisher, A.S., Alexander, G.E., Foster, N.L., Weiner, M.W., Koeppe, R.A., et al.: Categorical and correlational analyses of baseline fluorodeoxyglucose positron emission tomography images from the alzheimer's disease neuroimaging initiative (adni). Neuroimage 45(4), 1107–1116 (2009)
19. Liaw, A., Wiener, M.: Classification and regression by randomForest. R News 2(3), 18–22 (2002)
20. Louie, B., Mork, P., Martin-Sanchez, F., Halevy, A., Tarczy-Hornoch, P.: Data integration and genomic medicine. Journal of Biomedical Informatics 40(1), 5–16 (2007)
21. Marcus-Kalish, M.: Big data versus small data analysis towards personalized medicine practice. EPMA Journal 5(1), 1–2 (2014)
22. Marnette, B., et al.: ++Spicy: an OpenSource Tool for Second-Generation Schema Mapping and Data Exchange. PVLDB 4(12), 1438–1441 (2011)

23. McKhann, G.M., Knopman, D.S., Chertkow, H., Hyman, B.T., Jack, C.R., Kawas, C.H., Klunk, W.E., Koroshetz, W.J., Manly, J.J., Mayeux, R., et al.: The diagnosis of dementia due to Alzheimers disease: Recommendations from the National Institute on Aging-Alzheimers Association workgroups on diagnostic guidelines for Alzheimer's disease. Alzheimer's & Dementia 7(3), 263–269 (2011)
24. Organization, W.H., et al.: The ICD-10 classification of mental and behavioural disorders: clinical descriptions and diagnostic guidelines. World Health Organization, Geneva (1992)
25. Ovaska, K., Laakso, M., Haapa-Paananen, S., Louhimo, R., Chen, P., Aittomäki, V., Valo, E., Núñez-Fontarnau, J., Rantanen, V., Karinen, S., et al.: Large-scale data integration framework provides a comprehensive view on glioblastoma multiforme. Genome Med 2(9), 65 (2010)
26. Seoane, J., Dorado, J., Aguiar-Pulido, V., Pazos, A.: Data Integration in Genomic Medicine: Trends and Applications. Contribution of the IMIA Working Group on Informatics in Genomic Medicine. Yearbook of Medical Informatics 7(1), 117–125 (2012). http://europepmc.org/abstract/MED/22890352
27. Shadlen, M.F., Larson, E.B.: Evaluation of cognitive impairment and dementia. UpToDate, MA (2013)
28. Sherry, S.T., Ward, M., Sirotkin, K.: dbSNPdatabase for single nucleotide polymorphisms and other classes of minor genetic variation. Genome Research 9(8), 677–679 (1999)
29. Ženko, B., Džeroski, S., Struyf, J.: Learning predictive clustering rules. In: Bonchi, F., Boulicaut, J.-F. (eds.) KDID 2005. LNCS, vol. 3933, pp. 234–250. Springer, Heidelberg (2006)
30. Zhang, D., Shen, D., Initiative, A.D.N., et al.: Multi-modal multi-task learning for joint prediction of multiple regression and classification variables in Alzheimer's disease. Neuroimage 59(2), 895–907 (2012)

The Unsupervised Hierarchical Convolutional Sparse Auto-Encoder for Neuroimaging Data Classification

Xiaobing Han[1,5], Yanfei Zhong[1,5(✉)], Lifang He[2], Philip S. Yu[3,4], and Liangpei Zhang[1,5]

[1] State Key Laboratory of Information Engineering in Surveying, Mapping, and Remote Sensing, Wuhan University, Wuhan, People's Republic of China
zhongyanfei@whu.edu.cn
[2] Computer Vision Institute, School of Computer Science and Software Engineering, Shenzhen University, Shenzhen, People's Republic of China
[3] Department of Computer Science, University of Illinois at Chicago, Chicago, USA
[4] Institute for Data Science, Tsinghua University, Beijing, People's Republic of China
[5] The Collaborative Innovation Center of Geospatial Technology, Wuhan University, Wuhan 430079, People's Republic of China

Abstract. With the ongoing development of neuroimaging technology, neuroimaging classification has become a popular and challenging topic. The high dimension and small sample size characteristics pose many challenges to neuroimaging classification. The traditional neuroimaging classification solutions are tensor-based models, which may not fully consider the structural information and can't mine the essential features of the input data. Considering the complicated properties of the neuroimaging data, a deep learning based algorithm—the hierarchical convolutional sparse auto-encoder (HCSAE) considering all dimensional information together is proposed in this paper. The HCSAE treats different convolutional sparse auto-encoder (CSAE) in an unsupervised hierarchical mode, where the CSAE extracts the essential features of the input by the sparse auto-encoder (SAE) and encodes the inputs in a convolutional manner, which helps to extract efficient and robust features and conserve abundant detail information for the neuroimaging classification. The proposed algorithm was verified by three human brain fMRI classification datasets, and showed a great potential compared with the traditional classification algorithms.

Keywords: Deep learning · Hierarchical convolutional sparse auto-encoder (HCSAE) · Sparse auto-encoder (SAE) · Neuroimaging classification

1 Introduction

In recent years, with the rapid development of neuroimaging technology, to accurately diagnose the individual psychiatric patients based on the neuroimaging data structure is an urgent problem to be solved [1]. The traditional brain networks can't be easily utilized to recognize the brain activity because local spatial inferences on the voxel-based maps are not straightforward and the whole-brain interpretation results in

© Springer International Publishing Switzerland 2015
Y. Guo et al. (Eds.): BIH 2015, LNAI 9250, pp. 156–166, 2015.
DOI: DOI: 10.1007/978-3-319-23344-4_16

psychiatric disorders [2], [3]. However, with the development of knowledge mining and pattern recognition, various brain connectivity based methods can provide powerful predictions. Functional magnetic response imaging (fMRI) is a kind of neuroimaging modality utilized to identify the localized patterns of the brain activation based on the cerebral blood flow [4], and fMRI features are widely utilized to identify network based biomarkers of schizophrenia, Alzheimer's disease [3].

Neuroimaging classification has become a hot topic because of the potential to detect a variety of brain diseases. With the high dimensionality and small sample sizes, neuroimaging classification faces many challenges. Neuroimaging classification has been studied using vector-based models, such as Gaussian-RBF, K_{3rd} kernel, PCA+SVM, MPCA+SVM and linear kernel methods [5]. However, there are various neuroimaging data modalities, such as EEG, fMRI and DTI [6], which poses many challenges for vector-based neuroimaging classification. To solve the different modality classification problems with neuroimaging data, tensor-based methods have been proposed. The factor kernel, linear SHTM and the linear kernel are all tensor based methods [5]. The most effective tensor-based method is the dual structural-preserving kernel (DuSK) [5], which leverages the naturally available structures within the tensorial representation to encode prior in the kernel. Although DuSK considers the structure and nonlinearity of the tensor data, it doesn't automatically consider the abundant and complicated information of the neuroimaging data in an integral manner.

The traditional tensor-based neuroimaging classification methods are supervised based methods. However, a large amount of accurately labeled neuroimaging data is difficult to obtain. When facing with a large amount of unlabeled data, an efficient unsupervised method is needed. Deep learning [7],[8]is an effective feature extraction processing framework, where sparse auto-encoder (SAE) [9] is an excellent choice which extracts features based on all the categories and all the dimensional information of the neuroimaging data. The features extracted by the SAE containing abundant orientation information are robust and efficient. To apply the features extracted by the SAE for neuroimaging classification, the convolution mechanism was combined after the SAE. However, for the single-layer convolutional sparse auto-encoder (CSAE), the information of the input data is extracted and encoded for once, where the abundant information of the convolved feature maps is not utilized adequately.

In order to overcome the above problem, an unsupervised hierarchical convolutional sparse auto-encoder (HCSAE) is proposed in this paper, which treats the different CSAE in a hierarchical manner. Differing from the supervised convolutional neural network (CNN) hierarchical approach [10], the HCSAE adopts the efficient SAE as the feature extractors and exploits the full connection between the SAE features and the subsequent convolved images in an unsupervised manner, where the full connection can fully represent the original neuroimages and pass all the information to convolved feature maps. We note that the convolved feature maps of the former layer CSAE are a combination of the original neuroimaging data responding to different orientation features. To improve the computational efficiency, a pooling is added after the convolution, which just conserve significant and salient features of the convolved feature maps [11]. To elaborately represent the input data, HCSAE extracts and encodes the pooled feature maps of former layer CSAE once more in a hierarchical manner. The advantage of the HCSAE is that the latter layer CSAE extracts features which contain more abundant orientation, detail and structural information than the former layer CSAE, which is in favor of the final classification. Moreover, to further improve the performance of SAE, a "dropout" [12] strategy is introduced in this paper, which is different from the supervised network in [12].

The rest of the paper is organized as follows. Section 2 introduces the deep learning related work. Section 3 introduces HCSAE algorithm in detail. Section 4 presents the experiment results. In the final section, the conclusion is made.

2   Deep Learning Based Feature Extraction

2.1   Deep Learning

Deep learning [8], [13] has appeared in recent research work into neuroscience [14]. It is a feature extraction processing framework simulating the hierarchical information extraction mechanism of the human brain and handling the complex computation functions. Typical deep learning models include the auto-encoder (AE) [8], the sparse auto-encoder (SAE) [9], convolutional neural networks (CNNs) [10], and deep belief networks (DBNs) [15] et al.

2.2   Sparse Auto-encoder

The SAE is an excellent unsupervised feature learning choice [9], which is able to discover the essential features in unlabeled datasets. Similar to the AE [8], the SAE is an unsupervised symmetric network including encoding and decoding stages. The encoding stage attempts to map the unlabeled input data into hidden layers, while the decoding stage processes the hidden layer information into reconstructed data. The goal of the SAE is to extract a better hidden layer representation that can contain enough information of the input data. Figure 1 shows the SAE structure.

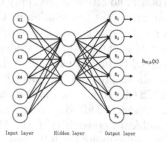

Fig. 1. The structure of the sparse auto-encoder

3   The Unsupervised Hierarchical Convolutional Sparse Auto-encoder

3.1   The Single-Layer Convolutional Sparse Auto-encoder

The single-layer CSAE [16] is an unsupervised feature extraction and classification algorithm, which consists of four stages: feature extraction, convolution, pooling and classification. The features extracted by SAE from the patches stochastically sampled on all categories of images are representative. In order to encode the original neuroimaging data with SAE features, convolution is utilized. Thus, significant detail and structural information is conserved on convolved feature maps, which are the combinations of the original neuroimaging data responding to abundant detail and structural features extracted by the SAE. The SAE has the ability to extract features of a high dimensionality by setting the hidden unit number. Thus, the convolution stage in the CSAE increases the data dimensionality and reduces the data size by traversing every dimension between the neuroimaging data and the SAE features. To reduce the storage volume and increase the computation velocity, max pooling [11] is utilized on the convolved feature maps to select the most salient and important features within the small receptive field. Finally, the softmax logistic regression [13] is added following the pooling stage to obtain the single-layer CSAE classification results.

The processing flowchart of the single-layer CSAE is shown in Figure 2.

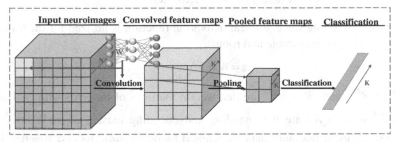

Fig. 2. The flowchart of the single-layer CSAE. To the left, the orange square denotes the feature extractors, and the large blue square denotes the original neuroimaging data.

3.2   The Unsupervised Hierarchical Convolutional Sparse Auto-encoder

Based on the single-layer CSAE, the pooled feature maps contain salient and significant features of the convolved feature maps. Therefore, feature extraction and feature encoding based on the pooled feature maps is again significant. To pass the information of the neuroimaging data to the final classifier in a way different to CNN [10], the unsupervised HCSAE is proposed in a hierarchical manner, where a full connection in HCSAE is performed between the features and the subsequent convolved feature maps via no labeled information. The HCSAE extracts different hierarchical and different abstract level features via the hierarchical CSAE, where the pooled feature maps of the former layer CSAE characterized with abundant detail and structural information are passed to the latter layer CSAE as input. After feature extraction in the latter layer CSAE, the features contain more abstract and more complicated orientation, structural, and detailed information. Therefore, the HCSAE can obtain the final pooled feature maps by encoding the former layer pooled feature maps via convolution for the classification. The HCSAE can be divided into three main stages: two hierarchical CSAE stages and a classification stage. To explicitly illustrate how each stage of the CSAE works, each CSAE stage is subdivided into three sub-stages, including feature extraction, convolution and pooling.

3.2.1   The First-Layer Convolutional Sparse Auto-encoder

For the first-layer CSAE, the original neuroimaging data are imported. As the patches have the characteristics of stationary properties, the features extracted at one part of the data can be applied to other parts of the data. To extract all the categories of image features by the SAE, the patches are sampled stochastically on each of the training image and each patch is represented by a vector with all the dimensions.

3.2.1.1   First-Layer CSAE Feature Extraction

In this stage, the reconstruction-oriented SAE is performed, where the hidden units conserve the most important features that can represent the input data. Suppose that the input patches $x \in R^N$ are processed by a nonlinear logistic sigmoid function. During the encoding stage, the input data are processed by equation (1).

$$a = f(W_1 x + b_1) \tag{1}$$

$$\text{where } f(x) = (1 + \exp(-x))^{-1} \tag{2}$$

During the decoding stage, a linear activation function is utilized for the training to make the SAE more applicable and robust.

$$z = W_2 a + b_2 \tag{3}$$

where $W_1 \in R^{K \times N}$ and $W_2 \in R^{N \times K}$ are tied weight matrices of the SAE with K features, and $b_1 \in R^K$ and $b_2 \in R^N$ are the encoding and decoding biases, where $W_1 = W_2^T$. The feature extractors of the input data are learned by optimizing the cost function in (4). By SAE, the number of features changes from N to K, where K is larger than N and the features have an increased dimension and contain more information.

$$J_{sparse}(X,Z) = \frac{1}{2} \sum_{i=1}^{m} \left\| x^i - z^i \right\|^2 + \frac{\lambda}{2} \sum_{l=1}^{n_l-1} \sum_{i=1}^{s_l} \sum_{j=1}^{s_{l+1}} (W_{ji}^{(l)})^2 + \beta \sum_{j=1}^{K} KL(\rho \| \hat{\rho}_j) \tag{4}$$

where X and Z denote the input and reconstructed data respectively. The first term of J_{sparse} is the reconstruction error between X and Z. λ is the weight decay coefficient and n_l is the layer number of the network. β is the sparsity penalization parameter and the sparse constraint was added by Kullback-Leibler divergence. Suppose that $\hat{\rho}_j = \frac{1}{m} \sum_{i=1}^{m} [a_i(x_i)]$ is the activation of hidden unit i averaged over the training set, and ρ is the sparsity parameter close to zero.

3.2.1.2   First-Layer CSAE Convolution

After feature extraction, a representative codebook $W \in R^{K \times N}$ can be obtained. Considering the SAE can extract robust and representative features of the whole categories, to better encode the neuroimaging data, convolution was combined after SAE. Suppose that the dimensionality of the neuroimaging data is $m \times n \times l$, and the patch dimensionality is $w \times w$, a $(m-w+1) \times (n-w+1) \times K$ convolved feature map from the original neuroimaging data is obtained. Each map of the K channel convolved feature maps conserves a kind of response to the extracted features, and the convolved feature maps contain abundant different orientation response features.

3.2.1.3 First-layer CSAE pooling
After convolution, to reduce the high dimensionality of the convolved feature maps and save memory, a max pooling strategy [11] is introduced in this stage to select the most representative information within the receptive field. Suppose that the stride is s, the pooled feature map $(n-w+1)/s\times(m-w+1)/s\times K$ is obtained.

3.2.2   The Second-Layer Convolutional Sparse Auto-encoder
In order to adequately utilize the abundant structural and detailed information conserved in pooled feature maps $(n-w+1)/s\times(m-w+1)/s\times K$ in the first layer, the feature extraction and encoding executed are once again needed. To extract the features of the pooled feature maps in first-layer CSAE, the SAE is utilized. After feature extraction by SAE for second-layer input $x_1 \in R^K$, a codebook $W \in R^{K\times M}$ is obtained by equations (5), (6), and (7).

$$a_1 = g(W_{11}x_1 + b_{11}) \tag{5}$$

$$z_1 = W_{22}a_1 + b_{22} \tag{6}$$

$$J_{sparse1}(X_1, Z_1) = \frac{1}{2}\sum_{i=1}^{m_1}\left\|x_1^i - z_1^i\right\|^2 + \frac{\lambda_1}{2}\sum_{l=1}^{n_{l_1}-1}\sum_{i=1}^{s_{l_1}}\sum_{j=1}^{s_{l_1+1}}(W_{ji}^{(l)'})^2 + \beta_1\sum_{j=1}^{M}KL(\rho_1 \| \hat{\rho}_{1j}) \tag{7}$$

where W_{11} and W_{22} are tied weights, $J_{sparse1}$ is the cost function of second-layer SAE.

After the second-layer SAE feature extraction, a codebook $W \in R^{K\times M}$ can be obtained. The convolved feature maps are obtained via convolution after the SAE feature extraction. Suppose that the patch size in the second-layer CSAE is $w_1 \times w_1$, the input of the second-layer SAE is $(m-w+1)/s\times(n-w+1)/s\times K$, the convolved feature maps $((m-w+1)/s-w_1+1)\times((n-w+1)/s-w_1+1)\times M$ are obtained. After max pooling in the second-layer CSAE, the pooled feature maps $((m-w+1)/s-w_1+1)/s_1\times((n-w+1)/s-w_2+1)/s_1\times M$ are obtained with stride s_1.

3.2.3   Classification of the Hierarchical Convolutional Sparse Auto-encoder
Pooled feature maps $((m-w+1)/s-w_1+1)/s_1\times((n-w+1)/s-w_2+1)/s_1\times M$ are imported to the final softmax logistic regression classifier in equation (8).

$$J(\theta) = -\frac{1}{m}\left[\sum_{i=1}^{m}\sum_{j=1}^{k}l(y^{(i)}=j)\log\frac{e^{\theta_j^T x^{(i)}}}{\sum_{l=1}^{k}e^{\theta_l^T x^{(i)}}}\right] + \frac{\lambda}{2}\sum_{i=0}^{k}\sum_{j=0}^{n}\theta_{ij}^2 \tag{8}$$

Finally, the HCSAE working mechanism is shown in Figure 3 step by step. The big blue grid and the orange squares in the left represent the original neuroimaging images and features extract by SAE respectively. The first dark gray gird stands for the convolved feature maps and the second blue grid stands for the pooled feature maps in first-layer HCSAE. The second grid stands for the convolved feature maps and the third gray grid stands for the pooled feature maps in the second-layer HCSAE. The last strip represents the vectors imported to the softmax classifier.

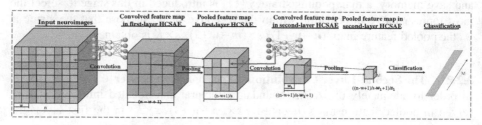

Fig. 3. The working mechanism of HCSAE

4   Experiments

4.1   Data Description

In this paper, HCSAE was evaluated on three real-world neuroimaging datasets of fMRI modality-attention deficit hyperactivity disorder (ADHD) collected from ADHD-200 global competition[1], Alzheimer's disease (ADNI) collected from the Alzheimer's disease Neuroimaging Initiative[2] and Human Immunodeficiency Virus Infection (HIV) collected from the Department of Radiology in Northwestern University [17]. For each dataset, we stochastically chose 80% of all the samples as the training, and the rest are set as the testing. Figure 4 shows some examples of ordered dimension from left-up to right-bottom for the three datasets.

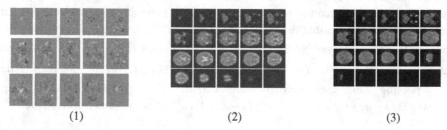

(1)   (2)   (3)

Fig. 4. (1), (2), (3) show some dimensions of the ADHD, ADNI, HIV respectively.

4.2   Experiments and Analysis

For all the three datasets, the patch size of the first-layer and the second-layer HCSAE were 8*8*n and 3*3*m, where n and m represent the third dimension. As the three datasets have different data structures, the parameters of the HCSAE for each dataset were different. According to [18], the hidden unit number deciding the network

---

[1] http://neurobureau.projects.nitrc.org/ADHD200/
[2] http://adni.loni.usc.edu/

structure was chosen as the primary element to train the network. The sparse constraint parameter is trained based on the fixed network structure. The classification results of the single-layer CSAE and the HCSAE are compared with the traditional neuroimaging data classification results in Table 1.

From Table 1, we can see that compared with the DuSK method for ADNI and HIV, the classification results of HCSAE increase 5% and 8% respectively, while ADHD keeps the similar results to the traditional methods. The experimental results confirm that HCSAE is effective for neuroimaging classification and the hierarchical manner is efficient. Figure 5 shows how parameters influence the network in detail.

Table 1. It shows the classification results of different methods on three fMRI datasets: mean (standard deviation)

Dataset	ADHD	ADNI	HIV
HCSAE	**0.65(0.05)**	**0.80(0.15)**	**0.82(0.06)**
Single-layer CSAE	0.63(0.02)	0.69(0.11)	0.77(0.03)
DuSK$_{RBF}$	**0.65(0.01)**	0.75(0.18)	0.74(0.00)
Gaussian RBF	0.58(0.00)	0.49(0.23)	0.70(0.00)
Factor kernel	0.50(0.00)	0.51(0.21)	0.70(0.01)
K$_{3rd}$ kernel	0.55(0.00)	0.55(0.14)	0.75(0.02)
Linear SHTM	0.51(0.03)	0.52(0.31)	0.70(0.01)
Linear SVM	0.51(0.01)	0.42(0.27)	0.74(0.01)
PCA+SVM	0.63(0.01)	0.50(0.02)	0.73(0.25)
MPCA+SVM	0.64(0.01)	0.51(0.02)	0.72(0.02)

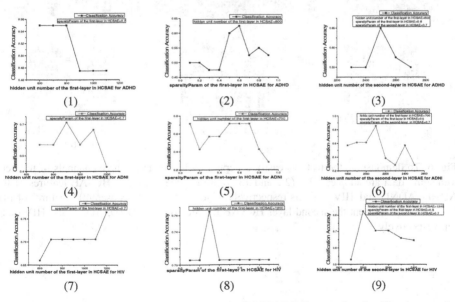

Fig. 5. These figures show how the parameters of HCSAE influence the classification results of three datasets. (1),(2), and (3);(4),(5), and (6);(7), (8), and (9) represent ADHD, ADNI and HIV respectively.

From Figure 5, when the hidden units number are set at 800,700,1200 and the sparsity is set as 0.6, 0.5, and 0.3 for ADHD, ADNI, and the HIV datasets respectively, the first layer of HCSAE achieves the satisfied classification results. Then, fixing the parameters of the first-layer HCSAE, when the second-layer hidden unit number are set at 2500,2100,and 2000 for ADHD, ADNI, HIV respectively, the second-layer of HCSAE achieves a satisfied classification accuracy. As the hidden unit number is a primary parameter deciding the network structure, only the hidden unit number of the second-layer HCSAE was tested. Meanwhile, we can see the hidden unit number of the second-layer HCSAE is nearly twice as that of the first-layer HCSAE, where the SAE increases the dimensionality of the features.

Figure 6 demonstrates the complicated SAE features in two layers of each dataset corresponding to the best classification results and the corresponding parameters, where each square (first line 8*8, second line 3*3) shows a kind of complicated orientation and structural information. Figure 7 shows some examples of the health and non-health neuroimaging data convolved in first-layer HCSAE for visualization.

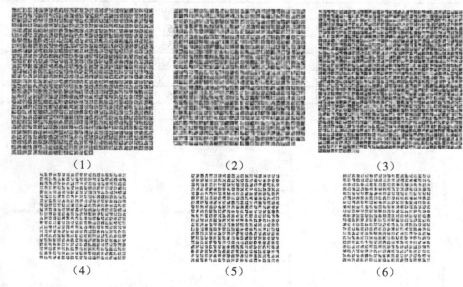

(1)   (2)   (3)

(4)   (5)   (6)

Fig. 6. To demonstrate the features easily accepted by human eyes, three channels of the neuroimaging data are adopted. (1), (2), and (3) represent the first-layer HCSAE features of the ADHD, ADNI, and HIV datasets respectively. The stochastically chosen 400 features of (4), (5), and (6) represent the second-layer HCSAE features of the ADHD, ADNI, and HIV datasets respectively.

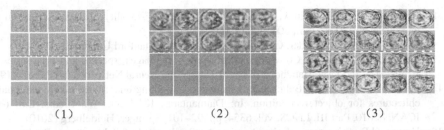

(1)   (2)   (3)

Fig. 7. (1), (2), (3) represent the first-layer convolved feature maps of ADHD, ADNI, HIV datasets respectively. The first two rows of each figure show some positive (health) samples, while the last two rows show some negative (non-health) samples.

5   Conclusions

This paper has provided an unsupervised deep learning based HCSAE algorithm for neuroimaging classification, which considers the whole dimension information in an integral manner. Compared with the traditional neuroimaging classification methods and the single-layer CSAE algorithm, the HCSAE achieves better classification results on the three neuroimaging datasets, which verifies that the abundant information in the former layer CSAE is passed to the latter layer CSAE in an unsupervised manner. In the future, a further research of the patch size and multiscale fMRI features will be carried out and the different modalities of neuroimaging data (BOLD, DTI, resting state functional interactions) will also be considered.

Acknowledgments. This work was supported by National Natural Science Foundation of China under Grant No. 41371344, the Fundamental Research Funds for the Central Universities under Grant No. 2042014 kf00231, and by NSF through grant CNS-1115234.

References

1. Craddock, R., James, G., Holtzheimer, P., Hu, X., Mayberg, H.: A whole brain fmri atlas generated via spatially constrained spectral clustering. Human Brain Mapping (2012)
2. Bihan, D.L., Breton, E., Lallemand, D., Grenier, P., Cabanis, E., Laval-Jeantet, M.: Brain, mind, and the evolution of connectivity. Radiology **161**(2), 401–407 (1986)
3. Basser, P., Pierpaoli, C.: Microstructural and physiological features of tissues elucidated by quantitative diffusion-tensor fmri. J. of Magnetic Resonance, Series B **111**(3), 209–219 (1996)
4. McKeown, M., Makeig, S., Brown, G., Jung, T., Kindermann, S., Bell, A., Sejnowski, T.: Analysis of fmri data by blind separation into independent spatial components. Human Brain Mapping **6**, 160–188 (1998)
5. He, L., Kong, X., Yu, P., Ragin, A., Hao, Z.: Dusk: a dual structure-preserving kernel for supervised tensor learning with applications to neuroimages. In: SDM (2014)
6. Sporns, O., Tononi, G., Kotter, R.: The human connectome: A structural description of the human brain. PLoS Computational Biology (2005)
7. Bengio, Y.: Learning Deep Architectures for AI, Foundations and Trends in Machine Learning (2009)

8. Hinton, G.E., Salakhutdinov, R.R.: Reducing the dimensionality of data with neural networks. Science **313**(5786), 504–506 (2006)
9. Ng, A.: Sparse autoencoder, CS294A Lecture notes on Stanford University (2010)
10. LeCun, Y., Bengio, Y.: Convolutional networks for images, speech, and time-series. In: Arbib, M.A. (ed.) The Handbook of Brain Theory and Neural Networks. MIT Press (1995)
11. Scherer, D., Müller, A., Behnke, S.: Evaluation of pooling operations in convolutional architectures for object recognition. In: Diamantaras, K., Duch, W., Iliadis, L.S. (eds.) ICANN 2010, Part III. LNCS, vol. 6354, pp. 92–101. Springer, Heidelberg (2010)
12. Hinton, G.E., Srivastava, N., Krizhevsky, A., Sutskever, I., Salakhutdinov, R.: Improving neural networks by preventing co-adaptation of feature detectors. CoRR, abs/1207.0580 (2012)
13. Krizhevsky, A., Sutskever, I., Hinton, G.E.: ImageNet classification with deep convolutional neural networks. In: Proc. Of NIPS (2012)
14. Lee, T.S., Mumford, D., Romero, R., et al.: The role of the primary visual cortex in higher level vision. Vision Research **38**(15–16), 2429–2454 (1998)
15. LeRoux, N., Bengio, Y.: Deep belief networks are compact universal approximations. Neural Comput. **22**(8), 2192–2207 (2010)
16. Zhang, F., Du, B., Zhang, L.: Saliency-Guided Unsupervised Feature Learning for Scene Classification. IEEE Transactions on Geoscience and Remote Sensing **53**, 2175–2184 (2014)
17. Wang, X., Foryt, P., Ochs, R., Chung, J., Wu, Y., Parrish, T., Ragin, A.: Abnormalities in resting-state functional connectivity in early human immunodeficiency virus infection. Brain Connectivity **1**(3), 207 (2011)
18. Coates, A., Ng, A.Y., Lee, H.: An analysis of single-layer networks in unsupervised feature learning. In: Proc .Int. Conf. Artificial Intelligence and Statistics, pp. 215–223 (2011)

A Personalized Method of Literature Recommendation Based on Brain Informatics Provenances

Ningning Wang[1,3]([✉]), Ning Zhong[1,3,4,5], Jian Han[1,3], Jianhui Chen[2],
Han Zhong[1,3], Taihei Kotake[5], Dongsheng Wang[1,6], and Jianzhuo Yan[3,7]

[1] International WIC Institute, Beijing University of Technology,
Beijing, China
{wangningning,hanjian0204}@emails.bjut.edu.cn,
zhong@maebashi-it.ac.jp, dswang@bjut.edu.cn
[2] Department of Computer Science and Technology,
Tsinghua University, Beijing, China
chenjhnh@mail.tsinghua.edu.cn
[3] Beijing International Collaboration Base on Brain Informatics and Wisdom
Services, Beijing, China
z.h0912@emails.bjut.edu.cn, yanjianzhuo@bjut.edu.cn
[4] Beijing Key Laboratory of MRI and Brain Informatics, Beijing, China
[5] Department of Life Science and Informatics,
Maebashi Institute of Technology, Maebashi, Japan
kotake@maebashi-it.org
[6] School of Computer Science and Engineering,
Jiangsu University of Science and Technology, Zhenjiang, China
[7] College of Electronic Information and Control Engineering,
Beijing University of Technology, Beijing, China

Abstract. Systematic Brain Informatics (BI) depends on a lot of prior knowledge, from experimental design to result interpretation. Scientific literatures are a kind of important knowledge source. However, it is difficult for researchers to find really useful references from a large number of literatures. This paper proposes a personalized method of literature recommendation based on BI provenances. By adopting the interest retention model, user models can be built based on the Data-Brain and BI provenances. Furthermore, semantic similarity is added into traditional literature vector modeling for obtaining literature models. By measuring similarity between the user models and literature models, the really needed literatures can be obtained. Results of experiments show that the proposed method can effectively realize a personalized literature recommendation according to BI researchers' interests.

1 Introduction

With the rapid development of Internet in information age, people often face with information overload when they retrieve information. As an effective means

© Springer International Publishing Switzerland 2015
Y. Guo et al. (Eds.): BIH 2015, LNAI 9250, pp. 167–178, 2015.
DOI: 10.1007/978-3-319-23344-4_17

to solve this problem, personalized recommendation systems focus on user preferences. They compute user interests automatically and recommend interested information or products to users in association with demand information. The literature recommendation system [8] is a kind of recommendation system. It recommends interested literatures for users according to their interests.

Brain Informatics (BI) [2] is an emerging interdisciplinary and multidisciplinary research field that focuses on studying the mechanisms underlying the human information processing system. It adopts the systematic methodology to study human information processing mechanism from macro and micro perspectives, for deep understanding of human intelligence eventually. Systematic BI researches are based on prior knowledge about similar experiments and analytical researches. Scientific literatures are a kind of important prior knowledge sources. Therefore, it is necessary for BI researchers to find related literatures from scientific literature databases and obtain necessary prior knowledge about experiments and analyses. However, BI researchers can't find really needed literatures because of information overload. For example, if they want to retrieve the literatures about cognitive function "Learning" from PubMed, the number of results is 240522. To solve this problem, this paper proposes a literature recommendation method called sLR-BIP. It builds user models base on the Data-Brain and BI provenances to capture users' interests accurately. Furthermore, semantic similarity is added into traditional lliterature vector modeling for obtaining literature models. Results of experiments show it expands the recommendation results and recommends more useful literatures to users.

The rest of the paper is organized as follows: Section 2 discusses the background and related work and Section 3 illustrates the details of the proposed method. Section 4 shows the experimental results and discussion. Finally, Section 5 gives conclusion and future work.

2   Background and Related Work

2.1   Data-Brain and BI Provenances

Aiming at complex brain science problems, BI adopts a systematic methodology, including four core issues: systematic investigation of human thinking centric mechanisms, systematic design of cognitive experiments, systematic human brain data management, systematic human brain data analysis and simulation [1]. In order to manage BI data for systematic BI study, BI needs a Data-Brain to integrate key data, information, and knowledge for various data requests of a systematic BI study. The Data-Brain is a domain-driven conceptual model of brain data, which represents multi-aspect relationships among multiple human brain data sources, with respect to all major aspects and capabilities of human information processing system (HIPS), for systematic investigation and understanding of human intelligence. The Data-Brain is divided into four dimensions, which corresponds to the four aspects of systematic methodology. By the domain-driven modeling method, the Data-Brain models the whole process of BI researches and includes all BI research interests. It can be used as a domain knowledge base about BI research interests for guiding the definition of users' interests.

BI provenances are the metadata describing the origin of BI data and successive processing. It involves multi-aspect experimental information, including subject, experimental process, measuring equipment, *etc*. In previous researches [3], a method based on Data-Brain has been proposed to construct BI provenances. Experiments and analysis-related information is extracted from various information sources, including scientific literatures, research reports, *etc*, and is integrated into provenance schemata, which is constructed based on the Data-Brain. Such BI provenances describe not only brain data but also related BI researches. They can be regarded as information sources, which record authors' previous researches, for defining authors' interests.

2.2   Literature Recommendation System

The literature recommendation system is a kind of important recommendation systems. It recommends literatures for users according to their research interests. Its cores are user interest modeling and literature modeling.

Many methods have been used to build user interest models, including TF-IDF, automatic clustering, bayes classifier, *etc*. However, only depending on the word frequency, some common words are mistaken for keywords with larger weights owing to their high frequencies, though they have nothing to do with user interests. This paper defines user interests based on the domain-driven Data-Brain and BI provenances, and constructs user models by using users forgetting curve based on frequency statistics [9], which can recognize users' recent interests transition. By taking recent interests transition into account, user interests can be captured exactly.

Vector space model (VSM) is a general means for modeling textual recommended objects. Traditional VSM only counts up the number of keywords in documents and can't reflect the real contents of documents. Yan Zhang [5] developed a weighted VSM, which considered not only the frequency of keywords, but also their positions in the documents. However, it can't represent the correlation between similar keywords because of lacking semantic information. Hence, we introduce semantic similarity to the literature model in this paper.

There are many ways of computing semantic similarity between words [6,7]. However, because most of methods use the semantic dictionary to compute the distance between words for the similarity measurement, all words have to be included in the dictionary. In our research, most of concepts in the Data-Brain are domain terminology, and there isn't such a domain dictionary to be used. Therefore this paper develops a new algorithm of semantic similarity for BI literature recommendation based on Yong Jiang's research [4].

3   Literature Recommendation Based on BI Provenances

As illustrated in Fig. 1, our method consists of three parts: modeling user interests, modeling literatures and matching user interests with literatures. The details will be discussed as follows.

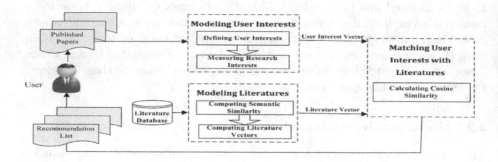

Fig. 1. A BI Provenances-based method for Literature Recommendation

3.1   Modeling User Interests

In order to provide precise recommendations for users, pervious research preferences and recent interests are taken into account to reflect real-time user preferences exactly and efficiently. Different BI research interests are defined based on the Data-Brain and measured by using the interest retention model [9].

Users' research interests are the basic elements for constructing user interest vectors. Hence, literature recommendation is based on user research interests. As mentioned, the Data-Brain model can be used as a domain knowledge base about BI research interests for guiding the definition of users' interests. In order to obtain users' research interests from BI provenances, some concepts are defined as follows:

An Interest Aspect, *denoted by e(k), is a sub-dimension in the Data-Brain, which describes a kind of user preferences for classifying users' research interests.*

An Interest, *denoted by $t_{e(k)}(i)$, is a class of interest aspects in the Data-Brain, which describes an interest point for indicating users' research interests.*

As mentioned in our previous researches, Data-Brain contains four dimensions and each dimension consists of one or more sub-dimensions. Based on domain experts' suggestions, this paper takes the following three sub-dimensions or types of concepts as interest aspects to describe users' research interests.

1. Cognitive function is the main part of function dimension. Human cognitive functions cover thinking centric cognitive functions, perception centric cognitive functions and other related cognitive functions from BI perspectives. Among them, thinking centric cognitive functions are the key point for BI

study. Cognitive function represents research objects or perspectives for BI, so it is an important interest aspect to describe users' research interests.

2. Device type is an important part of experiment dimension. Different device types decide different experimental research methods, brain data and analytical methods, so it is an important interest aspect to describe users' research interests.

3. Subject type is another important part of experiment dimension. Different subject types stand for different research emphases, which greatly influences device selection, feature recognition and result interpretation, so it is an important interest aspect to describe users' research interests.

In conclusion, user interest vector S is defined as follows:

$$S = (t_{e(1)}(i), t_{e(2)}(j), t_{e(3)}(l) | t_{e(1)}(i) \in e(1), t_{e(2)}(j) \in e(2), t_{e(3)}(l) \in e(3))$$

where $e(1)$, $e(2)$, $e(3)$ refer to cognitive function, device type and subject type, respectively.

Users may generate interests in some topics or decrease interests in them over a period of time, so their research interests change over time dynamically. This phenomenon is similar with the forgetting mechanism of cognitive memory. However, previous researches [8] just consider past user interests in the stage of modeling user interests, the effect of time on user's current interests is not taken into account. To solve this problem, this research adopts an interest retention model for user modeling.

A user research interest can be represented as a keyword. Assumed that the appearing times of an interest can be simply added together to reflect a user's overall interest on the specified keyword within a time interval, user's cumulative interest during n time intervals can be represented as:

$$CI\left(t_{e(k)}(i), n\right) = \sum_{j=1}^{n} y_{t_{e(k)}}(i), j \tag{1}$$

where $y_{t_{e(k)}(i),j}$ is the number of literatures in BI provenances that involved in interest $t_{e(k)}(i)$ during the time interval j, and i, j, k, n are positive integers.

Users' current interests are closely related to their previous interests. Hence, an interest retention model is used to calculate users' retained interests for modeling user interests. The retained interest of $t_{e(k)}(i)$ during n time intervals can be represented as:

$$RI\left(t_{e(k)}(i), n\right) = \sum_{j=1}^{n} y_{t_{e(k)}}(i), j \times AT_{t_{e(k)}(i)}^{-b} \tag{2}$$

where $T_{t_{e(k)}(i)}$ is the duration of interest $t_{e(k)}(i)$, $y_{t_{e(k)}(i),j}$ is the number of literatures in BI provenances that involved in interest $t_{e(k)}(i)$ during the time interval j. To adjust the value of retained interest, and keep maximum correlation between retained interest and current interest, we introduce parameters

"A" and "b". Based on our previous studies [9], their values are set as 0.855 and 1.295, respectively.

For each interest aspect, the retained interests of every interest are computed, and then the weighted vector V is defined as follows:

$$V = (RI(t_{e(1)}(i)), RI(t_{e(2)}(j)), RI(t_{e(3)}(l)))$$

where $t_{e(1)}(i)$ has the largest retained interest in $e(1)$, $t_{e(2)}(j)$ has the largest retained interest in $e(2)$ and $t_{e(3)}(l)$ has the largest retained interest in $e(3)$.

3.2   Modeling Literatures

To recommend suitable literatures for BI researchers, it is necessary to model literatures. This paper uses weighted VSM to model literatures and presents LR-BIP. Furthermore, semantic similarity is introduced into literature models and presents sLR-BIP.

Weighted VSM considers not only the frequency of keywords but also their positions in the documents. Different weight coefficients are assigned to the keywords in different positions. We define three position labels T_1, T_2, T_3, namely title, keywords and abstract, and give different weight coefficients to the keywords belonging to different position labels. According to the degree of importance, the weight ratio of these three position labels is $T_1: T_2 :T_3=3:2:1$. The weight of an interest keyword in literatures is represented as:

$$w_i = \sum_{p=1}^{3} N_p * C_p \tag{3}$$

$$C_p = \frac{T_p}{\sum_{j=1}^{3} T_j} \tag{4}$$

where w_i represents the weight of interest keyword t_i in literatures, N_p represents the appearing times of t_i in position label p, and C_p represents normalized weight of label p. Hence, the literature vector of literatures can be represented as:

$$W = (w_1, w_2, w_3)$$

where w_1, w_2, w_3 represent the weight of keyword according to cognitive function, device type and subject type, respectively.

However, the above literature model can't show the relevance between similar keywords because it lacks semantic information. For example, when a user retrieves literatures about cognitive function "Abduction" by matching the keyword, and the result is that there are few such literatures in the dataset. If semantic similarity is used, the result includes some literatures about cognitive function "Deduction", which belongs to "Reasoning" as with "Abduction" in the Data-Brain, and the user likely needs them.

Based on Yong Jiang's research [4], this research uses terminological similarity and structural similarity to calculate the semantic similarity between classes in the Data-Brain. Furthermore, this paper considers external structural similarity between two classes is determined by their own location and common father node, so Wu Z's method [10] is employed. The details are described as follows. With semantic similarity, the algorithm of literature vector is shown in Table 1.

Table 1. The algorithm of literature vector from sLR-BIP

The algorithm of literature vector with semantic similarity
1. For each interest aspect
2. If $(\exists\, t_{e(k)}(i))$ then
3. $w_i = w_{t_{e(k)}(i)} = 1.0 * \sum_{p=1}^{3} N_p * \frac{T_p}{\sum_{j=1}^{3} T_j}$
4.   If $(w_i > 1)$ then
5. $w_i = 1.0$
6.   End If
7. End If
8. Else
9. If $(\text{maxSemanticSimilarity}(t_{e(k)}(i),\, y) == sim(t_{e(k)}(i), t_{e(k)}(j))) then$
10. $w_i = w_{t_{e(k)}(j)} = sim(t_{e(k)}(i), t_{e(k)}(j)) * \sum_{p=1}^{3} N_p * \frac{T_p}{\sum_{j=1}^{3} T_j}$
11.   If $(w_i > sim(t_{e(k)}(i), t_{e(k)}(j)))$ then
12. $w_i = sim(t_{e(k)}(i), t_{e(k)}(j))$
13.   End If
14. End If
15. End For

Terminological Similarity, *denoted by* $sim_t(x, y)$, *which describes the characteristics relevance between classes.* The link weight $w(x, y)$ is used to compute terminological similarity, different from Yong Jiang's research, the PubMed dataset is used as data source instead of the Google search. It can be described as follows:

$$w(x, y) = \frac{f(x, y)}{f(y)}, \quad w(y, x) = \frac{f(x, y)}{f(x)} \tag{5}$$

From formula (5), $w(x, y)$ is not equal to $w(y, x)$ in most case, so the following rules should be adopted in practice:

If $0 < |w(x, y) - w(y, x)| < \delta$, *the word* x *and* y *are semantic correlated.*
where δ is a real number and describes the margin of errors. Based on previous study [4], the difference between $w(x, y)$ and $w(y, x)$ is within the margin of errors when δ is 0.1.

Internal Structural Similarity, *denoted by* $sim_{si}(x, y)$, *which describes the property relevance between classes in ontology, and is determined by the maximum similarity of properties between classes.*

As stated above, an interest aspect is a sub-dimension of the Data-Brain and each interest is a concept in the sub-dimension. Each dimension is constructed by relationship "is-a", so classes of each dimension in the Data-Brain have uniform properties and internal structural similarity of interests in the same interest aspect can be set as the value of 1.

External Structural Similarity, *denoted by* $sim_{se}(x, y)$, *which describes the superclass relevance between classes in ontology.*

It shows relevant location information of two classes based on the classification tree of ontology, which is determined by their own locations and common father node.

$$sim_{se}(x, y) = \frac{2H}{N_1 + N_2 + 2H} \tag{6}$$

where H represents the shortest path from C to the root node, and N_1, N_2 represent the shortest path from C to class x and y, respectively. C is the closest common father node of class x and y.

Hence, semantic similarity of classes x and y can be represented as:

$$sim(x, y) = \lambda_t \times sim_t(x, y) + \lambda_{si} \times sim_{si}(x, y) + \lambda_{se} \times sim_{se}(x, y) \tag{7}$$

In formula (7), $\lambda_t + \lambda_{si} + \lambda_{se} = 1$, and $\lambda_{si} = \lambda_{se}$ for that internal and external structural similarities have the same weight. Therefore, the overall semantic similarity can be expressed as follows:

$$sim(x, y) = \lambda \times sim_t(x, y) + \frac{1 - \lambda}{2} \times sim_{si}(x, y) + \frac{1 - \lambda}{2} \times sim_{se}(x, y)$$

$$= \lambda \times w(x, y) + \frac{1 - \lambda}{2} \times \left(\sum_{p_i \in P_x, p_j \in P_y} max\{w(p_i, p_j)\} + \sum_{s_i \in S_x, s_j \in S_y} max\{w(s_i, s_j)\} \right) \tag{8}$$

where λ is a weight coefficient used to weigh importance between terminological similarity and structural similarity, and $0 \leq \lambda \leq 1$. In this study, λ is set as 0.6 based on the previous study [4].

3.3   Outputting Recommended Literatures

Through the above steps, weighted vector V and literature vector W can be obtained, and then the similarity between V and W is measured by cosine similarity.

$$Sim(V, W) = \frac{\sum_{i=1}^{n} v_i * w_i}{\sqrt{\sum_{i=1}^{n} (v_i)^2} * \sqrt{\sum_{i=1}^{n} (w_i)^2}} \tag{9}$$

where v_i is the ith element of vector V as well as w_i, n is the number of elements of the vector.

From formula (9), varieties of literatures having different similarities with user interests can be obtained in descending order. The larger the value is , the more similar they are. Finally, the top-N literatures are recommended to user.

4   Experiments and Evaluation

4.1   Experiments Data

We selected PubMed dataset as a data source, because core theme of its periodicals is biomedicine. We first construct the neuroscience literatures dataset consisting of articles published in the journals of neuroscience from 2005 to 2007, and impact factor (IF) of these journals ranks top 10 in neuroscience. Then we randomly selected 500 articles from the dataset as test data. In our previous study, the Data-Brain has been constructed, as illustrated in Fig. 2.

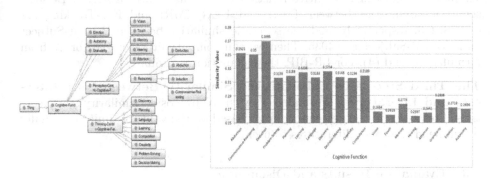

Fig. 2. The function dimension of the Data-Brain and the semantic similarity between "Induction" and the other classes

4.2   Experiment Process

The First Step is to Calculate user Interest Vectors. We treat Dr. Liang as a user, who is a BI researcher, and recommend literatures to him by the proposed method. We calculate retained interests according to formula (2). For example, for device type, we calculate all the retained interests in the interest aspect, and the results of "fMRI", "EEG", "Eye-Tracking" are 1.078, 0.535, 0.247, respectively. Hence, we know Dr. Liang is focusing on fMRI. Similarly, we can calculate other interests in other two interest aspects. Hence, user interest vector S is (Induction, fMRI, Normal-Subject) and weighted vector V is (1.546, 1.078, 1.448).

The Second Step is to Calculate Literature Vectors. For sLR-BIP, we need to compute semantic similarity between classes in the Data-Brain firstly.

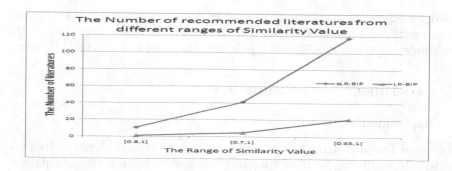

Fig. 3. Comparison of experiment results between sLR-BIP and LR-BIP

From formulas (5), (6) and (8), we can obtain semantic similarity between "Induction" and other cognitive function classes, as shown in Fig. 2. Besides, semantic similarities between fMRI and EEG, fMRI and Eye-Tracking are 0.3078, 0.3, respectively, and the semantic similarity between Patient-Subject and Normal-Subject is 0.4035. Then we can compute literature vector W from formulas (3) and (4). For LR-BIP, the calculation is similar.

The Third Step is to Calculate the Similarity Between User Interests and Literatures. We match V with W by cosine similarity, then sort these literatures in the descending order based on the value of similarity, finally recommend the top-N literatures to user.

4.3   Evaluation Results and Discussion

Experimental results show that sLR-BIP performs better than LR-BIP, it recommends more useful literatures for users. Fig. 3 is the comparison of experiment results between two methods. The X-axis is the range of semantic similarity and the Y-axis is the number of articles. This figure describes the number of recommended literatures during different ranges of similarity value. As shown in the figure, if the sLR-BIP is used, the number of literatures whose similarities matched with weighted vector are greater than 0.8 is 11; if the LR-BIP is used, the result is 1. The recommended literatures by the two methods are discussed for result evaluation.

Table 2 shows the results of LR-BIP. As shown in this table, the top ranking literatures are closer to Dr. Liang's research interests than behind. The first literature applies fMRI to study patient's learning with absence of functional FMRP, the last studies brain activities when people purchase various items. Hence, according to user interests model, we can know that the first one meets users' needs better.

Table 3 shows the results of sLR-BIP. As shown in this table, the first three literatures are recommended by sLR-BIP and the last three literatures are recommended by LR-BIP. In domain experts' opinion, the first three literatures

Table 2. Recommended literatures by LR-BIP

Article ID	Literature Vector	Similarity Value	Title
105	(0.167, 0.0, 0.167)	0.8907	Deletion of FMR1 in Purkinje cells enhances parallel fiber LTD, enlarges spines, and attenuates cerebellar.
151	(0.668, 0.0, 0.167)	0.7788	Multiple periods of functional ocular dominance plasticity in mouse visual cortex.
...	...	...	...
042	(0.0, 0.167, 0.0)	0.4536	Shopping centers in the brain.

Table 3. The first 3 articles with maximal matching degree

Article ID	Literature Vector	Similarity Value	Title
		sLR-BIP	
024	(0.220, 0.167, 0.167)	0.9932	Separate modulations of human V1 associated with spatial attention and task structure.
031	(0.181, 0.167, 0.167)	0.9922	Understanding emotions in others: mirror neuron dysfunction in children with autism spectrum disorders.
476	(0.132, 0.167, 0.067)	0.9078	Breakdown of functional connectivity in frontoparietal networks underlies behavioral deficits in spatial neglect.
		LR-BIP	
105	(0.167, 0.0, 0.167)	0.8907	Deletion of FMR1 in Purkinje cells enhances parallel fiber LTD, enlarges spines, and attenuates cerebellar eyelid conditioning in Fragile X syndrome.
151	(0.668, 0.0, 0.167)	0.7788	Multiple periods of functional ocular dominance plasticity in mouse visual cortex.
020	(0.0, 0.167, 0.167)	0.7515	Decoding human brain activity during real-world experiences.

apply fMRI to study some cognitive functions on subjects, and are closer to user interests than the last three. This indicates our method sLR-BIP is superior to the other.

5 Conclusion and Future Work

In this paper, we presented a personalized method of literature recommendation for researchers based on BI provenances. We consider both published papers and interests transition to construct the user interest model, and combine semantic similarity with VSM to construct the literature model. Experiment results show that our method is able to recommend interested literatures more effectively. In the future, we will consider all the interest aspects of different researchers, and thus the user interests can be got comprehensively.

Compared with other methods, our contributions are described below:

• The user interest model is used in association with a literature model to gain user interests and vector recommended objects, which improve the quality of literature recommendation.

• The semantic similarity is used to improve the unicity of recommendation and add semantic information to literature vectors, which allows users to get literatures not only belonging to their own research areas, but also related research areas.

• The issue on the data sparseness of traditional VSM is overcome, which makes articles can be described more accurately.

Acknowledgments. The work is supported by National Key Basic Research Program of China (2014CB744605), China Postdoctoral Science Foundation (2013M540096), International Science Cooperation Program of China (2013DFA32180), National Natural Science Foundation of China (61272345), Research Supported by the CAS/SAFEA International Partnership Program for Creative Research Teams, the Japan Society for the Promotion of Science Grants-in-Aid for Scientific Research (25330270).

References

1. Chen, J., Zhong, N.: Data-brain modeling for systematic brain informatics. In: Zhong, N., Li, K., Lu, S., Chen, L. (eds.) BI 2009. LNCS, vol. 5819, pp. 182–193. Springer, Heidelberg (2009)
2. Zhong, N., Bradshaw, J.M., Liu, J.M., Taylor, J.G.: Brain Informatics. IEEE Intelligent Systems, 16–20 (2011)
3. Chen, J.H., Zhong, N., Liang, P.P.: Data-Brain Driven Systematic Human Brain Data Analysis: A Case Study in Numerical Inductive Reasoning Centric Investigation. Cognitive Systems Research **15–16**, 17–32 (2012)
4. Jiang, Y., Wang, X.M., Zheng, H.T.: A semantic similarity measure based on information distance for ontology alignment. Information Sciences, 76–87 (2014)
5. Zhang, Y.: Applications of web mining in personalized search engine (2008). http://www.cnki.net/
6. Oliva, J., Serrano, J.I., Castillo, M.D., Iglesias, A.: SyMSS: A syntax-based measure for short-text semantic similarity. Data & Knowledge Engineering, 390–405 (2011)
7. Lee, M.C.: A novel sentence similarity measure for semantic-based expert systems. Expert Systems with Applications, 6392–6399 (2011)
8. Liu, Y.Y., Zhang, X.M.: Document Recommender Systems: Approaches to Increasing Infor-mation Retrieval Effectiveness. Library and Information Service, 11–19 (2007)
9. Zeng, Y., Zhong, N., Wang, Y., Qin, Y.L., Huang, Z.S., Zhou, H., Yao, Y.Y., Harmelen, F.V.: Us-er-centric query refinement and processing using granularity based strategies. Knowledge and Information Systems **27**(3), 419–450 (2011)
10. Wu, Z., Palmer, M.: Verb semantics and lexical selection. In: Proceedings of the 32nd Annual Meeting of the Associations for Computational Linguistics, pp. 133–138 (1994)

Brain-Inspired Technologies, Systems and Applications

Measuring Emotion Regulation with Single Dry Electrode Brain Computer Interface

C. Natalie van der Wal[1(✉)] and Mona Irrmischer[2]

[1] Department Computer Science, Vrije Universiteit, Amsterdam, The Netherlands
c.n.vander.wal@vu.nl
[2] Department Integrative Neurophysiology, Center for Neurogenomics
and Cognitive Research, Amsterdam, The Netherlands
m.irrmischer@vu.nl

Abstract. Wireless brain computer interfaces (BCI's) are promising for new intelligent applications in which emotions are detected by measuring brain activity. Applications, such as serious games and video game therapy, are measuring and using the user's emotional state in order to determine the intensity level of the game. This experimental study was designed to validate the measurement of emotion regulation with a single dry electrode wireless BCI during an emotion interference computer task by comparing it with the behavioural performance of this task. The behavioural measures showed significant main and interaction effects indicating that emotion regulatory mechanisms are present in the participants. The EEG measure Attention detected by the Myndplay Brainband XL showed a significant interaction indicating that type of training (meditation or laughter) increases or decreases attention during the emotion interference task. Overall, these results point in the direction of single electrode BCI's being able to detect emotion interference.

Keywords: Brain computer interface · Myndplay brainband · EEG · Emotion regulation · Affective computing

1   Introduction

In the field of artificial intelligence, a near future is envisioned filled with technology that can understand the emotions of humans, like companion or care robots and video game therapies. On the one hand, these systems are solutions to societal problems, like increasing healthcare costs and the growing need for healthcare workers due to people living longer and living unhealthy lifestyles. On the other hand these systems are developed from the different possibilities these new artificial intelligent technologies provide. For example, in the fields of medicine and entertainment, there are now video games and serious games for entertainment or therapy in which the user's emotional state is measured during the game in order to determine the intensity level of the game [1], [2], [3], [4], [5]. Examples of companion and care robots are: Jibo,

---

C.N. van der Wal and M. Irrmischer—Shared first authorship: equal contributions.

Y. Guo et al. (Eds.): BIH 2015, LNAI 9250, pp. 181–191, 2015.
DOI: 10.1007/978-3-319-23344-4_18

Softbank's Pepper, Intell's Jimmy, AMIGO, Care-O-Bot or PARO [6]. Robots will need to recognize and understand all human emotions and expressions to be able to interact and communicate with us in an effective, pleasant and smooth manner.

In the interdisciplinary field of affective computing, it is examined how the human-like capabilities of observation, interpretation and generation of emotions can be assigned to computers [7]. In human-computer interaction, multimodal data of humans, such as body gestures, facial features, speech and brain activity, is collected and processed in order to recognize human emotions. Wireless brain computer interfaces (BCI's) are promising for new intelligent applications in which emotions and emotion regulation are detected by measuring brain activity, because the possibility to make user-friendly miniature user interfaces and brain activity produces various phenomena which can be measured [8]. Studies of measuring emotional states with brain activities are increasing. Multiple findings indicate that frontal activity in terms of decreasing power in the alpha band is associated with emotional states [9]. Gamma activity has also been related to emotional processing, especially to negative emotions [10], [11]. There are no studies known to the authors in which emotion regulation mechanisms specifically are measured with a commercially available (dry) electrode BCI. Relevant research found are studies that determine the emotion recognition in data acquired from BCI's with only one or five electrodes [12], [13]. In the current study, effects of emotion interference on attention in all frequency bands (from alpha to theta) will be analysed and compared to the behavioural measures on a computer task that can measure emotion regulation. This work will be relevant for the affective computing community interested in the validity of commercially available BCI's.

A great number of studies examine attention toward affective stimuli, such as pain, threat, feeding and sexual behaviour [14], [15], [16]. From an evolutionary point of view, both pleasant and unpleasant situations have an importance for species survival, and greater motivational relevance compared with affectively neutral events [17]. The purpose of the current study presented here was to assess attentional resources allocation to different emotional contents by recording response times to acoustic tones occurring during picture viewing and measuring the brain activity. Attentional resources can be considered as a limited amount of processing capabilities or attentive availability, such that the greater the amount allocated to performing a task, the smaller the quota available for a second task to be performed concurrently [18]. The dual-task experimental paradigm has been used to estimate the amount of attentional resources allocated to a task (primary task) on the basis of the performance relative to another concurrent task (secondary task). The idea is that the secondary task is executed by using the resources left available by the performance of the primary task. In the current study, participants will perform the Emotion Interference Task, in which they have to respond to a tone (secondary task) presented during picture viewing (primary task) [19]. The time it takes to respond to the tone should reflect the extent of attention allocated to the picture, and thus the emotion interference.

As part of a bigger study, the participants followed a meditation or laughter training for one week and their performance on the EIT was measured before and after training. The primary focus of the bigger study was to determine the effect of meditation on attention, therefore the experimental group received meditation training and the control group received laughter training. In this way the control group did receive some form of training with similar characteristics, e.g. also in a group setting and with breathing exercises, but no attention regulation training like the experimental group. This control condition was chosen to overcome possible bias of waiting list control conditions: overestimating treatment effects. It was expected that after meditation training, persons can maintain their attention to the current moment better and are able to disengage their attention more rapidly from emotionally provocative stimuli, freeing up attentional resources to perform the simple cognitive task of responding to the tones. For the laughter training no effect of training on emotion regulation was expected because they did not receive the attention regulation training like the experimental group.

The current study is designed to measure emotion regulation with a single dry electrode wireless BCI, Myndplay Brainband XL [20], during an emotion regulation computer task and comparing it with the behavioural performance of this task. The main objectives of this study are to (1) understand the correlates of emotion regulation as detected with the Myndplay Brainband XL (BCI with two dry electrodes) and (2) comparing these with the behavioural measures of emotion regulation on the Emotion Interference Task. The rest of this paper is organised as follows: in Section 2 the experiment and its methods are described, followed by the results in Section 3. Section 4 concludes and discusses the results as well as future work.

2   Experiment

In this Section the methods of the current study are described.

2.1   Participants

Fifty-three students of the Vrije Universiteit Amsterdam were recruited from the campus through flyers and quasi-randomly assigned to the experimental (29 meditation training) or control condition (24 laughter training). Eight participants did not complete the study, due to moving house or unstated reasons, and were left out of the analysis. All participants are healthy, Dutch or English speaking, students 18–67 years old, without a history of neurological complications or substance abuse and no previous experience with meditation, yoga or laughter yoga. This study has been approved by the Scientific and Ethical Review Committee of the Faculty of Psychology and Education of the Vrije Universiteit, Amsterdam, Netherlands.

2.2   Measures and Materials

Emotion regulation is defined as an increased awareness of emotions and being less affected by these emotions through applying different emotion regulation strategies. An example emotion regulation strategy is to let affective stimuli have less interference by focussing attention back to the task goal or to another object (such as the breath). It is measured in the Emotion Interference Task by comparing average response times for neutral, negative and positive stimuli in a discrimination task (indicating if the pitch of the tone is high or low after seeing an affective picture). Response times are compared before and after meditation or laughter training. Moreover, neural correlates of emotion regulation were measured while performing the Emotion Interference Task, as measured by the Myndplay Brainband XL. Power in all frequency bands will be analysed.

Emotion Interference Task (EIT, Buodo et al. 2002): participants judged whether a tone is high- or low- pitched after viewing neutral, pleasant, or unpleasant pictures. Participants viewed 20 neutral and 20 arousing (10 pleasant and 10 unpleasant) scenes from the International Affective Picture System (IAPS) [21], in random order, for 6,000 ms each. At either 1,000 ms (1 s stimulus onset asynchrony (SOA)) or 4,000 ms (4 s SOA) after picture onset, a high- or low-pitched tone was presented. Participants had to press a button as quickly as possible to indicate whether the tone was high or low.

Stimulus Materials: forty-eight digitized colour pictures were chosen from the IAPS [21], depicting unpleasant (mutilated bodies), pleasant (nude erotic couples during intercourse) or neutral (household objects) stimuli. The positive and negative arousal categories were matched for normative mean arousal ratings (6.61 and 6.63, respectively). The neutral category had a mean arousal rating of 2.74. The IAPS picture numbers were as follows: mutilated bodies – 3010, 3030, 3053, 3059, 3060, 3063, 3100, 3101, 3102, 3120, 3130, 3168. ; erotic couples - 4652, 4659, 4660, 4664_1, 4668, 4670, 4680, 4681, 4687, 4694, 4695, 4698; household objects –7002, 7006, 7009, 7010, 7012, 7025, 7031, 7032, 7034, 7035, 7036, 7040, 7041, 7045, 7055, 7059, 7060, 7130, 7150, 7161, 7175, 7185, 7217, 7235. Twelve pictures were presented for each emotional category and 24 for the neutral one (in order to balance the number of pictures for each valence group).

Free Recall Task: at the end of the experiment, each participant performed a free recall of the pictures from the Emotion Interference Task.

Yogic Breathing Meditation Training and Laughter Yoga Training: Participants followed a yogic breathing and meditation training or a laughter yoga training. Each training consisted of 7 consecutive days starting Tuesday or Wednesday. Participants followed daily group sessions of 45 minutes (except for Saturday and Sunday). The group sessions of the meditation training consisted of breath manipulation exercises (called Pranayama in the eight-folded path of Ashtanga yoga), body scans and focused breathing meditation [22]. The Laughter Training group sessions consisted of yoga breathing exercises, laughing exercises and deep relaxation at the end of each session according to laughter yoga [23]. Participants of both trainings were also given daily homework exercises of 10-20 minutes per day consisting of exercises from the group sessions.

Myndplay Brainband XL: EEG data in this research was collected with a commercially available non-invasive BCI headset: the NeuroSky Myndplay Brainband XL. [20] The BCI uses a dry active sensor technology to read brain signals. Traditionally, standard medical electroencephalography devices use a conductive gel to facilitate the reading of the signals. Dry active sensor technology does not need such a gel and offer a more comfortable, easy-to-use alternative to the traditional gel electrode. The Brainband XL has two dry electrode contact points (1 reference) and a ear clip for the ear lobe (ground). The hardware used provides a sampling rate of up to 500 Hz in frequency bands ranging from delta waves (1-3Hz) up to mid-gamma (41-50Hz). A Fast Finite Fourier Transform is performed on the raw signal given the band powers which are then scaled using a proprietary algorithm to produce output which is only relative to each other.

2.3   Procedure

Pre-intervention: Each participant signed an informed consent after arrival at the test location and performed the experiment individually. The test leader sat in the same room as the participant behind a screen to collect the wireless signal of the Myndplay Brainband and be present if questions arose in the participant. As soon as the participant put on the Myndplay Brainband XL and the signal was received on the laptop of the test leader, the experiment began with a two minutes meditation to get calm and aware. Instructions were 'to sit up straight with your eyes closed and keep your mind empty'. Thereafter, the participants completed the Emotion Interference Task (EIT), which lasted 10 minutes. They were told that a series of pictures would be shown, and that each of the pictures should be carefully attended to, since a free-recall task would be performed later. This explicit information was given in order to assure they would actively attend to the pictures (primary task). During each picture the participant heard a tone and pressed a button to indicate if the tone had a high or low pitch. After the EIT, the participant completed a free recall of the pictures they saw in the EIT. The free recall task had two incentives: 1. It was meant to lead the participants into believing that this experiment was testing their memory instead of emotional interference, and 2. to increase actual attention allocated to the pictures, thus increasing the emotional effect of the stimuli.

Intervention: participants followed a 7-day yogic breathing and meditation training or a laughter yoga training.

Post-intervention: the participants completed the same tests as in pre-intervention. At the end of the experiment each participant was debriefed by explaining the goal of the study.

3   Results

Data of 45 participants that completed the study (20 laughter, 25 meditation training) was analysed with IBM SPSS Statistics 21. Mean reaction times (RTs) were collected for participant and entered into a 3x2x2 mixed-design analysis of variance (ANOVA) with Picture Valence (negative, positive, neutral) and Time (before or after intervention) as the within factors and Group (Meditation or Laughter Training) as the between factor. Incorrect responses and RTs greater or equal to 2000 msec were excluded from the analysis. Mauchly's Test of Sphericity indicated that the assumption of sphericity had not been violated for the repeated measure picture valence, $\chi 2(2) = 0.507, p = .776$, as well as for the interaction between time and picture valence, $\chi 2(2) = 3.743, p = .154$. Significant effects of Time, $F(2, 44) = 17.57, p < .0001$, and Picture Valence, $F(2, 44) = 5.05, p = .0016$, were found. Regardless of picture valence or the type of training participants received, the reaction times increased on the Emotion Interference Task after completing the training. The contrasts for the levels of Picture Valence show that the reaction times for the positive pictures differ significantly from the neutral pictures, but the negative pictures do not differ significantly from the neutral pictures. This indicates, that regardless of type of training or time of measurement, the participants generally attend longer to the positive pictures than the neutral or negative pictures. This was unexpected, since it was only expected for the experimental group and not for the control group. No significant interaction was found for the Time x Group interaction, indicating that both groups show the same increasing reaction times pattern before and after the training. The interaction between Time x Picture Valence was not significant as well, indicating there is no difference in reaction times for the picture valences when comparing before and after the trainings. A significant interaction was found for the Time x Picture Valence, $F(2, 44) = 7.70, p = .001$. Contrasts are significant both for positive versus neutral pictures over time, $F(2, 44) = 7.70, p < .001$, as well as for negative versus neutral pictures over time, $F(2, 44) = 7.70, p = .004$. Also, see Figures 1 and 2 for this pattern. This indicates that even though both groups generally increased their reaction times on all pictures valences after the training, compared to before the training, the increase for the neutral pictures is larger than those of the negative and positive pictures. This indicates that the participant in general can attend longer to all types of emotional stimuli after their training, but compared to neutral stimuli, they attend less longer to negative and positive stimuli, possibly due to the attentional deployment emotion regulation strategy. No significant interaction was found for the Time x Picture Valence x Group factors, indicating that the significant interaction between Time and Picture Valence does not differ between the groups. Finally, no significant main effect of Group was found, indicating that regardless of all other factors, the performances of both groups on the Emotion Interference Tasks do not differ significantly.

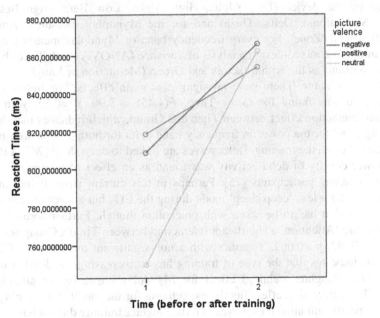

Fig. 1. Reaction Times Emotion Interference Task Laughter Group

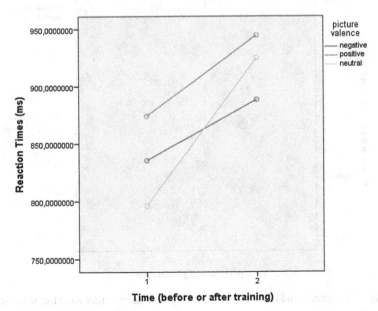

Fig. 2. Reaction Times Emotion Interference Task Meditation Group

The Myndplay processed EEG outcomes were analysed per frequency band that is outputted by the device (Low Alpha, High Alpha, Low Beta, High Beta, Low Gamma, Mid-gamma, Delta, Theta) and for the Myndplay measures 'Attention', 'Meditation' and 'Zone'. For every frequency band or Myndplay measure, data was entered into a 2x2 mixed-design analysis of variance (ANOVA) with Time (before or after intervention) as the within factors and Group (Meditation or Laughter Training) as the between factor. There were no significant main effects. For frequency band delta, a trend was found for factor Time, $F(1,45) = 3,90$, $p = 0.55$, with a non-significant interaction effect between Time and Group, which indicates that there is a decreasing trend for the power in frequency band delta for both groups after training, compared to before the training. Delta waves are linked to deep sleep [24]. A decrease in the power density of delta activity was found as an effect of taking caffeine, although in sleeping participants [25]. Perhaps in this current study it indicates that participants enter a less 'deep sleep' mode during the EIT, but a more attentive mode. This interpretation has to be taken with precaution though. Furthermore for Myndplay's measure 'Attention' a significant interaction between Time x Group was found, $F(1,45) = 10, 82$, $p = 0.002$. Together with a non-significant main effect of Time or Group, this indicates that the type of training has an increasing (meditation training) or decreasing (laughter training) effect for Myndplay's measure of attention, see Figure 4. This interaction effect fits the expectation for the meditation training which contained specific attentional exercises that the laughter training did not have.

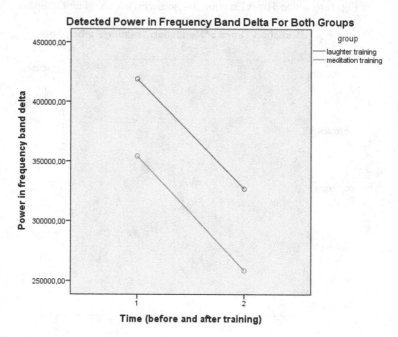

Fig. 3. Detected trend in power of frequency band delta before and after training

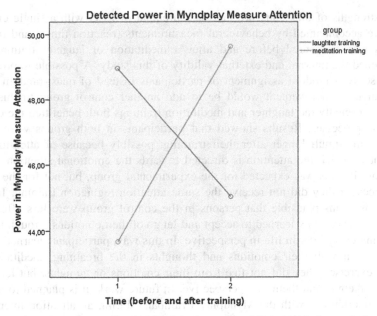

Fig. 4. Significant interaction effect in Myndplay's measure 'Attention' before and after training

4   Conclusions

The current study was designed to measure emotion regulation with a single dry electrode wireless BCI (Myndplay Brainband XL), during an emotion regulation computer task and comparing it with the behavioural performance of this task. The main objectives of this study were to (1) understand the correlates of emotion regulation as detected with the Myndplay Brainband XL (BCI with two dry electrodes) and (2) comparing these with the behavioural measures of emotion regulation on the Emotion Interference Task. The outcomes indicated that in the behavioural measures, unexpectedly, both experimental and control groups (meditation and laughter training) showed signs of being able to attend to all affective stimuli (positive, negative and neutral) longer after training which could be a sign of that the participants successfully learned to stay with their emotions and accept these. Although, compared to neutral stimuli, the increase in reaction times are larger for neutral stimuli than for positive and negative stimuli, indicating there are still emotion regulation strategies in use for negative and positive stimuli compared to neutral stimuli, such as attentional deployment. In the EEG measures a significant interaction was found for Time x Group for the Attention measure of Myndplay and a decreasing trend for factor Time in the delta frequency band of both groups after training, compared to before training. Overall these EEG outcomes point cautily in the direction of increased attention during the EIT after training. Together with the behavioural measures, it does seem there is an effect of training on emotion interference that can be detected in behavioural and EEG measures, although more research is needed to strengthen these results.

The strengths of this study are that measurement of EEG with a single electrode BCI were accompanied by behavioural measurements (reaction times) and that participants were measured before and after a meditation or laughter training. This strengthened the internal and external validity of this study. A possible improvement for this study is random assignment of participants instead of quasi-random assignment. Another improvement would be to add another control group to this study, since unexpectedly the laughter and meditation trainings both benefitted the emotion regulation processes. Results showed that participants in both groups were able to attend to all stimuli longer after their training, possibly because of attentional deployment in which the attention is directed towards the emotional situation and not away from it. This was expected for the experimental group, but not for the control group, because they did not receive the same attention regulation training. In retrospective, it seems plausible that persons in the control group were less affected by emotions, because they learned to accept and let go of their emotions through laughter and putting everything in life in perspective. In this way, participants learned to keep their attention with their emotions and thoughts in the breathing, meditation and laughter exercises; they did not flee from their emotions or thoughts, but learned to cope with them or put them into perspective. In future work, it is planned to measure emotion interference with the Myndplay Brainband during an attention interference task after viewing emotional film clips as done in [26].

References

1. Fernández-Aranda, F., Jiménez-Murcia, S., Santamaría, J.J., Gunnard, K., Soto, A., Kalapanidas, E., Penelo, E.: Video games as a complementary therapy tool in mental disorders: PlayMancer, a European multicentre study. Journal of Mental Health **21**(4), 364–374 (2012)
2. Baranowski, T., Buday, R., Thompson, D.I., Baranowski, J.: Playing for real: video games and stories for health-related behavior change. American Journal of Preventive Medicine **34**(1), 74–82 (2008)
3. Kato, P.M.: Video games in health care: Closing the gap. Review of General Psychology **14**(2), 113 (2010)
4. Susi, T., Johannesson, M., Backlund, P.: Serious games: An overview (2007)
5. Thompson, D., Baranowski, T., Buday, R., Baranowski, J., Thompson, V., Jago, R., Griffith, M.J.: Serious video games for health: how behavioral science guided the design of a Serious Video Game. Simulation & Gaming **41**(4), 587–606 (2010)
6. Examples of Companion and Care Robots. http://www.myjibo.com/, http://www.21stcenturyrobot.com/, http://www.bbc.com/news/technology-27709828, http://www.techunited.nl/en/amigo, http://www.care-o-bot.de/en/care-o-bot-3.html, http://www.parorobots.com/
7. Tao, J., Tan, T.: Affective computing: a review. In: Tao, J., Tan, T., Picard, R.W. (eds.) ACII 2005. LNCS, vol. 3784, pp. 981–995. Springer, Heidelberg (2005)
8. Garcia-Molina, G., Tsoneva, T., Nijholt, A.: Emotional brain–computer interfaces. International Journal of Autonomous and Adaptive Communications Systems **6**(1), 9–25 (2013)
9. Coan, J.A., Allen, J.J.B.: Frontal EEG asymmetry as a moderator and mediator of emotion. Biological Psychology **67**(1–2), 7–50 (2004)

10. Oathes, D.J., Ray, W.J., Yamasaki, A.S., Borkovec, T.D., Castonguay, L.G., Newman, M.G., Nitschke, J.: Worry, generalized anxiety disorder, and emotion: evidence from the EEG gamma band. Biological Psychological **79**, 165–170 (2008)
11. Muller, M.M., Keil, A., Gruber, T., Elbert, T.: Processing of affective pictures modulates right-hemispheric gamma band EEG activity. Clin. Neurophysiology **110**, 1913–1920 (1999)
12. de Man, J.: Analysing Emotional Video Using Consumer EEG Hardware. In: Kurosu, M. (ed.) HCI 2014, Part II. LNCS, vol. 8511, pp. 729–738. Springer, Heidelberg (2014)
13. Bos, D.O.: EEG-based emotion recognition. The Influence of Visual and Auditory Stimuli, 1–17 (2006)
14. Ohman, A., Soares, J.J.F.: On the automatic nature of phobic fear: Conditioned electrodermal responses to masked fear-relevant stimuli. Journal of Abnormal Psychology **102**, 121–132 (1993)
15. Soares, J.J.F., Ohman, A.: Preattentive processing, preparedness and phobias: Effects of instruction on conditioned electrodermal responses to masked and non-masked fear-relevant stimuli. Behaviour Research and Therapy **31**, 87–95 (1993)
16. Hansen, C.H., Hansen, R.D.: Finding the face in the crowd: An anger superiority effect. Journal of Personality and Social Psychology **54**, 917–924 (1988)
17. Derryberry, D., Rothbart, M.K.: Reactive and effortful processes in the organization of temperament. Development and Psychopathology **9**, 633–652 (1997)
18. Posner, M.I.: Chronometric explorations of mind. Erlbaum, Potomac (1978)
19. Buodo, G., Sarlo, M., Palomba, D.: Attentional Resources Measured by Reaction Times Highlight Differences Within Pleasant and Unpleasant. High Arousing Stimuli 1 **26**(2), 123–138 (2002)
20. Myndplay Brainband. http://myndplay.com/
21. Center for the Study of Emotion and Attention (CSEA-NIMH) (1999). The International Affective Picture System: Digitized photographsThe Center for Research in Psychophysiology, University of FloridaGainesville, FL
22. Swenson, D.: Ashtanga Yoga: The Practice Manual: An Illustrated Guide to Personal Practice (1999)
23. Laughter Yoga. http://www.laughteryoga.org
24. Amzica, F., Steriade, M.: Electrophysiological correlates of sleep delta waves. Electroencephalography and Clinical Neurophysiology **107**(2), 69–83 (1998)
25. Landolt, H.P., Dijk, D.J., Gaus, S.E., Borbély, A.A.: Caffeine reduces low-frequency delta activity in the human sleep EEG. Neuropsychopharmacology **12**(3), 229–238 (1995)
26. Dennis, T.A., Solomon, B.: Frontal EEG and emotion regulation: Electrocortical activity in response to emotional film clips is associated with reduced mood induction and attention interference effects. Biological Psychology **85**(3), 456–464 (2010)

Myndplay: Measuring Attention Regulation with Single Dry Electrode Brain Computer Interface

C. Natalie van der Wal[1](✉) and Mona Irrmischer[2]

[1] Department Computer Science, Vrije Universiteit, Amsterdam, The Netherlands
c.n.vander.wal@vu.nl
[2] Department Integrative Neurophysiology, Center for Neurogenomics and Cognitive Research, Amsterdam, The Netherlands
m.irrmischer@vu.nl

Abstract. Future applications for the detection of attention can be helped by the development and validation of single electrode brain computer interfaces that are small and user-friendly. The two objectives of this study were: to (1) understand the correlates of attention regulation as detected with the Myndplay Brainband XL and (2) compare these to existing neuroscientific literature. The Myndplay Brainband did succeed in highlighting the EEG frequency band Alpha as the main biomarker for sustained attention as measured with behavioral correlates. These results give an optimistic outlook to future applications that can detect mind wandering with single electrode brain computer interfaces.

Keywords: EEG · Brain computer interface · Myndplay brainband · Attention regulation · Mind wandering · Alpha power

1 Introduction

Wireless brain computer interfaces (BCI's) are a promising new development for intelligent applications, such as neuro-feedback for ADHD [1] or meditation training on your smartphone [2]. Advantages of wireless BCI's are the small size and wireless capability that make them easy to process in user-friendly interfaces. With possible future applications in mind, the current study was designed to validate the measurement of decreased attention with a single dry electrode wireless BCI: Myndplay Brainband XL. [3]. The two main objectives of this study are: (1) to test if it is possible to detect neural correlates of low attention and mind wandering with the Myndplay Brainband XL, and (2) compare these with biomarkers found in the existing neuro-scientific literature.

Everyone is familiar with mind wandering during some kind of task. Occasionally we are aware of it, at other times it happens unnoticed [4]. These are the moments when inner distraction is the most dangerous, as mind-wandering lacking meta-awareness often leads to mistakes [5], [6]. Especially when attention should be focused on a boring task, one is easily inclined to give in to subjectively more 'important' inner

---

C.N. van der Wal and M. Irrmischer–Shared first authorship: equal contributions.
Y. Guo et al. (Eds.): BIH 2015, LNAI 9250, pp. 192–201, 2015.
DOI: 10.1007/978-3-319-23344-4_19

strains of thought, as one might experience during a monotonous ride with the car in which one willingly (or unwillingly) ends up daydreaming. This interruption of attentional focus by task-unrelated thoughts is also known as "mind wandering", a state in which we spend nearly half of the waking time [7]. Intrusive thoughts, however, may also cause attention lapses in vital situations demanding sustained attention and potentially leading to hazardous conditions.

Investigating phenomena like attention regulation and mind-wandering experimentally has a problem: How would one measure an event which is happening inside a person, that has variable degrees of intensity and of which the participants themselves are often not fully aware? This is why in this study the attempt is drawn to use a wireless brain computer interface (BCI) to find neural correlates of attention regulation. Verifying the use of mobile devices can be important for the development of future online monitoring systems such as neuro-feedback or warning intelligent applications.

For this end, the study makes use of a body of research which demonstrated that mind-wandering is most prominent in situations of low cognitive control, like tiredness or boredom, as task irrelevant cognition or emotions can spontaneously interfere with the initial task at hand, for a review see: [8]. Even stronger, this interference is proportional to the difficulty of the task at hand [9]. Not surprising, highly routine and repetitive tasks are especially prone to mind wandering. The behavioral test used in this experiment makes use of exactly this phenomenon: The target presentation of the continuous temporal monitoring task is readily perceivable, if attended to. Every participant can obtain 100% accuracy, unless attention lapses cause misses in detection or delayed response times. The neural correlate that provided the strongest electrophysiological predictor of a lapse of attention with this task was an increased activity in the alpha band (8 –14 Hz) [10]. Therefore this frequency will be targeted as potential biomarker for low attention in this study. The rest of the paper is organized as follows: in Section 2, the methods and procedures of this experiment are explained. In Section 3, the results are shown and discussed in Section 4.

2   Experiment

In this Section the methods of the current study are described.

2.1   Participants

The 45 participants were healthy, Dutch or English speaking, students of the Vrije Universiteit Amsterdam and recruited from the campus through flyers. They were between 18–37 years old, with no history of neurological complications including ADHD, depression or substance abuse, and no previous experience with meditation. This study has been approved by the Scientific and Ethical Review Committee of the Faculty of Psychology and Education of the Vrije Universiteit, Amsterdam, Netherlands.

2.2   Measures and Materials

Design: as part of a bigger study, participants followed a meditation training or control group training for one week and their performance on multiple attention regulation tests was measured before and after training. The primary focus of the bigger study was to determine the effect of meditation on attention regulation. For the current study, only the performances of all participants on the Continuous Temporal Expectancy Task (CTET) before the training were analysed. In this way we would have a relative large sample to validate the measurements of the Myndplay Brainband XL on a task that can detect mind wandering.

Attention regulation is defined as the ability to focus the attention on a single object without mind wandering and to return quickly to this single object of attention when the mind does wander, and to maintain the focus even in a context which is repetitive, non-arousing and gives little external stimulation [11]. It is measured with behavioral indices, namely reaction times and lapses, as well as neural correlates, measured by the Myndplay Brainband XL.

Continuous Temporal Expectancy Task (CTET; [10]): participants completed a sustained attention task which was designed to measure lapses in attention such as mind wandering through the number and timing of errors the participants make. The task consists of a centrally presented stimulus (e.g. photos of different flowers), shown at regular intervals (700ms), resulting in a continuous stream of pictures. Participants are asked to monitor the temporal duration of each stimulus and to identify when a stimulus is presented longer (1400ms) than the standard duration. Longer durations occurred semi random (every 4th to 10th stimuli), resulting in a total of 80 targets. Identifying the target is unchallenging, but over time gets demanding when participants need to continuously perform these judgments over an extended period of time. This makes the CTET a measure of continuous deployment of attention to the time domain, i.e. time interval between events. The capability to monitor the time interval between two stimuli is increased when attention is actively oriented towards it [12], and decreases if top down attentional effort is diminishing. Lapses in identifying targets are therefore a direct correlate of decreased attention, a phenomenon seen in many everyday life applications. Different from conceptually similar attention tasks such as the go/no-go "Sustained attention to response task" (SART; [13]), every stimulus is a potential target and only discriminated by its longer presentation-time and not by perceptual features. This solves the problematic issue of target salience and automatically engaged exogenous attention interfering with the continuous attentional aspect which is targeted in this study [11]. Finally, it has been shown that performance declines after just 3 minutes of task performance, but there is no broader decline over blocks indicating that the CTET is a useful paradigm for tracing drifts in the level of attention over time [10]. Therefore in this study a single block of 7 continuous minutes was chosen to tap into long term sustained attention abilities of the participants. The actual stimuli were made of naturalistic pictures taken from the International Affective Picture System (IAPS; [14]), with pictures specifically chosen for their low arousal values. Additionally, the colour brightness, -saturation, and size of the scenes were standardized to decrease stimulus perception dependent differences.

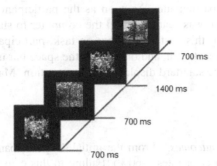

700 ms

1400 ms

700 ms

700 ms

Fig. 1. Example stimuli presentation sequence of the Continuous Temporal Expectancy Task (adapted from: [10])

Myndplay Brainband XL: EEG data in this research was collected with a commercially available non-invasive BCI headset: the NeuroSky Myndplay Brainband XL. [3]. The BCI uses a dry active sensor technology to read brain signals. Traditionally, standard medical electroencephalography devices use a conductive gel to facilitate the reading of the signals. Dry active sensor technology does not need such a gel and offers a more comfortable, easy-to-use alternative to the traditional gel electrode. The Brainband XL has two dry electrode contact points (1 reference) and an ear clip for the ear lobe (ground). The hardware used provides a sampling rate of up to 512 Hz to determine the power of the waves in frequency bands: Delta (1-3Hz), Theta (4-7Hz), Low Alpha (8-9HZ), High Alpha (10-12Hz), Low Beta (13-17Hz), High Beta (18-30Hz), Low Gamma (31-40Hz) and Mid-gamma (41-50Hz). Besides the power calculations of the waves in the frequency bands, it also reports a measurement for 'Attention'. A Fast Finite Fourier Transform is performed on the raw signal given the band powers which are then scaled using a proprietary algorithm to produce output which is only relative to each other.

Apparatus & Analysis: Data analysis was done using SPSS 21.0. For EEG waveband calculations, the original output of the Myndplay device was used. The reaction time averages were calculated as the time it took the participants to notice the target, from the moment it was displayed longer then the non-targets. The reaction time therefore includes both the time needed to notice and to react. Additionally, attention lapses were included in the reaction times in the form of time penalties, which were equal to the longest reaction time allowed (1400 ms). For example, if a person missed two targets, he would get two 'penalty' reaction times to account for the mistakes. This makes the resulting average reaction time a more comprehensive measure of actual performance, as misses are incorporated in the measure, diminishing the threat that bad performers in terms of lapses were identified as good performers due to possible faster average in the remaining responses.

2.3   Procedure

Each participant performed the experiment individually. The test leader sat behind a screen to collect the wireless signal of the Myndplay Brainband, and was present if questions arose in the participants. As soon as the participant put on the Myndplay Brainband XL, he or she was seated behind the computer to start the behavioral digitalized experiments. For this sustained attention task, participants were instructed to attend to the stimuli presentation, and only press the space bar upon noticing an object displayed longer than the standard display time (see section 'Materials').

3   Results

Behavioural and EEG outcomes: From the initial 45 participants, eight had to be excluded due to very high error rates (~60%). Failure to this extent, in such an easy task cannot be interpreted as low performance, but more likely as unwillingness to participate in a reasonable way. Inclusion of such data would flaw the analysis and therefore had to be excluded. (For completeness we ran the analysis without excluding these eight participants and the results were the same). Only participants who managed to successfully detect at least 70% of the target were included. This led to an average omission rate of 6, ranging from a minimum of 0 omissions in good performers to a maximum of 21 in bad performers. The overall performance of all participants was (average reaction time ± standard deviation): 795 ±102 ms, ranging from a minimum of 586 ms for the fastest responder to a maximum of 960 ms for the slowest responder.

The scaled EEG band powers used in this analysis were obtained by using the Myndplay output produced by a proprietary algorithm. The average values for all participants, per frequency band reported by the Myndplay Brainband are shown in table 1. There was no theoretical background for assuming other frequency bands to be relevant here (gamma, delta), and in the subsequent analysis these did not show any significant results, which is why they were not taken further into the results.

Table 1. Myndplay frequency bands output

Frequency Band	Low Alpha	High Alpha	Low Beta	High Beta	Attention
Average ± standard deviation	22894 ± 15081	17108 ± 8238	13259± 4389	18528 ± 11466	53 ± 7.7
Range	7111 to 81569	5633 to 37904	5279 to 21138	6986 to 52805	38 to 74

Correlation analysis: To determine whether there is a relation between reaction time and the alpha frequency bands output, correlation analyses were performed for both 'Low Alpha' and 'High Alpha', as outputted by the Myndplay Brainband. Both the power in the Low and High Alpha frequency bands are showing a positive correlation with reaction time (r_s =.371, p= 0.015 & r_s =.335, p= 0.026, respectively, one-tailed). This means that the power in the alpha frequency band increases as reaction time increases, i.e. subsequently performance gets worse (see Figure 2a & 2b).

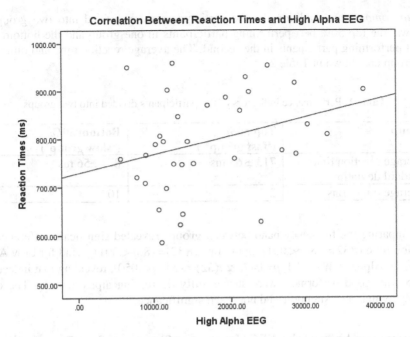

Fig. 2a. Correlation plots of participants' Low Alpha scores and reaction times, showing a positive relation between response time and EEG.

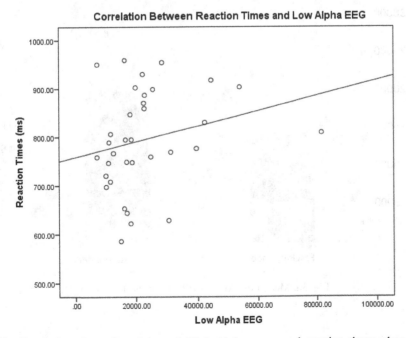

Fig. 2b. Correlation plots of participants' High Alpha scores and reaction times, showing a positive relation between response time and EEG.

Group comparison: Additionally, the participants were divided into two groups as follows: the top 50% best performing participants in one group and the bottom 50% worst performing participants in the second. The average reaction time and omissions per group are shown in Table 2.

Table 1. Performance indicators of the participants divided into two groups

Group	Top 50% ('fast group')	Bottom 50% ('slow group')
Average reaction time ± standard deviation	713 ± 63 ms	877 ±56 ms
Average omissions	2	10

Comparing the frequency band between groups revealed significant difference for reaction time ($t(32)$= -8, p<.001), omissions ($t(32)$= -8, p<.001),   and for Low Alpha and High Alpha ($t(32)$= -2.1, p=.047, & $t(32)$= -2.0, p=.050), revealing that indeed the group with good performers were successfully decreasing alpha activity. The other Myndplay marker 'Attention' did not reach significance.

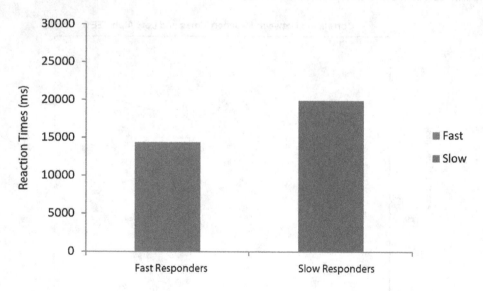

Fig. 3a. Mean Low Alpha for fast versus slow group

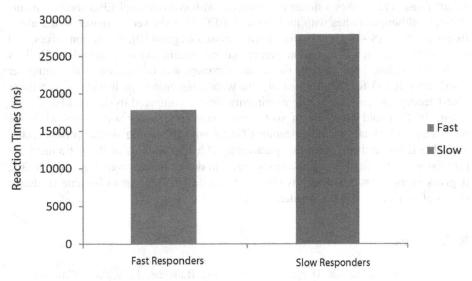

Fig. 3b. Mean High Alpha for fast versus slow group

4   Conclusion

The current study was designed to validate the measurement of decreased attention with a single dry electrode wireless BCI: the Myndplay Brainband XL. The two main objectives of this study were: (1) to test if it is possible to detect neural correlates of low attention and mind wandering with the Myndplay Brainband XL, and (2) compare these to biomarkers found in the existing neuro-scientific literature. Forty-five participants performed a task, called the CTET that can measure when participants wander their mind. Their behavioural performance, measured in reaction time and errors indicating mind wandering, were compared with their EEG measures produced by the Myndplay Brainband. The changes in the alpha frequency band (outputted as Low Alpha and High Alpha power by Myndplay Brainband) were targeted in the current study, based on findings in the neuro-scientific literature that indicates that mind-wandering influences the power in the alpha frequency band. Results show a positive correlation between the reaction time and power in the Low or High Alpha frequency band. When dividing the participants into two group: fast and slow responders, significant differences between the two groups were found for reaction time, errors and power in the Low and High Alpha frequency bands. This indicates that fast responders have less errors and a decrease in power in the Low and High Alpha frequency band. In accordance to earlier findings, e.g. [10], the Myndplay Brainband did succeed in highlighting the EEG frequency band alpha as the main biomarker for sustained attention as measured with behavioral correlates.

One of the strengths of this study is the comparison of behavioural measures (reaction times) with EEG measures of the Myndplay Brainband. A shortcoming of this study is the nontransparent algorithms used by Myndplay for the EEG waveforms calculations. This makes a direct comparison with conventional EEG measurements difficult, although studies with high density EEG also showed increases in the alpha frequency band (8–14 Hz) associated with missed targets [10], perception errors, and negatively correlated to temporal perceptual discrimination of 2 stimuli [15]. This study is therefore important for the future development of wireless brain computer interfaces (BCI's) for the problem of 'the wandering mind', as it introduces a more user-friendly and easy applicable monitoring device compared to standard EEG gear. Future BCI's could make use of such biomarkers to assist or warn users when the mind slips and attention is low. Amongst future work is: testing similar commercially available EEG hardware with this paradigm. The implications of these findings are promising for the field of applications that can detect mind wandering using BCI's, it gives an optimistic outlook, as single electrode BCI's seem to be able to detect lapses of performance and a wandering mind.

References

1. Lansbergen, M.M., van Dongen-Boomsma, M., Buitelaar, J.K., Slaats-Willemse, D.: ADHD and EEG-neurofeedback: a double-blind randomized placebo-controlled feasibility study. Journal of Neural Transmission 118(2), 275–284 (2011)
2. Carissoli, C., Villani, D., Riva, G.: Does a Meditation Protocol Supported by a Mobile Application Help People Reduce Stress? Suggestions from a Controlled Pragmatic Trial. Cyberpsychology, Behavior, and Social Networking 18(1), 46–53 (2015)
3. Myndplay Brainband. http://myndplay.com/
4. Schooler, J.W.: Re-representing consciousness: dissociations between experience and meta-consciousness. Trends in Cognitive Sciences 6(8), 339–344 (2002)
5. Weissman, D.H., Roberts, K.C., Visscher, K.M., Woldorff, M.G.: The neural bases of momentary lapses in attention. Nature Neuroscience 9(7), 971–978 (2006)
6. Christoff, K., Gordon, A.M., Smallwood, J., Smith, R., Schooler, J.W.: Experience sampling during fMRI reveals default network and executive system contributions to mind wandering. Proceedings of the National Academy of Sciences of the United States of America 106(21), 8719–8724 (2009)
7. Killingsworth, M.A., Gilbert, D.T.: A Wandering Mind Is an unhappy mind. Science (12), 79 (2010)
8. Mooneyham, B.W., Schooler, J.W.: The costs and benefits of mind-wandering: a review. Canadian Journal of Experimental Psychology/Revue Canadienne de Psychologie Expérimentale 67(1), 11 (2013)
9. McKiernan, K.A., Kaufman, J.N., Kucera-Thompson, J., Binder, J.R.: A parametric manipulation of factors affecting task-induced deactivation in functional neuroimaging. Journal of Cognitive Neuroscience 15(3), 394–408 (2003)
10. O'Connell, R.G., Dockree, P.M., Robertson, I.H., Bellgrove, M.A., Foxe, J.J., Kelly, S.P.: Uncovering the neural signature of lapsing attention: electrophysiological signals predict errors up to 20 s before they occur. The Journal of Neuroscience 29(26), 8604–8611 (2009)

11. Robertson, I.H., Garavan, H.: Vigilant attention. In: Gazzaniga, M.S. (ed.) The Cognitive Neurosciences, 3rd edn, pp. 631–640. MIT, Cambridge (2004)
12. Nobre, A., Correa, A., Coull, J.: The hazards of time. Curr. Opin. Neurobiol. **17**, 465–470 (2007)
13. Robertson, I.H., Manly, T., Andrade, J., Baddeley, B.T., Yiend, J.: Oops!: Performance correlates of everyday attentional failures in traumatic brain injured and normal subjects. Neuropsychologia **35**, 747–758 (1997)
14. Lang, P.J., Bradley, M.M., Cuthbert, B.N.: International affective picture system (IAPS): Technical manual and affective ratings (1999)
15. Baumgarten, T.J., Schnitzler, A., Lange, J.: Prestimulus Alpha Power Influences Tactile Temporal Perceptual Discrimination and Confidence in Decisions. Cerebral Cortex, p. bhu247 (2014)

Optimizing Performance of Non-Expert Users in Brain-Computer Interaction by Means of an Adaptive Performance Engine

André Ferreira, Athanasios Vourvopoulos[✉], and Sergi Bermúdez i Badia

Madeira-ITI, Universidade Da Madeira (UMa), 9000-390 Funchal, Madeira, Portugal
{andre.ferreira,athanasios.vourvopoulos,
sergi.bermudez}@m-iti.org

Abstract. Brain–Computer Interfaces (BCIs) are become increasingly more available at reduced costs and are being incorporated into immersive virtual environments and video games for serious applications. Most research in BCIs focused on signal processing techniques and has neglected the interaction aspect of BCIs. This has created an imbalance between BCI classification performance and online control quality of the BCI interaction. This results in user fatigue and loss of interest over time. In the health domain, BCIs provide a new way to overcome motor-related disabilities, promoting functional and structural plasticity in the brain. In order to exploit the advantages of BCIs in neurorehabilitation we need to maximize not only the classification performance of such systems but also engagement and the sense of competence of the user. Therefore, we argue that the primary goal should not be for users to be trained to successfully use a BCI system but to adapt the BCI interaction to each user in order to maximize the level of control on their actions, whatever their performance level is. To achieve this, we developed the Adaptive Performance Engine (APE) and tested with data from 20 naïve BCI users. APE can provide user specific performance improvements up to approx. 20% and we compare it with previous methods. Finally, we contribute with an open motor-imagery datasets with 2400 trials from naïve users.

Keywords: Brain-computer interfaces · Adaptive performance · Motor imagery

1 Introduction

Brain-computer interfaces (BCIs) are systems which aim at providing users with alternative communication channels. BCIs detect changes in brain signals and translate them into control commands [1]. Such systems utilize well defined underlying relationships between users' mental state and corresponding electrophysiological signals. In non-invasive BCI's, the use of electroencephalography (EEG) is commonly used for measuring brain activity. Currently, the 3 main techniques for user interaction and control include: (a) Steady State Visual Evoked Potentials (SSVEP), (b) P300 BCI and (c) Motor-Imagery (MI) or Event Related Synchronization/Desynchronization BCI. The use of these techniques in health are divided into two groups: (1) assistive

© Springer International Publishing Switzerland 2015
Y. Guo et al. (Eds.): BIH 2015, LNAI 9250, pp. 202–211, 2015.
DOI: 10.1007/978-3-319-23344-4_20

and (2) restorative [2]. An important distinction between the two strategies lies into the fact that assistive BCIs are based on "replacing" the damaged motor mechanisms, and restorative on "improving" existing motor function. Assistive BCI's can provide humans with motor impairments like tetraplegia, an alternative channel for communication or control by bypassing the affected corticospinal pathways. Examples include the control of functional electrical stimulation (FES) [3], orthotic devices [4], EEG wheelchair control [5], or BCI spelling devices [6]. On the other hand, restorative BCIs, target at mobilizing plastic changes of the brain in order to achieve reorganization of motor networks and enhance motor recovery [7]. MI training based on visuomotor imagination BCI is the most common type of BCI paradigm for motor function restoration. Results from previous studies have proven mental practice of action to be useful in MI-BCI [8], and have shown beneficial effects of MI practice during stroke recovery [9]. Overall, in neurorehabilitation, there is increasing evidence that technology-mediated therapy, like robotic and virtual reality based training [10], affects positively motor outcomes compared to standard rehabilitation techniques [11], [12]. So far, the combination of BCIs and virtual environments has gained popularity, and has been proven useful to train functional upper limb pointing movements [13], [14], although the use in clinical environment is limited [15] and hardly used outside laboratory environments [16]. This is mainly due to the fact that current BCI systems lack reliability and good performance in comparison with other types of interfaces [17]. As a result, there is no solid evidence on how BCI training needs to be designed and how improvements transfer to real life [18].

Additionally, within the last few years, the launch of low-cost EEG devices increased the user exposure and consequently the amount of BCI studies [19]. This rise in popularity led to the incorporation of BCIs as an alternative input to games, with early adoption by casual gamers. This has implications in terms of accessibility, level of control and BCI illiteracy [20]. Unfortunately, BCI training still requires long training periods resulting in user fatigue and low performance. This led Human-Computer Interaction researchers to work towards novel approaches to increase the communication bandwidth and quality of the BCI loop [21].

A comparative analysis on pure MI-BCI showed varying setups, algorithms and results [22]. Some studies report very different success rates using very similar approaches. Maximum performance scores of 89% were found on a bipolar montage (central electrodes over C3, Cz, C4) classified through a Bayes quadratic based on data from one healthy subject [23]. The lowest performance reached 61% with the same montage but using Linear Discriminant Analysis (LDA) tested with data from 2 healthy subjects [24]. Overall, all studies had very small training datasets with 2 users on average. In addition, most users had been previously trained on BCI use. Consequently, the risk of overfitting is very high, what results in poor predictive performance for the general user when it comes to actual online control. This imbalance between theoretical training performance and actual quality of the online control experienced by the general non-expert user suggests a shift in the interaction paradigm. Current MI-BCI interaction relies on time-constrained binary decisions – such as left vs. right arm motor imagery – and users undergo long, tiresome and complex periods of training so that EEG classification algorithms can reach *acceptable* performance rates. Here we propose to reverse the problem at hand and make MI-BCI interaction adaptive to the user, so that we can guarantee a _satisfactory_ performance rates by softening decisions – making them probabilistic and non-time-constrained – depending on our confidence on the user's EEG data. That is, we argue that the primary goal should not be for users to be trained to use a BCI system but to adapt the BCI interaction to each user in order to maximize the level of control on their actions. This will allow non-expert users and low-performing users to be able to increase their control, acceptance and motivation towards MI-BCI systems. To address the above limitations and improve MI-BCI based paradigms, with specific focus on motor rehabilitation, we have developed a MI-BCI Adaptive Performance Engine consisting on a Probabilistic Finite State Machine approach to increase sense of control as opposed to EEG classifier performance. Our system has been tested on 20 naïve healthy subjects, allowing for up to approx. 20% increase on performance when compared to standard EEG classification performance.

2   Methodology

2.1   Data Acquisition and Training Datasets

The BCI set up comprised 8 active electrodes equipped with a low-noise g.MOBIlab biosignal amplifier (gtec, Graz, Austria) and a 16-bit A/D converter (256 Hz). The spatial distribution of the electrodes followed the 10-20 system configuration [25] with the following electrodes over the sensory-motor areas: FC3, FC4, C3, C4, C5, C6, CP3, CP4. For all user data, a common spatial patterns filter was used for feature extraction, and LDA for the classification of MI from EEG data. The visual stimulation was based on the Graz-BCI paradigm [26] with a standard bars-and-arrows feedback on a binary (left vs. right) MI paradigm.

Experimental data consisted of a set of 20 EEG datasets consisting of 120 trials each, acquired from 20 healthy users (28 ± 4) performing standard MI training. Participants had no previous known neurological disorder and no previous experience in BCIs. Participants gave informed consent. Data from the MI datasets was processed in Matlab (MathWorks Inc., Massachusetts, US).

2.2   BCI - Adaptive Performance Engine

The BCI Adaptive Performance Engine (BCI-APE) is composed by 2 main components: (a) a Bayesian Inference Layer (BIL), simpler and more efficient as compared to other supervised learning techniques such as artificial neural networks, in order to formulate the input into a model, where we translate the continuous BCI classification data into probability. As for decision making, we made use of a (b) Finite State Machine (FSM) because of its efficiency and non-linear properties.

2.2.3   Bayesian Inference Layer
BIL works on top of the LDA EEG classifier, and is used to compute the likelihood of the classifier output for each MI class (left vs. right). This is done by modeling the data belonging to each class as a Gaussian distribution, where μ and σ indicate their

mean and standard deviation values $(MI_i(\mu, \sigma), i = [left, right])$. From it, we then compute the Likelihood of a specific LDA output belonging to each MI class with:

$$P(i|LDA\ output) = \frac{MI_i(\ LDA\ output, \mu_i, \sigma_i) * P_i}{\sum_j MI_j(\ LDA\ output, \mu_j, \sigma_j)} \tag{1}$$

Where P_i indicates the prior probability of action i (0.5 for left vs. right MI). μ and σ are updated at each iteration, taking into account all previous history of the user for the given i MI action. $LDA\ output$ indicates the output value of the LDA classifier.

2.2.2 Finite State Machine
Following the BIL, the likelihood of each MI classification forwarded into a FSM. The role of the FSM is to transform binary MI classifications – such as left vs. right – into evidence-based states (S_i). Is composed of 7 states, a neutral (S_0) and three for each MI class $(S_{1/-1}, S_{2/-2}, S_{3/-3})$. Each state has a transition threshold associated with it (w_1, w_2, w_3), and can only transition to one of the nearest neighbors or stay in the same state (see Fig. 1). As input, the FSM uses the difference of the posterior probabilities of left and right MI from eq. 1 and each state represents not only the class (negative and positive states represent left and right MI respectively), but also the confidence level associated to them (being $S_{3/-3}$ the most certain states).

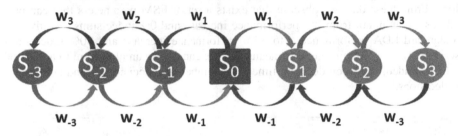

Fig. 1. State machine structure. S_0 represents the neutral state (indecision). The level of confidence of $S_{-3,3} > S_{-2,2} > S_{-1,1}$, and $W_{-3,-2,-1,1,2,3}$ are the state transition thresholds.

3   Results

3.1   Can Performance Be Improved by Means of the BCI-APE Approach?

In order to answer this, we used a dataset with MI training sessions of 15 naïve users to explore the parameter space of the aforementioned state machine thresholds (W_i) from 0 up to 0.3 on a 0.05 step, what resulted in 117649 FSM parameter combinations. For each combination we quantified the percentage of indecisions (S_0) and the correctness of decisions based on the remaining states. Results show that the FSM approach can increase performance over the original LDA classification (up to approx. 20%) at the expense of an increased amount of indecisions (Fig. 2). That is, less decisions are taken but with higher confidence.

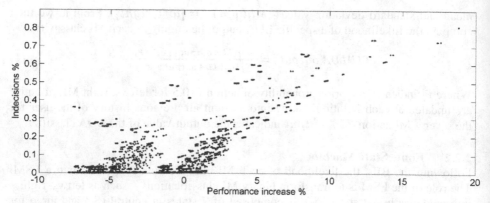

Fig. 2. Performance increase vs. indecisions percentage for the 117649 FSM parameter combinations on a MI dataset of 15 naïve users.

3.2   What Are the Tradeoffs of an Increased MI-BCI Performance?

Out of the above 117649 parameter combinations, we selected those combinations that provide the greater performance improvements with the minim number of indecisions. From these data we observe that exists a set of FSM parameters that can provide us a continuum from 0% performance increase and 0% indecisions – equivalent to standard LDA performance – to 20% performance increase and 80% indecisions (see Fig. 3). As consequence, this means that we can devise an algorithm to adjust the FSM to tradeoff between decision time – or number of indecisions – and confidence on decisions.

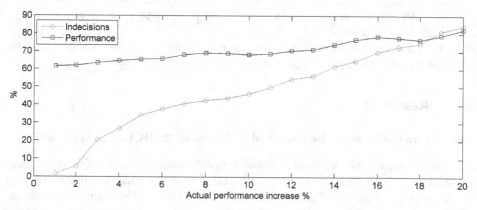

Fig. 3. Performance increase achieved with the FSM vs. indecisions.

3.3   Can APE Adjust Performance in Real Time?

Cross-referencing the best performing FSM thresholds values (W_i) with their resulting performance increase allows us to identify their relationship as illustrated in Fig. 4(a). This is a crucial step, due to only a few FSM weight combinations actually resulting in increased performance. It was also found that $W_{-1,-2,-3}$ should be kept 0 for maximal performance. That is, thresholds should be applied to transition from indecision to any decision state, but not to transition from any state to indecision. Further, it was also found that W_3 should be kept always constant at the highest value (0.3) and that W_1 increases with the overall performance. Interestingly, the evolution of W_2 with achieved performance shows that for low W_1 values – easy to transition from indecision to the lowest confidence level of decision – W_2 should be kept high whereas for high W_1 values – difficult to transition from indecision to the lowest confidence level of decision – W_2 should be low to facilitate the transition from low to mid confidence. We used a 3rd degree polynomial function to model how W_1 and W_2 change depending on the achieved performance increases (x) [Fig. 4(a)] (eq. 2):

$$W_1 = 114.42 * x^3 - 36.517 * x^2 + 4.7014 * x - 0.058208 \qquad (2)$$

$$W_2 = 87.662 * x^3 - 32.613 * x^2 + 2.4013 * x + 0.16366$$

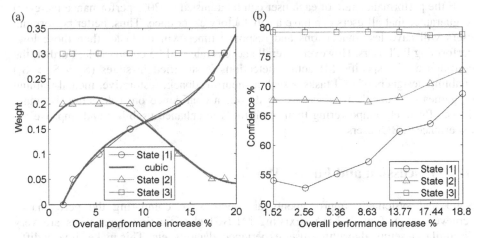

Fig. 4. (a) FSM threshold weight values vs. performance increase. (b) State confidence levels vs. performance increase.

Decisions taken at each state of the FSM have an associated performance level. That is, a MI detected based on S_3 should be more certain than in S_1. Fig. 4(b) illustrates the confidence level associated with each State ($S_3 > S_2 > S_1$), and how these change based on the FSM performance increase. In average, the confidence of S_3, S_2, and S_1 is 79.04% ± 0.25%, 68.76% ± 2.02% and 59.1% ± 5.88% respectively.

3.4   Evaluation of the Complete BCI-APE System

From the training data from 15 BCI naïve users we obtained the following results: Classification performance with standard LDA 58.70% ± 7.84%; Average improved performance of BCI-APE 70.46% ± 6.90%; Average maximum performance of BCI-APE 85.37% ± 10.09%; and indecisions of BCI-APE 48.25% ± 24.62%. Further, we implemented the complete BIL + FSM based on the above models of performance increase and we tested it against a dataset from 5 different BCI naïve users containing

5x120 MI trials. The previous results are confirmed with the test data: Classification performance with standard LDA 63.93% ± 6.28%; Average improved performance of BCI-APE 71.83% ± 6.64%; Average maximum performance of BCI-APE 88.37% ± 6.49%; and indecisions of BCI-APE 38.82% ± 19.60%.

4   Conclusions

BCI-APE was created from the need of ensuring satisfactory performances for non-expert and low-performing BCI users. BCI-APE provides a way to adapt performance accuracy on demand depending on the specific needs of users. By means of the presented model for online adjustment of the FSM transition weights (eq. 2), the accuracy of standard BCI classification algorithms such as LDA can be boosted up to 20% by clustering low confidence data as an indecision state S_0. Thus, for a specific BCI task a minimum acceptable performance rate can be stipulated, and by means of BCI-APE the performance rate of each user can be adjusted (0-20% performance increase) to guarantee that all users can have a satisfactory experience. Thus, better performing users will have less indecisions and response times will be faster than those low-performing BCI users. However, overall success rate will be comparable. Further, the confidence of a specific MI action detections is stratified in states ($S_3 > S_2 > S_1$) enabling designers of BCI tasks – such as neurofeedback, restorative, mental training or games – to decide what is best to do when confidence on a detection is small. Thus, effectively empowering them with tools to enhance usability and improve the experience of BCI users.

5   Discussion and Future Work

Solid and systematic improvements are seen when comparing the performance achieved by APE with LDA. Existing MI-BCI classification approaches are very dissimilar in setup, algorithms, user experience, datasets, etc. This makes it very difficult to assess if differences in performance arise from training, users, algorithms or setup. Thus, it results impossible to establish what the most appropriate MI-BCI classification approach is best. Nevertheless, when comparing BCI-APE to previous approaches – working on top of an LDA classifier and with naïve users – we observe a comparable performance with the best BCI classification algorithms (See Table 1). Further, we would expect even higher performances and lower indecisions if APE would be combined with more sophisticated and better performing classifiers than LDA.

The obtained results show interesting findings in several dimensions related with the use of adaptive performance for MI-BCI. Firstly, this system provides a real time performance (or task difficulty) adaptation. This is important in order to balance the difficulty in terms of user control and contribute positively on the interaction level by modulating user frustration/engagement related to a certain task. If used within a game, it can provide an enjoyable experience, but when used on a rehabilitation scenario, it is of a paramount importance. Many times, in rehabilitation exercises are not performed with the correct frequency or intensity because of lack of motivation and engagement of the patient. The BCI-APE approach can be used to tackle this issue, making the patient more prone to complete the rehabilitation task at hand.

Furthermore, we identified that there is an important trade-off for this performance increase, and it comes in the form of less decisions for the same time window. Thus, depending on the response time and accuracy required, with the help of the APE model we can adjust the performance levels in real-time. Finally, given the lack of availability of large MI datasets containing naïve subjects, we submitted our dataset (20 users x 120 trials) on PhysioNet[1] and made available under the Public Domain for dissemination and ex-change within the community.

Table 1. Classifier performance comparison, including APE. Adapted from Lotte et al.[22]

Protocol	Classification	Accuracy	electrodes / channels	# of subjects, trials/subject, training set, test set
on different EEG data	Gaussian SVM	86%	2 (C3, C4) at 128Hz	2, 1000 (500/side), 400 (200 random/side, remaining 600)
	LDA	61%		
	LDA	83.6%	6 –> 3 bipolar EEG channels	5 familiar with the Graz-BCI, 360, 240, remaining without artifacts
	Boosting wth MLP's	76.4%		
	LDA	80.6%		
	Boosting wth MLP's	80.4%		
	HMM	81.4% ± 12.8%	4 –> 2 bipolar EEG channels	4 (3 familiar and 1 naive), 880, some sessions where used to train other sessions
	LDA	72.4% ± 8.6%		
	MLP	85.97%	4 –> 2 bipolar EEG channels	3, 667±107, 60%, 20%
	FIR NN	87.4%		
	HMM	75.7%	2 bipolar EEG channels (C3, C4)	-, 160 (80/side), -, -
	HMM + SVM	78.15%		
	LDA	65% ± 3.3%	8 electrodes (FC3, FC4, C3, C4, C5, C6, CP3, CP4)	12, 120, -, -
	LDA + BCI-APE	up to 87.49 ± 7.13%	8 electrodes (FC3, FC4, C3, C4, C5, C6, CP3, CP4)	20, 120, 15 subjects, 5 subjects
on BCI competition 2003 data set III	Bayes quadratic integrated over time	89.3%	3 bipolar EEG channels (C3, Cz, C4)	1, 140, -, -
	BGN	83.57%	3 bipolar EEG channels (C3, Cz, C4)	1, 140, -, -
	MLP	84.29%		
	Bayes quadratic	82.86%		
	HMM	up to 77.5%	3 bipolar EEG channels (C3, Cz, C4)	1, 140, 100, 40
	Gaussian classifier	65.4%	3 bipolar EEG channels (C3, Cz, C4)	1, 140, 100, 40
	LDA	65.6%		
	Bayes quadratic	63.4%		
	Mahalanobis distance	63.1%		

As future work, new interaction paradigms need to be developed to embrace BCI-APE and to study its impact in users' perceived performance.

---

[1] http://physionet.org/

Acknowledgements. This work is supported by the European Commission through the RehabNet project - Neuroscience Based Interactive Systems for Motor Rehabilitation - EC (303891 RehabNet FP7-PEOPLE-2011-CIG), and by the Fundação para a Ciência e Tecnologia (Portuguese Foundation for Science and Technology) through SFRH/BD/97117/2013, and Projeto Estratégico - LA 9 - 2014-2015.

References

1. Wolpaw, J.R., Birbaumer, N., McFarland, D.J., Pfurtscheller, G., Vaughan, T.M.: Brain-computer interfaces for communication and control. Clin. Neurophysiol. Off. J. Int. Fed. Clin. Neurophysiol. **113**(6), 767–791 (2002)
2. Soekadar, S.R., Birbaumer, N., Cohen, L.G.: Brain–computer interfaces in the rehabilitation of stroke and neurotrauma. In: Kansaku, K., Cohen, L.G. (eds.) Systems Neuroscience and Rehabilitation, pp. 3–18. Springer Japan (2011)
3. Pfurtscheller, G., Müller-Putz, G.R., Pfurtscheller, J., Rupp, R.: EEG-Based Asynchronous BCI Controls Functional Electrical Stimulation in a Tetraplegic Patient. EURASIP J. Adv. Signal Process. **2005**(19), 628453 (2005)
4. Pfurtscheller, G., Guger, C., Müller, G., Krausz, G., Neuper, C.: Brain oscillations control hand orthosis in a tetraplegic. Neurosci. Lett. **292**(3), 211–214 (2000)
5. Carlson, T., Millan, J.D.R.: Brain-Controlled Wheelchairs: A Robotic Architecture. IEEE Robot. Autom. Mag. **20**(1), 65–73 (2013)
6. Birbaumer, N., Ghanayim, N., Hinterberger, T., Iversen, I., Kotchoubey, B., Kübler, A., Perelmouter, J., Taub, E., Flor, H.: A spelling device for the paralysed. Nature **398**(6725), 297–298 (1999)
7. Dobkin, B.H.: Brain-computer interface technology as a tool to augment plasticity and outcomes for neurological rehabilitation. J. Physiol. **579**(Pt 3), 637–642 (2007)
8. Prasad, G., Herman, P., Coyle, D., McDonough, S., Crosbie, J.: Applying a brain-computer interface to support motor imagery practice in people with stroke for upper limb recovery: a feasibility study. J. NeuroEngineering Rehabil. **7**(1), 60 (2010)
9. Pichiorri, F., Morone, G., Petti, M., Toppi, J., Pisotta, I., Molinari, M., Paolucci, S., Inghilleri, M., Astolfi, L., Cincotti, F., Mattia, D.: Brain-computer interface boosts motor imagery practice during stroke recovery. Ann. Neurol., February 2015
10. Cameirao, M.S., Badia, S.B.I., Oller, E.D., Verschure, P.F.: Neurorehabilitation using the virtual reality based Rehabilitation Gaming System: methodology, design, psychometrics, usability and validation. J. NeuroEngineering Rehabil. **7**, 48 (2010)
11. Laver, K., George, S., Thomas, S., Deutsch, J.E., Crotty, M.: Cochrane review: virtual reality for stroke rehabilitation. Eur. J. Phys. Rehabil. Med. **48**(3), 523–530 (2012)
12. Saposnik, G., Levin, M.: Outcome Research Canada (SORCan) Working Group, Virtual reality in stroke rehabilitation: a meta-analysis and implications for clinicians. Stroke J. Cereb. Circ. **42**(5), 1380–1386 (2011)
13. Cincotti, F., Pichiorri, F., Aricò, P., Aloise, F., Leotta, F., de Vico Fallani, F., Millán, J.D.R., Molinari, M., Mattia, D.: EEG-based Brain-Computer Interface to support post-stroke motor rehabilitation of the upper limb. In: Proc. Annu. Int. Conf. IEEE Eng. Med. Biol. Soc., vol. 2012, pp. 4112–4115 (2012)
14. Tung, S.W., Guan, C., Ang, K.K., Phua, K.S., Wang, C., Zhao, L., Teo, W.P., Chew, E.: Motor imagery BCI for upper limb stroke rehabilitation: An evaluation of the EEG recordings using coherence analysis. In: Proc. Annu. Int. Conf. IEEE Eng. Med. Biol. Soc., vol. 2013, pp. 261–264 (2013)

15. Ang, K.K., Guan, C.: Brain-Computer Interface in Stroke Rehabilitation. Journal of Computer Science and Engineering, June 2013
16. Lotte, F., Larrue, F., Mühl, C.: Flaws in current human training protocols for spontaneous Brain-Computer Interfaces: lessons learned from instructional design. Front. Hum. Neurosci., 7, September 2013
17. Lotte, F.: On the need for alternative feedback training approaches for BCI. presented at the Berlin Brain-Computer Interface Workshop (2012)
18. Silvoni, S., Ramos-Murguialday, A., Cavinato, M., Volpato, C., Cisotto, G., Turolla, A., Piccione, F., Birbaumer, N.: Brain-Computer Interface in Stroke: A Review of Progress. Clin. EEG Neurosci. 42(4), 245–252 (2011)
19. Marshall, D., Coyle, D., Wilson, S., Callaghan, M.: Games, Gameplay, and BCI: The State of the Art. IEEE Trans. Comput. Intell. AI Games 5(2), 82–99 (2013)
20. Allison, B.Z., Neuper, C.: Could anyone use a BCI? In: Tan, D.S., Nijholt, A. (eds.) Brain-Computer Interfaces, pp. 35–54. Springer, London (2010)
21. Tan, D., Nijholt, A.: Brain-computer interfaces and human-computer interaction. In: Tan, D.S., Nijholt, A. (eds.) Brain-Computer Interfaces, pp. 3–19. Springer, London (2010)
22. Lotte, F., Congedo, M., Lécuyer, A., Lamarche, F., Arnaldi, B.: A review of classification algorithms for EEG-based brain-computer interfaces. J. Neural Eng. 4(2), R1–R13 (2007)
23. Lemm, S., Schäfer, C., Curio, G.: BCI Competition 2003–Data set III: probabilistic modeling of sensorimotor mu rhythms for classification of imaginary hand movements. IEEE Trans. Biomed. Eng. 51(6), 1077–1080 (2004)
24. Garcia, G.N., Ebrahimi, T., Vesin, J.: Support vector EEG classification in the fourier and time-frequency correlation domains. In: Proceedings Of the First International IEEE EMBS Conference on Neural Engineering, pp. 591–594 (2003)
25. Report of the committee on methods of clinical examination in electroencephalography: 1957. Electroencephalogr. Clin. Neurophysiol., 10(2), 370–375, May 1958
26. Pfurtscheller, G., Neuper, C., Müller, G.R., Obermaier, B., Krausz, G., Schlögl, A., Scherer, R., Graimann, B., Keinrath, C., Skliris, D., Wörtz, M., Supp, G., Schrank, C.: Graz-BCI: state of the art and clinical applications. IEEE Trans. Neural Syst. Rehabil. Eng. Publ. IEEE Eng. Med Biol. Soc. 11(2), 177–180 (2003)

Movement Intention Detection
from Autocorrelation of EEG for BCI

Maitreyee Wairagkar$^{(\boxtimes)}$, Yoshikatsu Hayashi, and Slawomir Nasuto

University of Reading, Reading, UK
m.n.wairagkar@pgr.reading.ac.uk,
{y.hayashi,s.j.nasuto}@reading.ac.uk

Abstract. Movement intention detection is important for development of intuitive movement based Brain Computer Interfaces (BCI). Various complex oscillatory processes are involved in producing voluntary movement intention. In this paper, temporal dynamics of electroencephalography (EEG) associated with movement intention and execution were studied using autocorrelation. It was observed that the trend of decay of autocorrelation of EEG changes before and during the voluntary movement. A novel feature for movement intention detection was developed based on relaxation time of autocorrelation obtained by fitting exponential decay curve to the autocorrelation. This new single trial feature was used to classify voluntary finger tapping trials from resting state trials with peak accuracy of 76.7%. The performance of autocorrelation analysis was compared with Motor-Related Cortical Potentials (MRCP).

Keywords: Electroencephalography · Autocorrelation · Voluntary movement intention · Motor-Related Cortical Potentials · BCI

1 Introduction

Brain Computer Interface (BCI) provides a direct mode of interaction with computer and other external devices without utilising any motor pathways. Movement based BCI has a great potential for the use by patients with severe motor disabilities for operating robotic rehabilitation devices and for performing simple tasks intuitively. Thus, it is important to study underlying neural mechanisms of voluntary movement intention. This paper explores the fundamentals of movement intention by studying the temporal dynamics of EEG using novel feature.

Motor Related Cortical Potential (MRCP) and Event Related (De) synchronization (ERD/S) [1] are widely used movement correlates for movement detection from EEG. Although ERD can detect movement reliably [2,3] , it relies on the most responsive frequency band that vary from individual to individual. It is challenging to compute accurate instantaneous frequency distributions without compromising the temporal resolution and inducing delays. MRCP is a slow negative potential occurring from about 2s prior to the onset of the human voluntary movement [4], observed in frequencies lower than 1Hz [5]. Amplitude of MRCP

© Springer International Publishing Switzerland 2015
Y. Guo et al. (Eds.): BIH 2015, LNAI 9250, pp. 212–221, 2015.
DOI: 10.1007/978-3-319-23344-4_21

is extremely small (less than 8-10 μV)and hence, an average about 40-50 trials of repeated voluntary movements is used [5]. Single trial analysis is important for practical online BCI implementation. Although single trial variants of ERD [6] and MRCP [7,8] have been developed, these traditional principles are best suited for analysing averaged EEG over several trials [1], [9]. This creates a need for a robust feature for movement detection that can solely be obtained from a single trial and is independent of any particular frequency band besides providing different information related to movement. In this paper, we have proposed a new process related to motor command generation in the brain that compliments the information that is obtained from conventional ERD and MCRP processes. The new autocorrelation relaxation time feature was successfully used for classifying movement and resting state trials. The performance of the new single trial movement feature was compared rigorously with MRCP.

2   Materials and Methods

2.1   Experimental Procedure

Fourteen healthy participants (7 males and 7 females, ages 26±4) participated in this EEG experiment. Ethical approval for EEG experimentation on humans was obtained from School of Systems Engineering, University of Reading, UK. Written consent was obtained from all the participants. 12 participants were right handed and 2 were left handed. Participants did not have any previous experience of EEG experimentation.

This study was conducted to understand the neural correlates for detection of movement intention. A self-paced, asynchronous single finger tapping paradigm was developed to study EEG corresponding to motor command generation. Simple movement of index finger tapping was chosen as the task because it does not involve any complex hand gestures, directional reaching, grasping or trajectory planning.

The EEG experimental paradigm was developed in Simulink using the tools provided by BioSig toolbox [10]. A customised tapping device was developed using a programmable micro-controller for recording the finger taps from both index fingers. One channel of binary finger tapping signal was recorded simultaneously with EEG for each hand. EEG and finger tapping signals were co-registered using tools provided by TOBI framework [11].

Participants were seated on a chair with palms placed on the table in front. Index fingers of both the hands were placed in finger caps of the tapping device. A fixation cross was displayed on the screen for 2s at the beginning of each trial. It was followed by the instruction for right or left finger tap or resting state. A window of 10s was given to perform the instructed task voluntarily at the time of the participant's choice. Each trial was followed by a random break of 1s to 1.5s. 40 trials for each of the three conditions (right tap, left tap and rest)were recorded. 19 EEG channels in accordance with 10-20 international system were recorded using TruScan Deymed EEG amplifier. Ground and reference electrodes were placed at the centre and all the impedances were kept below 7kΩ.

2.2 EEG Pre-processing, Artefacts Removal and Segmentation

EEG was prepared for further analysis by performing pre-processing and arte-facts removal on all the EEG channels. DC offset was removed by subtracting the mean of each channel from the signal. All the EEG filtering was done using fourth order Butterworth filter. A notch filter at 50Hz was used to remove the power line noise. EEG was low-pass filtered with the cut-off frequency of 60Hz to eliminate high frequency noise.

Eye blinks and some movement artefacts were removed using Independent Component Analysis [12]. Independent components with artefacts were identified manually and were eliminated. EEG was segmented into time locked trials of length 6s by extracting 3s prior to the onset of finger tap and 3s after the onset of the finger tap. Channels F3, Fz, F4, C3, Cz, C4, P3, Pz and P4 over sensorimotor cortex were used for movement intention analysis.

2.3 Analysis of Movement-Related Cortical Potentials

MRCPs are obtained from lower frequencies by averaging several trials of EEG [5]. EEG was filtered between 0.1Hz to 0.5Hz to obtain movement related slow cortical potentials. Grand average MRCP was computed by averaging the all the trials from all the participants for nine channels. MRCP was also obtained for single trial.

2.4 Movement Intention Analysis Based on Exponential Decay of Autocorrelation

Autocorrelation gives an estimation of how EEG is related to itself over time. Previous research shows that the autocorrelation changes during movement [13,14]. Six virtual channels viz. F3-C3, Fz-Cz, F4-C4, C3-P3, Cz-Pz and C4-P4 were created using a longitudinal bipolar montage to enhance the movement related signal. EEG was band-pass filtered with cut-off frequencies 0.5Hz and 30Hz. Continuous autocorrelation was computed for each trial to determine the time development of the relaxation time of brain activity before, during and after the movement. Normalized autocorrelation was computed on 1s window shifted by 100ms from 6s trial.

Let the single window of a signal be represented by $A(t)$, the autocorrelation of $A(t)$ is defined by $C(\Delta t) = \langle A(t)A(t - \Delta t) \rangle$, where $\langle ... \rangle$ represents the average over time. At zero lag, the signal is perfectly correlated, giving $C(0) = \langle A^2 \rangle$, and as lag approaches infinity, the signal becomes completely uncorrelated, giving $C(\infty) = \langle A \rangle^2$. The trend of relaxation process of autocorrelation could be described by $C(t) = \langle A^2 \rangle e^{\frac{-t}{\tau}}$. Here, τ (decay constant) represents the relaxation time of autocorrelation. When autocorrelation is normalised, $\langle A^2 \rangle = 1$.

To get the relaxation time of autocorrelation by capturing the exponentially decaying trend of autocorrelation, the exponential decay curve $y = Ke^{\frac{-t}{\tau}}$ was fitted to the local maxima points of positive lags of autocorrelation of each window in the trial (see Fig. 1). The relaxation time τ was extracted as the

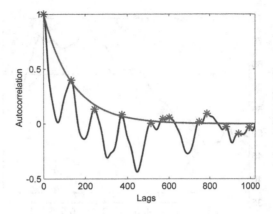

Fig. 1. Exponential curve fitting representing decay of autocorrelation (autocorrelation relaxation) for right finger tapping trial in F3-C3

feature at every 100ms in the 6s trial. The constant K was set to 1 as the autocorrelation was normalised. Changes in autocorrelation occurring during motor command generation were observed by studying the time progression of τ values.

2.5 Classification of Movement and Resting State Trials

Classification of MRCP Features. MRCP for each 6s trial was divided into 0.5s windows by shifting it by 100ms. Features for classification were obtained by averaging all the samples in each 0.5s window. Feature from first 0.5s window (-3s to -2.5s) was used as resting state feature for training the classifier. Linear discriminant analysis (LDA) classifier was trained for every window in the trial with two class corresponding features from all the trials. 10x10 cross-fold validation scheme was for this binary classification and percent classification accuracy was obtained. The threshold for classifier outcome was obtained from 95% confidence level ($p < 0.05$) for binary classification. The best performing channel was selected manually for each participant.

Classification of Autocorrelation Decay Features. Autocorrelation decay features (τ)were obtained for three classes viz. right finger tap, left finger tap and resting state. Classification was performed on each 1s window shifted by 100ms in 6s trial. LDA classifier was trained for each window with tap features and resting state features from the corresponding windows in all the trials. 10x10 cross-fold validation scheme was used for binary classification and percent classification accuracies were obtained. The classification accuracies for 6s trials for all the six virtual channels were plotted for all the participants (see Fig. 2).

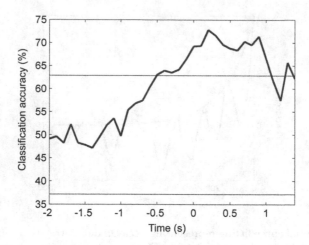

Fig. 2. Classification accuracies along the trial for left hand, participant 1 in virtual channel F3-C3. The horizontal line indicates statistical significance ($p < 0.05$)

3   Results

3.1   MRCP

Grand Average of MRCP. Grand average of MRCP is shown in the Fig. 3 for right and left hand trials. Negative potential peaks just before the actual onset of the finger tap in most of the channels. Thus, movement could be predicted from the grand average MRCP before its actual occurrence. The peak of the MRCP has small amplitude as expected.

Single Trial Classification of MRCP. (Table. 1) The classification accuracy crosses the threshold prior to the onset of movement indicating that movement could be predicted before its occurrence.

3.2   Decay of Autocorrelation Related to the Movement Intention

The trend of decay of autocorrelation which represents the relaxation time τ, changes during the voluntary movement. The τ value starts building-up prior to the onset of the motion. τ features in a single trial for right finger tap illustrated in Fig. 4 clearly show the increase prior to the movement onset. There is no such build-up of τ values in the resting state trials. Two sample t-tests were performed on finger tapping trials and resting state trials on six bipolar channels (with ($p < 0.05$)) to confirm the that difference around movement onset was statistically significant. Autocorrelation decays slower during intention and execution of movement and it decays faster otherwise. Table. 2 shows single trial classification results.

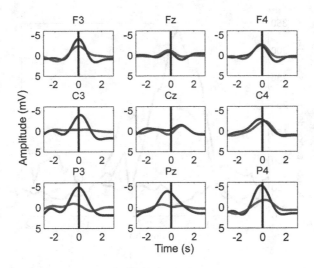

Fig. 3. Grand average of MRCP for nine channels. Red: right finger tapping, Blue: left finger tapping.

Table 1. Classification results for MRCP. Statistical significance ($p < 0.05$) is indicated in bold.

Participant ID	Right Finger Tapping			Left Finger Tapping		
	MRCP Classification Accuracy (%)	Channel	Time of threshold crossing (s)	MRCP Classification Accuracy (%)	Channel	Time of threshold crossing (s)
1	**70.25**	Pz	0.25	**68.63**	F3	-0.75
2	**64.08**	P3	0.30	**65.08**	P3	-0.80
3	**82.95**	C4	-1.60	**79.13**	P4	-1.60
4	**63.96**	P4	-1.35	**76.25**	P3	-1.75
5	**64.63**	F3	-0.90	**70.25**	F4	-0.50
6	**76.29**	P4	-0.90	**68.71**	F3	-0.20
7	**70.13**	F4	-0.95	**70.75**	Cz	-1.20
8	**66.25**	C4	-0.20	**77.50**	P4	-0.65
9	**66.25**	P3	-0.95	**64.63**	F4	-0.40
10	**70.38**	F3	-1.00	**67.75**	F3	-0.95
11	**64.50**	Cz	-1.20	59.88	C4	-
12	**67.13**	Fz	-1.10	**67.89**	Cz	0.60
13	**69.00**	C3	-1.95	**71.37**	P4	-0.90
14	**69.50**	F4	-0.25	**80.63**	C3	-0.25
Mean	68.95		-0.84	70.60		-0.72
SD	5.26		0.65	5.93		0.62

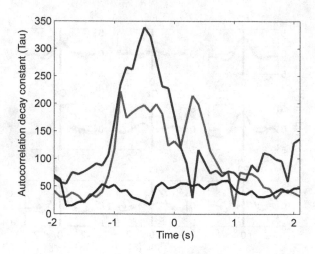

Fig. 4. Plot of changes in τ in virtual channel F3-C3 in a single trial for right finger tapping (red), left finger tapping (blue) and resting state (black) for participant 1

Table 2. Classification results for autocorrelation analysis. Statistical significance ($p <$ 0.05) is indicated in bold.

	Right Finger Tapping			Left Finger Tapping		
Participant ID	Autocorrelation Classification Accuracy (%)	Channel	Time of threshold crossing (s)	Autocorrelation Classification Accuracy (%)	Channel	Time of threshold crossing (s)
1	**71.00**	Cz-Pz	-0.20	**74.00**	C4-P4	-0.25
2	**76.70**	F4-C4	-0.25	**76.58**	F4-C4	-0.90
3	**65.75**	Fz-Cz	0.40	**66.63**	F4-C4	-0.60
4	**66.88**	F4-C4	-0.60	**69.00**	Fz-Cz	-0.55
5	**64.50**	F4-C4	-0.67	**65.38**	C3-P3	0.35
6	**69.57**	Cz-Pz	0.35	62.71	F4-C4	0.25
7	**69.25**	F3-C3	0.30	**72.50**	F3-C3	0.30
8	**66.13**	Cz-Pz	-0.20	63.00	F4-C4	0.10
9	**68.25**	F4-C4	-1.50	**65.38**	C3-P3	0.60
10	**64.38**	Cz-Pz	-0.75	58.88	Cz-Pz	-
11	**64.25**	F3-C3	0.35	**65.88**	F3-C3	0.10
12	**63.38**	C4-P4	0.75	**65.25**	C4-P4	-1.00
13	61.50	Fz-Cz	-	**65.38**	Fz-Cz	-1.00
14	**70.50**	C3-P3	0.40	**67.87**	C3-P3	-0.60
Mean	67.28		-0.12	67.03		-0.32
SD	3.92		0.63	4.71		0.57

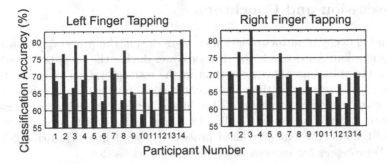

Fig. 5. Classification accuracies for autocorrelation and MRCP. Blue: Classification accuracies for Autocorrelation, Red: Classification accuracies for MRCP.

3.3   Comparison of Autocorrelation and MRCP Analysis

Classification Accuracies of Single Trial Autocorrelation and MRCP.
(Fig. 5) The classification accuracies of the newly proposed autocorrelation analysis method are very similar to the MRCP accuracies. The mean accuracies of autocorrelation and MRCP for right and left finger tapping are comparable (67.28% and 68.95% for right and 67.03% and 70.60% for left respectively). MRCP has higher maximum classification accuracy than autocorrelation but also greater SD (see Table 1 and 2).

Timings for Threshold Crossing of Classification Accuracies and Spatial Locations for Autocorrelation and MRCP. (Fig. 6) Like MRCP, autocorrelation analysis could also predict the movement before its onset in most cases and can be used for detection of movement intention. However, MRCP can predict the movement earlier than autocorrelation decay feature. Spatial locations of autocorrelation and MRCP analysis are different. Lateralization is not observed in both the cases. Different spatial locations suggests that the origin of the movement related information is distinct in both the cases.

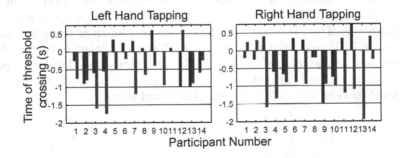

Fig. 6. Timings for threshold crossing for classification accuracies of autocorrelation and MRCP. Blue: Timings for autocorrelation, Red: Timings for MRCP.

4 Discussion and Conclusion

The trend in decay of autocorrelation changes during the process of motor command generation. Autocorrelation decays slower during the preparation and execution of the voluntary movement than in the resting state. Decay constant τ, representing the relaxation time of autocorrelation, proves to be a robust feature related to the movement detection. The change in τ is observed in the single trial and, hence, it could be used for online BCI applications. In this paper, we have validated the new movement related process to complement traditional MRCP and ERD processes for movement prediction and detection.

Classification accuracies for autocorrelation (mean 67% with peak accuracy of 76.7%) are similar to the mean accuracies (69.95% and 70.60%) obtained from single trial MRCP analysis. Similar results were obtained with modified single trial ERD analysis (paper currently in preparation). These classification accuracies are also comparable to the other work done for movement prediction and detection using MRCP and ERD [6–9], [15]. The accuracies obtained from the offline analysis using both the methods are not very high probably due to single finger tapping which involves fewer muscles. The results obtained from this task are purely based on movement intention and execution as opposed to other studies that used different full arm directional movements which can result to inclusion of cognitive information of trajectory planning and coordination.

This new feature is important because the information content on movement intention obtained from this feature is different from MRCP and ERD. This feature gives a third independent process related to movement in brain that complements MRCP and ERD. The advantage of this feature over ERD is that it does not require most responsive frequency band selection for individual and thus can be used more robustly. Unlike MRCP, this new feature provides information from a wide frequency range without eliminating any potential movement related information from higher frequencies. Further work on this autocorrelation feature could be used for modelling the oscillatory processes during movement intention generation in brain and thus understand methodically what happens in brain when an individual intends to move.

The single feature - autocorrelation relaxation time is capable of identifying the intention of movement from single trial with equally good performance as MRCP. Thus, this autocorrelation decay feature could be adapted for online BCI applications. The SD of autocorrelation was very small as compared to the SDs of other ERD and MRCP studies [7,8]. This is another indicator of the robustness and consistent performance of the autocorrelation. Thus, this paper introduces a new neural correlate of movement intention based on the temporal dynamics of EEG that is different from MRCP and ERD.

References

1. Pfurtscheller, G., Da Silva, F.L.: Event-related eeg/meg synchronization and desynchronization: basic principles. Clinical Neurophysiology 110(11), 1842–1857 (1999)
2. Blankertz, B., Losch, F., Krauledat, M., Dornhege, G., Curio, G., Muller, K.R.: The berlin brain-computer interface: accurate performance from first-session in bci-naive subjects. IEEE Transactions on Biomedical Engineering 55(10), 2452–2462 (2008)
3. Guger, C., Edlinger, G., Harkam, W., Niedermayer, I., Pfurtscheller, G.: How many people are able to operate an eeg-based brain-computer interface (bci)? IEEE Transactions on Neural Systems and Rehabilitation Engineering 11(2), 145–147 (2003)
4. Shibasaki, H., Hallett, M.: What is the bereitschaftspotential? Clinical Neurophysiology 117(11), 2341–2356 (2006)
5. Bai, O., Rathi, V., Lin, P., Huang, D., Battapady, H., Fei, D.Y., Schneider, L., Houdayer, E., Chen, X., Hallett, M.: Prediction of human voluntary movement before it occurs. Clinical Neurophysiology 122(2), 364–372 (2011)
6. López-Larraz, E., Montesano, L., Gil-Agudo, Á., Minguez, J.: Continuous decoding of movement intention of upper limb self-initiated analytic movements from premovement eeg correlates. Journal of Neuroengineering and Rehabilitation 11(1), 153 (2014)
7. Ibáñez, J., Serrano, J., Del Castillo, M., Monge-Pereira, E., Molina-Rueda, F., Alguacil-Diego, I., Pons, J.: Detection of the onset of upper-limb movements based on the combined analysis of changes in the sensorimotor rhythms and slow cortical potentials. Journal of Neural Engineering 11(5), 056009 (2014)
8. Xu, R., Jiang, N., Lin, C., Mrachacz-Kersting, N., Dremstrup, K., Farina, D.: Enhanced low-latency detection of motor intention from eeg for closed-loop brain-computer interface applications. IEEE Transactions on Biomedical Engineering 61(2), 288–296 (2014)
9. Lew, E.Y., Chavarriaga, R., Silvoni, S., Millán, J.D.R.: Single trial prediction of self-paced reaching directions from eeg signals. Frontiers in Neuroscience 8 (2014)
10. Vidaurre, C., Sander, T.H., Schlögl, A.: Biosig: the free and open source software library for biomedical signal processing. Computational Intelligence and Neuroscience (2011)
11. Breitwieser, C., Daly, I., Neuper, C., Muller-Putz, G.: Proposing a standardized protocol for raw biosignal transmission. IEEE Transactions on Biomedical Engineering 59(3), 852–859 (2012)
12. Jung, T.P., Makeig, S., Humphries, C., Lee, T.W., Mckeown, M.J., Iragui, V., Sejnowski, T.J.: Removing electroencephalographic artifacts by blind source separation. Psychophysiology 37(02), 163–178 (2000)
13. Hayashi, Y., Nagai, K., Ito, K., Nasuto, S.J., Loureiro, R.C., Harwin, W.S.: Analysis of eeg signal to detect motor command generation towards stroke rehabilitation. In: Converging Clinical and Engineering Research on Neurorehabilitation, pp. 569–573. Springer (2013)
14. Wairagkar, M., Daly, I., Hayashi, Y., Nauto, S.J.: Novel single trial movement classification based on temporal dynamics of eeg. In: Proceedings of 6th International Brain Computer Interface Conference, Gratz (2014)
15. Lew, E., Chavarriaga, R., Silvoni, S., Millán, J.D.R.: Detection of self-paced reaching movement intention from eeg signals. Front. Neuroeng. 5(13) (2012)

Time-Varying Parametric Modeling of ECoG for Syllable Decoding

Vasileios G. Kanas[1(✉)], Iosif Mporas[1,2], Griffin W. Milsap[3], Kyriakos N. Sgarbas[1], Nathan E. Crone[4], and Anastasios Bezerianos[5,6]

[1] Department of Electrical and Computer Engineering, University of Patras, Patras, Greece
vaskanas@upatras.gr
[2] Computer Informatics Engineering Department, TEI of Western Greece, Patras, Greece
[3] Department of Biomedical Engineering, Johns Hopkins University, Baltimore,
MD 21205, USA
[4] Department of Neurology, Johns Hopkins University, Baltimore, MD 21205, USA
[5] Department of Medical Physics, School of Medicine, University of Patras, Patras, Greece
[6] Singapore Institute for Neurotechnology, National University of Singapore,
Singapore, Singapore

Abstract. As a step toward developing neuroprostheses, the purpose of this study is to explore syllable decoding in a subject with implanted electrocorticographic (ECoG) recordings. For this study, we use ECoG signals recorded while a subject volunteered to perform a task in which the patient has been visually cued to speak isolated consonant-vowel syllables varying in their articulatory features. We propose a recursive estimation method to calculate the parametric model coefficients in each time instant and band power features from individual ECoG sites are extracted to decode the articulated syllables. Our findings may contribute to the development of brain machine interface (BMI) systems for syllable-level speech rehabilitation in handicapped individuals.

Keywords: Electrocorticography · Time-varying autoregressive model · Speech rehabilitation · Brain machine interface

1 Introduction

Speech decoding directly or indirectly from neural activity has been extensively studied for several years. The motivation of such approaches is, on the one hand, to examine the underlying functionality of the human brain during speech articulation and, on the other hand, to restore speech capabilities in severely handicapped individuals, such those suffering from disorders of consciousness [1]. Currently, electroencephalography (EEG), intracranial electrocorticography (ECoG), and intracortical microelectrode recordings have been utilized as neurophysiological recording techniques speech restoration.

Due to its non-invasive nature, EEG has been widely used in human studies to record brain activity for indirect control of spelling devices. In particular, approaches based on letter or word selection have been proposed utilizing specific brain waveforms, such as

© Springer International Publishing Switzerland 2015
Y. Guo et al. (Eds.): BIH 2015, LNAI 9250, pp. 222–231, 2015.
DOI: 10.1007/978-3-319-23344-4_22

slow cortical potentials [2-4], the P300 event-related potential (ERP) [5-8], steady state visual evoked potentials (SSVEP) [9, 10], sensorimotor rhythms (SMR) [11] and event-related (de)synchronization (ERD/ERS) [12-14]. On the contrary, relevant studies have focused on the challenging task of decoding continuous, dynamic speech, at various levels including formants [15], phonemes [12, 16], words [17], and even sentences [18]. However, speech decoding at the level of syllables has been paid less attention in the literature. In a related study [19], the authors support that speech rhythms can be identified using scalp-recorded EEG brain signals. In their work, Hilbert spectra are applied to decode three rhythmic structures for two different syllables (e.g. /ba/ and /ku/), without decoding the syllables itself. The aforementioned approaches for speech rehabilitation have been implemented using either time invariant parametric models, or filtering techniques, or short time spectral representations to isolate spectro-temporal features for classifying speech related events. In the current study, we focus on modeling the non-stationary ECoG brain activity proposing a time-varying autoregressive method (TVAR) for deriving ECoG spectral features to be used in the decoding of twelve individually spoken syllables.

Since brain signals are non-stationary containing numerous time-variant and transient components associated with underlying physiological activities, parametric modeling is usually used to study such data, as it allows the understanding of the underlying brain dynamics and mechanisms [20]. The main advantage of these models is that they avoid spectral leakage compared to non-parametric methods that use windowing like the fast Fourier transform. In addition, time-varying parametric models generate instantaneous estimates of power spectrum to perform non-stationary spectral analysis, providing higher time-frequency resolution [21]. While a detailed review of the methods for estimation and/or identification of time-varying model parameters can be found in [22], here, we describe briefly the main categories.

In general, the parametric methods can be categorized into three distinct classes according to the type of structure imposed on the evolution of the time-varying model parameters: 1) unstructured parameter evolution methods 2) stochastic parameter evolution methods and 3) deterministic parameter evolution methods (basis expansion modeling). The first category imposes no constraints to the parameter evolution, with short-time (sliding window based) and recursive approaches being prime methods within this class. However, the selection of the window size is vital to the performance of the sliding-window approach and, until now, there is no automatic method to guarantee an optimal selection. The second category of parameter estimation methods imposes stochastic smoothness constraints to the parameter evolution; approaches based on Kalman filtering constitute this category. Finally, the approaches belong to the third category aim to represent the evolution of the model parameters by deterministic functions belonging to known functional subspaces. In real-world applications, however, the model parameters of Kalman filtering or the basis functions in basis expansion modeling are often unknown and they have to be estimated or chosen by trial and error [23-25]. Therefore, the above categories are highly dependent on these parameters, and their performance will be considerably degraded when the parameters are inappropriately chosen. Motivated by this, in this paper, an adaptive unstructured approach, namely recursive maximum likelihood (RML), to estimate the parameters of the TVAR model is employed.

2   Materials and Methods

2.1   Neurosurgical Patient and Experimental Design

One patient with medically refractory epilepsy participated in this study. ECoG electrodes (Ad-Tech, Racine, Wisconsin; 2.3 mm exposed diameter, with 1 cm spacing between electrode centers) were surgically implanted on the brain surface (subdural, epipial) to map eloquent cortex and localize each patient's ictal onset zone prior to resective surgery. Electrode placement was dictated entirely by clinical needs. The patient provided informed consent to participate in the experimental protocol, which was approved by the Johns Hopkins Medicine Institutional Review Board. Localization of ECoG electrodes after surgery was performed using Bioimage by co-registration of pre-implantation volumetric MRI with post-implantation volumetric CT [26] (shown in Figure 1). An 8 x 8 grid of electrodes covered portions of the right frontal, temporal, and parietal lobes. There were no known auditory or language deficits in the patient.

The subject was seated in a hospital bed facing a laptop sitting on a hospital table in front of them. Textual representations of syllable stimuli (TAH, DEE, etc.) were presented to the patients using E-Prime software (Psychology Software Tools, Pittsburgh, PA) (Psychology Software Tools, Inc., Sharpsburg, Pennsylvania). The patients were instructed to speak each syllable as it was presented. The syllables were constructed from two vowels (/a/ and /i/) and six consonants (/p/, /b/, /t/, /d/, /g/, /k/) which varied by place of articulation and voiced or voiceless manner of articulation. Each of the 12 syllables was presented 10 times, for a total of 120 trials in each task. Between trials a fixation cross was displayed on the screen for 1,024 ms. Each syllable was presented for 3,072 ms.

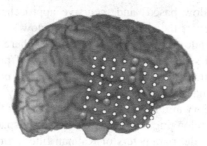

Fig. 1. ECoG electrode locations for the subject. The electrode grid covered areas of temporal, parietal, and frontal lobe in the right hemisphere that are analogues of language-processing areas in the left hemisphere. The blue circles represent the most informative channels as calculated by the Relief algorithm (see Section 4). The five best-ranked electrodes, are located in cortical areas relevant to the speech task.

2.2   ECoG Recording and Preprocessing

ECoG data was amplified and digitized with a sampling rate of 10 kHz using a 128-channel NeuroPort (Blackrock Microsystems, Salt Lake City, Utah). The ECoG recordings were pre-processed with a low-pass filter at 500 Hz before down-sampling to 1000 Hz. Notch filtering was also applied to attenuate interference at 60 Hz and its harmonics from power lines. Afterwards, the recorded signals were visually inspected for noise and motion artifacts. Noisy ECoG channels were excluded, leaving channels $M = 55$ (out of 64). To reduce the common-mode noise introduced by electrode referencing, the recordings were re-referenced by subtracting the mean of all commonly-referenced electrodes, a method called common average referencing (CAR) [27].

$$S_{CAR}^m[t] = S^m[t] - \frac{1}{M}\sum_{i=1}^{M} S^i[t]$$

S^n and S_{CAR}^n are the raw and CAR referenced ECoG amplitudes, respectively, on the m-th channel out of a total of M recorded channels. These re-referenced recordings were also normalized per-channel by subtracting the mean and dividing by the standard deviation of the time series [28]. Moreover, spoken responses were recorded in parallel through auxiliary Neuroport channels and a Zoom H2 recorder (Samson Technologies, Hauppauge, New York). Since the ECoG and speech recordings were time-aligned, the open source Praat software [29] was used by a speech technology engineer to manually segment each speech recording into intervals labeled as *silence*, *speech* and *noise*. The *noisy* intervals were excluded and the *speech* intervals, which corresponded to periods of articulation, were used for evaluating the classification models.

2.3   TVAR Model and RML Estimation Method

Parametric approaches assume the time series under analysis to be the output of a given linear mathematical model. As such, following the time-varying autoregressive moving average (TARMA) model, a nonstationary discrete-time signal $S_{CAR}^m[t]$ is modeled as follows:

$$S_{CAR}^m[t] = e[t] + \sum_{i=1}^{n_a} a_i[t]S_{CAR}^m[t-i] + \sum_{i=1}^{n_c} c_i[t]e[t-i]$$

with t designating discrete time, $e[t]$ an (unobservable) uncorrelated (white) noise sequence with zero mean and time-dependent variance $\sigma_e^2[t]$ that "generates" $S_{CAR}^m[t]$, and $a_i[t], c_i[t]$ the model's time-dependent AR and MA parameters, respectively. In this study, in order to estimate the TARMA model parameters at each time instant the recursive maximum likelihood is performed, imposing no structure on the signal dynamics. Here, the parameter n_c is set to zero. Let us denote the instantaneous parameter vector at time t as

$$\vartheta[t] = [\; a_1[t] \; \ldots \; a_{n_a}[t] \;]$$

then $\vartheta^t = [\; \vartheta^{Tr}[1] \; \ldots \; \vartheta^{Tr}[t] \;]$ stands for AR parameters up to time t, where transposition is designated by the superscript Tr. Based on the following exponentially weighted prediction error criterion,

$$\hat{\vartheta}[t] = \arg\min_{\vartheta[t]} \sum_{\tau=1}^{t} \lambda^{t-\tau} e^2[\tau, \vartheta^{\tau-1}]$$

$$e[t, \theta^{t-1}] = S_{CAR}^m[t] - \sum_{i=1}^{n_a} a_i[t-i] S_{CAR}^m[t-i]$$

the recursive estimation of $\vartheta[t]$ is accomplished via the RML method [30], with $\arg\min$ denoting the minimizing argument, and $e[t, \theta^{t-1}]$ the model's one-step-ahead prediction error (residual) made at time $t-i$ without knowing the parameter values at time t. The term $\lambda^{t-\tau}$, $\lambda \in (0,1)$ is a windowing function (known as the "forgetting factor") that assigns more weight to more recent errors. The AR parameter estimates are obtained using the RML method given as:

$$\hat{\vartheta}[t] = \hat{\vartheta}[t-1] + k \cdot \hat{e}[t \mid t-1]$$

$$\hat{e}[t \mid t-1] = S_{CAR}^m[t] - \xi^{Tr}[t] \cdot \hat{\vartheta}[t-1]$$

$$k[t] = \frac{P[t-1] \cdot \zeta[t]}{\lambda + \zeta^{Tr}[t] \cdot P[t-1] \cdot \zeta[t]}$$

$$P[t] = \frac{1}{\lambda}\left(P[t-1] - \frac{P[t-1] \cdot \zeta[t] \cdot \zeta^{Tr}[t] \cdot P[t-1]}{\lambda + \zeta^{Tr}[t] \cdot P[t-1] \cdot \zeta[t]} \right)$$

$$\zeta[t] + \hat{c}_1[t-1] \cdot \zeta[t-1] + \ldots + \hat{c}_{n_c}[t-n_c] \cdot \zeta[t-n_c] \triangleq \xi[t]$$

$$\xi[t] \triangleq [-S_{CAR}^m[t-1] \; \ldots \; -S_{CAR}^m[t-n_a] \; \vdots \; \hat{e}[t-1 \mid t-1] \; \ldots \; \hat{e}[t-n_c \mid t-n_c]]^{Tr}$$

$$\hat{e}[t \mid t] = S_{CAR}^m[t] - \xi^{Tr}[t] \cdot \hat{\vartheta}[t]$$

The term $S_{CAR}^m[t \mid t-1]$ indicates the one-step-ahead prediction of the signal at time t made at time t-1, and the term $\hat{e}[t \mid t-1]$ corresponds to the prediction error. For the initialization of the method it is customary to set $\hat{\vartheta}[0] = 0, P[0] = aI$ (where a stands for a large positive number and I the unity matrix), and the initial signal and a posteriori error values to zero. Finally, in order to reduce the effects of the arbitrary initial conditions, we applied the recursions on each signal in sequential phases (for instance a forward pass, a backward pass and a final forward pass). In general, the optimum order of the model can be considered as a tradeoff between maximizing the model's fitness while limiting its complexity. In this study, the model order and forgetting factor term are optimized for the recognition of task-related ECoG activity. Specifically, the model order and the forgetting factor are set to 30 and 0.999, accordingly.

3   Feature Extraction and Syllable Decoding

After estimating the model parameters, the power spectrum for each time instant t is defined as follows:

$$ PS = \left| \frac{1}{1 + \sum_{i=1}^{n_a} \hat{a}_i[t] e^{-j\omega T_s i}} \right|^2 \hat{\sigma}_e^2[t] $$

In this formulation, ω denotes frequency in rad/time unit, j the imaginary unit, and T_s the sampling period. Using the above model, we calculate spectral amplitudes between 0 and 200 Hz in 2 Hz bins. The calculated values (spectro-temporal ECoG features) in each time and frequency point result in a $T \times F$ representation, where T denotes the samples of the ECoG signal and F denotes the number of frequency bins. Afterwards, the spectro-temporal ECoG features were averaged across time and frequency (separately for each channel and trial). In the frequency domain, features were averaged over five ECoG frequency bands: delta-theta (1-7 Hz), alpha (8-12 Hz), beta (18-26 Hz), gamma (30-70 Hz) and high-gamma (80-200 Hz). Similar to our previous work [31], we used 80-200 Hz high gamma activity to track the spatiotemporal dynamics of word processing [32].

Finally, two classifiers were employed to decode the isolated spoken syllables from ECoG signals, namely the k-nearest neighbors kNN) algorithm [33], and support vector machines (SVM) using the sequential minimal optimization algorithm [34]. For the kNN classifier, the Euclidean distance was selected as the distance metric. After testing the parameter spacef, $k = 5$ was chosen empirically. Moreover, the Gaussian radial basis function (RBF) for the SVM kernel was used. Polynomial-based kernels were also considered, but their performance was considerably lower than the RBF kernel. The values of the soft margin parameter $C = 20.0$ and the scaling factor $\gamma = 1.0$ were found to offer optimal classification performance after a grid search at all combinations of $C = \{1.0, 5.0, 10.0, 20.0, 30.0\}$ and $\gamma = \{0.1, 0.5, 1.0, 2.0\}$. For evaluation of the results, a 5-fold cross validation was applied by utilizing 80% of the whole data to train our models and the remaining data for the test phase.

4   Experimental Results

Figure 2 depicts the syllable classification performance with respect to the individual frequency bands and the examined classifiers. The highest performance (19.5%) was achieved using features derived from the gamma band using the kNN classifier, while the second best accuracy (18.5%) achieved using the feature vector from the beta band and the SVM as classifier. These scores were higher than the chance decoding level (8.3%), as evaluated by a bootstrap resampling test with 20,000 repetitions while being statistically significant ($p < 0.009$). At this point, the Wilcoxon signed-rank test was applied to reject the null hypothesis that the two classifiers performed equally well on the whole collection of data sets. The null hypothesis was rejected with the Wilcoxon statistic being smaller than the critical value for a two-tailed test with a significance level of 0.05 ($p < 0.05$).

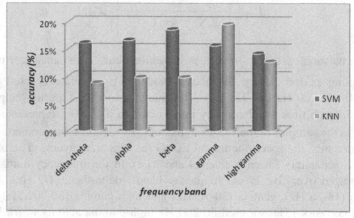

Fig. 2. Classification results (accuracy in percentage) for the subject with respect to each classifier and ECoG frequency band. Separately for each frequency band, each feature vector was used to drive our classification models.

In a further step, the Relief algorithm [35] is used to investigate the channels' significance in relationship to their location on the brain. The feature ranking scores depicted the discriminative ability of each ECoG feature for each frequency band. The feature ranking scores were averaged across each ECoG channel to reveal the most informative channels, as shown in Figure 1 (blue circles). The figure shows the five most informative ECoG sites (across frequency bands) for the syllable classification task. Our findings are consistent with the literature on the neuroanatomy of speech production. More specifically, the ECoG sites (as depicted in Figure 1) suggest that widely distributed areas, contain discriminative information for overtly articulated syllables [36]. Furthermore, many of the other most highly ranked electrodes (as calculated by the Relief algorithm) are located in cortical areas also relevant to speech processing, such as superior temporal gyrus (STG) and right ventral sensorimotor cortex (vSMC) [37-39].

5   Conclusion

Previous ECoG studies on speech decoding at levels including formants, phonemes, words, and even sentences. Here, the problem of syllable decoding from ECoG neural activity is studied. A recursive parameter estimation approach is proposed to calculate the time-varying autoregressive model coefficients and consequently to extract the power spectrum from the raw ECoG signal from different frequency bands. The highest accuracy achieved for classifying twelve overtly articulated syllables is 19.5%. In conclusion, to our best knowledge, this study has validated for the first time the feasibility of syllable classification from ECoG signals. Thus, no direct comparison with other approaches is feasible. Additional experiments on channel reduction, based on the information acquired from causal interactions between cortical areas, may also prove useful in the future.

Acknowledgement. This research has been co-financed by the European Union (European Social Fund, ESF) and Greek national funds through the Operational Program "Education and Lifelong Learning" of the National Strategic Reference Framework (NSRF); Research Funding Program: THALES. Investing in knowledge society through the European Social Fund.

References

1. Gosseries, O., Vanhaudenhuyse, A., Bruno, M.-A., Demertzi, A., Schnakers, C., Boly, M.M., et al.: Disorders of consciousness: coma, vegetative and minimally conscious states. In: States of Consciousness, pp. 29–55. Springer (2011)
2. Birbaumer, N., Ghanayim, N., Hinterberger, T., Iversen, I., Kotchoubey, B., Kübler, A., et al.: A spelling device for the paralysed. Nature **398**, 297–298 (1999)
3. Birbaumer, N., Hinterberger, T., Kubler, A., Neumann, N.: The thought-translation device (TTD): neurobehavioral mechanisms and clinical outcome. IEEE Transactions on Neural Systems and Rehabilitation Engineering **11**, 120–123 (2003)
4. Birbaumer, N., Kübler, A., Ghanayim, N., Hinterberger, T., Perelmouter, J., Kaiser, J., et al.: IV. Future Work. IEEE Transactions on rehabilitation Engineering **8**, 191 (2000)
5. Donchin, E., Spencer, K.M., Wijesinghe, R.: The mental prosthesis: assessing the speed of a P300-based brain-computer interface. IEEE Transactions on Rehabilitation Engineering **8**, 174–179 (2000)
6. Krusienski, D.J., Sellers, E.W., McFarland, D.J., Vaughan, T.M., Wolpaw, J.R.: Toward enhanced P300 speller performance. Journal of neuroscience methods **167**, 15–21 (2008)
7. Nijboer, F., Sellers, E., Mellinger, J., Jordan, M., Matuz, T., Furdea, A., et al.: A P300-based brain–computer interface for people with amyotrophic lateral sclerosis. Clinical neurophysiology **119**, 1909–1916 (2008)
8. Sellers, E.W., Donchin, E.: A P300-based brain–computer interface: initial tests by ALS patients. Clinical neurophysiology **117**, 538–548 (2006)
9. Cheng, M., Gao, X., Gao, S., Xu, D.: Design and implementation of a brain-computer interface with high transfer rates. IEEE Transactions on Biomedical Engineering **49**, 1181–1186 (2002)

10. Friman, O., Luth, T., Volosyak, I., Graser, A.: Spelling with steady-state visual evoked potentials. In: 3rd International IEEE/EMBS Conference on Neural Engineering, CNE 2007, pp. 354–357 (2007)
11. Vaughan, T.M., McFarland, D.J., Schalk, G., Sarnacki, W.A., Krusienski, D.J., Sellers, E.W., et al.: The wadsworth BCI research and development program: at home with BCI. IEEE Transactions on Neural Systems and Rehabilitation Engineering **14**, 229–233 (2006)
12. Pei, X., Barbour, D.L., Leuthardt, E.C., Schalk, G.: Decoding vowels and consonants in spoken and imagined words using electrocorticographic signals in humans. Journal of neural engineering **8**, 046028 (2011)
13. Neuper, C., Müller-Putz, G.R., Scherer, R., Pfurtscheller, G.: Motor imagery and EEG-based control of spelling devices and neuroprostheses. Progress in brain research **159**, 393–409 (2006)
14. Scherer, R., Muller, G., Neuper, C., Graimann, B., Pfurtscheller, G.: An asynchronously controlled EEG-based virtual keyboard: improvement of the spelling rate. IEEE Transactions on Biomedical Engineering **51**, 979–984 (2004)
15. Guenther, F.H., Brumberg, J.S., Wright, E.J., Nieto-Castanon, A., Tourville, J.A., Panko, M., et al.: A wireless brain-machine interface for real-time speech synthesis. PloS one **4**, e8218 (2009)
16. DaSalla, C.S., Kambara, H., Sato, M., Koike, Y.: Single-trial classification of vowel speech imagery using common spatial patterns. Neural Networks **22**, 1334–1339 (2009)
17. Kellis, S., Miller, K., Thomson, K., Brown, R., House, P., Greger, B.: Decoding spoken words using local field potentials recorded from the cortical surface. Journal of neural engineering **7**, 056007 (2010)
18. Zhang, D., Gong, E., Wu, W., Lin, J., Zhou, W., Hong, B.: Spoken sentences decoding based on intracranial high gamma response using dynamic time warping. In: Engineering in Medicine and Biology Society (EMBC), 2012 Annual International Conference of the IEEE, pp. 3292–3295 (2012)
19. Deng, S., Srinivasan, R., Lappas, T., D'Zmura, M.: EEG classification of imagined syllable rhythm using Hilbert spectrum methods. Journal of neural engineering **7**, 046006 (2010)
20. Bai, O., Nakamura, M., Ikeda, A., Shibasaki, H.: Nonlinear Markov process amplitude EEG model for nonlinear coupling interaction of spontaneous EEG. IEEE Transactions on Biomedical Engineering **47**, 1141–1146 (2000)
21. Ting, C.-M., Salleh, S.-H., Zainuddin, Z., Bahar, A.: Spectral estimation of nonstationary EEG using particle filtering with application to event-related desynchronization (ERD). IEEE Transactions on Biomedical Engineering **58**, 321–331 (2011)
22. Poulimenos, A., Fassois, S.: Parametric time-domain methods for non-stationary random vibration modelling and analysis—a critical survey and comparison. Mechanical Systems and Signal Processing **20**, 763–816 (2006)
23. Schlögl, A.: The electroencephalogram and the adaptive autoregressive model: theory and applications. Shaker, Germany (2000)
24. Khan, M.E., Dutt, D.N.: An expectation-maximization algorithm based Kalman smoother approach for event-related desynchronization (ERD) estimation from EEG. IEEE Transactions on Biomedical Engineering **54**, 1191–1198 (2007)
25. Niedzwiecki, M.: Identification of time-varying processes. Wiley, New York (2000)
26. Duncan, J.S., Papademetris, X., Yang, J., Jackowski, M., Zeng, X., Staib, L.H.: Geometric strategies for neuroanatomic analysis from MRI. Neuroimage **23**, S34–S45 (2004)

27. Goldman, D.: The clinical use of the "average" reference electrode in monopolar record-
    ing. Electroencephalography and clinical neurophysiology **2**, 209–212 (1950)
28. Pistohl, T., Schulze-Bonhage, A., Aertsen, A., Mehring, C., Ball, T.: Decoding natural
    grasp types from human ECoG. Neuroimage **59**, 248–260 (2012)
29. Boersma, P., Weenink, D.: Praat, a system for doing phonetics by computer (2001)
30. Ljung, L.: System identification: theory for the user. PTR Prentice Hall Information and
    System Sciences Series **198** (1987)
31. Kanas, V.G., Mporas, I., Benz, H.L., Sgarbas, K.N., Bezerianos, A., Crone, N.E.: Joint
    spatial-spectral feature space clustering for speech activity detection from ECoG signals.
    IEEE Transactions on Biomedical Engineering **61**, 1241–1250 (2014)
32. Canolty, R.T., Soltani, M., Dalal, S.S., Edwards, E., Dronkers, N.F., Nagarajan, S.S., et al.:
    Spatiotemporal dynamics of word processing in the human brain. Frontiers in neuroscience
    1, 185 (2007)
33. Aha, D.W., Kibler, D., Albert, M.K.: Instance-based learning algorithms. Machine learn-
    ing **6**, 37–66 (1991)
34. Platt, J.: Fast training of support vector machines using sequential minimal optimization.
    Advances in kernel methods—support vector learning **3** (1999)
35. Kononenko, I.: Estimating attributes: analysis and extensions of RELIEF. In: Bergadano, F.,
    De Raedt, L. (eds.) ECML 1994. LNCS, vol. 784, pp. 171–182. Springer, Heidelberg
    (1994)
36. Vigneau, M., Beaucousin, V., Herve, P.-Y., Duffau, H., Crivello, F., Houde, O., et al.:
    Meta-analyzing left hemisphere language areas: phonology, semantics, and sentence
    processing. Neuroimage **30**, 1414–1432 (2006)
37. Indefrey, P.: The spatial and temporal signatures of word production components: a critical
    update. Frontiers in psychology **2** (2011)
38. McGuire, P., Silbersweig, D., Frith, C.: Functional neuroanatomy of verbal self-
    monitoring. Brain **119**, 907–917 (1996)
39. Shergill, S.S., Brammer, M.J., Fukuda, R., Bullmore, E., Amaro, E., Murray, R.M., et al.:
    Modulation of activity in temporal cortex during generation of inner speech. Human brain
    mapping **16**, 219–227 (2002)

Classification Accuracy Improvement of Chromatic and High–Frequency Code–Modulated Visual Evoked Potential–Based BCI

Daiki Aminaka, Shoji Makino, and Tomasz M. Rutkowski[✉]

Life Science Center of TARA at University of Tsukuba,
1-1-1 Tennodai, Tsukuba, Ibaraki, Japan
tomek@bci-lab.info
http://bci-lab.info/

Abstract. We present results of a classification improvement approach for a code–modulated visual evoked potential (cVEP) based brain–computer interface (BCI) paradigm using four high–frequency flashing stimuli. Previously published research reports presented successful BCI applications of canonical correlation analysis (CCA) to steady–state visual evoked potential (SSVEP) BCIs. Our team already previously proposed the combined CCA and cVEP techniques' BCI paradigm. The currently reported study presents the further enhanced results using a support vector machine (SVM) method in application to the cVEP–based BCI.

Keywords: Brain–computer interfaces · ERP · cVEP · EEG classification

1 Introduction

A brain computer interface (BCI) is a technology that employs human neurophysiological signals for a direct brainwave–based communication of a brain with an external environment, and without dependence on any muscle or peripheral nervous system actions [9]. Particularly, in the case of patients suffering from locked–in–syndrome (LIS) [6], BCI could help them to communicate or complete various daily tasks (type letters or control their environments using Internet of Things technologies, etc). The BCI shall create a feasible option for amyotrophic lateral sclerosis (ALS) or coma patients to communicate with their families, friends or caretakers by using their trained, and properly classified, brainwaves only [9].

We propose to utilize and classify EEG brainwaves in response to a code–modulated visual evoked potential (cVEP). The cVEP is a natural response to the visual stimulus with specific code–modulated sequences [3,4]. It is generated by the brain when the user gazes at a light source which flashes with a specifically designed code–modulated sequence. The cVEP–based BCI belongs

© Springer International Publishing Switzerland 2015
Y. Guo et al. (Eds.): BIH 2015, LNAI 9250, pp. 232–241, 2015.
DOI: 10.1007/978-3-319-23344-4_23

to the stimulus–driven BCIs, which do not require a longer training comparing to the imagery–driven paradigms [9]. In this paper, we report EEG classification improvement results using a support vector machine (SVM) classification technique instead of the previously implemented by our team canonical correlation analysis (CCA) [1]. The CCA technique has been successfully used for classification of steady state visual evoked potentials (SSVEP) and it has resulted with good outcomes [5]. Next, a cVEP–based BCI has been also successfully implemented using the CCA [4]. We also successfully reproduced and further extended the above results based on a combination of cVEP stimuli and CCA–based classification [1]. A problem that raised in our previous research was related to a biased classification accuracy caused by the CCA towards some of the BCI commands. The training dataset for a classifier was created from cVEP responses when user gazed at the first flashing LED pattern (the top location in Figure 1). The remaining training patterns were created by applying circular shifts of the first LED cVEP's response. This method was responsible for the possible accuracy drop due to a limited number of training examples. We propose in this paper to use the linear SVM–based classifier to improve the cVEP BCI accuracy and to minimize any biases related to potential overfitting problems. In the presented project we also propose to use the RGB light–emitting diodes (LEDs) in order to evoke four types of cVEPs. We also utilize the higher flashing pattern carrier frequency of 40 Hz and compare our results with the classical setting of 30 Hz, of which refreshing rates has been chosen previously due to a limited computer display refresh rate of 60 Hz [2,3]. Moreover, we propose to use the chromatic green–blue stimulus [8] as a further extension in our project and we compare results with the classical monochromatic (white–black) set up.

From now on the paper is organized as follows. In the following section we describe materials and methods used in this study. Next, results and discussion are presented. Conclusions together with future research directions summarize the paper.

2   Materials and Methods

The experiments reported in this paper were performed in the Life Science Center of TARA, University of Tsukuba, Japan. All the details of the experimental procedures and the research targets of the cVEP–based BCI paradigm were explained in detail to the eight users, who agreed voluntarily to participate in the study. The electroencephalogram (EEG) cVEP–based BCI experiments were conducted in accordance with *The World Medical Association Declaration of Helsinki - Ethical Principles for Medical Research Involving Human Subjects*. The experimental procedures were approved and designed in agreement with the ethical committee guidelines of the Faculty of Engineering, Information and Systems at University of Tsukuba, Tsukuba, Japan (experimental permission no. 2013R7). The average age of the users was of 26.9 years old (standard deviation of 7.3 years old; seven males and one female).

2.1 Experimental Settings

The visual stimuli were presented to the subjects as flashing light sources delivered via the RGB LEDs. The LEDs were driven by square waves generated from *ARDUINO UNO* micro–controller board. The generator program was written by our team using *C*–language.

In this study we used $m-sequence$ encoded flashing patterns [4] to create four commands of the cVEP–based BCI paradigm. The $m-sequence$ is a binary pseudorandom string, which could be generated using the following equation,

$$x(n) = x(n-p) \oplus x(n-q), \quad (p > q), \tag{1}$$

where $x(n)$ is the nth element of the $m-sequence$ obtained by the exclusive–or (XOR) operation, denoted by $\oplus$ in the equation (1), using the two preceding elements indicated by their positions $(n-p)$ and $(n-q)$ in the string. In this project $p = 5$ and $q = 2$ were chosen. An initial binary sequence was decided, to create the final $m-sequence$, used in the equation (1), as follows,

$$\mathbf{x}_{initial} = [0, 1, 0, 0, 1]. \tag{2}$$

Finally, the 31 bits long sequence was generated based on the above initial sequence as in equation (2). The interesting $m-sequence$ feature, which is very useful for the cVEP–based BCI paradigm design, is an unique autocorrelation function. The autocorrelation function has only a single peak at the period sample value. If the $m-sequence$ period is N, the autocorrelation function will result with values equal to 1 at $0, N, 2N, \ldots$ and $1/N$ otherwise. It is also possible to introduce a circular shift of the $m-sequence$ denoted by τ, to create a set of $m-sequences$ with shifted autocorrelation functions, respectively. In this study, the shifted time length has been defined as $\tau = 7$ bits. Three additional sequences have been generated using shifting by $\tau, 2\cdot\tau$ and $3\cdot\tau$, respectively. During the online cVEP–based BCI experiments the four LEDs continued to flash simultaneously using the time–shifted $m-sequences$ as explained above. Two $m-sequence$ period lengths have been tested to investigate whether they would affect the cVEP responses. The conventional full $m-sequence$ period of $T = 516.7$ ms (based on the conventional computer screen refresh rate of 60 Hz and referred as "a low flashing frequency") and the proposed $T = 387.5$ ms (referred as "a high flashing frequency") have been tested. The experimental setting with four LEDs arranged on a square frame in front of a user is depicted in Figure 1.

2.2 EEG Signal Acquisition and Processing

During the cVEP–based BCI EEG experiments the users were seated on a comfortable chair in front of the LEDs (see Figure 1). The distance between user's eyes and LEDs was about $30 \sim 50$ cm (chosen by the users for a comfortable view of the all LEDs). An ambient light was moderate as in a typical office. The EEG signals were captured with a portable EEG amplifier system g.USBamp from g.tec Medical Engineering, Austria. Eight active wet (gel–based) g.LADYbird

EEG electrodes were connected to the head locations of O1, O2, PO3, PO4, P1, P2, Oz, and POz as in an extended 10/10 international system [9]. These positions were decided due to the visual cortex responses targeting experiment [9]. The ground electrode was attached to head location FPz and the reference to a left earlobe, respectively. Details of the EEG experimental set up are summarized in Table 1. An EEG sampling frequency was set to 512 Hz and a notch 4th–order Butterworth IIR filter at rejection band of $48 \sim 52$ Hz was applied to remove power line interference of 50 Hz. Moreover, the 8th–order Butterworth IIR band–pass filter at a pass band of $5 \sim 100$ Hz was applied to remove eye blinks and a high frequency noise.

The OpenViBE [7] bio–signal data acquisition and processing environment, together with in–house programmed in Python extensions, were applied to realize the online cVEP–based BCI paradigm. To avoid user's eye blinks, each trial to gaze at a single LED was separated with pauses during the experimental sessions (see details in Table 1).

In the data acquisition phase, first the users gazed at top flashing LED in order to collect classifier training dataset, as instructed verbally by the experimenter conducting the study. Twenty $m - sequence$ cycles were repeated in a single EEG capturing session. In short, sixty cVEPs to $m - sequence$ based flashing were collected for each direction in a single experimental trial. The triggers indicating the onsets of the $m - sequences$ were sent to g.USBamp directly from the *ARDUINO UNO* micro–controller to mark the beginning of each cVEP response. Finally, four experiment types were conducted for each user:

- the conventional low frequency;
- the proposed high frequency;
- and for the each above setting two color modes using white–black and green–blue flashing LEDs were applied.

Table 1. EEG experiment condition details

Number of users	8
Single session length	8 and 11 seconds
$m - sequence$ lengths T	516.7 and 387.5 ms
Shifts τ	116.7 and 87.5 ms
EEG recording system	g.USBamp by g.tec with active wet (gel–based) g.LADYbird electrodes
Number of EEG channels	8
Electrode locations	O1, O2, Po3, Po4, P1, P2, Oz and Poz
Reference electrode	Left earlobe
Ground electrode	FPz
Notch filter	Butterworth 4th order with a rejection band of $48 \sim 52$ Hz
Band–pass filter	Butterworth 8th order with a passband of $5 \sim 100$ Hz

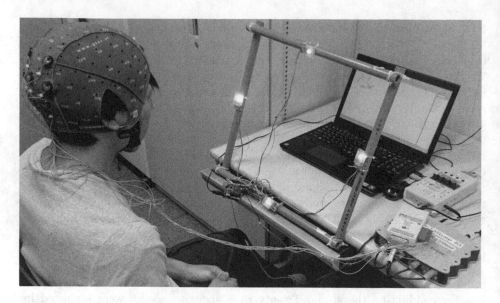

Fig. 1. The user is seating in front of a frame with four visual stimulation RGB LEDs used in this study. The top, bottom, right and left LEDs' flickering patterns correspond to the four different $m - sequences$, respectively. On the right side of the photograph there is the g.USBamp together with g.TRIGbox from g.tec Medical Engineering, Austria, used in the study. A laptop computer runs OpenViBE EEG data acquisition and processing environment.

2.3 The cVEP Responses Classification

A linear SVM classifier was used in this study to compare accuracies with a previously successfully implemented CCA method [1]. In the training session a single dataset containing the cVEP responses to top flashing LED was used. The remaining three cVEP responses were constructed by shifting the top LED response by τ, $2 \cdot \tau$ and $3 \cdot \tau$, where $\tau \in \{87.5 \text{ ms}, 116.7 \text{ ms}\}$. We used the linear SVM classifier to identify the intended by the user flickering patterns. The cVEP response processing and classification steps were as follows:

1. For the classifier training purposes, capturing the EEG cVEP $\mathbf{y}_1$ obtained in response to the first $m - sequence$. A procedure to construct the remaining training patterns $\mathbf{y}_i, (i = 2, 3, 4)$, based on the original recorded $\mathbf{y}_1$ sequence was as follows:

$$y_i(t) = y_1(t - (i - 1)\tau), \tag{3}$$

   where τ was the circular shift and t indicated a position in the sequence.
2. Averaging the captured j cVEPs as $y_{i,j}(t)$ for each target i separately. The averaged responses $\bar{\mathbf{y}}_i$ were used for the linear SVM classifier training. In this study, there were $N = 60$ training datasets and the number of averaged

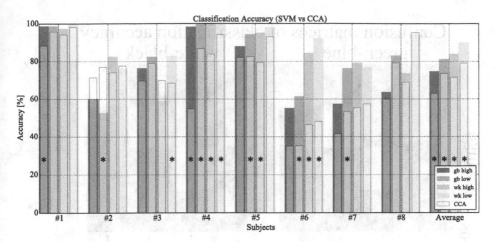

Fig. 2. The results of CCA and linear SVM–based classification from the eight users participating in the study presented in form of bar plots. There are four results depicted for each user, namely from the green–blue high frequency (green); green–blue conventional low frequency (light green); white–black higher frequency (orange); white–black lower frequency cases (yellow) bar color, respectively. The solid–colored bars resulted from the linear SVM application. On the other hand, the transparent bars, which overlap the solid counterparts, resulted from the CCA–based classification. The pairwise Wilcoxon–test was applied for each classification pair and the significant differences ($p < 0.05$) have been denoted with "*." The theoretical chance level of the experiments was of 25%.

responses was $M = 5$. The averaging procedure was as follows,

$$\bar{\mathbf{y}}_{i,l} = \frac{1}{M} \sum_{j=l}^{l+M-1} \mathbf{y}_{i,j}, \tag{4}$$

where $l = 1, 2, \ldots, N - M + 1$ was the dataset number.

3. For the test classification purposes, cVEPs from remaining BCI sessions, not used for the classifier training, to four target $m - sequences$ were applied.

The results of the above procedure applied to data recorded in the cVEP–based BCI experiments with eight users are discussed in the following section.

3   Results

Results of the conducted cVEP–based BCI paradigm experiments are summarized in form of accuracies as bar plots in Figure 2 and confusion matrices in Figures 3 and 4, respectively. The accuracies were calculated in experiments using the proposed green–blue high frequency, the green–blue conventional low frequency, the white–black high frequency, and the low frequency white–black

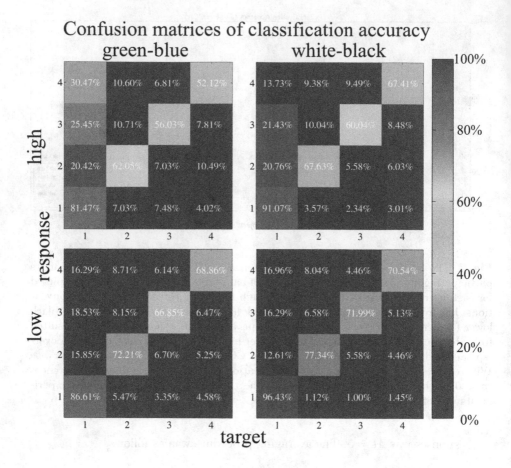

Fig. 3. The results of the linear CCA–based classification from the eight users depicted as confusion matrices from all the settings tested within the project.

flashing settings, respectively. The theoretical chance level of all experiments was of 25%.

To investigate command accuracy effects of cVEPs (discriminability) of CCA versus the proposed linear SVM, we applied pairwise Wilcoxon–test for a statistical analysis of median difference significances, because all the accuracy results were not normally distributed. The results of the classifiers' comparisons are presented in Table 2.

Next, a test was applied for a pairwise comparison of CCA versus linear SVM classification BCI accuracies for each frequency and color setting separately. The results presented in Figure 2 show individual bar plots, of which several have resulted with statistically significant differences (denoted with "∗"). Moreover, the averaged accuracies of all subjects resulted all with statistically significant

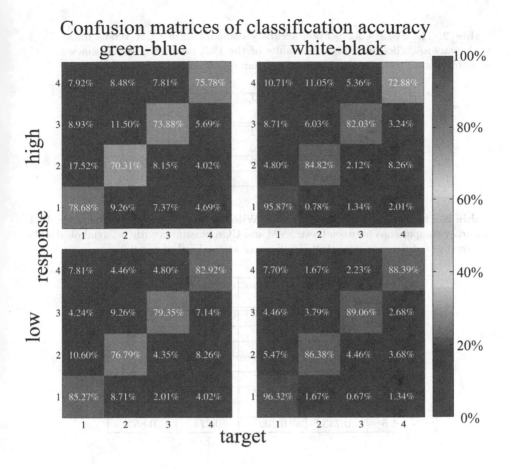

Fig. 4. The results of the linear SVM–based classification accuracy from the eight BCI experiments depicted as confusion matrices from all the settings tested within the project.

differences and the proposed linear SVM–based classification scored higher comparing to the CCA.

The accuracies for each command separately have been calculated and depicted in form of confusion matrices visualized in Figures 3 and 4, for CCA and linear SVM classifiers respectively. The results presented in the above mentioned figures have shown, that the biased classification result problem previously observed in the CCA case (command *one* scored relatively higher in the previous study) [1] was solved by the linear SVM application. Additionally, pairwise Wilcoxon–tests have been conducted for all users separately to evaluate differences of CCA versus linear SVM classifier accuracies in the four experimental settings. The resulting *p*–values are arranged in Table 3. There were significant

Table 2. The cVEP classification accuracy comparison of CCA versus linear SVM with pairwise Wilcoxon–test. The results of the BCI accuracy comparison with "*" symbols denote statistically significant median differences at a level of $p < 0.05$

Command number	green–blue high	white–black high	green–blue low	white–black low
#1	0.664	0.122	0.940	0.870
#2	0.327	0.005*	0.326	0.115
#3	0.067	0.009*	0.242	0.032*
#4	0.015*	0.385	0.036*	0.040*

Table 3. The cVEP classification pairwise Wilcoxon–test's p–value results of the BCI accuracy comparisons between linear SVM and CCA classifiers with "*" symbols denoting medians' difference statistical significances at the level of $p < 0.05$

User number	green–blue high	white–black high	green–blue low	white–black low
#1	0.028*	0.730	0.093	0.200
#2	0.122	0.167	0.001*	0.983
#3	0.245	0.194	0.522	0.034*
#4	0.000*	0.001*	0.001*	0.026*
#5	0.154	0.019*	0.014*	0.066
#6	0.105	0.006*	0.037*	0.006*
#7	0.082	0.060	0.036*	0.169
#8	0.743	0.702	0.374	0.853

pairwise differences observed in which the proposed linear SVM–based cVEP BCI classification accuracies scored also higher comparing to the CCA.

4   Conclusions

The proposed LED flashing and cVEP response–based BCI paradigm with the chromatic green–blue stimuli has been discussed in this paper. We tested linear SVM classification–based method in comparison to the classical already CCA case. The majority of the obtained linear SVM accuracy results scored higher comparing to CCA outcomes. We also resolved biased accuracies problem observed previously by our group in case of the CCA. The linear SVM classification cVEP BCI accuracies scored very good for all commands comparing to the CCA. The conducted experiments to verify the feasibility of the proposed method confirmed successfully our research hypothesis based on the results obtained from the eight healthy users. All of the cVEP–based BCI accuracies resulted well above the theoretical chance levels and there were also 100% outcomes observed.

For the future research, we plan to investigate upper limits of the stimulus frequency and an optimization of the $m - sequences$ in order to create the even better code–modulated visual BCI.

Acknowledgments. We would like to thank Dr. Andrzej Cichocki from RIKEN Brain Science Institute, Japan, and Dr. Koichi Mori from Research Institute of National Rehabilitation Center for Persons with Disabilities, Japan, for very stimulating discussions about chromatic SSVEP–based BCI which stimulated this project. This research was supported in part by the Strategic Information and Communications R&D Promotion Program (SCOPE) no. 121803027 of The Ministry of Internal Affairs and Communication in Japan, and by KAKENHI, the Japan Society for the Promotion of Science, grant no. 24243062.

References

1. Aminaka, D., Makino, S., Rutkowski, T.M.: Chromatic and high-requency cVEP-based BCI paradigm. In: 2015 37th Annual International Conference of the IEEE Engineering in Medicine and Biology Society (EMBC). IEEE Engineering in Medicine and Biology Society, August 25–29, 2015. (accepted, in press)
2. Bakardjian, H., Tanaka, T., Cichocki, A.: Optimization of SSVEP brain responses with application to eight-command brain-computer interface. Neuroscience Letters **469**(1), 34–38 (2010)
3. Bin, G., Gao, X., Wang, Y., Hong, B., Gao, S.: VEP-based brain-computer interfaces: time, frequency, and code modulations [Research Frontier]. IEEE Computational Intelligence Magazine **4**(4), 22–26 (2009)
4. Bin, G., Gao, X., Wang, Y., Li, Y., Hong, B., Gao, S.: A high-speed BCI based on code modulation VEP. Journal of Neural Engineering **8**(2), 025015 (2011)
5. Bin, G., Gao, X., Yan, Z., Hong, B., Gao, S.: An online multi-channel SSVEP-based brain-computer interface using a canonical correlation analysis method. Journal of Neural Engineering **6**(4), 046002 (2009)
6. Plum, F., Posner, J.B.: The Diagnosis of Stupor and Coma. FA Davis, Philadelphia (1966)
7. Renard, Y., Lotte, F., Gibert, G., Congedo, M., Maby, E., Delannoy, V., Bertrand, O., Lécuyer, A.: Openvibe: an open-source software platform to design, test, and use brain-computer interfaces in real and virtual environments. Presence: Teleoperators and Virtual Environments **19**(1), 35–53 (2010)
8. Sakurada, T., Kawase, T., Komatsu, T., Kansaku, K.: Use of high-frequency visual stimuli above the critical flicker frequency in a SSVEP-based BMI. Clinical Neurophysiology (2014). (online first)
9. Wolpaw, J., Wolpaw, E.W. (eds.): Brain-Computer Interfaces: Principles and Practice. Oxford University Press (2012)

Investigation of Familiarity Effects
in Music-Emotion Recognition Based on EEG

Nattapong Thammasan[✉], Koichi Moriyama, Ken-ichi Fukui,
and Masayuki Numao

Institute of Scientific and Industrial Research (ISIR),
Osaka University, Ibaraki-shi 567-0047, Japan
{nattapong,koichi,fukui,numao}@ai.sanken.osaka-u.ac.jp

Abstract. Familiarity is a crucial subjectivity issue in music perception
that is often overlooked in neural correlate studies and emotion recognition research. We investigated the effects of familiarity to brain activity
based on electroencephalogram (EEG). In our research, we focused on
self-reporting and continuous annotation based on the hypothesis that
the emotional state in music experiencing is subjective and changes over
time. Our methodology allowed subjects to select 16 MIDI songs, comprised of 8 familiar and 8 unfamiliar songs. We found evidence that
music familiarity induces changes in power spectral density and brain
functional connectivity. Furthermore, the empirical results suggest that
using songs with low familiarity could slightly enhance EEG-based emotion classification performance with fractal dimension or power spectral
density feature extraction algorithms and support vector machine, multi-
layer perceptron or C4.5 classifiers. Therefore, unfamiliar songs would be
most appropriate for emotion recognition system construction.

Keywords: Electroencephalogram · Music · Emotion · Familiarity

1 Introduction

Emotion recognition based on electroencephalogram (EEG) has become a highly
active research area recently due to the prominence of EEG with high temporal resolution but low cost. Based on EEG correlates study of emotion [1,2],
a great number of efforts to estimate human emotional state have been proposed [3]. Emotion recognition in music listening is an appealing research since
music experience is pleasurable and music itself is a fascinating material to evoke
emotion because of its capability to elicit strong and wide variety of emotions [4].

Nevertheless, the subjective nature of human perception still challenges music
emotion detection. Music perception is influenced by various factors such as cul-
tural background, age, gender, training, and also familiarity with the music [5].
Listening to familiar music involves expectation and prediction based on prior
knowledge to musical excerpts, therefore memory factor could play an important role in the emotional state during music listening. Previously, the number

© Springer International Publishing Switzerland 2015
Y. Guo et al. (Eds.): BIH 2015, LNAI 9250, pp. 242–251, 2015.
DOI: 10.1007/978-3-319-23344-4_24

of works investigating the relevance between music familiarity and brain activity was relatively limited. Plailly *et al.* [6] reported that the feeling of familiarity of music and odors induced activation in the deep left hemisphere while the feeling of unfamiliarity induces activation in the right hemisphere. They concluded that there were neural processes, likely related to the semantic memory system, specific to feeling of familiarity regardless of the types of triggering stimuli. Daltrozzo *et al.* [7] observed larger negativity of event-related potentials (ERP) along fronto-central scalp and suggested that the feeling of familiarity could involve in conceptual processing. Pereira *et al.* [8] reported the role of familiarity in the brain correlates of music appreciation using fMRI, and suggested that familiarity is related to limbic, paralimbic and reward circuitries. Bosch *et al.* [9] found the evidence from electrodermal activity that some levels of expectation and predictability caused by familiarity play an important role in the experience of emotional arousal in response to music.

To the best of our knowledge, however, the effect of music background knowledge to music perception based on EEG spectra and connectivity has not been explored. Furthermore, the previous researches to identify emotion in music listening based on EEG data often neglected familiarity effects. If music familiarity actually has influence to brainwave, ignoring familiarity would degrade EEG-based emotion recognition. In this study, we investigate neural correlates of music familiarity by focusing on the disparity of brain responses at the different levels of familiarity. In addition, we constructed a model to classify emotion in response to music in a similar way to traditional approaches but taking familiarity into account. To construct an emotion recognition model, we relied on the continuous emotion self-annotation approach based on the assumption that emotion in music experiencing is subjective and changes over time.

One of the typical model to describe human emotion systematically is the arousal-valance emotion space proposed by Russell [10]. This *dimensional* approach defines emotion as corresponding points in two-dimensional space. The valence is represented as a horizontal axis indicating positivity of emotion while arousal is denoted as a vertical axis that indicates activation of emotions. We employed the arousal-valence emotion model to represent emotions in this research as it enables continuous acquiring emotional feedback in response to music and it has been found to be a simple but highly reliable model in recent works [3,5].

2 Research Methodology

2.1 Experimental Procedure

Fifteen male subjects between 22 and 30 years of age (mean = 25.52, SD = 2.14) participated in the study. All subjects were students of Osaka University and had minimal formal musical education. Each subject selected 16 music clips from 40-song MIDI library and indicated the familiarity to each selected song on a scale from 1 to 6. Eight of selected songs were the songs that he/she felt familiar with (i.e., 4–6 familiar levels), and the others were the unfamiliar songs (i.e., 1–3 familiar levels). Our data collection software also provides a function to play short(<10s) samples of songs to facilitate familiarity indication.

To avoid cognitive load in emotion reporting, annotating was conducted separately from music listening and brainwave recording. The selected songs were presented as sounds synthesized by the Java Sound API's MIDI package[1]. The song sequences opened with 4 familiar songs which were then followed by 4 unfamiliar songs, 4 familiar songs, and 4 unfamiliar songs. The songs were two minutes long on average. A 16-second silent rest was inserted between the musical excerpts in order to reduce effects from previous song listening. After listening to the 16 songs and taking a short rest, the subject annotated his/her emotion perceived in the previous session without EEG recording, while the songs were presented again in the same order. Emotion reporting was performed by continuously specifying a corresponding point in the arousal-valence emotion space shown on a monitor screen. Arousal and valence were recorded independently as numerical values that ranged from –1 to 1. Finally, the subject was asked to confirm or change his/her familiarity with the songs and indicate confidence that the annotated emotions were consistent with the perceived emotion during EEG recording sessions on a discrete scale from 1 to 3.

2.2   Data Acquisition and Recording

Electrical brain activities were recorded from 12 electrodes (Fp1, Fp2, F3, F4, F7, F8, Fz, C3, C4, T3, T4, and Pz) mounted in the Waveguard EEG cap[2] and placed in accordance with the 10-20 international system. The ground electrode was located on the forehead, and the electrode Cz was used as the reference electrode. Sampling frequency was 250 Hz. Impedance of each electrode was kept below 20 kΩ throughout the experiment. Notch filter, a band-stop filter with a narrow stopband, was applied to remove 60Hz power line noise. To reduce unrelated artifacts, the subjects were instructed to close their eyes and minimize their movement throughout brainwave recording. EEG signals were amplified by Polymate AP1532[3] amplifier and visualized on APMonitor[4].

2.3   Data Preprocessing

EEG signals were filtered between 0.5–60 Hz by a bandpass filter. We employed EEGLAB[5], an EEG processing framework under MATLAB, to remove artifacts mainly caused by unintentional body movement. Then, we applied the independent component analysis (ICA), also provided in EEGLAB, to remove eye-movement artifacts. Finally, we associated the artifact-corrected EEG signals to the subject's ground-truth emotional annotation via timestamps.

---

[1] http://docs.oracle.com/javase/7/docs/technotes/guides/sound/
[2] http://www.ant-neuro.com/products/waveguard
[3] http://www.teac.co.jp/industry/me/ap1132/
[4] Software developed for Polymate AP1532 by TEAC Corporation.
[5] Open source environment for electrophysiological signal processing developed by the University of California, San Diego: http://sccn.ucsd.edu/eeglab/

3   Investigation of Neural Correlates of Familiarity

The question of whether music familiarity has any detectable association with EEG signals is still unanswered. To demonstrate brainwave characteristics of music familiarity, we performed two different types of analysis mainly used in EEG-based systematic brain function examination. To minimize label ambiguities resulting from the subjective familiarity scores, we performed analysis only to the songs with highest (i.e., familiar level 6) and lowest (i.e., familiar level 1) music familiarity. Therefore, we ignored data from Subject No. 8 and Subject No. 13 because they did not report the level 6 at all. Furthermore, we disregarded data from Subject No. 1 and Subject No. 3 due to reports of drowsiness during EEG recording. As Subject No. 12 misunderstood the instruction related to familiarity, data from this subject was also omitted.

3.1   Single-Electrode-Level Power Spectral Density Analysis

To demonstrate EEG characteristic, the power spectral density (PSD) technique was applied to analyze signals in the frequency domain. This technique is based on the fast Fourier transform (FFT). In this research, EEG signals from 12 electrodes were decomposed into 5 distinct frequency bands: delta (0–4 Hz), theta (4–8 Hz), alpha (8–13 Hz), beta (13–30 Hz), and gamma (30–40 Hz). MATLAB Signal Processing Toolbox[6] and its *avgpower* function were used to derive the average power in every frequency band. To obtain higher amount of data for analysis, we applied a sliding window segmentation technique, where the window size was defined as 1000 samples, equivalent to 4–s length. In this work, non-overlapping consecutive time windows were used.

Statistical Analysis. We performed 2-way analysis of variance (ANOVA) with replication examining the effect of familiarity (high and low) and subject individuality. For each frequency range and electrode, we collected multiple PSD values from every subject and divided them into two groups: low and high familiarity. The replication, i.e., the multiple observations, was derived from multiple PSD samples from each subject. However, as the number of PSD samples from each subject was not equal because of the variety of the number of highest (or lowest) familiar songs and their lengths, unified number of replication was needed. We defined the number of replication as the minimum size of available data across subjects and familiarity. We then collected data from each subject by randomly selecting available data up to the replication number. Then, 2-way ANOVA was applied to test the hypotheses whether the main effects of familiarity and subjectivity are significant. Post-hoc analyses were calculated using Tukey tests.

Results. We performed ANOVA at the significant level $p < 0.05$ to explore the significant difference of PSD affected by familiarity. According to results, inter-subject variability resulted in the most significance disparities in PSD. However,

---

[6] http://www.mathworks.com/products/signal/

Table 1. Significance values p of difference between familiar and unfamiliar songs across subjects in single-electrode EEG data; bold characters represent that power spectra in music with high familiarity are greater than that in music with low familiarity.

Band	Significant results of Tukey Test for familiarity ($p<0.05$)							
δ	Fz	0.0005	**F7**	0.0357	**T3**	0.0377		
θ	Fz	0.0002						
α	**Fp1**	0.0153	**Fp2**	0.0260	**Pz**	0.0292	**T4**	0.0007
β	Fz	0.0047	T3	0.0315	T4	0.0005		
γ	C4	0.0105	Pz	0.0003	**F8**	0.0019	T4	0.0006

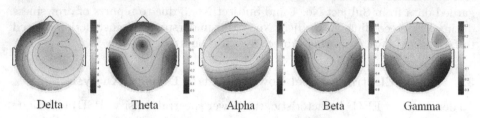

Delta   Theta   Alpha   Beta   Gamma

Fig. 1. Topological plot of the difference of averaged power spectra between songs with high and low familiarity over all participants (familiarity power – unfamiliarity power); positive areas represent that high familiarity produce higher power than low familiarity, and negative areas depict that unfamiliarity produce higher power.

we still found the significant difference of PSD caused by familiarity as shown in Table 1. We then averaged the power spectra over subjects in high and low music familiarity. We topologically plotted the difference of the averages (familiarity − unfamiliarity) from every electrode to frontal scalp and illustrated in Fig. 1. For instance, positive areas represent the electrodes where familiar songs produced higher averaged power spectra over subjects than unfamiliar songs.

It has been found that listening to unfamiliar songs relates to the recollection, an ability to recall the former context associated with a musical excerpt utilizing *episodic memory* [11]. We hypothesized subjects might recollect past experience from episodic memory to figure out what song it was during listening to novel music. Previous research [12] showing the greater gamma power over parietal scalp during recollection in comparison to familiarity is consistent with our results that showed marginally higher gamma bandwaves in Pz electrode during listening to unfamiliar song. In addition, Hsieh and Ranganath [13] also reported an implication of Fmθ in working memory and episodic memory, where these memories could possibly be relevant to unfamiliar song listening. Moreover, the increase of Fz theta power in our results also corresponds with previous report of enhance of frontal midline theta rhythm (Fmθ) during focused attention [14]. A plausible underlying reason was that unfamiliar songs in our study required a higher level of attention in listening in order to be able to annotate emotion subsequently.

3.2 Functional Connectivity Analysis

Brain activities are likely to involve functional circuits, therefore examining interrelated activities among multiple brain sites would be promising in reflecting brain function. In addition to the analyses at the single-electrode level, we investigated functional connectivity in the brain in association with music familiarity. While brain functional connectivity could be estimated by various algorithms, we used three different approaches: correlation, coherence, and the phase synchronization index (PSI) between each pair of EEG electrodes. These three approaches had been actively used in studies of brain correlates, especially in emotional researches [15]. In order to analyze on specific EEG frequency bands, we applied the second order bandpass Butterworth filter to extract delta, theta, alpha, beta and gamma bands. We calculated connectivity index among all pairs of 12 electrode in each frequency band separately by utilizing MATLAB Statistics and Machine Learning Toolbox[7].

Correlation corresponds to a relationship between two signals from the different sites. Given signals x and y, the correlation at each frequency (f) is a function of cross-covariance C_{xy}^f and auto-covariances, C_{xx}^f and C_{yy}^f, of x and y: $R_{xy}(f) = C_{xy}^f / \sqrt{C_{xx}^f C_{yy}^f}$.

Coherence includes the covariation between two signals as a function of frequency. It indicates that two brain sites are working more closely together at a specific frequency band. Given signals x and y, coherence is a function of the power spectral densities, $P_{xx}(f)$ and $P_{yy}(f)$, of x and y, and the cross-power spectral density, $P_{xy}(f)$, of x and y: $Coh_{xy}(f) = |P_{xy}(f)|^2 / P_{xx}(f) P_{yy}(f)$.

Phase Synchronization Index (PSI) is a nonlinear measure of connectivity. PSI among regions in the brain indicates connectivity in terms of phase difference between two signals. PSI can be restricted to certain frequency bands reflecting specific brain rhythms. For two signals x and y with data length L, the phase synchronization index is defined as: $PSI_{xy} = |\frac{1}{L} \sum_{t=0}^{L} e^{i[\phi_x(t) - \phi_y(t)]}|$, where $\phi_x(t) = \arctan \tilde{x}(t) / x(t)$ is the Hilbert phase of signal x, and $\phi_y(t)$ is the phase of signal y, while $\tilde{x}(t)$ is the Hilbert transform of $x(t)$.

Statistical Analysis. To identify the significance of EEG functional connectivity disparity due to music familiarity, we performed 1-way ANOVA for each frequency band. The main factor within subject was familiarity (high and low). Firstly, the connectivity indexes were calculated from EEG signals of each subject-song pair. Then, the indexes were separated into two groups according to familiarity. After that, the indexes of all subject-song pairs were unified into the respective overall indexes. Since coherence and PSI ranged from 0 to 1 and correlation ranged from −1 to 1, we applied the arithmetic mean to derive overall coherence and overall PSI, and quadratic mean to derive overall correlation across songs. Post-hoc analyses were done by Tukey test.

---

[7] http://www.mathworks.com/products/statistics/

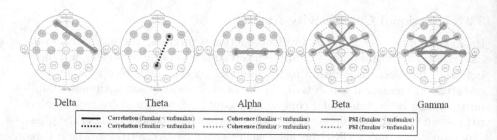

Delta   Theta   Alpha   Beta   Gamma

———— Correlation (familiar < unfamiliar)   ———— Coherence (familiar < unfamiliar)   ———— PSI (familiar < unfamiliar)
•••••••• Correlation (familiar > unfamiliar)   •••••••• Coherence (familiar > unfamiliar)   •••••••• PSI (familiar > unfamiliar)

Fig. 2. Functional connectivity with significant different values ($p<0.05$) due to music familiarity; lines indicate significant higher (solid) and lower (dash) connectivity index in unfamiliar songs compared to familiar songs

Results. Significantly different connectivity are illustrated in Fig. 2. We found increase of connectivity in delta, alpha, beta, and gamma bands when subjects listened to unfamiliar songs. Burgess and Ali [12] reported greater functional connectivity in the gamma band during an experience of recollection compared to that during familiarity experiencing. Our results agree with this study because we found higher connectivity in unfamiliar songs, especially in gamma band. Imperatori *et al.* [16] reported higher delta and gamma band connectivity during an autobiographical memory task. Based on our hypothesis related to episodic memory during unfamiliar song listening, our results correspond with their findings.

4   Familiarity Effects in Emotion Recognition Systems

According to our results in EEG correlates regarding music familiarity, we constructed an emotion recognition system by considering music familiarity. Firstly, EEG data were separated in accordance with familiarity level (high and low familiar), then we trained emotion recognition models independently and compared recognition results with the models using original data. Percentage of EEG data from familiar songs to total data of each subject was 52.46% on average.

4.1   Feature Extraction Algorithms

First, we extracted informative features from EEG signals. We applied two different methods: fractal dimension (FD) and PSD. FD values reveal the complexity of EEG signals and have been used in emotion recognition from EEG [17]. In this work, we applied Higuchi algorithm [18] to calculate FD values. PSD reflects characteristics of signals in the frequency domain and has been widely employed in recent emotion recognition researches [3]. The sliding window technique with 1000-sample length was employed to retrieve a large amount of data without overlapping between consecutive windows. Associated emotions continuously annotated by subjects were unified with the majority method to label emotional tags for each window.

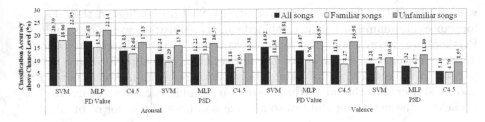

Fig. 3. Comparison among data from familiar/unfamiliar/all songs in arousal and valence classification showing enhancement above the chance level

4.2 Emotion Classification

EEG features from each subject were used to classify arousal and valence independently. Emotion recognition was turned to binary classification by separating arousal into high and low classes and valence into positive and negative classes. We applied three different algorithms to classify emotional states: support vector machine (SVM) based on Pearson VII kernel function (PUK) kernel, multilayer perceptron (MLP) with one hidden layer, and C4.5. The classification was performed with WEKA[8]. Overall performance of emotion recognition on each subject was evaluated by 10-fold cross-validation method.

4.3 Results of Emotion Classification

Due to the reports of drowsiness from two subjects and misunderstanding from one subject, we disregarded data from these three subjects and analyzed data from 12 remaining subjects. Averaged confidence level of consistency in annotation over remained subjects was 2.4063 ($SD = 0.6565$) which reflects that annotated data were applicable. As we relied on self-annotation from the subjects, the imbalance of dataset could mislead the interpretation of results. Therefore, we defined a new baseline, the *chance level*, which is the majority class of data. For instance, given a training dataset is composed by 60% of positive and 40% negative arousal samples, the chance level is 60%. Classification accuracies from each model were compared to the chance level to evaluate the performance of emotion recognition over majority-voting classification.

The averaged classification results over subjects compared to chance levels are illustrated in Fig. 3. In the arousal recognition, data from unfamiliar song sessions enhanced classification over the chance level more than data from all songs, while familiar songs achieved poor performance. The best result over chance level was from classifying FD features with SVM using unfamiliar song data that achieved 87.80% ($SD = 7.73\%$), while the chance level was 64.86% ($SD = 7.04\%$). In the valence recognition, unfamiliar song data achieved slightly better results than all song data did. FD value classification with SVM reached highest relative accuracy, 86.91% ($SD = 8.13\%$), and the chance-level accuracy

---

[8] http://www.cs.waikato.ac.nz/ml/weka/

was 68.10% ($SD = 11.79\%$). However, statistical *t-test* indicated that the performances of unfamiliar versus combined song classification were not significant. Furthermore, when using data from the same set of the subjects in Section 3, unfamiliar song data still achieved higher over-chance-level performance in comparison to the other types of data. The superior performance of FD over PSD and SVM over the other algorithms were also found in previous researches [3,17] because of the better capabilities to analyze non-linear behavior of brain.

5   Discussion

According to EEG correlate evidence, familiarity affected brain activities reflected in dissimilarities of power spectra and functional connectivity. Compared to emotion driven effects [15], the number of significantly different functional connectivity due to familiarity was relatively low. This could suggest that emotion would be more influential in brain activities than familiarity.

As familiarity is a key factor in the interaction between music and listeners, emotion recognition would suffer from heterogeneous familiarity levels to songs. Our results suggested that using only unfamiliar songs could provide better classification in emotion recognition from EEG data based on continuous self-annotation. In summary, homogeneous familiarity to songs is a factor to be considered in constructing better and valid emotion recognition systems.

The real underlying mechanisms of music familiarity effects on brainwaves are warrants further investigation. Since the work [8] reported the association of familiar musical excerpts and the reward system in the brain, it is worth it to examine whether the results we obtained are related to their findings. It is noticeable that annotation played an important role in this study. The question if emotion annotation is affected by second-time listening and/or attention is also a worthy focus for future work. Further experiments with higher number of participants, study on female subjects, and another sophisticated analyses such as event-related potentials, are required to gain a clearer understanding of familiarity. An automatic familiarity detection system would be yielded as an example of application from this work.

6   Conclusion

Familiarity is an essential subjective factor in music perception that was frequently neglected in previous emotion recognition researches. Our EEG correlate evidences indicated significant difference of brain activities due to music familiarity, reflected in single-electrode-level power spectra and functional connectivity. Based on self-reporting continuous emotion annotation approach, constructing emotion classifiers by typical algorithms would benefit from controlling familiarity levels to music. Data from only unfamiliar songs could produce better emotion classification results than data from a combination of familiar and unfamiliar songs. Therefore, unfamiliar songs are more appropriate for use in constructing emotion recognition systems.

References

1. Schmidt, L.A., Trainor, L.J.: Frontal brain electrical activity (EEG) distinguishes valence and intensity of musical emotions. Cogn. Emot. **15**(4), 487–500 (2001)
2. Sammler, D., Grigutsch, M., Fritz, T., Koelsch, S.: Music and emotion: Electrophysiological correlates of the processing of pleasant and unpleasant music. Psychophysiology **44**(2), 293–304 (2007)
3. Kim, M.K., Kim, M., Oh, E., Kim, S.P.: A Review on the Computational Methods for Emotional State Estimation from the Human EEG. Comput. Math. Methods Med. **2013**, article 573734 (2013)
4. Koelsch, S.: Brain and Music. John Wiley & Sons (2012)
5. Yang, Y.H., Chen, H.H.: Music Emotion Recognition. CRC Press (2011)
6. Plailly, J., Tillmann, B., Royet, J.P.: The feeling of familiarity of music and odors: the same neural signature? Cereb. Cortex **17**(11), 2650–2658 (2007)
7. Daltrozzo, J., Tillmann, B., Platel, H., Schon, D.: Temporal aspects of the feeling of familiarity for music and the emergence of conceptual processing. J. Cogn. Neurosci. **22**(8), 1754–1769 (2010)
8. Pereira, C.S., Teixeira, J., Figueiredo, P., Xavier, J., Castro, S.L., Brattico, E.: Music and Emotions in the Brain: Familiarity Matters. PLoS ONE **6**(11), e27241 (2011)
9. van den Bosch, I., Salimpoor, V.N., Zatorre, R.J.: Familiarity mediates the relationship between emotional arousal and pleasure during music listening. Front. Hum Neurosci. 2013 **7**, 534 (2013)
10. Russell, J.A.: A circumplex model of affect. J. Pers. Soc. Psychol. **39**(6), 1161–1178 (1980)
11. Platel, H.: Functional neuroimaging of semantic and episodic musical memory. Ann. N. Y. Acad. Sci. **1060**, 136–147 (2005)
12. Burgess, A.P., Ali, L.: Functional connectivity of gamma EEG activity is modulated at low frequency during conscious recollection. Int. J. Psychophysiol. **46**(2), 91–100 (2002)
13. Hsieh, L.T., Ranganath, C.: Frontal midline theta oscillations during working memory maintenance and episodic encoding and retrieval. Neuroimage **85**(2), 721–729 (2014)
14. Aftanas, L.I., Golocheikine, S.A.: Human anterior and frontal midline theta and lower alpha reflect emotionally positive state and internalized attention: high-resolution EEG investigation of meditation. Neurosci. Lett. **310**(1), 57–60 (2001)
15. Lee, Y.Y., Hsieh, S.: Classifying different emotional states by means of EEG-based functional connectivity patterns. PLoS ONE **9**(4), e95415 (2014)
16. Imperatori, C., Brunetti, R., Farina, B., Speranza, A.M., Losurdo, A., Testani, E., Contardi, A., Della Marca, G.: Modification of EEG power spectra and EEG connectivity in autobiographical memory: a sLORETA study. Cogn. Process. **15**(3), 351–361 (2014)
17. Sourina, O., Liu, Y., Nguyen, M.K.: Real-time EEG-based emotion recognition for music therapy. J. Multimodal User Interfaces **5**, 27–35 (2012)
18. Higuchi, T.: Approach to an irregular time series on the basis of the fractal theory. Physica D **31**, 277–283 (1988)

A Neural Network Based Model for Predicting Psychological Conditions

Filip Dabek[✉] and Jesus J. Caban

National Intrepid Center of Excellence (NICoE), Walter Reed National Military
Medical Center, Bethesda, MD, USA
filip.j.dabek.ctr@mail.mil

Abstract. Preventive care attempts to inform individuals and clinicians
of potential complications or conditions a patient might encounter. With
the recent interest on leveraging big data in the healthcare domain to better design data-driven models for preventive medicine and the increased
awareness of the long-lasting effects of concussions, being able to predict
psychological conditions post concussion can have a paramount effect
on mild traumatic brain injury patients. We present a neural network
model that is able to predict the likelihood of developing psychological
conditions such as anxiety, behavioral disorders, depression, and post-
traumatic stress disorder. We analyzed the effectiveness of our model
against a dataset of 89,840 patients. Our results show that we are able
to achieve accuracies ranging from 73% to 95% for each of the clinical
conditions under consideration, with an overall accuracy of 82.35% for
all conditions.

Keywords: Big data · Machine learning · Concussion · Informatics ·
Mild traumatic brain injury · Psychological conditions

1 Introduction

Preventive care attempts to provide an early diagnosis by seeking to inform the
patient and their physician of potential complications and diagnoses to expect.
With the recent increase in big data present in the healthcare domain [1,2], from
medical organizations modernizing their operations through electronic health
records (EHRs) and deploying new health information technology (HIT) systems,
there exists an opportunity for applying predictive models on this vast amount
of EHR data to increase the potential for preventive care to be applied.

During the last decade a significant amount of attention has been given to
the acquisition of clinical data from patients suffering from mild traumatic brain
injury (mTBI) and psychological health (PH) problems after a concussion. The
increased awareness has been in part driven by the Department of Defense (DoD),
the National Football League (NFL), and many other government and private
organizations that have been leading different efforts to raise awareness about the
short- and long-term effects of concussions. With this increased concentration on

© Springer International Publishing Switzerland 2015
Y. Guo et al. (Eds.): BIH 2015, LNAI 9250, pp. 252–261, 2015.
DOI: 10.1007/978-3-319-23344-4_25

concussions, applying machine learning onto the big data available is a natural step in improving the livelihood of these patients and furthering the research.

Firstly, a traumatic brain injury (TBI) is defined and indicated by "Any period of loss of or a decreased level of consciousness, Any loss of memory for events immediately before or after the injury, Any alteration in mental state at the time of the injury, Neurological deficits that may or may not be transient, or intracranial lesion following the traumatic event" [3]. In the United States alone, an estimated 1.7 million TBIs occur each year, leading to more than 1.3 million emergency room visits, a quarter million hospitalizations, and 52 thousand deaths [4]. The leading causes of TBIs are falls, physical assault/injury, and motor vehicle accidents. In the U.S. Military, over 307,000 cases of TBI have been diagnosed since 2000, 80% of which were in a non-deployed setting [5].

Patients who have been screened positive with mTBI are at increased risk of psychological problems that can have a significant impact in the recovery time. Early detection of psychological conditions such as anxiety, depression, PTSD, and various behavioral conditions following a concussion might improve the overall outcome of a patient and could potentially reduce the cost associated with treatment. Advances in big data and scalable analytical techniques open new opportunities by creating new tools that use the patient's pre-existing conditions and longitudinal clinical trajectories to determine the likelihood of a patient developing psychological conditions. This paper presents a neural network model that uses longitudinal clinical data of thousands of patients that have been diagnosed with a concussion to build a model that predicts the likelihood of a diagnosis related to various psychological disorders after a concussion, most specifically anxiety, behavioral conditions, depression, and PTSD. Section 2 describes some of the previous work, Section 3 describes our dataset and how diagnoses are transformed into feature vectors, Section 4 describes our approach to build a model that can be used to predict psychological conditions months in advance, Section 5 discusses some of our results, and Section 6 concludes the paper and describes some of the future work.

2   Background

Existing clinical literature has shown that a strong association exists between mTBI and PTSD and that several factors play a role in the development of PTSD. Bryant et al. argued that the stress reaction caused by a concussion is a key factor in developing PTSD [6,7]. Another study found that soldiers that lose consciousness and subsequently were diagnosed with mTBI while deployed in Iraq were strongly associated with developing PTSD three to four months after returning home from combat [8]. In addition, research has found that patients with a concussion are susceptible to developing anxiety, depression, and other neuropsychological conditions [9,10].

With the knowledge that there exists a strong association between mTBI and various psychological conditions [11], research on predictive models have shown the possibility of being able to estimate the likelihood of a patient developing such conditions. Hoogendoorn et al. used Electronic Medical Records (EMRs) to build a Chi-squared Automatic Interaction Detection (CHAID) decision tree learner for predicting colorectal cancer, and subsequently leading to an early diagnosis and increased survival rates [12]. Another recent study used support vector machines and random forest classifiers to try to predict cancer diagnosis using different types of patient data [13], and based on recent review papers, cancer and heart disease are two of the more commonly researched diseases with respect to predictive modeling techniques in healthcare [14]. These trends show the opportunity to build predictive analytical models using EHR data and most specifically the gap in studying psychological conditions that needs to be addressed.

In the machine learning field, popular algorithms such as support vector machines (SVMs), random forest classifiers, and decision trees have been used to predict and classify future events. For example, an approach used a Target Information Equivalence Algorithm (TIE) to identify the most important features to input to an SVM in order to improve the prediction of PTSD in trauma patients [15]. In our own previous work [16], we have used SVMs and a set of rules to create a hybrid system which predicts a diagnosis of PTSD in patients using EHR data. However, with the black box approach of SVMs removing the ability to optimize and improve the algorithm, an approach such as a neural network allows for a fine tuning of network for the data that is available. In addition, being able to predict multiple diagnoses using SVMs would have required a separate SVM for each diagnosis which would have been highly inefficient compared to that of a single neural network.

Research has shown that neural networks can be applied to enormous and active datasets to predict future events and outcomes, such as the area of stock markets. Artificial Neural Networks (ANNs) have also been used in basic prediction of the chance of a patient's survival following an mTBI [17]. With the power of neural networks, we hope to improve upon our previous work that used SVMs to be able to predict multiple psychological conditions in a single, efficient network.

3   Dataset

The dataset used for this paper was a subset of our larger clinical collection that consists of over 15 million patients and billions of clinical encounters. We extracted a dataset of 8.7 million clinical diagnoses from 98,342 mTBI patients for our analysis. The data was organized using various TeraData/Aster services and retrieved using MapReduce. The original dataset of 98,342 patients was further filtered to only include patients with more than thirty days of data and no history of moderate or severe TBI. The resulting subsets of 89,840 patients had 5.3 million TBI-related clinical encounters and 8.7 million clinical diagnoses. In this study, a TBI-related encounter was defined as a visit to the doctor regardless of inpatient/outpatient where the patient is treated with one or more of the conditions that are commonly known to be related to concussions such as behavioral disorder, sleep problems, cognitive deficiencies, and audiology complaints. Figure 1(a) shows a diagram illustrating the longitudinal properties of clinical encounters. Note that only TBI-related encounters were taken into consideration. The patients under consideration had an average of 59.06 encounters.

To build our model the dataset was defined to be $P = \{P_1, P_2, \ldots, P_n\}$ where P is a set containing each patient P. Each patient P_i had an associated sequence of encounters $E_i \in \{E_1, E_2, \ldots, E_m\}$ representing unique clinical appointments or hospital visits. Each encounter E_i had an associated set of diagnoses represented by $D \in \{D_1, D_2, \ldots, D_k\}$. The set of possible diagnoses was: Alzheimer's, Anxiety, Audiology, Behavioral, Cognitive deficits, Depression, Endocine dysfunction, Headache, NonSkull Fracture/mTBI, Neurology, Post Concussion Syndrome (PCS), PTSD, Parkinson's, Seizure, Sleep, Speech, Stress, Vcode, Vision, Late Effect NonSkull Fracture.

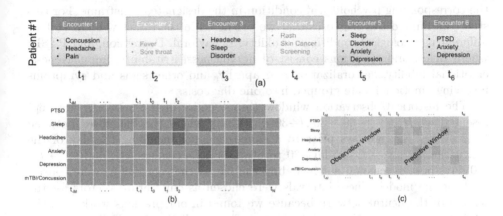

Fig. 1. (a) Illustration of the longitudinal properties of clinical encounters. Note that only TBI-related encounters were taken into consideration in this study. (b) The encounters and diagnoses are transformed into a sparse matrix representation where each row corresponds to a TBI-related diagnosis and each column corresponds to a different time point. The colors of each cell give an example of the importance of each diagnosis in that encounter, which could be studied further and applied to a future approach of a network. (c) Once the data is aligned based on the first occurrence of a concussion, two features are created: *the observation window* and *the predictive window*.

The key step in developing an approach to predicting psychological conditions in mTBI patients was to transform the encounters and diagnoses of each patient into feature vectors that could be input as nodes to a neural network. First the encounters / diagnosis tuples were transformed into a sparse matrix representation where each row was a TBI-related diagnosis and each column corresponded to a different time point. Figure 1(b) shows the general idea. Note that since all the 89,840 patients under consideration had a concussion, all patients were aligned based on the date of their first mTBI event. The date of this event is represented as t_0, pre-existing encounters are represented as t_i (with $i < 0$), and all encounters and diagnosis after the concussion are represented as t_i (with $i > 0$).

As we will attempt to predict diagnoses post concussion, we are able to split the data of each patient at the first occurrence of a concussion resulting in two features being formed: *an observation window* and *a predictive window*. We define the observation window as consisting of the diagnoses corresponding to a patient prior to their first diagnosis of a concussion, and we define the predictive window to be whether or not they were diagnosed with a psychological condition within one year after their concussion. Figure 1(c) shows a visual representation of the windows on either side of a concussion. The timeframes of both of these windows are flexible, as the historical window could be a month or even up to a year prior to the concussion, while the target window could be evaluated for 30 days or up to a year post concussion. The target window for each patient contains a "0" or "1" indicating whether or not a patient was diagnosed with the corresponding psychological condition in the designated timeframe. For this study we limited the diagnoses that we predicted in the target window to four different psychological conditions: Anxiety, Behavioral, Depression, and PTSD; where Behavioral conditions consist of nervousness, irritability, impulsiveness, emotional lability, demoralization and apathy, and other signs and symptoms involving emotional state grouped into one diagnosis.

The historical/observation window (input nodes in the network) was represented as $H = \langle (-60, -30], (-30, 0], [0, 30) \rangle$ where the diagnoses between $t_{-30} \rightarrow t_{-1}$ (i.e. 30 days prior to a concussion not including the day of the concussion), $t_{-60} \rightarrow t_{-30}$ (days 30 to 60 prior to a concussion), and $t_1 \rightarrow t_{30}$ (30 days post concussion not including the day of the concussion) were considered for the model. These intervals were chosen as our feature vectors for the testing of the neural network because we found in our previous work that the 30 days after a concussion were most crucial in predicting future diagnoses, the 60 days prior provided us with enough information to provide accurate results, and that these intervals allowed for a sense of time to be incorporated into the feature vector [16]. In addition, the psychological conditions were predicted over the target window of $T = \langle [30, 365] \rangle$ where a patient having a diagnosis of the corresponding condition between $t_{30} \rightarrow t_{365}$ evaluated to "true".

4   Approach

With our clinical data transformed into a sparse matrix and the feature vectors generated, we began constructing our neural network in order to evaluate its effectiveness at predicting behavioral diagnoses.

We constructed a feed forward neural network with the input layer consisting of 60 nodes, representing each cell of the sparse matrix of diagnosis counts (20 diagnosis counts for three time intervals) as was described in Section 3 with the historical/observation window of H, and the output layer consisting of 4 nodes, representing each diagnosis being predicted (Anxiety, Behavioral, Depression, and PTSD) as was described with the target window of T. Typically when using a neural network for classification, each of the output nodes represent a class and after the network finishes its computations, the node with the highest activation classifies the datapoint as its respective class. However, in our scenario patients may have multiple diagnoses and thus all of the nodes need to be taken into account. Therefore, for each output node we needed to identify the cutoff point in its activation for which a patient would be classified as either having or not having a diagnosis.

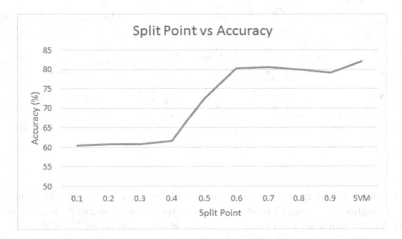

Fig. 2. This graph shows the accuracy of splitting the activation, a number from 0 to 1, at each output node for the training data at the various values, as well as using an SVM. Due to the variability in the optimal split point varying between runs of the network and the flexibility of SVMs, we ultimately chose to use an SVM at each output node in our final model.

Initially, we ran the network with one hidden layer of size 100 and analyzed the various split points for the output nodes' activations in order to identify which point would provide the maximum accuracy. Upon running the network, we found that each diagnosis had a different split point and that the split points varied between runs of the network, due to the nature of a network learning the data. Therefore, we decided to place a support vector machine (SVM) at each output node with the intention of it identifying the optimal split point. Even though SVMs are normally used for complex data they were beneficial in this case as they provided a quick approach to splitting the data. We used the SVMs in such a way that once the network was finished being trained the training data was passed through the network, and the activation at the node and the corresponding label of whether or not the patient received the diagnosis was passed to the SVM as training data. Due to the varying split points caused by the nature of neural networks in which each node's activation varies between runs, our approach allows for our model to dynamically adjust to the varying split points and have proven to be effective in our analyses as can be seen in Figure 2.

Figure 3 shows an example of our constructed neural network which will be fine tuned and optimized in the following section.

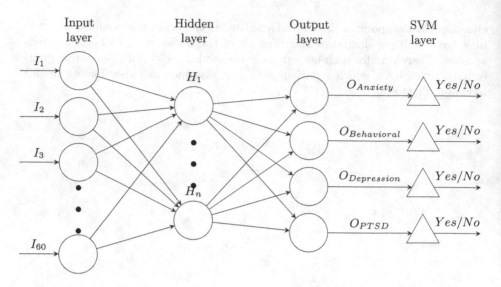

Fig. 3. Example of the neural network created where the input layer takes the sparse matrix of diagnosis counts (20 diagnosis counts for three time intervals), the output layer has an activation for each condition which is routed to an SVM to identify if the patient was ("Yes") or was not ("No") diagnosed with the corresponding psychological condition.

5   Results

Using our extensive dataset of 89,840 patients, we were able to effectively evaluate and optimize our neural network model through several methods of analysis. First we looked at the number of epochs needed to train the data, followed by the number of hidden layers and number of nodes in each hidden layer. Finally, we aggregated all of our optimizations to identify the overall accuracy that our model will be able to achieve. It should be noted that we only considered patients that had enough data to span the windows that were defined in Section 3: $H = \langle(-60, -30], (-30, 0], [0, 30)\rangle$ for the historical window and $T = \langle[30, 365]\rangle$ for the target window.

First, we ran our network with varying epochs and found that the optimal epoch for each diagnosis varied. However, we found that the value of 10 produced the most consistent and relatively best performance for each diagnosis and thus our subsequent tests used this value. In addition, all subsequent tests were run three times with the mean and standard deviation being recorded across the runs.

Second, we ran our network with one hidden layer and varied the amount of nodes that were present in this layer. The size of the hidden layer impacts the amount of variation in the data that can be detected by the network, which means that more nodes should be able to discern more patterns. Figure 4 shows the effect of the number of nodes on the mean accuracy of the network. Analyzing

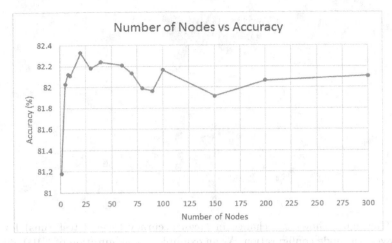

Fig. 4. This graph shows the change in mean accuracy as the number of nodes in a single hidden layer is varied.

this graph shows that the accuracy peaked at 20 and 100 nodes, with 20 nodes resulting in the highest accuracy. However, even though 20 nodes produced a higher accuracy we chose to use 100 nodes due to the standard deviation of the 100 node test runs to be significantly smaller than the 20 node test runs (0.2% versus 0.3%). The same analysis was seen with the configuration of 40-60 node counts as their standard deviation was also greater than that of the 100 nodes.

Third, we optimized our network on varying numbers of layers and varying sizes of each subsequent layer. We quickly found by running our network with one, two, and three hidden layers (all of node size 100) that as the number of hidden layers increased, the mean accuracy decreased. Furthermore, using a wide variety of various layer and node configurations, we were not able to beat the mean accuracy of using a single hidden layer consisting of 100 nodes, as can be seen in Figure 5. Analyzing the layer configurations from the standpoint of standard deviations showed that there existed points where the single hidden layer did not perform better. However, even with a slightly higher standard deviation for a single hidden layer the better mean accuracy results in a more optimal confidence interval than the various other configurations that we tested.

Combining all of the optimizations made to our network we were able to achieve high prediction accuracies for each diagnosis, as can be seen in Table 1, along with an area under the curve (AUC) value of 75.59%. These prediction accuracies are relatively high compared to the random chance of predicting correctly and in addition we were able to achieve these accuracies using a single, efficient network rather than a separate network for each, further improving the benefit of our model.

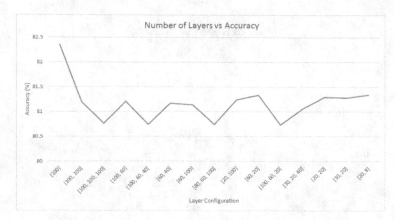

Fig. 5. This figure shows the change in mean accuracy (over 3 test runs) for each hidden layer and node configuration. As an example, a configuration of "[100, 60, 40]" represents three hidden layers where the first layer consists of 100 nodes, followed by a layer of 60 nodes, and finally the last hidden layer of 40 nodes.

Table 1. The final mean accuracy and standard deviation in predicting each psychological condition.

	Mean Accuracy	Standard Deviation
Anxiety	73.35%	±0.17%
Behavioral	95.27%	±0.10%
Depression	76.96%	±0.41%
PTSD	83.82%	±0.20%
Overall	82.35%	±0.22%

6   Conclusion

In this paper we have presented a neural network model that is able to correctly predict psychological conditions, specifically anxiety, behavioral, depression and PTSD, in patients that have suffered a mild traumatic brain injury with accuracies ranging from 73% to 95% for each condition, an overall accuracy 82.35%, and a total of 3,130 out of the 6,629 patients (47.2%) in the test data being correctly predicted for all diagnoses. These results are paramount in working towards the goal of providing physicians and patients valuable information concerning the future to allow for better preparedness and early diagnosis.

Comparing our neural network model to that of our previous SVM approach (85% in our previous approach), we have been able to achieve similar results in the prediction of PTSD, while also being able to predict various other psychological conditions simultaneously with little overhead. In our previous approach we would have required an SVM for each diagnosis and a set of pre-defined rules for each SVM, whereas in our new approach we have been able to use one neural network for all of our computations. For future work, we look to expand our prediction model to a recurrent neural network (RNN) as these networks will be able to capture the longitudinal aspect of patient diagnoses better with the recurrent connection that exists in them.

References

1. Murdoch, T.B., Detsky, A.S.: THe inevitable application of big data to health care. JAMA **309**(13), 1351–1352 (2013)
2. Margolis, R., Derr, L., Dunn, M., Huerta, M., Larkin, J., Sheehan, J., Guyer, M., Green, E.D.: The National Institutes of Health's Big Data to Knowledge (BD2k) initiative: capitalizing on biomedical big data. Journal of the American Medical Informatics Association : JAMIA **21**(6), 957–958 (2014)
3. O'Neil, M.E., Carlson, K., et al.: Definition of mTBI from the VA/DOD Clinical Practice Guideline for Management of Concussion/Mild Traumatic Brain Injury, U.S. Department of Veterans Affairs (2009)
4. Faul, M., Xu, L., Wald, M., Coronado, V.: CDC - TBI in the US Report - Traumatic Brain Injury - Injury Center, Centers for Disease Control and Prevention
5. DoD Worldwide Numbers for TBI. http://dvbic.dcoe.mil/dod-worldwide-numbers-tbi
6. Bryant, R.A., Marosszeky, J.E., Crooks, J., Gurka, J.A.: Posttraumatic Stress Disorder After Severe Traumatic Brain Injury. American Journal of Psychiatry
7. Bryant, R.A., Nickerson, A., Creamer, M., et al.: Trajectory of post-traumatic stress following traumatic injury: 6-year follow-up. The British Journal of Psychiatry (2015). bjp.bp.114.145516
8. Hoge, C.W., Auchterlonie, J.L., Milliken, C.S.: Mental health problems, use of mental health services, and attrition from military service after returning from deployment to iraq or afghanistan. JAMA **295**(9), 1023–1032 (2006)
9. Anxiety and depression after mild head injury: a case control study **51**
10. Kay, T.: Neuropsychological treatment of mild traumatic brain injury. The Journal of Head Trauma Rehabilitation **8** (3)
11. Caban, J., Riedy, G., Oakes, T., Grammer, G., DeGraba, T.: Understanding the effects of concussion using big data. In: 2014 IEEE International Conference on Big Data (Big Data), pp. 18–23(2014). doi:10.1109/BigData.2014.7004387
12. Hoogendoorn, M., Moons, L.M.G., Numans, M.E., Sips, R.-J.: Utilizing data mining for predictive modeling of colorectal cancer using electronic medical records. In: Ślzakę, D., Tan, A.-H., Peters, J.F., Schwabe, L. (eds.) BIH 2014. LNCS, vol. 8609, pp. 132–141. Springer, Heidelberg (2014)
13. Statnikov, A., Aliferis, C.F.: Are Random Forests Better than Support Vector Machines for Microarray-Based Cancer Classification? AMIA Annual Symposium Proceedings **2007**, 686–690 (2007)
14. Yoo, I., Alafaireet, P., Marinov, M., et al.: Data Mining in Healthcare and Biomedicine: A Survey of the Literature. Journal of Medical Systems **36**(4), 2431–2448 (2011)
15. Karstoft, K.-I., Galatzer-Levy, I.R., Statnikov, A., Li, Z., Shalev, A.Y.: Bridging a translational gap: using machine learning to improve the prediction of PTSD. BMC Psychiatry **15** (1)
16. Dabek, F., Caban, J.: Leveraging big data to model the likelihood of developing psychological conditions after a concussion. In: 2015 INNS International Conference on Big Data (Big Data) (2015)
17. Rughani, A.I., Dumont, T.M., Lu, Z., et al.: Use of an artificial neural network to predict head injury outcome. Journal of Neurosurgery **113**(3), 585–590 (2009)

Application to Women's Healthcare of Health Management System Using a Tablet Phone

Hiroyuki Okazaki[1]([✉]), Hiroki Matsumoto[1], Yoshiki Shibata[1],
Shinichi Motomura[1], and Naoyuki Masada[2]

[1] Maebashi Institute of Technology, 460-1 Kamisadori-Cho,
Maebashi-City 371-0816, Japan
{okazaki_g,matsumoto,shibata,motomura}@maebashi-it.ac.jp
[2] Development Planning Division, Nakayo, Inc.,
1-3-2 Soja-Machi, Maebashi-City 371-0853, Japan
masada@nyc.co.jp

Abstract. The World Health Organization (WHO) is promoted utilization of information technology (IT) including the Internet as e-Health to provide information and services which are useful in health promotion. However, in countries which use Chinese characters, there is a relatively short history since the establishment of keyboards that supported these character systems, and this is resulting in delays in the popularization of e-Health. In these regions, it is desirable to utilize systems which can be used by simple screen operations without requiring the use of a keyboard.

Accordingly, Maebashi City which is a core Japanese city formerly known for its silk production located a little over 100km north of Tokyo, has been implementing activities for a project in cooperation with the Maebashi Institute of Technology and other organizations. This project aims to resolve the various issues facing the region by utilizing Information and Communication Technology (ICT) using a tablet-type device which does not require keyboard operation. Meanwhile, the Maebashi Institute of Technology and Nakayo, Inc. had already been building a health management system for elderly persons which used ICT utilizing a tablet-type device that does not require keyboard operation. Accordingly, in this study, investigation was carried out regarding an efficient women's healthcare management system that combines these two activities, and a mechanism was proposed which would centrally unite both. In this paper, the validity of the women's healthcare management realized by linking this system with the Women's Healthcare Portal is confirmed using field trials, and the necessity of building a system that unifies both is confirmed.

Keywords: Women's healthcare · Tablet phone · Countries which use chinese characters · Health management server

1 Introduction

By the World Health Organization (WHO), all people throughout the world should maintain a satisfactory condition of health, both physical and mental,

Y. Guo et al. (Eds.): BIH 2015, LNAI 9250, pp. 262–271, 2015.
DOI: 10.1007/978-3-319-23344-4_26

and it is promoted utilization of information technology (IT) including the Internet as e-Health to provide information and services which are useful in health promotion. Continuous information exchanges on e-Health are promoted in workshops held by the International Telecommunication Union (ITU) and WHO, and the necessity of implementing e-Health worldwide is recognized [1]. Further, a variety of related research is conducted globally [2–5]. For example, research of telemedicine and e-Health is presented in ref.1. In ref.2, it is presented an application of the e-Health in the plural chronic situation.

However, in countries which use Chinese characters, even in regions where high-speed Internet is widely used, there is a relatively short history since the establishment of keyboards that supported these character systems, and there is reputed to be a 100-year disparity in the popularization of keyboards compared to the West, where people have been familiar with the use of keyboards since the era of typewriters. For this reason, older persons will be more likely to state that they have never used a keyboard, are unable to type well, or find keyboard operation troublesome, which is delaying the popularization of e-Health. Accordingly, in these regions it is desirable to utilize systems that can be used by simple screen operations without requiring the use of a keyboard. In this study, consideration and verification were carried out with regard to a remote health management system that was built taking these types of regional aspects as preconditions. Specifically, verification is carried out taking Maebashi City which is a core Japanese city formerly known for its silk production located a little over 100km north of Tokyo, as an example.

In Maebashi City, for local problems such as health, economy, the employment, we built "a project" for the purpose of solving it by ICT using the tablet terminal where keyboard operation was unnecessary. The project was named "Maebashi ICT Silk Project" and was carried out about the health, Women's Healthcare Portal was built with the cooperation of Maebashi Institute of Technology. This portal enabled grasp such as the information of the vaccination, the consultation information of the medical institution by consolidating health condition and a taking medicine history before dying from birth. The final aim of this portal is effective treatment and reduction of medical related expenses. The first step to realize this was to build a unified management system for the health information relating to children from the time of birth until their graduation from elementary school. First, IC cards were given to mothers with children who were cooperating in the evaluation of this system in order to provide them with the authorization necessary to enable them to use the system, in other words, for personal identification. Next, by establishing their personal portal sites with their IC card, they were allowed to use contents such as physical records of the mother from the beginning of pregnancy to childbirth and of their child after birth, inoculation records, and electronic medical records.

Meanwhile, effective health management could be realized by applying the Health Management System that was developed by the Maebashi Institute of Technology and Nakayo, Inc., which uses a tablet phone that automatically measures and manages a person's vital signs including body weight and blood pressure. This has been confirmed using field trials targeting elderly persons, and the validity of the system has been verified [6].

In this study, it was determined to apply the above-mentioned Health Management System to women's healthcare. The Health Management System, which automatically measures the mother and child's vital signs (body weight, pulse, and blood pressure), has been built by the Maebashi Institute of Technology and Nakayo, Inc. It uses the GRANYC Android™ tablet phone (known below as the tablet phone) developed by Nakayo which supports use of the Hikari high speed optical fiber Internet connection service and can be installed in ordinary homes. This Health Management System was originally built as a system for implementing health management and medication management by independently carrying out health promotion and prevention of illnesses to enable elderly persons to enjoy their old age in good health. However, because it was believed that the system could also be applied to women's healthcare by linking the Women's Healthcare Portal with the health management function of this system, field trials were conducted to confirm the necessity and validity. Further, physicians had already suggested the necessity and validity of a medication management function for mothers with children. However, because the main objective of this study was to confirm the validity and necessity of integrating both systems, it was decided in this study to apply only the electronic medical record information of the Women's Healthcare Portal this time, and to set the investigation of the physicians' suggestion as an issue for the future.

In this paper, evaluations were carried out regarding the linking of both systems, and investigations were carried out based on these evaluations to determine the ideals for women's healthcare systems using ICT in the future. In the evaluations, nine mothers with children who had been invited to participate in the Maebashi ICT Silk Project were given introductions to both systems and were provided with an opportunity to actually use the machines. In addition, two mothers as monitors were allowed to utilize the system for a fixed period, and together with the results obtained by conducting interviews with two MD, confirmation was made of the necessity and validity of linking both systems. Below, explanations are given of the confirmation methods in section 2, and of the evaluations and results in section 3, while consideration is made of the evaluation results in section 4, and a summary of this paper is given in section 5.

2   Methods

The evaluation was carried out by linking the personal Women's Healthcare Portal site using IC cards created in the Maebashi ICT Silk Project, with a Health Management System. This system, developed by the Maebashi Institute of Technology and Nakayo, Inc., consists of a Health Management Server (Figure 1).

In this Women's Healthcare Portal site, a system was built that enables unified management of data such as information from the currently utilized Maternal and Child Health Handbook and information from physical examinations of children at elementary schools. Using this data, it will be possible for example

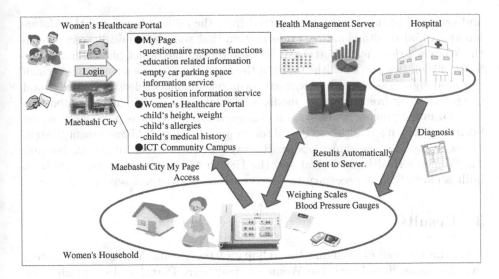

Fig. 1. Configuration diagram of the Women's Healthcare Portal and the Health Management System

for mothers when investigating their own resistance to German measles to view the Women's Healthcare Portal site to obtain information such as their past inoculation information and patient information.

The Health Management System is linked to this Women's Healthcare Portal site using a tablet phone which automatically measures the mother and child's vital signs. The Health Management System consists of an Android™ application that allows use of various health management and medication management system functions by installing a health management application in the tablet phone, and a Health Management Server that enables management of the vital sign measurement results and setting information utilizing the Google App Engine (GAE) service provided by Google. The Health Management System comprises a health management function and a medication management function, and an explanation is given below of each function. In the health management function, the results of measurements made by the vital sign sensors such as weighing scales and blood pressure gauges incorporating Bluetooth communications functions are automatically sent to and recorded in the Health Management Server. The medication management function enables support of the measured person's medicine-taking using a medication confirmation function, remaining medicine confirmation function, a medication alarm function, and a notification mail function. Additionally, using the calendar function, all of the measurement results and the medication situation in a day can be confirmed. However, as described in section 1, in this study it was determined not to use this function. In the field trials, it was to be confirmed that the new functions, in which the vital sign measurement results can be automatically and electronically recorded and arranged so that they can be viewed from the tablet phone, and the Maternal and Child Health Handbook information that was electronically recorded in the Women's Healthcare Portal can be viewed from the tablet phone, enable the more efficient women's healthcare than the health management system in which the vital signs are manually recorded on paper media or electronic media and the information from the paper media Maternal and Child Health Handbook is used for management. In the system linkage in this study, it is possible to access both the Women's Healthcare Portal server and the Health Management System server using only one tablet phone. However, in the current situation, because the Women's Healthcare Portal and the Health Management Server have been built separately, it is necessary to access each of the systems separately.

3   Results

With the purpose of verifying the validity of the Health Management System that had been linked with the Women's Healthcare Portal and confirming the remaining issues, evaluations were implemented by mothers with babies and by physicians who had been invited to participate in the Maebashi ICT Silk Project with regard to the items described below.

(1) After it was tried to use the Health Management System by nine mothers (the 30-year-old first half from 20 years old) with the baby, we evaluated the system by the questionnaire
(2) After the system was used for two pregnant mothers (Expectant mother A:20-year-old first half, Expectant mother B:20-year-old second half) for approximately one month, we interviewed
(3) Interviews with two MD

(1) The introduction of the Health Management System to mothers with babies was coordinated by Maebashi City. At the "Hiyoko (Chick) Class" childcare-related social gathering attended by nine mothers with children aged two to three months held at the Maebashi Health Center on February 20, 2013, an explanation was made of the Women's Healthcare Portal, and an introduction was given to the Health Management System, during which demonstrations were made of the actual machines. Afterwards, a questionnaire and interviews were implemented to carry out evaluation, and the participants' opinions were collected regarding the necessity of the Health Management System in women's healthcare and issues for its improvement. With regard to the questionnaire, in order to analyze the degree of completion of the women's healthcare in the Health Management System, a numerical representation was made using the contents of the question items (Table 1). Each item was given a maximum of five points, and the averaged results are shown in Figure 2 and Figure 3.

Table 1. Question Items

Item	Standards (Evaluation: From 5: Good to 3: Normal and 1: Poor)
1	Do you feel that a function for managing your body weight, blood pressure, and pulse is necessary?
2	How did you feel about the screen layout, the text size, and the ease of viewing?
3	How did you feel about the operability, including the touch operation and the ease of pressing the buttons?
4	How did you feel about the ease of viewing the graphs and figures that can be seen in the Health Information Service?
5	Was the operation up to the viewing of the information in the Health Information Service appropriate?
6	For the health information, it is possible to use the Internet to show your daily condition during medical examinations. Do you consider that this service is effective?
7	Do you think that you would like to actually try using the Health Management Service?

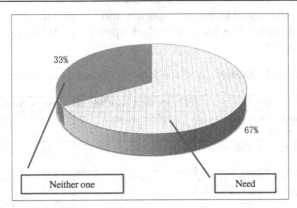

Fig. 2. View of the Women's Healthcare Portal Explanatory Meeting

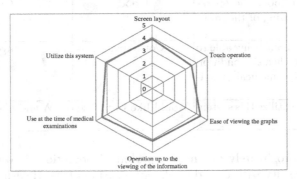

Fig. 3. View of the Women's Healthcare Portal Explanatory Meeting

60% of the mothers with babies responded that there was a need for managing body weight, blood pressure, and pulse in women's healthcare, and none of the mothers responded that this was unnecessary. In addition, in the questionnaire conducted after the explanation had been given of the system and the mothers had actually used the tablet phone, although a low evaluation was received regarding the screen operation, it was possible to confirm the necessity of the other items. The low evaluation given to the operability of the screens can be explained by the fact that the screens were designed for use by elderly persons, and it is believed that one of the causes was also the complication of having to separately access two systems. It is thought that this suggests the necessity of optimizing the screens for each age group and of building one system by integrating both systems.

(2)Tablet phones incorporating the health management applications were installed and operated for an approximately one month period in the homes of two expectant mothers who were acting as monitors. Afterwards, interviews were implemented regarding the contents of the question items to collect the opinions of the subjects with regard to problem points and improvement points that they became aware of during the fixed period of operation (Table 1). These results are shown in Table 2.

Table 2. Evaluation of the Health Management System

Question Items	Expectant mother A	Expectant mother B
How do you feel about the necessity of health management?	Necessary	Would be good if available
How do you feel about the screen layout?	Good	Good
How do you feel about the touch operation and button operability?	Good	Good
How do you feel about the ease of viewing the graphs and figures?	Good	Good
How do you feel about the operation up to the viewing of the information?	Good	Good
How do you feel about being able to utilize your daily health condition information during medical examinations?	Convenient	Convenient
Would you like to utilize this system in the future?	Would like to utilize	Would like to utilize

Even in the approximately one month period of operation, it was possible to confirm the necessity with regard to the application of the Health Management System to mothers with children.

(3) In the interviews with the two MD that were realized due to the cooperation of the Maebashi Medical Association, the opinions described below were obtained with regard to the Women's Healthcare Portal site and the Health

Management System. Since both physicians offered nearly the same opinions, their opinions were summarized and shown in Table 3.

Table 3. Results of interviewing the physicians

Item	Opinion
Favorable aspects	It is possible to confirm the person's vital sign information from home during medical examinations.
	In addition to elderly persons and mothers with children, the system might be able to be applied to all age groups.
	Depending on the situation, it will be possible to confirm the person's condition at their home by viewing the Health Management Server.
Aspects requiring improvement	For mothers with children, the measurement of body temperature is important, so it will be necessary to allow connection of a basal thermometer.
	The system consists of a Women's Healthcare Portal site and Health Management Server. Depending on the situation it is troublesome to view two servers, so it is possible that the system cannot be applied to our work.

4 Considerations

From the verification carried out this time, it was possible to confirm the necessity and validity of applying the Health Management System that was developed for elderly persons also to women's healthcare linked with the Women's Healthcare Portal. Below is a description of specific opinions and considerations.

In the interviews of the mothers with babies and expectant mothers, it is believed that the fact that many of those interviewed answered that it was convenient to be able to display their daily vital sign information during medical examinations and to have a physician confirm their health condition while at home indicates the validity of this study. With regard to the evaluation of the system, it is thought that the fact that the results of the evaluation items other than for the screen operation showed a high degree of satisfaction indicates the validity in relation to the practical implementation. Regarding the screen operation, this application was created for use by elderly persons and thus there was no problem with operability. However, it is thought that the unfavorable evaluation was received because persons from younger generations, who are used to operating smartphones, found the operation unsatisfactory. It is therefore believed that it will be necessary to resolve the problem such as by customizing the screens for the age group that is using it. As an additional problem of the screen operation, it is also thought that the complication with regard to having to separately access two systems was one of the causes of the unfavorable evaluation, and it is believed that this suggests the necessity of building one system by integrating both systems. Further, the mothers expressed the opinions that "I feel reluctant to use a service that I'm unfamiliar with while bringing up my child" and "It would be good if the system would allow me to consult with a medical institution in an emergency". It is thought that these opinions indicate the necessity of providing services that avoid giving stress to the user, and of expanding the services such as by including an ability to consult with medical institutions using the videophone function that is already incorporated in the tablet phone, and by realizing these it is believed that the convenience would be improved. In the interviews with the physicians, in addition to requesting the connection of a basal thermometer similarly to the opinions given by the mothers with babies, the importance was understood of providing a full lineup of vital sign sensors including basal thermometers based on the Continua Health Alliance standards which have the objective of allowing seamless communications with the tablet phone. Currently, investigations are made into the seamless connection of basal thermometers. In the study this time, the necessity and validity of the health management function of the Health Management System linked with the Women's Healthcare Portal was confirmed. Regarding the medication management, this was set as an issue for consideration in the future.

From the above, it was confirmed that efficient women's healthcare could be realized by linking the Women's Healthcare Portal with the Health Management System to apply the Health Management System to mothers with children. As can be understood from these verifications, and particularly from Table 3, it was possible to confirm the necessity of building a system that improves the functional aspects without adding to the workload on physicians and without increasing the burden on mothers with children of applying the system.

5   Summary

By linking with the Women's Healthcare Portal, it was possible to confirm the validity of the Health Management System developed for elderly persons also for women's healthcare using field trials. Further, the fact that there is a high necessity to integrate both systems, the Women's Healthcare Portal and the Health Management System, was also confirmed from the field trials. Currently, in addition to coordinating the integration of both systems with the cooperation of Maebashi City, investigation is made with regard to the connection of the various vital sign sensors, including basal thermometers.

Going forward, the first stage will be the expansion of the services to cover women's healthcare that considers the full lineup of vital sign sensors and linkages with medical institutions. As well as further improving the convenience, such as by applying the system to commercially available smartphones, it is planned to build a health management system that contributes to health management not only for elderly persons and mothers with children, but for all the people throughout their entire lives. Furthermore, we increase the number of the monitors and are going to perform an accurate evaluation.

In addition, because the type of remote health management system described in this study, utilizing a tablet-type device that does not require keyboard operation, has a compact device size, it will enable the provision of high quality services to all people, including not only elderly persons who are unfamiliar with keyboard use, but also persons who are accustomed to keyboard operation. Therefore, it is believed that this system can contribute to maintaining people's health as an e-Health system which can be used by people throughout the world, not just by people living in countries using Chinese characters.

References

1. Joint ITU-WHO Workshop on e-Health Standards and Interoperability. http:// www.itu.int/en/ITU-T/Workshops-and-Seminars/e-Health/201204/Pages/ default.aspx
2. Jordanova, M., Lievens, F.: Global telemedicine and eHealth (A synopsis). In: E-Health and Bioengineering Conference (EHB), pp. 1–6, November 2011
3. Zulman, D.M., Jenchura, E.C., Cohen, D.M., Lewis, E.T., Houston, T.K., Asch, S.M.: How Can eHealth Technology Address Challenges Related to Multimorbidity? Perspectives from Patients with Multiple Chronic Conditions. Journal of General Internal Medicine, February 2015)
4. Choi, N.G., DiNitto, N.G.: The Digital Divide Among Low-Income Homebound Older Adults: Internet Use Patterns, eHealth Literacy, and Attitudes Toward Computer/Internet Use. J. Med. Internet Res. **15**(5), e93 (2013)
5. Rolim, C.O., Koch, F.L., Westphall, C.B., Werner, J., et al.: A cloud computing solution for patient's data collection in health care institutions. In: Second International Conference on eHealth, Telemedicine, and Social Medicine, ETELEMED 2010, pp. 95–99, February 2010
6. Matsumoto, H., Ogashiwa, N., Masada, N., Koyahara, T., Sato, M., Okazaki, H., Kobayashi, M.: Development of medication management and health management systems using a tablet phone. Japanese Telemedicine and Telecare Association **9**(2), 173–175 (2013). (in Japanese)

Special Session on Neuroimaging Data Analysis and Applications

GN-SCCA: GraphNet Based Sparse Canonical Correlation Analysis for Brain Imaging Genetics

Lei Du[1], Jingwen Yan[1], Sungeun Kim[1], Shannon L. Risacher[1],
Heng Huang[2], Mark Inlow[3], Jason H. Moore[4], Andrew J. Saykin[1],
and Li Shen[1]([✉]), for the Alzheimer's Disease Neuroimaging Initiative

[1] Radiology and Imaging Sciences, Indiana University School of Medicine,
Indianapolis, IN, USA
shenli@iu.edu
[2] Computer Science and Engineering, University of Texas at Arlington,
Arlington, TX, USA
[3] Mathematics, Rose-Hulman Institute of Technology, Terre Haute, IN, USA
[4] Biomedical Informatics, School of Medicine, University of Pennsylvania,
Philadelphia, PA, USA

Abstract. Identifying associations between genetic variants and neuroimaging quantitative traits (QTs) is a popular research topic in brain imaging genetics. Sparse canonical correlation analysis (SCCA) has been widely used to reveal complex multi-SNP-multi-QT associations. Several SCCA methods explicitly incorporate prior knowledge into the model and intend to uncover the hidden structure informed by the prior knowledge. We propose a novel structured SCCA method using Graph constrained Elastic-Net (GraphNet) regularizer to not only discover important associations, but also induce smoothness between coefficients that are adjacent in the graph. In addition, the proposed method incorporates the covariance structure information usually ignored by most SCCA methods. Experiments on simulated and real imaging genetic data show that, the proposed method not only outperforms a widely used SCCA method but also yields an easy-to-interpret biological findings.

1 Introduction

Brain imaging genetics, which intends to discover the associations between genetic factors (e.g., the single nucleotide polymorphisms, SNPs) and quanti-

L. Shen—This work was supported by NIH R01 LM011360, U01 AG024904 (details available at http://adni.loni.usc.edu), RC2 AG036535, R01 AG19771, P30 AG10133, and NSF IIS-1117335 at IU, by NSF CCF-0830780, CCF-0917274, DMS-0915s228, and IIS-1117965 at UTA, and by NIH R01 LM011360, R01 LM009012, and R01 LM010098 at Dartmouth.
ADNI—Data used in preparation of this article were obtained from the Alzheimer's Disease Neuroimaging Initiative (ADNI) database (adni.loni.usc.edu). As such, the investigators within the ADNI contributed to the design and implementation of ADNI and/or provided data but did not participate in analysis or writing of this report. A complete listing of ADNI investigators can be found at: http://adni.loni. usc.edu/wp-content/uploads/how_to_apply/ADNI_Acknowledgement_List.pdf.

© Springer International Publishing Switzerland 2015
Y. Guo et al. (Eds.): BIH 2015, LNAI 9250, pp. 275–284, 2015.
DOI: 10.1007/978-3-319-23344-4_27

tative traits (QTs, e.g., those extracted from neuroimaging data), is an emerging research topic. While single-SNP-single-QT association analyses have been widely performed [17], several studies have used regression techniques [9] to examine the joint effect of multiple SNPs on one or a few QTs. Recently, bi-multivariate analyses [6,7,12,18], which aim to identify complex multi-SNP-multi-QT associations, have also received much attention.

Sparse canonical correlation analysis (SCCA) [14,19], a type of bi-multivariate analysis, has been successfully used for analyzing imaging genetics data [6,12], and other biology data [4,5,14,19]. To simplify the problem, most existing SCCA methods assume that the covariance matrix of the data to be the identity matrix. Then the Lasso [14,19] or group Lasso [6,12] regularizer is often solved using the soft-thresholding method. Although this assumption usually leads to a reasonable result, it is worth pointing out that the relationship between those variables within either modality have been ignored. For neuroimaging genetic data, correlations usually exist among regions of interest (ROIs) in the brain and among linkage disequilibrium (LD) blocks in the genome. Therefore, simply treating the data covariance matrices as identity or diagonal ones will limit the performance of identifying meaningful structured imaging genetic associations.

Witten *et al.* [19,20] proposed an SCCA method which employs penalized matrix decomposition (PMD) to yield two sparse canonical loadings. Lin *et al.* [12] extended Witten's SCCA model to incorporate non-overlapping group knowledge by imposing $l_{2,1}$-norm regularizer onto both canonical loadings. Chen *et al.* [3] proposed the ssCCA approach by imposing a smoothness penalty for one canonical loading of the taxa based on their relationship on the phylogenetic tree. Chen *et al.* [4,5] treated the feature space as an undirected graph where each node corresponds to a variable and r_{ij} is the edge weight between nodes i and j. They proposed network based SCCA which penalizes the l_1 norm of $|r_{ij}|(u_i - sign(r_{ij})u_j)$ to encourage the weight values u_i and u_j to be similar if $r_{ij} > 0$, or dissimilar if $r_{ij} < 0$. A common limitation of these SCCA models is that they approximate $\mathbf{X^T X}$ by identity or diagonal matrix. Du *et al.* [7] proposed an S2CCA algorithm that overcomes this limitation, and requires users to explicitly specify non-overlapping group structures. Yan *et al.* [21] proposed KG-SCCA which uses l_2 norm of $r_{ij}^2(u_i - sign(r_{ij})u_j)$ to replace that in Chen's model [4,5]. KG-SCCA also requires the structure information to be explicitly defined. Note that an inaccurate sign of r_{ij} may introduce bias [10].

In this paper, we impose the Graph-constrained Elastic Net (GraphNet) [8] into SCCA model and propose a new GraphNet constrained SCCA (GN-SCCA). Our contributions are twofold: (1) GN-SCCA estimates the covariance matrix directly instead of approximating it by the identity matrix $\mathbf{I}$; (2) GN-SCCA employs a graph penalty using data-driven technique to induce smoothness by penalizing the pairwise differences between adjacent features. Thorough experiments on both simulation and real imaging genetic data show that our method outperforms a widely used SCCA implementation [19][1] by identifying stronger imaging genetic associations and more accurate canonical loading patterns.

2   Preliminaries

2.1   Sparse CCA

We use the boldface lowercase letter to denote the vector, and the boldface uppercase letter to denote the matrix. The i-th row and j-th column of $\mathbf{M} = (m_{ij})$ are represented as $\mathbf{m}^i$ and $\mathbf{m}_j$. Let $\mathbf{X} = \{\mathbf{x}^1; ...; \mathbf{x}^n\} \subseteq \mathbb{R}^p$ be the SNP data and $\mathbf{Y} = \{\mathbf{y}^1; ...; \mathbf{y}^n\} \subseteq \mathbb{R}^q$ be the QT data, where n, p and q are the subject number, SNP number and QT number respectively.

The SCCA model presented in [19,20] is as follows:

$$\max_{\mathbf{u},\mathbf{v}} \mathbf{u}^T \mathbf{X}^T \mathbf{Y} \mathbf{v} \qquad s.t. \ ||\mathbf{u}||_2^2 \leq 1, ||\mathbf{v}||_2^2 \leq 1, ||\mathbf{u}||_1 \leq c_1, ||\mathbf{v}||_1 \leq c_2, \qquad (1)$$

where the two terms $||\mathbf{u}||_2^2 \leq 1$ and $||\mathbf{v}||_2^2 \leq 1$ originate from the equalities $||\mathbf{u}||_2^2 = 1$ and $||\mathbf{v}||_2^2 = 1$, where $||\mathbf{u}||_2^2 = 1$ and $||\mathbf{v}||_2^2 = 1$ approximate $||\mathbf{X}\mathbf{u}||_2^2 = 1$ and $||\mathbf{Y}\mathbf{v}||_2^2 = 1$ to simplify computation. This simplification approximates the covariance matrices $\mathbf{X}^T\mathbf{X}$ and $\mathbf{Y}^T\mathbf{Y}$ by the identity matrix $\mathbf{I}$ (or sometimes a diagonal matrix), assuming that the features are independent. Most SCCA methods employ this simplification [3–5,12,19,20]. Besides, $||\mathbf{u}||_1 \leq c_1$ and $||\mathbf{v}||_1 \leq c_2$ induce sparsity to control the sparsity of canonical loadings. In addition to the Lasso (l_1-norm), the fused Lasso can also be used [5,14,19,20].

2.2   Graph Laplacian

The Graph Laplacian, also called the Laplacian matrix, has been widely used in the spectral clustering techniques and spectral graph theory [2], owing to its advantage in clustering those correlated features automatically. We denote a weighted undirected graph as $G = (V, E, W)$, where V is the set of vertices corresponding to features of $\mathbf{X}$ or $\mathbf{Y}$, E is the set of edges with $e_{i,j}$ indicating that two features $\mathbf{v}_i$ and $\mathbf{v}_j$ are connected, and $w_{i,j}$ is the weight of edge $e_{i,j}$. Here we consider G as a complete graph and thus every two vertices are connected.

Formally, the adjacency matrix of G is defined as:

$$A(i, j) = \begin{cases} w_{i,j}, & \text{if } i \neq j, \text{and} \\ 0, & \text{otherwise.} \end{cases} \qquad (2)$$

Generally, $w_{i,j}$ is set to $|r_{i,j}|^d$, where $r_{i,j}$ is the sample correlation between the i-th and j-th variables. In this work, for simplicity, we set $d = 2$, i.e. $w_{i,j} = r_{i,j}^2$. It can also be decided by domain experts in other applications.

---

[1] SCCA in the PMA software package is widely used as a benchmark algorithm. Here we simply use SCCA to denote the SCCA method in this software package. See http://cran.r-project.org/web/packages/PMA/ for details.

Let $\mathbf{D}$ be a diagonal degree matrix with the following diagonal entries: $D(i,i) = \sum_j A(i,j)$. Then the Laplacian matrix $\mathbf{L}$ is defined as $\mathbf{L} = \mathbf{D} - \mathbf{A}$ [8]. $\mathbf{L}$ has many merits such as the symmetry and the positive semi-definite structure. Most importantly, it can map a weighted graph onto a new space such that connected vertices stay as close as possible.

3 GraphNet Based SCCA (GN-SCCA)

Inspired by the Graph Laplacian [11] and the GraphNet [8] technique, we define the penalty $P(\mathbf{u})$ and $P(\mathbf{v})$ as follows:

$$P(\mathbf{u}) = ||\mathbf{u}||_{GN} = \mathbf{u}^T \mathbf{L}_1 \mathbf{u} \le c_1,$$
$$P(\mathbf{v}) = ||\mathbf{v}||_{GN} = \mathbf{v}^T \mathbf{L}_2 \mathbf{v} \le c_2. \tag{3}$$

where $\mathbf{L}_1$ and $\mathbf{L}_2$ are the Laplacian matrices of two complete undirect graphs defined by the sample correlation matrices of the SNP and QT training data, respectively. The terms $\mathbf{u}^T \mathbf{L}_1 \mathbf{u}$ and $\mathbf{v}^T \mathbf{L}_2 \mathbf{v}$ make each feature fair be penalized smoothly according to the correlation between the two features.

Applying the two penalties above, the GN-SCCA model takes the form:

$$\min_{\mathbf{u},\mathbf{v}} -\mathbf{u}^T \mathbf{X}^T \mathbf{Y} \mathbf{v} \tag{4}$$

$s.t.$ $||\mathbf{X}\mathbf{u}||_2^2 \le 1, ||\mathbf{Y}\mathbf{v}||_2^2 \le 1, P(\mathbf{u}) \le c_1, P(\mathbf{v}) \le c_2, ||\mathbf{u}||_1 \le c_3, ||\mathbf{v}||_1 \le c_4,$

where the terms $||\mathbf{u}||_1 \le c_3$ and $||\mathbf{v}||_1 \le c_4$ are used to induce sparsity; and the $P(\mathbf{u})$ and $P(\mathbf{v})$ are Graph Laplcaian based GraphNet constraints [8]. Note that we use $||\mathbf{X}\mathbf{u}||_2^2 \le 1$ instead of $||\mathbf{X}||_2^2 \le 1$, which is typically used in other models, and thus our model takes into consideration the full covariance information.

Using Lagrange multiplier and writing the penalties into the matrix form, the objective function of GN-SCCA is as follows:

$$\mathcal{L}(\mathbf{u},\mathbf{v}) = -\mathbf{u}^T\mathbf{X}^T\mathbf{Y}\mathbf{v} + \frac{\lambda_1}{2}||\mathbf{u}||_{GN} + \frac{\lambda_2}{2}||\mathbf{v}||_{GN} + \frac{\beta_1}{2}||\mathbf{u}||_1 + \frac{\beta_2}{2}||\mathbf{v}||_1 + \frac{\gamma_1}{2}||\mathbf{X}\mathbf{u}||_2^2 + \frac{\gamma_2}{2}||\mathbf{Y}\mathbf{v}||_2^2 \tag{5}$$

where $(\lambda_1,\lambda_2,\beta_1,\beta_2)$ are tuning parameters, corresponding to (c_1,c_2,c_3,c_4).

Take the derivative regarding $\mathbf{u}$ and $\mathbf{v}$ separately and let them be zero:

$$(\lambda_1\mathbf{L}_1 + \beta_1\mathbf{D}_1 + \gamma_1\mathbf{X}^T\mathbf{X})\mathbf{u} = \mathbf{X}^T\mathbf{Y}\mathbf{v}, \tag{6}$$
$$(\lambda_2\mathbf{L}_2 + \beta_2\mathbf{D}_2 + \gamma_2\mathbf{Y}^T\mathbf{Y})\mathbf{v} = \mathbf{Y}^T\mathbf{X}\mathbf{u}, \tag{7}$$

where $\mathbf{D}_1$ is a diagonal matrix with the k_1-th element as $\frac{1}{2||u^{k_1}||_1}$ ($k_1 \in [1,p]$), and $\mathbf{D}_2$ is a diagonal matrix with the k_2-th element as $\frac{1}{2||v^{k_2}||_1}$ ($k_2 \in [1,q]$)[2].

Since $\mathbf{D}_1$ relies on $\mathbf{u}$ and $\mathbf{D}_2$ relies on $\mathbf{v}$, we introduce an iterative procedure to solve this objective. In each iteration, we first fix $\mathbf{v}$ and solve for $\mathbf{u}$, and then fix $\mathbf{u}$ and solve for $\mathbf{v}$. The procedure stops until it satisfies a predefined stopping criterion. Algorithm 1 shows the pseudocode of the GN-SCCA algorithm.

---

[2] If $||u^{k_1}||_1 = 0$ or $||v^{k_2}||_1 = 0$, we approximate it with $\sqrt{||u^{k_1}||_2^2 + \zeta}$ or $\sqrt{||v^{k_2}||_2^2 + \zeta}$, where ζ is a very small non-zero value. According to [13], this regularization will not affect the result when $\zeta \to 0$.

Algorithm 1. GraphNet based Structure-aware SCCA (GN-SCCA)

Require:
$\quad\mathbf{X} = \{\mathbf{x}_1, ..., \mathbf{x}_n\}^T,\ \mathbf{Y} = \{\mathbf{y}_1, ..., \mathbf{y}_n\}^T$
Ensure:
$\quad$ Canonical vectors $\mathbf{u}$ and $\mathbf{v}$.
1: Initialize $\mathbf{u} \in \mathbb{R}^{p \times 1}$, $\mathbf{v} \in \mathbb{R}^{q \times 1}$; $\mathbf{L}_1 = D_u - A_u$ and $\mathbf{L}_2 = D_v - A_v$ only from the training data;
2: **while** not converged **do**
3: $\quad$ **while** not converged regarding $\mathbf{u}$ **do**
4: $\quad\quad$ Calculate the diagonal matrix $\mathbf{D}_1$, where the k_1-th element is $\frac{1}{2||u^{k_1}||_1}$;
5: $\quad\quad$ Update $\mathbf{u} = (\lambda_1 \mathbf{L}_1 + \beta_1 \mathbf{D}_1 + \gamma_1 \mathbf{X}^T \mathbf{X})^{-1} \mathbf{X}^T \mathbf{Y} \mathbf{v}$;
6: $\quad$ **end while**
7: $\quad$ **while** not converged regarding $\mathbf{v}$ **do**
8: $\quad\quad$ Calculate the diagonal matrix $\mathbf{D}_2$, where the k_2-th element is $\frac{1}{2||v^{k_2}||_1}$;
9: $\quad\quad$ Update $\mathbf{v} = (\lambda_2 \mathbf{L}_2 + \beta_2 \mathbf{D}_2 + \gamma_2 \mathbf{Y}^T \mathbf{Y})^{-1} \mathbf{Y}^T \mathbf{X} \mathbf{u}$;
10: $\quad$ **end while**
11: **end while**
12: Scale $\mathbf{u}$ so that $||\mathbf{X}\mathbf{u}||_2 = 1$;
13: Scale $\mathbf{v}$ so that $||\mathbf{Y}\mathbf{v}||_2 = 1$.

3.1 Convergence Analysis of GN-SCCA

We first introduce Lemma 1 described in [13].

Lemma 1. *The following inequality holds for any two nonzero vectors $\tilde{\mathbf{u}}$, $\mathbf{u}$ with the same length,*

$$||\tilde{\mathbf{u}}||_2 - \frac{||\tilde{\mathbf{u}}||_2^2}{2||\mathbf{u}||_2} \leq ||\mathbf{u}||_2 - \frac{||\mathbf{u}||_2^2}{2||\mathbf{u}||_2}. \tag{8}$$

Lemma 2. *For any real number $\tilde{u}$ and any nonzero real number u, we have*

$$||\tilde{u}||_1 - \frac{||\tilde{u}||_1^2}{2||u||_1} \leq ||u||_1 - \frac{||u||_1^2}{2||u||_1}. \tag{9}$$

Proof. The proof is obvious, given Lemma 1, $||\tilde{u}||_1 = ||\tilde{u}||_2$ and $||u||_1 = ||u||_2$.

Theorem 1. *In each iteration, Algorithm 1 decreases the value of the objective function till the algorithm converges.*

Proof. The proof consists of two phases. (1) Phase 1: For Steps 3-6, $\mathbf{u}$ is the only variable to estimate. The objective function Eq. (5) is equivalent to

$$\mathcal{L}(\mathbf{u}, \mathbf{v}) = -\mathbf{u}^T \mathbf{X}^T \mathbf{Y} \mathbf{v} + \frac{\lambda_1}{2}||\mathbf{u}||_{GN} + \frac{\beta_1}{2}||\mathbf{u}||_1 + \frac{\gamma_1}{2}||\mathbf{X}\mathbf{u}||_2^2$$

From Step 5, we denote the updated value as $\tilde{\mathbf{u}}$. Then we have

$$-\tilde{\mathbf{u}}^T \mathbf{X}^T \mathbf{Y} \mathbf{v} + \lambda_1 \tilde{\mathbf{u}}^T \mathbf{L}_1 \tilde{\mathbf{u}} + \beta_1 \tilde{\mathbf{u}}^T \mathbf{D}_1 \tilde{\mathbf{u}} + \gamma_1 \tilde{\mathbf{u}}^T \mathbf{X}^T \mathbf{X} \tilde{\mathbf{u}}$$
$$\leq -\mathbf{u}^T \mathbf{X}^T \mathbf{Y} \mathbf{v} + \lambda_1 \mathbf{u}^T \mathbf{L}_1 \mathbf{u} + \beta_1 \mathbf{u}^T \mathbf{D}_1 \mathbf{u} + \gamma_1 \mathbf{u}^T \mathbf{X}^T \mathbf{X} \mathbf{u}$$

According to the definition of $\mathbf{D}_1$, we obtain

$$-\tilde{\mathbf{u}}^T \mathbf{X}^T \mathbf{Y} \mathbf{v} + \lambda_1 \tilde{\mathbf{u}}^T \mathbf{L}_1 \tilde{\mathbf{u}} + \beta_1 \sum_{k_1} \frac{||\tilde{u}^{k_1}||_1^2}{2||u^{k_1}||_1} + \gamma_1 \tilde{\mathbf{u}}^T \mathbf{X}^T \mathbf{X} \tilde{\mathbf{u}}$$
$$\leq -\mathbf{u}^T \mathbf{X}^T \mathbf{Y} \mathbf{v} + \lambda_1 \mathbf{u}^T \mathbf{L}_1 \mathbf{u} + \beta_1 \sum_{k_1} \frac{||u^{k_1}||_1^2}{2||u^{k_1}||_1} + \gamma_1 \mathbf{u}^T \mathbf{X}^T \mathbf{X} \mathbf{u} \tag{10}$$

Then summing Eq. (9) and Eq. (10) on both sides, we obtain

$$-\tilde{\mathbf{u}}^T\mathbf{X}^T\mathbf{Y}\mathbf{v} + \lambda_1\tilde{\mathbf{u}}^T\mathbf{L_1}\tilde{\mathbf{u}} + \beta_1||\tilde{\mathbf{u}}||_1 + \gamma_1||\mathbf{X}\tilde{\mathbf{u}}||_2^2 \leq -\mathbf{u}^T\mathbf{X}^T\mathbf{Y}\mathbf{v} + \lambda_1\mathbf{u}^T\mathbf{L_1}\mathbf{u} + \beta_1||\mathbf{u}||_1 + \gamma_1||\mathbf{X}\mathbf{u}||_2^2$$

Let $\lambda_1^* = 2\lambda_1$, $\gamma_1^* = 2\gamma_1, \beta_1^* = 2\beta_1$, we arrive at

$$-\tilde{\mathbf{u}}^T\mathbf{X}^T\mathbf{Y}\mathbf{v} + \frac{\lambda_1^*}{2}||\tilde{\mathbf{u}}||_{GN} + \frac{\beta_1^*}{2}||\tilde{\mathbf{u}}||_1 + \frac{\gamma_1^*}{2}||\mathbf{X}\tilde{\mathbf{u}}||_2^2 \leq -\mathbf{u}^T\mathbf{X}^T\mathbf{Y}\mathbf{v} + \frac{\lambda_1^*}{2}||\mathbf{u}||_{GN} + \frac{\beta_1^*}{2}||\mathbf{u}||_1 + \frac{\gamma_1^*}{2}||\mathbf{X}\mathbf{u}||_2^2.$$

$$(11)$$

Thus, the objective value decreases during Phase 1: $\mathcal{L}(\tilde{\mathbf{u}}, \mathbf{v}) \leq \mathcal{L}(\mathbf{u}, \mathbf{v})$.

(2) Phase 2: For Steps 7-10, $\mathbf{v}$ is the variable to estimate. Similarly, we have

$$-\tilde{\mathbf{u}}^T\mathbf{X}^T\mathbf{Y}\tilde{\mathbf{v}} + \frac{\lambda_2^*}{2}||\tilde{\mathbf{v}}||_{GN} + \frac{\beta_2^*}{2}||\tilde{\mathbf{v}}||_1 + \frac{\gamma_2^*}{2}||\mathbf{Y}\tilde{\mathbf{v}}||_2^2 \leq -\tilde{\mathbf{u}}^T\mathbf{X}^T\mathbf{Y}\mathbf{v} + \frac{\lambda_2^*}{2}||\mathbf{v}||_{GN} + \frac{\beta_2^*}{2}||\mathbf{v}||_1 + \frac{\gamma_2^*}{2}||\mathbf{Y}\mathbf{v}||_2^2$$

$$(12)$$

Thus, the objective value decreases during Phase 2: $\mathcal{L}(\tilde{\mathbf{u}}, \tilde{\mathbf{v}}) \leq \mathcal{L}(\tilde{\mathbf{u}}, \mathbf{v})$.

Applying the transitive property of inequalities, we obtain $\mathcal{L}(\tilde{\mathbf{u}}, \tilde{\mathbf{v}}) \leq \mathcal{L}(\mathbf{u}, \mathbf{v})$. Therefore, Algorithm 1 decreases the objective function in each iteration.

We set the stopping criterion of Algorithm 1 as $\max\{|\delta| \mid \delta \in (\mathbf{u}_{t+1} - \mathbf{u}_t)\} \leq \tau$ and $\max\{|\delta| \mid \delta \in (\mathbf{v}_{t+1} - \mathbf{v}_t)\} \leq \tau$, where τ is a desirable estimate error. In this paper, $\tau = 10^{-5}$ is empirically chosen in the experiments.

4   Experimental Results

4.1   Results on Simulation Data

We used four simulated data sets to compare the performances of GN-SCCA and a widely used SCCA implementation [19]. We applied two different methods to generate these data with distinct structures to assure diversity. The first two data sets (both with $n = 1000$ and $p = q = 50$, but with different built-in correlations) were generated as follows: 1) We created a random positive definite group structured covariance matrix $\mathbf{M}$. 2) Data set $\mathbf{Y}$ with covariance structure $\mathbf{M}$ was calculated by Cholesky decomposition. 3) Data set $\mathbf{X}$ was created similarly. 4) Canonical loadings $\mathbf{u}$ and $\mathbf{v}$ were created so that the variables in one group share the same weights based on the group structures of $\mathbf{X}$ and $\mathbf{Y}$ respectively. 5) The portion of the specified group in $\mathbf{Y}$ were replaced based on the $\mathbf{u}$, $\mathbf{v}$, $\mathbf{X}$ and the assigned correlation. The last two data sets (with different n, p, q and built-in correlations) were created using the simulation procedure described in [5]: 1) Predefined structure information was used to create $\mathbf{u}$ and $\mathbf{v}$. 2) Latent vector z was generated from $N(\mathbf{0}, \mathbf{I}_{n \times n})$. 3) $\mathbf{X}$ was created with each $\mathbf{x}_i \sim N(z_i\mathbf{u}, \mathbf{I}_{p \times p})$ and $\mathbf{Y}$ with each $\mathbf{y}_i \sim N(z_i\mathbf{v}, \sum_y)$ where $(\sum_y)_{jk} = \exp^{-|v_j - v_k|}$.

According to Eqs. (6-7), six parameters need to be decided for GN-SCCA. Here we choose the value of tuning range based on two considerations: 1) Chen and Liu [4] showed that the results were insensitive to γ_1 and γ_2 in a similar study; 2) The major difference between traditional CCA and SCCA is the penalty terms. Thus their results will be the same if small parameters are used.

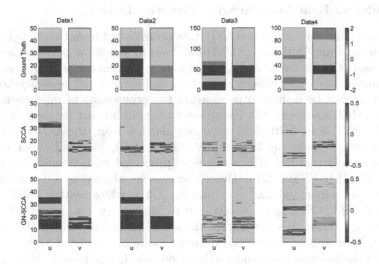

Fig. 1. Comparisons on estimated canonical loadings using 5-fold cross-validation on synthetic data. The ground truth (the top row), SCCA results (the middle row) and GN-SCCA results (the bottom row) are all shown. For each panel pair, the 5 estimated **u**'s are shown on the left panel, and the 5 estimated **v**'s are shown on the right.

With this observation, we tune γ_1 and γ_2 from small range of $[1,10,100]$, and tune the remaining ones from 10^{-1} to 10^3 through **nested** 5-fold cross-validation.

The true signals and estimated **u** and **v** are shown in Fig. 1. The estimated canonical loadings **u** and **v** of GN-SCCA were consistent with the ground truth on all simulated data sets, while SCCA only found an incomplete portion of the true signals. Shown in Table 1 are the cross-validation performances of the two methods. The left part of the table shows that GN-SCCA outperformed SCCA consistently and significantly, and it has better test accuracy than SCCA on testing data. The right part of Table 1 presents the area under ROC (AUC), where GN-SCCA also significantly outperformed SCCA on all data sets. These results demonstrated that GN-SCCA identifies the correlations and signal locations more accurately and more stably than SCCA.

Table 1. 5-fold nested cross-validation results on synthetic data: Mean±std. is shown for estimated correlation coefficients and AUC regarding the estimated canonical loadings. p-values of paired t-test between GN-SCCA and SCCA are also shown.

True	Correlation Coefficient (CC)			Area under ROC (AUC)					
CC	SCCA	GN-SCCA	p	SCCA:u	GN-SCCA:u	p	SCCA:v	GN-SCCA:v	p
Data1(0.80)	0.48±0.03	0.80±0.01	1.52E-05	0.65±0.02	1.00±0.00	1.44E-06	0.81±0.04	1.00±0.00	2.65E-04
Data2(0.90)	0.56±0.04	0.90±0.01	8.38E-06	0.66±0.01	1.00±0.00	3.15E-07	0.79±0.04	1.00±0.00	1.79E-04
Data3(0.92)	0.55±0.15	0.89±0.06	1.54E-03	0.67±0.01	0.89±0.04	2.49E-04	0.81±0.04	1.00±0.00	2.23E-04
Data4(0.98)	0.97±0.01	0.98±0.01	6.82E-02	0.89±0.05	0.98±0.03	3.45E-03	0.69±0.01	1.00±0.00	1.88E-07

4.2   Results on Real Neuroimaging Genetics Data

We used the real neuroimaging and SNP data downloaded from the Alzheimer's Disease Neuroimaging Initiative (ADNI) database to assess the performances of GN-SCCA and SCCA. One goal of ADNI is to test whether serial MRI, positron emission tomography, other biological markers, and clinical and neuropsychological assessment can be combined to measure the progression of mild cognitive impairment (MCI) and early AD. Please see www.adni-info.org for more details.

Both the SNP and MRI data were downloaded from the LONI website (adni.loni.usc.edu). There are 204 healthy control (HC), 363 MCI and 176 AD participants. The structural MRI scans were processed with voxel-based morphometry (VBM) in SPM8 [1,15]. Briefly, scans were aligned to a T1-weighted template image, segmented into gray matter (GM), white matter (WM) and cerebrospinal fluid (CSF) maps, normalized to MNI space, and smoothed with an 8mm FWHM kernel. We subsampled the whole brain and yielded 465 voxels spanning all brain ROIs. These VBM measures were pre-adjusted for removing the effects of the baseline age, gender, education, and handedness by the regression weights derived from HC participants. We investigated SNPs from the top 5 AD risk genes [16] and APOE e4. In total we have 379 SNPs in this study. Our task was to examine correlations between the voxels (GM density measures) and genetic biomarker SNPs.

Table 2. 5-fold nested cross-validation results on real data: The models learned from training data were used to estimate the correlation coefficients for both training and testing cases. p-values of paired t-tests between GN-SCCA and SCCA are shown.

Correlation coefficients	SCCA						GN-SCCA						p
	F1	F2	F3	F4	F5	mean±std.	F1	F2	F3	F4	F5	mean±std.	
Training	0.22	0.23	0.24	0.20	0.21	0.22±0.02	0.28	0.27	0.28	0.26	0.27	0.27±0.01	2.25E-4
Testing	0.07	0.04	0.09	0.05	0.16	0.07±0.03	0.21	0.28	0.24	0.31	0.27	0.26±0.04	9.14E-4

Shown in Table 2 are the 5-fold cross-validation results of GN-SCCA and SCCA. GN-SCCA significantly and consistently outperformed SCCA in terms of identifying stronger correlations from the training data. For the testing performance, SCCA did not do well possibly due to over-fitting, while GN-SCCA consistently outperformed SCCA. Fig. 2 shows the heat maps of the trained canonical loadings learned from cross-validation. We could observe that both weights, i.e. $\mathbf{u}$ and $\mathbf{v}$, estimated by GN-SCCA were quite sparse and presented a clear pattern which could be easier to interpret. However, SCCA identified many signals which could be harder to explain. The strongest genetic signal, identified by GN-SCCA, was the APOE e4 SNP rs429358; and the strongest imaging signals came from the hippocampus. They were negatively correlated with each other. This reassures that our method identified a well-known correlation between APOE and hippocampal morphometry in an AD cohort. These results show the capability of GN-SCCA to identify biologically meaningful imaging genetic associations.

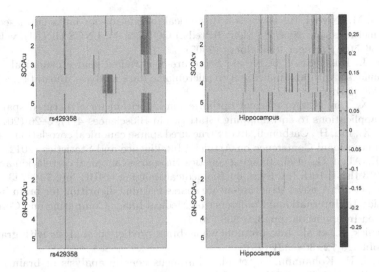

Fig. 2. Comparisons on estimated canonical loadings using 5-fold cross-validation on real data. The SCCA results (the top row) and GN-SCCA results (the bottom row) are shown. For each panel pair, the 5 estimated **u**'s are shown on the left panel, and the 5 estimated **v**'s are shown on the right.

5 Conclusions

We proposed a GraphNet constrained SCCA (GN-SCCA) to mine imaging genetic associations, and incorporated the covariance information ignored by many existing SCCA methods. The GraphNet term induces smoothness by penalizing the pairwise differences between adjacent features in a complete graph or an user-given graph (correlation matrix used in this study). Our experimental study showed that GN-SCCA accurately discovered the true signals from the simulation data and obtained improved performance and biologically meaningful findings from real data. In this work, we only did comparative study between GN-SCCA and a widely-used SCCA method [19]. We have observed many recent developments in structured SCCA models. Some (e.g., [6,12,14,18,19]) ignored the covariance structure information of the input data, which was usually helpful to imaging genetics applications. A few other models (e.g., [7,21]) overcome this limitation but impose different sparsity structures. Work is in progress to compare the proposed GN-SCCA with these structured SCCA models. Given the mathematically simple formulation of GN-SCCA, we feel it is a valuable addition which is complementary to the existing SCCA models.

References

1. Ashburner, J., Friston, K.J.: Voxel-based morphometry-the methods. Neuroimage **11**(6), 805–821 (2000)

2. Belkin, M., Niyogi, P.: Towards a theoretical foundation for laplacian-based manifold methods. In: Auer, P., Meir, R. (eds.) COLT 2005. LNCS (LNAI), vol. 3559, pp. 486–500. Springer, Heidelberg (2005)
3. Chen, J., Bushman, F.D., et al.: Structure-constrained sparse canonical correlation analysis with an application to microbiome data analysis. Biostatistics **14**(2), 244–258 (2013)
4. Chen, X., Liu, H.: An efficient optimization algorithm for structured sparse cca, with applications to eqtl mapping. Statistics in Biosciences **4**(1), 3–26 (2012)
5. Chen, X., Liu, H., Carbonell, J.G.: Structured sparse canonical correlation analysis. In: International Conference on Artificial Intelligence and Statistics (2012)
6. Chi, E., Allen, G., et al.: Imaging genetics via sparse canonical correlation analysis. In: 2013 IEEE 10th Int. Sym. on Biomedical Imaging (ISBI), pp. 740–743 (2013)
7. Du, L., et al.: A novel structure-aware sparse learning algorithm for brain imaging genetics. In: International Conference on Medical Image Computing and Computer Assisted Intervention, pp. 329–336 (2014)
8. Grosenick, L., et al.: Interpretable whole-brain prediction analysis with graphnet. NeuroImage **72**, 304–321 (2013)
9. Hibar, D.P., Kohannim, O., et al.: Multilocus genetic analysis of brain images. Front. Genet. **2**, 73 (2011)
10. Kim, S., Xing, E.P.: Statistical estimation of correlated genome associations to a quantitative trait network. PLoS Genetics **5**(8) (2009)
11. Li, C., Li, H.: Network-constrained regularization and variable selection for analysis of genomic data. Bioinformatics **24**(9), 1175–1182 (2008)
12. Lin, D., Calhoun, V.D., Wang, Y.P.: Correspondence between fMRI and SNP data by group sparse canonical correlation analysis. Med. Image Anal. (2013)
13. Nie, F., Huang, H., Cai, X., Ding, C.H.: Efficient and robustfeature selection via joint 2, 1-norms minimization. In: Advances inNeural Information Processing Systems, pp. 1813–1821 (2010)
14. Parkhomenko, E., Tritchler, D., Beyene, J.: Sparse canonical correlation analysis with application to genomic data integration. Statistical Applications in Genetics and Molecular Biology **8**(1), 1–34 (2009)
15. Risacher, S.L., Saykin, A.J., et al.: Baseline MRI predictors of conversion from MCI to probable AD in the ADNI cohort. Curr. Alzheimer Res. **6**(4), 347–361 (2009)
16. Shah, R.D., Samworth, R.J.: Variable selection with error control: another look at stability selection. Journal of the Royal Statistical Society: Series B (Statistical Methodology) **75**(1), 55–80 (2013)
17. Shen, L., Kim, S., et al.: Whole genome association study of brain-wide imaging phenotypes for identifying quantitative trait loci in MCI and AD: A study of the ADNI cohort. Neuroimage **53**(3), 1051–1063 (2010)
18. Vounou, M., Nichols, T.E., Montana, G.: Discovering genetic associations with high-dimensional neuroimaging phenotypes: A sparse reduced-rank regression approach. NeuroImage **53**(3), 1147–1159 (2010)
19. Witten, D.M., Tibshirani, R., Hastie, T.: A penalized matrix decomposition, with applications to sparse principal components and canonical correlation analysis. Biostatistics **10**(3), 515–534 (2009)
20. Witten, D.M., Tibshirani, R.J.: Extensions of sparse canonical correlation analysis with applications to genomic data. Statistical Applications in Genetics and Molecular Biology **8**(1), 1–27 (2009)
21. Yan, J., Du, L., et al.: Transcriptome-guided amyloid imaging genetic analysis via a novel structured sparse learning algorithm. Bioinformatics **30**(17), i564–i571 (2014)

B-Spline Registration of Neuroimaging Modalites with Map-Reduce Framework

Pingge Jiang and James A. Shackleford[✉]

Electrical and Computer Engineering Department,
Drexel University, Philadelphia, PA 19104, USA
shack@drexel.edu

Abstract. In this paper, we propose an improved B-spline registration algorithm for feature fusion of images from different neuroimaging techniques. The current B-spline registration method generally consists of several steps: initial curve estimation, similarity estimation between the warped image and fixed image, gradient computation, optimization and curve re-estimation. We improved the accuracy and efficiency of gradient computation by introducing a map-reduce framework which partitions the volume into multiple subregions and each subregion can be processed independently and efficiently. Experimental results show that our method achieves higher accuracy than the traditional registration algorithm and computational burden is released for large scale neuroimages.

Keywords: B-spline · Deformable registration · Map-reduce · Multi-modal · Image fusion · Neuroimaging

1 Introduction

The modern study of neurodegenerative disorders has benefited greatly from a number of imaging modalities enabling in-depth qualitative assessment and quantitative modeling. In the study of Alzheimer's disease (AD) and schizophrenia, Magnetic resonance imaging (MRI) based neuroimaging techniques have provided means of directly visualizing and detecting abnormal tissues, thereby increasing the throughput and quality of clinical trials. Specifically, MRI has provided vital insight regarding the advancement of understanding age-related degenerative diseases [1]. Diffusion Weighted Imaging (DWI) and Diffusion Tensor Imaging (DTI) have found an increased popularity due to their ability to quantify the diffusion of molecules within or across voxels. This has enabled researchers with the ability to characterize the orientation and integrity of white matter tracts [2], which allows for the examination of alterations in anisotropy [3], the study of hemispheric differences in microscopic fiber characteristics [4], the monitoring of changes in cortico-cortical connectivity [5] and more. Due to disparities in tissue response between various imaging modalities as well as inhomogeneities exhibited by certain perturbation methods, acquired images may exhibit non-linear geometric inaccuracies when imaging the same

© Springer International Publishing Switzerland 2015
Y. Guo et al. (Eds.): BIH 2015, LNAI 9250, pp. 285–294, 2015.
DOI: 10.1007/978-3-319-23344-4_28

underlying objects [6]. Consequently, a method for correlating anatomical features collected from differing imaging modalities is required to spatially correlate, and thereby fuse, such images to form robust functional models. B-spline deformable registration method is quite popular in this field due to its flexibility and robustness. However, the state-of-art B-spline algorithm introduces a significant computational burden.

In this paper, we propose a solution that allows for the B-spline registration process to be computed in a time-efficient manner by leveraging the map-reduce framework. Experiments are performed on clinical images obtained from several imaging techniques with a performance evaluation is focusing on computational efficiency and registration quality. Our method provides an innovative and practical idea of large scale image registration, which not only improves the registration quality but also reduced the computational burden.

2   Related Work

Registration plays an important role in neuroimaging by establishing a spatial correspondence for common biomarkers between images. Practical usage includes the alignment of images within a temporal series, the quantification of tissue movement, or the fusion of multiple imaging modalities. Yushkevich *et al.* uses the combination of global rigid registration with deformable registration to measure longitudinal brain atrophy [7]. The Symmetric Normalization (SyN) approach and B-spline based Free-Form deformation (FFD) were applied in his experiment to compare the bias attributions to spatial alignment of baseline image and followup images. Motivated by the time-consuming and labor-intensive nature of performing large-scale hippocampal atrophy studies, Carmichael *et al.* [8] compared several registration methods for obtaining the desired spatial transformation between the atlas image to the subject image. Kubichi *et al.* used registration to obtain structural correlation; thus, allowing for the results of DTI and MTR to be compared between controls and patients with schizophrenia [9]. Jahanshad *et al.* register the fractional anistropy (FA) maps to the target subject to generate the deformation fields that put all the anisotropy maps in the study into the same coordinate space [4].

The goal of our experiment is similar to Jahanshad's work. MRI and FA maps are acquired, while voxel-level registration is required for structural correlation. Cubic B-spline registration is applied on the FA maps to generate the deformation fields. However, the traditional B-spline algorithm contributes high computational burden for large scale images. Here, we aim to improve algorithmic efficiency and accuracy by using a map-reduce framework to rapidly solve an analytic formulation of the B-spline algorithm.

3   Theory

Given a three dimensional moving image M having voxel coordinates $\theta = x, y, z$ with voxel intensity $m = M(\theta)$ and a corresponding fixed image F having voxel coordinates $\delta = x_2, y_2, z_2$ with voxel intensity $f = F(\delta)$, a pixel-wise deformation vector field v providing an anatomomical mapping from F to M can be derrived by optimizing a similarity metric C that expresses a global extrema for the $v = v*$ most accruately describing the deformation differentiating the two images. When solving this optimization problem, the dense deformation v is paramaterized using the uniform cubic B-spline basis, which provides a sparse representation of v in terms of the B-spline basis coefficients P while introducing first order continuity into the deformation model. The vector field at any given voxel is determined by the 64 B-spline control points have overlapping local support regions at the voxel coordinate. Thus the deformation field can be found by solving the optimization problem $v* = \arg\max_P C(F, T(M, P))$, where $T(M, P)$ represents the image M transformed into the coordinate system of F given the spare paramerization of v provided by P. The relation between the control point parameterization P and the vector field v is given by:

$$v(x) = \sum_{l=0}^{3} \sum_{m=0}^{3} \sum_{n=0}^{3} B_l(u) B_m(v) B_n(w) P_{i+l, \, j+m, \, k+n} \tag{1}$$

in the x-direction, and similarly for the remaining dimensions. Here, (i, j, k) denote the coordinates for a group of voxels that are supported by a common set of 64 control points, which we refer to as a *tile* of voxels within the volume. Additionally, (u, v, w) are the local coordinates of the voxel within its housing tile normalized between $[0, 1]$, e.g., $i = \left[\frac{x}{n_x}\right] - 1, j = \left[\frac{y}{n_y}\right] - 1, k = \left[\frac{z}{n_z}\right] - 1$, $u = \frac{x}{n_x} - \left[\frac{x}{n_x}\right], v = \frac{y}{n_y} - \left[\frac{y}{n_y}\right], w = \frac{z}{n_z} - \left[\frac{z}{n_z}\right]$, where n_x, n_y and n_z denote the distance between control points. Finally, B_l for $l \in [0, 3]$ is the piecewise uniform cubic B-spline basis function in the x-dimension; likewise, B_m and B_n provide support in the remaining dimensions.

3.1   The Traditional Procedure

The optimization of the similarity metric $C(F, T(M, P))$ can be performed efficiently using a quasi-Newtonian method to search for P^* given an analytic expression for the cost function gradient [10]:

$$\frac{\partial C}{\partial P} = \sum_{(x, \, y, \, z)} \frac{\partial C}{\partial v(x, \, y, \, z)} \frac{\partial v(x, \, y, \, z)}{\partial P} \tag{2}$$

Here, the first term describes how the similarity function changes with respect to the deformation field and is independent of the parameterization provided by the B-spline basis. The second term describes how the deformation field changes with the B-spline basis function coefficients and can be easily calculated by taking the derivative of (1) with respect to P:

$$\frac{\partial v(x, \, y, \, z)}{\partial P} = \sum_{l=0}^{3} \sum_{m=0}^{3} \sum_{n=0}^{3} B_l(u) B_m(v) B_n(w) \tag{3}$$

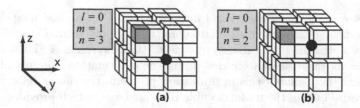

Fig. 1. A single tile experiencing different B-spline tensor product weights with respect to the control points influencing it. (a) The tile will be weighted by the tensor product of the B-spline basis function pieces (0, 1, 3), whereas in (b) the same tile will be weighted by pieces (0, 1, 2) for a different control point in the computation of (2)

Note that $\partial v/\partial P$ is simply the B-spline basis function tensor product evaluated at the relative location of a specific voxel within a tile. Since the B-spline control points are uniformly spaced, the normalized coordinates (u, v, w) used to evaluate the 64 B-spline tensor products will be the same for every tile in the volume. Consequently, $\partial v/\partial P$ can be precomputed and stored as a lookup table (LUT) for later use in the computation of (2).

The traditional approach to computing the similarity metric gradient given by (2) is to iterate across the control grid and solve for $\partial C/\partial P$ at each control point directly. However, due to the local support region overlap of control points influencing a single tile (Figure 1), computing the gradient in this way results in 63 redundant loads of the $\partial C/\partial v$ values defined at each voxel coordinate for each tile, which results in serious performance deficiency. In this paper, we introduce a map-reduce framework that loads each tile of $\partial C/\partial v$ values only once, applies all 64 possible B-spline tensor products, and then maps these intermediate results to the appropriate control points so that $\partial C/\partial P$ can subsequently be computed via a simple reduction. This procedure not only overcomes the redundant reload problem but also performs the calculation of $\partial C/\partial P$ in a tiered magnitude fashion that reduces floating point precision error introduced by machine epsilon.

3.2 The Map-Reduce Framework

The method we proposed in this paper uses a two stage map-reduce framework. Map-reduce is a programming model that typically used for parallizing the process of huge amount of datasets by a working cloud. Map step emits multiple $< key, data >$ pairs based on the predefined functions and reduce step will process each group of data in parallel based on the key value. In our experiment, the first stage is a tile-based process, every tile in the volume is analyzed by different workers in the working cloud independently. The second stage is a volume-based process, which uses the information we get from each tile to perform a high efficiency calculation.

Stage 1. The first stage starts with $\partial C/\partial v$ values having been computed for every voxel in the volume. Here, each tile of $\partial C/\partial v$ values is assigned to a compute unit, which loads the tile of data only once and applies the 64 different B-spline coefficient combinations to produce 64 intermediate results. Each result contributes to a different control point's computation of $\partial C/\partial P$, where each control point will ultimately require intermediate results from a different unique set of 63 tiles to complete.

The map function in this stage pairs $\partial C/\partial v$ at each voxel with the appropriate piecewise B-spline basis tensor product using an index between 0 to 63, which will later be used by the reduce function to determine the control point association with the produced intermediate result. After all voxels have been processed, $64 \times N_x \times N_y \times N_z$ pairs will be generated for reducing. The reduce function then sums up the pairs generated from same influential control points based on the index that map function gave, resulting in just 64 vectors per tile and give all the information needed from each tile for the second stage. The solution for each tile can be in the form of:

$$Z_{tile,\, l,\, m,\, n} = \sum_{z=0}^{N_z} \sum_{y=0}^{N_y} \sum_{x=0}^{N_x} \frac{\partial C}{\partial v\,(x,\, y,\, z)} B_l\,(u)\, B_m\,(v)\, B_n\,(w) \qquad (4)$$

Stage 2. In the second stage, the map function pairs each Z value to its corresponding control point to finally emit a sequence of $< P_i, Z_j >$ pairs throughout the volume. Where, P is defined as the control point index and Z is one of the 64 intermediate solutions computed for each tile in the first stage. Ideally, the registration volume can be partitioned into tiles and distributed across the working cloud. Thus every tile in the volume can be processed in parallel. The shuffling procedure groups together all the Z values associated with a common control point P into one slot and passes them to the reduce procedure. The reduce function iterates over the data and performs summation across all the Z values within the slot to obtain the $\partial C/\partial P$ for a given control point. Once all slots have been processed, the partial cost gradients are merged to acquire the final cost gradient.

Finally, since the addition of floating point numbers of differing orders of magnitudes results in rounding error attributable to the machine epsilon, this pyramidal approach to partitioning and accumulating the gradient calculation structures the computation for reduced errors in precision. Furthermore, the necessary data bandwidth and memory resources decrease as we traverse the reduction pyramid because data is loaded only once and reduced into more compact and meaningful representations as the computation progresses. The entire map-reduce framework for cost function gradient computation is in Figure 2.

4   Fusing Imaging Modalities

Here we apply our algorithm to recovering the deformable coordinate system transform necessary to fuse T-1 weighted MRI and fractional anisotropy (FA) diffusion tensor images of the brain. Specifically, we fuse the FA image into the T-1 weighted MRI; thus, making the MRI the fixed image F and the FA image the

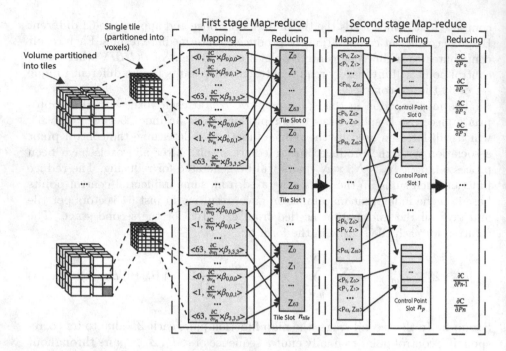

Fig. 2. Proposed map-reduce framework for cost-function gradient calculation

moving image M. Since MRI imaging suffers from susceptibility related distortions at natural interfaces (such as the skull base) as well as geometric distortions induced by gradient field non-linearities, deformable registration can be used to recover these local non-linear deformations necessary to acquire an anatomically accurate mapping to corresponding tissue locations in the FA image.

Mutual Information (MI) is the employed similarity metric for evaluating the fusion of the MRI and FA images subject to the deformation field. Specifically, evaluation of the shared mutual information begins with obtaining a potential deformation vector field v corresponding to each voxel θ in the MRI image. Partial volume interpolation is then performed in the FA image for the point corresponding to θ determined by v. These partial volumes are used to construct the probability mass function (pmf) of voxel intensities for the FA image as well as the joint pmf of corresponding pixel values between the MRI and FA images as determined by the mapping imposed by v. These probability mass functions, in combination with an additional pmf for the MRI image voxel intensity values, are used to calculate the gradient of the MI similarity metric required by the optimization procedure used to evolve the optimal v.

These three pmfs are passed to mapping workers to calculate tile based gradients individually and in parallel. Referring to [11], the $\partial C/\partial v$ values for MI are calculated by:

$$\frac{\partial C}{\partial v} = \sum_{n=1}^{8} \frac{\partial C}{\partial p_j\left(f,\, M\left(n\right)\right)} \times \frac{\partial w_n}{\partial v} \tag{5}$$

The mapping workers then load all $\partial C/\partial v$ values to produce 64 Z vectors for each voxel in the tiles. Using a control point LUT to assign $< P_i, Z_j >$ pairs for each control point slot. Reduction workers acquire all the pairs with same control point index and accumulate the Z_j values in that control point slot. This process is performed iteratively, where the B-spline coefficients will be evolve to maximize the mutual information between the MRI and FA images based on the similarity score and its gradient after all the reduce workers have completed. Here, we use the L-BFGS-B quasi-Newtonian optimizer to arrive at the final mapping v.

5   Results

The experimental tests reported in this section were performed on a machine equipped with a 3.5GHz Intel Core i7-3770K processor and 32GB of RAM. Registration quality and execution time are evaluated to analyze the performance of our algorithm. Control point spacing is used as the partition unit for data distribution.

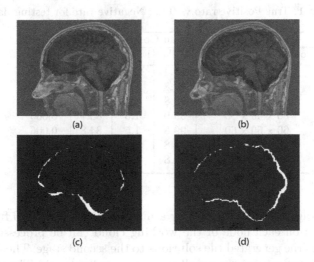

Fig. 3. (a) A 368 x 256 x 256 MRI volume superimposed with a 256 x 256 x 80 FA map prior registration. (b) FA superimposed on the MRI after registration. B-spline control-point grid spacing is 40 x 40 x 40. (c) Brain contour difference before registration (d) Misregistered brian contour after registration

Figure 3 shows the registration results produced by the proposed B-spline method. The MRI image is a $368 \times 256 \times 256$ voxel volume and the corresponding

FA map is a $256 \times 256 \times 80$ voxel volume. Figure 3(a) shows the FA image superimposed on the MRI image before the registration and Figure 3(b) shows the overlapping volume after the registration. Figures 3(c) & (d) show the false positive and false negative region for the overall brain contour, respectively, before and after registration. Here the voxel intensity pmfs are computed as 32 bin histograms for each of the volumes. The results shown are for a deformation field v obtained after 10 L-BFGS-B optimizer iterations and a control point spacing of $40 \times 40 \times 40$.

Registration quality is highly affected by the size of control point spacing. Complex local deformation cannot be captured with increasing control point spacing, whereas more complex motion may be recovered with decreased spacing due to the increased degrees of freedom afforded to the transform. Table 1 details the true positive and false positive rates for the contour of the brain and the corpus callosum after registration. As expected, coarse control point spacing performs well in registering the general shape of the whole brain, while recovering the local details of the corpus callosum suffers. Conversely, recovering the large deformations of the brain contour exhibit slightly poorer results for fine control point configurations, where as the corpus callosum exhibits improved results. This suggests that a multi-stage registration starting with a coarse control spacing and ending with a finer spacing may provide optimal results.

Table 1. True Positive rate vs True Negative rate for testing data

	Brian Contour		Corpus Callosum	
Control Point Spacing	TP(%)	FP(%)	TP(%)	FP(%)
20 x 20 x 20	99.4	2.0	87.2	0.006
30 x 30 x 30	99.8	1.7	86.6	0.005
40 x 40 x 40	99.8	1.8	86.1	0.004
50 x 50 x 50	99.9	1.5	85.7	0.005
60 x 60 x 60	99.8	1.5	84.8	0.006
70 x 70 x 70	99.8	1.5	84.5	0.007
80 x 80 x 80	99.8	1.4	83.7	0.006

The first stage can be processed by a multi-node system. Map function and reduce function on each node of the working cloud can be processed independently and pass the generated tile solutions to the second stage. Then the second stage map-reduce function process all the data simultaneously. The average processing time for first stage and second stage is shown in Figure 4(b). For a tile size of 20 x 20 x 20, it takes approximately 6 ms for the first stage map and reduce function to emit the Z vectors and approximately 15 ms for the second stage functions combine all the data for the volume. With the increasing of tile size, the burden of first stage map-reduce increases, while the second stage map-reduce can process less data in less time.

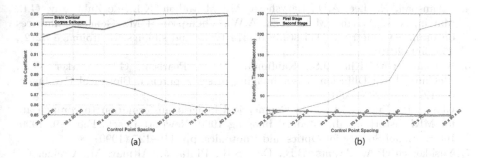

Fig. 4. (a) Registration quality of corpus callosum (b) Single iteration execution time vs control-point spacing

6   Conclusions

We have developed a map-reduce based B-spline deformable registration algorithm for feature fusion of multiple neuroimaging techniques. The implementation of map-reduce framework makes it possible for large scale MRI or DTI images to be partitioned into independent small subregions and registered separately. We have evaluated the implementation of map-reduce based B-spline in terms of accuracy and efficiency. Experimental results indicate that our map-reduce based B-spline implementation arrives at an anatomically correct transform about the corpus callosum given a single stage registration with constant control spacing. Future work involves extending the implementation to leverage a pyramidal or simultaneous multi-resolution B-spline control grid in order to prevent the parameter optimization process from converging up a local extrema; thereby providing deformation solutions that more accurately describe both fine and course non-linear deformations with higher accuracy.

References

1. Dickerson, B.C., Goncharova, I., Sullivan, M., Forchetti, C., Wilson, R., Bennett, D., Beckett, L., et al.: MRI-derived entorhinal and hippocampal atrophy in incipient and very mild Alzheimers disease. Neurobiology of Aging **22**(5), 747–754 (2001)
2. Sexton, C.E., Mackay, C.E., Lonie, J.A., Bastin, M.E., Terrière, E., O'Carroll, R.E., Ebmeier, K.P.: MRI correlates of episodic memory in Alzheimer's disease, mild cognitive impairment, and healthy aging. Psychiatry Research: Neuroimaging **184**(1), 57–62 (2010)
3. Kalus, P., Slotboom, J., Gallinat, J., Federspiel, A., Gralla, J., Remonda, L., Strik, W.K., Schroth, G., Kiefer, C.: New evidence for involvement of the entorhinal region in schizophrenia: a combined MRI volumetric and DTI study. Neuroimage **24**(4), 1122–1129 (2005)

4. Jahanshad, N., Lee, A.D., Barysheva, M., McMahon, K.L., de Zubicaray, G.I., Martin, N.G., Wright, M.J., Toga, A.W., Thompson, P.M.: Genetic influences on brain asymmetry: a DTI study of 374 twins and siblings. Neuroimage **52**(2), 455–469 (2010)

5. Kanaan, R.A., Kim, J.S., Kaufmann, W.E., Pearlson, G.D., Barker, G.J., McGuire, P.K.: Diffusion tensor imaging in schizophrenia. Biological Psychiatry **58**(12), 921–929 (2005)

6. Chang, H., Fitzpatrick, J.M.: Geometrical image transformation to compensate for MRI distortions. In: Medical Imaging 1990, Newport Beach, Feb 4–9, 1990. International Society for Optics and Photonics, pp. 116–127 (1990)

7. Yushkevich, P.A., Avants, B.B., Das, S.R., Pluta, J., Altinay, M., Craige, C., Initiative, A.D.N., et al.: Bias in estimation of hippocampal atrophy using deformation-based morphometry arises from asymmetric global normalization: an illustration in ADNI 3 T MRI data. Neuroimage **50**(2), 434–445 (2010)

8. Carmichael, O.T., Aizenstein, H.A., Davis, S.W., Becker, J.T., Thompson, P.M., Meltzer, C.C., Liu, Y.: Atlas-based hippocampus segmentation in Alzheimer's disease and mild cognitive impairment. Neuroimage **27**(4), 979–990 (2005)

9. Kubicki, M., Park, H., Westin, C., Nestor, P., Mulkern, R., Maier, S., Niznikiewicz, M., Connor, E., Levitt, J., Frumin, M., et al.: DTI and MTR abnormalities in schizophrenia: analysis of white matter integrity. Neuroimage **26**(4), 1109–1118 (2005)

10. Shackleford, J.A., Kandasamy, N., Sharp, G.: On developing B-spline registration algorithms for multi-core processors. Physics in Medicine and Biology **55**(21), 6329 (2010)

11. Shackleford, J., Kandasamy, N., Sharp, G.: Accelerating MI-based B-spline registration using CUDA enabled GPUs. In: Int. Conf. Med. Image Comput. Comput. Assist. Interv. (2012)

Integrated Visualization of Human Brain Connectome Data

Huang Li[1,2], Shiaofen Fang[1]([✉]), Joaquin Goni[2], Joey A. Contreras[2],
Yanhua Liang[2,4], Chengtao Cai[2,5], John D. West[2], Shannon L. Risacher[2],
Yang Wang[2], Olaf Sporns[3], Andrew J. Saykin[2],
and Li Shen[1,2]([✉]), for the ADNI

[1] Computer and Information Science,
Purdue University Indianapolis, Indianapolis, IN, USA
sfang@cs.iupui.edu, shenli@iu.edu
[2] Radiology and Imaging Sciences,
Indiana University School of Medicine, Indianapolis, IN, USA
[3] Psychological and Brain Sciences,
Indiana University Bloomington, Bloomington, IN, USA
[4] Electrical and Control Engineering,
Heilongjiang University of Science and Technology, Harbin, China
[5] College of Automation, Harbin Engineering University, Harbin, China

Abstract. Visualization plays a vital role in the analysis of multi-modal
neuroimaging data. A major challenge in neuroimaging visualization is
how to integrate structural, functional and connectivity data to form a
comprehensive visual context for data exploration, quality control, and
hypothesis discovery. We develop a new integrated visualization solution for brain imaging data by combining scientific and information
visualization techniques within the context of the same anatomic structure. New surface texture techniques are developed to map non-spatial
attributes onto the brain surfaces from MRI scans. Two types of non-
spatial information are represented: (1) time-series data from resting-
state functional MRI measuring brain activation; (2) network properties
derived from structural connectivity data for different groups of subjects,
which may help guide the detection of differentiation features. Through
visual exploration, this integrated solution can help identify brain regions
with highly correlated functional activations as well as their activation
patterns. Visual detection of differentiation features can also potentially
discover image based phenotypic biomarkers for brain diseases.

Keywords: Brain connectome · MRI · DTI · fMRI · Visualization

S. Fang and L. Shen—This work was supported by NIH R01 LM011360, U01
AG024904, RC2 AG036535, R01 AG19771, P30 AG10133, and NSF IIS-1117335.
ADNI—Data used in preparation of this article were obtained from the Alzheimer's
Disease Neuroimaging Initiative (ADNI) database (adni.loni.usc.edu). As such, the
investigators within the ADNI contributed to the design and implementation of
ADNI and/or provided data but did not participate in analysis or writing of this
report. A complete listing of ADNI investigators can be found at: http://adni.loni.
usc.edu/wp-content/uploads/how_to_apply/ADNI_Acknowledgement_List.pdf.

© Springer International Publishing Switzerland 2015
Y. Guo et al. (Eds.): BIH 2015, LNAI 9250, pp. 295–305, 2015.
DOI: 10.1007/978-3-319-23344-4_29

1 Introduction

Human connectomics [1] is an emerging field that holds great promise for a systematic characterization of human brain connectivity and its relationship with cognition and behavior. The analysis of human brain connectome networks faces two major challenges: (1) how to reliably and accurately identify connectivity patterns related to cognition, behaviour and also to neurological conditions based on an unknown set of network characterization and features; (2) how to seamlessly integrate computational methods with human knowledge and how to translate this into user-friendly, interactive software tools that optimally combines human expertise and machine intelligence to enable novel contextually meaningful discoveries. Both challenges require the development of highly interactive and comprehensive visualization tools that can guide researchers through a complex sea of data and information for knowledge discovery.

Scientific visualization has long been playing an important role in neuroimaging data analysis, by rendering detailed 3D anatomic structures from modalities such as magnetic resonance imaging (MRI) and diffusion tensor imaging (DTI) scans. Example studies include DTI fiber tract visualization [2,3,4,5,6,7], network visualization [8,9,10,11], and multi-modal data visualization [12,13,14]. In this context, recent development in information visualization provides new ways to visualize non-structural attributes or in-depth analysis data, such as graph/network visualization and time-series data visualization. These, however, are usually separate visual representations away from the anatomic structures. In order to maximize human cognitive abilities during visual exploration, we propose to integrate the visual representations of the connectome network attributes onto the surfaces of the anatomical structures of human brain. Multiple visual encoding schemes, combined with various interactive visualization tools, can provide an effective and dynamic data exploration environment for neuroscientists to better identify patterns, trends and markers.

2 Brain Imaging Data and Connectome Construction

The MRI and DTI data used in the preparation of this article were obtained from the Alzheimers Disease Neuroimaging Initiative (ADNI) database (adni.loni.usc.edu). The ADNI was launched in 2003 as a public-private partnership, led by Principal Investigator Michael W. Weiner, MD. The primary goal of ADNI has been to test whether serial MRI, positron emission tomography (PET), other biological markers, and clinical and neuropsychological assessment can be combined to measure the progression of mild cognitive impairment (MCI) and early Alzheimers disease (AD). For up-to-date information, see www.adni-info.org.

We downloaded the baseline 3T MRI (SPGR) and DTI scans together with the corresponding clinical data of 134 ADNI participants, including 30 cognitively normal older adults without complaints (CN), 31 cognitively normal older adults with significant memory concerns (SMC), 15 early MCI (EMCI), 35 late

MCI (LMCI), and 23 AD participants. In our multi-class disease classification experiment, we group these subjects into three categories: Healthy Control (HC, including both CN and SMC participants, N=61), MCI (including both EMCI and LMCI participants, N=50), and AD (N=23).

Using their MRI and DTI data, we constructed a structural connectivity network for each of the above 134 participants. Our processing pipeline is divided into three major steps described below: (1) Generation of regions of interest (ROIs), (2) DTI tractography, and (3) connectivity network construction.

(1) ROI Generation. Anatomical parcellation was performed on the high-resolution T1-weighted anatomical MRI scan. The parcellation is an automated operation on each subject to obtain 68 gyral-based ROIs, with 34 cortical ROIs in each hemisphere, using the FreeSurfer software package (http://freesurfer.net/). The Lausanne parcellation scheme [15] was applied to further subdivide these ROIs into smaller ROIs, so that brain networks at different scales (e.g., $N_{roi} = $ 83, 129, 234, 463, or 1015 ROIs/nodes) could be constructed. The T1-weighted MRI image was registered to the low resolution b0 image of DTI data using the FLIRT toolbox in FSL, and the warping parameters were applied to the ROIs so that a new set of ROIs in the DTI image space were created. These new ROIs were used for constructing the structural network.

(2) DTI tractography. The DTI data were analyzed using FSL. Preprocessing included correction for motion and eddy current effects in DTI images. The processed images were then output to Diffusion Toolkit (http://trackvis.org/) for fiber tracking, using the streamline tractography algorithm called FACT (fiber assignment by continuous tracking). The FACT algorithm initializes tracks from many seed points and propagates these tracks along the vector of the largest principle axis within each voxel until certain termination criteria are met. In our study, stop angle threshold was set to 35 degree, which meant if the angle change between two voxels was greater than 35 degree, the tracking process stopped. A spline filtering was then applied to smooth the tracks.

(3) Network Construction. Nodes and edges are defined from the previous results in constructing the weighted, undirected network. The nodes are chosen to be N_{roi} ROIs obtained from Lausanne parcellation. The weight of the edge between each pair of nodes is defined as the density of the fibers connecting the pair, which is the number of tracks between two ROIs divided by the mean volume of two ROIs [16,17]. A fiber is considered to connect two ROIs if and only if its end points fall in two ROIs respectively. The weighted network can be described by a matrix. The rows and columns correspond to the nodes, and the elements of the matrix correspond to the weights.

To demonstrate our visualization scheme for integrative exploration of the time-series of resting-state fMRI (rs-fMRI) data with brain anatomy, we employed an additional local (non-ADNI) subject, who was scanned in a Siemens PRISMA 3T scanner (Erlangen Germany). A T1-weighted sagittal MP-RAGE was obtained (TE =2.98 ms, TR partition = 2300ms, TI = 900ms, flip angle = 9, 128 slices with 111mmvoxels). A resting-state session of 10 minutes was also obtained. Subject was asked to stay still and awake, and to keep eyes closed.

BOLD acquisition parameters were: TE = 29ms, TR = 1.25s, Flip angle = 79, 41 contiguous interleaved 2.5 mm axial slices, with in-plane resolution = 2.5 2.5 mm. BOLD time-series acquired were then processed according to the following steps (for details see [18]): mode 1000 normalization; z-scoring and detrending; regression of 18 detrended nuisance variables (6 motion regressors [X Y Z pitch jaw roll], average gray matter (GM), white matter (WM) and cerebral spinal fluid (CSF) signals, and all their derivatives computed as backwards difference); band-pass filter of 0.009 to 0.08 Hz using a zero-phase 2nd order Butterworth filter; spatial blurring using a Gaussian filter (FWHM=2mm); regression of the first 3 principal components of WM (mask eroded 3 times) and CSF (ventricles only, mask eroded 1 time). The Desikan-Killiany Atlas (68 cortical ROIs, as available in the Freesurfer software) was registered to the subject. The resulting processed BOLD time-series where then averaged for each ROI. Note that the Lausanne parcellation scheme (mentioned above) at the level of $N_{roi} = 83$ consists of the above 68 cortical ROIs together with the brain stem (as 1 ROI) and 14 subcortical ROIs. As a result, we will use 68 time series (one for each cortical ROI) in our time series visualization experiments.

3   Information Visualization: Methods and Results

In this section, we propose a few information visualization methods. Using the VTK (www.vtk.org) C++ library, we have implemented and packaged these methods into a software tool named as BECA, standing for Brain Explorer for Connectomic Analysis. A video has been made to demonstrate the proposed methods and is available at http://www.iu.edu/~beca/bih15_demo.mp4.

3.1   Visualizing Structural Connectivity Networks

3D visualization of a connectivity network within an anatomical structure can provide valuable insight and better understanding of the brain networks and their functions. In a brain connectome network, we render nodes as ROI surfaces, which are generated using an iso-surface extraction algorithm from the MRI voxel sets of the ROIs. Drawing the network edges is, however, more challenging since straight edges will be buried inside the brain structures. We apply the cubic Bezier curves to draw curved edges above the brain structure. The four control points of each edge are defined by the centers of the ROI surfaces and the extension points from the centroid of the brain, as shown in Figure 1a. Figure 2 shows visualization examples of a connectome network, along with the cortical surface, the ROIs, and the DTI fibers.

3.2   Visualizing Network Attributes with Textural Mapping

Brain connectivity networks obtained through the above pipeline can be further taken into complex network analysis. Network measures (e.g., node degree,

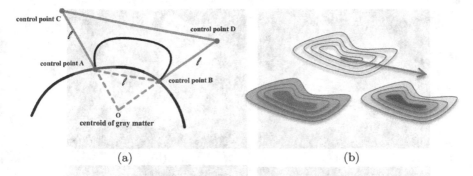

Fig. 1. (a) Building a Bezier curve connecting two ROIs. (b) Offset contours with different colors or different shades of the same color.

betweenness, closeness) can be calculated from individuals or average of a population. Different measures may characterize different aspects of the brain connectivity [19]. In order to visualize these network attributes, we propose a surface texture based approach. The main idea is to take advantage of the available surface area of each ROI, and encode the attribute information in a texture image, and then texture-map this image to the ROI surface. Since the surface shape of each ROI (as a triangle mesh) is highly irregular, it becomes difficult to assign texture coordinates for mapping the texture images. We apply a simple projection plane technique. A projection plane of an ROI is defined as the plane with a normal vector that connects the center of the ROI surface and the centroid of the entire brain. The ROI surface can then be parallelly projected onto its projection plane, and the reverse projection defines the texture mapping process. Thus, we can define our attribute-encoded texture image on this project plane to depict a visual pattern on the ROI surface. Visually encoding attribute information onto a texture image is an effective way to represent multiple attributes or time-series attributes. Below we will demonstrate this idea in two different scenarios: Time-series data from rs-fMRI and multi-class disease classification.

3.3 Visualizing fMRI Data and Functional Connectivity

As a functional imaging method, rs-fMRI can measure interactions between ROIs when a subject is resting [20]. Resting brain activity is observed through changes in blood flow in the brain which can be measured using fMRI. The resting state approach is useful to explore the brain's functional organization and to examine if it is altered in neurological or psychiatric diseases. Brain activation levels in each ROI represent a time-series that can be analyzed to compute correlations between different ROIs. This correlation based network represents the functional connectivity networks and, analogously to structural connectivity, it may be represented as a square symmetric matrix.

Using the surface texture mapping approach, we need to first encode this time-series data on a 2D texture image. We propose an offset contour method

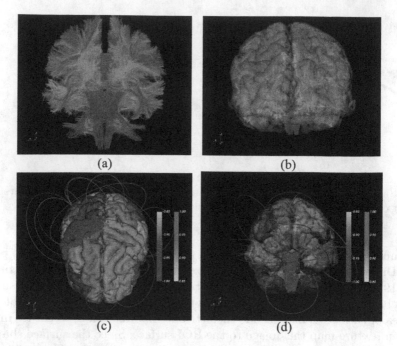

Fig. 2. (a) DTI fiber tracts; (b) Transparent cortical ROIs and DTI fibers; (c,d) Network edges as Bezier curves (thresholded by edge intensity)

to generate patterns of contours based on the boundary of each projected ROI. The offset contours are generated by offsetting the boundary curve toward the interior of the region, creating multiple offset boundary curves (Figure 1b). There are several offset curve algorithms available in curve/surface modeling. Since in our application, the offset curves do not need to be very accurate, we opt to use a simple image erosion algorithm [21] directly on the 2D image of the map to generate the offset contours.

In time-series data visualization, the time dimension can be divided into multiple time intervals and represented by the offset contours. Varying shades of a color hue can be used to represent the attribute changes over time. Figure 3 shows the steps for constructing the contour-based texture. First, we map each ROI onto a projection plane perpendicular to the line connecting the centroid of the brain and the center of this ROI. The algorithm then iteratively erodes the mapped shape and assigns colors according to the activity level of this ROI at each time point. Lastly we overlay the eroded regions to generate a contour-based texture. We also apply a Gaussian filter to smooth the eroded texture image to generate more gradual changes of the activities over time. Figure 4 shows a few examples of the offset contours mapped to the ROIs. The original data has 632 time points, which will be divided evenly across the contours depending on the number of contours that can be fitted in to the available pixels within the projected ROI.

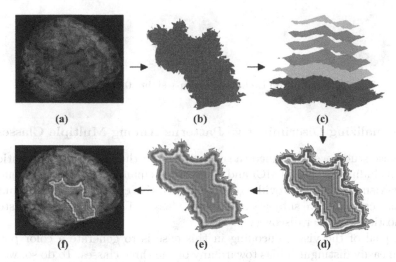

Fig. 3. (a) Original ROI (b) ROI mapping (c) Iterative erosion (d) Overlaying (e) Gaussian blurring (f) Applying the texture

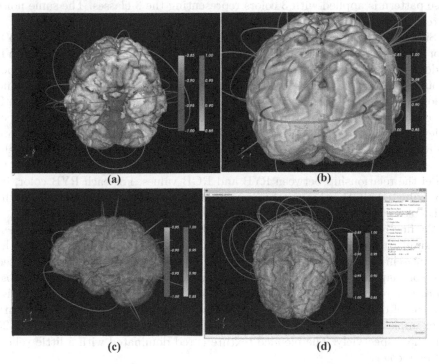

Fig. 4. Visualization of time-series data and the functional connectivity network. (a)(b) 100% gray matter opacity (c)(d)70% gray matter opacity

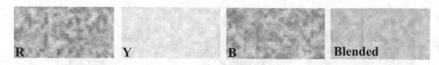

Fig. 5. Blending RYB channels with weights 0.5, 0.25 and 0.25

3.4   Visualizing Discriminative Patterns Among Multiple Classes

In this case study, we performed the experiment on the ADNI cohort mentioned before, including 61 HC, 50 MCI and 23 AD participants. The goal is to generate intuitive visualization to provide cognitively intuitive evidence for discriminating ROIs that can separate subjects in different classes. This can be the first step of a diagnostic biomarker discovery process.

The goal of the visual encoding in this case is to generate a color pattern that can easily distinguish bias toward any of the three classes. To do so, we first assign a distinct color to each class. Various color patterns can be generated using different color blending and distribution methods. In our experiment, a noise pattern is applied with 3 colors representing the 3 classes. The same noise pattern approach can also accommodate more colors.

Since color blending is involved in a noise pattern, we choose to use an RYB color model, instead of the RGB model. This is because color mix using RYB model is more intuitive in a way that the mixed colors still carry the proper amount of color hues of the original color components. For example, Red and Yellow mix to form Orange, and Blue and Red mix to form Purple. Thus, RYB model can create color mixtures that more closely resemble the expectations of a viewer. Of course these RYB colors still need to be eventually converted into the RGB values for display. For the conversion between these two color models, we adopt the approach proposed in [22,23], in which a color cube is used to model the relationship between RYB and RGB values. For each RYB color, its approximated RGB value can be computed by a trilinear interpolation in the RYB color cube.

We first construct noise patterns to create a random variation in color intensity, similar to the approach in [22]. Different color hues are used to represent the attributes in different classes of subjects. Any network measurement can be used for color mapping. In our experiment, we use the node degrees averaged across subjects in each class. A turbulence function [24] is used to generate the noise patterns of different frequencies (sizes of the sub-regions of the noise pattern). An example is shown in Figure 5, we blend RYB channels with weights 0.5, 0.25 and 0.25 respectviely. The blended texture is red-dominated with a little yellow and blue color.

Figure 6 shows some examples of the texture mapped views of the three classes: HC (Red), MCI (Yellow) and AD (Blue). The colors of the edges also represent the blended RYB color values, based on the average edge weights in the three classes. From the resulting images, we can identify a specific ROI that exhibits bias toward one or two base colors. This can be a potential indication

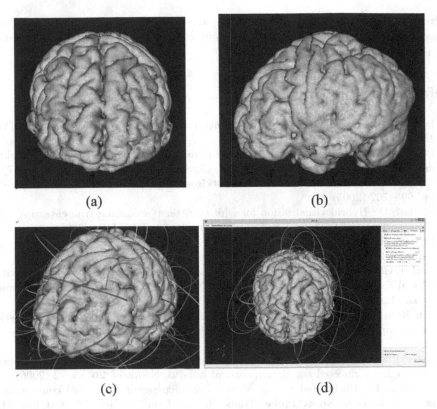

(a)   (b)

(c)   (d)

Fig. 6. Examples of connectome networks with noise patterns: (a)(b) ROIs with noise textures; (c)(d) ROIs with noise textures and color bended edges.

that this ROI may be a good candidate for further analysis as a potential imaging phenotypic biomarker.

4   Conclusions

We have presented an integrated visualization solution for human brain connectome data. Multiple modalities of images are involved including MRI, DTI and fMRI. Our focus is on the integration of analysis properties of the connectome networks into the anatomical brain structures. We apply a surface texture based approach to encode network properties and attributes onto the surfaces of the brain structures to establish visual connections and context. Surface texture is an effective approach to integrate information visualization and scientific visualization since scientific data typically have spatial structures containing surface areas, which can be taken advantage of for visual encoding.

In the future, we would like to continue developing the integrated visualization tool for public domain distribution, and the proposed BECA software tool will be available at http://www.iu.edu/~beca/. We would also like to study interesting visual analytic topics to compare multiple networks from different network construction procedures, in particular, between structural networks and functional networks.

References

1. Behrens, T.E., Sporns, O.: Human connectomics. Curr. Opin. Neurobiol. **22**(1), 144–153 (2012)
2. Petrovic, V.: Visualizing whole-brain DTI tractography with GPU-based tuboids and LoD management. IEEE Trans. Vis. Comput. Graph. **13**, 1488–1495 (2007)
3. Stoll, C., et al.: Visualization with stylized line primitives. In: IEEE Vis., pp. 695–702 (2005)
4. Merhof, D.: Hybrid visualization for white matter tracts using triangle strips and point sprites. IEEE Trans. Vis. Comput. Graph. **12**, 1181–1188 (2006)
5. Peeters, T.H.J.M., et al.: Visualization of DTI fibers using hair-rendering techniques. Proc. ASCI, 66–73 (2006)
6. Parker, G.J.: A framework for a streamline-based probabilistic index of connectivity (PICo) using a structural interpretation of MRI diffusion measurements. J. Magn. Reson. Imaging **18**, 242–254 (2003)
7. von Kapri, A., et al.: Evaluating a visualization of uncertainty in probabilistic tractography. In: Proc. SPIE Medical Imaging Vis. Image-Guided Procedures and Modeling, p. 7625 (2010)
8. Achard, S.: A resilient, lowfrequency, small-world human brain functional network with highly connected association cortical hubs. J. Neurosci. **26**, 63–72 (2006)
9. Salvador, R.: Undirected graphs of frequency-dependent functional connectivity in whole brain networks. Philos. Trans. R. Soc. Lond. B Biol. Sci. **360**, 937–946 (2005)
10. Schwarz, A.J.: Negative edges and soft thresholding in complex network analysis of resting state functional connectivity data. NeuroImage **55**, 1132–1146 (2011)
11. van Horn, J.D.: Mapping connectivity damage in the case of Phineas Gage. PLoS One **7**, e37454 (2012)
12. Schurade, R., et al.: Visualizing white matter fiber tracts with optimally fitted curved dissection surfaces. In: EurographicsWorkshop on Vis. Comp. for Biol. and Med., pp. 41–48 (2010)
13. Eichelbaum, S.: LineAO improved threedimensional line rendering. IEEE Trans. Vis. Comput. Graph. **19**, 433–445 (2013)
14. Svetachov, P., et al.: DTI in context: illustrating brain fiber tracts in situ. In: EuroVis, pp. 1023–1032 (2010)
15. Hagmann, P., et al.: Mapping the structural core of human cerebral cortex. PLoS Biol **6**(7) (2008)
16. Hagmann, P.: Mapping human whole-brain structural networks with diffusion MRI. PLoS One **2**, 7 (2007)
17. Cheng, H.: Optimization of seed density in dti tractography for structural networks. J. Neurosci. Methods **203**(1), 264–272 (2012)
18. Power, J.D.: Methods to detect, characterize, and remove motion artifact in resting state fMRI. Neuroimage **84**, 320–341 (2014)
19. Rubinov, M., Sporns, O.: Complex network measures of brain connectivity: uses and interpretations. Neuroimage **52**(3), 1059–69 (2010)

20. Biswal, B.B.: Resting state fMRI: A personal history. Neuroimage **62**(2), 938–944 (2012)
21. Rosenfeld, A.: Digital Picture Processing. Academic Press, New York (1982)
22. Nathan, G., Baoquan, C.: Paint inspired color mixing and compositing for visualization. In: IEEE Sym. on Info. Vis., pp. 113–118 (2004)
23. Liang, Y.D., et al.: Brain Connectome Visualization for Feature Classification. In: Proc. of IEEE Vis. (2014)
24. Perlin, K.: An image synthesizer. In: Proc. of SIGGRAPH, pp. 287–296 (1985)

Sleep Stages Classification Using Neural Networks with Multi-channel Neural Data

Zhenhao Ge[(✉)] and Yufang Sun

Purdue University, West Lafayette, IN, USA
{zge,sun361}@purdue.edu

Abstract. Recent studies on sleep reveal its importance not only on body functioning but also in brain and cognition health. As the development of wearable smart devices, neural data such as electroencephalogram (EEG) becomes commonly accessible. Developing good algorithm for sleep classification is more urgent and necessary than before. This paper presents a new and robust 5-stage sleep classification algorithm based on feedforward neural network, with flexible model structure using normalized Power Spectral Density (PSD) collected from multi-channel neural data. The algorithm is described with detailed mathematical elaboration. It utilizes the power of deep learning and provides average accuracy close to 90% which is competitive, compared with previous researches.

Keywords: Sleep stages · Neural networks · Neural data · EEG · EOG · EMG

1 Introduction

Modern fast-paced lifestyle causes more health problems, among which sleep is one of the most important concerns people encounter. Because not only help to recover the body functions, sleep also keeps brain clear and toxin-free, and subconsciously help to filter/organize knowledge in memory and consolidate daytime learning [5]. Lack of sleep leads to various nasty conditions, including headaches, depression, heart disease, diabetes, etc. and eventually shorten human lifespan.

Companies, such as Withings and Fitbit, produce devices to track sleep duration and quality, while some other companies even personalize neural data, such as electroencephalogram (EEG), which is used to be only accessible from neural science laboratories, by inventions such as *Mindwave* from NeuroSky, *muse* from InteraXon, normally with an inexpensive price.

With the raising popularity of sleep measurement, developing effective sleep stages classification algorithm becomes more urgent and essential. K. Susmakova et al. classified waking, sleep onset and deep sleep by measuring electrophysiological signals, including electroencephalogram (EEG), electooculogram (EOG), electrocardiogram (ECG) and electromyogram (EMG) with Fisher quadratic classifier and obtained various accuracy rates for different characteristics [20].

© Springer International Publishing Switzerland 2015
Y. Guo et al. (Eds.): BIH 2015, LNAI 9250, pp. 306–316, 2015.
DOI: 10.1007/978-3-319-23344-4_30

Table 1. Sleep database profile

Dataset	S1_BSL	S1_REC	S2_BSL	S2_REC
Duration (hours)	10.55	17.37	10.46	18.46
No. of sleep stages	1265	2083	1255	2215

E. Estrada et al. proved that EOG and EMG are both important to improve the sleep classification performance [7].

Recently, with the increased accessibility of massive data and the growth of computational power, compared with other classification methods such as Support Vector Machine [17], neural networks especially deep learning regains its popularity and has significantly improved performance in many applications [4] including speech recognition [16], natural language processing, object recognition, anomaly detection and trend prediction. Farideh Ebrahimi et al. feeds wavelet packet coefficients of EEG into an artificial neural network for 4-stage sleep classification, including wake, NREM1+REM, NREM2 and Slow Wave Sleep (SWS), and achieve around 93% total accuracy [6]. M. Emin Tagluk et al. built a feedforward network directly for 5-stage sleep classification using raw EEG, EOG, EMG signals and achieved 72%∼78% accuracy for each stage [21].

This paper proposes a new 5-stage sleep classification algorithm using feedforward networks, which has demonstrated its success in many classification applications, such as handwritten digit recognition [18]. The network structure is similar to [6] but with more flexibility and achieves better performance.

The paper is organized as follows: Sec. 2 and 3 describe the data and feature preparation; training, testing and optimization of sleep classifier using neural networks is demonstrated in Sec. 4; followed by results and analysis in Sec. 5; finally, we conclude the paper and propose the future work in Sec. 6.

2   Data Exploration

The sleep data used here (Table 1 and Fig. 1) contains 4 datasets, provided by Dr. Carskadon's Sleep Research Lab in Brown University, collected from 9 channels, including 4-channel electroencephalogram (EEG), 2-channel electrooculography (EOG) and 3-channel Electromyogram (EMG) from 2 subjects (S1, S2), each of which has a baseline night (BSL) of rested sleep and a recovery night (REC) following sleep deprivation[1][3]. These signals are collected at a sampling rate of 128 samples/second and are labeled with corresponding stages at 30-second duration. For later sleep stage classification, each of the 4 datasets are randomly divided into training, development and test sets with ratio 3:1:1.

As shown in Fig. 1a, there are 7 types of sleep stages, among which sleep with Rapid Eye Movement (REM) and Non-Rapid Eye Movement (NREM) form the major 2 categories. NREM is originally subdivided into 4 stages based on

---

[1] The original database contains 4 subjects, however only 2 of them are used here due to the sleep stage label missing and mismatch issues in the rest 2 subjects.

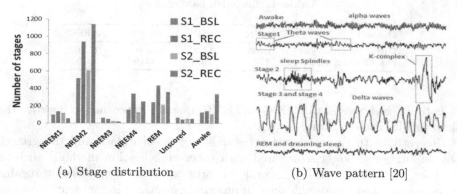

(a) Stage distribution   (b) Wave pattern [20]

Fig. 1. Distribution and pattern of sleep stages

Table 2. Sleep stages used in classification

stage 1	stage 2	stage 3	stage 4	stage 5
NREM1	NREM2	NREM3	REM	Others (unscored, awake)

sleep depth. By the American Academy of Sleep Medicine (AASM) new criteria, NREM3 and NREM4 are now combined as NREM3. Since this paper aims to classify the major sleep stages, the other stages such as "unscored" and "awake" are also combined. Table 2 shows the finalized stages used for classification.

Table 3 and Fig. 1b describe the meaning of EEG in each stage. EEG is enough to identify 3 stages of NREM [1,20], while EOG and EMG are necessary to distinguish REM from NREM1 and identify awakeness. [7].

3 Feature Generation

Similar to other signal processing applications, such as speech recognition, 1D signal is commonly converted from time domain to frequency domain to reveal its frequency characteristics [9,10]. In this paper, EEG, EOG and EMG signals are also converted to frequency domain as Power Spectral Density (PSD) via Welch's method [22] with parameters including 1) windowing type (Hanning), 2) 256 points of Fast Fourier Transform (N_{fft}) and 3) 0 point of overlap samples ($N_{overlap}$). Fig. 2a is an example of PSD of EEG signals.

To visualize the frequency changes in time, 2D spectrogram with duration of 10 stages (300 seconds), computed using the same parameter settings as PSD, is also demonstrated in Fig. 2b. Since the sampling rate $f_{sampling}$ is 128 Hz, the representable frequency range is $[0, 64]$ Hz. By observing the frequency amplitude in Fig. 2, frequency range $[0, 32]$ Hz should be more than enough to represent the dynamics in PSD. Thus in this implementation, we set up cutoff frequency

Table 3. Sleep stage description based on EEG [1,20]

Stage	Description	Explanation
Awake	Low voltage (10-30 μv), continuity of alpha activity	
NREM1	Low voltage, mixed frequency EEG with highest amplitude in 2-7 Hz	Light sleep, eye closed, but easy to wake up
NREM2	Sleep spindles (12-14 Hz) and k-complexes (a sharp negative wave followed by a positive one) occurs	Light sleep, heart rate slows, body temperature drops, ready for deep sleep
NREM3	More than 20% of delta activity	Deep sleep, harder to rouse, feel disoriented if someone wake you up
REM	Low voltage and mixed frequency, sawtooth wave pattern is oftern present, similar to NREM1	Heart rate and breathing quikens, intense dreams, brain is more active

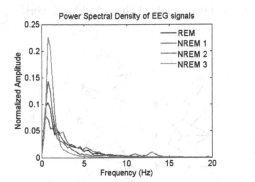

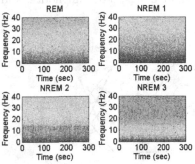

(a) Example of Power Spectral Density distribution of sleep stages

(b) Example of Spectrogram of sleep stages in 10 sleep stages

Fig. 2. Example of Power Spectral Density and spectrogram

$f_0 = 32$ Hz to save computational cost, and the corresponding number of frequency component (dimension) N_{freq} to represent $[0, 32]$ Hz should be:

$$N_{freq} = N_{fft} * \frac{f_0}{f_{sampling}} + 1 = 256 * \frac{32}{128} + 1 = 65 \qquad (1)$$

where "+1" in Eq. (1) means to include to 0-frequency component. The 65-dimensional PSD feature X_{PSD} are computed at stage level and used as feature to train and classify sleep into various stages. X_{PSD} are also normalized to X_{NPSD} by its local maximum within the same stage in Eq. (2) to compensate the undesired amplitude variation due to measurement setup difference.

$$X_{NPSD}^{(i)} = X_{PSD}^{(i)} / \max(X_{PSD}^{(i)}), \quad i: \text{current stage index} \qquad (2)$$

Since there are 9 channels of signals including EEG, EOG and EMG, the final feature X used for classification is the concatenation of PSD of these signals and its dimension N is actually 585 (65×9).

4   Classification Using Neural Networks

Neural network (NN)-based classifier builds a multi-layer feedforward network which transforms input PSD features into prediction values indicating the possibility of each sleep stage. There are parameters need to be specified for classifier training like a) number of layers L, which includes input/output layers, and the layers between them (hidden layers), b) number of nodes N_i in each layer L_i.

In this implementation, there are 585 input nodes (65 P_{NPSD} frequency dimension $\times$ 9 channels) and 5 output nodes, since it is a 5-stage classification problem. The number of nodes in each hidden layer are restricted to be identical for simplicity. For example, structure $585 : 25 \times 3 : 5$ means a 5-layer model with 585 input nodes, 5 output nodes, and 25 nodes in each of the 3 hidden layers.

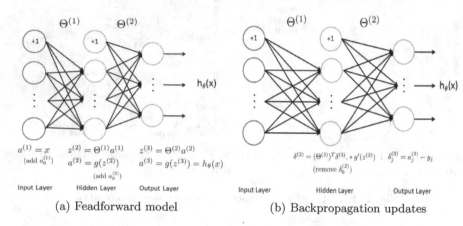

(a) Feadforward model   (b) Backpropagation updates

Fig. 3. Example of a 3-layers neural network model

4.1   Model Representation and Feedfoward Propagation

Fig. 3a shows an example of 3-layer neural network model with variables:

- $a^{(l)}$: output from the l-th layer , when $l = 1$, $a^{(1)} = x$,where x is the input feature, while when $l = L$, where L is the last layer, $a^{(L)} = h_\theta(x)$;
- $z^{(l)}$: input to the l-th layer, there is no $z^{(1)}$ since the network starts from 1st layer output;
- $\Theta^{(l)}$: weight matrix between layer l to $l + 1$ with dimension $[N_{l+1} \times N_l + 1]$, where N_l and N_{l+1} are the size of l-th and $l + 1$-th layers. There are only $L - 1$ weight matrices from $\Theta^{(1)}, \Theta^{(1)}, ..., \Theta^{(L-1)}$ in a L-layer network;

- $z^{(l)}, l \in [2, L]$ can be computed by $z^{(l+1)} = \Theta^{(l)} a^{(l)}$, while $a^{(l)}, l \in [2, L]$ can be computed by $a^{(l)} = g(z^{(l)})$, where $g(z)$ is the node (neuron) sigmoid function, which defines as $g(z) = 1/(1 + e^{-z})$;
- $h_\theta(x)$: classifier function, which can be computed through forward propagation: $x = a^{(1)} \to z^{(2)} \to a^{(2)} \to \cdots \to z^{(L)} \to a^{(L)} = h_\theta(x)$.

We use example with only 1 hidden layer in Fig. 3a for simplicity in algorithm description, however, the general philosophy applies to networks with any number of hidden layers. If there are 25 nodes in Fig. 3a and the model structure is $585 : 25 : 5$, the cost function with regularization given m samples should be:

$$J(\theta) = \frac{1}{m} \sum_{i=1}^{m} \sum_{k=1}^{5} \left[-y_k^{(i)} \log((h_\theta(x^{(i)}))_k) - (1 - y_k^{(i)}) \log(1 - (h_\theta(x^{(i)}))_k) \right] \quad (3)$$

$$+ \frac{\lambda}{2m} \left[\sum_{j=1}^{25} \sum_{k=1}^{585} (\Theta_{j,k}^{(1)})^2 + \sum_{j=1}^{5} \sum_{k=1}^{25} (\Theta_{j,k}^{(2)})^2 \right],$$

In Eq. (3), $y_k^{(i)}$ is the target label for sample i, where $y_k^{(i)} = 1$ if sample i belongs to the k-th class, otherwise 0. The 2nd term is the regularization term, which prevents model over-fitting. $\Theta^{(1)} = [\theta_{j,k}^{(1)}], j \in [1, 25], k \in [0, 585]$ and $\Theta^{(2)} = [\theta_{j,k}^{(2)}], j \in [1, 5], k \in [0, 25]$. Please note that the k index starts from 0, but 0th column is not included in Eq. (3), since the bias term in each layer except the final layer (there is no bias term in the final layer) is added into its weight matrix but it does not need to be regularized.

4.2 Weights Initialization and Backward Propagation

Given m samples with target labels $(x^{(t)}, y^{(t)})$, where $t \in [1, m]$, the general idea to train a L-layer neural network model with optimal weights is: first randomly initialize weights in $\Theta^{(l)}$, where $l \in [1, L-1]$, then update them toward the direction which minimize the cost, i.e. the "downhill" direction of $\partial J/\partial \theta_{i,j}^{(l)}$ through forward and backward propagation, where $i \in [1, N_{l+1}], j \in [0, N_l]$ and $\theta_{i,j}^{(l)}$ is the weight from jth node in layer l to ith node in layer $l + 1$. Fig. 3b provides a framework for backpropagation weight updates with some terminologies used below for derivation.

We first randomly initialize the weight matrices $\Theta_1, \Theta_2, \ldots, \Theta_{L-1}$ with uniform distributed numbers in $[-\epsilon_0, \epsilon_0]$, ϵ_0 is normally within $[0, 1]$ and $\epsilon_0 = 0.12$ is used here. Then, perform forward pass to compute activations from $z^{(2)}$ to $a^{(L)}$. Third, start backward propagating $\partial J/\partial \theta_{i,j}^{(l)}$ by defining

$$\delta_j^{(l)} = m \cdot \frac{\partial J}{\partial z_j^{(l)}}, \quad (4)$$

as the error derivative w.r.t $z_j^{(l)}$. Since $h_\theta(x_j)^{(L)} = a_j^{(L)}$,

$$\frac{\partial J}{\partial a_j^{(L)}} = -\frac{1}{m}\left(\frac{y_j}{a_j^{(L)}} + \frac{1-y_j}{1-a_j^{(L)}}(-1)\right) = \frac{1}{m}\frac{a_j^{(L)} - y_j}{(1-a_j^{(L)})a_j^{(L)}}. \tag{5}$$

Also since

$$\frac{\partial J}{\partial z_j^{(L)}} = \frac{\partial J}{\partial a_j^{(L)}}\frac{da_j^{(L)}}{dz_j^{(L)}} = \left(\frac{1}{m}\frac{a_j^{(L)} - y_j}{(1-a_j^{(L)})a_j^{(L)}}\right)\left((1-a_j^{(L)})a_j^{(L)}\right) = \frac{a_j^{(L)} - y_j}{m}, \tag{6}$$

thus,

$$\delta_j^{(L)} = m \cdot \frac{\partial J}{\partial z_j^{(L)}} = a_j^{(L)} - y_j \implies \delta^{(L)} = a^{(L)} - y. \tag{7}$$

Next, to backpropagate $\delta_j^{(l)}$ (i.e. $\frac{\partial J}{\partial z_j^{(l)}}$) from $\delta_j^{(l+1)}$ (i.e. $\frac{\partial J}{\partial z_j^{(l+1)}}$), let node index in layer l be $(1, 2, \ldots, j, \ldots, s_l)$, and node index in layer $l+1$ be $(1, 2, \ldots, i, \ldots, s_{l+1})$. Since

$$\frac{\partial J}{\partial z_j^{(l)}} = \frac{\partial J}{\partial a_j^{(l)}} \cdot \frac{da_j^{(l)}}{dz_j^{(l)}} = \left[\sum_i \left(\frac{\partial z_i^{(l+1)}}{\partial a_j^{(l)}} \cdot \frac{\partial J}{\partial z_i^{(l+1)}}\right)\right]\frac{da_j^{(l)}}{dz_j^{(l)}}, \tag{8}$$

and

$$z_i^{(l+1)} = \sum_{j=0}^{s_l} \theta_{ij}^{(l)} a_j^{(l)} \implies \frac{\partial z_i^{(l+1)}}{\partial a_j^{(l)}} = \theta_{ij}^{(l)}, \text{ and } \frac{da_j^{(l)}}{dz_j^{(l)}} = g'(z_j^{(l)}), \tag{9}$$

then, Eq. (8) can be simplified to

$$\frac{\partial J}{\partial z_j^{(l)}} = \left[\sum_i \left(\theta_{ij}^{(l)}\frac{\partial J}{\partial z_i^{(l+1)}}\right)\right]g'(z_j^{(l)}) = (\Theta_j^{(l)})^T\frac{\partial J}{\partial z^{(l+1)}}g'(z_j^{(l)}) \tag{10}$$

Similarly to Eq. (8) - Eq. (10), weight gradient can be computed by:

$$\delta^{(l)} = m\frac{\partial J}{\partial \theta^{(l)}} = m\frac{\partial J}{\partial z^{(l+1)}}(a^{(l)})^T = \delta^{(l+1)}(a^{(l)})^T. \tag{11}$$

Initialize $\Delta^{(l)} = 0$ and use it to accumulate weight error derivative through all samples ($\delta_0^{(l)}$ is ignored since it corresponds to the bias term):

$$\Delta^{(l)} = \Delta^{(l)} + \delta^{(l+1)}(a^{(l)})^T \tag{12}$$

Finally with the consideration of regularization,

$$\frac{\partial J}{\partial \theta_{i,j}^{(l)}} = \frac{1}{m}\Delta_{i,j}^{(l)} \text{ for } j = 0 \text{ and } \frac{\partial J}{\partial \theta_{i,j}^{(l)}} = \frac{1}{m}\Delta_{i,j}^{(l)} + \frac{\lambda}{m}\theta_{i,j}^{(l)} \text{ for } j \geq 1 \tag{13}$$

In summary, the backpropagation is an efficient way to compute gradient of parameters θ_{ij}, it back-propagates $\frac{\partial J}{\partial z_j^{(l)}}$ (i.e. $\frac{1}{m}\delta^{(l)}$) $\frac{\partial J}{\partial a_j^{(l)}}$ (i.e. $\frac{1}{m}(\Theta_j^{(l-1)})^T\delta^{(l)}$), and then $\frac{\partial J}{\partial \theta_{ij}^{(l-1)}}$ (i.e. $\frac{1}{m}a_j^{(l-1)}\delta_i^{(l)}$).

4.3 Model Parameter Optimization

This algorithm is implemented in MATALB with vectorization of for-loop, which turns online training (one sample at a time) into batch training, and significantly improved computational efficiency. Given the cost function and weight gradients computed from forward and back propagation, the weights are optimized using the 'fmincg.m' function developed by Carl Edward Rasmussen [19]. It automatically handles parameters optimization through training, such as learning rate.

To find the network model providing best accuracy in the evaluation set, multiple models with parameters in certain range are trained. These parameters (with searching range) include a) number of layers (3,4,5,6), b) number of nodes in each hidden layer (25, 50, 100, 200), c) regularization factor λ (0, 0.01, 0.03, 0.1, 0.3, 1), d) number of training iterations (100, 200, ..., 800). Performances on training and development sets are monitored to ensure training to be terminated before getting overfit.

5 Results and Analysis

Table 4 shows classification accuracies for 3 types of experiments: a) train/test on single set; b) train/test on multiple sets; c) train on multiple sets, test on single set. Models in the 1st part are trained from a specific dataset, and tested

Table 4. 5-stage sleep classification accuracy using neural networks

| Hidden layers | Dataset | | Accuracy (%) | |
(λ, iterations)	Train	Dev.+Test	Dev.	Test
$100 \times 4(0, 700)$	S1_BSL$_{train}$	S1_BSL$_{dev,test}$	85.4	82.6
$50 \times 3(0.01, 700)$	S1_REC$_{train}$	S1_REC$_{dev,test}$	84.9	89.0
$100 \times 2(0.03, 600)$	S2_BSL$_{train}$	S2_BSL$_{dev,test}$	86.9	92.4
$100 \times 3(0, 400)$	S2_REC$_{train}$	S2_REC$_{dev,test}$	91.6	90.5
$100 \times 3(0.03, 700)$	S1&S2_BSL$_{train}$	S1&S2_BSL$_{dev,test}$	87.1	87.3
$50 \times 2(0.3, 800)$	S1&S2_BSL&REC$_{train}$	S1&S2_BSL&REC$_{dev,test}$	87.5	88.1
$50 \times 2(0.3, 800)$	S1&S2_BSL&REC$_{train}$	S1_BSL$_{dev,test}$	87.0	82.6
$50 \times 2(0.3, 800)$	S1&S2_BSL&REC$_{train}$	S1_REC$_{dev,test}$	85.9	88.5
$50 \times 2(0.3, 800)$	S1&S2_BSL&REC$_{train}$	S2_BSL$_{dev,test}$	87.3	89.4
$50 \times 2(0.3, 800)$	S1&S2_BSL&REC$_{train}$	S2_REC$_{dev,test}$	89.4	90.1

Table 5. Classified v.s. actual stages on training/testing with general datasets

		Actual Stage				
		1	2	3	4	5
Classified Stage	1	70	12	0	17	4
	2	50	846	31	14	2
	3	0	19	422	1	0
	4	10	25	1	376	4
	5	18	4	0	0	289

using samples from the same dataset. They provide slightly better fit for data from the same dataset as training, but may not generalize well. In contrast, models in part 3 are more context (subject, sleep type) independent, which may not provide best fit for each of these individual set, but they are constantly provide good accuracy for all testsets in general. Results in part 2 are from all datasets using general model, which serve as average of the results in part 3.

Table 5 shows the confusion matrix for actual and classified stages trained and tested using all datasets (the 6-th experiment in Table 4). Due to the unbalance of the actual number of each stage (the number of stage 2 is significantly more than the number of stage 1), most of mis-classifications fall to the stage 2, especially for samples from stage 1. This phenomenon indicates that the results can be further improved once larger training set is obtained and the characteristics for stages other than 2 got better captured.

6   Conclusion and Future Work

This paper proposed a NN-based 5-stage sleep classifier, including 3 stages of NREM, plus REM, awake, etc. with normalized PSD as input features. It was trained and tested using relatively small but comprehensive database with multiple subjects and sleep types, and achieved close to 90% in average on a challenging task (e.g. more confused and narrower ranges of sleep types), compared with [6,21]. With consideration of accuracy limitation on human manual scoring on sleep stage, achieving close to 90% overall accuracy is good enough. The core feedforward neural network algorithm including forward and backward propagation are described in details with solid mathematical derivation.

The software/scripts for current implementation is available online from [8]. For future work, the classification performance may be improved further, if model parameters such as number of nodes and regularization parameter λ can be hierarchically refined similar to the parameter optimization technique used in [11, 14], or if given larger database with more data sources, such as electrocardiogram (ECG) for heart rate measurement, and more flexible network structure, such as hidden layers with different sizes. In addition, current algorithm trains and tests with stage characteristics without consideration of historical trends, but a) sleep stages are more likely going deeper gradually in the sequence of NREM1 $\rightarrow$ NREM2 $\rightarrow$ NREM3 $\rightarrow$ REM than vice versa, or b) REM is more likely to occur in later stage of sleep rather than at the very beginning. Thus, combining current model with stage transition matrix in Markov chain which evolves in time might be helpful. Furthermore, feature can also be improved with higher frequency resolution and dimension reduction and optimization techniques such as Principle Component Analysis (PCA), Linear Discriminant Analysis (LDA) [12,13], or Sparse Matrix Transform (SMT) [2,15].

Lots of analysis become more feasible with high accuracy of sleep classification. For example, one can score people's sleep quality based on the percentages of sleep stages and the pattern of sleep stage change through the night; examine how the amount of time in each sleep stage change between well-rested night and the sleep-deprived night; or investigate the variation of each sleep stage between different subjects, etc.

Acknowledgments. We would like to thank Lecturer Monica Linden and Dr. Carskadon from Brown University for providing the sleep data for developing the classification algorithm.

References

1. What are REM and non-REM sleep? http://www.webmd.com/sleep-disorders/guide/sleep-101 (accessed June 01, 2015)
2. Cao, G., Guo, Y., Bouman, C.A.: High dimensional regression using the sparse matrix transform (SMT), pp. 1870–1873 (2010)
3. Carskadon, M.A., Dement, W.C., et al.: Normal human sleep: an overview. Principles and Practice of Sleep Medicine **2**, 16–25 (2000)
4. Deng, L., Yu, D.: Deep learning: methods and applications. Foundations and Trends in Signal Processing **7**(3–4), 197–387 (2014)
5. Durrant, S.J., Cairney, S.A., Lewis, P.A.: Overnight consolidation aids the transfer of statistical knowledge from the medial temporal lobe to the striatum. Cerebral Cortex **23**(10), 2467–2478 (2013)
6. Ebrahimi, F., Mikaeili, M., Estrada, E., Nazeran, H.: Automatic sleep stage classification based on eeg signals by using neural networks and wavelet packet coefficients. In: 30th Annual International Conference of the IEEE Engineering in Medicine and Biology Society, EMBS 2008, pp. 1151–1154. IEEE (2008)
7. Estrada, E., Nazeran, H., Barragan, J., Burk, J., Lucas, E., Behbehani, K.: Eog and emg: two important switches in automatic sleep stage classification. In: 28th Annual International Conference of the IEEE Engineering in Medicine and Biology Society, EMBS 2006, pp. 2458–2461. IEEE (2006)
8. Ge, Z.: Zhenhao Ge's academic homepage - software (2015). https://sites.google.com/site/gezhenhao/software
9. Ge, Z.: Development of Automatic Speech Evaluation System. Ph.D. thesis, Purdue University Indianapolis (2008)
10. Ge, Z.: Mispronunciation detection for language learning and speech recognition adaptation (2013)
11. Ge, Z., Sharma, S.R., Smith, M.J.: Adaptive frequency cepstral coefficients for word mispronunciation detection. In: 2011 4th International Congress on Image and Signal Processing (CISP), vol. 5, pp. 2388–2391. IEEE (2011)
12. Ge, Z., Sharma, S.R., Smith, M.J.: PCA method for automated detection of mispronounced words. In: SPIE Defense, Security, and Sensing, pp. 80581D–80581D. International Society for Optics and Photonics (2011)
13. Ge, Z., Sharma, S.R., Smith, M.J.: PCA/LDA approach for text-independent speaker recognition. In: Society of Photo-Optical Instrumentation Engineers (SPIE) Conference Series, vol. 8401, p. 7 (2012)
14. Ge, Z., Sharma, S.R., Smith, M.J.: Improving mispronunciation detection using adaptive frequency scale. Computers & Electrical Engineering **39**(5), 1464–1472 (2013)
15. Guo, Y., Depalov, D., Bauer, P., Bradburn, B., Allebach, J.P., Bouman, C.A.: Binary image compression using conditional entropy-based dictionary design and indexing. In: Proc. SPIE, Color Imaging: Displaying, Processing, Hardcopy, and Applications, vol. 8652 (2013)

16. Hinton, G., Deng, L., Yu, D., Dahl, G.E., Mohamed, A.R., Jaitly, N., Senior, A., Vanhoucke, V., Nguyen, P., Sainath, T.N., et al.: Deep neural networks for acoustic modeling in speech recognition: The shared views of four research groups. IEEE Signal Processing Magazine **29**(6), 82–97 (2012)
17. Lu, C., Allebach, J.P., Wagner, J., Pitta, B., Larson, D., Guo, Y.: Online image classification under monotonic decision boundary constraint. In: Proc. SPIE, Color Imaging: Displaying, Processing, Hardcopy, and Applications, vol. 9395 (2015)
18. Ng, A.: Cousera course: Machine learning. https://www.coursera.org/learn/machine-learning/home/info (accessed June 01, 2015)
19. Rasmussen, C.E.: Gaussian processes for machine learning (2006)
20. Šušmáková, K.: Human sleep and sleep eeg. Measurement Science Review **4**(2), 59–74 (2004)
21. Tagluk, M.E., Sezgin, N., Akin, M.: Estimation of sleep stages by an artificial neural network employing eeg, emg and eog. Journal of Medical Systems **34**(4), 717–725 (2010)
22. Welch, P.D.: The use of fast fourier transform for the estimation of power spectra: A method based on time averaging over short, modified periodograms. IEEE Transactions on Audio and Electroacoustics **15**(2), 70–73 (1967)

Unveil the Switching Deficits in Depression by the Dwelling Time in Dominant Community of Resting-State Networks

Maobin Wei[1], Jiaolong Qin[1], Rui Yan[2], Kun Bi[1], Chu Liu[1], Zhijian Yao[2,3], and Qing Lu[1,4(✉)]

[1] Key Laboratory of Child Development and Learning Science,
Research Center of Learning Science, Southeast University, 2 Sipailou, Nanjing 210096, China
luq@seu.edu.cn
[2] Academic Department of Psychiatry, Nanjing Brain Hospital, Nanjing Medical University,
249 Guangzhou Road, Nanjing 210029, China
[3] China Medical School, Nanjing University, 22 Hankou Road, Nanjing 210093, China
[4] Suzhou Research Institute of Southeast University, 399 Linquan Street,
Suzhou 215123, China

Abstract. The exploration of the dynamics of intrinsic activity has been documented and some breakthrough reports emerge in healthy volunteer. However, the dynamic research on the depression remains unclear. This study was to investigate dynamic anomaly of the resting-state networks (RSNs) in depression. Forty-seven RSNs were extracted from Resting-state functional magnetic resonance imaging data of the 40 depressed patients and 40 matched healthy controls. The dynamic functional connectivities were calculated for constructing multislice networks, whose modular structures were detected by the multislice community detection method. The dwelling time in the dominant community with significant difference distributed in the posterior cingulated cortex (PCC), middle cingulated cortex (MCC), insula, thalamus, and middle temporal gyrus networks. The PCC network with increased dwelling time, together with the MCC and insula networks with decreased dwelling time, were associated with the imbalance between the internal-directed and external-directed behavior, indicating the switching deficits in the depressed patients.

Keywords: Depression · Multislice community · Resting-state fMRI · Dynamic · Dominant community

1 Introduction

Brain activity dynamics is very attractive to neuroscientists for its serviceability to better explore how the brain works, even in the resting-state time and under disease-related status. Constructing dynamic functional connectivity through sliding time windows was one dominant method for tracking such dynamics in neuroimaging research. It has been documented that the dynamic functional connectivity underlying the functional magnetic resonance imaging (fMRI) data could be described as a

© Springer International Publishing Switzerland 2015
Y. Guo et al. (Eds.): BIH 2015, LNAI 9250, pp. 317–324, 2015.
DOI: 10.1007/978-3-319-23344-4_31

succession of separated states through clustering method [1], or as a combination of multiple patterns through principal component analysis [2]. Measuring the variability of the functional connectivity could help our understanding of the functional coordination between different brain regions over the time, which might be disturbed in mental disorders. The schizophrenia was reported to exhibit dysconnectivities between the sub-cortical nuclei and sensorimotor cortex and within the default mode network by exploring the dynamic functional connectivity [3, 4]. Similar to the schizophrenia, the depressed patients experienced dynamic pattern of momentary mental states that might contribute mechanistically to the development of psychopathology. Thus, the exploration of the dynamics of intrinsic activity in patients with depressive symptoms could excavate more valuable information associated with the emotional and cognitive dysfunction.

In order to keep the orders of the time-windows, we applied the multislice community detection method to investigate the abnormal intrinsic brain networks implicated in the depression. This method was valuable for the time-dependent networks, and could detect the modular attributions of the resting-state networks (RSNs) change over the time. The acquired modular structures linked the different RSNs at the different times, and mirrored the different types of functional module in which the RSNs participated. We hypothesized that a resting-state network might change the functional patterns for the adaptability over the resting time, but tend to undertake a certain function and be attributed to a fixed function community with maximum probability, which was defined as the dominant community of each resting-state network. Therefore, the study was to explore the abnormal RSNs implicated in the depression-related affect dysregulations and cognitive deficits via the dwelling time in the dominant community.

2   Materials and Methods

2.1   Participants

Forty right-handed, native Chinese-speaking depressed patients (20 females; age mean ± standard deviation: 32.9 ± 8.1; education years mean ± standard deviation: 14.1 ± 2.3) were recruited from in-patient facilities at the hospital and 40 matched healthy controls (20 females; age mean ± standard deviation: 31.4 ± 7.9; education years mean ± standard deviation: 14.9 ± 1.8) participated in the study.

Psychiatric diagnosis was based on DSM-IV criteria and Structure Clinical Interview for DSM-IV, and determined by an expert psychiatrist. All patients were rated on 17-item Hamilton Rating Scale for Depression on the day of scanning and scored higher than 17. All participants met the following inclusive criteria: no current comorbidity with other major psychiatric, neurological or medical illness (e.g., learning disability, brain injury, psychotic symptoms, bipolar disorder); no history of dependency on or recent abuse of alcohol and/or drugs; no physical contraindications for fMRI. After a complete description of the study to all subjects, written informed consent was obtained via forms approved by the Research Ethics Review Board.

2.2   Image Acquisition

All images were collected on a 3-Tesla Siemens verio scanner with an 8-channel radio frequency coil. High resolution T1-weighted structural images were acquired by magnetization-prepared rapid acquisition gradient-echo sequence with the following scan parameters: repetition time (TR) = 1900 ms, echo time (TE) = 2.48 ms, flip angle (FA)= 9°, number of slices = 176, slice thickness = 1 mm, in plane voxel resolution = 1 mm × 1 mm, field of view (FOV)= 250 × 250 mm2, acquisition time = 4 min 18 s. Resting-state fMRI data were acquired using a gradient-echo EPI sequence with TE = 40 ms, TR = 3000 ms, flip angle = 90°, slice thickness = 4 mm, no slice gap, number of slices=32, field of view 240×240 mm2, matrix size = 64 × 64, in plane voxel resolution = 3.75 mm × 3.75 mm,. Resting-state scans were 6 min 45 s in duration (133 volumes). Subjects were instructed to keep their eyes closed and not to think of anything particular during the resting-state scans.

2.3   Data Preprocessing

For each subject, the first five functional volumes were discarded to account for T1 saturation effects. The standard preprocessing steps were performed via the SPM8 software package (http://www.fil.ion.ucl.ac.uk/spm/software/spm8), including slice-timing, motion correction, spatial normalization and spatial smoothing (6 mm full width at half maximum (FWHM) Gaussian kernel). No participant had head motion >3 mm of translation or >1.5 degree of rotation in any direction. The frame-wise displacement exhibited no significant difference between the depression patients and controls groups (p = 0.25).

2.4   The Calculation of Dynamic Functional Connectivity

Spatial ICA was conducted for all 80 participants using the Informax algorithm in the Group ICA of fMRI Toolbox (GIFT) software (http://icatb.sourceforge.net). Subject-specific data reduction principal components analysis retained 120 principal components. The relatively large number of subject-specific principal components has been shown to stablize subsequent back-reconstruction. Group ata reducation retained 100 components, and subject-specific spatial components were estimate by GICA3 back-reconstruction method. ICA was repeated 20 times using ICASSO toolbox to validate the number of independent components (ICs) and determine the robustness and reliability of ICA algorithm. Forty-seven ICs were selected by visual inspection as anatomically relevant areas across subjects, potentially depicting functionally relevant RSNs.

Similar to the calculation of the dynamic functional connectivity in previous reports [1], we split the time series of each RSNs with a sliding Gaussian window (width=30 TRs, σ = 3 TRs, step=1 TR), resulting in 98 windows. The functional connectivity in each window was estimated from the regularized precision matrix and using the graphical LASSO method with a penalty on the L1 norm of the precision matrix to promote the sparsity.

2.5   Multislice Community Detection

The dynamic connectivity networks were linked by connecting each node in one window to itself in the adjacent windows to form the multislice network. Inter-slice coupling parameter was introduced to describe the links of the same node in adjacent the windows, and to concatenate the different slices in sequence. In our experiment, the coupling parameters with 0 indicated no interslice links, while 1 indicated presence of interslice links. The community structure of the multislice network was detected by the multislice community detection method [5] with the "generalized Louvain" MATLAB code [6], as well as custom scripts run in MATLAB (R2012b; MathWorks, Natick, MA, USA).

The dwelling time in each attributed community of the RSNs was calculated to find their dominant community, in which each network located with the largest percent of time. Then, we conducted between-group statistical test to compare the dwelling time of each RSN in its dominant community.

3   Results

The 47 RSNs identified by group ICA were similar to the RSNs observed in previous studies [1] . The communities calculated by the multislice community detection method were mainly distributed in the range of two to six. One subject was randomly taken for illustrating the communities to which the 47 nodes (RSNs) were assigned across the scanning time (Figure 1).

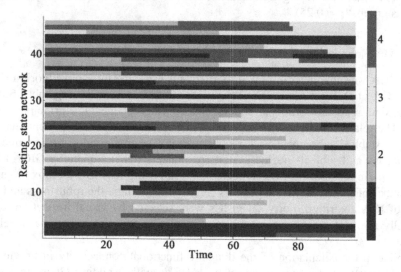

Fig. 1. The communities to which the 47 nodes (resting-state networks) were assigned across the resting period. The different color indicated the different communities.

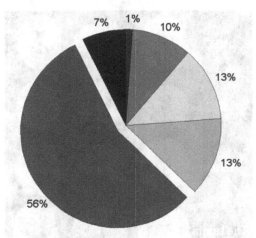

Fig. 2. Illustration of the dominant community of a randomly selected resting-state network. The percentage around denoted the occupancy of the dwelling time of each community (corresponding to the different color) over the whole period.

Figure 2 depicted the distribution of the dwelling time over all possible communities for a randomly selected RSN. The dwelling time of a RSN in its dominant community was selected to conduct statistical comparison of differences between the depressed and controls groups. Figure 3 showed the differences of the dwelling time of all the RSNs between the two groups. Two sub-networks of the cognitive control networks involved in the core brain regions of the bilateral middle cingulate cortex (MCC) and insula showed reduced dwelling time in their corresponding dominant community in depression. One sub-networks of the default mode networks including the posterior cingulated cortex (PCC) exhibited increased dwelling time in their corresponding dominant community as compared with that of the controls. Other two networks with core regions of the thalamus middle temporal gyrus (MTG) dwelled longer in the dominant community in the depressed patients. The spatial distribution mapping of the RSNs with significant difference in dwelling time were illustrated in Figure 4.

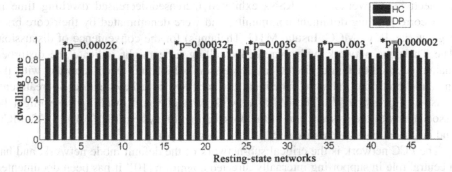

Fig. 3. The differences of the dwelling time of all the resting-state networks between controls and depressed groups. * p-values denotes the significant difference after FDR correction, HC, healthy controls; DP, depression patients.

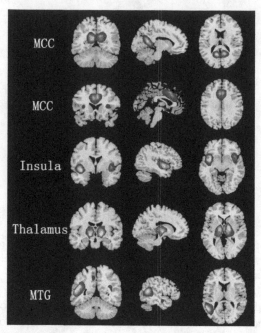

Fig. 4. The spatial distribution mapping of the RSNs with significant difference in dwelling time. PCC, Posterior cingulated cortex; MCC, Middle cingulate cortex; MTG, Middle temporal gyrus.

4   Discussion

Exploring the dynamics of intrinsic functional networks associated with depression-related dysfunction was critical for elucidating the neurobiological mechanisms of depression. In the present study, we examined the function pattern of the RSNs via the dwelling time in the dominant community that was obtained by applying the multislice community detection method to the time-dependent resting-state functional connectivity networks. Five RSNs exhibited increased/decreased dwelling time in their corresponding dominant community, and were denominated by their core brain regions (i.e. PCC, MCC, Insula, MTG, Thalamus) for the convenience of discussion. The Thalamus network with increased dwelling time might indicate the disturbed thalamo-cortico-thalamic circuits in depression, which has been reported with the impaired prefronto-thalamic functional connectivity as a key feature of treatment-resistant depression [7]. The MTG network with elevated dwelling time might be associated with the dysfunction of the dorsal attention system [8, 9]. The PCC, MCC and insula networks were discussed in the following part.

The PCC network is the critical sub-network of the default mode network, and has a central role in supporting internally directed cognition [10]. It has been documented that the PCC shows increased activity when individuals retrieve autobiographical memories or plan for the future [11], and abnormal PCC functional connectivity emerges in major depression [12, 13]. In depression, the PCC network dwelled longer in the dominant community, which was speculated that the overactive PCC spend more time on the dominant community, resulting in the persistent negative bias [14]. The Insula network was the center of salience processing across multiple sensory and cognitive domains and responsible for the dynamic switching between the internally and externally directed actions [15]. The function of the MCC has been reported to be associated with the nociceptive inputs [16], but its other function remains uncertain. We found that the Insula and MCC network dwelled in the dominant community with decreased values in depression, implying their critical roles in the cognitive control dysfunction. The spontaneous negative bias and depressive rumination led to the difficulties in regulating self-focused thinking in order to engage in more goal-directed behavior at any time in depressed patients [17], and switching deficits, which was indicated by the decreased dwelling time of the Insula and MCC networks in the study. Taking account of the other function role of PCC network , which was reported to control the balance between the internal and external attention [18], actively involving in maintaining a vigilant attentional state [19] or in signalling behaviourally relevant changes in the environment [20], it was conjectured that the depressed patients exhibited the disturbed switching function between the default mode network and cognitive control network while associated with the persistent negative bias. Intriguingly, the abnormal dwelling time in the community of the PCC, MPC and Insula network just verified such speculation.

In conclusion, the study explored the dynamic connectivity of RSNs via multislice community detection method, and obtained the dysfunctional RSNs described by the dwelling time in the dominant community under depressive status. The findings of the PCC network with increased dwelling time, together with the MCC and Insula networks with decreased dwelling time, were associated with the imbalance between the internal-directed and external-directed behavior, indicating the switching deficits in the depressed patients.

Acknowledgements. This work was supported by the National Natural Science Foundation of China (81371522, 61372032), Jiangsu Clinical Medicine Technology Foundation (BL2012052, BL2014009), Jiangsu Natural Science Foundation (BK2012740, BK20131074), Nanjing Science and Technology Development Project Foundation (201402016), and the Fundamental Research Funds for the Central Universities (CXLX13_11). All authors report no biomedical financial interests or potential conflicts of interest.

References

1. Allen, E.A., Damaraju, E., Plis, S.M., Erhardt, E.B., Eichele, T., Calhoun, V.D.: Tracking Whole-Brain Connectivity Dynamics in the Resting State. Cereb. Cortex **24**(3), 663–676 (2012)
2. Leonardi, N., Richiardi, J., Gschwind, M., Simioni, S., Annoni, J., Schluep, M., Vuilleumier, P., Van De Ville, D.: Principal components of functional connectivity: A new approach to study dynamic brain connectivity during rest. NeuroImage **83**, 937–950 (2013)

3. Sakoğlu, Ü., Pearlson, G., Kiehl, K., Wang, Y., Michael, A., Calhoun, V.: A method for evaluating dynamic functional network connectivity and task-modulation: application to schizophrenia. MAGMA 23(5–6), 351–366 (2010)

4. Damaraju, E., Allen, E.A., Belger, A., Ford, J.M., McEwen, S., Mathalon, D.H., Mueller, B.A., Pearlson, G.D., Potkin, S.G., Preda, A., Turner, J.A., Vaidya, J.G., van Erp, T.G., Calhoun, V.D.: Dynamic functional connectivity analysis reveals transient states of dys-connectivity in schizophrenia. NeuroImage: Clin. 5, 298–308 (2014)

5. Mucha, P.J., Richardson, T., Macon, K., Porter, M.A., Onnela, J.: Community Structure in Time-Dependent, Multiscale, and Multiplex Networks. Science 328(5980), 876–878 (2010)

6. Jutla, I.S., Jeub, L.G., Mucha, P.J.: A generalized Louvain method for community detection implemented in MATLAB (2011–2012). http://netwiki.amath.unc.edu/GenLouvain

7. Li, C.T., Chen, L.F., Tu, P.C., Wang, S.J., Chen, M.H., Su, T.P., Hsieh, J.C.: Impaired pre-fronto-thalamic functional connectivity as a key feature of treatment-resistant depression: a combined MEG, PET and rTMS study. PLoS One 8(8), e70089 (2013)

8. Ma, C., Ding, J., Li, J., Guo, W., Long, Z., Liu, F., Gao, Q., Zeng, L., Zhao, J., Chen, H.: Resting-state functional connectivity bias of middle temporal gyrus and caudate with altered gray matter volume in major depression. PLoS One 7(9), e45263 (2012)

9. Fox, M.D., Corbetta, M., Snyder, A.Z., Vincent, J.L., Raichle, M.E.: Spontaneous neuronal activity distinguishes human dorsal and ventral attention systems. Proc. Natl. Acad. Sci. 103(26), 10046–10051 (2006)

10. Buckner, R.L., Andrews-Hanna, J.R., Schacter, D.L.: The Brain's Default Network: anatomy, function, and relevance to disease. Ann. N. Y. Acad. Sci. 1124, 1–38 (2008)

11. Addis, D.R., Wong, A.T., Schacter, D.L.: Remembering the past and imagining the future: Common and distinct neural substrates during event construction and elaboration. Neuropsychologia 45(7), 1363–1377 (2007)

12. Zhu, X., Wang, X., Xiao, J., Liao, J., Zhong, M., Wang, W., Yao, S.: Evidence of a Dissociation Pattern in Resting-State Default Mode Network Connectivity in First-Episode, Treatment-Naive Major Depression Patients. Biol. Psychiatry 71(7), 611–617 (2012)

13. Berman, M.G., Misic, B., Buschkuehl, M., Kross, E., Deldin, P.J., Peltier, S., Churchill, N.W., Jaeggi, S.M., Vakorin, V., McIntosh, A.R., Jonides, J.: Does resting-state connectivity reflect depressive rumination? A tale of two analyses. NeuroImage 103, 267–279 (2014)

14. O'Nions, E.J., Dolan, R.J., Roiser, J.P.: Serotonin transporter genotype modulates subgenual response to fearful faces using an incidental task. J. Cogn. Neurosci. 23(11), 3681–3693 (2011)

15. Uddin, L.Q.: Salience processing and insular cortical function and dysfunction. Nat. Rev. Neurosci. 16(1), 55–61 (2015)

16. Frot, M., Vioux, H., Garcia-Larrea, L.: Operculo-insular and mid-cingulate gyrus functional coupling after painful laser stimulation: An intra-cerebral EEG coherence study. European Journal of Pain 11(S1), S95–S96 (2007)

17. Belleau, E.L., Taubitz, L.E., Larson, C.L.: Imbalance of default mode and regulatory networks during externally focused processing in depression. Soc. Cogn. Affect. Neurosci., pii:nsu117 (2014)

18. Leech, R., Sharp, D.J.: The role of the posterior cingulate cortex in cognition and disease. Brain 137(P11), 12–32 (2014)

19. Hahn, B., Ross, T.J., Stein, E.A.: Cingulate Activation Increases Dynamically with Response Speed under Stimulus Unpredictability. Cereb. Cortex 17(7), 1664–1671 (2007)

20. Pearson, J.M., Heilbronner, S.R., Barack, D.L., Hayden, B.Y., Platt, M.L.: Posterior cingulate cortex: adapting behavior to a changing world. Trends Cogn. Sci. 15(4), 143–151 (2011)

Visual Object Categorization from Whole to Fine: Evidence from ERP

Haiyan Zhou[1,2,3](✉), Sanxia Fan[1,2,3], Jialiang Guo[1,2,3], Xiaomeng Ma[1,2,3], Jianzhuo Yan[4], Yulin Qin[1,5], and Ning Zhong[1,2,3,6](✉)

[1] International WIC Institute, Beijing University of Technology,
Beijing 100024, China
zhouhaiyan@bjut.edu.cn
[2] Beijing International Collaboration Base on Brain Informatics and Wisdom
Services, Beijing, China
[3] Beijing Key Laboratory of MRI and Brain Informatics, Beijing, China
[4] College of Electronic Information and Control Engineering,
Beijing University of Technology, Beijing, China
[5] Department of Psychology, Carnegie Mellon University, Pittsburgh, USA
[6] Department of Life Science and Informatics, Maebashi Institute of Technology,
Maebashi-City 371-0816, Japan
zhong@maebashi-it.ac.jp

Abstract. The phenomenons of basic-level advantage and its reversal to the superordinate level during visual object categorization suggest the flexible and widely automatic semantic activation in human being, which would permit the actions to be consistent with goals and environment. However the under mechanism and the neural relation of visual object categorization is still not clear. By using the technique of ERP (Event-related Potential), with a word-picture matching task, we observed a superordinate-level advantage both in the behavioral reaction time (RT). The ERP activities showed that for the condition of superordinate-level condition, there was a shortest peak latency in the early visual attentional ERP component of P2; then in the middle semantic processing component of N400, there was a strongest amplitude; and finally there was a weakest amplitude in the component of late waveform in the late response period. These results suggest that there would be a processing from whole to fine during visual object categorization.

1 Introduction

Human being shows a flexible ability to response the external information in different abstract level. For example, there is a basic-level advantage during visual object categorization [1]. When a picture of collie is shown to name it, participant would probably answer it with the concept of "dog" (an intermediate level of specificity), while not "collie" (a subordinate level) or "animal" (a superordinate level). The result suggests the different levels of category concepts could be the right responses, (e.g. "collie", "dog", "animal", even "pet"), but the intermediate level seems to be a preferred cognitive status in human mind. This phenomenon was first reported by Rosch in 1976 and named basic-level advantage [1].

© Springer International Publishing Switzerland 2015
Y. Guo et al. (Eds.): BIH 2015, LNAI 9250, pp. 325–334, 2015.
DOI: 10.1007/978-3-319-23344-4_32

The basic-level advantage effect could be a result of information processing based on the experience and even the evolution for a long time for human being. It is argued that the category names in the basic-level was more frequently used than other terms [2,3], and usually the first nouns children typically acquired were also at this level [4]. So the information in this level seemed more readily to access than others and could be retrieved more quickly [4].

However, it is another story for semantic dementia (SD). When SD patient is asked to name a picture of object, like a collie as above, the response is typically more general, such as animal [5,6]. Patients with SD exhibit a deterioration of knowledge about meanings of world, together with a remarkable sparing of many other cognitive abilities. It can be seen that a damaged knowledge system led to the preferred cognitive status being changed from the intermediate level to more general level, and thus a reversal of the basic-level advantage effect is appeared. But to be noted, the reversal advantage effect to more general level is also appeared in healthy people. Rogers and colleagues [4] asked college students to judge whether picture and object name matched or not in a very limited time. The participants showed a superordinate level advantage effect, but not the advantage of intermediate basic level.

Based on the parallel distributed processing (PDP) theory, Rogers and Patterson [4] proposed that the meaning of words and objects were emerged from the interactive activation of perceptual, motor and linguistic representations across different modalities, and the intermediate level of semantic had the balance between the similarity and differential with other semantic representations. However, during the activation of semantic representation, the general names were the first to pass through the region of the semantic space and they were the earliest to begin to activate; while the activation of the intermediate basic names speeded rapidly since they were similarity-based generalization and with minimum interference, and it was showed the basic-level advantage effect; as to the subordinate specific names, they were the last one to activate until the internal state was very close to the correct representations. It is also observed in some other studies that the concept names in the superordinate level had the similar processing advantage in fast name tasks [7,8]. The results suggest that the fastest did not necessarily means the first. But a recent study [9] indicates that the superordinate-level categories are not automatic and obligatory process with a stroop-like paradigm. The conflicting results suggest the mechanism and the neural relation of the visual object categorization is still not clear.

The technique of ERP has a good temporal resolution, and it is noninvasive to record the time-locked response to a stimuli. By recording the ERP activity, Large and colleagues [10] observed that categorical names in the superordinate level were the first to be activated and the advantage ERP back to the basic level, which is consistent with the hypothesis proposed based on the PDP theory. However, they manipulated the similarity between target and nontarget, which might led the participant to pay heavy attention about the visual stimuli and enhance the advantage processing in the superordinate level. In this study, with the technique of ERP, we used a word-picture matching paradigm, a more natural task, to investigate the time course of visual categorization. Based on the prior word priming, we expected that there would be a superordinate-level advantage both in behavior and ERP data.

2   Methods

2.1   Participants

Twenty undergraduate and graduate students (10 males and 10 females) from Beijing University of Technology participated in the behavioral experiment, and fifteen (8 males and 7 females) additional students participated in the ERP experiment. The participants were from 20 to 26 years old and right-handed. All of them reported normal or corrected-to-normal vision, and with no history of neurological or psychiatric disorders. Written informed consent was obtained from each of them.

2.2   Materials

Thirty-two color pictures of animals and transportation in superordinate level were used as stimuli. There were 8 specific categories in subordinate level: water buffalo, milk cows, goat, jumbuck goat, bus, truck, sailboat and steamboat, and there were four different photographs for each of specific categories. They made up to 4 sets of cows, sheep, vehicles and boats for classification in the intermediate level. All of the pictures were selected after an assessment of familiarity by additional 15 college students. There was no familiarity different between the animal and transportation (P = 0.829).

2.3   Task and Procedure

For the word-picture matching task, as shown in Figure 1, there was little difference for the behavioral and ERP experiments. In both experiments , for each trial, after a fixation star appearing in the center of the screen for 500 ms, a category word was appeared in the screen for 1000 ms, and then a color picture was appeared for 1000 ms. For the behavioral experiment, participants were asked to response whether the picture matched the prior word or not when the picture appeared. The participants were demanded to response in 2000 ms. While for the ERP experiment, after the appearance of picture, a question mark for 1000 ms was appeared finally in the screen reminding the participant to make the matching judge. In this way, it is avoided the effect of key-press during ERP recording during the picture processing. In the superordinate condition, nontargets were selected from a different superordinate category. For instance, if the word stimulus was "animal", the nontarget was a photograph of any kind of transportation. In the intermediate condition, nontargets were always from the same superordinate category as the target, for the word stimulus of "sheep", the nontarget was always another kind of animal. In the subordinate conditions, nontargets were always items from the same intermediate category; for instance, if the word stimulus was "water buffalo", the distracter was a photograph of a different kind of "cow". There were totally three sessions and 48 trials in each session. The psychological software tool of E-prime 2.0 (http://www.pstnet.com/eprime.cfm) was used to present stimuli and record response.

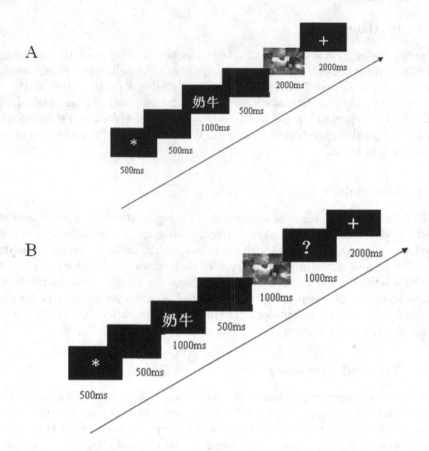

Fig. 1. Procedure of word-picture matching task. A for the behavioral experiment and B for the ERP experiment.

2.4   ERP Recording and Analysis

Brain electrical activity was recorded referentially against left mastoid and off-line re-referenced to linked mastoids, by a 32-channel amplifier with a sampling frequency of 500 Hz (Brain Products, Gilching, Germany). Besides two referential and two electro-oculogram (EOG)electrodes, a 28-channel electroencephalography (EEG) data was collected with electrode impedances kept below $5k\Omega$. The data analysis in this study were performed using Vision Analyzer 1.05

(Brain Products, Gilching, Germany) and SPSS Statistics 18.0 (IBM, Somers, USA). The recorded EEG data were filtered with a 0.01−60 Hz finite impulse response (FIR) filter with zero phase distortion, followed by epoch segmentation. Filtered data were segmented in association with the picture appearance, beginning 200 ms prior to the stimulus onset and lasting for 1200 ms. All epochs were baseline corrected with respect to the mean voltage over the 200 ms preceding stimulus-onset. Epochs containing obvious EOG were rejected. Data from two participants were kicked out in the further analysis because their data were out of the range from -80uV to 80 uV in the data inspection, and finally data from 13 participants totally were included in the further analysis. A repeated measures analysis of variance (ANOVA) was performed to investigate the main effect of category level, and then a post-hoc comparison with the Bonferroni test was performed if the main effect was significant.

3 Results

3.1 Behavioral Performance

Reaction times (RTs) and accuracy rate (ACC) was used to estimate the behavioral performance. RT was beginning with the appearance of the picture and ending with the response of key-press. ACC was calculated by the number of the correct responses (including the right YES and NO responses) divided by the total number of the trials in each category condition. The correct responses included the response of Hit (picture in word category and participant says YES) and Correct Reject (picture not in word category and participant says NO). Except for the responses of the Miss (picture in word category and participant says NO) and False Alarm (picture not in word category and participant says No), the incorrect responses included the No response during the permitted 2000 ms and the responses with RTs out of the range of 3 standard deviation (SD). The details of the RTs and ACCs in the three category conditions are shown in Figure 2. A repeated measures ANOVA performed both on reaction times (RTs) and accuracy rate (ACC) with the category level (subordinate, basic and superordinate) as a within-subject factor.

ANOVA revealed a main effect of concept level ($F(2, 38) = 12.072$, $P < 0.01$) on ACC. The mean accuracy rate to intermediate basci level was significantly higher than that in the superordinate level ($P < 0.05$), and the mean accuracy rate of superordinate level was also significantly higher than that in the subordinate level ($P < 0.01$).

There was also a significant main effect of category level on RT ($F(2, 38) = 27.988$, $P < 0.05$). The mean reaction time to the superordinate level was significantly faster than the intermediate basic level ($P < 0.05$), and the RT in the basic level was significantly faster than that in the subordinate level ($P < 0.05$), suggesting an advantage processing effect in the superordinate level.

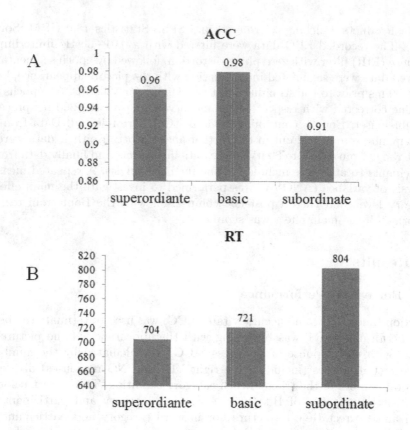

Fig. 2. Mean ACC (A) and RT (B) for word-picture matching task.

3.2   ERP Results

To investigate the timecourse of visual object processing, we analyzed the relative early and late periods during the appearance of pictures. We divided the ERP data into 4 time windows to analyze the ERP components of N1, P1, N400 and late negative waveform (LNW) with the time windows of 100–150 ms, 150–250 ms, 400–500 ms and 700–800 ms, respectively. Both the peak latencies and the maximal amplitudes were conducted in a repeated measure ANOVA with with the category level (subordinate, basic and superordinate) as a within-subject factor. The ERP patterns in the conditions of subordinate, basic and superordinate were show in Figure 3.

- Time window 100–150 ms (N1 component)

The repeated measures ANOVA (superordinate, intermediate basic, subordinate) indicated that the main effect of category level for the latency was not reached the significant level ($P = 0.229$), but there was an effect for the amplitudes ($F(2, 24) = 1.710$, $P < 0.05$). From Figure 3, it is clear that the amplitudes in the subordinate level were larger than those in the superordinate and intermediate basic levels categorizations (both $P < 0.05$), and there was no

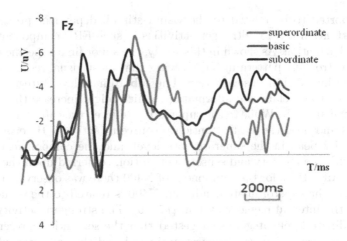

Fig. 3. ERP waveforms during the picture epoch for superordinate, basic and subordinate level category conditions in the Fz electrode.

differences between the superordinate and the intermediate levels for the amplitudes.

• Time window 150–250 ms (P2 component)

The ANOVA indicated there was a main effect of concept level for the latencies. The same analysis on amplitudes showed there was a main effect of category ($F(2, 24) = 0.181$, $P < 0.05$), with the latency in the superordinate level shorter than those in the intermediate and subordinate levels (both $P < 0.05$). Also there was a main effect of the category level for the amplitude ($F(2, 24) = 0.232$, $P < 0.05$), and the amplitude in the subordinate was larger than those in the superordinate and the intermediate levels (both $P < 0.05$).

• Time window 400–500 ms (N400 component)

The ANOVA indicated there was no main effect of the concept level for the latency, but there was a main effect for the amplitude ($F(2, 24) = 0.362$, $P < 0.05$). The amplitude in the superordinate level was larger than those in the intermediate and subordinate levels (both $P < 0.05$).

• Time window 700–800 ms (late waveform)

The ANOVA indicated there was no main effect of the concept level for the latency, but also there was a main effect for the amplitude ($F(2, 24) = 1.635$, $P < 0.05$). The amplitude in the subordinate level was larger than those in the intermediate and superordinate levels (both $P < 0.05$).

4   Discussion

As expected, in the task of word-picture matching, the reaction time for the superordinate level was the fastest. Such advantage processing was also observed in the ERP data, and there was minor amplitude in N1 and shortest latency in P2 in the condition of superordinate level. The early ERP components of N1 and

P2 are reported to be related to the visual stimuli dependent processing and selective attention [11–15]. Stronger activities in such ERP components suggest more visual attention. As shown in this study, the subordinate specific categories activated a strongest pattern in N1, showing that most visual resource and processing were included in this condition. The subordinate-level categories contain the most exact and elaborate information, which might increase the processing load of visual analysis. While to the superordinate level, the categories are highly generalized and need the least attention resource to activate. Here we observed an earliest P2 peak in the superordinate level, and the component of P2 was reflected with the memory and sensory perception conferred upon the attention [13, 15, 16]. After that, for the component of N400 there was observed a strongest amplitude in the superordinate condition. N400 is related to the semantic integration in the internal memory system [17–19]. The strongest activity of N400 in superordinate-level categories suggested that the semantic representation in this condition was the most strongest activated and the semantic information were integrated with the prior word concept, which were stored in the working memory. Together with the earlier N1, P2, and N400, it is showed the visual object categorization might be the processing from the whole to the fine, which is consistent with the hypothesis of Rogers and Patterson [4].

In the later period of the time course, a weakest amplitude of the late negative waveform (Time window 700–800 ms) was observed in the superordinate level, indicating a smallest processing load in this condition. This result verifies the behavioral RT patterns in this study, and it is also consistent with the related previous research [10]. However, according to the hypothesis of Rogers and Patterson [4], we did not observed a back to basic-level advantage, which might be related to the task paradigm. In our previous ERP study [20], with same materials in a picture-word matching task, there is a similar earlier superordinate-level advantage, but the advantage processing shifted back to the basic level in the late period. By comparing to that task paradigm, the picture-word matching task might be involved in more semantic processing, while the word-picture matching task here might be involved more in the visual processing. A prior appeared word activates the semantic representation in mind and more visual identification are needed to satisfy the task demand. Another study in our group [21] with the technique of functional magnetic resonance imaging (fMRI), there observed a different activity patterns for these two tasks in the inferior prefrontal cortex, which is related to the information retrieval.

However, it seems that there exists difference within the three category levels in the time window of 250 to 350 ms, which is related to the component of N200. This component is located from the the external driven processing to the internal driven processing, which is thought to be relate to the mismatching, executive control and language processing. It seems that there is the shortest latency in the subordinate level, and the weakest amplitude in the superordinate level, which is consistent with the inference based in the components of N1 and P1. It needs statistical analysis to test the reliability, which would be considered in our future study.

5 Conclusion

In this study, with a relative more natural word-picture matching task, we investigated the time course of visual object categorization by analysis the ERP data. Both the behavioral and ERP patterns suggested a superordinate-level advantage. Based on the activity patterns in the early visual attention components N1 and P2, the middle semantic activation components of N400, and the late response components of late negative waveform, it is showed that there might be a processing from whole to fine in the visual object categorization.

Acknowledgements. This work was supported by the National Basic Research Program of China (2014CB744600), International Science & Technology Cooperation Program of China (2013DFA32180), National Natural Science Foundation of China (61272345), and also supported by Beijing Municipal Commission of Education, Beijing International Collaboration Base on Brain Informatics and Wisdom Services and Beijing Key Laboratory of Magnetic Resonance Imaging and Brain Informatics.

References

1. Rosch, E., Mervis, C.B., Gray, W.D., Johnson, D.M., Boyes-Braem, P.: Basic objects in natural categories. Bulletin of the Psychonomic Society **6**(NB4), 415–415 (1976)
2. Markman, A., Wisniewski, E.: Similar and different: The differentiation of basic-level categories. Journal of Experimental Psychology: Learning, Memory, and Cognition **23**(1), 54–70 (1997)
3. Wisniewski, E., Murphy, G.: Superordinate and basic category names in discourse: A textual analysis. Discourse Processes **12**(2), 245–261 (1989)
4. Rogers, T., Patterson, K.: Object categorization: Reversals and explanations of the basic-level advantage. Journal of Experimental Psychology: Gerneral **136**(3), 51–69 (2007)
5. Hodges, J., Graham, N., Patterson, K.: Charting the progression in semantic dementia: Implications for the organization of semantic memory. Memory **3**, 463–495 (1995)
6. Warrington, E., James, M.: Visual Object and Space Perception Battery. Thames Valley Test Company, Edmunds (1975)
7. Mack, M., Wong, A., Gauthier, I., Tanaka, J., Palmeri, T.: Time course of visual object categorization: Fastest does not necessarily mean first. Vision Research **49**, 1961–1968 (2009)
8. VanRullen, R., Thorpe, S.J.: Is it a bird? Is it a plane? Ultra-rapid visual categorization of natural and artifactual objects. Perception **30**(6), 655–668 (2001)
9. Greene, M., Li, F.: Visual categorization is automatic and obligatory: Evidence from stroop-like paradigm. Journal of Vision **14**(1), 1–11 (2014)
10. Large, M., Kiss, I., McMullen, J.: Electrophysiological correlates of objects categorization: Back to basics. Cognitive Brain Research **20**(3), 415–426 (2004)
11. Wascher, E., Hoffman, S., Sanger, J., Grosjean, M.: Visuo-spatial processing and the N1 component of the ERP. Psychophysiology **46**(6), 1270–1277 (2009)
12. Luck, S.J., Woodman, G.E., Vogel, E.K.: Event-related potential studies of attention. Trends in Cognitive Sciences **4**(11), 432–440 (2000)

13. Mangun, G., Hillyard, S.: Mechanisms and models of selective attention. In: Coles, M., Mangun, G. (eds.) Electrophysiology of the Mind, pp. 340–385. Oxford University Press, Oxford (1996)

14. Rugg, M.D., Milner, A.D., Lines, C.R., Phalp, R.: Modulations of visual event-related potentials by spatial and non-spatial visual selective attention. Neuropsychologia 25(9), 85–96 (1987)

15. Hillyard, S., Picton, T.: Event-related potentials and selective information processing in man. In: Desmedt. J. (ed.) Cognitive Components in Cerebral Event-Related Potentials and Selective Attention. Clinical Neurophysiology, pp. 1–52 (1979)

16. Lawrence, V., Houghton, S., Tannock, R., Douglas, G., Durkin, K., Whiting, K.: ADHD outside the laboratory: boys' executive function performance on tasks in videogame play and on a visit to the zoo. Journal of Abnormal Child Psychology 30(5), 447–462 (2002)

17. Brown, C., Hagoort, P.: The processing nature of the N400: Evidence from masked priming. Journal of Cognitive Neuroscience 5(1), 34–44 (1993)

18. Holcomb, P.: Semantic priming and stimulus degradation: Implications for the role of the N400 in language processing. Psychophysiology 30(1), 47–61 (1993)

19. Lau, E., Phillips, C., Poeppel, D.: A cortical network for semantics: (de)constructing the N400. Nature Review Neuroscience 9, 920–933 (2008)

20. Fan, S., Wang, X., Liao, Z., Long, Z., Zhou, H., Qin, Y.: Basic level advantage during information retrieval: an erp study. In: Zanzotto, F.M., Tsumoto, S., Taatgen, N., Yao, Y. (eds.) BI 2012. LNCS, vol. 7670, pp. 27–37. Springer, Heidelberg (2012)

21. Zhou, H., Liu, J., Jing, W., Qin, Y., Lu, S., Yao, Y., Zhong, N.: The role of lateral inferior prefrontal cortex during information retrieval. In: Hu, B., Liu, J., Chen, L., Zhong, N. (eds.) BI 2011. LNAI, vol. 6889, pp. 53–63. Springer, Heidelberg (2011)

Special Session on Interactive Machine Learning with the Human-in-the-Loop: Cognitive Computing at its Best

Joint Decision Making on Two Perception Systems Using Diversity Rank-Score Function Graph

Darius Mulia[1], Kilby Sanchez[1], Christina Schweikert[2(✉)], and D. Frank Hsu[1]

[1] Laboratory of Informatics and Data Mining, Department of Computer and Information Science, Fordham University, Bronx, USA
{dmulia,kisanchez}@fordham.edu, hsu@cis.fordham.edu
[2] St John's University, Queens, NY, USA
schweikc@stjohns.edu

Abstract. Joint decision making on multiple visual perception systems have been studied extensively. However, the issues of what to choose (single decision or combination of more than one decision) and how to combine (average, weighted average, score, rank, or other fusion techniques) remain a challenging problem, even in the case of two systems. In this paper, we utilize the combinatorial fusion approach which treats a perception system, in this case human perception, as a scoring system and uses the notion of cognitive diversity to measure the dissimilarity of a pair of scoring patterns (or behavior). In particular, a diversity rank-score function graph is used as a visualization tool to decide which pairs of systems are good candidates to combine. Our work provides a general framework for joint decision making on visual perception systems and a powerful visualization tool for the combination of pairs of decision makers.

1 Introduction

In our daily life, as well as in critical situations, many decisions are made based on our human senses. For example, based on visual input, one will make a decision whether it is safe to cross the street, a referee at a tennis match will decide if a ball lands out of the court bounds, or a pilot will decide how to navigate through a storm. Of course, decision-making usually involves the combination of a variety of factors – visual, as well as other sensory inputs including sounds, touch, etc. In this paper, we focus on visual perception, and we investigate the conditions under which it is possible to improve accuracy by combining the observations of more than one person.

There is existing research, on the neurological level, into how fusion takes place within a sensory system [9, 10, 25], in addition to how visual information is combined with information obtained from other senses [5, 6, 7, 8, 20]. There is also research into the effect of combining multiple visual systems [1, 7, 15]. From another perspective, the works of Bahrami et al [1], Ernst and Banks [5], and Kepecs et al [15] research how visual-based decisions can be improved when two people make the decisions interactively. A study conducted by Koriat [16] suggests that it may not be necessary to combine the decisions of two people - since it may be best to simply take the decision of the more confident one. Our focus here is on the combination of the

© Springer International Publishing Switzerland 2015
Y. Guo et al. (Eds.): BIH 2015, LNAI 9250, pp. 337–346, 2015.
DOI: 10.1007/978-3-319-23344-4_33

decisions / observations made by individual visual systems – specifically, combining the visual observations of two people in a controlled setting. The aim is to gain insight into how we can improve decisions made based on visual perception by fusing the decisions of two people.

In this project, we apply an innovative information fusion method, known as combinatorial fusion [12, 13, 14], to combine visual perception systems. Combinatorial fusion has been successfully applied to other domains, for example: sensors [3, 4], information retrieval [12], text categorization [17], protein structure prediction [18], image recognition [19], target tracking [21], ChIP-seq peak detection [24], and virtual screening [28]. A main finding of combinatorial fusion applications is that, in many cases, the combined scoring system outperforms individual systems when each individual system has relatively good performance and there is diversity between the systems [2, 12, 13, 14, 22, 23]. An advantage of the combinatorial fusion approach is that we can test the performance of different kinds of combination, by score or by rank, and determine which is best, depending on diversity.

In this paper, we treat each perception system as a scoring system, A, which consists of a score function, s_A, and a rank function, r_A, derived from sorting the score function. A rank-score characteristic (RSC) function, f_A, is defined in terms of s_A, and r_A. Cognitive diversity between two scoring systems A and B, d(A, B), is measured in terms of f_A and f_B, $d(f_A, f_B)$.

The novelty of our approach is the use of the diversity rank-score characteristic (RSC) function $f_{(A,B)}$, in terms of the diversity score function $s_{(A,B)}$ and the diversity rank function $r_{(A, B)}$, to rank the set of diversity scores. Moreover, the diversity rank-score function graph is plotted and used to visualize the behavior of the diversity scores between two scoring systems (and hence two perception systems) A and B. Our approach of using the diversity rank-score function graph as a visualization tool is extremely useful, particularly when the number of pairs or visual perception systems is very large.

In the future, it can be incorporated into larger-scale systems for domains in which visualization plays an important role. Another area of research, which focuses on interactive data visualization, has shown recent advances [11, 26, 27].

2   Methods for Combining Visual Perception Systems

2.1   Statistical Mean

If we consider a person making a decision based on visual input, this person's final decision is based on a selection from a range of choices. To bring this into the context of a scoring system, we will consider each one of these possible choices as the items to be scored. There are several different approaches to combining scoring systems to arrive at the best result [1, 5, 7, 15, 20]. If we have a set of scores on a common set of items, we can compute a joint decision based an average, or a weighted average. The mean of two decisions, P and Q, is calculated as [2]:

$$M_i = (P/\sigma_1{}^i + Q/\sigma_2{}^i) / (1/\sigma_1{}^i + 1/\sigma_2{}^i) , \text{ for i } =0,1,2 \qquad (1)$$

where P and Q are the two decisions of the individual scoring systems, and σ_1 and σ_2 represent the respective confidence measurements.

2.2   Scoring System Approach

The visual perception experiment was conducted in a similar manner to previous experiments by our research group [2]. We recruited a series of volunteers in pairs to witness the toss of a metal object in a grassy area of a park; each participant was asked to indicate where the object landed, along with the confidence of their observation. The subject's observation is captured as an x,y coordinate, and the confidence is given by specifying a radius around the point. The smaller the radius, the higher the confidence. Each pair of participants is considered a trial where each individual is represented by a scoring system: P and Q. The confidence radius, r, is used to represent the standard deviation of the distribution around the proposed landing point of the object, or σ. Here, we compute σ as 0.5r.

Since we want P and Q to be compatible scoring systems, we need to create a common set of items to be scored. The items in this case are intervals within an established "common visual space". The σ values are used to compute the means described above: M_0, M_1, and M_2. The performance of each M_i is computed as the distance between M_i and A, computed as $m_i = d(M_i, A)$, where A is the actual site of the tossed object. P, Q, and A are x- and y- coordinates on a grid representing the grassy field. The M_i coordinate would be located between points P and Q.

To create a larger observation area, the line PQ is extended to points P' and Q', where M_i is the midpoint of the new line P'Q'. This new line segment P'Q' is referred to as the common visual space (Fig. 1).

Fig. 1. Common visual space with P, Q, M, P', and Q'

The line segment P'Q', of length d(P',Q'), is partitioned into 63 intervals. Each interval i, where i = 1, 2, ..., 63, has a midpoint d_i and length d(P',Q')/63. The midpoint of the center interval, in this case, d_{32}, contains M_i.

The scores for each middle point d_i, i = 1 to 63, of the 63 intervals along the common visual space between P' and Q' are generated for scoring systems P and Q. A normal distribution is used to compute the score function, as shown in formula (2) and (3). The score function for P is shown, and will be similar for Q.

$$s_p(d_i) = \frac{1}{\sigma\sqrt{2\pi}} \int_{-\infty}^{di} e^{\frac{-(x-dm)^2}{(2\sigma^2)}} \, dx \text{, if } d_i \le d_m,$$

(2)

$$s_p(d_i) = \frac{1}{\sigma\sqrt{2\pi}} \int_{di}^{\infty} e^{\frac{-(x-dm)^2}{(2\sigma^2)}} \, dx \text{, if } d_i > d_m,$$

(3)

The standard deviation, σ, is obtained from the confidence factor for P, d_j also represents the value at the center of the interval, and d_m is the midpoint of the interval that P or Q is in. Each of the midpoint d_i of the 63 intervals has a score given by P, $s_p(d_i)$ and a score given by q, $s_q(d_i)$. These are the score functions s_p and s_q that will be used in the combinatorial fusion framework. To obtain the rank function r, we sort the score function s from highest to lowest and assign ranks so that the d_i with the lowest rank has the highest score.

2.3   Combining Two Visual Scoring Systems Using Combinatorial Fusion Analysis (CFA)

The scoring systems s_P and s_Q will be used as the score functions in the combinatorial fusion framework. A scoring system A consists of a score function s_A and a rank function r_A on the set D of possible n positions (here, $D = \{d_i | i = 1, 2, ..., 63\}$). Let $N=[1,n]$ be the set of integers from 1 to n and R be the set of real numbers. The Rank-Score Characteristic (RSC) function, f_A, is a composite function of s_A and the inverse of r_A, defined by Hsu et al. [13, 14]. The RSC is a mapping from ranks to scores, f_A : $N \rightarrow R$, defined by (also see ref [2, 14, 23]):

$$f_A(i)=(s_A \circ r_A^{-1})(i) = s_A(r_A^{-1}(i)) . \tag{4}$$

To implement a system combination, we can either combine by score, or by rank. The score combination (SC), or rank combination (RC), of the two scoring systems, P and Q, is computed as the average of the scores, or ranks, for each d_i.

Here, d_i is in D, and s_A and r_A are the score function and rank function of the scoring system A - in this project, A= P or Q. We will refer to the score combination of systems P and Q as C, and the rank combination of systems P and Q as D.

The score function of C, $s_C(d_j)$, is sorted in descending order to obtain the rank function of the score combination, $r_C(d_j)$. Then, $s_D(d_i)$ is sorted in ascending order to obtain the rank function of the rank combination, $r_D(d_i)$. The top ranked d_i's in C and D are considered the optimal points for the combination. The performance of these points (p, q, M_i, C, and D) is determined by the numerical distance from the point to the target A. The point with the shortest distance to the target is the highest performing point.

2.4   Cognitive Diversity and Diversity Rank-Score Function

In addition to analyzing the results of combination by score and by rank, we are also interested in finding a way to determine which combination will yield the best performance in a particular situation. We can measure the diversity between two scoring systems and investigate the relationship between diversity and the performance of the score or rank combinations. The diversity between two scoring systems, d(P, Q), can be computed, as defined by Hsu et al [13], to be the diversity between two rank-score functions f_P and f_Q, $d(f_P, f_Q)$. The diversity score function, $d(P,Q)$, for the scoring systems P and Q is defined as:

$$d(P,Q) = d(f_P, f_Q) = \left(\sum_{i=1}^{63} (f_P(i) - f_Q(i))^2 / 63 \right)^{1/2} \qquad (5)$$

The diversity score function is referred to as $s_{(P,Q)}$. Given this, we can now simply compute the diversity rank function by sorting $s_{(P,Q)}$ in ascending order and assigning ranks accordingly, to generate $r_{(P,Q)}$. The diversity rank-score function is computed, across 16 trials, by using the diversity score function and corresponding diversity rank function, giving us the following [18]:

$$f_{(P,Q)}(i) = (s_{(P,Q)} \circ r_{(P,Q)}^{-1})(i) = s_{(P,Q)}(r_{(P,Q)}^{-1}(i)) \qquad (6)$$

The diversity rank-score graph visualizes the diversity rank-score function, as can be seen in section 3.2.

3 Trials and System Combination Analysis

3.1 Results of Analysis

Table 1 includes the information and analysis for 16 trials, including the coordinates, confidence radius rank for M_0, M_1, and M_2, as well as rank for score and rank combinations, C and D, respectively.

Table 1. Results for 16 trials.

Trial	(a): Per (P,Q)	(b): Conf.Rad(P,Q)	(c): Rank			(d):Rank(P,Q,Mi,C,D) for i=0,1,2														
			M_0	M_1	M_2	P	Q	M_0	C	D	P	Q	M_1	C	D	P	Q	M_2	C	D
Trial 1	(28.1,17.6)	(12,6)	2	1	3	4	2	1	2	4	4	3	1	4	2	4	3	1	4	2
Trial 2	(16,5.7)	(8,6)	3	2	1	4	1	3	1	4	4	3	1	4	2	4	3	1	4	2
Trial 3	(101.7,47.4)	(18,10)	3	2	1	4	1	3	1	4	4	1	3	4	2	4	1	3	4	2
Trial 4	(21.6,34.5)	(10,16)	3	1	2	2	5	1	2	2	3	4	1	4	2	3	4	1	4	2
Trial 5	(27.4,23.1)	(14,16)	1	2	3	3	1	2	3	3	5	1	2	3	3	5	1	2	3	3
Trial 6	(133.3,169.1)	(16,12)	1	2	3	1	4	3	4	1	1	5	3	1	4	1	5	3	1	4
Trial 7	(18,25.2)	(16,8)	1	2	3	1	4	3	4	1	1	5	2	3	3	1	5	2	3	3
Trial 8	(42.8,20)	(12,6)	3	1	2	4	2	1	2	4	4	3	1	4	2	4	3	1	4	2
Trial 9	(5.1,16.1)	(12,12)	1	1	1	1	4	3	4	1	1	4	3	4	1	1	5	4	1	1
Trial 10	(242.2,267.1)	(8,10)	3	2	1	1	5	4	1	2	4	3	4	1	2	4	1	3	4	2
Trial 11	(96,26.5)	(20,16)	3	2	1	4	1	3	1	4	4	1	3	4	2	4	1	3	4	2
Trial 12	(7.2,9)	(10,8)	1	2	3	2	4	1	4	2	2	4	1	5	3	2	5	1	3	3
Trial 13	(9.2,15.2)	(10,8)	1	2	3	2	4	1	4	2	2	4	1	5	3	2	5	1	3	3
Trial 14	(23.8,32.6)	(10,8)	1	2	3	2	4	1	4	2	2	5	1	2	4	2	5	1	2	4
Trial 15	(21.1,15.8)	(18,12)	3	2	1	4	1	3	1	4	5	1	4	1	1	5	1	4	2	2
Trial 16	(10,19)	(10,10)	1	1	1	2	3	1	3	3	2	3	1	3	3	2	3	1	3	3

The first column, Trial, is the specific trial that was analyzed. Column (a) provides the performances of P and Q in inches, which is the distance between P and the actual A, and the distance between Q and actual A. Column (b) provides the confidence radii of P and Q. In (b), there are green and white cells which indicate the success or failure of Koriat's Criteria, respectively. The green cells indicate that choosing the more confident system would lead to the more optimal decision. The white cells indicate that there will be no optimal decision made regardless of choosing the systems based on their confidence.

In column (c), we rank the relative performance of weighted means M_0, M_1, and M_2 against each other, within the scope of each trial. A yellow cell indicates that the weighted mean is the highest ranked performer among P, Q, M_i, C, and D. White cells indicate that the weighted mean is not the highest ranked performer among its respective values of P, Q, M_i, C, and D.

Column (d), is divided up into three sub-columns. Each sub-column ranks P, Q, M_i, C, and D in descending order of performance for $i = 0, 1$, and 2. The number 1 indicates the best (or closest) performance to actual A, while the number 5 indicates the worst or the farthest performance from A. Multiple occurring values imply that a tie has occurred for a performance ranking. If, for example, if both C and D have the same interval di as their optimal decision, then they will share the same performance. Subsequently, they share the same performance rank. Red cells indicate when the score combination (C) and rank combinations (D) are superior to or tied with the best performing individual system.

3.2   Role of Diversity Rank-Score Graph

The following Fig. 2, 3, and 4, depict the diversity rank-score graphs for the three different methods to compute the mean: M_0, M_1, and M_2, respectively.

When using different computations for M_i, the diversity between the two systems, P and Q, will vary. In Fig. 2, 3, 4, we can see the visualization of the diversity rank-score functions under the three conditions: M_0, M_1, and M_2, respectively. Table 2 shows where the trials, d_i, are ranked according to diversity, with respect to M_0, M_1, and M_2. By examining the diversity rank-score graphs, we can see that in Fig. 2, M_0, there is a sharp drop in cognitive diversity after rank 4. In Fig. 3, M_1, there is a big drop after rank 5. In Fig. 4, M_2, there is a sharp decrease in diversity after ranks 3 and 5. Given the results in Fig. 2, 3, 4, and Table 1, we can see a general trend that when there is a relatively high cognitive diversity, it is likely that we will see more consistently improved performance when combining by score or rank, particularly in the case of M_1.

In a more general setting, even if we do not know how well the score combinations or rank combinations would perform, by visualizing the diversity rank-score function graph, we can get a sense of the relative diversity of the system pairs. Based on this diversity, and on the area of application, we can make predictions as to which type of combination (score or rank) would be most suitable for two systems, whether it be input from human perception, sensors, or other scoring/ranking systems.

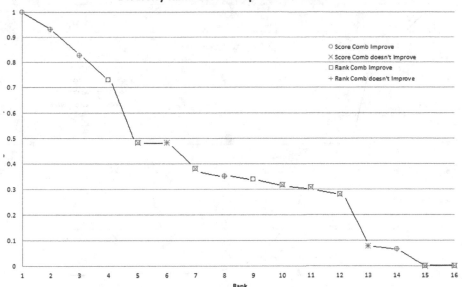

Fig. 2. Diversity Rank-Score Graph Based on M_0

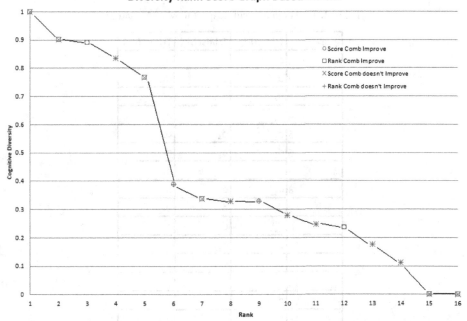

Fig. 3. Diversity Rank-Score Graph Based on M_1

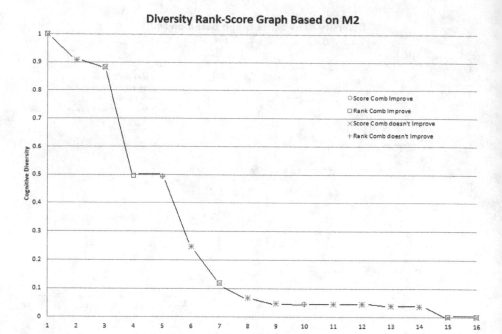

Fig. 4. Diversity Rank-Score Graph Based on M_2

Table 2. Trials ranked with respect to M_0, M_1, and M_2

Rank	Trials(M_0)	Trials(M_1)	Trials(M_2)
1	d_1	d_1	d_1
2	d_8	d_8	d_3
3	d_3	d_2	d_4
4	d_4	d_3	d_2
5	d_6	d_4	d_6
6	d_2	d_6	d_5
7	d_{13}	d_{10}	d_8
8	d_{11}	d_{11}	d_7
9	d_{10}	d_{14}	d_{10}
10	d_4	d_7	d_{14}
11	d_{12}	d_{13}	d_{11}
12	d_7	d_{15}	d_{15}
13	d_5	d_{12}	d_{13}
14	d_{15}	d_5	d_{12}
15	d_9	d_{16}	d_{16}
16	d_{16}	d_9	d_9

4   Conclusions and Future Directions

This project continues our previous studies on the combination of multiple visual perception systems, specifically human perception. Our current approach utilizes Combinatorial Fusion Analysis to facilitate the system combination using the diversity rank-score graph as a visualization tool. Before applying combinatorial fusion, we generated scoring functions for a participant's observations, which enabled us to generate rank functions, as well as rank-score functions. CFA provides a method to compute cognitive diversity between two systems.

By examining the diversity rank-score graphs, we can see the influence of cognitive diversity on the two types of scoring system combinations – by score or by rank, in terms of which results in an improved performance compared to the individual systems. In this case, we analyze the result of the score combinations under different computation of the mean, including weighted means, denoted as M_0, M_1, and M_2. Under the condition M_0, the top 2 trials, when ranking by cognitive diversity, showed improvement using sore combination. When using M_1, the top 3 trials by rank showed improvement with the rank combination. Also, when using M_2, 2 of the top 3 trials, when ranked by cognitive diversity, showed improvement under rank combination.

In future experiments, we will further examine the role of cognitive diversity and system combination methods. In particular, we will take advantage of the visualization property of the diversity rank-score function graphs, which is extremely useful when the number of pairs of scoring systems becomes very large.

References

1. Bahrami, B., Olsen, K., Latham, P., et al.: Optimally interacting minds. Science **329**. 5995, 1081–1085 (2010)
2. Batallones, A., Sanchez, K., Mott, B., et al.: On the combination of two visual cognition systems using combinatorial fusion. Brain Informatics **2**, 21–32 (2015)
3. Deng, Y., Hsu, D.F., Wu, Z., et al.: Combining Multiple Sensor Features for Stress Detection using Combinatorial Fusion. Journal of Interconnection Networks 13(03n04) (2012)
4. Deng, Y., Wu, Z., Chu, C.H., et al.: Sensor Feature Selection and Combination for Stress Identification Using Combinatorial Fusion. International Journal of Advanced Robotic Systems 10 (2013)
5. Ernst, M.O., Banks, M.S.: Humans integrate visual and haptic information in a statistically optimal fashion. Nature **415**, 429–433 (2002)
6. Ernst, M.O.: Learning to integrate arbitrary signals from vision and touch. Journal of Vision **7**(5):7, 1–14 (2007)
7. Ernst, M.O.: Decisions made better. Science 329. 5995, 1022–1023 (2010)
8. Gepshtein, S., Burge, J., Ernst, O., et al.: The combination of vision and touch depends on spatial proximity. J. Vis. **5**(11), 1013–1023 (2009)
9. Gold, J.I., Shadlen, N.: The neural basis of decision making. Annual Review of Neuroscience **30**, 535–574 (2007)
10. Hillis, J.M., Ernst, M.O., Banks, M.S., et al.: Combining sensory information: mandatory fusion within, but not between, senses. Science **298**(5598), 1627–1630 (2002)

11. Holzinger, A., Bruschi, M., Eder, W.: On Interactive Data Visualization of Physiological Low-Cost-Sensor Data with Focus on Mental Stress. In: Cuzzocrea, A., Kittl, C., Simos, D.E., Weippl, E., Xu, L. (eds.) CD-ARES 2013. LNCS, vol. 8127, pp. 469–480. Springer, Heidelberg (2013)

12. Hsu, D.F., Taksa, I.: Comparing rank and score combination methods for data fusion in information retrieval. Information Retrieval 8(3), 449–480 (2005)

13. Hsu, D.F., Chung, Y.S., Kristal, B.S.: Combinatorial Fusion Analysis: methods and practice of combining multiple scoring systems. In: Hsu, H.H. (ed.) Advanced Data Mining Technologies in Bioinformatics, pp. 1157–1181. Idea Group Inc. (2006)

14. Hsu, D., Kristal, B.S., Schweikert, C.: Rank-Score Characteristics (RSC) Function and Cognitive Diversity. In: Yao, Y., Sun, R., Poggio, T., Liu, J., Zhong, N., Huang, J. (eds.) BI 2010. LNCS, vol. 6334, pp. 42–54. Springer, Heidelberg (2010)

15. Kepecs, A., Uchida, N., Zariwala, H., et al.: Neural correlates, computation and behavioural impact of decision confidence. Nature 455, 227–231 (2008)

16. Koriat, A.: When are two heads better than one. Science, 360–362 (April 20, 2012)

17. Li, Y., Hsu, D.F., Chung, S.M.: Combination of Multiple Feature Selection Methods for Text Categorization by Using Combinatorial Fusion Analysis and Rank-Score Characteristic. International Journal on Artificial Intelligence Tools 22(02) (2013)

18. Lin, K.L., Lin, C.Y., Huang, C.D., et al.: Feature selection and combination criteria for improving accuracy in protein structure prediction. IEEE Transactions on NanoBioscience 6(2), 186–196 (2007)

19. Liu, H., Wu, Z.H., Zhang, X., et al.: A skeleton pruning algorithm based on information fusion. Pattern Recognition Letters 34(10), 1138–1145 (2013)

20. Lunghi, C., Binda, P., Morrone, C.: Touch disambiguates rivalrous perception at early stages of visual analysis. Current Biology 20(4), R143–R144 (2010)

21. Lyons, D.M., Hsu, D.F.: Combining multiple scoring systems for target tracking using rank–score characteristics. Information Fusion 10(2), 124–136 (2009)

22. Ng, K.B., Kantor, P.B.: Predicting the effectiveness of naive data fusion on the basis of system characteristics. J. Am. Soc. Inform. Sci. 51(12), 1177–1189 (2000)

23. Paolercio, E., McMunn-Coffran, C., Mott, B., et al.: Fusion of two visual perception systems utilizing cognitive diversity. In: Proceedings of the 12th IEEE International Conference on Cognitive Informatics and Cognitive Computing, pp. 226–236 (July 2013)

24. Schweikert, C., Brown, S., Tang, Z., et al.: Combining multiple ChIP-seq peak detection systems using combinatorial fusion. BMC Genomics 13(suppl. 8), S12 (2012)

25. Tong, F., Meng, M., Blake, R.: Neural basis of binocular rivalry. Trends in Cognitive Sciences 10(11), 502–511 (2006)

26. Turkay, C., Jeanquartier, F., Holzinger, A., Hauser, H.: On Computationally-Enhanced Visual Analysis of Heterogeneous Data and Its Application in Biomedical Informatics. In: Holzinger, A., Jurisica, I. (eds.) Interactive Knowledge Discovery and Data Mining in Biomedical Informatics. LNCS, vol. 8401, pp. 117–140. Springer, Heidelberg (2014)

27. Wong, B., Xu, K., Holzinger, A.: Interactive Visualization for Information Analysis in Medical Diagnosis. In: Holzinger, A., Simonic, K.-M. (eds.) USAB 2011. LNCS, vol. 7058, pp. 109–120. Springer, Heidelberg (2011)

28. Yang, J.M., Chen, Y.F., Shen, T.W., et al.: Consensus scoring for improving enrichment in virtual screening. Journal of Chemical Information and Modeling. 45, 1134–1146 (2005)

Interactive and Iterative Annotation for Biomedical Entity Recognition

Seid Muhie Yimam[1], Chris Biemann[1(✉)], Ljiljana Majnaric[2],
Šefket Šabanović[2], and Andreas Holzinger[3,4]

[1] CS Department, FG Language Technology, TU Darmstadt,
64289 Darmstadt, Germany
{yimam,biem}@cs.tu-darmstadt.de
[2] Faculty of Medicine, Josip Juraj Strossmayer University of Osijek, Osijek, Croatia
ljiljana.majnaric@gmail.com
[3] Research Unit HCI-KDD, Institute for Medical Informatics, Statistics and
Documentation, Medical University Graz, Auenbruggerplatz 2, 8036 Graz, Austria
a.holzinger@hci-kdd.org
[4] CBmed - Center for Biomarker Research in Medicine, Stiftingtalstrasse 5,
8010 Graz, Austria

Abstract. In this paper, we demonstrate the impact of interactive machine learning for the development of a biomedical entity recognition dataset using a human-into-the-loop approach: during annotation, a machine learning model is built on previous annotations and used to propose labels for subsequent annotation. To demonstrate that such interactive and iterative annotation speeds up the development of quality dataset annotation, we conduct two experiments. In the first experiment, we carry out an iterative annotation experimental simulation and show that only a handful of medical abstracts need to be annotated to produce suggestions that increase annotation speed. In the second experiment, clinical doctors have conducted a case study in annotating medical terms documents relevant for their research. The experiments validate our method qualitatively and quantitatively, and give rise to a more personalized, responsive information extraction technology.

Keywords: Interactive annotation · Machine learning · Knowledge discovery · Data mining · Human in the loop · Biomedical entity recognition

1 Introduction and Motivation

The biomedical domain is increasingly turning into a data-intensive science, and one challenge with regard to the ever-increasing body of medical literature is not only to extract meaningful information from this data, but to gain knowledge, insight, and to make sense of the data [1]. Text is a very important type of data within the biomedical domain. For example, patient records contain large amounts of text which has been entered in a non-standardized format, consequently posing a lot of challenges to processing of such data and for the clinical

© Springer International Publishing Switzerland 2015
Y. Guo et al. (Eds.): BIH 2015, LNAI 9250, pp. 347–357, 2015.
DOI: 10.1007/978-3-319-23344-4_34

doctor the written text in the medical findings is still the basis for any decision making [2,3]. Further, scientific results are communicated in text form, consequently for the biomedical domain text is an indispensable data type for gaining knowledge [4].

Modern automated information extraction (IE) systems usually are based on machine-learning models, which require large amount of manually annotated data to specify the model according to the task at hand. Unfortunately, particularly in the medical domain, experts have obligations with higher priorities, thus it is very expensive and cumbersome to annotate a large number of training examples. In order to alleviate this problem, there is a need for an approach where human annotators are facilitated to annotate faster than the traditional way, in order to produce required annotations in less time.

In this paper, we tackle the extractions of entity mentions from biomedical texts, specifically from MEDLINE abstracts (www.ncbi.nlm.nih.gov/pubmed), using a recent human-into-the-loop automation strategy that has not been applied in the medical domain before. Unlike named entity recognition (NER) systems on e.g. the news domain, entity recognition on medical domains comprises of extractions of technical terms in the broader medical and biological arena such as name of diseases, proteins, substances and so on, see e.g. [5,6].

Such an automation approach is specifically very important for the medical domain, as a full manual annotation is extremely expensive. Medical professionals in turn, however, are willing to perform this task only diligently if it matches their current field of interest. The human-into-the-loop automation approach enables users to start the automation process without pre-existing annotations, and works by suggesting annotations as soon as the users have annotated a rather small number of documents. This annotate-little and predict-little strategy is deemed adequate for Biomedical domains as it 1) produce quality annotation in a very short period of time, and 2) the approach is adaptive in such a way that newly evolving concepts or entities will not be ignored by an old and static prediction classification model. Note that while models trained on a small number of entity mentions cannot be expected to produce high-quality automatic labels, however their annotation suggestions might still be useful for the task at hand.

We conduct two experiments to exemplify and evaluate our human-into-the-loop approach of entity mention annotation for the medical domain. In the first aspect, we simulate the interactive machine learning approach by incrementally processing the BioNLP/NLPBA 2004 named entity annotated data set [7]. During the simulation, a classifier model is first trained on very few annotations and we measure the number and quality of correctly predicted annotations in the next chunk of the data, which subsequently is added to the training, simulating the annotation process. With this simulation, we can learn whether annotating very few documents already produces reasonable and faithful predictions so that it relieves users from annotating every document in the data set.

In the second experiment, we put our approach to practice and apply it in a use case where medical professionals annotate documents in order to support research on their particular question of interest. Specifically, the task used for this study is focused towards the investigations of the causes of the B-chronic lymphocytic leukemia (B-CLL) on MEDLINE abstracts.

In the experiment, we compare two setups where annotators are presented, or not presented with suggestions from the classifier in the interactive annotation interface. This experiment sets out to clarify whether medical professionals perceive our human-in-the-loop approach as appropriate and helpful in quantitative terms and in a qualitative assessment.

2   Related Work

Human into the Loop: Automated machine learning algorithms work well in certain environments. However, biomedical data are full of probability, uncertainty, incompleteness, vagueness, noise, etc., which makes the application of automated approaches difficult, yet often impossible. Moreover, the complexity of current machine learning algorithms has discouraged medical professionals from the application of such solutions. However, for increasing the quality of such approaches, the integration of the expert's domain knowledge is indispensable. The interaction of the domain expert with the data would greatly enhance the whole knowledge discovery process chain. Interactive Machine Learning (iML) puts the human into the loop to enable what neither a human nor a computer could do on their own, cf. [1].

Interactive/Adaptive Learning: Static machine learning assumes that the actual state of the "domain universe" can be sufficiently acquired by listing all available data sets at particular time. In the contrast, adaptive machine learning assumes the possibility that there might exist unrecorded facts at particular time, which can only be appear at some point in the future. Authors of [8] address an industrial case study (tile manufacturing process) and found out that the classical machine learning setup faced difficulties such as 1) feedback is usually obtained after a process is completed, which might help the system, 2) some variables can change through time, and 3) error correction is always done after observation. The research by [9] on clustering a large number of documents using an interactive recommender system shows that users can sort documents into clusters significantly faster with an interactive recommender system than correcting the output of a static automated method. On top of simple user feedback in [10], such as accepting and rejecting suggestions, complex feedback like choosing the best features, suggestions for the re-weighting of features, proposing new features and combining features remarkably improve the system. Moreover, experiments in [11] examine the effect of allowing end users to do feature labeling, instead of annotating instances of training data: Especially for small amounts of training, the feature labeling approach was shown to be effective. In our work, we do not incorporate feature labeling, but we will consider it in our future work.

NER for Medical Domains: Recent years have seen a surge on Biomedical text processing (see [12] for a survey), most of which rely on the GENIA corpus [13], which is a collection of biomedical abstracts. It is mainly annotated for linguistic structures such POS tagging and syntax annotation, semantic annotation of entities and so on [14,15]. The work of [16] focuses on the automatic detections of multiple biomedical entities using a single-word classification approach in contrast to earlier works in the area focusing on single entity types such as proteins or genes. In this approach, they use features such as word attributes and contextual information. To alleviate the bottleneck of manual named entity annotation for medical texts, [17] have set up a crowdsourcing project on Amazon Mechanical Turk (www.mturk.com) to annotate three entity types. The research shows that using crowdsourcing is a viable alternative to annotate medical texts at scale for entity types that are understood by laymen like "medication". However, for a more complex and fine-grained distinction that requires domain knowledge, medical professionals are required.

3   Methodology

Annotation Learning: The development of large amounts of high quality training data at one shot is hard and even undesirable [18]. Instead, an interactive machine learning methodology is more applicable where the machine-learning model is enhanced not using the prevailing train-learn-evaluate technique, but improving the model in a more iterative fashion.

Interactive learning focuses on enhancing an existing machine-learning model based on newly acquired information, which is not possible in a classical machine learning setting. The benefit of interactive learning is many-fold, such as 1) the classifier model gets better and better as new training examples are added to the training data, 2) when there is a sudden change to the underlying data set, what is known as *concept drift*, the machine-learning model gets updated accordingly [19], and 3) it largely reduces the total annotation time required to annotate the whole dataset. Most importantly, such approach will not require a pre-existing annotation dataset so that it is truly responsive and incremental, fully adaptive to the user's need, and it makes such approach more affordable when integrated into a larger information extraction system.

As the machine-learning model can be enriched incrementally, applications employing this model will not be affected, as the system can still draw suggestions from the old model while building the new model. This approach overcomes the limitations where systems have to wait until full training and prediction cycles are completed, decreasing deployment time.

Medical NER Tagging: Medical named entity mention recognition is a well-researched area with a large number of datasets used in competitions [7,20–23]. These mainly focus on entity/mention and chunk detections and relation extraction. Unfortunately, Biomedical annotation task is still challenging unlike other language processing tasks due to the fact that most of the annotations require highly experienced professional annotators, as discussed above.

To demonstrate the effect of interactive learning on Biomedical entity tagging, we used thee BioNLP/NLPBA 2004 corpus and train a classifier using a rather generic sequence tagging system developed for German named entity recognition [24] based on CRFsuite [25]. The system is highly configurable regarding features and data formats. For this study, we use basic standard features to characterize the text: Character and word features, which consists of the first and last character ngrams (n=3) of the current token as affixes, considered in a time-shifted window of two tokens around the word token in focus. We also incorporated automatically induced part-of-speech (POS) tag clusters as features, which are based on the system by [26] trained on a MEDLINE 2004 dataset. For unseen tokens in the cluster, the Pretree multi-purpose word classifier tool from the ASV toolbox [27] is used to approximate the unsupervised POS tags. Furthermore, word shape features that reflect capitalization and character classes (e.g. numbers vs. letters), were found to be relevant for biomedical mentions, as the shape of such entities often differs from non-entity tokens.

4 Annotation Problem Use Case

In this section, the use case of our medical research professionals is laid out. It focuses on understanding the interplay between risk factors and genetic presuppositions with a leukemia cancer.

B-chronic lymphocytic leukemia (B-CLL), a malignant hematopoetic neoplasm of B-lymphocytes (B cells), is the most common leukemia in the westernized world [28]. Yet, its risk factors and underlying mechanisms are still unknown. Some features of this malignancy, such as the incidence increasing with age and low proliferative capacity combined with impaired apoptosis (homeostatic cell death), categorize this disorder more as a chronic aging disease, than as a "real" leukemia, known to arise from the primary genetic defect and the subsequent block in immune cell differentiation [29]. On the other hand, accumulated evidence indicate that the pathogenesis of some commonly occurring cancers, such as breast, or colon cancer, as well as of some types of lymphomas (malignant neoplasms of the lymphoid tissue), can be explained by the complex interplay of age-related and lifestyle-related mechanisms, operating mainly through chronic inflammation and impaired insulin dependent metabolism, known as insulin resistance condition (decreased insulin action in target tissues followed by chronic hyperglycemia) [30–32].

Biological links towards cancerogenesis and lymphomagenesis go via impaired cell homeostasis mechanisms, including apoptosis and proliferation, as well as inter-cellular and intra-cellular signaling [33, 34]. Medical expert posed a hypothesis that the same risk factors and mechanisms stay also in the background of the pathogenesis of B-CLL. Exact evidence in the literature is absent. Literature search and reasoning could be demanding, because of the need to revealing many complex relationships between the numerous sets of entities and the syntagmatic constructs.

In order to alleviate the efforts of meaningful literature searching, we used the tool of adaptive annotation learning. Firstly, the medical expert prepared a set of selected abstracts, downloaded from the MEDLINE. Then, based on a limited number of specific medical entities, including CELL, CONDITION, DISORDER, GENE, MOLECULE, PROTEIN, MOLECULAR PATHWAY and

SUBSTANCE, she annotated the important structures throughout the entire text body and made them visible.

5   Experiment and Evaluation

Simulating Interactive Learning: In order to prove that interactive machine learning can yield a quality-annotated data set in a short training loop, we conduct our first experiment based on the BioNLP/NLPBA 2004 data set. The data set is divided into an increasing size of documents simulating interactive annotation. As it can be seen from Table 2 and Figure 1, a (simulated) annotation of only 40 sentences already predicted an adequate amount of suggestions where users can quickly accept or modify and proceed to the next iteration. Aiming at maximizing F-score as the harmonic mean of Precision and Recall, we can clearly observe in Tab. 1 that, after simulated annotating of about 500 sentences, the gain in performance decreases, which implies that only annotating small portion of the sentences produces reasonable suggestions that are mostly acceptable by the annotator. Also, we can see that more annotations beyond 5,000-10,000 sentences are subject to diminishing returns, i.e. it takes an increasing number of annotations to achieve the same amount of relative improvements, the more annotations are used for training. In a human-in-the-loop setting, this can be detected during the process, and could be a sign for requiring more advanced features in the machine learning setup.

Qualitative Assessment: In addition to the quantitative experimental simulation done in Section 5, we have conducted practical annotation and automation experiments using a total of 10 MEDLINE abstracts that were chosen in the context of our use case described in Section 4. For this, we have used the annotation and automation component [35] of the WebAnno web-based annotation

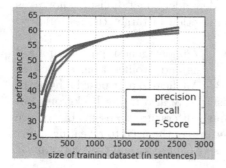

Fig. 1. Learning curve showing the performance of interactive automation for BioNLP/NLPBA 2004 data set using different sizes of training data

Table 2. Evaluation result for the BioNLP/NLPBA 2004 task using an interactive online learning approach with different sizes of training dataset tested on the fixed development dataset.

Sentences	Recall	Precision	F-score
40	27.27	39.05	32.11
120	37.74	44.01	40.63
280	46.68	51.39	48.92
600	53.23	54.89	54.05
1240	57.83	57.74	57.78
2520	59.35	61.26	60.29
5080	62.32	64.03	63.16
10200	66.43	67.50	66.96
18555	69.48	69.16	69.32

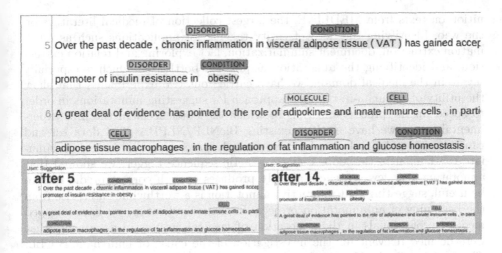

Fig. 2. Automation suggestions using the WebAnno automation component after annotating 5 initial resp. 9 additional abstracts. Correct suggestions are marked in grey, while wrong suggestions are marked in red.

tool. WebAnno [36] features a split-pane visualization, where annotation is performed in the upper pane by selecting text and choosing a label. In the lower pane, suggestions are displayed, which can be accepted and appear as annotations in the upper pane upon clicking on them, cf. Fig. 2. The experiment was conducted in two rounds. In the first round, medical experts have annotated 5 abstracts comprising a total of 86 sentences for specific medical entities as described in Section 4. Once the first round of annotations was completed, the automation was started using WebAnno's automation component in order to provide initial suggestions. As displayed in Fig. 2, the automation component already suggests some entity annotations immediately after the first round. Using the automation suggestions, the expert continued annotating. After another 9 annotated abstracts that serve as training for the sequence tagging model, the quality and quantity of suggestions have again increased, see Fig. 2.

Qualitatively, annotators found that using the automation component, they perceived a significant increase in annotation speed. This confirms results in [37], where adaptive annotation automation in WebAnno can speed up the annotation process by a factor of 3 to 4 in comparison to a traditional annotation interface without suggestions. On a further note, the WebAnno tool was perceived as adequate and useable by our medical professionals, requiring only very limited usage instructions.

6   Conclusion and Future Outlook

In this work, we investigated the impact of adaptive machine learning for the annotation of quality training data. Specifically, we tackled medical entity recognition on texts from MEDLINE, the largest collection of medical literature on the web. Identifying the need of entity tagging for applications such as information extraction, document summarization, fact exploring and relation extraction, and identifying the annotation acquisition bottleneck which is especially severe in the medical domain, we have carried out two experiments that show the utility of a human-in-the-loop approach for suggesting annotations in order to speed up the process and thus to widen the bottleneck. In the first experimental setup, we have used an existing BioNLP/NLPBA 2004 data set and run experimental simulation by incrementally processing the dataset to simulate the human in the loop. Using a generic sequence tagger, we showed that annotating very few sentences already produces enough correct predictions to be useful, suggesting that interactive annotation is a worthwhile enterprise from the beginning of an annotation project. In the second setup, we have engaged medical professionals in the annotation of medical entities in documents that were deemed relevant for the investigation of the cause of malignant B-CLL. The freely available WebAnno annotation tool (github.com/webanno) has been used for the annotation and automation process and annotators found that the adaptive annotation approach 1) makes it fast and easy to annotate medical entities, and 2) useful entity suggestions were already obtained after the annotation of only 5 MEDLINE abstracts, and suggestions subsequently improved tremendously after having annotated another 9 abstracts, reducing the annotation effort.

On a larger perspective, our results demonstrate that a paradigm change in machine learning is feasible and viable. Whereas the mantra of the past has been 'there is no (annotated) data like more (annotated) data' for supervised machine learning, suggesting large annotation efforts involving many human annotators, it becomes clear from our experiments that these efforts can be sped up tremendously by switching to an approach where the human can continuously improve the model by annotation while using the model to extract information, with the especially good news that the largest model improvements are achieved already very early in the process, as long as the domain is confined.

While such an adaptive approach to machine learning that factors in the user into the equation still calls for new evaluation methodologies to be assessed in all its aspects, it is deemed more adequate, more immediate and quicker deployable. It also fits better the shift towards an interactive, more natural, more adaptive, more contextualized and iterative approach under the umbrella of cognitive computing.

Acknowledgments. Parts of this work have been carried out with the K1 COMET Competence Center CBmed, which is funded by the Austrian Federal Ministry of Transport, Innovation and Technology (BMVIT); the Austrian Federal Ministry of Science, Research and Economy (BMWFW); Land Steiermark (Department 12, Business and Innovation); the Styrian Business Promotion Agency (SFG); and the Vienna Business Agency. The COMET program is executed by the FFG. The development of WebAnno and the research on adaptive machine learning was supported by the German Federal

Ministry of Education and Research (BMBF) as part of the CLARIN-D infrastructure and by German Research Foundation (DFG) as part of the SEMSCH project.

References

1. Holzinger, A.: Human-Computer Interaction and Knowledge Discovery (HCI-KDD): What Is the Benefit of Bringing Those Two Fields to Work Together? In: Cuzzocrea, A., Kittl, C., Simos, D.E., Weippl, E., Xu, L. (eds.) CD-ARES 2013. LNCS, vol. 8127, pp. 319–328. Springer, Heidelberg (2013)
2. Holzinger, A., Schantl, J., Schroettner, M., Seifert, C., Verspoor, K.: Biomedical Text Mining: State-of-the-Art, Open Problems and Future Challenges. In: Holzinger, A., Jurisica, I. (eds.) Interactive Knowledge Discovery and Data Mining in Biomedical Informatics. LNCS, vol. 8401, pp. 271–300. Springer, Heidelberg (2014)
3. Holzinger, A., Geierhofer, R., Modritscher, F., Tatzl, R.: Semantic information in medical information systems: Utilization of text mining techniques to analyze medical diagnoses. JUCS **14**, 3781–3795 (2008)
4. Holzinger, A., Yildirim, P., Geier, M., Simonic, K.M.: Quality-based knowledge discovery from medical text on the web. In: Pasi, G., Bordogna, G., Jain, L.C. (eds.) ISRL, vol. 50, pp. 145–158. Springer (2013)
5. Ghiasvand, O., Kate, R.: UWM: Disorder mention extraction from clinical text using CRFs and normalization using learned edit distance patterns. In: Proc. SemEval 2014, Dublin, Ireland (2014)
6. Leser, U., Hakenberg, J.: What makes a gene name? named entity recognition in the biomedical literature. Briefings in Bioinformatics **6**, 357–69 (2005)
7. GuoDong, Z., Jian, S.: Exploring deep knowledge resources in biomedical name recognition. In: Proc. NLPBA/BioNLP at COLING 2004, Geneva, Switzerland, pp. 99–102 (2004)
8. Ludl, M.C., Lewandowski, A., Dorffner, G.: Adaptive machine learning in delayed feedback domains by selective relearning. Appl. Artif. Intell., 543–557 (2008)
9. Drucker, S.M., Fisher, D., Basu, S.: Helping Users Sort Faster with Adaptive Machine Learning Recommendations. In: Campos, P., Graham, N., Jorge, J., Nunes, N., Palanque, P., Winckler, M. (eds.) INTERACT 2011, Part III. LNCS, vol. 6948, pp. 187–203. Springer, Heidelberg (2011)
10. Stumpf, S., Rajaram, V., Li, L., Burnett, M., Dietterich, T., Sullivan, E., Drummond, R., Herlocker, J.: Toward harnessing user feedback for machine learning. In: Proc. 12th IUI, pp. 82–91 (2007)
11. Das, S., Moore, T., Wong, W.K., Stumpf, S., Oberst, I., Mcintosh, K., Burnett, M.: End-user feature labeling: Supervised and semi-supervised approaches based on locally-weighted logistic regression. Artif. Intell. **204**, 56–74 (2013)
12. Cohen, A.M., Hersh, W.R.: A survey of current work in biomedical text mining. Briefings in Bioinformatics **6**, 57–71 (2005)
13. Ohta, T., Tateisi, Y., Kim, J.D.: The GENIA corpus: An annotated research abstract corpus in molecular biology domain. In: Proc. Human Language Technology Research, HLT 2002, San Francisco, CA, USA, pp. 82–86 (2002)
14. Tateisi, Y., Tsujii, J.: Part-of-speech annotation of biology research abstracts. In: Proc. LREC 2004, Lisbon, Portugal, pp. 1267–1270 (2004)
15. Tateisi, Y., Yakushiji, A., Ohta, T., Tsujii, J.: Syntax annotation for the GENIA corpus. In: Proc. IJCNLP 2005, Lisbon, Portugal, pp. 222–227 (2005)

16. Lee, C., Hou, W.J., Chen, H.H.: Annotating multiple types of biomedical entities: A single word classification approach. In: Proc. Int'l Joint Workshop on NLP in Biomedicine and Its Applications, pp. 80–83 (2004)
17. Yetisgen-Yildiz, M., Solti, I., Xia, F., Halgrim, S.R.: Preliminary experience with amazon's mechanical turk for annotating medical named entities. In: Proc. NAACL HLT 2010 Workshop on Creating Speech and Language Data with Amazon's Mechanical Turk, pp. 180–183 (2010)
18. Vidulin, V., Bohanec, M., Gams, M.: Combining human analysis and machine data mining to obtain credible data relations. Information Sciences 288, 254–278 (2014)
19. Hoens, T.R., Chawla, N.V.: Learning in non-stationary environments with class imbalance. In: Proc. 18th ACM SIGKDD, New York, NY, USA, pp. 168–176 (2012)
20. Uzuner, Ö., Luo, Y., Szolovits, P.: Evaluating the state-of-the-art in automatic de-identification. J Am. Med. Inform. Ass. 14, 550–563 (2007)
21. Uzuner, Ö., Solti, I., Xia, F., Cadag, E.: Community annotation experiment for ground truth generation for the i2b2 medication challenge. J Am. Med. Inform. Ass. 17, 561–570 (2010)
22. Kim, J.D., Ohta, T., Pyysalo, S., Kano, Y., Tsujii, J.: Overview of BioNLP 2009 shared task on event extraction. In: Proc. BioNLP 2009, pp. 1–9 (2009)
23. Kim, J.D., Pyysalo, S., Ohta, T., Bossy, R., Nguyen, N., Tsujii, J.: Overview of bionlp shared task 2011. In: Proc. BioNLP, pp. 1–6 (2011)
24. Benikova, D., Yimam, S.M., Santhanam, P., Biemann, C.: GermaNER: free open german named entity recognition tool. In: Proceedings of the GSCL 2015, Duisburg, Germany (2015)
25. Okazaki, N.: CRFsuite: a fast implementation of Conditional Random Fields (CRFs) (2007)
26. Biemann, C.: Unsupervised Part-of-Speech Tagging in the Large. Res. Lang. Comput., 101–135 (2009)
27. Biemann, C., Quasthoff, U., Heyer, G., Holz, F.: Asv toolbox - a modular collection of language exploration tools. In: Proc. LREC 2008, pp. 1760–1767 (2008)
28. Brown, J.R.: Inherited susceptibility to chronic lymphocytic leukemia: evidence and prospects for the future. Ther Adv Hematol 4, 298–308 (2013)
29. Nieto, W.G., Teodosio, C., López, A, Rodríguez-Caballero, A., Romero, A., Bárcena, P., Gutierrez, M.L., Barez Hernandez, P., Carreño Luengo, M.T., Casado Romo, J.M., Cubino Luis, R., De Vega Parra, J.: Non-cll-like monoclonal b-cell lymphocytosis in the general population: Prevalence and phenotypic/genetic characteristics. Cytometry Part B 78B, 24–34 (2010)
30. Larsson, S.C., Wolk, A.: Obesity and risk of non-Hodgkin's lymphoma: A meta-analysis. International Journal of Cancer 121, 1564–1570 (2007)
31. Tsugane, S., Inoue, M.: Insulin resistance and cancer: Epidemiological evidence. Cancer Science 101, 1073–1079 (2010)
32. Bastard, J.P., Maachi, M., Lagathu, C., Kim, M.J., Caron, M., Vidal, H., Capeau, J., Feve, B.: Recent advances in the relationship between obesity, inflammation, and insulin resistance. European Cytokine Network 17, 4–12 (2006)
33. Ginaldi, L., De Martinis, M., Monti, D., Franceschi, C.: The immune system in the elderly. Immunologic Research 30, 81–94 (2004)
34. Le Marchand-Brustel, Y., Gual, P., Grémeaux, T., Gonzalez, T., Barrès, R., Tanti, J.-F.: Fatty acid-induced insulin resistance: role of insulin receptor substrate 1 serine phosphorylation in the retroregulation of insulin signalling. Biochem. Soc. Trans. 31, 1152–1156 (2003)

35. Yimam, S., Eckart de Castilho, R., Gurevych, I., Biemann, C.: Automatic annotation suggestions and custom annotation layers in WebAnno. In: Proc. ACL 2014 System Demonstrations, Baltimore, MD, USA, pp. 91–96 (2014)
36. Yimam, S., Gurevych, I., Eckart de Castilho, R., Biemann, C.: WebAnno: A flexible, web-based and visually supported system for distributed annotations. In: Proc. ACL 2013 System Demonstrations, Sofia, Bulgaria, pp. 1–6 (2013)
37. Yimam, S.M.: Narrowing the loop: Integration of resources and linguistic dataset development with interactive machine learning. In: Proc. HLT-NAACL: Student Research Workshop, Denver, Colorado, pp. 88–95 (2015)

Analysis of Patient Groups and Immunization Results Based on Subspace Clustering

Michael Hund[1][✉], Werner Sturm[2], Tobias Schreck[2], Torsten Ullrich[3],
Daniel Keim[1], Ljiljana Majnaric[4], and Andreas Holzinger[5,6]

[1] Data Analysis and Visualization Group,
University of Konstanz, Konstanz, Germany
michael.hund@uni-konstanz.de
[2] Institute for Computer Graphics and Knowledge Visualization,
Graz University of Technology, Graz, Austria
[3] Fraunhofer Austria Reseach GmbH, Vienna, Austria
[4] Faculty of Medicine, JJ Strossmayer University of Osijek, Osijek, Croatia
[5] CBmed - Center for Biomarker Research in Medicine, Graz, Austria
[6] Research Unit HCI-KDD, Institute for Medical Informatics,
Statistics and Documentation, Medical University Graz, Graz, Austria

Abstract. Biomedical experts are increasingly confronted with what
is often called *Big Data*, an important subclass of high-dimensional
data. High-dimensional data analysis can be helpful in finding relationships between records and dimensions. However, due to data complexity,
experts are decreasingly capable of dealing with increasingly complex
data. Mapping higher dimensional data to a smaller number of relevant
dimensions is a big challenge due to the *curse of dimensionality*. Irrelevant, redundant, and conflicting dimensions affect the effectiveness and
efficiency of analysis. Furthermore, the possible mappings from high-
to low-dimensional spaces are ambiguous. For example, the similarity
between patients may change by considering different combinations of
relevant dimensions (subspaces). We show the potential of subspace analysis for the interpretation of high-dimensional medical data. Specifically,
we analyze relationships between patients, sets of patient attributes, and
outcomes of a vaccination treatment by means of a subspace clustering
approach. We present an analysis workflow and discuss future directions
for high-dimensional (medical) data analysis and visual exploration.

Keywords: Knowledge discovery and exploration · Subspace clustering · Subspace analysis · Subspace classification · Classification
explanation

1 Introduction

Today, experts in Life Sciences are not only confronted with large amount of
data, but particularly with high-dimensional data e.g., by the trend towards
personalized medicine [1]. A big challenge of biomedical informatics research is

© Springer International Publishing Switzerland 2015
Y. Guo et al. (Eds.): BIH 2015, LNAI 9250, pp. 358–368, 2015.
DOI: 10.1007/978-3-319-23344-4_35

to gain knowledge from these complex high-dimensional data sets [2]. Within such data, relevant *structural* and/or *temporal* patterns ("knowledge") are often hidden and not accessible to the expert. While automatic data analysis can provide candidate patterns for user exploration, it is not always clear which analysis methods are suitable for a given problem. Often, methods which consider the full data space are applied. However, these may fail to deliver useful results due to the *curse of dimensionality* [3]. We present a case study on the applicability of full- and subspace-based analysis methods on a real-world immunization data set. We present a potentially effective analysis workflow, which can help to understand the relationship of clusters of patients in context of attribute similarities and outcomes of an immunization treatment. We also provide a discussion of limitations and possible extensions to subspace analysis in this domain.

2 Related Work

We briefly survey related work in the area of clustering including subspace methods and interactive data exploration.

Cluster Analysis. Cluster analysis is a widely known tool to reduce large data sets to a smaller number of clusters, which can be compared with each other and in relation to some target attribute of interest [4]. Traditional clustering approaches such as *k-means* or *hierarchical clustering* [4] take all dimensions into account. However, it has been shown that for many dimensions the so-called *curse of dimensionality* may prevent effective cluster analysis, as the similarity measure may become less discriminant [3,5]. To this end, subspace cluster algorithms search for clusters not in the whole data space, but within different subsets of dimensions (called *subspaces*) in which discriminating clusters can be found [6].

Interactive Data Exploration. Data analysis algorithms typically require parameters to be set, and often, multiple solutions need to be considered before arriving at a satisfactory result. To this end, methods of interactive and visual exploration of the data and the analysis outputs can be very helpful. Specifically, many visualization techniques have been developed for exploration of high-dimensional data and clusterings. For example, Parallel Coordinate Plots [7] map high-dimensional data to Polylines, allowing the user to discern groups in data and potentially relevant relationships, effective for moderate numbers of dimensions. Another standard approach is to reduce data dimensionality and show relationships of data points by their positions in a data projection [8]. In [9], users could compare data clusterings with constituent data dimensions.

The latter approaches have in common to consider all input data dimensions at once. In other work, visualizations to explore clusters in subspaces, by a combination of heatmap and glyph representations in the so-called ClustNails approach [10] were proposed. The system was applicable to any subspace clustering approach. In [11], 2D projections of the data in alternative subspaces were applied, to identify complementary, orthogonal or redundant subspaces; again,

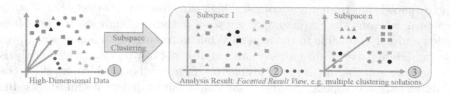

Fig. 1. Subspace clustering: algorithms compute multiple, alternative solution in different subspaces, i.e. clustering by color (subspace 1) or by shape (subspace 2).

the approach was applicable to different subspace selection methods. Another system to rely on subspace cluster comparison is VISA [12], which implement a simple glyph alternative to represent and compare subspace clusters. In [13], visual comparison of data groups across dimensions using linked views in an encompassing system was presented.

3   Data Analysis with Subspace Clustering

As discussed in Section 2, subspace clustering can be a promising tool for analysis of high-dimensional data with respect to multiple different groups in data and their relationships to dimensions. Its main idea is illustrated in Fig. 1. The goal is to understand data in terms of (a) groups of similar records (clusters), and (b) the underlying dimensions (subspaces). As an outcome of subspace cluster analysis applied on a high-dimensional data ①, depending on the parametrization and/or subspace cluster method, clusterings in multiple *different subspaces* may be found, constituting different notions of similarity; e.g. grouping according to color ② or shape ③. Each subspace cluster may give rise to a different interpretation. Depending on the underlying algorithm, we can state that all cluster members are similar to each other w.r.t. the dimensions of the subspace. The main difference to *feature selection* [14] is that subspace analysis aims for different patterns in different subspaces while feature selection typically determine a single subspace to optimize a quality criterion such as the classification error.

For our experiments in Section 4.3, we rely on a subspace clustering approach called *Proclus* (Projected Clustering) [15]. Proclus is similar to *k-means* [4] as it generates, by an iterative process, a *partition* of the data. Each data point can belong to one cluster, and each cluster is represented by a prototype point (medoid). Proclus needs two parameters: the number of clusters C and the average dimensionality per subspace D. The subspace computation starts by a random initialization of medoids. In a refinement step, for each of the C medoids a well-fitting subspace of average dimensionality D is found. This is achieved by finding dimensions that show a low variance of the distances between the respective medoid and its cluster members. The resulting subspace contains dimensions in which the values of the cluster members are similar. While other subspace clustering methods are available [6], we chose Proclus for its simplicity, efficiency, and robustness to noise, using the *OpenSubspace Framework* [16] implementation.

4 Use Case: Explanations for Vaccination Outcomes

We study the potential of a subspace clustering-based analysis on a real-world medical analysis problem. We introduce a relevant dataset from a clinical research, describe our analysis goals, present results of initial experiments, and interpret them from the domain perspective.

4.1 Considered Data Set and Analysis Goal

Data Set Used. The examined data set is based on a real patient data which describes volunteers vaccinated against influenza. Patients were selected to represents a high-risk population for influenza complications. All subjects were suffering of multiple (age-related) chronic medical conditions which interfere with the immune system. The investigated group of subjects consists of 35 male and 58 female persons aged between 50 and 89 years. The data set contains 61 dimensions describing clinical parameters such as sex, age, anthropometric measures, hematological, and biochemical tests. In addition to that, dimensions containing diagnosis results of common chronic diseases are included. Finally, a single target attribute representing the positive or negative vaccination outcome (36 positive, 57 negative) is included. Further details about the dataset and the underlying influenza vaccination can be found in [17].

Analysis Perspectives. According to the domain expert (medical physician and researcher) who created the dataset, the reasons for a positive or negative vaccination outcome can neither be described by a single dimension, nor by a fixed combination of dimensions. Instead, a variety of different reasons may cause the positive or negative outcome. In the remainder of this paper, we analyze the above described dataset by means of a subspace clustering based method in order to discover multiple reasons for different outcomes. Our idea is to apply a subspace clustering algorithm to the dataset in order to find similarities of patients of the same outcome class. The subspace dimensions can be interpreted as possible explanations for an outcome.

Data Preprocessing. As shown above, the considered dataset is heterogeneous as it contains both numerical and nominal dimensions. Existing subspace clustering algorithms typically work on numerical data only. Also, for existing implementations there is no description how missing values are treated. As a consequence, we preprocessed the dataset in the following way: (1) We removed all patient records that have a missing value in any of its dimension. Afterwards the resulting dataset contains 29 patients with a positive and 42 patients with a negative outcome. (2) We transformed all nominal dimensions such as *sex*, *hypert*, or *statins* into a numerical representation. Due to the fact that all nominal dimension (except for diabetes mellitus (DM)) consist of only two different values (mainly *yes* and *no*), we converted the values to either 0 or 1. Finally, we normalized all dimensions linearly in the range $[0, 1]$. After this, all dimensions are numerical in the range of $[0, 1]$, enabling further analysis with equally weighted dimensions.

4.2   Experiments in Full-Space Analysis

In our initial experiments on the dataset, we found that a full-space analysis is not useful. We used data mining tools such as KNIME [18] to cluster patients into different groups, or applied different classification algorithms to correctly predict the vaccination outcome of a patient.

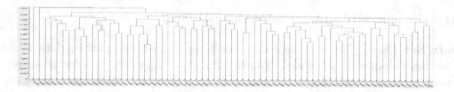

Fig. 2. Dendrogram illustrating the hierarchical clustering of our dataset (*Euclidean distance* and *average linkage* type). The x-axis represents the individual patients, while the y-axis indicate the dissimilarity between two patients or patients with clusters.

Full-Space Clustering: A hierarchical clustering was applied. The results are illustrated as a Dendrogram in Fig. 2. The x-axis is mapped to the individual patients, the y-axis represents the dissimilarity between two patients or a patient cluster. A large y-value corresponds to a high dissimilarity. From Fig. 2 we see that none of the patients are considered similar and, as a consequence, no useful grouping of patients can be identified. We assume the reasons as: (1) Patients are typically similar to each other only in a subset of dimensions, (2) a similarity in one dimension can be countered by a dissimilarity in another dimension, and (3) the *concentration effect* [5] affects the similarity computation in high-dimensional spaces.

Full-Space Classification: For the classification task, did not remove missing values but rather replace them by the average value of the dimension. We applied several classification algorithms to find useful predictors for the vaccination outcomes. Our experiments comprised e.g., *Decision-Trees, Bayes Classification,* and *Random Forest.* We split the dataset into a training set (80% of the records) and a validation set (20% of the records). For the validation, we measured the percentage of correctly classified patients after the model training. While the accuracy of the classification of the training dataset performs very well (approx. 84% for decision tree), the accuracy for the validation dataset dropped below 50% for some algorithm; which is worse than random classification. We assume the poor classification performance is caused by (1) the size of the training dataset which is too small, and (2) there are no global aspects allowing a classification into the two outcome classes. Instead, different combinations of features may be of relevance to predict the outcome properly.

4.3   Subspace Analysis: Initial Experiments and Results

To search for local explanations of the vaccination outcome, subspace analysis techniques are beneficial. In the following, we describe three different

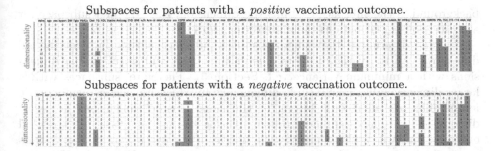

Subspaces for patients with a *positive* vaccination outcome.

Subspaces for patients with a *negative* vaccination outcome.

Fig. 3. Subspaces detected by experiment 2: subspace clustering (*Proclus*) applied separately to patients with a positive, or negative outcome. The columns represent the different dimensions (green indicate that dimension belongs to subspace). Each row represents a clustering result of different dimensionality.

experiments that we conducted. The experiments apply the subspace clustering algorithm *Proclus* to different subsets of the data. We interpret the discovered subspaces as a mean to describe the similarity between a subset of patients and, as a consequence, as possible reasons for a vaccination outcome. Supplementary material of the experiments and the attribute description can be found on our website (http://files.dbvis.de/bih2015/).

Experiment 1. In the first experiment, we apply Proclus to the preprocessed dataset and aim for subspace clusters that contain mainly patients of a single outcome. The dimensions of these clusters and the respective values of the cluster members are a means to describe the specific outcome. For this experiment, we vary Proclus' parameters (#clusters: 2-8; avg. #dimensions: 3-14). We evaluate each cluster with the *Entropy score* [16] which measures the purity of a cluster w.r.t. a specified class label. The supplementary material on our website provides an overview of the results. We can see that almost none of the detected clusters contain patients of only one specific class, but rather a mixture of both classes without a significant majority of a positive or negative outcome. We believe that this result is caused by (1) the computation strategy of Proclus which aims for large clusters, and (2) the dataset contains dimensions in which many patients are similar to each other - independent of their class label. These dimensions dominate the detected clusters and prevent Procus from finding clusters relevant for the description of the vaccination outcome (c.f. experiment 2).

Experiment 2. To find descriptive clusters for each vaccination outcome, we split the dataset into subsets according to the outcome class. Further analysis is applied to the individual subsets. In the first part, we configure *Proclus* to detect subspaces containing a *single cluster*. The dimensions of the subspace indicate global similarities of a class. For each subset the average number of dimensions varies between 3 and 14. The results can be found in Fig. 3. The different dimensions are indicated as columns while each row represents a subspace cluster with a different dimensionality. The cells of a row are marked with a green background, if the subspace contains the dimension. E.g., the first subspace for a positive outcome contains the dimensions: *HbA1c*, *COPB*, and *RF*.

Proclus determines the dimensions of a subspace cluster by ordering all dimensions by the variance of its cluster members, and selecting the dimensions with a minimum variance (c.f. Section 3). Therefore, subspaces with a larger dimensionality may include dimensions in which its cluster members are less similar. As all records belong to the same cluster, dimensions in lower-dimensional subspaces are more descriptive for an outcome class (w.r.t. global outcome similarity). Consequently, the height of the green bars in Fig. 3 illustrates the importance of a dimension for an outcome class. Except for *HPA* and *PRL*, the globally descriptive dimension are identical for both outcomes. This result is in-line with the detected subspaces of the first experiment (see supplementary material), i.e. the following set of dimensions is discriminative for all patients from a global perspective: *HbA1c*, *COPB*, *aller d*, *HPA*, *CRP*, *RF*, *INS*, *PRL*, *TSH*, *ANA*, and *IGE*. Most patients in our dataset are similar in these dimensions, however, we do not get much knowledge about the patients w.r.t. the vaccination outcome. This observation is confirmed by the second part of experiment 2. In addition to the first part, we also varied the #clusters between 2-4. The complete result can be found in the supplementary material. In summary, we can see that even for results with 4 clusters, the majority of dimensions is from the given set above. From the second experiment, we can conclude that subspace clustering helps to find dimensions in which patients of a specific class are similar to each other, hence these dimensions may be an indicator for the reason of the classification. However, experiment 2 shows, that dimensions in which most patients are similar to each other, highly influence the clustering results. As a consequence the subspaces for both outcome classes are similar to each other.

Experiment 3. In our last experiment, we concentrate on *more local patterns*. From the previous experiments, we know that all patients, and in particular all patients of one outcome class are similar to each other in the dimensions described above. To find more local patterns, we remove these dimensions from both subsets and re-apply Proclus. Afterwards, a heuristic is used to search for a result in which all patients are assigned to any subspace cluster, the cluster sizes are similar, and the number of dimensions is rather high. For both outcome classes, we selected a result with four different clusters and an average number of dimensions of 14. A table of the subspaces and the assigned cluster members for each outcome class can be found in the supplementary material. From these results, we can make the following observations: (1) The patients belonging to a subspace cluster are similar in all of the dimensions of the subspace; (2) For one outcome class, we found subspaces that differ significantly in their dimensions; (3) The relevant subspaces for a positive and a negative outcome class are different. We provided our results to the domain-expert who created the dataset. The expert liked the result very much and provided some insights into our findings:

Fig. 4. Our proposed workflow to discover relations between patients, relevant dimensions and different class labels (here vaccination outcomes).

Positive Vaccination Outcome: One subspace shows a group of patients that is homogeneous in all dimensions of the subspace. Based on the following dimension and its values, we can state that the group of patients is rather healthy, i.e. a positive vaccination outcome: The patients do not have hypertension, CVD, neoplasm, (attribute noo), psychiatric disorders and do not have adverse reaction to drugs (attribute dr aller). Furthermore, the patients do not use any of the following medications: statins, anticoagulants, or analgesics which results in preserved renal function (dimension CLEAR).

Negative Vaccination Outcome: One subspace show a clear reason for a negative vaccination outcome: although not having *DM*, adverse reactions on drugs (*dr aller*), not having increased *Fglu* values, not having anaemia (*E, HB*), patients can have negative vaccination outcoume due to impairment in some relevant pathophysiologic mechanisms, including slightly increased *MCV* (a sign of decreased *VITB12* and/or *FOLNA*), and decreased cortisol (*CORTIS*). Further examples for both outcome classes are described in the supplementary material.

4.4 Proposed Subspace Analysis Workflow

Based on our findings in the experiments described above, we propose a subspace clustering-based workflow (c.f. Fig. 4) to find relations between data records, dimensions, and associated class labels. The workflow consists of the main steps Ⓐ and Ⓒ as well as an optional step Ⓑ improving local similarity aspects.

The first step of the workflow is to separate all data records based on their class label Ⓐ. The subsequent steps are applied to each record subset individually. The optional step Ⓑ is in-line with the findings of the second experiment. In many datasets, there are dimensions that highly influence the detection of subspace clusters. On the one hand, these dimensions are interesting as they show the global similarity between data records. On the other hand, such dimensions can distort the results, e.g. a dataset with non-relevant dimensions in which all records are similar. Subspace clustering consider these dimensions as a relevant and add them to most clusters. In such a case, step Ⓑ can be applied to remove such dimensions. In Ⓒ, a subspace clustering is applied to the remaining dimensions to finally determine the similarities between records, dimensions, class labels.

5   Discussion

The explorative analysis of patient treatment data is a challenging task. As our experiments show, subspace clustering can be a valuable tool to discover relevant groups of patients w.r.t. different medical subspaces and their relationship to the treatment (here: vaccination outcome). As a key finding of our experiments, an analysis in the full attribute space may not be the best choice, but subspace methods can be an interesting tool, especially if used in an appropriate analysis workflow. We proposed one workflow, considered as promising starting point.

We also identify a number of extension possibilities to our approach. For one, we may need heuristic criteria which could select, from a large number of parameters (e.g., input dimensions, number of clusters, distance thresholds etc.) a small number of results which are not redundant but can be meaningfully interpreted. To this end, we need a formalization how to measure what alternative or complementary means in terms of dimensions, cluster size, and attribute subsets. We need to include additional medical background into such a specification. Visual interfaces may be particularly beneficial to this end. A key issue in visualization is how to effectively map patient records, cluster, and attribute properties to visual displays. Regarding data size, scalability of the cluster analysis may become an issue, which could be addressed by efficient implementations.

We considered Proclus which considers all dimensions of a subspace as equally important for the subspace. However, there may also exist non-linear relationships between attributes which might be relevant. Alternative analysis tools like non-linear multivariate regression could be considered to optimize attribute selection. Also on the preprocessing side, how to appropriately treat categorical and binary attributes in the analysis is a problem. We here chose standard approaches, but the expert may be needed to specify how to treat such attributes.

While often, analysis is handled by ad-hoc approaches, it would be desirable to have a software framework to allow a flexible, interactive specification of analysis workflows, to easily apply and re-use proven workflows. We imagine a workflow editor which could support the analysis process in a scalable way, and at the same time, allow experts to document which and why analysis steps were taken.

6   Conclusion and Future Outlook

The life sciences, biomedicine and health care are turning into a data intensive science, where we face not only increased volumes and a diversity of highly complex, multi-dimensional and often weakly-structured and noisy data, but also the growing need for integrative analysis and modeling [1]. Considering that analysis in the full attribute (feature) space may not be effective, we here explored subspace cluster analysis to study the relationship between patient data and immunization treatment outcome on a specific research data set. We found that a segmentation of the patients for treatment outcome followed by subspace clustering allowed to identify relevant patient groups and respective medical attributes, which can be a basis to generalize medical knowledge. Our proposed workflow is only a first step, and we identified a number of interesting challenges and extensions for future work in the area. The grand vision for the future is to effectively support human learning with machine learning - visualization is close to the end-user, hence indispensable within this approach.

Acknowledgments. We thank Ines Färber of RWTH Aachen for fruitful discussions on subspace clustering algorithms.

References

1. Holzinger, A., Dehmer, M., Jurisica, I.: Knowledge discovery and interactive data mining in bioinformatics - state-of-the-art, future challenges and research directions. BMC Bioinformatics **15**, I1 (2014)
2. Holzinger, A.: Biomedical Informatics: Discovering Knowledge in Big Data. Springer, New York (2014)
3. Hinneburg, A., Aggarwal, C.C., Keim, D.A.: What is the nearest neighbor in high dimensional spaces? In: Proc. Int. Conference on Very Large Data Bases. Morgan Kaufmann Publishers Inc., pp. 506–515 (2000)
4. Han, J., Kamber, M., Pei, J.: Data Mining: Concepts and Techniques. 3rd edn. Morgan Kaufmann Publishers Inc
5. Beyer, K., Goldstein, J., Ramakrishnan, R., Shaft, U.: When is "nearest neighbor" meaningful? In: Proc. Int. Conference on Database Theory, pp. 217–235 (1999)
6. Kriegel, H.P., Kröger, P., Zimek, A.: Clustering high-dimensional data: A survey on subspace clustering, pattern-based clustering, and correlation clustering. ACM Transactions on Knowledge Discovery from Data (TKDD) **3**, 1–58 (2009)
7. Fua, Y.H., Ward, M., Rundensteiner, E.: Hierarchical parallel coordinates for exploration of large data sets. In: Proc. Conference on Visualization, pp. 43–50. IEEE CS Press (1999)
8. Buja, A., Swayne, D.F., Littman, M.L., Dean, N., Hofmann, H., Chen, L.: Data visualization with multidimensional scaling. Journal of Computational and Graphical Statistics **17**, 444–472 (2008)
9. Seo, J., Shneiderman, B.: Interactively exploring hierarchical clustering results. Computer **35**, 80–86 (2002)
10. Tatu, A., Zhang, L., Bertini, E., Schreck, T., Keim, D., Bremm, S., von Landesberger, T.: Clustnails: Visual analysis of subspace clusters. Tsinghua Science and Technology **17**, 419–428 (2012)
11. Tatu, A., Maaß, F., Färber, I., Bertini, E., Schreck, T., Seidl, T., Keim, D.: Subspace search and visualization to make sense of alternative clusterings in high-dimensional data. In: Proc. IEEE Conf. Visual Analytics Science and Technology, pp. 63–72 (2012)
12. Assent, I., Krieger, R., Müller, E., Seidl, T.: Visa: visual subspace clustering analysis. SIGKDD Explor. Newsl. **9**, 5–12 (2007)
13. Turkay, C., Lex, A., Streit, M., Pfister, H., Hauser, H.: Characterizing cancer subtypes using dual analysis in caleydo StratomeX. IEEE Computer Graphics and Applications **34**, 38–47 (2014)
14. Liu, H., Motoda, H.: Computational Methods of Feature Selection. Chapman & Hall/CRC (2007)

15. Aggarwal, C., Procopiuc, C., Wolf, J., Yu, P., Park, J.: Fast algorithms for projected clustering. In: Proc. ACM Int. Conf. on Management of Data, pp. 61–72 (1999)
16. Müller, E., Günnemann, S., Assent, I., Seidl, T.: Evaluating clustering in subspace projections of high dimensional data 2, 1270–1281 (2009)
17. Trtica-Majnaric, L., Zekic-Susac, M., Sarlija, N., Vitale, B.: Prediction of influenza vaccination outcome by neural networks and logistic regression. Journal of Biomedical Informatics 43, 774–781 (2010)
18. Berthold, M., Cebron, N., Dill, F., Gabriel, T., Kötter, T., Meinl, T., Ohl, P., Sieb, C., Thiel, K., Wiswedel, B.: KNIME: The Konstanz Information Miner. In: Studies in Classification, Data Analysis, and Knowledge Organization. Springer (2007)

Witnesses for the Doctor in the Loop

Peter Kieseberg[1,2,3]([✉]), Johannes Schantl[2,3], Peter Frühwirt[1], Edgar Weippl[1], and Andreas Holzinger[2,3]

[1] SBA Research, Favoritenstr. 16, A-1040 Vienna, Austria
pkieseberg@sba-research.org
[2] Research Unit HCI-KDD, Institute for Medical Informatics,
Statistics and Documentation, Medical University Graz,
Auenbruggerplatz 2, 8036 Graz, Austria
[3] CBmed - Center for Biomarker Research in Medicine,
Stiftingtalstrasse 5, 8010 Graz, Austria

Abstract. The "doctor in the loop" is a new paradigm in information driven medicine, picturing the doctor as authority inside a loop supplying an expert system with information on actual patients, treatment results and possible additional (side-)effects, as well as general information in order to enhance data driven medical science, as well as giving back treatment advice to the doctor himself. While this approach offers several positive aspects related to P4 medicine (personal, predictive, preventive and participatory), it also relies heavily on the authenticity of the data and increases the reliance on the security of databases, as well as on the correctness of machine learning algorithms. In this paper we propose a solution in order to protect the doctor in the loop against responsibility derived from manipulated data, thus enabling this new paradigm to gain acceptance in the medical community.

Keywords: P4 medicine · Fingerprinting · Data driven science

1 Introduction and Motivation

While the concept of the "doctor in the loop" seems to be a logical consequence of the application of machine learning technologies and derived knowledge into medical science, one major problem arises: The doctor in question is forced to trust the results derived from algorithms based on the authenticity of stored data to a large extent, while being seen as the primary responsible party during information provisioning, as well as during treatment, i.e. the doctor retains responsibility or, in case he/she is involved in the selection of the source data, even gains more, while loosing control over the process. With the technology available to tackle large amounts of complicated data in real time through Big-Data techniques, results derived from such processes may even become more uncontrollable. This opens up the problem of acceptance of the "doctor in the loop" approach by medical personal: The question is the trustworthiness of the underlying data and execution chains, especially considering manipulation, e.g. in the aftermath of a wrong treatment. Thus, in order to mitigate this risk for the

© Springer International Publishing Switzerland 2015
Y. Guo et al. (Eds.): BIH 2015, LNAI 9250, pp. 369–378, 2015.
DOI: 10.1007/978-3-319-23344-4_36

overall concept, manipulations in the underlying database need to be detected, as well as control over the information entered by the doctor needs to be safeguarded against subsequent manipulation. This also includes the manipulation-secure logging of execution chains of enrichment and analytics algorithms and workflows. The contribution of this work can be summarized as follows:

- We provide a model of the "doctor in the loop concept" including an abstract architecture of its entities with respect to security.
- Attack scenarios and attacker models against this approach are devised.
- Based on these models, strategies for mitigation are defined.

2   Background and Related Work

The problem of securing infrastructures relying on human behaviour has been discussed throughout the last decade and more, being on of the very fundamental problems for computer security [1]. The problem is often related to the issues of awareness [2] or missing usability in security [3], as well as other subtopics, also including the sharing of data between different entities [4]. This is also often related to the issues of providing health related information to other clinicians [5] or to automated systems [6].

2.1   Chained Witnesses

The term "chained witnesses" was coined in [7], where the authors propose a technique for securing internal mechanisms of databases against manipulation. The main advantage of this approach over the multitude of approaches described in the literature was resilience against an attacker model that included the database administrator as possible adversary. While this is discussable in most real-life systems where the database administrator is seen as a trusted entity, this is especially interesting in the "doctor in the loop" concept.

The main principle of this approach lies in appending a so-called *witness* for each transaction that is issued against the database to the internal logging mechanisms: The database storing the information is considered as untrusted, furthermore, even file system administrator rights are assumed for the attacker. Let D_i be the ith data record written to the database at time t_i. Furthermore, we assume that $\mathcal{H}$ is a cryptographically secure one-way hash function, $\mathcal{T}$ is a trusted third party and $\mathcal{R}$ is a secure pseudo random number generator (PRNG) and r_i is the result of its ith iteration. The witness for transaction D_i is calculated as

$$w_i = \mathcal{H}(w_{i-1}||D_i||t_i||r_i) = \mathcal{H}(w_{i-1}||D_i||t_i||\mathcal{R}(r_{i-1}))$$

with $||$ denoting string concatenation. The tuple (t_i, w_i) is then called the *signature* of the record D_i. In order to start the hash-chain, an initialization phase is required: A trusted third party $\mathcal{T}$ selects a random number s as seed for the PRNG and thus generates r_0 by using the PRNG on s. Furthermore, the initial witness is defined as $w_0 := \mathcal{H}(r_0)$.

Due to the definition of the witnesses as chained hashes, any changes in older data sets lead to cascading changes in all subsequent witnesses (Figure 1 shows the chaining). For the verification, the data of the protected internal logging mechanisms is executed against an old trusted backup under the premise of T and compared to the investigated database instance. In [7] the authors propose several mechanisms for achieving this kind of manipulation security in real-life environments, especially targeting internal database mechanisms for providing rollbacks (so-called *transaction logs*[1]). Furthermore, the database management system (DBMS) must be modified in a way to provide the calculation of the respective witness as an atomic action, invisible to the administrator, i.e. the mechanism for writing the transaction log needs to be modified directly in order to fetch the random numbers r_i and calculate the witness immediately, without leaking r_i to the administrator. As shown in [7] the implementation of such a process can be done for MySQL, furthermore, the authors pointed out solutions for closed source DBMSs based on the database replication logs.

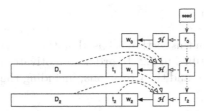

Fig. 1. Chained Witnesses ([7]).

2.2 The Doctor in the Loop

The concept of the "doctor in the loop" is an extension of the increasingly frequent use of knowledge discovery for the enhancement of medical treatments together with the "human in the loop" concept: The expert knowledge of the doctor is incorporated into "intelligent" systems (e.g. using interactive machine learning) and enriched with additional information and expert know-how. Using machine learning algorithms, medical knowledge and optimal treatments are identified. This knowledge is then fed back to the doctor to assist him/her (see Figure 2).

While general techniques regarding data driven research have their own problems with respect to privacy protection (see e.g. [8]), an additional major problem for the doctor in the loop lies in guaranteeing the trustworthiness of the data provided by other entities and by analysis workflows. Furthermore, the data provided by the doctor needs to be secured against subsequent manipulation in the case of a cover-up, either by the system, or by the doctor himself. In this work we will solely focus on this problem and leave the problems of privacy protection and data leakage discovery to the literature [4,9].

---

[1] It must be noted that the term "logs" is slightly misleading, since these are not human readable log files, but internal mechanisms for ensuring transaction safety.

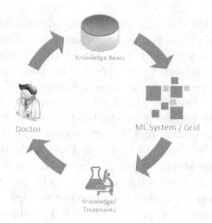

Fig. 2. The doctor in the loop.

3   The Approach

The approach outlined in this section is based on the generic concept of the "doctor in the loop" as described in 2.2. In order to motivate the chaining approach, we will define the entities and their relations, including the chaining mechanism.

3.1   Entities and Relations

For our analysis, we define a more specific model for the doctor in the loop. Figure 3 gives an overview on the components:

- The **Doctor**, who is the main expert in the cycle, collects data from patients, including their reactions to individual treatments and eventual other effects. Furthermore, he/she provides additional knowledge from his/her experience and sanity-checks results. All data he/she provides to the system is sent to the Knowledge Base, which also provides him/her with the relevant feedback.
- The **Knowledge Base** provides the store for the data and all results of workflows and external resources, as well as the only means for communication between the doctor and the other entities. This entity is the primary target for our chained witnesses approach, since all data that is transferred between the relevant entities for the "doctor in the loop" approach utilize it. The knowledge base may also host stored procedures for the analysis of the data, i.e. parts of the ML-grid are implemented as stored procedures inside the knowledge base.
- The **Grid** serves as a generic model for a machine learning / reasoning structure that takes input data and returns results using analytics algorithms. The grid may be implemented as external mediation tool, as well as in the form of internal stored procedures inside the knowledge base. In our concept, the exact definition of the grid will be kept on an abstract level, since securing will be done on the side of the underlying database of the knowledge base.

- **Interfaces** from other entities to the knowledge base are logged by the underlying DBMS. This includes all transactions changing data or structures in the database, as well as the change and invocation of stored procedures that may implement part of the grid.
- The entity **Medical Research** denotes external knowledge bases that serve as external data input to the grid, or to the knowledge base.
- **ML Research** provides the grid with new algorithms for the analysis of the data stored in the knowledge base.

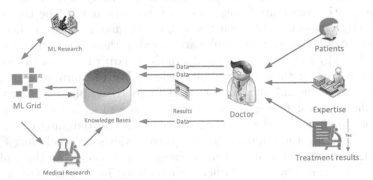

Fig. 3. Entities and Relations.

3.2   Interaction and Chaining

For the abstract approach we only consider a general scenario where a generic data receiving decision maker $\mathfrak{M}$ (e.g. the doctor) sends data to a generic data store $\mathfrak{S}$ (e.g. the knowledge base). Furthermore, an entity $\mathfrak{P}$, the data provider, operates on the same database and delivers a result to $\mathfrak{S}$. $\mathfrak{M}$ takes a result (e.g. a treatment) based on the results and returns additional information, especially on the reaction of the patient and other (side-)effects. Furthermore, $\mathfrak{M}$ controls the results stored in $\mathfrak{S}$ with respect to sanity-checks based on his background knowledge and issues respective corrections to $\mathfrak{S}$ that are subsequently used by $\mathfrak{P}$. From a security point of view this especially implies that the exact order of the transactions with respect to the knowledge base is of vital importance in order to guarantee authenticity.

Data Provider: The model of $\mathfrak{P}$ is selected to be as generic as possible and covers all single data providing entities except the decision maker. This especially includes all parts of the grid, as well as additional data sources with respect to 3.1. Due to the assumption that $\mathfrak{P}$ might be some proprietary entity, incorporating additional mechanisms for controlling the decision provider(s) is not reasonable. Furthermore, $\mathfrak{P}$ might in reality consist of several different entities (internal stored procedures and external workflow engines), i.e. $\mathfrak{M}$ might provide data to and receive information from several different $\mathfrak{P}_i, i \in \mathbb{N}$ data providers. Thus, the $\mathfrak{P}$ only needs to fulfill the following prerequisites:

1. All results are written to $\mathfrak{S}$, there is no additional side channel to $\mathfrak{M}$, i.e. $\mathfrak{M}$ and $\mathfrak{P}$ are independent.
2. Everything sent to $\mathfrak{S}$ by $\mathfrak{P}$ is signed using state of the art cryptographic technologies and is therefore assumed to be unforgeable.

Especially requirement two seems to be strong, still this is standard in many current communication protocols.

Data Store: The data store possesses an internal table structure for storing all collected data, invoked enrichment algorithms, as well as the received data, protected with the chained witnesses approach: For each entry in the transaction log D_i, the respective signature (t_i, w_i) is stored (see [7]). It must be kept in mind that the only connection between two entries D_i and D_j lies in their timely succession, i.e. all changes in all tables are stored in the same transaction mechanism, ordered by the time of entering t_i. In the **setup phase**, the initialization is done by a trusted third party $\mathfrak{T}$ (see below). We furthermore assume that the data store is run independently from the underlying physical server, i.e. $\mathfrak{S}$ possess administrator privileges over all tables, as well as full access to the file system for enrichment and processing of incoming and outgoing data, as well as for restructuring the database layout (tables, views ...), including full control over log settings. Still, it does not possess root privileges on the underlying machine, which is run by $\mathfrak{T}$ or another trusted entity. In addition, the data store frequently sends a backup to $\mathfrak{T}$, which is validated as shown below. The newly validated database image iteratively serves as the new base point for the next validation cycle.

Decision Maker: The decision maker $\mathfrak{M}$ is independent from the data store, i.e. it does not have any control over $\mathfrak{S}$. Furthermore, it is also independent from all data providers (see there). In this approach we assume that the decision maker is honest in general (see data insertion).

Trusted Third Party: The trusted third party $\mathfrak{T}$ controls and manages the random values needed in the chained witnesses approach for the data store. During the setup phase, a new random seed s is selected and the first random value r_0 is generated using the cryptographically secure pseudo random number generator (PRNG). Furthermore, the first witness $w_0 = \mathfrak{H}(r_0)$ is sent to $\mathfrak{M}$. Additionally, $\mathfrak{T}$ can be the entity responsible for running the physical server for $\mathfrak{S}$, including root privileges. While $\mathfrak{T}$ is thus in a very powerful position, $\mathfrak{T}$ must be independent from all other entities, especially from all data providing parties, thus possessing no interest in data manipulation. Furthermore, interaction between $\mathfrak{S}$ and $\mathfrak{T}$ is limited to the setup phase and during the verification of authenticity.

Network Providers: The network provider is responsible for enabling the communication between the data provider and the decision maker. We assume that all traffic is protected by end-to-end encryption against eavesdropping, other attacks by a malicious network provider, e.g. denial of service, are not inside the scope of this paper. This also holds true for the underlying public key infrastructure that is needed in order to facilitate the encrypted communication.

Data Insertion: The decision maker is modeled to receive data from outside machine based systems, especially by the patients during personal consultation. As outlined later in the attacker model 4.1, we assume that the decision maker is in principle honest, i.e. at the time of consultation, no harm towards the patient is intended from his/her side. This also means that the data entered into the database is correct at the time of insertion. All data received by the patients is immediately stored to $\mathfrak{S}$.

Verification of Authenticity: In the verification step, $\mathfrak{T}$ extracts the internal transaction logs (this is possible using a method provided in [10]) and uses a trusted backup as starting point for consecutive execution of the log entries, thus verifying the witness for each transaction by using the secret initialisation vector s and the PRNG. The first encountered invalid witness provides the position of a manipulation of the log. Furthermore, the result of the verification is compared bit-wise to the current database, thus being able to uncover changes done directly in the underlying file system.

4 Evaluation

4.1 Attacker Models and Attack Vectors

In this section we give a description of the attacker models and attack vectors with respect to the assets of the "doctor in the loop" approach.

Data Provider and Decision Maker: Both entities could have the interest of manipulating data on the data store in case of cover-ups, e.g. manipulating previously delivered incorrect data. The main attack vector of the decision maker lies in updating data on the data store, either provided by itself, or result (treatment) data from the data provider. The data provider possesses the same attack vectors, in addition, he/she might try to manipulate and/or re-execute stored procedures that operate on the data in order to cover up wrong results. In order to keep the concept as simple and strong as possible, we assume that there is no dedicated secure application controlling access to and from the database by the entities, i.e. the entities write their changes directly into the data store. This is especially important in order to be secure against SQL-injections or related attacks by default.

Data Store: The data store itself is an important entity in the overall concept, since it serves as the central data exchange platform and is thus vital for providing trust into the "doctor in the loop" concept. The database administrator controls all access to the database, including the possibility to undo logs, as well as change arbitrary data and structures. Furthermore, not only the database itself, but also the underlying file system, can be of interest for an attacker: As outlined in related work [10], file carving techniques can be used in order to retrieve or manipulate data by directly accessing the database files on the file system. In this evaluation we thus concentrate on these two fundamental attack vectors:

- The **Database Administrator (DBA)** possesses administrator privileges on the database itself, including the ability to change logging routines and user rights, as well as read access to the underlying file system.
- The **File System Administrator (FSA)** can modify arbitrary files on the server, including the files belonging to the database, as well as the OS (system) logs. He has no access to the database query interface though.

Neither of the two attackers possesses root privileges on the respective database server.

4.2   Security Evaluation

In this Section we will analyze the respective assets that could be targeted by the attackers modelled in the previous section.

Manipulation through the database (All except FSA): Both, the data provider, as well as the decision maker could be interested in reissuing incorrectly entered data. In case they act with their own privileges, i.e. as data provider or decision maker, every modification of data is stored in the internal logs, together with the respective timestamp of the change, making it easily detectable. In case the attacker possesses administrator privileges on the DBMS (DBA), the internal log mechanisms are under the full control of the attacker, except for the chaining: Since the attacker still does not possess root privileges on the server, it is impossible for him/her to read the value r_i from the RAM, which is then used in the generation of the witness with $\mathfrak{H}$. Since $\mathfrak{H}$ is a cryptographic hash function, when given $h := \mathfrak{H}(\mathfrak{h}')$, h' cannot be deduced from h.

Targeting stored procedures (DBA): The database administrator can execute and modify every stored procedure on any stored data set. Still, in case executions change any data in any table on the whole database, the changes are logged in order to retain transaction safety.

Manipulation through database files (FSA): The file system administrator could bypass all logging mechanism by manipulating data directly in the underlying database files. This includes the transaction log and other rollback mechanisms, which have to be invoked by the DBMS. Using the witnesses these changes remain detectable, since the resulting database in the verification step will be different from the one currently on the server. Still, the attacker could insert data via the file system and remove it right before the validation, making this manipulation undetectable. As a countermeasure, the validation process should be done frequently at random times. Furthermore, we propose to use the chaining witnesses approach with respect to special logs containing checksums of the database files.

Manipulation of the DBMS: The attacker could remove the chaining witnesses from the source code of the DBMS and install a recompiled version. While this is possible, this action would require root privileges on the server. Furthermore, modifications on the binary could be easily detected via frequent comparison of checksums of the respective code to the originally issued version.

Modification of the transaction mechanism (DBA): The authenticity of the information in the transaction mechanism/log is protected by the chained witnesses approach, so every manipulation can be detected under the given attacker model and the manipulated record can be identified. This could only be circumvented by deleting the whole log, which itself is an highly obvious manipulation pointing to the database administrator.

Combined attackers: In the above examples we split the attacker between the DBA and the FSA, still, the resilience of the approach is retained even in case the attacker possesses both privileges. This can be directly inferred from this section, since the chaining is done on DBMS level, without the involvement of either, the DBA or the FSA.

4.3 Limitations

The limitations of the proposed approach can mainly be attributed to limitations of the original chained witnesses approach, especially regarding the lifetime of the internal transaction logs and problems related to an attacker possessing root privileges. Furthermore, the approach only works with DBMSs that actually provide transaction safety and thus provide the respective mechanisms.

More specific to the architecture provided in this paper, the main limitation lies in the assumption of independence of the different entities, which in reality may not be guaranteed due to the setup of the overall environment (e.g. a hospital running a "doctor in the loop" approach might control the doctor, the database and parts of the grid, as well as $\mathfrak{T}$).

5 Conclusion and Future Outlook

In this work we provided an approach for protecting decision relevant data in a generic "doctor in the lop" setup against manipulation targeting the underlying database. This is especially needed in order to increase trust in the "doctor in the loop" concept for both sides, the involved medical personal, as well as external partners and research labs providing results based on the data. The work is based on the chained witnesses approach outlined in [7]. Future work is especially needed in the area of usability in order to effectively incorporate the architecture into the daily routines without introducing even more overhead for the medical personal, thus enabling the "doctor in the loop" to use the benefits of machine supported medicine. Future work from our side includes the development of a prototype implementation in order to test the effects of introducing this concept into real-life environments.

Acknowledgments. Parts of this work have been carried out with the K1 COMET Competence Centers SBA Research and CBmed, which are funded by the Federal Ministry of Transport, Innovation and Technology (BMVIT); the Federal Ministry of Science, Research and Economy (BMWFW); Land Steiermark (Department 12, Business and Innovation); the Styrian Business Promotion Agency (SFG); and the Vienna Business Agency. The COMET program is executed by the FFG.

References

1. Smith, S.W.: Humans in the loop: Human-computer interaction and security. IEEE Security & Privacy, **1**, 75–79 (2003)
2. Lupiana, D.: Development of a framework to leverage knowledge management systems to improve security awareness (2008)
3. Clark, S., Goodspeed, T., Metzger, P., Wasserman, Z., Xu, K., Blaze, M.: Why (special agent) johnny (still) can't encrypt: A security analysis of the apco project 25 two-way radio system. In: USENIX Security Symposium, Citeseer (2011)
4. Kieseberg, P., Hobel, H., Schrittwieser, S., Weippl, E., Holzinger, A.: Protecting Anonymity in Data-Driven Biomedical Science. In: Holzinger, A., Jurisica, I. (eds.) Interactive Knowledge Discovery and Data Mining in Biomedical Informatics. LNCS, vol. 8401, pp. 301–316. Springer, Heidelberg (2014)
5. Randeree, E.: Secure health knowledge: Balancing security, privacy and access. In: AMCIS 2005 Proceedings, 287 (2005)
6. Warkentin, M., Johnston, A., Adams, A.: User interaction with healthcare information systems: Do healthcare professionals want to comply with hipaa? AMCIS 2006 Proceedings, 326 (2006)
7. Frühwirt, P., Kieseberg, P., Krombholz, K., Weippl, E.: Towards a forensic-aware database solution: Using a secured database replication protocol and transaction management for digital investigations. Digital Investigation **11**, 336–348 (2014)
8. Hobel, H., Schrittwieser, S., Kieseberg, P., Weippl, E.: (Anonymity and pseudonymity in data-driven science)
9. Heurix, J., Zimmermann, P., Neubauer, T., Fenz, S.: A taxonomy for privacy enhancing technologies. Computers & Security (2015)
10. Fruehwirt, P., Kieseberg, P., Schrittwieser, S., Huber, M., Weippl, E.: Innodb database forensics: Reconstructing data manipulation queries from redo logs. In: The Fifth International Workshop on Digital Forensics (WSDF) (2012)

Detection of Diabetic Retinopathy and Maculopathy in Eye Fundus Images Using Fuzzy Image Processing

Sarni Suhaila Rahim[1,2(✉)], Vasile Palade[1], Chrisina Jayne[1], Andreas Holzinger[3], and James Shuttleworth[1]

[1] Faculty of Engineering and Computing, Coventry University,
Priory Street, Coventry CV1 5FB, UK
rahims3@uni.coventry.ac.uk, sarni@utem.edu.my,
{vasile.palade,ab1527,csx239}@coventry.ac.uk
[2] Faculty of Information and Communication Technology, Universiti Teknikal Malaysia Melaka, Hang Tuah Jaya, 76100 Durian Tunggal, Melaka, Malaysia
[3] Institute for Medical Informatics, Medical University Graz, Graz, Austria
a.holzinger@hci-kdd.org

Abstract. Diabetic retinopathy is a damage of the retina and it is one of the serious consequences of the diabetes. Early detection of diabetic retinopathy is extremely important in order to prevent premature visual loss and blindness. This paper presents a novel automatic detection of diabetic retinopathy and maculopathy in eye fundus images using fuzzy image processing. The detection of maculopathy is essential as it will eventually cause loss of vision if the affected macula is not timely treated. The developed system consists of image acquisition, image preprocessing with a combination of fuzzy techniques, feature extraction, and image classification by using several machine learning techniques. The fuzzy-based image processing decision support system will assist in the diabetic retinopathy screening and reduce the burden borne by the screening team.

Keywords: Diabetic retinopathy · Eye screening · Colour fundus images · Fuzzy image processing · Machine learning · Classifiers

1 Introduction

Diabetic Retinopathy (DR) is a complication of diabetes and it is the leading cause of blindness and visual disability. Regular eye examination is essential for an early detection of retinopathy in order to reduce visual loss and blindness caused by DR. The main purpose of diabetic retinopathy screening is to detect whether the individuals require follow-up referral for further treatment or not [1]. Therefore, an accurate and robust retinal screening system is required to assist the retinal screeners to classify the retinal images effectively and with high confidence.

An international clinical diabetic retinopathy and diabetic macula oedema disease severity scale was proposed by Wilkinson and others [2] to assist in the grading the fundus images into distinct categories based on retinal appearances. The scale is based on the Early Treatment Diabetic Retinopathy Study (ETDRS) on the classification of

© Springer International Publishing Switzerland 2015
Y. Guo et al. (Eds.): BIH 2015, LNAI 9250, pp. 379–388, 2015.
DOI: 10.1007/978-3-319-23344-4_37

DR [3]. The DR lesions can be categorized into the so-called retinopathy stages, namely, mild DR, moderate DR, severe DR, proliferative DR and Advanced Diabetic Eye Disease (ADED).

Maculopathy is represented by yellow lesions near the macula and is a disease in the macula region of the retina. Macula is the centre of the retina and provides our central vision. The macula region is a very sensitive area where the centre of the macula, called fovea, a tiny area which is responsible for detailed vision as well as colour vision [1]. Therefore, the detection of maculopathy is very important because the loss of vision at the fovea alone causes legal blindness. Maculopathy is present when there are any exudates, haemorrhages or microaneurysms in the macula region. However, the visible signs of maculopathy are only indirect markers for the possible presence of macula oedema, which is the swelling of the retina [1]. The presence or absence of the maculopathy will determine the need for treatment or referral. The referral to the ophthalmologist is assigned if the maculopathy is present, while referral is not required and the screening is repeated in one year time, if the maculopathy is absent. Therefore, the combined detection of diabetic retinopathy and maculopathy is vital in order to effectively assist the management of the diabetic retinopathy screening.

In our earlier work, we have proposed a preliminary system for the diabetic retinopathy screening [4], which classified images into two main categories; normal (no apparent retinopathy) or abnormal (retinopathy presence) using non-fuzzy techniques. Then, we continued by presenting an automatic screening system to detect the earliest visible signs of retinopathy, i.e., microaneurysms, by using fuzzy image processing [5]. Four variants of microaneurysms detection systems, which utilize different techniques, with or without the implementation of fuzzy image processing, were presented and comparisons were made. For example, the second system variant, implementing the greyscale conversion, Fuzzy Histogram Equalisation and Circular Hough Transform was proven to produce better results compared to the first system variant which implemented the greyscale conversion, histogram equalisation and Circular Hough Transform techniques. The overall results show that the implementation of the fuzzy preprocessing techniques provides better contrast enhancement as well as other improvements for colour fundus images, and, hence, it greatly helps microaneurysms detection to be more efficient and reliable. However, we proposed individual system variants implementing different fuzzy processing techniques. In this paper, we are proposing a novel detection system for diabetic retinopathy and maculopathy by combining several consecutive fuzzy image preprocessing techniques in one system, based on the previous encouraging results on using fuzzy image processing obtained in [5]. In addition, the proposed system is following the current practice observed by the ophthalmologist in the classification and grading of diabetic retinopathy and maculopathy, which classifies into ten main classes, as explained under the proposed system section in [5] and outlined below in Section 6.

The paper is organized as follows. Section 2 presents the related work on the diabetic retinopathy and maculopathy detection, followed by Section 3, which details the proposed detection system. Section 4 describes the image preprocessing stage, while Section 5 explains the feature extraction part. Section 6 describes the classification, while Section 7 presents the results of the system and, finally, Section 8 details some conclusions of the work and a future plan.

2 Related Work on Diabetic Retinopathy and Maculopathy Detection

Grading of diabetic retinopathy is a challenging task for both automatic systems and medical doctors. Detection of normal and other two main classes of diabetic retinopathy, which are non-proliferative and proliferative diabetic retinopathy, was proposed by Mookiah et al. [6] and Priya et al. [7] by implementing certain preprocessing techniques. Meanwhile, the detection of maculopathy was proposed by Vimala and Kajamohideen [8], where some morphological operations were implemented. In addition, an automatic system which grades the maculopathy into severity levels was developed by Tariq et al. [9], Siddalingaswamy and Prabhu [10] also Punnolil [11]. An automatic diagnosis which highlighted the referable maculopathy in retinal images for diabetic retinopathy screening was proposed by Hunter et al. [12], while Chowriappa et al. [13] proposed an ensemble selection method for features and, later, performed the classification of the images into the corresponding classes of disease severity. However, fuzzy processing has not been implemented during the preprocessing stage within the maculopathy detection systems reported earlier in the literature.

Fuzzy image processing uses fuzzy techniques in the various stages of an image processing task. Fuzzy processing can help produce better representation of images and eventually improve the performance analysis. Fuzzy image processing has been used on medical and also non-medical images. The fuzzy histogram equalisation technique called the Brightness Preserving Dynamic Fuzzy Histogram Equalisation (BPDFHE) was proposed by Sheet et al. [14], and later was used in digital pathology images by Garud et al. [15]. Fuzzy filtering is another fuzzy image processing method that can be performed on images. Among the fuzzy filtering techniques, we can mention those proposed by Patil and Chaudhari [16], Toh et al. [17] and also Kwan [18]. In addition, fuzzy edge detection can be used as a preprocessing technique to enhance the image quality.

3 Proposed System

The proposed system implements a combination of fuzzy techniques in the image preprocessing part, which involves fuzzy filtering, followed by the fuzzy histogram equalization and finally the fuzzy edge detection. In order to test the system performance, the system is evaluated with the combination of normal and diabetic retinopathy fundus images from a novel data set, which was collected from the Eye Clinic, Department of Ophthalmology, Hospital Melaka, Malaysia. The dataset consists of 600 colour fundus images of size 3872 x 2592 pixels in JPEG format. The detailed explanation of the dataset is presented in [5].

The proposed screening system has been developed using Matlab R2014a. The system starts with the image acquisition process, where the system selects images for further processing (using the *imgetfile* followed by *imread* function). The selected images undergo preprocessing in order to improve the image contrast as well as perform other enhancements with the combination of fuzzy techniques. After that, the preprocessed images are used for feature extraction, where three features, namely, the area, the mean and the standard deviation of on pixels are extracted. Finally, in the classification phase, some machine learning classifiers are trained using these features to classify the images into the respective classes.

Figure 1 presents the block diagram of the proposed system for automatic screening and classification of the diabetic retinopathy using fuzzy image processing techniques. The individual stages are discussed in more detail in the following sections.

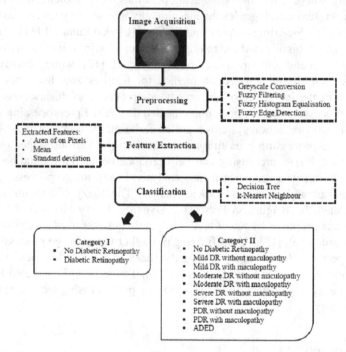

Fig. 1. Block diagram of the proposed automatic detection of diabetic retinopathy and maculopathy using fuzzy image processing

4   Image Preprocessing

Image preprocessing is the operation of improving the image data quality. Fuzzy approaches are implemented in this paper in the preprocessing stage. The image preprocessing techniques involved in the present work include greyscale conversion, Fuzzy Filtering, Fuzzy Histogram Equalisation and Fuzzy Edge Detection.

4.1   Greyscale Conversion

The greyscale conversion, which converts the original colour fundus images from the developed dataset into a greyscale image, is the first preprocessing technique used. The *rgb2gray* function is used to convert the colour image to the greyscale intensity image by eliminating the hue and saturation information while retaining the luminance.

4.2   Fuzzy Filtering

The second preprocessing technique is the implementation of the fuzzy approach in image filtering. Digital image filtering helps to improve the image quality or restore the digital image that is corrupted by noise. The original fundus images may be affected with some noise in its acquisition or transmission process. Thus, noise removal is required to enhance the image quality and it is an important step before any processing task. The proposed system implemented the median filter by employing fuzzy techniques. The Fuzzy Switching Median (FSM) filter by Toh et al. [17] was working well in removing salt-and-pepper noise while preserving image details and textures, by incorporating fuzzy reasoning in correcting the detected noisy pixels. However, this technique was not very well able to detect microaneurysms in fundus images, as presented by Rahim et al. [5]. The technique is used once again in this paper in order to investigate its performance in detecting diabetic retinopathy and maculopathy at the same time.

4.3   Fuzzy Histogram Equalisation

After filtering the image from noise, the histogram equalisation is performed. This is used to enhance the contrast of images by transforming the values in an intensity image to produce the output image that approximately matches a specified histogram. Since the colour fundus images are more challenging compared to another two modes of fundus photography examination which are angiography and red-free, therefore fuzzy approach is proposed to be used in the histogram equalisation technique in order to generate better contrast for the visualisation and detection. Rahim et al. [5] used the Brightness Preserving Dynamic Fuzzy Histogram Equalisation (BPDFHE) technique, which was proposed by Sheet et al. [14] for colour fundus images, while Garud et al. [15] used the same technique for pathology images. Due to the good performance of this technique for both types of medical images, it has been chosen as a preprocessing technique for the proposed diabetic retinopathy and maculopathy detection presented in this paper.

4.4   Fuzzy Edge Detection

An edge detection method sometimes produces small intensity differences between two neighbouring pixels which do not always represent an edge or which might represent a shading effect. Therefore, the use of membership functions would overcome such problems by defining the degree with which a pixel belongs to an edge or a uniform region. A Fuzzy Inference System (FIS) using a Mamdani-type system is proposed here for edge detection. The image gradient along the x-axis and y-axis of the image are the inputs for the FIS. For each input, a zero-mean Gaussian membership function is specified, where if the gradient value for a pixel is 0 (region), then it belongs to the zero membership function with a degree of 1. Another membership function is added which specifies the standard deviation for the zero membership function for the gradient inputs. For the output, which is the intensity of the edge-detected image, a triangular membership function is specified. Next, the two FIS rules are added to make a pixel white if it belongs to a uniform region where both inputs are zero, or otherwise the black pixel is presented if one of the inputs is not zero. In order to calculate the white pixels from the edge-detected image, the output image is converted or inversed to produce the black and white image. Figure 2 shows the membership functions of the inputs and outputs for the edge detection, while Figure 3 (a)-(f) shows the output after each of the preprocessing operations on the selected image, as explained previously.

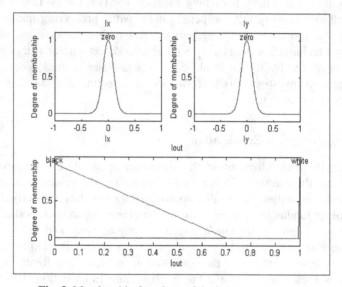

Fig. 2. Membership functions of the inputs and outputs

5   Feature Extraction

After performing the preprocessing techniques, feature extraction takes place to obtain the features from the preprocessed images. Three preliminary features are proposed, namely, the area of on pixels, the mean and the standard deviation are extracted for the detection purposes. The first feature is the number of white pixels on the black and white image, while the second and third features are the mean value and the standard deviation of on pixels, respectively. Other more sophisticated features could be extracted in addition to these three proposed features in order to improve the classification performance, and we will address this in our future work.

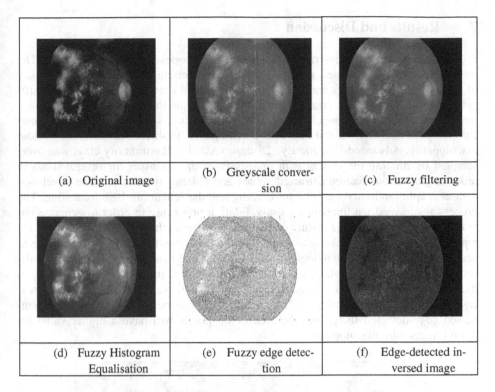

(a) Original image	(b) Greyscale conversion	(c) Fuzzy filtering
(d) Fuzzy Histogram Equalisation	(e) Fuzzy edge detection	(f) Edge-detected inversed image

Fig. 3. Preprocessing the output image

6   Classification

The extracted feature values were used in the classification stage, where the PRTools Matlab toolbox [19] for pattern recognition has been employed for this task. In order to generate a variety of results and performance analysis of the system, two types of classification were considered. First, the images have been classified into two classes, i.e., normal (276 images) and diabetic retinopathy (324 images). In addition, with the use of several machine learning classifiers, the images are then classified into ten classes which provide more details, i.e., No Diabetic Retinopathy (DR) with 276 images, and the other nine detailed classes of the DR cases, which are: Mild DR without maculopathy (72 images), Mild DR with maculopathy (27 images), Moderate DR without maculopathy (85 images), Moderate DR with maculopathy (83 images), Severe DR without maculopathy (23 images), Severe DR with maculopathy (11 images), Proliferative DR without maculopathy (6 images), Proliferative DR with maculopathy (10 images) and Advanced Diabetic Eye Disease (ADED, with only 7 images). Several machine learning classifiers, such as the binary decision tree classifier and the 1-nearest neighbour classifier have been selected to train and classify images into these categories.

7   Results and Discussion

Figure 4 shows the user interface snapshot of the proposed developed system. The performance of the proposed system, including the misclassification error, accuracy of the individual classifiers and also the specificity and sensitivity of the two classifiers for both categories are presented in Table 1 based on the confusion matrix generated. Since the dataset is hugely imbalanced for some classes, i.e., mild DR with maculopathy, severe DR without and with maculopathy, proliferative with and without maculopathy, Advanced Diabetic Eye Disease (ADED), the minority class was oversampled by running the system with images from these classes for several times in order to get various feature extracted values and balance the dataset. The developed dataset is split randomly into 90% for training and the remaining 10% for testing. The process is repeated ten times in a cross-validation procedure in order to generate unbiased results. The average results on the ten runs for each of the two classifiers are reported. The experimental results show that the two classifiers, and especially the k-nearest neighbour, are able to identify well for both main categories. The two classifiers identified much better the diabetic retinopathy cases, in the two classes' case, as there were more examples of such images in the database compared to ten classes' case for some of the ten classes. The maculopathy can be seen clearly from the inversed edge-detected image and the area of on pixels will have a higher value for those images with maculopathy.

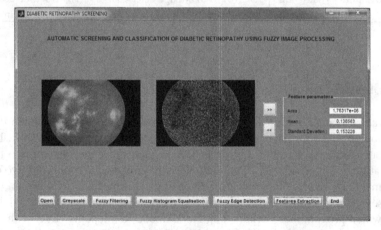

Fig. 4. Snapshot of the proposed system user interface

Table 1. Average results when using the classifiers

	Category I : 2 classes		Category II : 10 classes	
	Binary decision tree	k-nearest neighbour	Binary decision tree	k-nearest neighbour
Misclassification error	0.2539	0.2139	0.4395	0.2975
Accuracy	0.7461	0.7861	0.5605	0.7025
Specificity	0.4536	0.5572	0.4500	0.6500
Sensitivity	0.8403	0.8598	0.5956	0.7297

8 Conclusions and Future Work

An automatic system for the detection of diabetic retinopathy and maculopathy in colour fundus images using fuzzy image processing techniques has been developed in this paper. The system can be enhanced by implementing different other combinations of preprocessing techniques including those based on fuzzy approaches. The proposed developed system could be a benchmark for the development of other retinopathy signs' detection systems, such as for microaneurysms, exudates, hemorrhages and neovascularisation. As a conclusion, employing fuzzy image processing can help produce a more reliable screening system. In addition, it helps achieve the overall aim of the screening, which is to detect earlier the sight threatening diseases and to ensure a timely treatment in order to prevent vision loss. There are manifold future possibilities on other machine learning research on this, e.g. by including the human-in-the-loop [20] concept. For any such approach, one would first need a relevant and robust digital content representation from the image data. However, traditional pixel-based image analysis techniques do not effectively extract and represent the content. Consequently, a promising approach would be to extract graphs from images [21], which would enable a lot of other experiments, e.g. with evolutionary algorithms [22].

Acknowledgements. This project is part of a PhD research currently being carried out at the Faculty of Engineering and Computing, Coventry University, UK. The deepest gratitude and thanks go to the Universiti Teknikal Malaysia Melaka (UTeM) and Ministry of Education Malaysia for sponsoring this PhD research. The authors are thankful to the Ministry of Health Malaysia and the Hospital Melaka, Malaysia, for providing the database of retinal images and also for the manual grading done by three experts.

References

1. Taylor, R., Batey, D.: Handbook of retinal screening in diabetes: diagnosis and management. John Wiley & Sons Ltd., England (2012)
2. Wilkinson, C.P., Ferris, F.L., Klein, R.E., Lee, P.P., Agardh, C.D., Davis, M., Dills, D., Kampik, A., Pararajasegaram, R., Verdaguer, J.T.: Proposed International Clinical Diabetic Retinopathy and Diabetic Macula Edema Disease Severity Scales. American Academy of Ophthalmology 110(9), 1677–1682 (2003)
3. Early Treatment Diabetic Retinopathy Study Research Group.: Grading diabetic retinopathy from stereoscopic color fundus photographs- an extension of the modified Airlie House classification. ETDRS report number 10. Ophthalmology 98(5 suppl.), 823–833 (1991)
4. Jayne, C., Rahim, S.S., Palade, V., Shuttleworth, J.: Automatic Screening and Classification of Diabetic Retinopathy Fundus Images. In: Mladenov, V., Jayne, C., Iliadis, L. (eds.) EANN 2014. CCIS, vol. 459, pp. 113–122. Springer, Heidelberg (2014)
5. Rahim, S.S., Palade, V., Shuttleworth, J., Jayne, C., Raja Omar, R.N.: Automatic detection of microaneurysms for diabetic retinopathy screening using fuzzy image processing. In: Iliadis, L. et al. (eds.) Engineering Applications of Neural Networks. CCIS, vol. 517. Springer, Heidelberg (2015)

6. Mookiah, M.R.K., Acharya, U.R., Martis, R.J., Chua, C.K., Lim, C.M., Ng, E.Y.K., Laude, A.: Evolutionary algorithm based classifier parameter tuning for automatic diabetic retinopathy grading: a hybrid feature extraction approach. Knowledge-Based Systems **39**, 9–22 (2013)

7. Priya, R., Aruna, P.: Review of automated diagnosis of diabetic retinopathy using the support vector machine. International Journal of Applied Engineering Research **1**(4), 844–863 (2011)

8. Vimala, A.G.S.G., Kajamohideen, S.: Detection of diabetic maculopathy in human retinal images using morphological operations. Online J. Biol. Sci. **14**, 175–180 (2014)

9. Tariq, A., Akram, M.U., Shaukat, A., Khan, S.A.: Automated detection and grading of diabetic maculopathy in digital retinal images. J. Digit Imaging **26**(4), 803–812 (2013)

10. Siddalingaswamy, P.C., Prabhu, K.G.: Automatic grading of diabetic maculopathy severity levels. In: 2010 International Conference on Systems in Medicine and Biology, pp. 331–334. IEEE, New York (2010)

11. Punnolil, A.: A novel approach for diagnosis and severity grading of diabetic maculopathy. In: 2013 International Conference on Advances in Computing, Communications and Informatics, pp. 1230–1235. IEEE, New York (2013)

12. Hunter, A., Lowell, J.A., Steel, D., Ryder, B., Basu, A.: Automated diagnosis of referable maculopathy in diabetic retinopathy screening. In: Annual international of the IEEE Engineering in Medicine and Bilogy Society, EMBS, pp. 3375–3378. IEEE, New York (2011)

13. Chowriappa, P., Dua, S., Rajendra, A.U., Muthu, R.K.M.: Ensemble selection for feature-based classification of diabetic maculopathy images. Computers in Biology and Medicine **43**(12), 2156–2162 (2013)

14. Sheet, D., Garud, H., Suveer, A., Mahadevappa, M., Chatterjee, J.: Brightness preserving dynamic Fuzzy Histogram Equalization. IEEE Transactions on Consumer Electronics **56**(4), 2475–2480 (2010)

15. Garud, H., Sheet, D., Suveer, A., Karri, P.K., Ray, A.K., Mahadevappa, M., Chatterjee, J.: Brightness preserving contrast enhancement in digital pathology. In: 2011 International Conference on Image Information Processing (ICIIP 2011), pp. 1–5. IEEE, New York (2011)

16. Patil, J., Chaudhari, A.L.: Development of digital image processing using Fuzzy Gaussian filter tool for diagnosis of eye infection. International Journal of Computer Applications **51**(19), 10–12 (2012)

17. Toh, K.K.V., Mat Isa, N.A.: Noise adaptive Fuzzy switching median filter for salt-and-pepper noise reduction. IEEE Signal Processing Letters **17**(3), 281–284 (2010)

18. Kwan, H.K.: Fuzzy filters for noisy image filtering. In: IEEE International Symposium on Circuits and Systems 2003 (ISCAS 2003), vol. 4, pp. 161–164. IEEE, New York (2003)

19. Duin, R.P.W., Juszczak, P., Paclik, P., Pekalska, E., de Ridder, D., Tax, D.M.J., Verzakov, S.: PRTools4.1, A Matlab Toolbox for Pattern Recognition, Delft University of Technology (2007)

20. Holzinger, A.: Human-Computer Interaction and Knowledge Discovery (HCI-KDD): What Is the Benefit of Bringing Those Two Fields to Work Together? In: Cuzzocrea, A., Kittl, C., Simos, D.E., Weippl, E., Xu, L. (eds.) CD-ARES 2013. LNCS, vol. 8127, pp. 319–328. Springer, Heidelberg (2013)

21. Holzinger, A., Malle, B., Giuliani, N.: On Graph Extraction from Image Data. In: Slezak, D., Peters, J.F., Tan, A.-H., Schwabe, L. (eds.) Lecture Notes in Artificial Intelligence, LNAI 8609, pp. 552–563. Springer, Heidelberg, Berlin (2014)

22. Holzinger, A., Blanchard, D., Bloice, M., Holzinger, K., Palade, V., Rabadan, R.: Darwin, Lamarck, or Baldwin: Applying Evolutionary Algorithms to Machine Learning Techniques. In: The 2014 IEEE/WIC/ACM International Conference on Web Intelligence (WI 2014), pp. 449–453. IEEE (2014)

A Domain-Expert Centered Process Model for Knowledge Discovery in Medical Research: Putting the Expert-in-the-Loop

Dominic Girardi[1]([☒]), Josef Kueng[2], and Andreas Holzinger[3]

[1] Research Unit Medical Informatics, RISC Software GmbH,
Johannes Kepler University Linz, Linz, Austria
dominic.girardi@risc.uni-linz.ac.at
[2] Institute for Application Oriented Knowledge Processing,
Johannes Kepler University Linz, Linz, Austria
[3] Institute for Medical Informatics, Statistics and Documentation,
Medical University of Graz, Graz, Austria

Abstract. Established process models for knowledge discovery see the domain expert in a customer-like, supervising role. In the field of bio-medical research, it is necessary for the domain experts to move into the center of this process with far-reaching consequences for their research work but also for the process itself. We revise the established process models for knowledge discovery and propose a new process model for domain-expert driven knowledge discovery. Furthermore, we present a research infrastructure which is adapted to this new process model and show how the domain expert can be deeply integrated even into the highly complex data mining and machine learning tasks.

Keywords: Expert-in-the-loop · Interactive machine learning · Process model · Knowledge discovery · Medical research

1 Introduction

Scientists in the life sciences are confronted with increasingly large, complex and high-dimensional data sets [17]. Consequently the application of machine learning techniques for knowledge discovery is indispensable. However, auto-mated machine learning algorithms work well in lower dimensional spaces and well-defined environments, but in the biomedical domain we are confronted with probability, uncertainty, incompleteness, vagueness, noise, etc., which makes the application of automated approaches difficult and the complexity of machine learning algorithms have kept away non-experts from the application of such solutions. However, a smooth interaction of the domain expert with the data would greatly enhance the whole knowledge discovery process chain [18]. In everyday clinical research the actual process differs significantly from estab-lished process descriptions. In the commonly known definitions (see [21] for a

© Springer International Publishing Switzerland 2015
Y. Guo et al. (Eds.): BIH 2015, LNAI 9250, pp. 389–398, 2015.
DOI: 10.1007/978-3-319-23344-4_38

good overview) the domain expert is seen in a super-vising, consulting and customer role. A person that is outside the process and assists in crucial aspects
with domain knowledge and receives the results. All the other steps of the process are performed by so called data analysts, who are supported by the domain
experts in understanding the domain and interpreting the results. However, for
the analysis of medical data, detailed and explicit medical expert knowledge and
knowledge of clinical processes is urgently required. Roddick et al. [29] point
out that data mining in medical domain requires significant domain expertise
and can not be performed without the intense cooperation of medical domain
experts. This clearly distinguishes data mining in the medical domain from data
mining in market basket or financial trading data. Furthermore, Roddick et al.
suggest the findings of data mining in medical research should only be interpreted
as suggestions for further research. Cois and Moore [7] stress the uniqueness of
medical data mining, caused by the nature of its data and other aspects. This is
also supported by Bellazi and Zupan [3], who stress the safety aspect of medical
knowledge discovery and is an often neglected part, as the expert-in-the-loop (in
the biomedical sciences we speak of a "doctor-in-the-loop") is a new paradigm
in information driven medicine, seating the expert as authority inside a loop
supplying him/her with information on the actual patient data [20].

To integrate the domain expert more deeply into the machine learning and
data mining tasks is a very recent approach, however, data mining is only one
of many steps of the knowledge discovery process chain (see Figure 2 in [18]).
Consequently, it is mandatory to investigate which tasks arise for the domain
experts as central actors of the whole knowledge discovery process and what
consequences this paradigm shift has for the process itself. In this paper we
focus on aspects of a novel process model.

2   Related Research

There is not much research yet on this hot topic. A recent work by Mirchevska et
al (2014) [25], presents a method for combining domain knowledge and machine
learning for classifier generation and online adaptation, which exploits advantages in domain knowledge and machine learning as complementary information
sources. The authors state that whilst machine learning methods may discover
patterns in domains that are too subtle for humans to detect, domain knowledge of an expert may contain information on a domain even not present in the
available domain data! This has essential influences for medical research.

The essence is that knowledge elicitation from domain experts and empirical
machine learning are two completely distinct approaches for knowledge discovery
with different and mutually complementary capabilities [33].

3   A New Process Model

3.1   Established Process Models

In 1996 Usama Fayyad, Gregory Piatetsky-Shapiro, and Padhraic Smyth published a number of articles [9], [10], [8] which build the base for what we call now

the process of knowledge discovery in databases. Soon, further process models were published with different focus and degree of detail [30], [6], and many more. Generally, there is a big consensus among these process models. In their review paper from 2006 Kurgan et al. [21, Table1onpage6] even managed to extract a generic process model out of the most established process model.

Aside from the significant consensus concerning the steps of these process models, there is also a huge agreement about the roles within these processes. The process is executed by a so-called data analyst, a person who's profile varies from computer scientist, to statistician or data mining expert. The domain expert is always seen in an external position, as a customer and/or supervisor. This fact is clearly reflected by the first steps of the generic process model (and hereby of most other process models): *1 - Understanding the Domain* and *2 - Understanding the data*. Both steps would be unnecessary for domain-experts within the process loop.

3.2 A New Process Model

When kept in mind, that medical domain experts are required to be deeply involved into the process of medical knowledge discovery [7], the known process models are hardly suitable. A new process model is needed, which regards the central role of the domain-experts.

We present a new process model for domain-expert centered knowledge discovery in (bio-)medical research — see Figure 1. It is, of course, closely related to and derived from existing models, but differs in crucial aspects. The major different to established definitions can not be seen in this process description, it takes place at another level. It is the switched role of the medical domain experts from the edge of the process to the center. Subsequently, the first significant difference is the absence of the step 'Understanding of the Problem', which is of course caused by the new major player of the process, who does no longer need invest time in getting into the research matter. So, the steps of the new process are defined as follows:

1. **Data Modeling.** This step is closely related to the step 'Understanding of the data' in the definitions of [27]. It is necessary for the researcher(s) to be aware what kind of data is needed to be able to answer the research questions. What data entities from my research domain are relevant for the current research projects, which of their attributes are needed and in what kind of relation are they in. This data definition, which will be called the domain ontology from now on, builds the base for all further data-based operations and differs from research project to research project and from domain to domain. This distinguishes this process definition from many conventional definitions, where only available data — data which is produced in every day routines — is analyzed. For being able to answer medical research questions it is necessary to overcome the bias of using only what is easily available.

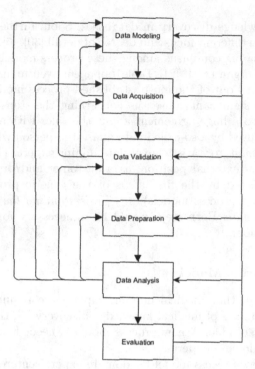

Fig. 1. A new process model for domain-expert centered knowledge discovery in (bio-)medical research

2. **Data Acquisition.** Especially in medical, scientific research it is often necessary to acquire the data of need. Data which is stored in electronic hospital information systems (HIS) is hardy suitable for scientific research because it is often semi-structured, textual data [5] or contains data mostly for billing and documentation purposes [22]. Especially medical diagnoses and interpretations of medical test are often stored as free text. Furthermore, redundant and contradictory data also occurs. Although data mining has already been performed directly on HIS, its results are less scientifically applicable than for management purposes [31], [32]. The missing or insufficient re-usability of data stored in clinical information system has already been identified as a major challenge to medical informatics [28].

3. **Data Validation.** The quality of the outcome of a research projects strongly depends on the quality of the underlying data. As already mentioned above, data quality is a widely underestimated issue in medical data sets, and even data from electronic sources (hospital information systems, etc.) are erroneous and inconsistent. Considering the complexity and amount of medical data needed for medical research the need for an automatic data validation becomes obvious. Data quality is known to be a generally underrepresented topic in medical publications [4].

4. **Data Preparation.** Data analysis rarely performed directly on the whole data set directly. Usually, data set of interest are created for certain hypothesis and erroneous or implausible data is removed from these sets. Furthermore, in medicine, very often changes or differences (functions on data values) rather than raw data contains valuable information [29]. Consequently, it is necessary to define these desired functions on the data and make their result accessible as new calculated variables.

5. **Data Analysis.** In this phase the actual step of knowledge discovery is performed, using either conventional statistics or methods of data mining, machine learning or means of visual analytics.

6. **Evaluation.** In a final step, the gain knowledge must be clinically evaluated and verified.

The steps of this process are not aligned in a strict sequence. On the one hand, steps happen in parallel or are strongly interwoven with each other. So, it is possible to see the steps data acquisition and data validation in a sequential order, where validation is performed as soon as all the data is acquired. Alternatively, data acquisition and data validation can occur in parallel where each newly entered piece of data is immediately checked. Furthermore, it is of course possible to already perform data preparation and subsequent analysis while the data acquisition is still in progress. On the other hand there exist a number of feedback loops, such as from almost any step of the process to data modeling. This means at any of these steps it may become necessary to adapt the actual domain ontology. Furthermore, insights gained from data validation and data analysis may cause re-acquisition or revision of existing data. And results from first data analysis may reveal systematic data errors which results in a revision of the data validation rules or the data preparation algorithms.

3.3   Consequences and Challenges

The researching medical domain experts face a number of challenges and obstacles when they try to perform medical research and knowledge discovery. The situation is worsened by the fact that research projects with limited funding often complete lack an explicit IT support. So the researchers find themselves in a situation where they have to deal with both, the complexity of their research domain and the complexity of their own data and data structures with all its consequences.

The selection, setup and maintenance of a research data infrastructure has already been identified as a major obstacle in biomedical research [12]. In 2007, a survey among biomedical researchers [1] found out that data handling in general had become a major barrier in a number of bio-medical research projects. Furthermore, biomedical researchers are often hardly able to cope with the complexity of their own data. The fact that many researchers use general-purpose office applications, which do not provide any support in data handling, worsens the situation.

Although highly sophisticated data mining (DM) and machine learning (ML) algorithms have been used in other domains for decades, their usage in the field of medical research is still limited. A survey from 2012 among hospitals from Germany, Switzerland, South Africa, Lithuania, and Albania [26] showed that only 29% of the medical personnel of responders were familiar with a practical application of DM. Although the survey is sure not globally representative, it clearly shows the trend that medical research is still widely based on basic statistical methods. One reason for this rather low acceptance rate is the relatively high technical obstacle that needs to be taken in order to apply these algorithms combined with the limited knowledge about the algorithms themselves and their output. A view that is shared by [16] who states that *'the grand challenge is to combine these diverse fields to support the expert end users in learning to interactively analyze information properties thus enabling them to visualize the relevant parts of their data'*.

Since the medical domain itself is a very complex one and data acquisition is usually done by multiple persons over a certain period of time, it is crucial for subsequent data analysis to check the plausibility and validity of the collected data. Simple recording errors can usually be detected by simple rules, but systematic and procedural errors, which are known to cause severe bias to the study outcome [2], can rather be detected by high complex rules. In general, data quality in medical research project is not a well researched topic [4].

4   Application and Implementation

In order to address all these challenges we developed a generic, ontology-centered research infrastructure. The main principle is the following: By modeling the actual research domain in form of a domain-ontology (Step 1 of the process) the domain-experts builds the base for all subsequent steps. The whole research infrastructure derives its structure and behavior from the central domain ontology — at run-time. Changes to the ontology have immediate effects on the whole system, which consists of three main modules. Firstly, a management tool, which allows the user to model and maintain the domain ontology, but also process and analyze the research data. The other two components are an ontology-derived electronic data interface based upon and open-source ETL (Extract-Transform-Load) suite, and an ontology-derived web interface for manual data input and processing. Wherever possible the elaborate structural meta-information is used to actively support the user in data handling, processing and analyzing. The system always appears to the user as if it was especially tailored for his domain. For a more detailed information on the infrastructure itself, the reader is kindly referred to [13], [14], [15].

Based on one particular example we now want to show how this process in combination with an appropriate software system can enable the domain expert to utilize advanced machine learning algorithms. Given the following situation: The researcher used the above-mentioned research infrastructure for collecting his research data and now wants to investigate a (possibly non-linear) influence of a number of features on a target class. Experts in the field of computer science will recognize this problem as a binary classification problem. In order to answer this question to the researcher, the following approach was made: After the user selects the potential features and the desired target class for a given data set, a number of classification algorithms in numerous configurations are launched parallelly in background. The whole data transformation and pre-processing is performed automatically by using the extensive structural meta-information from the current domain ontology. For all resulting classification models a 10-fold cross validation is performed and the area under the RoC curve of each classification algorithm and configuration is calculated. As a result, the best area under RoC of each algorithm are consolidated and presented in a user-friendly way. In this way the research gets an indication whether the assumed influence is measurable or not. This approach is based upon the following assumptions:

1. The quality of the classification model that is developed by a classification algorithm in a reasonable (default) configuration or an automatically optimized configuration provides an indication whether a reliable classification is possible at all or not. E.g. if such a classification model shows an area under the ROC curve of something close to 0.5 then it is rather unlikely to increase the quality of the classification model to a satisfying level just by adjusting and tuning the algorithms parameters. It is way more promising to adjust the input set of input variables.
2. If none of the applied classification algorithms in any of the used configuration is able to yield a satisfying classification model then it is assumed that there is no measurable influence of the input features on the target class within the available data set.

It has to be kept in mind, that this approach shows a number of limitations and restrictions: The yielded result is an indication whether an influence can be assumed, not a classification model. The models themselves are only a mean to get a result. The result doesn't provide any information an statistical significance of the discovered phenomena. The result doesn't provide any information on causalities and reasons for the discovered phenomena. This approach does not (yet) take into account the correlations among the input features. This approach does not (yet) provide any information whether a subset of the chosen features would have been sufficient to predict the class label. This approach does not provide any explanation component on how strong or in which way the features influence the target class. Nonetheless, it does yield an easy to use and easy to interpret indication whether the assumed (even non-linear) influence can be measured in the data.

For a first test set up the following algorithms were used: A Naive Bayes classifier, a Random Forest, a Logistic Regression, a Support Vector Machine with Grid Search optimization [19], and a Multi-Layer Perceptron. The ontology-guided meta-classifier was tested with the following publically available test data sets: The Iris flower data set [11], a randomly generated numeric data set, a heart disease data set, and a diabetes data set from lima indians. The real-word data set were provided by the UCI Machine Learning Repository[23].

Table 1. Area under ROC curve for the test data sets for all selected algorithms. NB = Naive Bayes, RF = Random Forest, MLP = Multi Layer Perceptron, LR = Logistic Regression, SVM = Support Vector Machine

Data Set	Target	NB	RF	MLP	LR	SVM	Median	Variance
Iris	Setosa	1.00	1.00	1.00	1.00	1.00	1.00	0.000
Iris	VersiColor	0.98	0.99	0.99	0.81	0.97	0.98	0.005
Iris	Virginica	0.98	0.98	0.99	0.99	0.97	0.98	0.00003
Random	Target	0.64	0.70	0.55	0.55	0.50	0.55	0.004
Heart	Diagnose	0.88	0.93	0.90	0.91	0.84	0.90	0.0003
Diabetes	Class variable	0.82	0.88	0.82	0.83	0.80	0.82	0.0006

First test results clearly showed, that the classification algorithms show a big degree of consensus in their results and were able to identify the already known influences of the features on the target class variables and were able to reject a possible influence in the random number data set. The most remarkable fact is that all these results were yielded without any IT-expert driven parametrization of the algorithms. All the user did, was selecting the target class, features and data sets of interest. The whole pre-processing was done automatically by using the meta-information from the domain ontology, and the algorithm parametrization was either not necessary or done by automatic optimization.

5   Results and Discussion

All known and relevant process models for knowledge discovery see the (medical) domain expert in a customer-like, supervising role [21], [24]. While the scientific community is slowly realizing what benefits can be gained when the domain expert is deeply integrated into the data mining and machine learning loop, no accordingly research on the knowledge discovery process could be found.

We propose a new process model for expert driven knowledge discovery in medical research. It eliminates the frequent task *Understanding the Domain* and *Understanding the Data* from known models and replaces this tasks by the tasks: *Data Modeling, Data Acquisition*, and *Data Validation*. For the software support of this new process model, an ontology-centered approach was chosen. In the first step of the new process (Data Modeling) the domain experts defines what data (structures) are necessary for the current research questions to be answered. This definition is stored in the form of a domain-ontology, which is subsequently used to actively support the user in all the tasks of the process.

In this paper we demonstrated how the extensive use of ontology-originated, structural meta-information can help to allow medical domain-expert using advanced machine learning algorithms — algorithms that are usually preserved for IT and machine-learning experts. By automatizing the data pre-processing and algorithm parametrization to a very high degree, it is possible for a Non-IT user to apply these algorithms and answer research questions.

References

1. Anderson, N.R., Lee, E.S., Brockenbrough, J.S., Minie, M.E., Fuller, S., Brinkley, J., Tarczy-Hornoch, P.: Issues in biomedical research data management and analysis: Needs and barriers. Journal of the American Medical Informatics Association 14(4), 478–488 (2007). http://jamia.bmj.com/content/14/4/478. abstract
2. Baigent, C., Harrell, F.E., Buyse, M., Emberson, J.R., Altman, D.G.: Ensuring trial validity by data quality assurance and diversification of monitoring methods. Clinical Trials 5(1), 49–55 (2008). http://ctj.sagepub.com/content/5/1/49. abstract
3. Bellazzi, R., Zupan, B.: Predictive data mining in clinical medicine: current issues and guidelines. International Journal of Medical Informatics 77(2), 81–97 (2008)
4. Van den Broeck, J., Cunningham, S.A., Eeckels, R., Herbst, K.: Data cleaning: detecting, diagnosing, and editing data abnormalities. PLoS Medicine 2(10), e267 (2005)
5. Bursa, M., Lhotska, L., Chudacek, V., Spilka, J., Janku, P., Huser, M.: Practical Problems and Solutions in Hospital Information System Data Mining. In: Böhm, C., Khuri, S., Lhotská, L., Renda, M.E. (eds.) ITBAM 2012. LNCS, vol. 7451, pp. 31–39. Springer, Heidelberg (2012)
6. Cios, K.J., Teresinska, A., Konieczna, S., Potocka, J., Sharma, S.: Diagnosing myocardial perfusion from pect bull-eye maps-a knowledge discovery approach. IEEE Engineering in Medicine and Biology Magazine 19(4), 17–25 (2000)
7. Cios, K.J., William Moore, G.: Uniqueness of medical data mining. Artificial Intelligence in Medicine 26(1), 1–24 (2002)
8. Fayyad, U., Piatetsky-Shapiro, G., Smyth, P.: The kdd process for extracting useful knowledge from volumes of data. Communications of the ACM 39(11), 27–34 (1996)
9. Fayyad, U., Piatetsky-shapiro, G., Smyth, P.: From data mining to knowledge discovery in databases. AI Magazine 17, 37–54 (1996)
10. Fayyad, U.M., Piatetsky-Shapiro, G., Smyth, P., Uthurusamy, R.: Advances in knowledge discovery and data mining (1996)
11. Fisher, R.A.: The use of multiple measurements in taxonomic problems. Annals of Eugenics 7(2), 179–188 (1936)
12. Franklin, J.D., Guidry, A., Brinkley, J.F.: A partnership approach for electronic data capture in small-scale clinical trials. Journal of Biomedical Informatics 44(suppl. 1), S103–S108 (2011)
13. Girardi, D., Arthofer, K.: An ontology-based data acquisition infrastructure - using ontologies to create domain-independent software systems. In: KEOD 2012, Proceedings of the International Conference on Knowledge Engineering and Ontology Development, Barcelona, Spain, October, 4-7, pp. 155–160. SciTePress, Barcelona (2012)
14. Girardi, D., Dirnberger, J., Trenkler, J.: A meta model-based web framework for domain independent data acquisition. In: ICCGI 2013, The Eighth International Multi-Conference on Computing in the Global Information Technology, pp. 133–138. International Academy, Research, and Industry Association, Nice, France (2013)
15. Girardi, D., Küng, J., Giretzlehner, M.: A Meta-model Guided Expression Engine. In: Nguyen, N.T., Attachoo, B., Trawiński, B., Somboonviwat, K. (eds.) ACIIDS 2014, Part I. LNCS, vol. 8397, pp. 1–10. Springer, Heidelberg (2014)

16. Holzinger, A.: On knowledge discovery and interactive intelligent visualization of biomedical data-challenges in human-computer interaction & biomedical informatics. In: DATA (2012)
17. Holzinger, A., Dehmer, M., Jurisica, I.: Knowledge discovery and interactive data mining in bioinformatics - state-of-the-art, future challenges and research directions. BMC Bioinformatics 15(S6), I1 (2014). http://www.biomedcentral.com/1471-2105/15/S6/I1
18. Holzinger, A., Jurisica, I.: Knowledge Discovery and Data Mining in Biomedical Informatics: The Future Is in Integrative, Interactive Machine Learning Solutions. In: Holzinger, A., Jurisica, I. (eds.) Interactive Knowledge Discovery and Data Mining in Biomedical Informatics. LNCS, vol. 8401, pp. 1–18. Springer, Heidelberg (2014)
19. Hsu, C.W., Chang, C.C., Lin, C.J., et al.: A practical guide to support vector classification (2003)
20. Kieseberg, P., Schantl, J., Frhwirt, P., Weippl, E., Holzinger, A.: Witnesses for the doctor in the loop. In: Brain and Health Informatics BIH 2015, Lecture Notes in Artificial Intelligence LNAI. Springer, Heidelberg (in print, 2015)
21. Kurgan, L.A., Musilek, P.: A survey of knowledge discovery and data mining process models. The Knowledge Engineering Review 21(01), 1–24 (2006)
22. Leiner, F., Gaus, W., Haux, R., Knaup-Gregori, P.: Medical Data Management - A Practical Guide. Springer (2003)
23. Lichman, M.: UCI machine learning repository (2013). http://archive.ics.uci.edu/ml
24. Mariscal, G., Marbán, Ó., Fernández, C.: A survey of data mining and knowledge discovery process models and methodologies. The Knowledge Engineering Review 25(2), 137–166 (2010)
25. Mirchevska, V., Lustrek, M., Gams, M.: Combining domain knowledge and machine learning for robust fall detection. Expert Systems 31(2), 163–175 (2014)
26. Niakšu, O., Kurasova, O.: Data mining applications in healthcare: Research vs practice. Databases and Information Systems Baltic DB&IS 2012, p. 58 (2012)
27. Pal, N.R., Jain, L.: Advanced techniques in knowledge discovery and data mining. Springer, New York (2004)
28. Prokosch, H.U., Ganslandt, T.: Perspectives for medical informatics. Methods Inf. Med. 48(1), 38–44 (2009)
29. Roddick, J.F., Fule, P., Graco, W.J.: Exploratory medical knowledge discovery: experiences and issues. SIGKDD Explor. Newsl. 5(1), 94–99 (2003). http://doi.acm.org/10.1145/959242.959243
30. Shearer, C.: The crisp-dm model: the new blueprint for data mining. Journal of Data Warehousing 5(4), 13–22 (2000)
31. Tsumoto, S., Hirano, S.: Data mining in hospital information system for hospital management. In: ICME International Conference on Complex Medical Engineering, CME 2009, pp. 1–5 (April 2009)
32. Tsumoto, S., Hirano, S., Tsumoto, Y.: Information reuse in hospital information systems: A data mining approach. In: 2011 IEEE International Conference on Information Reuse and Integration (IRI), pp. 172–176 (August 2011)
33. Webb, G.I.: Integrating machine learning with knowledge acquisition through direct interaction with domain experts. Knowledge-Based Systems 9(4), 253–266 (1996)

Symposium on Computational Psychophysiology

The Research of Depression Based on Power Spectrum

Ming-Hou Sun, Qing-Lin Zhao, Bin Hu$^{(\boxtimes)}$, Yan Chen,
Li-Juan Xu, and Hong Peng

School of Information Science and Engineering, Lanzhou University,
Lanzhou 730000, Gansu, China
bh@lzu.edu.cn

Abstract. Depression is a common emotional disease endangering human health [1], however, there is no objective and precise method for the diagnosis of depression at present both at home and overseas. Through power spectrum analysis for two leads EEG signals of the depression group and the control group, we extracted the relative power and gravity frequency, two characteristic parameters of the EEG signals each rhythm, and studied the differences between the two groups' characteristic parameters. The results of SPSS statistical analysis demonstrate that the EEG characteristic parameters have a strong correlation with the degree of depression. Specifically speaking, the relative power of depression group's left and right brain α rhythm is asymmetric, and the relative power of depression group's δ rhythm is higher than the control group, while the relative power of α rhythm is lower than the control group. In addition, the gravity frequency of depression group migrates to the low frequency compared with the control group. Relative power and gravity frequency reflect the suppressive state of the body objectively and accurately, compared with the clinical diagnosis method and the rating scale, can be more objective diagnosis of depression.

Keywords: Depression · Power spectrum · Relative power · Gravity frequency

1 Introduction

Depression, also known as depressive disorders, with significant and lasting low mood as the main clinical features, is a common emotional disorder endangering human health disease [1]. According to the world health organization (WHO)

Supported by the National Basic Research Program of China (973 Program) (No.2014CB744600, No.2011CB711000), the Program of International S&T Cooperation of MOST (No.2013DFA11140), the National Natural Science Foundation of China (grant No.61210010, No.61300231), and Natural Science Foundation of Gansu Province, China (1208RJZA127), Central Universities Fundamental Research Funds (Grant No.lzujbky-2015-k07).

Y. Guo et al. (Eds.): BIH 2015, LNAI 9250, pp. 401–409, 2015.
DOI: 10.1007/978-3-319-23344-4_39

report NO.369 in October 2012, the global incidence of depression is about 11%, the current estimated 350 million people worldwide suffer from depression. Reports reveal that 65%~80% of the depression patients can appear suicide ideation, while 45%~55% of the patients actually carry out suicidal behaviors, and 15% of patients with severe depression even commit suicide. The number of suicide estimates up to 1 million people every year. According to the results of the global burden of disease (GBD) study conducted by Harvard University in the United States, the world health organization and the world bank cooperation, disability-adjusted life year (DALY) was taken as index, depression for high burden of disease can expect to be second by 2020.

The WHO experts noted that the earlier detection and treatment of depression, as other diseases, the better. If intervention at high-risk state of depression, the treatment effect will be more satisfactory, and we can also save a lot of health care costs at the same time. For the quality of susceptible high-risk groups, if not as early as possible warning, intervention, it may develop into major depressive disorder (MDD)[2], bipolar disorder and other serious mental illnesses, this kind of diseases have a high relapse rate, high suicide rate and other characteristics, and will eventually bring serious burden to individuals, families and the whole society.

At present, the main method of diagnosis of depression at home and abroad are clinical diagnosis method [3], rating scale [4] and the interview [5]. However, these methods are difficult to accurately determine whether patients suffered from depression, main reasons are: (1)At the time of treatment, people with mental disorders do not want others to know they are suffering from depression, and vigorously to downplay their symptoms, or to the physician to introduce some irrelevant issues, such as sleep problems, physical discomfort issues while hiding the core symptoms, leading to misdiagnosis and missed diagnosis [6]; (2)The doctor to the recognition rate of depression is still relatively low. A WHO multicenter cooperative research data shows that Shanghai physicians for the recognition rate of depression is only 21%. (3)Less public health human resources. With the large increase in demand for mental health services, the lack of technology of psychiatric hospital staff is more prominent; (4)Clinical diagnostic methods and rating scales can only take effect when diagnosis threshold is reached, together with the patient's subjective factors, making the diagnosis rate is relatively low. In order to eliminate subjective factors influence of patients, this study is based on the rating scale, and then collect the EEG that objective, accurate and non-invasive evaluation methods to explore a more accurate method of diagnose depression.

Resting state EEG is reflecting the resting state of the objective index of brain activity, compared with the task state EEG, with the features of easy collection, less interference factors, which is widely used, including research on EEG power spectrum is becoming the current hot spots. Therefore, this article is in the resting state EEG power spectrum of each rhythm variation and characteristics, and then explore a more accurate method of diagnose depression.

2 Methods

2.1 Subjects

The 22 subjects are selected in this study, 11 of them are patients with depression, another 11 as the control group, which of age and income match with depression group. The average age of subjects is about 30 years old, and there is no history of major diseases. Participants shall sign a written informed consent form before the experiment, and a week before the experiment without taking any psychiatric drugs, after the experiment to be given a certain reward.

Every subject of this study need through self-rating scale and MINI scale screening. Self-rating Scale include Eysenck Personality Questionnaire (EPQ)[7], the Pittsburgh Sleep Quality Index (PSQI)[8], Life Event Scale [9], Generalized Anxiety Disorder Scale [10], the Patient Health Questionnaire [11], Childhood Abuse Questionnaire [12], Simplified Coping Style Questionnaire [13], Amount of Social Support Composition [14]. MINI scale is tested by psychiatrists and subjects of the interview.

2.2 EEG Collection

The EEG acquisition instrument in this article was developed 3 leads the EEG acquisition instrument by our team, as shown in Fig.1, and compared with the equipment, such as ERP and BP has simple operation, convenient carrying and the characteristics of strong adaptability. Electrode placement in accordance with international 10-20 system (Fig.2), and the earlobe as the reference electrode, record the resting state of FP2, FPz and FP1 leads of EEG signals. During the experiment, the subjects need eyes closed, put the peace of mind and body can not take any action. The experiment of sampling rate is 250 hz and sampling time is 90 s.

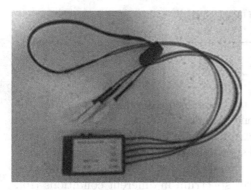
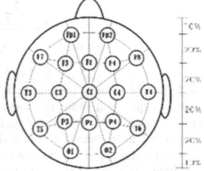

Fig. 1. EEG acquisition instrument   Fig. 2. National 10-20 electrode system

3   Data Preprocessing and Analysis

3.1   Data Preprocessing

In this article, FP2 and FP1 leads of EEG signals are analyzed, each lead of the
EEG data first through 0.5∼30 hz of FIR band-pass filter, shown in Fig.3, and
then excluding the first 300 samples of data, the rest of the sampling data as
the research object in this paper.

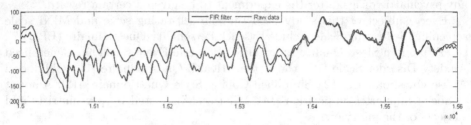

Fig. 3. Data preprocessing

3.2   Algorithm of the Relative Power and Gravity Frequency

In this paper, we adopt Welch periodogram to estimate the EEG power spectrum
[15], then use Hanning window to reduce side lobe leaked effects, next, use FFT
to calculate power spectrum of 1000 sampling data points, finally, calculate of
EEG rhythm δ (0.5∼4 hz), θ (4∼8 hz), α (8∼16 hz) and β (16∼30 hz) power
spectrum values of total power spectrum (0.5∼30 hz) ratio respectively, and this
ratio is the relative power. In order to compare different mental state migration
situation of gravity of the EEG power spectrum, we calculate gravity frequency
of within the scope of 0.5 to 30 hz power spectrum, computation formula is as
follows:

$$f_g = \frac{\sum_{f=f_1}^{f_2} [P(f) \times f]}{\sum_{f=f_1}^{f_2} P(f)}, \tag{3.1}$$

where f_g for the gravity frequency, f_1 to f_2 for frequency range, $P(f)$ for the
signal power spectrum, f for the frequency values.

The gravity frequency of power spectrum can not only better response signal
power spectral density distribution, and shows that the frequency spectrum component of the larger the frequency of the signal components, can also be reflected
in the whole migration of the EEG power spectrum in different conditions [16].

3.3 Analysis

3.3.1 Symmetry of Alpha Rhythm Relative Power

Calculating the relative power and gravity frequency of δ (0.5~4 hz), θ (4~8 hz), α (8~14 hz) and β (14~30 hz) rhythms of two leads EEG FP2, FP1, as shown in Table 1. Using SPSS19.0 software packages to do paired sample T-test of the left and right brain α rhythm of two groups, respectively, as shown in Table 2.

Statistical analysis shows that a significant difference is found in the relative power of left and right brain signals α rhythm of the depression group of the α rhythm, with statistical significance. While the difference of relative power of the control group α rhythm do not reach the significant level, no statistical significance.

Table 1. Data of EEG's relative power in different rhythm and gravity frequency

Group	δ		θ		α		β		fg	
	FP2	FP1	FP2	FP1	FP2	FP1	FP2	FP1	FP2	FP1
Depression	0.6592	0.6471	0.066	0.0607	0.2395	0.2561	0.0353	0.0361	4.4428	4.5588
	0.6207	0.6782	0.1241	0.1355	0.0465	0.0513	0.2088	0.1351	6.877	5.2599
	0.853	0.8501	0.0626	0.0625	0.0482	0.051	0.0362	0.0363	2.5436	2.5473
	0.8133	0.8134	0.0922	0.091	0.0466	0.0483	0.048	0.0473	3.1337	3.1084
	0.7072	0.689	0.209	0.2236	0.0574	0.0615	0.0264	0.0259	3.7424	3.895
	0.6978	0.6565	0.2045	0.2284	0.0479	0.0543	0.0499	0.0508	3.8107	4.1732
	0.7422	0.6841	0.1092	0.1343	0.0992	0.1248	0.0494	0.0568	3.5333	4.0586
	0.7895	0.8018	0.1103	0.0997	0.0647	0.0584	0.0355	0.0401	2.898	2.8787
	0.4016	0.3896	0.4519	0.4624	0.0954	0.0955	0.051	0.0525	5.1968	5.2848
	0.4012	0.383	0.5622	0.5789	0.0234	0.0246	0.0132	0.0134	4.039	4.1359
	0.7643	0.7524	0.1021	0.104	0.0803	0.0875	0.0533	0.0561	3.4661	3.5744
Contol	0.5362	0.5366	0.1758	0.1756	0.2575	0.2576	0.0305	0.0301	5.0808	5.0754
	0.6341	0.6393	0.2095	0.2075	0.1349	0.1326	0.0215	0.0206	4.0157	3.9774
	0.2102	0.1909	0.4052	0.4124	0.3541	0.3691	0.0303	0.0276	7.1041	7.203
	0.5899	0.5505	0.0925	0.0864	0.1022	0.1064	0.2154	0.2566	6.6824	7.4245
	0.6205	0.6368	0.0783	0.0713	0.1942	0.1989	0.107	0.0929	5.3433	5.0788
	0.8128	0.8391	0.0742	0.0638	0.0573	0.048	0.0557	0.0491	3.1123	2.8057
	0.2652	0.5009	0.6305	0.4297	0.0761	0.0521	0.0283	0.0172	5.4612	3.8614
	0.5412	0.4944	0.1676	0.1763	0.1506	0.1906	0.1406	0.1387	6.1065	6.6143
	0.2021	0.2058	0.6771	0.6685	0.0904	0.0893	0.0358	0.0364	6.1898	6.1756
	0.664	0.6829	0.1219	0.1086	0.1728	0.1714	0.0043	0.0371	4.0278	3.831
	0.5412	0.4944	0.1676	0.1763	0.1506	0.1906	0.1406	0.1387	6.1065	6.6143

Table 2. Paired Sample T-test

| | Pair Differences | | | | | | | |
| | | | | 95% Confidence Interval of The Difference | | | | |
	Mean	Std. Deviation	Std.Error Mean	Lower	Upper	t	df	Sig(2-tailed)
FP2_d-FP1-d	.0058364	.0086067	.002595	0.0116184	.000543	2.249	10	.048
FP2_c-FP1_c	.0108909	.0316988	.0095576	0.0321865	.0104047	1.140	10	.281

FP2_d and FP1_d represent left and right EEG signals of the depression group, FP2_c and FP1_c represent left and right EEG signals of the control group.

For a normal person, the frequency of α rhythm on both sides of the cerebral hemispheres are the same at any time, slight difference should be suspected of being abnormal, lower side is generally abnormal parts, differences of amplitude in the frontal bilateral does not exceed 20% [17]. Therefore, asymmetry of relative power of left and right brain α rhythm represents the lesions, showing that the depression is related with the asymmetry of relative power of left and right brain α rhythm, which provides powerful basis for exploring the risk theory and methods of the potential depression. The research results of emotional brain lateralization done by Jiang Yuan of Beijing normal university also pointed out that depression is associated with asymmetric abnormalities of frontal lobe [18].

3.3.2 Analysis of the Relative Power of EEG in Different Rhythm

In order to reduce the influences of the relative power fluctuations of each rhythm, we will average the relative powers of each rhythm of two leads EEG as the relative power and gravity frequency of each EEG rhythm. Sorting the two groups' the relative power of each EEG rhythm, respectively, then we draw the comparison chart, as shown in Fig.4. Using SPSS19.0 packages for the processed relative power of EEG each rhythm to do independent sample T-test (Levene homogeneity of variance analysis), the results are shown in Table 3.

From the statistical results in Table 3, we can obtain that two groups' relative power of δ and α rhythm have a significant difference, statistically significant, while the difference of the relative power of the θ and β rhythm did not reach significant level, not statistically significant. As can be seen from Fig.4, the relative power of δ rhythm of depression group is significantly bigger than the control group, the relative power of α rhythm of control group is significantly bigger than the depression group, and the relative power of the two groups' θ and β rhythm is not obvious different, which is consistent with the results of statistical analysis.

Since α and β high frequency fast wave is generally considered is the main wave when the cerebral cortex is excited, which reflects the degree of brain neurons. high amplitude slow waves are main performances when the cerebral cortex

Table 3. Independent Samples T-test

| | Levene's Test for Equality of Variances | | T-test for Equality of Means | | | | | 95% Confidence Interval of The Difference | |
	F	Sig.	t	df	Sig.	Mean Difference	Std.Error Difference	Lower	Upper
δ	1.129	.301	2.245	18.8444	.037	.16842727	.07503234	.01129502	.3255595
θ	.656	.427	-.571	19.275	.574	-.0455909	.079809	-.2124726	.1212908
α	4.016	.059	-2.574	14.939	.021	-.1034182	.0401843	-.1890994	-.017737
β	3.190	.089	-.851	16.802	.407	-.0200909	.0236186	-.0699665	.0297847

is in a suppressive state, which reflects the degree of brain neurons inhibition [19]. Therefore, the above results show that reducing the level of excitement, which is also consistent with the subject's subjective feeling. Brain inhibition degree is increased of depression group than the normal group, the degree of excitement is reduced, which is also consistent with subjective feeling of the subjects.

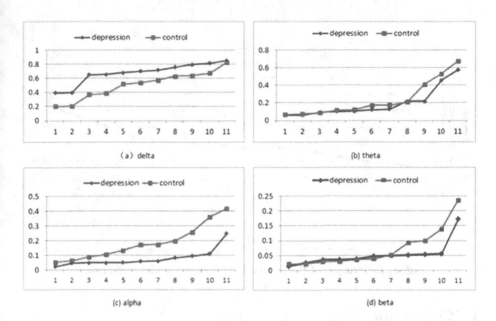

Fig. 4. Differences of EEG's average relative power in different rhythm under two groups

3.3.3   Comparison and Analysis of Gravity Frequency

Sorting the the gravity frequency of two groups, respectively, and we draw the comparison as shown in Fig.5. Then doing the independent sample T-test (Lenvene homogeneity of variance analysis), the statistical results are shown in Table 4. Statistical analysis shows that the gravity frequency of two groups have a significant difference, statistical significant. And Fig.4 shows that the gravity frequency of depression group is obviously lower than the control group, suggesting that the gravity frequency of EEG power spectrum of patients with depression migrated to low frequency, and the frequency of larger signal components of frequency spectrum is reduced, which is consistent with previous analysis of relative power of each rhythm. The relative power of δ high amplitude slow wave of depression group significantly increased than the control group, while the relative power of the high frequency fast wave significantly reduced, which caused the gravity frequency of whole power spectrum migrated to low frequency, showing that the the excitability of the brain is reduced, the inhibition degree is increased.

Table 4. Independent Samples T-test

		Levene's Test for Equality of Varianc		T-test for Equality of Means					95% Confidence Interval of The Difference	
		F	Sig.	t	df	Sig.	Mean Difference	Std.Error Difference	Lower	Upper
fg	Equal variance assumed	3.125	.092	-2.741	20	.013	-1.4971409	.5464563	-2.636611	-.3576702
	Equal variance not assumed	.656	.427	-2.741	17.696	.014	-1.4971409	.5462563	-2.646200	-.3480818

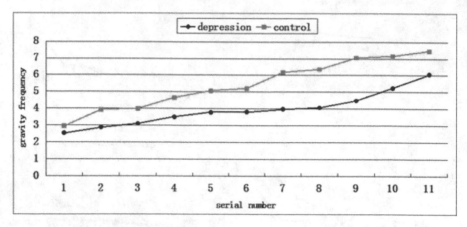

Fig. 5. Differences of EEG's gravity frequency under two groups

4 Conclusion

Through collecting FP2 and FP1 leads of resting-state EEG of 22 subjects in the depression group and the control group and performing power spectrum analysis, we extracted relative power and gravity frequency in different rhythm of the raw EEG. Afterwards we made a further discussion within and between groups. First, statistical analysis of the relative power of the left and right brain alpha rhythms in two groups respectively were made. And significant differences were found in the relative power of the left and right brain in depression group, indicating that in what situation the subjects are in the depression, which also provides us with a more reliable judgment standard for diagnosis of depression. Second, by means of comparative and statistical analysis in relative power and gravity frequency between two groups, it can be concluded that the delta relative power of depression group is higher than the control group, whereas the relative power of rhythm and gravity frequency are significantly lower than the control group. And then it suggests that the body is in a state of depression, the level of excitement reduces while the degree of inhibition increases.

The main limitation of the study is that the number of the subjects is low and the ages of the selected subjects mainly ranging from 25 to 35 is narrow. In our future study, we will expand the number of subjects, choose the subjects of different ages, and adopt more comprehensive approach to explore the diagnosis of depression, so as to give the medical staff more objective criteria to diagnose depression.

References

1. Merson, M., Black, RE., Mills, A.J.: International health: disease, programs, systems and policies, pp. 331–372. Jones, Bartlett, Sudbury Massachusetts (2005)
2. Yanping, Z., Xianyun, L., Zhiqing, W.: A survey of 50 general hospital outpatient depression discorder in Beijing. Chin. J. Psychiatry **39**, 161–164 (2006)
3. Zeping, X., Shifu, X.: Research of comprehensive hospital outpatient depression disorder. J. Clin. Psychol. Med. **11**, 95–96 (2001)
4. Fava, M., Kendler, K.S.: Major Depressive Discorder. Neuron. **28**, 335–341 (2000)
5. Jimin, J., Junmian, X.: Clinical study of depression diagnostic classification. J. Clin. Psychol. Med. **11**, 95–96 (2001)
6. Xin, M., Shuran, L.: The prevalence of depression in Beijing. Chin. J. Psychiatry, 40100-40103 (2007)
7. Zhonggeng, C.: Eysenck Personality Questionnaire analysis of the project. Acta Psychologica Sinica, 183–218 (1983)
8. Xianchen, L., Maoqin, T.: Reliability and validity of the Pittsburgh Sleep Quality Index. Chin. J. Psychiatry **29**, 103–107 (1996)
9. Zhenguo, F., Jiamei, C., Shengli, L.: The study of elderly depression compared with life events and social support. Chinese Mental Health Journal, 230–231 (1993)
10. Spitzer, R.L., Kroenke, K., Williams, J.B.W., et al.: A brief measure for assessing generalized anxiety disorderthe GAD7. Arch Intern Med
11. Xu, Y., Wu, H.S., Xu, Y.F.: The reliability and validity of patient health questionnaire depression module in Chinese elderly. Shanghai Archives of Pay-chiatry (2007)
12. Zhao, X.F., Zhang, Y.L., Li, L.F.: Reliability and validity of Chinese version of Child-hood trauma questionnaire. Chinese Journal of Clinical Rehabilitation (2005)
13. Xie, Y.N.: Reliability and validity of Simple Coping Strategy Questionnaire. Chinese Journal of Clinical Psychology (1998)
14. Xiangdong, W., Xilin, W., Hong, M.: Mental health Assessment scale of mental health. Chinese Mental Health Journal, 194–197 (1999)
15. Fengying, W., Lili, Z.: Power Spectrum Density Estimation and the simulation in Matlab. Chinese Core Journal (2002)
16. Zhang, C., Zheng, C.X., Pei, X.M.: Power Spectrum Analysis on the Multiparam-eter Electroencephalogram Features of Physiological Mental Fatigue. Journal of Biomedical Engineering 26, 162–172 (2009)
17. Jianzhong, W., Chongde, L., Yu, P.: Development Characteristics of 13 to 18 year olds EEG alpha rhythm. Journal of Beijing Normal University **37**, 825–831 (2001)
18. Jiang, Y., Chongde, L.: Emotional Brain lateralization progress. Studies of Psychology and Behavior 312–318 (2010)
19. Wang, J.L., Gao, G.D., Jian, Z., et al.: Nonlinear characters of neuronal discharge of globus pallidus in Parkinsons disease. Chin. J. Clin. Rehabilitation (2005)

Modelling Uncertainty in Health Care Systems

Philip Moore[✉] and Hong Liu

Shandong Normal University, Jinan, Shandong, China
ptmbcu@gmail.com, lhsdcn@126.com

Abstract. Computer science research has seen a paradigm change in respect of it's attitude to uncertainty. The traditional view is that science strives for certainty in all its manifestations the developing view considers uncertainty to be a potentially important aspect which, far from being a negative influence, may provide significant utility. We consider uncertainty, introduce fuzzy set theory, and discuss health care systems which are characterized by uncertainty. Fuzzy set theory has provided a basis upon which uncertainty may be addressed and we conclude that fuzzy set theory provides significant research potential for decision-support systems in the medical domain.

Keywords: Uncertainty · Decision support · Health care systems · Fuzzy sets · Iintuitionistic fuzzy sets

1 Background

In the field of computer science, developments over many years in the understanding of *uncertainty* have been profound. These developments have been manifested in a gradual transition from the traditional view (which argues that uncertainty is undesirable in science to an alternative (or modern) view which asserts that in science it is unavoidable [10] and, if effectively modelled, may indeed provide significant potential utility in managing inconsistency [5].

The challenge lies in the development of methods by which optimal levels of allowable (and controlled) uncertainty can be achieved for each modelling problem [5]. These developments are discussed in this paper with consideration of an implementation strategy predicated on Fuzzy Set Theory (FST) to address the challenges faced in accommodating uncertainty. Health care systems are typically characterized by dynamic uncertainty and imprecision, the medical domain being a domain in which the utility of *Fuzzy Set Theory* (FST) has been demonstrated [5]. We conclude that the application of FST provides an effective basis upon which uncertainty in the medical decision-support systems may be addressed in both 'face-to-face' consultations and in remote on-line triage.

The remainder of this paper is structured as follows: in Section 2 uncertainty in the medical domain is discussed. In Section 3 set theory is introduced with consideration of intuitionistic fuzzy sets and membership functions. Implementation strategy is introduced in Section 5 Section 6 sets out a discussion where challenges, open research questions, and future work are discussed. The paper concludes with closing observations in Section 7.

© Springer International Publishing Switzerland 2015
Y. Guo et al. (Eds.): BIH 2015, LNAI 9250, pp. 410–419, 2015.
DOI: 10.1007/978-3-319-23344-4_40

2 Uncertainty in the Medical Domain

Uncertainty is an inherent characteristic of health care systems and the diagnostic process. When faced with a patient presenting with a health problem, a clinician or health care professional must try to identify a diagnosis based on the patients reported symptoms along with test results where appropriate. The diagnostic process may be viewed in terms of degrees of uncertainty with clinicians being: (1) certain of a diagnosis $\langle x \rangle$, (2) be unsure of a diagnosis $\langle x \rangle$ or $\langle y \rangle$, or (3) be certain that diagnosis $\langle y \rangle$ is not applicable. Moreover, a single symptom may be indicative of several different diseases, and the presence of several conditions in a single patient may disrupt the expected symptom pattern of any one of the possible conditions or diseases.

While knowledge concerning the symptom-disease relationship constitutes one source of *uncertainty* [in the diagnostic process] knowledge concerning the state of the patient constitutes another. Clinicians base diagnostic decisions on knowledge of the patient which may include: past history and lifestyle (which may be subjective, exaggerated, underestimated, or incomplete) a physical examination, and a range of test results including cognitive function [in possible cases of e.g., depression] using Electroencephalography (EEG).

The desire to better understand the diagnostic process has prompted attempts to model it using fuzzy sets. These models vary in the degree to which they attempt to deal with different complicating aspects of medical diagnosis such as the relative importance of symptoms, the varied symptom patterns of different disease stages, and the relationships between diseases. For example, a symptom may be quite likely to occur with a given disease but may also commonly occur with several other diseases, therefore limiting its power as a discriminating factor among them. Another symptom, on the other hand, may be relatively rare with a given disease, but its presence may nevertheless constitute almost certain confirmation of the presence of the disease. To address the uncertainty in the diagnostic process a fertile field of study has been the use of FST.

3 Set Theory

Research into the theory of fuzzy set theory can be dated back to the mid-1960's where the original concept was presented in the seminal paper by Lotfi Zadeh [10]. There exists a very large body of documented research appertaining to the theory with reported results demonstrating success [of the concept] in the 'real-world' in domains as diverse as: medicine, economics, fuzzy systems with genetic algorithms, fuzzy regression, and interpersonal communication [5]. Building on the early work into traditional sets (hereafter termed a *Crisp* sets), developments in *Fuzzy Sets* have extended fuzzy set theory to include *Intuitionistic Fuzzy Sets* (IFS) [1], Soft Sets (SS) [6], and *Picture Fuzzy Sets* (PFS) [2]. In this paper we focus on the use of IFS.

Crisp sets) are defined in such a way as to dichotomize individuals in some given universe of discourse into two groups: (1) full-members of a set, and (2) non-members of a set). A *characteristic function* assigns values in the range $\langle 1 \rangle$ or $\langle 0 \rangle$ to each individual in the universal set where $\langle 1 \rangle$ equates to a member of a set and $\langle 0 \rangle$ equates to a non-member of a set under consideration. Fuzzy sets are a generalization of crisp sets and provide for a gradual transition from full membership to non-membership. For example, if we are considering the concept of 'high temperature' the representative fuzzy set would be markedly different for 'weather' and 'cooking' while retaining the concepts: 'low', 'medium', and 'high' temperature ranges generally normalized to values in 'real-number' $(\Re)$ values in the range $[0, 1]$.

Consider a fuzzy set where $\langle A \rangle$ is a fuzzy set and $\langle x \rangle$ is a relevant object; the proposition: $\langle x \rangle$ is a member of $\langle A \rangle$ may be neither *true* or *false* as is required by two-valued logic. It may be that $\langle x \rangle$ is a member of $\langle A \rangle$ is *true* only to some degree. It is most common (but not required) to express degrees of set membership using 'real-number' $(\Re)$ values in the closed interval between $[0, 1]$. A membership function for a fuzzy set $\langle A \rangle$ is denoted by (μ_A) as shown in (1):

$$\mu_A : X \to [0, 1] \tag{1}$$

The concept of a crisp set can be considered as a restricted case of the more general concept of a fuzzy set for which only these two grades of membership are allowed. A fuzzy set can be defined mathematically by assigning to each object in the universe of discourse a value representing its grade of membership in the fuzzy set. This grade corresponds to the degree to which that individual is similar or compatible with the concept represented by the fuzzy set. Thus, objects may belong in the fuzzy set to a greater or lesser degree as indicated by a larger or smaller membership grade.

FST has been shown to be capable of describing uncertainty by attributing the degree to which an object is a member of a set. However, in reality it may not always be true that the degree of non-membership of an element in a fuzzy set is equal to 1 minus the membership degree because there may be some *degree of hesitation*, also termed the *hesitation margin* or *hesitation degree*. To address this issue an extension of the traditional fuzzy set theory termed IFS has been proposed, an IFS (A) on a universe (X) is an object in the form (2):

$$A = (x.\mu_A(x), \nu_A(x) | x \varepsilon X) \tag{2}$$

where: $(\mu_A(x) \epsilon [0, 1])$ is termed the degree of *positive* membership of $\langle x \rangle$ in $\langle A \rangle$ and $\{\nu_A(x) \epsilon [0.1]\}$ is termed the degree of *negative* membership of $\langle x \rangle$ in $\langle A \rangle$, and where (μ_A) and (ν_A) satisfy the following conditions as shown in equation (3):

$$\mu_A(x) + \nu_A(x) \le 1 \tag{3}$$

However, it may not always be true that the degree of non-membership of an element in a fuzzy set is equal to 1 minus the *positive* membership degree (or the *intuitionistic index*). Extending the foregoing discussion to consider a use case where equation (2) is not equal to 1, this is expressed as in (4):

$$(\forall x \epsilon X) (1 - (u_A(x) + \nu_A(x))) \tag{4}$$

In considering IFS and the degree of hesitation, it can be seen that an IFS provides a basis upon which the modelling of hesitation (or uncertainty) may be realized using an additional degree of membership which may be expressed as (5):

$$(u_A(x) + \nu_A(x) + \eta_A(x)) = 1 \tag{5}$$

where $(\mu_A(x))$ represents the degree of positive membership of a set, $(\nu_A(x))$ represents the degree of negative membership of a set, and $(\eta_A(x))$ represents the degree of hesitation or uncertainty. Thus, the negation of the non membership degree w.r.t. the standard fuzzy negation $((\eta_A(x)))$ can be seen as a degree of membership.

3.1   Membership Functions

While for crisp sets the values (1) or (0) identify an object as a member or non-member respectively of a set. This function can be generalized with the values assigned to objects of a universal set falling within a specified range which identifies the membership grade of the objects in the universal set, larger values denote higher degrees of set membership. Such a function is termed a *Membership Function* (MF) and the set defined by a MF is a fuzzy set. The range of values is not arbitrary and may be designed to suit the domain of discourse with each MF mapping elements of a given universal set $\langle X \rangle$ (which is always a crisp set) into real numbers in $[0, 1]$. MF are denoted as: $\mu_A : X \to [0, 1]$.

A central role for a MF is *defuzzification* as in practice, the fuzzy relation will, during defuzzification, resolve to a *Crisp* set with the delineation being achieved using the α cut and the *strong* α^+ cut [5]. The role of the *a-cut* and the *strong a-cut* is central to the relationship that exists between fuzzy sets and crisp sets as the final result of defuzzification will be a crisp set where a Boolean decision will be achieved which identifies set membership. Consider a fuzzy set A defined on X and any number within the range $[0, 1]$, the *a-cut* $(^a A)$ and *strong a-cut* $(^{a+} A)$ in respect of $\langle A \rangle$ are *crisp* sets as denoted in (6) and (7) respectively:

$$^a A = \{x | A(x) \geq a\} \tag{6}$$

$$^{a+} A = \{x | A(x) > a\} \tag{7}$$

a-cuts and the *strong a-cuts* are central in the relationship that exists between fuzzy and crisp sets such that $(^{a+} A \subseteq^a A)$ applies where a set defined by a *strong a-cut* is a subset of a set defined by an *a-cut*.

A diverse range of symmetric and asymmetric MF's are presented in the literature including: (1) *triangular*, (2) *trapezoidal*, and (3) *linear* MF's. A Typical MF shown in Figure 1 is a *trapezoidal* MF which is *symmetric* and is based on a normal (Gaussian) distribution. However, while a MF may also be *asymmetric* it may also adopt many other configurations to suit the domain of discourse. There are MF's which incorporate significantly increased complexity however, as noted by Klir & Yuan [5]: *"It turns out [however] that many applications are not overly sensitive to variations in the shape. In such cases, it is convenient to use a simple shape such as a 'trapezoidal or triangular membership function".*

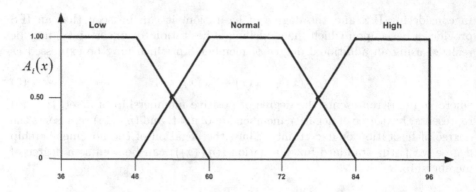

Fig. 1. A typical symmetrical trapezoidal membership function

In considering medical diagnosis, intuitively there are two general classifications of MF: (1) for individual symptom(s), and (2) for the overall diagnosis. In the case of (1) a diagnosis will use a range of metrics (each of which will have it's individual defined MF. For example, a MF for symptoms / test results where the metrics will be in the typical ranges: *normal*, *low*, and *high*, these types of symptom will generally employ a *trapezoidal* MF. For (2), a diagnosis is the result of a combination of metrics and will be the result of data processing (this is discussed under implementation in Section 5).

A diagnosis will in actuality be a fuzzy relation between the symptoms for specific diseases $(S(s_i)\,|\,s_i \epsilon S)$ and the symptoms reported by the patient along with the results of the medical tests $\langle s_i \rangle$. Using IFS, we can identify the probability of a specific disease or condition being the correct one or the inverse according to equations (1), (2), (3), and (4) (see Section 3). In practice there is a requirement to define graduations for each symptom along with specific discrete membership functions.

4   Data Modelling

An important objective of model creation is the maximization of it's usefulness and effectiveness. This objective is closely connected to the relationship among three key characteristics of every systems model namely: *complexity*, *credibility*, and *uncertainty*. This relationship is not fully understood [5], however, it is known that the concept of *uncertainty* plays a pivotal role in efforts to maximize the usefulness of systems models which must attempt to match human cognitive processes. Clearly, data processing requires a data structure capable of storing data and information on diseases and the related symptoms. Additionally, such a data structure must accommodate semantic and linguistic descriptors along with quantitative parameters along with the capability to accommodate multiple parameters (frequently in a list format) for the majority of properties (e.g., symptoms and diseases). Such a data structure must be machine readable but importantly should also be human readable.

As discussed in [7] and [8] the traditional *Relational Database Management Systems* (RDMS), whilst historically successful, has significant limitations given the traction being generated in respect of unstructured data (generally referred to as *NoSQL*). Moreover, Interesting research documented in [3] has investigated NoSQL systems with a ontologies where an ontology is 'layered' onto a NoSQL approach to provide a semantic capability; this research has reported interesting and potentially useful methods of data modelling in many domains of interest including importantly the medical domain where semantic representation forms an important feature.

The current optimal approach to the creation of such a data structure is Ontology-Based Context Modelling (OBCM) as the approach provides an effective cross platform approach with the ability to search, access, and update the data and properties in an ontology. Additionally, when built using the Semantic Web technologies with the W3C *Web Ontology Language* (OWL) OBCM enables the creation of a simple data structure plus the capability to implement inference and reasoning where the domain of discourse demands such an approach. Research into OBCM in a medical context has demonstrated the utility of the approach in respect of physiological signals knowledge representation and as an emotion reasoning model for mental health monitoring.

Developing a suitable domain specific data structure demands the skills of computer scientists (who generally have limited medical knowledge) and the expertise of clinicians (who generally have limited computer science skills). Thus, we must employ a multidisciplinary approach with collaboration between computer scientists and health care professionals (clinicians) where both *explicit* and *tacit* knowledge is leveraged to create a data structure which provides the information required by *Context Processing* (CP).

To create a data structure we propose to use an ontology where the *Crisp* sets define the *patient* ($P(p_i) \in P$), disease ($D(d_i) \in D$), and symptoms ($S(s_i) \in S$) which may include both presenting physical symptoms and the results obtained from tests which may include pathology and cognitive test results. A specific disease is characterized by a number of symptoms $\langle s_i \rangle$ which characterize a disease or condition, and a patient presenting for a consultation with a clinician will report symptoms $\langle s_i \rangle$ which, when combined with the results derived from medical tests (such as blood pressure, temperature, and pulse rate) will point the clinician towards a diagnosis (result) $\langle r \rangle$ where ($r_i \in R$).

5   Implementation Strategy

Thus far uncertainty, set theory with the related topic of MF's, and the data structure with data modelling has been discussed. In this section an implementation strategy is introduced with a discussion around what has historically been thought of as data fusion. Studies have investigated data processing (contextual information) using CP which implements *Context Matching* (CM), Figure 2 shows a high level conceptual view of the CM which is an extension of the concept of data fusion. CM provides an effective basis upon which *Partial Matching*

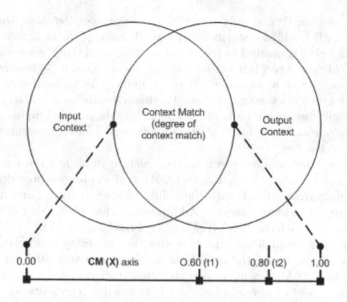

Fig. 2. A conceptual high-level view of CM. The model shows the relationship between the *input* and *output* contexts where PM is implemented with *defuzzification* using defined thresholds (decision boundaries)

(PM) [predicated on degrees of set membership based on fuzzy set theory] while accommodating [or at least mitigating violations of] *Constraint Satisfaction and Preference Compliance* (CS) may be achieved as discussed in [9].

CP and CM is in summary, an event driven fuzzy rule-based system with OBCM. The approach is in effect a deterministic search where $\langle u \rangle$ is a member of a set $\langle U \rangle$, this process is essentially a linear 'brute-force' search of the hypothesis space $\langle U \rangle$ with the objective of identifying a context match. In thinking about medical diagnostics, we aim to match patients observed symptoms and test results to specific conditions. In this case the information will be the tacit and explicit knowledge derived from clinicians in collaborative systems development. Patient monitoring essentially involves two processes:

- Compare changes in a patient's context at time (t_0) and (t_1). The evaluation is designed to identify relative change (i.e., no change or positive / negative change) in a patient's context and implement appropriate intervention(s) as required.
- Compare a patient's presenting symptoms (the *input* context) against the symptoms that classify specific diseases (the *output* context) in the diagnostic process. This demands that multiple symptoms and test results are evaluated and a recommendation made (decision-support)

These processes can be viewed in terms of iterative CP as modelled in Figure 3 where the *input* context is a set of reported symptoms $(S(s_i) \, \epsilon S)$ is matched to

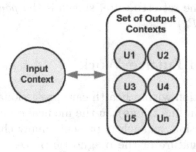

Fig. 3. Context processing for iterative context matching is shown where the *input* context is matched to the *output* context(s) shown as $(U_1...U_n)$ where the *input* context is a set of symptoms plus medical test results (metrics) and $(U_1...U_n)$ represents potential diseases to be matched to the reported metrics

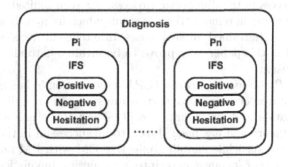

Fig. 4. A conceptual model showing the relationship between the Power set, the Family set of properties, and the IFS used in the modelling of each feature

the *output* context(s) (a disease or condition which may range from a physical ailment to a mental disorder such as depression) $(D(d_i) \epsilon D))$ shown as $(U_1...U_n)$. The diagnosis (or result) of the CM $(r_i \epsilon R)$ will be a quantitative result (normalized to a value in the range $[0,1]$) which identifies the probability of a specific disease or condition $(r_i \epsilon R)$ being the correct diagnosis.

In terms of fuzzy set theory the problem involves: (1) a power set which represents the overall result in terms of the diagnosis, and (2) a *Family* (or level 2) set of properties that relate to specific medical symptoms. As we have discussed, multiple symptoms (e.g., symptoms that require a symmetric or asymmetric MF) which are used by clinicians and decision-support systems to arrive at a diagnosis.

The result of CP and CM may be viewed on two levels: the matching of individual symptoms and the overall recommendation as to the correct diagnosis (or a range of potential diagnoses with levels of confidence) for a clinician to consider. For a discussion on IFS set membership see Section 3. Figure 4 shows a conceptual model of the set structure, shown is the *power set* and *family sets* for the properties $(P_1...P_n)$.

6   Challenges and Future Work

Diagnosis [in a consultation with a health care professional either face-to-face or in remote telephone or on-line triage)] in the medical domain is characterized by uncertainty and imprecision, as such it presents many challenges largely driven by the highly dynamic nature of the diagnostic process and the inherent complexity of the relationship between symptoms reported by a presenting patient (including test results) and the related symptoms which characterize specific diseases and conditions.

Thus it is clear that implementing decision-support in the medical domain represents a significant challenge which to date, while expert systems have provided limited success in the diagnostic process, has seen limited success. This is evidenced by the issues in remote triage systems which frequently use of adviser's who are not medically trained, in such cases an intelligent decision support system as proposed in this paper may prove to be invaluable to all stakeholders in health-care provision.

The *Context Processing Algorithm* (CPA) (see Section 5) has been developed to implement data processing in context-aware systems, for a discussion on the CPA with evaluation and test results see [9]. The CPA is predicated on traditional fuzzy set theory and has been shown to be successful in the processing of contextual information while enabling effective CM with PM and CS [9]. The CPA enables the use of semantic descriptors, semiotics, linguistics in data modelling using qualitative, and quantitative methods along with the capability to implement valence modelling (single, bi-directional, and tri-directional methods) and *Euclidean distance* [4].

However, the CPA has limitations where decision-support in the medical domain is concerned. This limitation is the result of the complexities in the processing of symptom metrics which are not a simple Boolean match between the *input* and *output* contexts. Consider mental disorders and depression, identification and diagnosis of the condition must be considered in relation to its degree of severity measured on a spectrum which ranges from normal a persons normal state to clinical depression which may also include suicide risks.

To address the limitations in the CPA identified it is proposed that the CPA be extended to produce the *Extended Context Processing Algorithm* (ECPA). The ECPA will be designed to implement IFS [as proposed in this paper] in a rule-based system created using OBCM. A central consideration in the ECPA will be the capability to incorporate emotive response and cognitive features in the data processing to attempt to model the human brain and cognitive function which forms a central component in identifying and implementing emotive response to a broad and diverse range of stimuli.

7   Conclusion

Within health-care systems globally there are significant challenges related to *uncertainty*, this is particularly true for clinicians and health care professionals where a vital task is the diagnosis of patients. In this paper we have considered the medical domain and the challenges in reaching a definitive diagnosis, these challenges are most prevalent in the diagnosis and treatment of mental disorders such as depression and psychosis which rely on the use of both objective and subjective data plus cognitive functions. Limitations in space have restricted a detailed discussion on this topic however the approach presented in this paper has, we argue, the capability to implement the diagnosis and treatment of mental disorders which may be triggered by both physical and cognitive problems.

The approach proposed in this paper is posited as an effective approach to enable the effective provision of decision-support in intelligent context-aware systems in the medical domain for both face-to-face consultations and remote triage. The development challenges identified are non-trivial and will require intensive, long term, and multidisciplinary collaborative research however the potential results present exciting solutions to the global health-care systems.

References

1. Atanassov, K.T.: Intuitionistic fuzzy sets. Fuzzy sets and Systems **20**(1), 87–96 (1986)
2. Cuong, B.C., Kreinovich, V.: Picture fuzzy sets-a new concept for computational intelligence problems. In: Proceedings of the Third World Congress on Information and Communication Technologies (WICT 2013), pp. 1–6 (December 2013)
3. Curé, O., Lamolle, M., Duc, C.L.: Ontology based data integration over document and column family oriented nosql. arXiv preprint arXiv:1307, 2603 (2013)
4. Gower, J.C.: Euclidean distance geometry. Mathematical Scientist **7**(1), 1–14 (1982)
5. Klir, G., Yuan, B.: Fuzzy sets and fuzzy logic: theory and applications, vol. 4. Prentice Hall, New Jersey (1995)
6. Molodtsov, D.: Soft set theory–first results. Computers & Mathematics with Applications **37**(4), 19–31 (1999)
7. Moore, P., Hu, B., Zhu, X., Campbell, W., Ratcliffe, M.: A survey of context modelling for pervasive cooperative learning. In: IEEE Proceedings of the First International Symposium on Information Technologies and Applications in Education (ISITAE 2007), pp. K5-1–K5-6. IEEE (November 2007)
8. Moore, P., Qassem, T., Xhafa, F.: Nosql and electronic patient records: Opportunities and challenges. In: Proc of the 9th International Conference on P2P, Parallel, Grid, Cloud, and Internet Computing (3PGCIC 2014), Track 13: e-Health Technologies for Patient Monitoring (ETPM). IEEE (2014)
9. Moore, P., Pham, H.V.: Personalization and rule strategies in human-centric data intensive intelligent context-aware systems. The Knowledge Engineering Review **30**(2), 1–16 (2015)
10. Zadeh, L.A.: Fuzzy sets. Information and control **8**(3), 338–353 (1965)

Brief Discussion on Current Computerized Cognitive Behavioral Therapy

Hanshu Cai[1], Shixin Wei[1], Xue Han[1], Lijuan Xu[2], Xiaocong Sha[1], and Bin Hu[1(✉)]

[1] UAIS Lab, The School of Information Science and Engineering Lanzhou University,
Lanzhou 730000, China
{caihsh13,weishx13,hanx13,shaxc14,bh}@lzu.edu.cn
[2] Institute of Automation Chinese Academy of Science, Beijing 100190, China
cttwork@163.com

Abstract. Computerized cognitive-behavioral therapy (CCBT) has been given a great amount of expectation in depression treatment as an alternative or addition to antidepressant drug. Therefore CCBT has been the subject of extensive research and trial since early 1990's. This paper aims to provide a background and primer to fellow researchers who wish to contribute in future development of CCBT. In this paper, we necessarily cannot give the complete full coverage, instead we seek to provide a brief review of CCBT's effectiveness and main drawback, complemented by discussions about possible improvement that takes advantage of latest technology in sensor and data mining.

1   Background

Depression has become a major health problem in the 21st century. In US, around 10 percent of the population suffers from depression [1]; while UK alone spends £77 billion annually towards the cost of depression related mental health issues [2]. The world Health Organization (WHO) estimates about 25% of world's population will experience some episodes of depression in their life time, and has already declared depression as the fourth largest burden of disease [3], as well as the second largest cause of disability in the world by 2020 [4].

Surely, one most commonly used method to fight depression is antidepressant drugs. They are very effective, but come with adverse effects such as inducing mania, restlessness, agitation and confusion. Furthermore, once the medication ends, the therapeutic effects end as well, which results in a high rate of relapse.

Beside traditional medication treatment, a form of psychotherapy, cognitive behavioral therapy (CBT) was introduced [5]. The therapy is based upon a combination of basic behavioral and cognitive principles [6]. It does not require either detailed review of patients' history, nor the time-consuming face-to-face diagnosing. Patients could be helped after just a few sessions [7]. And the effectiveness of CBT is clinically proved [8]. However, CBT also has its drawbacks. It is a face-to-face therapy, which some patients choose to avoid from fear of stigma. And it is not cost-effective, which means it is difficult to apply in a large scale.

© Springer International Publishing Switzerland 2015
Y. Guo et al. (Eds.): BIH 2015, LNAI 9250, pp. 420–431, 2015.
DOI: 10.1007/978-3-319-23344-4_41

With help from the internet and the computer technology, we may overcome CBT's main drawbacks. The idea of computerized cognitive behavioral therapy (CCBT), also known as internet-delivered cognitive behavioral therapy (ICBT), was surfaced. Instead of face-to-face with a therapist, CBT can be delivered over internet via interfaces such as computer or mobile phone. CCBT has been found to overcome the prohibitive costs compare to the usual care[9]. As a consequence, in February 2006, the British National Institute for Clinical Excellence (NICE) recommended that CCBT be made available for use across England and Wales for depression patients [10]. A few examples of available products at present are 'Beating the Blues'[11], 'Help4Mood'[12], 'Colour Your Life' [13] and 'MoodGym'[14].

Despite the high expectation and over a decade of clinical implementation, CCBT never reach the level of coverage in neither public awareness nor clinical adaptation. So what went wrong? Is CCBT not effective at all? Or are there usability issues? Most importantly, how could we improve it? We go through the hundreds of research publications and clinical meta-reviews for answers, and following are results that we conclude.

2   Effectiveness

Cognitive behavioral therapy (CBT) is well studied and there are substantial evidence to support its effectiveness in the treatment of depression. However, it is a face-to-face psychotherapy, which means it is expensive and there will be a long waiting list. With the limited therapists, CBT is nearly impossible to be carried out in large population. Computerized CBT (CCBT) is computer based, which requires less therapist involvement and most population may use it with little computer skills.

Although CCBT follow the same principle and procedures of CBT, without the skilled therapist, whether CBT remains the same effectiveness as its predecessor remains as a popular research interest in the interdisciplinary domain of psychiatry, psychology and computer science.

2.1   Clinical Effectiveness

The earliest paper publish on the subject of clinical effectiveness of CCBT in treatment of depression is by Selmi in 1990 [15], which is using randomized controlled trial (RTC) as its experiment method. RTC is often considered the gold standard for clinical trial of effectiveness or efficacy of new medical interventions. To date, majority publications on analysis and review of CCBT are using RTC as choice of method. Table 1 shows some of these RTC based articles which all conclude the outcome of depression treatment using CCBT are effective.

Meta-analyses [19, 38-43] are also consistent with the results that CCBT helps to reduce the symptoms of depression. In systematic review from Kaltenthaler et al. [44-47], there are evidence that suggest CCBT is as effective as therapist-led cognitive

Table 1. List of trails suggest CCBT is clinical effective

Study	Country	Number of Participants	Study Duration
Clark et al.,2002 [16]	US	299	12 month
Andersson et al., 2005 [17]	Sweden	117	9 month
Wright et al., 2005 [18]	US	45	9 month
Spek et al., 2007 [19]	Netherlands	301	14 month
Warmerdamet al. 2008 [20]	Netherlands	263	15 month
de Graaf et al., 2009 [21]	Netherlands	303	15 month
Kessler et al., 2009 [22]	UK	297	12 month
Titov et al.,2010 [23]	Australia	141	9 month
Vernmark et al., 2010 [24]	Sweden	88	9 month
Berger et al., 2011 [25]	Germany	76	9 month
Farrer et al., 2011 [26]	Australia	188	9 month
Levin et al., 2011 [27]	US	191	9 month
Griffiths et al., 2012 [28]	Australia	355	15 month
Johansson et al., 2012 [29]	Sweden	121	8 month
Moritz et al., 2012 [30]	Germany	210	2 month
Carlbring et al., 2013 [31]	Sweden	80	5 month
Glozier et al., 2013 [32]	Australia	562	3 month
Lintvedt et al., 2013 [33]	Norway	163	2 month
William et al., 2013 [34]	Australia	297	3 month
O'Mahen et al., 2014 [35]	UK	249	6 month
Wagner et al., 2014 [36]	Switzerland	62	3 month
Imamura et al., 2015 [37]	Japan	381	12 month

behavioral therapy and CCBT may be more effective than treatment as usual (TAU). Griffiths et al. [28, 48, 49] conclude that most CCBT interventions were reported to be effective in reducing risk factors or improving symptoms and CCBT offers promise for use.

2.2   Cost Effectiveness

We fail to find any publication that performed an economic analysis of CCBT due to the fact that almost all of the CCBT programs that general population are facing are developed by commercial companies. As a result, all these products are in market for sales and profits. All publications are intentionally excluded the 'commercially-sensitive' information to prevent revealing their cost and profit margin. For that reason, we may never be able to access the necessary information that needed to calculated exact cost of each CCBT program nor compare the relative cost-effectiveness of rival products.

The only figure we find is from Kaltenthaler et al. [44], who illustrated the cost for 'Beating the Blues' program, per quality-adjusted life-year is estimated to be £1250. Look at the amount itself, we may feel it is a lot. However, compare to the thousands of dollars cost for CBT and drug therapy, it is significantly cheaper. Traditional therapy requires patient to take time off, in order to do face-to-face session with practitioner; on the other hand, patient could choose to start their CCBT session at their time of convenience. While CBT would put patient in a wait list first, CCBT could start as soon as needed. Therefore CCBT is a better choice for depressed patients in economic aspects.

2.3   Available Products Review

There are around a hundred products of CCBT available currently in various language. About half of them are specialty in treatments for depression. Some of the top contestants are 'Beating the Blues'[11], 'Help4Mood'[12], 'Colour Your Life' [13] and 'MoodGym'[14]. There are various studies published in measuring the effectiveness of the CCBT programs against the treatment as usual (TAU) by CBT, which delivered by general practitioners. Our four products that is given for example are among those most commonly studied.

'Beating the Blues' is developed by 'Ultrasis' in UK. It is one of the most successful CCBT system by far. In February 2006, the National Institute for Health and Clinical Excellence (NICE) recommended that 'Beating the Blues' should be made available across the NHS. It consists of eight one hour sessions. Kaltenthaler et al. have concluded that 'Beating the Blues' was effective in reducing the symptoms of depression [44-47, 50].

'Help4Mood' is a project inside 7th European Framework Programme (FP7) for developing a computational distributed system to support remotely the treatment of patients with major depression at home. 'Help4Mood' is also one of the very few CCBT system that uses interactive virtual agent. Wolters et al. suggest 'Help4Mood' is effective in improving of patients with depression [51-54].

'Colour Your Life' is based on the Dutch version of 'The Coping with Depression Course' of Lewinsohn [55, 56]. It is originally developed for patients who are over 50 years old[57] and later was adapted for general adult populations. It consists of eight 30-min sessions and a ninth booster session. Richards et al. compared 'Colour Your Life' with TAU by general practitioners, found it is just as effective as TAU [21, 58, 59].

'MoodGym' is another web based intervention system, which is designed by National Institute for Mental Health Research at The Australian National University. It consists of five modules, an interactive game, anxiety and depression assessments, downloadable relaxation audio, a workbook and feedback assessment. Griffiths et al. also found 'MoodGym' is effective in sense of overcoming depression [40, 44, 46, 48, 58, 60, 61].

At present there are quite a few papers published on the effectiveness of CCBT, which indicates above products are effective in treatment of depression. However there is no specific one product that are universally refer to, therefore comparison between these products are difficult. And so far we fail to find evidence to prove any product are superior over another for depression. Also, to our knowledge, there is no evidence to show any particular CCBT programs that are more effective than usual general practitioner (GP) care.

3   Concerns

While CCBT is treated as a new super star of depression treatment. Fellow researchers are also addressing their concerns, such as So et al. [62] address the issue of high drop-out rate as well as the excessive use of self-rating scales as measurement of outcome at the endpoints.

3.1   Attrition Rate

Although, we fail to find any publications which research solely on the subject of the acceptability or drop-out of CCBT programs. However, there are relatively large attrition rate reported in numerous studies. Table 2 is a list of attrition rate reported in some of the trials for CCBT.

Table 2. List of attrition rate reported in CCBT trials

Study	Number of Participants	Attrition Rate
Clarke et al. 2002 [16]	299	41%
Andersson et al. 2005 [17]	117	27%
Spek et al. 2007 [19]	301	40%
Warmerdam et al. 2008	263	40%
de Graaf et al. 2009 [21]	303	5%
Venrnmark et al. 2010 [24]	88	14%
Wagner et al., 2014 [36]	62	22%
O'Mahen et al., 2014 [35]	249	women 63%
Imamura et al., 2015 [37]	381	30%

Besides stunning 63% in particular women group, average attrition rate of higher 30% still puts CCBT in a much higher drop-out rate compare to other therapies. After all, CCBT is an unsupervised and computer-based treatment, which breaks doctor-patient relationship as in traditional therapy. And support and guidance from the practitioner is essential in therapeutic progress. How to re-bridge the connection or how to make the patient to be self-motivated is yet a challenge for future development of CCBT.

3.2   Excessive Use of Self-rating Scale

The second issue is that self-rating scale such as Beck Depression Inventory (BDI) is used as measurement of outcome in all CCBT programs that we find. BDI is a

21-question multiple-choice self-report inventory, and it is one of the most widely used instruments for measuring the severity of depression [63]. However, despite BDI is academically reliable as a screening tool, repeating and excessive use may not give the definitive estimate. Prusoff et al. suggest that self-report ratings from acutely depressed patients are not a reliable estimate of the severity of their symptoms [64].

On the other hand, CCBT is design to adjust and reform cognitive behavior, which may significantly influence the characteristic of self-rating scale, such as BDI by cognitive factors rather than other instrumentals due to the different conceptualization of depression among scales [62, 65, 66]. Although there is no publication to address and test whether repeating use of BDI during the CCBT progress would compromise the accuracy in what extend, we have to keep in mind the risk of overestimation of self-rating scales in current CCBT programs.

4   Discussion

Since CCBT first introduced in earlier 1990's, information technology has been advancing rapidly in both hardware and software. CCBT could take advantage of these new development to overcome its drawbacks.

Mobile devices, such as cell-phone and iPad, have gradually become necessary for everybody's daily life. Hu and Wan et al. [67, 68] used intelligent mobile computing to assist in the treatment of depression. Non-invasive Electroencephalography (EEG) system is another potential choice. As EEG is a mixture of multiple types of brain waves, how to de-noising the signal has always been a challenge. Peng and Hu et al. [69, 70] presented an approach to remove noise, such as ocular artifacts in EEG, which clears way for multiple promising applications. For instance, Zhao, Liu and Hu et al. [71, 72] applied EEG into a biometric solution for security identification; Zhao and Peng et al. used EEG for schizophrenia diagnosis [73-75] and stress monitoring [76, 77]. Depression detection using EEG is also experimented by Zhang and Peng et al. [69, 78] and prototype wearable EEG system was developed by Hu and Peng et al. [69, 79]. Although EEG-based assessment might not be as accurate as current self-rating scales, it is undeniable a very good potential option, which may either replace or work with current scales as measurement tool for severity of depression. After all, EEG signal cannot be forged and would not be influenced by cognitive factors.

Besides hardware, software such as data mining and sharing platforms could also assist. Chen, Su and Zhang et al. [80-83] developed an ontology, which defines the domain variables and relationships that could be used for automatic depression detection using the EEG system. Data mining could as well be applied to analysis patient's diary and therapy log to better diagnose the progress of the therapy. Better graphic software could design more vivid virtual agents, which may bring more human-like support to the patient. All these small improvement would eventually add up and keep patient self-motived.

5   Conclusions

In this paper, we have shown that there are sufficient evidence to show CCBT is clinical effective, and some researchers even conclude CCBT is even more effective than treatment as usual (TAU). Evidences also suggest that use of CCBT results in reduction of therapist time in comparison with traditional CBT. However, studies noticed high drop-out rate, and some expressed the concern of excessive use of self-rating scales as primary outcome assessment tool in current CCBT. We believe the evolving technology could contribute to the future development of CCBT. Non-invasive sensor system, such as electroencephalograph (EEG), could be the integrated to make better and more advanced measurement instrument, while data mining and better presentation could help to keep patient self-motivated to complete the treatment.

Acknowledgment. This work was supported by the National Basic Research Program of China (973 Program) (No.2014CB744600, No.2011CB711000), the Program of International S&T Cooperation of MOST (No.2013DFA11140), the National Natural Science Foundation of China (grant No.61210010, No.61300231).

References

1. Robins, L.N., Regier, D.A.: Psychiatric disorders in America: the epidemiologic catchment area study. Free Press (1991)
2. Minister, O.o.t.D.P.: Mental health and social exclusion. Social Exclusion Unit report. ODPM London (2004)
3. Organization, W.H.: The World health report: 2001: Mental health: new understanding, new hope (2001)
4. Murray, C.J., Lopez, A.D.: Alternative projections of mortality and disability by cause 1990–2020: Global Burden of Disease Study. The Lancet **349**, 1498–1504 (1997)
5. Beck, A.T.: Depression: Clinical, experimental, and theoretical aspects. Hoeber Medical Division, Harper & Row (1967)
6. Beck, J.S.: Cognitive behavior therapy: Basics and beyond. Guilford Press (2011)
7. Excellence, N.I.f.C., Health, N.C.C.f.M.: Depression: management of depression in primary and secondary care. National Institute for Clinical Excellence (2004)
8. Driessen, E., Hollon, S.D.: Cognitive behavioral therapy for mood disorders: efficacy, moderators and mediators. Psychiatric Clinics of North America **33**, 537–555 (2010)
9. Musiat, P., Tarrier, N.: Collateral outcomes in e-mental health: a systematic review of the evidence for added benefits of computerized cognitive behavior therapy interventions for mental health. Psychological medicine **44**, 3137–3150 (2014)
10. Excellence, N.I.f.C.: Computerised cognitive behaviour therapy for depression and anxiety: Technology Appraisal 97. National Institute for Clinical Excellence, London (2006)
11. See: www.ultrasis.com
12. See: www.help4mood.info
13. See: www.colouryourlife.net
14. See: www.moodgym.anu.edu.au

15. Selmi, P.M., Klein, M.H., Greist, J.H., Sorrell, S.P., Erdman, H.P.: Computer-administered cognitive-behavioral therapy for depression. The American journal of psychiatry **147**, 51 (1990)
16. Clarke, G., Reid, D.E., O'Connor, E., DeBar, L.L., Kelleher, C., Lynch, F., Nunley, S.: Overcoming depression on the Internet (ODIN): a randomized controlled trial of an Internet depression skills intervention program. Journal of Medical Internet Research **4** (2002)
17. Andersson, G., Bergström, J., Holländare, F., Carlbring, P., Kaldo, V., Ekselius, L.: Internet-based self-help for depression: randomised controlled trial. The British Journal of Psychiatry **187**, 456–461 (2005)
18. Wright, J.H., Wright, A.S., Albano, A.M., Basco, M.R., Goldsmith, L.J., Raffield, T., Otto, M.W.: Computer-assisted cognitive therapy for depression: maintaining efficacy while reducing therapist time. American Journal of Psychiatry (2005)
19. Spek, V., Cuijpers, P., Nyklícek, I., Riper, H., Keyzer, J., Pop, V.: Internet-based cognitive behaviour therapy for symptoms of depression and anxiety: a meta-analysis. Psychological medicine **37**, 319–328 (2007)
20. Warmerdam, L., van Straten, A., Twisk, J., Riper, H., Cuijpers, P.: Internet-based treatment for adults with depressive symptoms: randomized controlled trial. Journal of Medical Internet Research **10** (2008)
21. de Graaf, L.E., Gerhards, S., Arntz, A., Riper, H., Metsemakers, J., Evers, S., Severens, J., Widdershoven, G., Huibers, M.: Clinical effectiveness of online computerised cognitive–behavioural therapy without support for depression in primary care: randomised trial. The British Journal of Psychiatry **195**, 73–80 (2009)
22. Kessler, D., Lewis, G., Kaur, S., Wiles, N., King, M., Weich, S., Sharp, D.J., Araya, R., Hollinghurst, S., Peters, T.J.: Therapist-delivered Internet psychotherapy for depression in primary care: a randomised controlled trial. The Lancet **374**, 628–634 (2009)
23. Titov, N., Andrews, G., Davies, M., McIntyre, K., Robinson, E., Solley, K.: Internet treatment for depression: a randomized controlled trial comparing clinician vs. technician assistance. PloS one **5**, e10939 (2010)
24. Vernmark, K., Lenndin, J., Bjärehed, J., Carlsson, M., Karlsson, J., Öberg, J., Carlbring, P., Eriksson, T., Andersson, G.: Internet administered guided self-help versus individualized e-mail therapy: A randomized trial of two versions of CBT for major depression. Behaviour research and therapy **48**, 368–376 (2010)
25. Berger, T., Hämmerli, K., Gubser, N., Andersson, G., Caspar, F.: Internet-based treatment of depression: a randomized controlled trial comparing guided with unguided self-help. Cognitive behaviour therapy **40**, 251–266 (2011)
26. Farrer, L., Christensen, H., Griffiths, K.M., Mackinnon, A.: Internet-based CBT for depression with and without telephone tracking in a national helpline: randomised controlled trial. PloS one **6**, e28099 (2011)
27. Levin, W., Campbell, D., McGovern, K., Gau, J., Kosty, D., Seeley, J., Lewinsohn, P.: A computer-assisted depression intervention in primary care. Psychological medicine **41**, 1373–1383 (2011)
28. Griffiths, K.M., Mackinnon, A.J., Crisp, D.A., Christensen, H., Bennett, K., Farrer, L.: The effectiveness of an online support group for members of the community with depression: a randomised controlled trial. PLoS One **7**, e53244 (2012)
29. Johansson, R., Sjöberg, E., Sjögren, M., Johnsson, E., Carlbring, P., Andersson, T., Rousseau, A., Andersson, G.: Tailored vs. standardized internet-based cognitive behavior therapy for depression and comorbid symptoms: a randomized controlled trial. PLoS One **7**, e36905 (2012)

30. Moritz, S., Schilling, L., Hauschildt, M., Schröder, J., Treszl, A.: A randomized controlled trial of internet-based therapy in depression. Behaviour research and therapy **50**, 513–521 (2012)
31. Carlbring, P., Hägglund, M., Luthström, A., Dahlin, M., Kadowaki, Å., Vernmark, K., Andersson, G.: Internet-based behavioral activation and acceptance-based treatment for depression: a randomized controlled trial. Journal of Affective Disorders **148**, 331–337 (2013)
32. Glozier, N., Christensen, H., Naismith, S., Cockayne, N., Donkin, L., Neal, B., Mackinnon, A., Hickie, I.: Internet-delivered cognitive behavioural therapy for adults with mild to moderate depression and high cardiovascular disease risks: a randomised attention-controlled trial (2013)
33. Lintvedt, O.K., Griffiths, K.M., Sørensen, K., Østvik, A.R., Wang, C.E., Eisemann, M., Waterloo, K.: Evaluating the effectiveness and efficacy of unguided internet-based self-help intervention for the prevention of depression: a randomized controlled trial. Clinical psychology & psychotherapy **20**, 10–27 (2013)
34. Williams, A.D., Blackwell, S.E., Mackenzie, A., Holmes, E.A., Andrews, G.: Combining imagination and reason in the treatment of depression: a randomized controlled trial of internet-based cognitive-bias modification and internet-CBT for depression. Journal of consulting and clinical psychology **81**, 793 (2013)
35. O'Mahen, H., Richards, D., Woodford, J., Wilkinson, E., McGinley, J., Taylor, R., Warren, F.: Netmums: a phase II randomized controlled trial of a guided Internet behavioural activation treatment for postpartum depression. Psychological medicine **44**, 1675–1689 (2014)
36. Wagner, B., Horn, A.B., Maercker, A.: Internet-based versus face-to-face cognitive-behavioral intervention for depression: A randomized controlled non-inferiority trial. Journal of affective disorders **152**, 113–121 (2014)
37. Imamura, K., Kawakami, N., Furukawa, T., Matsuyama, Y., Shimazu, A., Umanodan, R., Kawakami, S., Kasai, K.: Does Internet-based cognitive behavioral therapy (iCBT) prevent major depressive episode for workers? A 12-month follow-up of a randomized controlled trial. Psychological medicine **45**, 1907–1917 (2015)
38. Gellatly, J., Bower, P., Hennessy, S., Richards, D., Gilbody, S., Lovell, K.: What makes self-help interventions effective in the management of depressive symptoms? Meta-analysis and meta-regression. Psychological medicine **37**, 1217–1228 (2007)
39. Barak, A., Hen, L., Boniel-Nissim, M., Shapira, N.A.: A comprehensive review and a meta-analysis of the effectiveness of internet-based psychotherapeutic interventions. Journal of Technology in Human Services **26**, 109–160 (2008)
40. Andersson, G., Cuijpers, P.: Internet-based and other computerized psychological treatments for adult depression: a meta-analysis. Cognitive behaviour therapy **38**, 196–205 (2009)
41. Andrews, G., Cuijpers, P., Craske, M.G., McEvoy, P., Titov, N.: Computer therapy for the anxiety and depressive disorders is effective, acceptable and practical health care: a meta-analysis. PloS one **5**, e13196 (2010)
42. Foroushani, P.S., Schneider, J., Assareh, N.: Meta-review of the effectiveness of computerised CBT in treating depression. BMC psychiatry **11**, 131 (2011)
43. Grist, R., Cavanagh, K.: Computerised cognitive behavioural therapy for common mental health disorders, what works, for whom under what circumstances? A systematic review and meta-analysis. Journal of Contemporary Psychotherapy **43**, 243–251 (2013)

44. Kaltenthaler, E., Brazier, J., De Nigris, E., Tumur, I., Ferriter, M., Beverley, C., Parry, G., Rooney, G., Sutcliffe, P.: Computerised cognitive behaviour therapy for depression and anxiety update: a systematic review and economic evaluation. Health technology assessment **10**, 1–186 (2006)
45. Kaltenthaler, E., Parry, G., Beverley, C.: Computerized cognitive behaviour therapy: a systematic review. Behavioural and Cognitive Psychotherapy **32**, 31–55 (2004)
46. Kaltenthaler, E., Parry, G., Beverley, C., Ferriter, M.: Computerised cognitive–behavioural therapy for depression: systematic review. The British Journal of Psychiatry **193**, 181–184 (2008)
47. Kaltenthaler, E., Shackley, P., Stevens, K., Beverley, C., Parry, G., Chilcott, J.: A systematic review and economic evaluation of computerised cognitive behaviour therapy for depression and anxiety (2002)
48. Griffiths, K.M., Christensen, H.: Review of randomised controlled trials of Internet interventions for mental disorders and related conditions. Clinical Psychologist **10**, 16–29 (2006)
49. Griffiths, K.M., Farrer, L., Christensen, H.: The efficacy of internet interventions for depression and anxiety disorders: a review of randomised controlled trials. Medical Journal of Australia **192**, S4 (2010)
50. Ferriter, M., Kaltenthaler, E., Parry, G., Beverley, C.: Computerised CBT: a review. Mental health today (Brighton, England), pp. 30–31 (2008)
51. Wolters, M.K., Burton, C.D., Matheson, C., Breso, A., Szentagotai, A., Martinez-Miranda, J., Rosell, J., Fuster, E., Pagliari, C., McKinstry, B.: Help4Mood supporting joint sense making in the treatment of major depressive disorder. In: WISH 2013 Workshop on Interactive Systems in Healthcare (2013)
52. de Cerio, D.P.-D., Valenzuela, J., Ruiz, S., Garcia-Lozano, M., Colome, J.: Help4Mood: A computational distributed system to support the treatment of patients with major depression. COST IC1004, TD (11) 1039 (2011)
53. Martínez-Miranda, J., Bresó, A., García-Gómez, J.M.: Modelling therapeutic empathy in a virtual agent to support the remote treatment of major depression. In: ICAART, vol. 2, pp. 264–269 (2012)
54. Burton, C., McKinstry, B., Tătar, A.S., Serrano-Blanco, A., Pagliari, C., Wolters, M.: Activity monitoring in patients with depression: a systematic review. Journal of affective disorders **145**, 21–28 (2013)
55. Cuijpers, W.J.M.J., Bonarius, M., van den Heuvel, A.: De'omgaan met depressie'cursus: een handreiking voor begeleiders en organisatoren. NcGv/LOP (1995)
56. Lewinsohn, P.M.: The coping with depression course: A psychoeducational intervention for unipolar depression. Castalia (1984)
57. Spek, V., Nyklíček, I., Smits, N., Cuijpers, P., Riper, H., Keyzer, J., Pop, V.: Internet-based cognitive behavioural therapy for subthreshold depression in people over 50 years old: a randomized controlled clinical trial. Psychological medicine **37**, 1797–1806 (2007)
58. Wade, A.G.: Use of the internet to assist in the treatment of depression and anxiety: a systematic review. Primary Care Companion to the Journal of Clinical Psychiatry **12** (2010)
59. Richards, D., Richardson, T.: Computer-based psychological treatments for depression: a systematic review and meta-analysis. Clinical psychology review **32**, 329–342 (2012)
60. Titov, N.: Internet-delivered psychotherapy for depression in adults. Current Opinion in Psychiatry **24**, 18–23 (2011)
61. Christensen, H., Griffiths, K.M., Jorm, A.F.: Delivering interventions for depression by using the internet: randomised controlled trial. Bmj. **328**, 265 (2004)

62. So, M., Yamaguchi, S., Hashimoto, S., Sado, M., Furukawa, T.A., McCrone, P.: Is compu-terised CBT really helpful for adult depression?-A meta-analytic re-evaluation of CCBT for adult depression in terms of clinical implementation and methodological validity. BMC psychiatry **13**, 113 (2013)

63. Beck, A., Ward, C., Mendelson, M., Moctc, J., Erbaugh, J.: An inventory for measuring depression. Archives of General Psychiatry **4**(6), 561–571 (1961)

64. Prusoff, B.A., Klerman, G.L., Paykel, E.S.: Concordance between clinical assessments and patients' self-report in depression. Archives of General Psychiatry **26**, 546–552 (1972)

65. Lambert, M.J., Hatch, D.R., Kingston, M.D., Edwards, B.C.: Zung, Beck, and Hamilton Rating Scales as measures of treatment outcome: a meta-analytic comparison. Journal of Consulting and Clinical Psychology **54**, 54 (1986)

66. Moran, P.W.: A review of current assessment tools for monitoring changes in depression (1982)

67. Hu, B., Moore, P., Wan, J.: Ontology Based Mobile Monitoring and Treatment against Depression. Wireless Communications and Mobile Computing, Special Issue on Pervasive Computing Technology and its Applications, 1–16 (2008)

68. Wan, J., Hu, B., Moore, P., Ashford, R.: Intelligent Mobile Computing to Assist in the Treatment of Depression. In: 2008 Third International Conference on Pervasive Compu-ting and Applications. (2008)

69. Peng, H., Hu, B., Liu, Q., Dong, Q., Zhao, Q., Moore, P.: User-centered depression pre-vention: An EEG approach to pervasive healthcare. In: 2011 5th International Conference on Pervasive Computing Technologies for Healthcare (PervasiveHealth), pp. 325–330. IEEE (2011)

70. Peng, H., Hu, B., Qi, Y., Zhao, Q., Ratcliffe, M.: An improved EEG de-noising approach in electroencephalogram (EEG) for home care. In: 2011 5th International Conference on Pervasive Computing Technologies for Healthcare (PervasiveHealth), pp. 469–474. IEEE (2011)

71. Zhao, Q., Peng, H., Hu, B., Li, L., Qi, Y., Liu, Q., Liu, L.: Towards an efficient and accu-rate EEG data analysis in EEG-based individual identification. In: Yu, Z., Liscano, R., Chen, G., Zhang, D., Zhou, X. (eds.) UIC 2010. LNCS, vol. 6406, pp. 534–547. Springer, Heidelberg (2010)

72. Zhao, Q., Peng, H., Hu, B., Liu, Q., Liu, L., Qi, Y., Li, L.: Improving individual identifica-tion in security check with an EEG based biometric solution. In: Yao, Y., Sun, R., Poggio, T., Liu, J., Zhong, N., Huang, J. (eds.) BI 2010. LNCS, vol. 6334, pp. 145–155. Springer, Heidelberg (2010)

73. Zhao, Q., Hu, B., Li, Y., Peng, H., Li, L., Liu, Q., Li, Y., Shi, Q., Feng, J.: An Alpha rest-ing EEG study on nonlinear dynamic analysis for schizophrenia. In: 2013 6th International IEEE/EMBS Conference on Neural Engineering (NER), pp. 484–488. IEEE (2013)

74. Peng, H., Hu, B., Li, L., Ratcliffe, M., Zhai, J., Zhao, Q., Shi, Q., Li, Y., Liu, Q.: A study on validity of cortical alpha connectivity for schizophrenia. In: 2013 35th Annual Interna-tional Conference of the IEEE Engineering in Medicine and Biology Society (EMBC), pp. 3286–3290. IEEE (2013)

75. Zhao, Q., Hu, B., Liu, L., Ratcliffe, M., Peng, H., Zhai, J., Li, L., Shi, Q., Liu, Q., Qi, Y.: An EEG based nonlinearity analysis method for schizophrenia diagnosis. Biomedical En-gineering **9**, 136 (2012)

76. Zhao, G., Hu, B., Li, X., Mao, C., Huang, R.: A pervasive stress monitoring system based on biological signals. In: 2013 Ninth International Conference on Intelligent Information Hiding and Multimedia Signal Processing, pp. 530–534. IEEE (2013)

77. Peng, H., Hu, B., Zheng, F., Fan, D., Zhao, W., Chen, X., Yang, Y., Cai, Q.: A method of identifying chronic stress by EEG. Personal and ubiquitous computing 17, 1341–1347 (2013)
78. Zhang, X., Hu, B., Zhou, L., Moore, P., Chen, J.: An EEG based pervasive depression detection for females. In: Zu, Q., Hu, B., Elçi, A. (eds.) ICPCA 2012 and SWS 2012. LNCS, vol. 7719, pp. 848–861. Springer, Heidelberg (2013)
79. Hu, B., Majoe, D., Ratcliffe, M., Qi, Y., Zhao, Q., Peng, H., Fan, D., Zheng, F., Jackson, M., Moore, P.: EEG-based cognitive interfaces for ubiquitous applications: Developments and challenges. IEEE Intelligent Systems 26, 46–53 (2011)
80. Zhang, X., Hu, B., Chen, J., Moore, P.: Ontology-based context modeling for emotion recognition in an intelligent web. World Wide Web 16, 497–513 (2013)
81. Su, Y., Hu, B., Xu, L., Cai, H., Moore, P., Zhang, X., Chen, J.: EmotionO+: physiological signals knowledge representation and emotion reasoning model for mental health monitoring. In: 2014 IEEE International Conference on Bioinformatics and Biomedicine (BIBM), pp. 529–535. IEEE (2014)
82. Chen, J., Hu, B., Moore, P., Zhang, X., Ma, X.: Electroencephalogram-based emotion assessment system using ontology and data mining techniques. Applied Soft Computing 30, 663–674 (2015)
83. Zhang, X., Hu, B., Ma, X., Moore, P., Chen, J.: Ontology driven decision support for the diagnosis of mild cognitive impairment. Computer methods and programs in biomedicine 113, 781–791 (2014)

Symposium on Modelling Brain Information

A Middleware for Integrating Cognitive Architectures

Karina Jaime[1]($\boxtimes$), Armando Cervantes[1], Ory Medina[1], Felix Ramos[1],
Jonathan-Hernando Rosales[1], Gustavo Torres[2], and Marco Ramos[3]

[1] Department of Computer Science, Cinvestav Unidad Guadalajara,
Zapopan, Mexico
{ajaime,acervantes,omedina,framos,jrosales}@gdl.cinvestav.mx
[2] Department of Computer Science, Universidad Autonoma de Guadalajara,
Zapopan, Mexico
gustavo.blanco@edu.uag.mx
[3] Department of Computer Science, Universidad Autonoma del Estado de Mexico,
Toluca, Mexico
marco.corchado@gmail.com

Abstract. The features of distributed systems help to solve problems in different research areas like fault tolerance, use of distributed resources, etc. The relevant cognitive architectures (CA) use middleware (distributed systems concept) to test its models and propose new theories. Thanks to a middleware, the researchers may conceive CAs as a whole, not as a set of components. However, most of the middlewares used in present CAs are modifications of generic ones, which leads to extra processing affecting the whole performance. In this research, we propose a middleware designed and developed taking into account the requirements of CAs. Our middleware allows us the integration of different cognitive functions, like memory and attention developed independently in an easily and incrementally. Also our middleware allows us test the cognitive functions integrated in the CA. To test our proposal, the middleware simulates an attention-novelty handling cognitive process.

Keywords: Middleware · Cognitive architectures · Developing tool

1 Introduction

A CA is a theoretical structure with a set of mechanisms for human cognition [1]. CAs provide the required infrastructure for an intelligent system [2]. A middleware is an abstraction layer that offers a way to communicate software over a network regardless of the hardware or platform [3]. Some CAs use middlewares as developing and testing tool.

In particular, our research group is developing a cognitive architecture based on neuroscience results. Such architecture has eight cognitive functions: memory, attention, emotion, perception, motor, motivation, planning and decision-making. Each cognitive functions is being developed by one or two researchers.

© Springer International Publishing Switzerland 2015
Y. Guo et al. (Eds.): BIH 2015, LNAI 9250, pp. 435–444, 2015.
DOI: 10.1007/978-3-319-23344-4_42

We needed a tool for integrating all the knowledge generated by the group. We believed a middleware could solve this problem. There are many general purpose middlewares and a few specific middlewares for develop CAs. Below, we describe the most notable middlewares.

CORBA [4,5] is a general propose middleware designed to solve the recurrent issues of distributed system as transparent location, language interaction, interface descriptions and concurrent access. CORBA uses a mechanism to communicate and invoke methods on objects that can be at different locations and in a different language in an entirely transparent way to the user. CORBA is a robust system, full of security mechanisms. These mechanism are not necessary for because the lost of information is not a issue for our model.

BALT & CAST [6] is a tool designed to solve recurrent problems in cognitive robot implementations. It follows the CoSy Architecture Schema (CAS)[7], which is based in the intercommunication between sub-architectures. Each subarchitecture has an individual working memory and a task manager. BALT & CAST works with an abstraction layer on top of CORBA and has a software called CAS Toolkit that provides abstract classes to create key components of a CAS architecture. However, BALT & CAST is documented insufficiently and has a very restrictive construction for our purposes.

Yet Another Robot Platform (YARP) [8] is a middleware developed with the purpose of making it easier for the researchers to implement their algorithms in real time, without infrastructure issues. The cognitive architecture for humanoid robots iCub [9] uses YARP for its implementation. YARP runs in a cluster of network-connected computers and distributes the work over them. YARP works whit the Observer patron. Since YARP is oriented to robotics, it provides many features that we do not need and affect the system's performance.

LIDA [10] is a framework for general artificial intelligence. In LIDA, any agent acts based on its current status. LIDA divides the agent's behaviours into cognitive cycles. LIDA force the agents to work under its cognitive cycle, which is not compatible with our approach.

[11] proposed a middleware based on interconnected modules that represent brain areas, and each module is a node running in the network. Each brain area can communicate with any other. This middleware provides a set of tools to test cognitive function models. The middleware makes the communication processes transparent to the researchers, allowing them to focus on the modelling stage. [11] has a central component (MAINMIDDLEWARE). If the component crashes, the entire system breaks down. They proposal is the closest one to the desired tool. However, its centralized architecture is against our distributed approach.

In this paper, we present a middleware for the development of cognitive architectures with a fully distributed approach. This middleware abstracts the components of the brain and their communication, providing a platform to segment behaviours allowing an effortless integration. Section 2 describes the proposal middleware. Section 3 presents the implementation of a simple cognitive architecture using the middleware as its core. It also shows the results obtained with a neuroscience experiment. Section 4 discusses the middleware by giving an overview of the results and the goals. It also lists the future work.

2   Middleware for Cognitive Architecures

There are three important and complementary ways to describe distributed systems: physical models, architectural models, and fundamental models [12]. We chose the architectural model because it separately describe distributed system components and its interrelationships [12]. The middleware followed the object-oriented design for distributed system architectures. It is message-oriented, asynchronous, and no-wait send. It is also small-scale and in the way to be open. The security is not essential in the current middleware stage. The middleware is heterogeneous; it runs on different operating systems thanks to the multi-platform features of Java.

The proposed middleware took the principles from [11]. Each process is a node. Each node represents a brain area. The nodes run on different platforms, and they send messages with their generated information.

2.1   Communication Entities

The system has two primary structures (see Figure 1): big nodes (BN) and small nodes (SN). The BNs are computational abstractions of brain areas. The SNs are sub-process solving the petitions made to the big nodes.

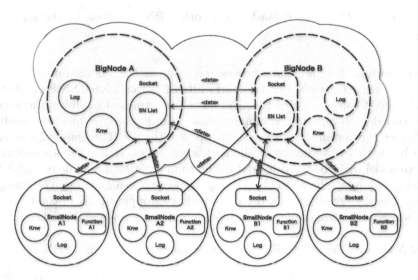

Fig. 1. MW Communication Entities. The circles with continuous line are big node. The circles with dashed lines are the small nodes.

Big Nodes. A cognitive architecture (CA) is a theoretical structure with a set of A BN is node/process running in the middleware. Each BN is independent of the others. BNs are computational abstractions of a brain structure; they can only represent one brain area at the time, and only one BN represents a brain area at the time. For example, a BN could represent the brain area Perirhinal Cortex. The BNs send and receive messages inspired by neuron synapses process. The sum of these messages could cause an action. The combination of actions generates behavior or other action. In [13], the BNs are the CA3, CA1, among others. The BNs together identify objects from a virtual environment.

BNs have three principal modules (see Figure 1): the logger, the knowledge storage, and the communication module. The logger registers all the events that happen in the BN. The knowledge storage has a list with the known nodes addresses. It has the knowledge of what to make with the data. The communication module manages the incoming requests. The BNs use peer-to-peer and multicast communication. The multicast communication is only used for searches and registers; the rest of their communication is peer-to-peer. BNs are concurrent servers; they pass the request to an external process (SN), after which it immediately waits for the next incoming request [14]. They also act as clients in some situations. Next, the BN's functions as servers and as clients are listed.

Big Node as a Server A BN registers other BN's addresses. It registers only its SNs. It has a list with the available SNs. It creates SNs for solving petitions. It stores information pieces temporally until they are sent to SNs. It deletes useless SNs. It searches BNs on its internal registers.

Big Node as a Client A BN asks for another BN's address to the multicast group.

Small Nodes. SNs are node/process running in the middleware. Each SN always belongs to one BN and does part of its BN's work. Each SN is created by its BN, and it can be deleted too. SNs have four principal modules: the logger, the knowledge storage, the communication module and the function module. The logger register all the events that happen in the SN. The knowledge storage has a list with the addresses of all the known nodes. It has the knowledge of what to make with the incoming data. The communication module manages the incoming requests. The SNs only use peer-to-peer communication. The function module has the definition of a BN process. For example, A SN in the CA3 [13] creates new codes from others. The SNs function as servers and as clients.

Small Node as a Server An SN does one or more functions of its BN.

Small Node as a Client An SN is registered on its BN and some other SN. It can ask for big node addresses. It can ask for another small node address. It lets its big node know when it is available.

Naming. Every node in the middleware has a four bytes unique identifier (besides the IP and the Port). The first two bytes in the identifier have a counter with the number of the BN, the other two bytes contain nothing when the identifier belongs to a BN. In the SN case, they have a counter with the number of the SN. The identifier serves two purposes: it differentiates one node from other, it discriminates a BN from an SN. Thanks to the distinction between BNs and SNs identifiers. A BNs chooses if stores or not the address of an SN because an SN can disappear after sending the message.

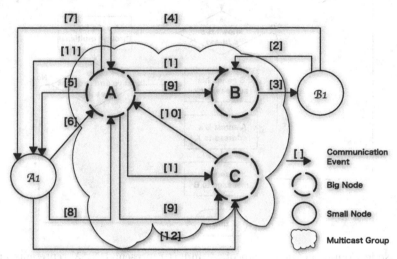

Fig. 2. MW Interaction Example. [1] A is presented in the multicast group. [2] B_1 ask for A's address. [3] B responds with A's address. [4] B_1 sends information to A as B. [5] A creates a new small node and temporally stores the received data. [6] A_1 is presented to A. [7] A re-sends the data to A_1 and remove the data from the storage. [8] A_1 asks for C's address. [9] A asks for C's address to the multicast group. [10] C responds with its address. [11] A sends C's address to A_1. [12] A_1 sends the data to C as A.

Node Communication Protocols. A BN is mainly a message commutator. Once the BN starts, it opens a peer-to-peer and multicast socket. The BN connects to a multicast group and sends his peer-to-peer address. The multicast group is hard-coded in the middleware, this is the way the middleware keeps location transparent. Only the BNs register in the multicast group to avoid a router overload and keep a simple architecture. When a BN receives a package, it reads the operation code in the header to choose what to do with the package. The package can be processed, stored, forwarded to an SN or dropped. The data package structure has a operation code, data type (type of information), and the data. Almost the rest of the package only contains the operation code.

The human brain can suffer the loss of information (packets) during communication [15]; for that reason, the loss of packets in our middleware is irrelevant. This fact allows us to use the UDP paradigm for peer-to-peer communication between the nodes.

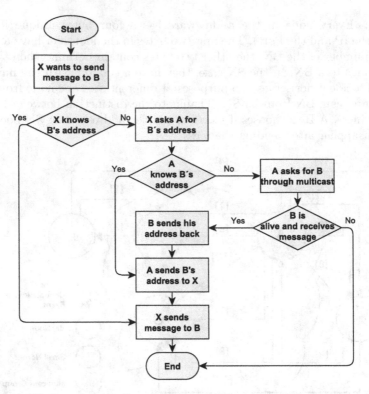

Fig. 3. Node Communication Protocol. A and B represent BN. X represents an SN that belongs to A.

The middleware allows communication between any pair of nodes, as long as they know each others address. In order to ensure this, they follow a protocol for address discovery. The protocol is described in Figure 3.

There are three main types of messages: search, find and data. The search messages are for requesting a node's address. The find messages are to communicate a node's address. The data messages contains generated information for the SN. This type of encapsulation helps to have a transparent communication layer to the end user. Figure 2 shows a communication example.

3   Habituation to Novelty

[16] presents an agent cognitive architecture based on neuroscientific evidence, said architecture simulates the processes of visual attention and novelty handling of the human brain. The architecture is divided into three sections or processing stages: A)Visual Processing, B)Novelty Handling and C)Attentional Selection, each section is formed by a set of modules which abstract each a brain structure. This section describes the abstraction necessary to implement the *Novelty Handling* (Figure 4) processing stage in the middleware. This section also describes the results obtained from testing the architecture on a case study, which is based on the experiment used on [17].

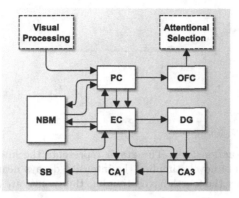

Fig. 4. Model of visual attention and response to novelty. Processing stage: Novelty handling [16].

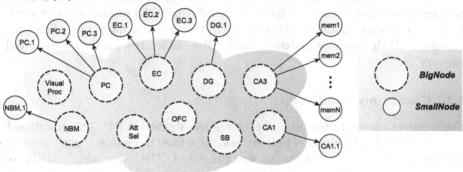

Fig. 5. Cognitive architecture implemented in the middleware. Certain nodes like *VisualProc* and *SB* do not require SmallNodes; *PC, EC, DG, CA1 and NBM* use SmallNodes as process nodes; *CA1* uses SmallNodes as process units, as well as storage units.

3.1   Implementation

In order to implement the cognitive architecture using the middleware, every module and process needs to be abstracted to the middleware standard, assuming a BigNode for each module and SmallNodes for the processes of each module (Figure 5). In some cases, a process can be implemented at BigNode level

The node VisalProc is used as the beginning point of the architecture, this node runs the experiment. SB and OFC are used solely as information relays, their only job is to relay the data received to the next structure/module. PC and EC have both a relay function, this allows to relay the information received from the visual processing module directly to the next structure without smallNodes, however, they also need to perform certain tasks when the information is coming from a different structure, these tasks are performed in smallNodes. DG, CA1 and NBM have only one task, however this task must be performed simultaneously for every received stimulus, this is done by creating a new smallNode

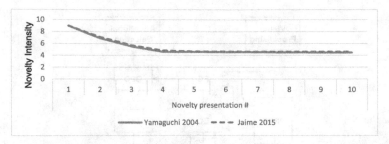

Fig. 6. Novelty habituation level. The graph represents the intensity of the novelty after 10 presentations of novel stimulus, the intensity decays near to half the original and then stabilizes after the fourth novel stimulus, this results are consistent with those obtained by [17].

every time the node receives data. CA3 uses the smallNodes as storage units, each smallNode stores a single "memory". Each time CA3 receives data, it sends it to all of it's smallNodes, which compare the received data with their own "memory". If the memory matches, the small node sends a packet of "retrieved memory".

3.2 Case Study and Results

The architecture was tested using the experiment defined in [17]. The experiment consists of a bi-field visual selection task, in which the subject must press a button each time a target stimulus was presented. The experiment consists of six sessions with an inter-session period of 5 minutes. Each session consists of 5 blocks with a duration of 36 seconds each. Each block starts with an arrow that indicates the visual field to attend (left or right), followed by a set of stimuli presented semi-randomly. The stimuli set consists of three kind of stimulus, the standard stimulus (an equilateral triangle), the target stimulus (a tilted equilateral triangle) and novel stimuli (images that have never been seen by the subject). It is necessary to mention that this experiment only observes the levels of habituation to novel stimulus.

The experiment was performed 30 times and the results averaged. The scale used to measure the novelty is the same used by Yamaguchi [17]. The results were compared to those obtained by [17] regarding novelty habituation (Fig 6).

This implementation along with the middleware and manuals can be found at http://niclab.com/portal/mw

4   Discussion and Conclusions

To test our proposal and show it in this article, we used the middleware to implement the attention-novelty handling architecture as was described in the previous section. The results prove that our middleware allows the researchers to focus entirely on the design and modeling of each cognitive function of the cognitive architecture, releasing them from the hassle of handling communication and platform issues. However, the middleware has been used in several master thesis and published articles ([18] [13] [19] [20] [21] [22] [23] [24]) and each time it allows the user to focus on the cognitive function it proposes.

On the other hand, despite the fact that the proposed middleware is designed to meet the specific requirements of CAs, the experiences prove that its use is not a restricted for CAs. It is useful for different applications like multi-agent systems. The middleware's behavior based on the type nodes, enable the middleware to be used in solutions based on instance on agents. For example in the case of agents the little nodes can behave as neurons for neural networks or classifiers, or in the case of pervasive services the small nodes can behave as mobile services and BNs as managers. These characteristics mean that our proposal is not limited to CAs but can be useful for different applications, and even more, a CA running in the middleware can connect with external applications that represent the world.

Finally, we continue working to offer a complete tool that frees the users (CA designers) from trivial work. This tool will get at the level of just drawing the connections graphically. That means that our tool will abstract: communications, message types between components, and different types of small nodes. The tool will also use a descriptive language to describe the connections.

Acknowledgments. We would like to thank CINVESTAV and CONACyT for the support provided to the realization of this research project.

References

1. Kieras, D.E., Meyer, D.E.: An overview of the epic architecture for cognition and performance with application to human-computer interaction. Hum.-Comput. Interact. **12**, 391–438 (1997)
2. Langley, P.: Cognitive architectures and general intelligent systems. AI Magazine **27**, 33–44 (2006)
3. Coulouris, G., Dollimore, J., Kindberg, T., Blair, G.: Characterization of distributed systems. In: Distributed Systems. Concepts and Designs, 5 edn., pp. 1–36. Addison Wesley (2012)
4. OMG: The common object request broker: Architecture and specification. OMG Document Number 91.12.1 (1991)
5. Puder, A., Romer, K., Pilhofer, F.: Introduction. In: Distributed Systems Architecture A Middleware Approach, pp. 1–6. Elsevier Morgan Kaufmann Publishers (2006)
6. Hawes, N., Zillich, M., Wyatt, J.: Balt & cast: middleware for cognitive robotics. In: The 16th IEEE International Symposium on Robot and Human interactive Communication, RO-MAN 2007, pp. 998–1003, August 2005
7. Hawes, N., Wyatt, J., Sloman, A.: An architecture schema for embodied cognitive systems. School of Computer Science Research Reports-University of Birmingham CSR 12 (2006)
8. Metta, G., Fitzpatrick, P., Natale, L.: Yarp: Yet another robot platform. International Journal of Advanced Robotic Systems (2006)

9. Sandini, G., Metta, G., Vernon, D.: The *iCub* cognitive humanoid robot: an open-system research platform for enactive cognition. In: Lungarella, M., Iida, F., Bongard, J.C., Pfeifer, R. (eds.) 50 Years of Aritficial Intelligence. LNCS (LNAI), vol. 4850, pp. 358–369. Springer, Heidelberg (2007)
10. Franklin, S., Patterson Jr, F.G.: The lida architecture adding new models of learning to an intelligent, autonomous software agent. Integrated Design and Process Technology **703**, 764–1004 (2006)
11. Torres, G., Jaime, K., Ramos, F.: Brain architecture for visual object identification. International Journal of Cognitive Informatics and Natural Intelligence (IJCINI) **7**(1), 75–97 (2013)
12. Coulouris, G., Dollimore, J., Kindberg, T., Blair, G.: System models. In: Distributed Systems. Concepts and Designs, 5 edn., pp. 37–80 Addison Wesley (2012)
13. Jaime, K., Torres, G., Ramos, F., Garcia, G.: A proposed model for visual memory identification. In: 2012 IEEE 11th International Conference on Cognitive Informatics Cognitive Computing (ICCI*CC), pp. 35–42, August 2012
14. Tanenbaum, A.S., Steen, M.V.: Processes. In: Distributed Systems Principles and Paradigms, 2nd edn., pp. 69–114. Pearson Prentice Hal (2007)
15. Siegelbaum, S.A., Kandel, E.R.: Overview of synaptic transmission. number 8. In: Principles of Neural Science, 5th edn., pp. 177–188. Mc Graw Hill Medical (2013)
16. Ávila-Contreras, C., Medina, O., Jaime, K., Ramos, F.: An agent cognitive model for visual attention and response to novelty. In: Jezic, G., Kusek, M., Lovrek, I., J. Howlett, R., C. Jain, L. (eds.) Agent and Multi-Agent Systems: Technologies and Applications. AISC, vol. 296, pp. 27–36. Springer, Heidelberg (2014)
17. Yamaguchi, S., Hale, L.A., D'Esposito, M., Knight, R.T.: Rapid prefrontal-hippocampal habituation to novel events. The Journal of Neuroscience **24**, 5356–5363 (2004)
18. Jaime, A.K.: Modelo de memoria semantica para crituaturas virtuales basado en neurociencias. Master's thesis, CINVESTAV del IPN Unidad Guadalajara, Zapopan, Jalisco, August 2011
19. Torres, G.A.: Metodología para el desarrollo de arquitecturas cognitivas basada en neurociencias. PhD thesis, CINVESTAV del IPN Unidad Guadalajara, Zapopan, Jalisco, Octubre 2013
20. Rosales, J.H., Jaime, K., Ramos, F., Ramos, M.: An emotional regulation model with memories for virtual agents. In: IEEE 12th International Conference on Cognitive Informatics and Cognitive Computing (ICCI*CC), pp. 260–267, July 2013
21. Rosales, J.H.: Sistema de regulacion emociones para criaturas virtuales. Master's thesis, CINVESTAV del IPN Unidad Guadalajara, Zapopan, Jalisco, August 2013
22. Avila-Contreras, C.: Arquitectura cognitiva de atencion selectiva bimodal: vision y somatosensacion. Master's thesis, CINVESTAV del IPN Unidad Guadalajara, Zapopan, Jalisco, August 2014
23. Medina, O., Vargas, S., Madrigal, D., Ramos, F., Torres, G.: A bio-inspired architecture of the vestibular system for body balance of a humanoid robot. In: 2014 IEEE 13th International Conference on Cognitive Informatics Cognitive Computing (ICCI*CC), pp. 73–79 (2014)
24. Medina, O.D.: Sistema de memoria no declarativa para criaturas virtuales: Aprendizaje no asociativo. Master's thesis, CINVESTAV del IPN Unidad Guadalajara, Zapopan, Jalisco, August 2014

Four Ways to Evaluate Arguments According to Agent Engagement

Pierre Bisquert[1]([⊠]), Madalina Croitoru[2], and Florence Dupin de Saint-Cyr[3]

[1] INRA, Montpellier, France
pierre.bisquert@supagro.inra.fr
[2] University of Montpellier, Montpellier, France
croitoru@lirmm.fr
[3] IRIT, Toulouse, France
florence.bannay@irit.fr

Abstract. In this paper we are interested in the computational and formal analysis of the persuasive impact that an argument can have on a human. We present a preliminary account of the listener mental process (representation and reasoning mechanisms of the dual process cognitive model) as well as her engagement based on the ELM model. This engagement determines the reasoning process that the agent will adopt in order to evaluate and incorporate the uttered argument.

Keywords: Cognitive bias · Dual process · Argumentation · Artificial intelligence

1 Introduction

Several decades worth of empirical studies have clearly shown that human responses often deviate from the expected rational response on many reasoning tasks. We study the link between attitudes and persuasion, a central point of social psychology [2,18]. While important methodological and theoretical issues regarding the consistency between attitudes and behaviors were made early on [1,8] no agreement between different modalities was achieved. The ELM model [15,16] is one of the first models to generalise a theory of attitude change in persuasion. ELM distinguishes between two "routes" that govern the reception of persuasive communications and the outcomes concerning attitude changes: the *central route*, that involves a large amount of cognition and that has the tendency to be more rational concerning the logical quality of the received argument, and the *peripheral route*, that involves little cognition and where arguments are more likely to be evaluated thanks to simple cues such as the political view on the advocated position, the liking of the speaker, etc.

The art of persuasion is intimately connected with the psychological process of perception. In [5] the author presents the relationship between mental processes that psychologists label cognitive biases and legal arguments. Arguments built on this relationship contain what philosophers label informal fallacies.

© Springer International Publishing Switzerland 2015
Y. Guo et al. (Eds.): BIH 2015, LNAI 9250, pp. 445–456, 2015.
DOI: 10.1007/978-3-319-23344-4_43

By using legal arguments that contain informal fallacies, the lawyer can play upon the listeners inherent cognitive biases to persuade them to see things in a way that favors its goals. Argumentation in a large sense is not to be identified with rational persuasion as some arguments are not addressing the rational part of the listener [3].

To bridge the different communities working on argumentation, in [10] the authors distinguish between the three meanings of the word argument: argument as a reason, argument as a structured sequence of reasons and claims, and argument as a social exchange. All three meanings are integral to a complete understanding of human reasoning and cognition. We follow in their foot steps by integrating different aspects of what an argument is in our preliminary model. The core of our approach is to propose a model of cognitive biases and their role in persuasion and argumentation.

In their seminal article [22] Tversky and Kahneman explain how supposedly "rational" judgments are based on data with limited validity, processed according to heuristic rules. They illustrate their thesis with a number of biases empirically demonstrated (such as the illusion of validity, retrievability of instances, anchoring, framing, etc.). The ancient idea that cognitive processes can be partitioned into two main families (traditionally called intuition and reason) is now widely embraced under the general label of dual-process theories [6,7,12,19]. According to Kahneman [22], human reasoning takes place in two systems: System 1 (S1) and System 2 (S2). The first system deals with quick and instinctive thoughts and is based on associations such as cause-effect, resemblance, valence etc. The second system, used as little as possible, is a slow and conscious process that deals with what we commonly call reason.

In this paper, after defining a new cognitive model and two reasoning processes based on [12] as well as [15] in Section 2, we present how an argument might be evaluated and its effect on the agent's mind in Section 3. Finally, some properties are shown in Section 4.

2   Towards a Computational Model of Cognitive Evaluation

2.1   Cognitive Model

In this paper, our aim is to define a computational cognitive model of the evaluation of an argument. Based on Kahneman's theory we propose to define an agent cognitive model on two components AT (an association table linking a formula to an ordered set of formulae and to a flag encoding an appreciation) and KB (a logical knowledge base) in order to encode S1 and S2 respectively.[1] Formally, we consider a logical language and we denote by $\mathcal{L}$ the set of well formed formulae of this language given the usual connectives $\wedge$, $\vee$, $\rightarrow$, $\neg$ and the constants $\perp$ and $\top$. The set of terms in the language is denoted by $\mathcal{T}$. $\vdash$ denotes classical inference. The fact that a term t appears in a formula φ is denoted by $t \in \varphi$.

---

[1] Note that S1 and S2 are linked as we will see in (1) of Definition 2.

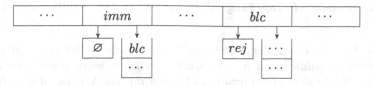

Fig. 1. *Partial representation of Alex's associative table.*

Definition 1 (Association table). *An agent's association table AT is a set of triples of the form $(\varphi, (S, \succ_S), f)$ where:*

- *$\varphi \in \mathcal{L}$ is a well formed formula representing a piece of knowledge,*
- *$S \subseteq \mathcal{L}$ is a set of well formed formulae associated to φ endowed with a total strict order $\succ_S \subseteq S \times S$, the pair $(S, \succ_S)$ is called a stack (when there is no ambiguity, the total ordered will be omitted),*
- *$f \in \{acc, rej, \varnothing\}$ is a flag stating that φ is respectively accepted, rejected or not informed in the association table.*

The set of all well formed formulae in the association table is denoted by $\mathcal{L}_{AT}$, i.e., $\mathcal{L}_{AT} = \bigcup_{(\varphi, S, f) \in AT} \varphi$. Given a formula $\varphi \in \mathcal{L}_{AT}$, the stack S associated with φ in AT will be denoted by $AT(\varphi)$, and the top element of this stack is denoted $\mathsf{Top}(\varphi)$. Formally, $\mathsf{Top}(\varphi) = \varphi_0$ s.t. $\forall \varphi' \neq \varphi_0 \in AT(\varphi), \varphi_0 \succ_S \varphi'$. The flag f associated to φ is denoted by $\mathsf{flag}(\varphi)$. If f is a flag then $-f$ is a flag such that $-acc = rej, -rej = acc$ and $-\varnothing = \varnothing$. Note that AT is implicit in the definitions of Top and flag.

A cognitive model is based on AT and on a knowledge base KB which contains Beliefs, Appreciations (*i.e.* associations of formulae to flags) and a set of Appreciation Rules[2] called *a-rules*. An a-rule has the form $\varphi \rightsquigarrow (\psi, f)$ where $\varphi, \psi \in \mathcal{L}$ and $f \in \{acc, rej\}$. Due to space constraints, we will not detail how an operator $\mid\sim$ is built such that $KB \mid\sim (\varphi, f)$ iff the appreciation of φ is $f \in \{acc, rej, \varnothing\}$ wrt KB.

Definition 2 (Cognitive model). *A cognitive model is a tuple $\kappa = (KB, AT, \lambda, i)$:*

- *$KB = (K, F, R)$ s.t. $K \subseteq \mathcal{L}, F \subseteq \mathcal{L} \times \{acc, rej, \varnothing\}$ and R is a set of a-rules.*
- *AT is an association table such that $\forall \varphi \in K, \forall t, t' \in T, \forall f \in \{acc, rej, \varnothing\}$*

$$((t, t' \in \varphi) \Rightarrow t \in AT(t')) \quad and \quad ((\varphi, f) \in F \Rightarrow \mathsf{flag}(\varphi) = f) \qquad (1)$$

- *$\lambda \in \mathbb{N}$ is an integer value representing the threshold above which the agent feels to be enough aware about the topic of a formula to be able to reason rationally,*
- *$i : \mathcal{L} \to \{0, 1, 2\}$ is a three value marker that gives the interest level of the agent relatively to a formula.*

In other words, (1) expresses the link between KB and AT, more precisely, every pair of terms belonging to a given formula in K are associated in AT and the flags in AT comply with F. In case of ambiguity about the current cognitive

---

[2] Inspired from the Desire-Generation rules (of Rahwan and Amgoud [17]).

model, the symbols AT, Top, flag will be indexed by the cognitive model κ they refer to.

Example 1. *Let us consider a fictional human agent called Alex. Alex has a keen interest in politics and he has started to learn more about immigration (imm). He thinks that immigration will bring the much required workforce in domains that lack attractiveness. He also thinks that it will mean a better living for everybody as the local economy will be relaunched. His KB contains rules such as $imm \rightarrow extraWork$, $extraWork \rightarrow moreMoney$, $moreMoney \rightarrow \neg lJobs$.*

Recently, Alex has also watched a documentary about immigration that presented the horrible living conditions of certain immigrants. While he still does not know whether to accept or reject the notion of immigration, the first thing he now associates immigration with is the bad living condition (blc) of immigrants, something he disapproves of. This is represented in Fig. 1.

2.2   System 1 and System 2 Reasoning

Let us see how to use this representation framework in order to reason. In this paper, we call *reasoning* the process of evaluating the acceptability of a formula $\varphi \in \mathcal{L}$, *i.e.*, mapping φ to a flag in $\{acc, rej, \varnothing\}$. The reasoning is not the same in S1 and S2. In S1, reasoning is based on the association table AT while in S2 it is based on an inference principle. We propose to encode S1-reasoning as follows: if the current formula has a non-empty flag, then this flag is returned; else, the head of the stack associated to the current formula becomes the current formula. The agent does this procedure until she is not able to reach new formulae in her S1 system anymore.

Definition 3 (S1-reasoning). *Given a cognitive model $\kappa = (KB, AT, \lambda, i)$, we define S1-reasoning, about a formula φ, denoted $\mathrm{eval}_1(\varphi, \kappa)$, as follows:*

$$\mathrm{eval}_1(\varphi, \kappa) = \mathrm{evalr}(\varphi, \{\varphi\})$$

$$\mathrm{evalr}(\varphi, R_\varphi) = \begin{cases} \mathbf{flag}(\varphi) & \textit{if } \mathbf{flag}(\varphi) \neq \varnothing, \\ \mathrm{evalr}(\mathrm{Top}(\varphi), R_\varphi \cup \{\mathrm{Top}(\varphi)\}) & \textit{if } \mathbf{flag}(\varphi) = \varnothing \textit{ and } \mathrm{Top}(\varphi) \notin R_\varphi, \\ \varnothing & \textit{otherwise.} \end{cases}$$

where R_φ is the set of formulae visited by evalr.

Example 2. *Given the association table shown in Fig. 1, the result of $eval_1(imm)$ is rej. Indeed, since the formula imm has the flag $\varnothing$, the S1-reasoning gets the top formula of the stack associated to imm, which is blc. The flag of blc being different than $\varnothing$, it is the result of the evaluation.*

Definition 4 (S2-reasoning). *Given a cognitive model $\kappa = (KB, AT, \lambda, i)$, S2-reasoning is defined by:*

$$\mathrm{eval}_2(\varphi, \kappa) = f \ s.t. \ KB \mathrel{\vert\!\sim} (\varphi, f)$$

3   Argument Evaluation

3.1   Argument and Profiles

We first give a (restrictive[3]) definition of an argument: it is an entity containing a source (which is a formula and represents the speaker), a premise (which is a formula and can be itself a conjunction of more basic premises), a warrant (an *a-rule*) and a conclusion associated with an acceptance flag.

Definition 5 (Argument). *An* argument *is a tuple* $(s, h, w, (c, f))$ *where* s *is the speaker enunciating the argument,* h *is a formula (the hypothesis of the argument),* w *(the warrant) is an a-rule,* c *is a formula (the conclusion) and* $f \in \{acc, rej\}$ *is a flag stating that the argument conclusion should be accepted or rejected.*

In the ELM model [15], the determination of the "route" is made thanks to two main factors: the *interest* in processing the message and the *ability* (wrt knowledge and cognitive availability) to process it. We use these factors in order to define different profiles of agents (note that we leave the cognitive availability for future work). Such profiles represent typical (and extreme) dispositions wrt the evaluation of an argument.

- **Interest**, given by the function i (see Def. 2). An agent may be not interested by a formula φ ($i(\varphi) = 0$), interested ($i(\varphi) = 1$) or "fanatic" ($i(\varphi) = 2$).
- **Knowledge**, represented by the size of the stack related to φ in AT. This size is compared to the agent's threshold λ (see Def. 2) in order to link the quantity of information the agent has to his feeling about being sufficiently aware on φ.

These two parameters are used to determine the agent profile. We introduce four level of engagement: unconcerned, enthusiastic, quiescent or engaged with increasing involved level of cognition (see Definitions 8, 9, 10, 11).

Definition 6 (Profile). *The* profile *of an agent is a function that maps a formula* $\varphi \in \mathcal{L}$ *and a cognitive model* $\kappa = (KB, AT, \lambda, i)$ *to an element of* $\{unc, ent, qui, eng\}$:

$$\texttt{profile}(\varphi, \kappa) = \begin{cases} unc & \text{if } i(\varphi) = 0 \\ qui & \text{if } i(\varphi) = 1 \text{ and } |AT(\varphi)| < \lambda \\ eng & \text{if } i(\varphi) = 1 \text{ and } |AT(\varphi)| \geq \lambda \\ ent & \text{if } i(\varphi) = 2 \end{cases}$$

The following postulate expresses that if an agent is **enthusiastic** about a formula φ, then she has an opinion about φ.

Postulate 1. $\texttt{profile}(\varphi, \kappa) = ent$ *implies* $\texttt{flag}_\kappa(\varphi) \neq \varnothing$

The next section details the value of the function $\texttt{evalarg}$ defined below.

---

[3] Here, we only consider arguments in favor of appreciations and not in favor of beliefs.

Definition 7. *Given a cognitive model $\kappa = (KB, AT, \lambda, i)$, an argument $a = (s, h, w, (c, f))$ and a profile $p = \texttt{profile}(c, \kappa)$, let $\texttt{evalarg}$ be a function that maps a and p to an evaluation of the argument in $\{acc, rej, \varnothing\}$, denoted as $\texttt{evalarg}(a, p)$.*

3.2   Argument Evaluation According to Profiles

In this section, we introduced the four profiles and we define formally how the evaluation is done with respect to a profile.

Unconcerned. As its name implies, the unconcerned profile represents the fact that no interest is given by the agent in the received argument. Hence, an unconcerned agent will not bother trying to evaluate this argument and will just discard it.

Definition 8. *Given an argument $a = (s, h, w, (c, f))$, the evaluation of a by an unconcerned agent unc is never done.*

Enthusiastic. The enthusiastic profile represents the fact that an agent is already convinced. As such, she does not feel the need to evaluate rationally the argument and will just check if the flag of the argument's conclusion correspond to the flag in her AT.

Definition 9. *Given an argument $a = (s, h, w, (c, f))$, the evaluation of a by an enthusiastic agent $\texttt{evalarg}(a, ent) = acc$ iff $eval_1(c) = f$ else $\texttt{evalarg}(a, ent) = rej$.*

Quiescent. A quiescent profile represents an "ideally instinctive" agent evaluating an argument thanks to her S1. More precisely, when receiving an argument, the agent evaluates the argument's conclusion and the speaker. She will accept the argument if she agrees with the conclusion and does not reject the speaker, or vice-versa.

Definition 10. *Given an argument $a = (s, h, w, (c, f))$, the evaluation of a by a quiescent agent with a cognitive model κ is defined as follows:*

$$\texttt{evalarg}(a, qui) = \begin{cases} acc & if\ (eval_1(c, \kappa) = f\ and\ eval_1(s, \kappa) \neq rej)\ or \\ & (eval_1(c, \kappa) \neq -f\ and\ eval_1(s, \kappa) = acc), \\ rej & if\ (eval_1(c, \kappa) = -f\ and\ eval_1(s, \kappa) \neq acc)\ or \\ & (eval_1(c, \kappa) \neq f\ and\ eval_1(s, \kappa) = rej), \\ \varnothing & otherwise \end{cases}$$

In future work, we plan to take into account the extra sources of persuasion such as the context created by the source of information including trustworthiness and charisma of the source, the contextual mood of the agent, etc.

Example 3. *After a hard day's work, when Alex's wife said that "since immigration leads to less jobs, which would be dreadful, immigration has to be rejected", he did not have the cognitive availability to rationally consider* *this argument. While he would not have agreed with a deeper analysis, he instead relied on his S1, where immigration is associated with something he rejects (see Fig. 1), and therefore accepted the argument.*

Engaged. An engaged profile represents an "ideally rational" agent evaluating an argument exclusively thanks to her knowledge base. In this work, we suppose that an engaged agent evaluates an argument in a way similar to critical questions (see [23]). More precisely, given an argument $a = (s, h, (w_h \rightsquigarrow (w_c, w_f)), (c, f))$, an engaged agent has to use her S2 in order to check that:

- The premises are consistent with the knowledge of the agent ($K \nvdash \neg h$),
- There is no exception to the warrant in the context h ($KB \cup \{h \wedge w_h\} \nvdash (w_c, -w_f)$),
- The premises and the warrant entail the conclusion $(({\{h\}, \varnothing, \{w\}}) \mathrel{|\!\sim} (c, f))$.

Note that we also have to check that the conclusion of the argument is not already deducible in order to ensure that the premises and the warrant are well required and are well related to the conclusion. In our particular case, it amounts to check if it is not always accepted or rejected (*i.e.* $(\varnothing, \varnothing, \varnothing) \mathrel{|\!\not\sim} (c, f)$). This leads us to the following:

Definition 11. *Given an argument $a = (s, h, (w_h \rightsquigarrow (w_c, w_f)), (c, f))$, the evaluation of a by an engaged agent with a cognitive model $\kappa = (KB, AT, \lambda, i)$ with $KB = (K, F, R)$ is defined as follows:*

$$
\mathsf{evalarg}(a, eng) = \begin{cases} acc & if \begin{cases} K \nvdash \neg h \text{ and} \\ \mathsf{eval}_2(w_c, KB \cup \{h \wedge w_h\}) \neq -w_f \text{ and} \\ (\mathsf{eval}_2(c, (\{h\}, \varnothing, \{w\})) = f \text{ and } \mathsf{eval}_2(c, (\varnothing, \varnothing, \varnothing)) = \varnothing) \end{cases} \\ rej & if \begin{cases} KB \vdash \neg h \text{ or} \\ \mathsf{eval}_2(w_c, KB \cup \{h \wedge w_h\}) = -w_f \text{ or} \\ (\mathsf{eval}_2(c, (\{h\}, \varnothing, w)) = -f \text{ or } \mathsf{eval}_2(c, (\varnothing, \varnothing, \varnothing)) \neq \varnothing) \end{cases} \\ \varnothing & otherwise \end{cases}
$$

Example 4. *Several days after the discussion with his wife, Alex thought of her argument again. The argument premise contains $imm \wedge (imm \rightarrow lJobs)$. Now that he is able to analyse the argument more rationally, he logically deduces from his knowledge that immigration does not lead to less jobs (i.e. $K \vdash imm \rightarrow \neg lJobs$), which means that the premises of the argument are inconsistent with Alex's knowledge. Hence, Alex rejects the argument.*

3.3 Argument Influence on the Agent's Mind

Once the argument has been evaluated by an agent, her cognitive model may have to be modified to account for the persuasive impact of the argument. Such modifications can either be the change of a flag value, the addition of a new association or the addition of an appreciation rule. Def. 12 gives the functions representing these modifications.

Definition 12 (Update operations). *Given two cognitive states $\kappa = (KB, AT, \lambda, i)$ with $KB = (K, F, R)$ and κ', two formulas $x, y \in \mathcal{L}$ and a flag $f \in \{acc, rej, \varnothing\}$, we define:*

- $\mathtt{setflag}(\kappa, x, f) = \kappa'$ *where* $\kappa' = ((K, F', R), AT', \lambda, i)$ *with*
  - $L_{AT'} = L_{AT}$,
  - $\forall \varphi \in L_{AT}$ *s.t.* $\varphi \neq x$, $\mathtt{flag}_{\kappa'}(\varphi) = \mathtt{flag}_{\kappa}(\varphi)$ *and* $AT'(\varphi) = AT(\varphi)$,
  - $flag_{\kappa'}(x) = f$ *and* $F' = F \cup \{(x, f)\}$ *and* $AT'(x) = AT(x)$.
- $\mathtt{push}(\kappa, (x, y)) = \kappa'$ *where* $\kappa' = (KB', AT', \lambda, i)$ *with*
  - *if* $x \notin L_{AT}$ *then* $AT' = AT \cup \{(x, S_x, \varnothing)\}$ *with* $S_x = \{y\}$,
  - *else*
    - $\forall \varphi \in L_{AT}$ *s.t.* $\varphi \neq x$, $\mathtt{flag}_{\kappa'}(\varphi) = \mathtt{flag}_{\kappa}(\varphi)$ *and* $AT'(\varphi) = AT(\varphi)$,
    - $\mathtt{flag}_{\kappa'}(x) = \mathtt{flag}_{\kappa}(x)$ *and* $AT'(x) = AT(x) \cup \{y\}$ *with* $\mathtt{Top}(x) = y$,
- $\mathtt{addrule}(\kappa, r) = \kappa'$ *where*
  - $\kappa' = \kappa$ *if* $r \in R$,
  - *else* $\forall t, t' \in r, \kappa' = \mathtt{push}(((K, F, R \cup \{r\}), AT, \lambda, i), (t, t'))$.

Depending on the profile, the cognitive model will be modified in different ways. These differences aim at representing the fact that the persuasion may be deeper depending on the cognitive involvement of the agent. Table 1 gives the functions to apply to κ in order to update it, according to the possible evaluations of an argument by an agent and her profile. The "$\times$" in the *ent* and *unc* lines corresponds to impossible cases due to, respectively, Postulate 1 and Def. 8. Concerning the *eng* line, "$\times$" indicates the fact that an engaged agent is not influenced by what she hears when she does not accept the argument.

4   Properties

Let us first notice that after receiving an argument, the knowledge of an agent can only increase: more precisely, among the formulae that were already present, the number of flags that are not empty decreases (however some new formula may

Table 1. *Update of a cognitive state κ.*

	$evalarg((s, h, w, (c, f)))$		
$\mathtt{profile}(c, \kappa)$	$\varnothing$	rej	acc
unc	$\mathtt{push}(\kappa, (c, h))^4$	$\times$	$\times$
ent	$\times$	$\mathtt{push}(\kappa, (c, h))$ $\mathtt{setflag}(\kappa, s, rej)$	$\mathtt{push}(\kappa, (h, c))$ $\mathtt{push}(\kappa, (c, h))$ $\mathtt{setflag}(\kappa, s, acc)$
qui	$\mathtt{push}(\kappa, (c, h))$	$\mathtt{push}(\kappa, (c, h))$ $\mathtt{setflag}(\kappa, c, -f)$ $\mathtt{setflag}(\kappa, s, rej)$	$\mathtt{push}(\kappa, (h, c))$ $\mathtt{push}(\kappa, (c, h))$ $\mathtt{setflag}(\kappa, c, f)$ $\mathtt{setflag}(\kappa, s, acc)$
eng	$\times$	$\times$	$\mathtt{addrule}(\kappa, w)$ $\mathtt{addrule}(\kappa, (h \rightsquigarrow (c, f)))$ $\mathtt{setflag}(\kappa, c, f)$

be added with an empty flag) and the number of associations grows. Moreover some rules can also be added in the case of an engaged profile.

Proposition 1. *Let $\kappa = ((K, F, R), AT, \lambda, i)$, $\kappa' = ((K', F', R'), AT', \lambda', i')$ such that κ' is the cognitive model obtained from κ after the utterance of an argument. It holds that $L_{AT} \subseteq L_{AT'}$, $\forall \varphi \in L_{AT}, AT(\varphi) \subseteq AT'(\varphi)$, and $K = K'$ and $R \subseteq R'$ and $\lambda = \lambda'$ and $i = i'$.*

The flag values are non-monotonic since a formula can obtain either an accepted, rejected or empty flag depending on the engagement profile.

According to [24], the model of how information is transformed in public opinion follows four axioms mentioned below. Our proposal satisfies these axioms:

Reception axiom: *The greater the level a person's level of cognitive engagement with an issue the more likely he / she will be exposed to and comprehend political messages concerning that issue.* It holds since an unconcerned agent does not evaluate the argument, an enthusiastic agent takes it into account if she agrees with the conclusion, a quiescent agent evaluates it with S1-reasoning and an engaged agent evaluates it with S2-reasoning. Hence, the more engaged an agent is, the more information she takes into account (in the following order: unconcerned, enthusiastic, quiescent, engaged).

Resistance axiom: *People tend to resist arguments that are inconsistent with their political predispositions but they do so only to the extent that they posses the contextual information necessary to perceive a relationship between the message and their predispositions.* Unconcerned, enthusiastic and engaged agents may resist an argument since they are not influenced by its flag. A quiescent agent resists arguments that are against her opinion or uttered by a source she rejects (see Definition 10).

Accessibility axiom: *The more recently a consideration has been called to mind, or thought about, the less time it takes to retrieve that consideration or related considerations from memory and bring them to the top of the head for use.* This axiom is satisfied concerning the association table AT since every kind of profile add the new piece of information at the top of the stack (see Table 1).

Response axiom: *Individuals answer survey questions by averaging across the considerations that are immediately salient or accessible to them.* It holds for quiescent and enthusiastic: a quiescent agent evaluates a formula by considering the most immediately accessible information and an enthusiastic agent evaluates only the immediate value of a formula. However, it does not hold for unconcerned and engaged agents: one does not evaluate the formula, and the other evaluates the formula with her knowledge base.

---

[4] An argument is never evaluated by an unconcerned agent. We represent the fact that, like enthusiastic and quiescent agents, she is unconsciously influenced by what she hears.

5   Conclusion

In this paper, we have shown a preliminary formal account of dual process theory and its link with persuasion. Based on a classic model of persuasion, ELM, we defined four profiles evaluating an argument in different ways. In particular, one of the profiles aims at representing the cognitive biases that may arise with error prone reasoning. Moreover, each of these profiles implies different types of update of the cognitive model. This allows us to represent that, when an argument is accepted, the more cognition was involved in its evaluation, the more persuasive content will take root in the mind of the agent.

Related Work. To tackle general artificial intelligence problems several cognitive architectures inspired by dual process theories have recently been implemented. [9] presents an extension of the CLARION problem solving architecture that relies on two modules: a bottom-level module allowing to handle implicit knowledge and a top-level module managing explicit knowledge, which recall respectively the S1 and S2 systems of dual process theory. More directly connected to dual process theory, [21] proposes a general intelligence cognitive architecture based on [11]. This architecture is composed of a long-term memory that is independent of specific tasks and a working memory that is a capacity-limited list of elements of the long-term memory in accordance with the context. The S1 and S2 systems are represented thanks to two binary relations on the element of the long-term memory and two propagation processes. This allows them to distinguish between perception and imagination. In an approach similar to ours, some works aim at explaining purely human processes. For instance, [14] studies the emergence of emotions thanks to a three-levels cognitive architecture based on an extension of dual process theory [20]. In this architecture, S1 (the *reactive* level) is responsible for fast and instinctive behaviours while S2 is subdivided into the *algorithmic* level, used for cognitive control, and the *reflective* level, handling rational behaviour. [13] proposes a cognitive architecture called mReasoner aiming at reasoning on syllogistic arguments by relying on three systems. The S0 computes *intentions* which are representations of the meaning of the premises. S1 uses these intentions to create a model representing the different possible subjects the premises may refer to; the S1 then reasons heuristically by drawing a conclusion that is true in this model. Finally, the S2 looks for other models that may contradict the initial model, which is a slow process that may confirm or invalidate the S1 conclusion. It is interesting to note that S1 and S2 of [13] are similar to S1 and S2 of [22]. However, none of the existing work are specifically interested in the analysis of persuasion through cognitive biases.

Perspectives. Our work is a preliminary step in the study of the link between persuasion and cognitive biases, and, as such, opens numerous perspectives. In particular, we are interested in taking into account the cognitive availability in order to determine which system will be used to reason. Such study would benefit from the definition of a profile corresponding to a continuum between the quiescent and the engaged profiles. This new profile might better represent human reasoning and might allow us to study the link between persuasion and bounded rationality, together with the influence of S1 on S2-reasoning. Moreover, we do not take explicitly into account influence between agents such as social proof, authority, etc. Yet, being instinctive, a quiescent agent is naturally drawn to follow non-rational cues. As such, work such as [4] and rhetoric could prove very promising in our formalization. Finally, even if we have shown the correspondence between our work and the public opinion axioms of [24], a study in collaboration with psychologists would indubitably be useful to check the soundness of our approach.

References

1. Ajzen, I., Fishbein, M.: Attitude-behavior relations: A theoretical analysis and review of empirical research. Psychological Bulletin **84**(5), 888 (1977)
2. Allport, G.: Attitudes. In: Handbook of Social Psychology. Clark Univ. Press (1935)
3. Blair, J.A.: Argumentation as rational persuasion. Argumentation **26**(1), 71–81 (2012)
4. Cialdini, R.: Influence: Science and Practice. Allyn and Bacon (2001)
5. Clements, C.S.: Perception and Persuasion in Legal Argumentation: Using Informal Fallacies and Cognitive Biases to Win the War of Words. BYU Law Review 319, March 2013
6. Epstein, S.: Integration of the cognitive and the psychodynamic unconscious. American Psychologist **49**(8), 709 (1994)
7. Evans, J.S.B., Over, D.E., et al.: Rationality and reasoning. Psychology Press (2013)
8. Fazio, R.H., Zanna, M.P.: Direct experience and attitude-behavior consistency. Advances in Experimental Social Psychology **14**, 161–202 (1981)
9. Hélie, S., Sun, R.: Incubation, insight, and creative problem solving: a unified theory and a connectionist model. Psychological Review **117**(3), 994–1024 (2010)
10. Hornikx, J., Hahn, U.: Reasoning and argumentation: Towards an integrated psychology of argumentation. Thinking & Reasoning **18**(3), 225–243 (2012)
11. Kahneman, D.: A perspective on judgment and choice: Mapping bounded rationality. American Psychologist **58**(9), 697–720 (2003)
12. Kahneman, D., Frederick, S.: Representativeness revisited: Attribute substitution in intuitive judgment. Heuristics and biases: The Psychology of Intuitive Judgment **49** (2002)
13. Khemlani, S., Johnson-Laird, P.N.: The processes of inference. Argument & Computation **4**(1), 4–20 (2013)
14. Larue, O., Poirier, P., Nkambou, R.: Emotional emergence in a symbolic dynamical architecture. In: Chella, A., Pirrone, R., Sorbello, R., Jóhannsdóttir, K.R. (eds.) Biologically Inspired Cognitive Architectures 2012. AISC, vol. 196, pp. 199–204. Springer, Heidelberg (2013)
15. Petty, R., Cacioppo, J.: The Elaboration Likelihood Model of Persuasion. Advances in Experimental Social Psychology **19**(C), 205 (1985)
16. Petty, R.E., Cacioppo, J.T., Goldman, R.: Personal involvement as a determinant of argument-based persuasion. Journal of Personality and Social Psychology **41**(5), 847 (1981)

17. Rahwan, I., Amgoud, L.: An argumentation based approach for practical reasoning. In: Proc. of Int. J. Conf. on Autonomous Agents and MultiAgent Systems, pp. 347–354 (2006)
18. Ross, E.A.: Social psychology: An introduction and source book. Macmillan (1908)
19. Sloman, S.A.: The empirical case for two systems of reasoning. Psychological Bulletin **119**(1), 3 (1996)
20. Stanovich, K.: Rationality and the Reflective Mind. Oxford University Press (2010)
21. Strannegård, C., von Haugwitz, R., Wessberg, J., Balkenius, C.: A cognitive architecture based on dual process theory. In: Kühnberger, K.-U., Rudolph, S., Wang, P. (eds.) AGI 2013. LNCS, vol. 7999, pp. 140–149. Springer, Heidelberg (2013)
22. Tversky, A., Kahneman, D.: Judgment under uncertainty: Heuristics and biases. Science **185**(4157), 1124–1131 (1974)
23. Walton, D., Reed, C., Macagno, F.: Argumentation Schemes. Cambridge University Press, Cambridge (2008)
24. Zaller, J.: The Nature and Origins of Mass Opinion. Cambridge Studies in Political Psychology Series. Cambridge University Press (1992)

Author Index